Honda ST1300 Pan European
Service and Repair Manual

by Matthew Coombs

Models covered

ST1300 Pan European. 1261cc. 2002 to 2011
ST1300A Pan European. 1261cc. 2002 to 2011

(4908-336)

© Haynes Publishing 2011

ABCDE
FGHIJ
KLMNO
PQRS

A book in the Haynes Service and Repair Manual Series

All rights reserved. No part of this book may be reproduced or transmitted in any form or by any means, electronic or mechanical, including photocopying, recording or by any information storage or retrieval system, without permission in writing from the copyright holder.

ISBN: 978 1 84425 908 3

Library of Congress Control Number 2010934575

Printed in the USA

Haynes Publishing
Sparkford, Yeovil, Somerset BA22 7JJ, England

Haynes North America, Inc
861 Lawrence Drive, Newbury Park, California 91320, USA

Haynes Publishing Nordiska AB
Box 1504, 751 45 Uppsala, Sweden

Contents

LIVING WITH YOUR HONDA ST1300 PAN EUROPEAN

Introduction
The Birth of a Dream	Page	0•4
Acknowledgements	Page	0•8
About this manual	Page	0•8
Model development and Bike Spec	Page	0•9
Identification numbers	Page	0•10
Buying spare parts	Page	0•10
Safety first!	Page	0•11

Pre-ride checks
Coolant level	Page	0•12
Brake fluid levels	Page	0•12
Engine oil level	Page	0•14
Clutch fluid level	Page	0•15
Suspension, steering and final drive	Page	0•15
Tyres	Page	0•16
Legal and safety checks	Page	0•16

MAINTENANCE

Routine maintenance and servicing
Specifications	Page	1•2
Lubricants and fluids	Page	1•2
Maintenance schedule	Page	1•3
Component locations	Page	1•4
Maintenance procedures	Page	1•6

Contents

REPAIRS AND OVERHAUL

Engine, transmission and associated systems

Engine, clutch and transmission	Page	**2•1**
Cooling system	Page	**3•1**
Engine management system	Page	**4•1**

Chassis components

Frame and suspension	Page	**5•1**
Brakes, wheels and final drive	Page	**6•1**
Bodywork	Page	**7•1**

Electrical system

	Page	**8•1**

Wiring diagrams

	Page	**8•30**

REFERENCE

Tools and Workshop Tips	Page	**REF•2**
Security	Page	**REF•20**
Lubricants and fluids	Page	**REF•23**
Conversion factors	Page	**REF•26**
MOT Test Checks	Page	**REF•27**
Storage	Page	**REF•32**
Fault Finding	Page	**REF•35**
Technical Terms Explained	Page	**REF•44**

Index

	Page	**REF•48**

Introduction

The Birth of a Dream

by Julian Ryder

There is no better example of the Japanese post-war industrial miracle than Honda. Like other companies which have become household names, it started with one man's vision. In this case the man was the 40-year old Soichiro Honda who had sold his piston-ring manufacturing business to Toyota in 1945 and was happily spending the proceeds on prolonged parties for his friends. However, the difficulties of getting around in the chaos of post-war Japan irked Honda, so when he came across a job lot of generator engines he realised that here was a way of getting people mobile again at low cost.

A 12 by 18-foot shack in Hamamatsu became his first bike factory, fitting the generator motors into pushbikes. Before long he'd used up all 500 generator motors and started manufacturing his own engine, known as the 'chimney', either because of the elongated cylinder head or the smoky exhaust or perhaps both. The chimney made all of half a horsepower from its 50 cc engine but it was a major success and became the Honda A-type.

Less than two years after he'd set up in Hamamatsu, Soichiro Honda founded the Honda Motor Company in September 1948. By then, the A-type had been developed into the 90 cc B-type engine, which Mr Honda decided deserved its own chassis not a bicycle frame. Honda was about to become Japan's first post-war manufacturer of complete motorcycles. In August 1949 the first prototype was ready. With an output of three horsepower, the 98 cc D-type was still a simple two-stroke but it had a two-speed transmission and most importantly a pressed steel frame with telescopic forks and hard tail rear end. The frame was almost triangular in profile with the top rail going in a straight line from the massively braced steering head to the rear axle. Legend has it that after the D-type's first tests the entire workforce went for a drink to celebrate and try and think of a name for the bike. One man broke one of those silences you get when people are thinking, exclaiming 'This is like a dream!' 'That's it!' shouted Honda, and so the Honda Dream was christened.

> 'This is like a dream!'
> 'That's it'
> shouted Honda

Mr Honda was a brilliant, intuitive engineer and designer but he did not bother himself with the marketing side of his business. With hindsight, it is possible to see that employing Takeo Fujisawa who would both sort out the home market and plan the eventual expansion into overseas markets was a masterstroke. He arrived in October 1949 and in 1950 was made Sales Director. Another vital new name was Kiyoshi Kawashima, who along with Honda himself, designed the company's first four-stroke after Kawashima had told them that the four-stroke opposition to Honda's two-strokes sounded nicer and therefore sold better. The result of that statement was the overhead-valve 148 cc E-type which first ran in July 1951 just two months after the first drawings were made. Kawashima was made a director of the Honda Company at 34 years old.

The E-type was a massive success, over 32,000 were made in 1953 alone, a feat of mass-production that was astounding by the

Honda C70 and C90 OHV-engined models

standards of the day given the relative complexity of the machine. But Honda's lifelong pursuit of technical innovation sometimes distracted him from commercial reality. Fujisawa pointed out that they were in danger of ignoring their core business, the motorised bicycles that still formed Japan's main means of transport. In May 1952 the F-type Cub appeared, another two-stroke despite the top men's reservations. You could buy a complete machine or just the motor to attach to your own bicycle. The result was certainly distinctive, a white fuel tank with a circular profile went just below and behind the saddle on the left of the bike, and the motor with its horizontal cylinder and bright red cover just below the rear axle on the same side of the bike. This was the machine that turned Honda into the biggest bike maker in Japan with 70% of the market for bolt-on bicycle motors, the F-type was also the first Honda to be exported. Next came the machine that would turn Honda into the biggest motorcycle manufacturer in the world.

The C100 Super Cub was a typically audacious piece of Honda engineering and marketing. For the first time, but not the last, Honda invented a completely new type of motorcycle, although the term 'scooterette' was coined to describe the new bike which had many of the characteristics of a scooter but the large wheels, and therefore stability, of a motorcycle. The first one was sold in August 1958, fifteen years later over nine-million of them were on the roads of the world. If ever a machine can be said to have brought mobility to the masses it is the Super Cub. If you add in the electric starter that was added for the C102 model of 1961, the design of the Super Cub has remained substantially unchanged ever since, testament to how right Honda got it first time. The Super Cub made Honda the world's biggest manufacturer after just two years of production.

The CB250N Super Dream became a favorite with UK learner riders of the late seventies and early eighties

Honda's export drive started in earnest in 1957 when Britain and Holland got their first bikes, America got just two bikes the next year. By 1962 Honda had half the American market with 65,000 sales. But Soichiro Honda had already travelled abroad to Europe and the USA, making a special

The GL1000 introduced in 1975, was the first in Honda's line of GoldWings

Introduction

Carl Fogarty in action at the Suzuka 8 Hour on the RC45

An early CB750 Four

point of going to the Isle of Man TT, then the most important race in the GP calendar. He realised that no matter how advanced his products were, only racing success would convince overseas markets for whom 'Made in Japan' still meant cheap and nasty. It took five years from Soichiro Honda's first visit to the Island before his bikes were ready for the TT. In 1959 the factory entered five riders in the 125 class. They did not have a massive impact on the event being benevolently regarded as a curiosity, but sixth, seventh and eighth were good enough for the team prize. The bikes were off the pace but they were well engineered and very reliable.

The TT was the only time the West saw the Hondas in '59, but they came back for more the following year with the first of a generation of bikes which shaped the future of motorcycling – the double-overhead-cam four-cylinder 250. It was fast and reliable – it revved to 14,000 rpm – but didn't handle anywhere near as well as the opposition. However, Honda had now signed up non-Japanese riders to lead their challenge. The first win didn't come until 1962 (Aussie Tom Phillis in the Spanish 125 GP) and was followed up with a world-shaking performance at the TT. Twenty-one year old Mike Hailwood won both 125 and 250 cc TTs and Hondas filled the top five positions in both races. Soichiro Honda's master plan was starting to come to fruition, Hailwood and Honda won the 1961 250 cc World Championship. Next year Honda won three titles. The other Japanese factories fought back and inspired Honda to produce some of the most fascinating racers ever seen: the awesome six-cylinder 250, the five-cylinder 125, and the 500 four with which the immortal Hailwood battled Agostini and the MV Agusta.

When Honda pulled out of racing in '67 they had won sixteen rider's titles, eighteen manufacturer's titles, and 137 GPs, including 18 TTs, and introduced the concept of the modern works team to motorcycle racing. Sales success followed racing victory as Soichiro Honda had predicted, but only because the products advanced as rapidly as the racing machinery. The Hondas that came to Britain in the early '60s were incredibly sophisticated. They had overhead cams where the British bikes had pushrods, they had electric starters when the Brits relied on the kickstart, they had 12V electrics when even the biggest British bike used a 6V system. There seemed no end to the technical wizardry. It wasn't that the technology itself was so amazing but just like that first E-type, it was the fact that Honda could mass-produce it more reliably than the lower-tech competition that was so astonishing.

When in 1968 the first four-cylinder CB750 road bike arrived the world of motorcycling changed for ever, they even had to invent a new word for it, 'Superbike'. Honda raced again with the CB750 at Daytona and won the

World Endurance title with a prototype DOHC version that became the CB900 roadster. There was the six-cylinder CBX, the CX500T – the world's first turbocharged production bike, they invented the full-dress tourer with the GoldWing, and came back to GPs with the revolutionary oval-pistoned NR500 four-stroke, a much-misunderstood bike that was more a rolling experimental laboratory than a racer. Just to show their versatility Honda also came up with the weird CX500 shaft-drive V-twin, a rugged workhorse that powered a new industry, the courier companies that oiled the wheels of commerce in London and other big cities.

It was true, though, that Mr Honda was not keen on two-strokes – early motocross engines had to be explained away to him as lawnmower motors! However, in 1982 Honda raced the NS500, an agile three-cylinder lightweight against the big four-cylinder opposition in 500 GPs. The bike won in its first year and in '83 took the world title for Freddie Spencer. In four-stroke racing the V4 layout took over from the straight four, dominating TT, F1 and Endurance championships with the RVF750, the nearest thing ever built to a Formula 1 car on wheels. And when Superbike arrived Honda were ready with the RC30. On the roads the VFR V4 became an instant classic while the CBR600 invented another new class of bike on its way to becoming a best-seller. The V4 road bikes had problems to start with but the VFR750 sold world-wide over its lifetime while the VFR400 became a massive commercial success and cult bike in Japan. The original RC30 won the first two World Superbike Championships is 1988 and '89, but Honda had to wait until 1997 to win it again with the RC45, the last of the V4 roadsters. In Grands Prix, the NSR500 V4 two-stroke superseded the NS triple and became the benchmark racing machine of the '90s. Mick Doohan secured his place in history by winning five World Championships in consecutive years on it.

In yet another example of Honda inventing a new class of motorcycle, they came up with the astounding CBR900RR FireBlade, a bike with the punch of a 1000 cc motor in a package the size and weight of a 750. It became a cult bike as well as a best seller, and with judicious redesigns continues to give much more recent designs a run for their money.

When it became apparent that the high-tech V4 motor of the RC45 was too expensive to produce, Honda looked to a V-twin engine to power its flagship for the first time. Typically, the VTR1000 FireStorm was a much more rideable machine than its opposition and once accepted by the market formed the basis of the next generation of Superbike racer, the VTR-SP-1.

One of Mr Honda's mottos was that technology would solve the customers' problems, and no company has embraced

The CX500 – Honda's first V-Twin and a favorite choice of dispatch riders

cutting-edge technology more firmly than Honda. In fact Honda often developed new technology, especially in the fields of materials science and metallurgy. The embodiment of that was the NR750, a bike that was misunderstood nearly as much as the original NR500 racer. This limited-edition technological tour-de-force embodied many of Soichiro Honda's ideals. It used the latest techniques and materials in every component, from the oval piston, 32-valve V4 motor to the titanium coating on the windscreen, it was – as Mr Honda would have wanted – the best it could possibly be. A fitting memorial to the man who has shaped the motorcycle industry and motorcycles as we know them today.

The ST Pan European

The definition of a successful motorbike, or any product, is one that perfectly fulfils its design criteria. By that measure the Honda Pan European has been an unqualified success. The original 1100cc was around for thirteen years and barely changed as it became a cult machine for the long-distance rider. Actually, that's not fair – the word 'cult' implies some sort of small-scale group on the fringes of society. Pan European riders are

The VFR400R was a cult bike in Japan and a popular grey import in the UK

Introduction

The 2002 ST1300

The 2006 ST1300A

both numerous and right in the centre of the motorcycling spectrum.

The bike set out to fill a gap, one that many thought didn't really exist, between the Gold Wing tourer and the CBR1000F. The Gold Wing had grown to be an enormous, flashy six-cylinder behemoth while the CBR, despite being less than hi-tech with its steel frame and heavy at 520lb (235kg), was Honda's flagship. This, remember, was before the advent of the FireBlade. With hindsight, we can agree that the CBR1000 was a sports tourer not a true sportster, so what was the new V4? On the road it was a true all-rounder, capable of commuting and also carrying two people and their luggage across continents in comfort without the compromises of the Wing or the discomfort of a true sportster. If the Pan were a car it would be called a GT – Gran Turismo.

The Pan European certainly fared better than the other all-rounder Honda introduced in the late-1980s, the Pacific Coast. Intended mainly for the USA, the all-enclosed V-twin was a little ahead of its time – it now looks like the granddaddy of all the superscooters that are so popular in big European cities

The original 1100cc Pan European stayed in the Honda range almost unchanged for over a decade, and developed a loyal following of repeat buyers. But even a design that gets it so right first time has a natural lifetime. Honda hung on for as long as they could but in 2002 the 1300cc Pan was born. It was, of course, still a transverse V4 but the new bike shared only its concept with the original. It should also be mentioned that despite being a V4, the Pan European has nothing in common with the VF range, Honda's first V4s, or the VFR. And there's part of the reason for the Pan's success, it was developed as a stand-alone project and didn't have to compromise with a motor intended for a different type of machine.

However, the original carburetted engine in a steel frame was considered to have run its race, so in 2002 the new pan European arrived with twin-beam aluminium chassis, fuel injection and chain drive to the camshafts rather than the original belts. It also looked a good deal more aggressive with styling seemingly influenced by the X-Wing concept bike exhibited at the Tokyo Show.

The 1100cc Pan was the first Honda to feature an ABS system and the linked brake system – DCBS – has always been a feature of the bike. However, the 1300cc version quietly did away with the traction control that was part of the earlier bike's system. The new Pan European is lower, shorter and lighter than the old bike and has an almost infinitely adjustable seat and a screen that can be adjusted on the move. No doubt the ditching of the traction control helped in the lightning process, but it is an interesting little detail in the rush towards electronic control of everything. Presumably Honda decided this was one bit of complexity owners could do without.

So the Pan European goes on into its third decade doing what it was meant to do and with the backing of the sort of customer loyalty rarely seen today. Very few designs can boast that sort of longevity or devotion.

Acknowledgements

Our thanks are due to Fowlers of Bristol who supplied the machine featured in the illustrations throughout this manual. We would also like to thank NGK Spark Plugs (UK) Ltd for supplying the colour spark plug condition photographs, the Avon Rubber Company for supplying information on tyre fitting and Draper Tools Ltd for some of the workshop tools shown.

Thanks are also due to Julian Ryder who wrote the introduction 'The Birth of a Dream' and to Honda (UK) Ltd. who supplied model photographs.

About this Manual

The aim of this manual is to help you get the best value from your motorcycle. It can do so in several ways. It can help you decide what work must be done, even if you choose to have it done by a dealer; it provides information and procedures for routine maintenance and servicing; and it offers diagnostic and repair procedures to follow when trouble occurs.

We hope you use the manual to tackle the work yourself. For many simpler jobs, doing it yourself may be quicker than arranging an appointment to get the motorcycle into a dealer and making the trips to leave it and pick it up. More importantly, a lot of money can be saved by avoiding the expense the shop must pass on to you to cover its labour and overhead costs. An added benefit is the sense of satisfaction and accomplishment that you feel after doing the job yourself.

References to the left or right side of the motorcycle assume you are sitting on the seat, facing forward.

We take great pride in the accuracy of information given in this manual, but motorcycle manufacturers make alterations and design changes during the production run of a particular motorcycle of which they do not inform us. No liability can be accepted by the authors or publishers for loss, damage or injury caused by any errors in, or omissions from, the information given.

Illegal copying

It is the policy of Haynes Publishing to actively protect its Copyrights and Trade Marks. Legal action will be taken against anyone who unlawfully copies the cover or contents of this Manual. This includes all forms of unauthorised copying including digital, mechanical, and electronic in any form. Authorisation from Haynes Publishing will only be provided expressly and in writing. Illegal copying will also be reported to the appropriate statutory authorities.

Model development and bike spec

Twelve years after the launch of the original ST1100 Pan European in 1990 comes the all new ST1300 Pan European. While maintaining the design principal of the original Pan, but striving also to improve and modernise, the ST1300 features new components throughout, including a completely new engine.

The engine retains the longitudinal mounting and 16 valve V-Four layout, but has become more compact by introducing chain drive to the double-overhead camshafts to replace the previous belt drive, and by moving the alternator from the back of the engine to between the cylinder banks. To maintain a good centre of gravity the crankshaft now sits lower than before, and smooth running is ensured using twin balancer shafts. Lightweight aluminium composite cylinder liners house aluminium pistons with a surface coating to reduce friction. Drive to the rear wheel from the five-speed gearbox is by shaft.

Honda's PGM-FI fuel injection system supplies fuel and air to the engine via 36 mm throttle bodies and two inlet valves per cylinder, with exhaust gases exiting via another two valves per cylinder into a four-into-two exhaust system with closed-loop catalytic converter. Fuel is sourced from two tanks – the main tank in the conventional position and an additional tank, housing the fuel pump, located below the seat, spreading the weight and increasing overall capacity. An electronic engine management system controls both the injection system and the ignition system. All European models feature Honda's immobiliser system (HISS).

The engine sits in a new twin-beam aluminium frame which uses the engine as a stressed member. Front suspension is by non adjustable oil-damped 45 mm forks with cartridge dampers. Rear suspension is by single shock absorber with adjustable rebound damping and spring pre-load, and a lightweight aluminium swingarm with the right-hand section housing the driveshaft.

The hydraulic braking system has two triple piston calipers acting on 310 mm discs at the front, and one triple piston caliper acting on a 316 mm disc at the rear. All models feature Honda's combined braking system, whereby operating the front brake lever also activates a proportion of the rear caliper, and operating the rear brake pedal also activates a proportion of each front caliper. Two versions are available, either with or without Honda's anti-lock braking system (ABS).

The new models feature an adjustable seat that can be raised and lowered through three positions, and an adjustable windshield.

Since its launch in 2002 the ST1300 has changed very little, with modifications only to the design of the swingarm pivot, the brake calipers, the engine protection bars, the side covers and a radiator bracket.

Available in red, silver and green in 2002 and 2003, with blue replacing the green in 2004, and black replacing the blue in 2006.

Dimensions and weights

Overall length	2270 mm
Overall width	860 mm
Overall height	
Standard	1485 mm
Windshield adjustment low to high	1390 to 1630 mm
Wheelbase	1490 mm
Seat height	790 ± 15 mm
Footrest height	286 mm
Ground clearance	135 mm
Weight (dry)	
Standard models	281 kg
ABS models	287 kg
Weight (wet)	
Standard models	315 kg
ABS models	321 kg
Maximum weight capacity	196 kg

Engine

Type	Four-stroke 90° V-four
Capacity	1261 cc
Bore	78.0 mm
Stroke	66.0 mm
Compression ratio	10.8:1
Cooling system	Liquid cooled
Clutch	Wet multi-plate, hydraulic
Transmission	Five-speed constant mesh
Final drive	Shaft
Camshafts	DOHC, chain-driven
Fuel system	PGM-FI fuel injection, 36 mm throttle bodies
Exhaust system	Four-into-two
Ignition system	Computer-controlled digital transistorised with electronic advance

Chassis

Frame type	Twin spar aluminium box section
Rake and trail	26°, 98 mm
Fuel tank	
Capacity (including reserve)	29 litres
Reserve volume	approx. 5 litres
Front suspension	
Type	45 mm oil-damped cartridge-type telescopic forks
Travel	120 mm
Adjustment	none
Rear suspension	
Type	Single shock absorber, aluminium swingarm
Travel (at axle)	123 mm
Adjustment	Spring pre-load, rebound damping
Wheels	
Front	18 inch 3-spoke alloy
Rear	17 inch 3-spoke alloy
Tyres	
Front	120/70-ZR18 (59W)
Rear	170/60-ZR17 (72W)
Front brake	Twin 310 mm floating discs with triple piston sliding calipers
Rear brake	Single 316 mm disc with triple piston sliding caliper

Identification numbers

Frame and engine numbers

The frame serial number is stamped into the right-hand side of the steering head. The engine number is stamped into the cylinder block on the right-hand side. Both of these numbers should be recorded and kept in a safe place so they can be given to law enforcement officials in the event of a theft. The VIN plate is on the left-hand side of the steering head. There is a colour code label on the top of the right-hand rear sub-frame rail. The throttle bodies also have an ID number stamped into them.

The frame serial number, engine serial number, and colour code should also be kept in a handy place (such as with your driver's licence) so they are always available when purchasing or ordering parts for your machine.

Where necessary models are identified using a model code that corresponds to their model type and production year, e.g. ST1300-3 for a 2003 standard model, or ST1300A-3 for a 2003 ABS-equipped model. Refer to the accompanying table.

Model	Year
ST1300-2/A-2	2002
ST1300-3/A-3	2003
ST1300-4/A-4	2004 and 2005
ST1300-6/A-6	2006 and 2007
ST1300-8/A-8	2008
ST1300-9/A-9	2009 to 2011

The colour code label is on the top of the rear sub-frame on the right-hand side

The engine number is stamped into the right-hand side of the cylinder block

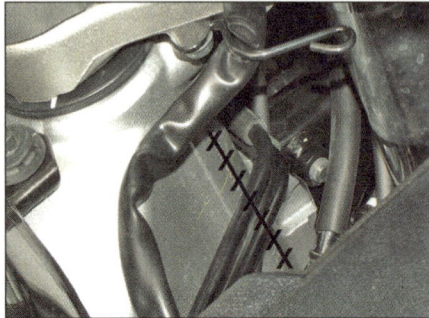

The frame number is stamped into the right-hand side of the steering head

The VIN plate (arrowed) is riveted to the left-hand side of the steering head

Buying spare parts

Once you have found all the identification numbers, record them for reference when buying parts. Since the manufacturers change specifications, parts and vendors (companies that manufacture various components on the machine), providing the ID numbers is the only way to be reasonably sure that you are buying the correct parts for your model.

Whenever possible, take the worn part to the dealer so direct comparison with the new component can be made. Along the trail from the manufacturer to the parts shelf, there are numerous places that the part can end up with the wrong number or be listed incorrectly.

The two places to purchase new parts for your motorcycle – the franchised or main dealer and the parts/accessories store – differ in the type of parts they carry. While dealers can obtain every single genuine part for your motorcycle, the accessory store is usually limited to normal high wear items such as brake pads, spark plugs and filters. Rarely will an accessory outlet have major suspension components, camshafts, transmission gears, or engine cases.

Used parts can be obtained from breakers for roughly half the price of new ones, but you can't always be sure of what you're getting. Once again, take your worn part to the breaker for direct comparison, or when ordering by mail order make sure that you can return it if you are not happy.

Whether buying new, used or rebuilt parts, the best course is to deal directly with someone who specialises in your particular make.

Safety First! 0•11

Professional mechanics are trained in safe working procedures. However enthusiastic you may be about getting on with the job at hand, take the time to ensure that your safety is not put at risk. A moment's lack of attention can result in an accident, as can failure to observe simple precautions.

There will always be new ways of having accidents, and the following is not a comprehensive list of all dangers; it is intended rather to make you aware of the risks and to encourage a safe approach to all work you carry out on your bike.

Asbestos

● Certain friction, insulating, sealing and other products - such as brake pads, clutch linings, gaskets, etc. - contain asbestos. Extreme care must be taken to avoid inhalation of dust from such products since it is hazardous to health. If in doubt, assume that they do contain asbestos.

Fire

● Remember at all times that petrol is highly flammable. Never smoke or have any kind of naked flame around, when working on the vehicle. But the risk does not end there - a spark caused by an electrical short-circuit, by two metal surfaces contacting each other, by careless use of tools, or even by static electricity built up in your body under certain conditions, can ignite petrol vapour, which in a confined space is highly explosive. Never use petrol as a cleaning solvent. Use an approved safety solvent.

● Always disconnect the battery earth terminal before working on any part of the fuel or electrical system, and never risk spilling fuel on to a hot engine or exhaust.
● It is recommended that a fire extinguisher of a type suitable for fuel and electrical fires is kept handy in the garage or workplace at all times. Never try to extinguish a fuel or electrical fire with water.

Fumes

● Certain fumes are highly toxic and can quickly cause unconsciousness and even death if inhaled to any extent. Petrol vapour comes into this category, as do the vapours from certain solvents such as trichloro-ethylene. Any draining or pouring of such volatile fluids should be done in a well ventilated area.
● When using cleaning fluids and solvents, read the instructions carefully. Never use materials from unmarked containers - they may give off poisonous vapours.
● Never run the engine of a motor vehicle in an enclosed space such as a garage. Exhaust fumes contain carbon monoxide which is extremely poisonous; if you need to run the engine, always do so in the open air or at least have the rear of the vehicle outside the workplace.

The battery

● Never cause a spark, or allow a naked light near the vehicle's battery. It will normally be giving off a certain amount of hydrogen gas, which is highly explosive.

● Always disconnect the battery ground (earth) terminal before working on the fuel or electrical systems (except where noted).
● If possible, loosen the filler plugs or cover when charging the battery from an external source. Do not charge at an excessive rate or the battery may burst.
● Take care when topping up, cleaning or carrying the battery. The acid electrolyte, evenwhen diluted, is very corrosive and should not be allowed to contact the eyes or skin. Always wear rubber gloves and goggles or a face shield. If you ever need to prepare electrolyte yourself, always add the acid slowly to the water; never add the water to the acid.

Electricity

● When using an electric power tool, inspection light etc., always ensure that the appliance is correctly connected to its plug and that, where necessary, it is properly grounded (earthed). Do not use such appliances in damp conditions and, again, beware of creating a spark or applying excessive heat in the vicinity of fuel or fuel vapour. Also ensure that the appliances meet national safety standards.
● A severe electric shock can result from touching certain parts of the electrical system, such as the spark plug wires (HT leads), when the engine is running or being cranked, particularly if components are damp or the insulation is defective. Where an electronic ignition system is used, the secondary (HT) voltage is much higher and could prove fatal.

Remember...

✗ **Don't** start the engine without first ascertaining that the transmission is in neutral.
✗ **Don't** suddenly remove the pressure cap from a hot cooling system - cover it with a cloth and release the pressure gradually first, or you may get scalded by escaping coolant.
✗ **Don't** attempt to drain oil until you are sure it has cooled sufficiently to avoid scalding you.
✗ **Don't** grasp any part of the engine or exhaust system without first ascertaining that it is cool enough not to burn you.
✗ **Don't** allow brake fluid or antifreeze to contact the machine's paintwork or plastic components.
✗ **Don't** siphon toxic liquids such as fuel, hydraulic fluid or antifreeze by mouth, or allow them to remain on your skin.
✗ **Don't** inhale dust - it may be injurious to health (see Asbestos heading).
✗ **Don't** allow any spilled oil or grease to remain on the floor - wipe it up right away, before someone slips on it.
✗ **Don't** use ill-fitting spanners or other tools which may slip and cause injury.
✗ **Don't** lift a heavy component which may be beyond your capability - get assistance.

✗ **Don't** rush to finish a job or take unverified short cuts.
✗ **Don't** allow children or animals in or around an unattended vehicle.
✗ **Don't** inflate a tyre above the recommended pressure. Apart from overstressing the carcass, in extreme cases the tyre may blow off forcibly.
✔ **Do** ensure that the machine is supported securely at all times. This is especially important when the machine is blocked up to aid wheel or fork removal.
✔ **Do** take care when attempting to loosen a stubborn nut or bolt. It is generally better to pull on a spanner, rather than push, so that if you slip, you fall away from the machine rather than onto it.
✔ **Do** wear eye protection when using power tools such as drill, sander, bench grinder etc.
✔ **Do** use a barrier cream on your hands prior to undertaking dirty jobs - it will protect your skin from infection as well as making the dirt easier to remove afterwards; but make sure your hands aren't left slippery. Note that long-term contact with used engine oil can be a health hazard.
✔ **Do** keep loose clothing (cuffs, ties etc. and long hair) well out of the way of moving mechanical parts.

✔ **Do** remove rings, wristwatch etc., before working on the vehicle - especially the electrical system.
✔ **Do** keep your work area tidy - it is only too easy to fall over articles left lying around.
✔ **Do** exercise caution when compressing springs for removal or installation. Ensure that the tension is applied and released in a controlled manner, using suitable tools which preclude the possibility of the spring escaping violently.
✔ **Do** ensure that any lifting tackle used has a safe working load rating adequate for the job.
✔ **Do** get someone to check periodically that all is well, when working alone on the vehicle.
✔ **Do** carry out work in a logical sequence and check that everything is correctly assembled and tightened afterwards.
✔ **Do** remember that your vehicle's safety affects that of yourself and others. If in doubt on any point, get professional advice.
● If in spite of following these precautions, you are unfortunate enough to injure yourself, seek medical attention as soon as possible.

Pre-ride checks

Coolant level

Before you start:
✔ Make sure you have a supply of coolant available (a mixture of 50% distilled water and 50% corrosion inhibited ethylene glycol anti-freeze is needed). Premix coolant is readily available from motorcycle dealers.
✔ Always check the coolant level when the engine is at normal working temperature. Take the motorcycle on a short run to allow it to reach normal temperature.
Caution: Do not run the engine in an enclosed space such as a garage or workshop.

✔ Stop the engine. Support the motorcycle on the centrestand on level ground.
✔ The coolant reservoir is located behind the left-hand fairing side panel – remove the access panel and the engine guard cover (see Chapter 7).

Bike care:
● Use only the specified coolant mixture. It is important that the correct proportion of anti-freeze is used in the system all year round, and not just in the winter. Do not top

> **Warning: DO NOT remove the radiator pressure cap to add coolant. Topping up is done via the coolant reservoir tank filler. DO NOT leave open containers of coolant about, as it is poisonous.**

the system up using only water, as the system will become too diluted.
● Do not overfill the reservoir tank. If the coolant is significantly above the UPPER level line at any time, the surplus should be siphoned or drained off to prevent the possibility of it being expelled out of the overflow hose.
● If the coolant level falls steadily, check the system for leaks (see Chapter 1). If no leaks are found and the level continues to fall, it is recommended that the machine is taken to a Honda dealer for a pressure test.

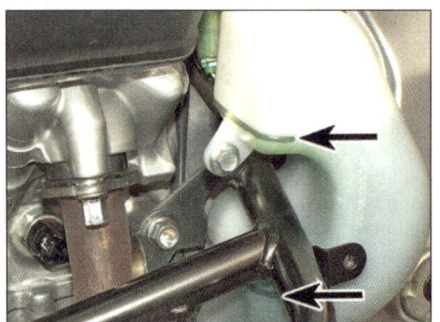

1 The coolant level should lie between the UPPER and LOWER level lines (arrowed) that are marked on the reservoir.

2 If the coolant level is on or below the LOWER line, remove the reservoir filler cap.

3 Top the reservoir up with new coolant to the UPPER level line, using a suitable funnel if required. Fit the cap. Install the engine guard cover and access panel (see Chapter 7).

Brake fluid levels

> **Warning: Brake hydraulic fluid can harm your eyes and damage painted surfaces, so use extreme caution when handling and pouring it and cover surrounding surfaces with rag. Do not use fluid that has been standing open for some time, as it is hygroscopic (absorbs moisture from the air) which can cause a dangerous loss of braking effectiveness.**

Before you start:
✔ The front brake fluid reservoir is on the right-hand handlebar. The rear brake fluid reservoir is located behind the right-hand side cover.
✔ Make sure you have some DOT 4 hydraulic fluid.
✔ Wrap a rag around the reservoir being worked on to ensure that any spillage does not come into contact with painted surfaces.
✔ Support the bike on the centrestand on level ground. When checking the fluid in the front reservoir, turn the handlebars to the left so the reservoir is level.

Bike care:
● The fluid in the front and rear brake master cylinder reservoirs will drop very gradually as the brake pads wear down. If the fluid level is low check the brake pads for wear (see Chapter 1), and replace them with new ones if necessary (see Chapter 6). Do not top the reservoir(s) up until the new pads have been fitted, and then check to see if topping up is still necessary – when the caliper pistons are pushed back to accommodate the extra thickness of the pads some fluid will be displaced back into the reservoir.

● If either fluid reservoir requires repeated topping-up there is a leak somewhere in the system, which must be investigated immediately (see Chapter 1).
● Check for signs of fluid leakage from the hydraulic hoses and/or brake system components – if found, rectify immediately (see Chapter 6).
● Check the operation of both brakes before taking the machine on the road; if there is evidence of air in the system (spongy feel to lever or pedal), it must be bled (see Chapter 6).

Pre-ride checks

FRONT BRAKE

1 The front brake fluid level is visible through the window in the reservoir body – it must be above the LOWER level line (arrowed).

2 If the level is on or below the LOWER line, undo the reservoir cover screws and remove the cover, diaphragm plate and diaphragm.

3 Use new DOT 4 hydraulic fluid to top up to the upper level line (arrowed) inside the reservoir. Do not overfill and take care to avoid spills (see **Warning**). Note that a white plastic float (as shown here) may be fitted to certain models.

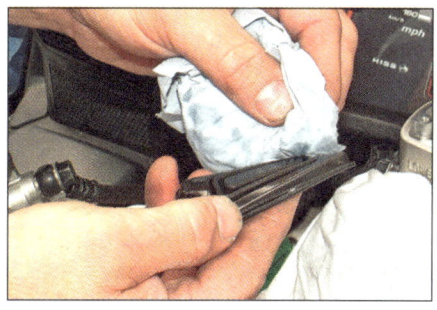

4 Wipe any moisture off the diaphragm with a tissue.

5 Ensure that the diaphragm is correctly seated before installing the plate and cover. Secure the reservoir cover with its screws.

REAR BRAKE

1 Remove the right-hand side cover (see Chapter 7). The rear brake fluid level is visible through the reservoir body – it must be between the UPPER and LOWER level lines (arrowed).

2 If the level is on or below the LOWER line, unscrew the reservoir cap, then remove the diaphragm plate and diaphragm.

3 Top up with new clean DOT 4 hydraulic fluid, until the level is up to the UPPER line. Do not overfill and take care to avoid spills (see **Warning**).

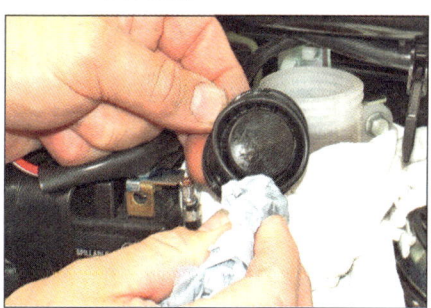

4 Wipe any moisture off the diaphragm with a tissue.

5 Ensure that the diaphragm is correctly seated before installing the plate and cap. Install the side cover.

Pre-ride checks

Engine oil level

Before you start:
✔ Start the engine and let it idle for 3 to 5 minutes.
Caution: Do not run the engine in an enclosed space such as a garage or workshop.
✔ Stop the engine. Support the motorcycle on the centrestand on level ground. Allow it to stand undisturbed for 2 to 3 minutes to allow the oil level to stabilise.
✔ The oil level inspection window is located on the right-hand side of the engine and is visible via the aperture in the lower fairing. If necessary wipe the window so that it is clean.

Bike care:
● If you have to add oil frequently, check whether there are any oil leaks from the engine joints, oil seals and gaskets. If not, the engine could be burning oil, in which case there will be white smoke coming out of the exhaust (see *Fault Finding*).

The correct oil:
● Modern, high-revving engines place great demands on their oil. It is very important that the correct oil is used.
● Always use a good quality motorcycle oil of the specified type and viscosity and do not overfill the engine.
Caution: Do not use chemical additives or oils labelled "ENERGY CONSERVING". Such additives or oils could cause clutch slip.

Oil type	API grade SG or higher JASO MA
Oil viscosity	Europe – SAE 10W40 US and Canada 2003 to 2006 – SAE 10W40 US and Canada 2007-on – SAE 10W30

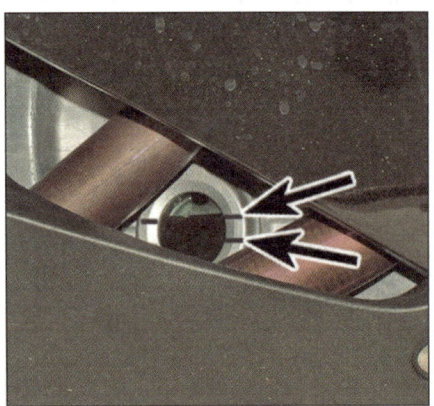

1 With the motorcycle vertical, the oil level should lie between the upper and lower level lines (arrowed). If the level is on or below the lower line, remove the access panel from the right-hand fairing side panel and the trim cover from the top of the valve cover (see Chapter 7).

2 Unscrew the oil filler cap.

3 Top up the engine with the recommended grade and type of oil to bring the level almost up to the upper line on the inspection window. Do not overfill.

4 Make sure the filler cap O-ring (arrowed) is in good condition and correctly seated before fitting the cap. Install the trim cover and access panel (see Chapter 7).

Pre-ride checks

Clutch fluid level

Before you start:
✔ The clutch fluid reservoir is on the left-hand handlebar.
✔ Make sure you have some DOT 4 hydraulic fluid.
✔ Wrap a rag around the reservoir to ensure that any spillage does not come into contact with painted surfaces.
✔ Support the bike on the centrestand on level ground. Turn the handlebars to the right so the reservoir is level.

Bike care:
● The clutch fluid reservoir shouldn't require repeated topping-up, but it is still important to check the level.
● Check for signs of fluid leakage from the hydraulic hose and release system components – if found, rectify immediately (see Chapter 2).
● Check the operation of the clutch before taking the machine on the road; if there is evidence of air in the system (spongy feel to lever, difficulty selecting gears and clutch drag), it must be bled (see Chapter 2).

> **Warning:** Clutch hydraulic fluid can harm your eyes and damage painted surfaces, so use extreme caution when handling and pouring it and cover surrounding surfaces with rag. Do not use fluid from an opened container as it is hygroscopic (absorbs moisture from the air) which can cause a loss of clutch operating effectiveness.

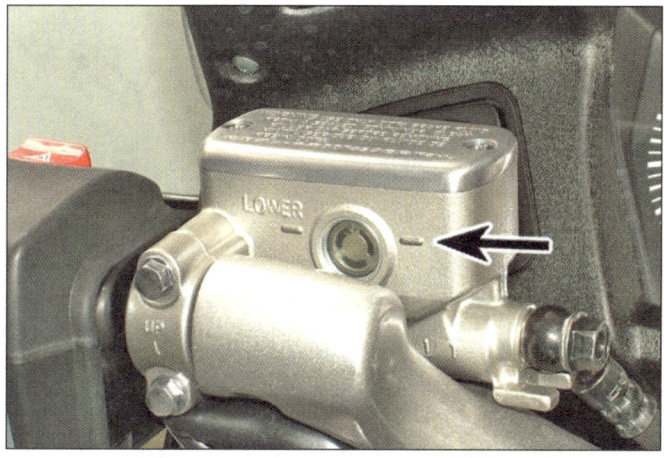

1 The clutch fluid level is visible through the window in the reservoir body – it must be above the LOWER level line (arrowed).

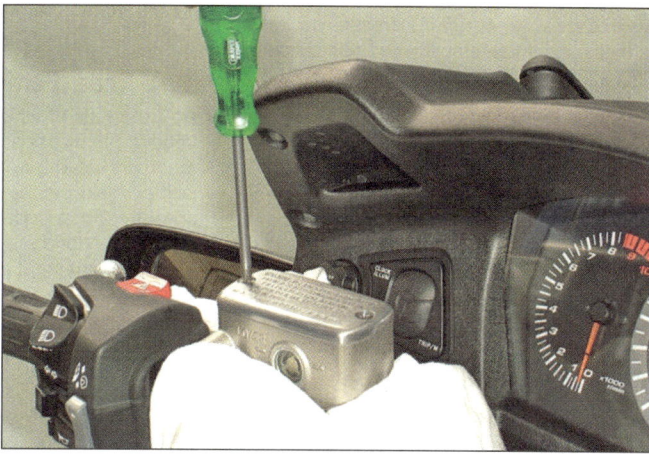

2 If the level is on or below the LOWER line, undo the reservoir cover screws and remove the cover, diaphragm plate and diaphragm.

3 Top up with new clean DOT 4 hydraulic fluid, until the level is up to the upper level line inside the reservoir. Do not overfill and take care to avoid spills (see **Warning** above).

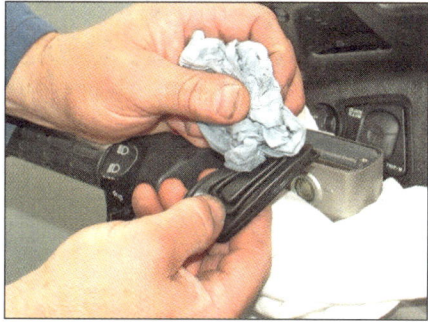

4 Wipe any moisture off the diaphragm with a tissue.

5 Ensure that the diaphragm is correctly seated before installing the plate and cover. Secure the reservoir cover with its screws.

Suspension, steering and final drive

Suspension and Steering:
● Check that the front and rear suspension operates smoothly without binding (see Chapter 1).
● Check that the suspension is adjusted as required (see Chapter 5).
● Check that the steering moves smoothly from lock-to-lock.

Final drive:
● Check for signs of oil leakage around the final drive housing. If any is evident, check the final drive oil level (Chapter 1).

Pre-ride checks

Tyres

The correct pressures:
- The tyres must be checked when **cold**, not immediately after riding. Note that tyre pressure is affected by both ambient temperature and atmospheric pressure and so can change daily.
- Incorrect tyre pressures will cause abnormal tread wear and unsafe handling. An extremely low tyre pressure may cause the tyre to slip on the rim or come off.
- Use an accurate pressure gauge. Many forecourt gauges are wildly inaccurate. If you buy your own, spend as much as you can justify on a quality gauge.
- Proper air pressure will increase tyre life and provide maximum stability and ride comfort.

Front	Rear
42 psi (2.9 Bar)	42 psi (2.9 Bar)

Tyre care:
- Check the tyres carefully for cuts, tears, embedded nails or other sharp objects and excessive wear. Operation of the motorcycle with excessively worn tyres is extremely hazardous, as traction and handling are directly affected.
- Pick out any stones or nails which may have become embedded in the tyre tread. If left, they will eventually penetrate through the casing and cause a puncture.
- Ensure the dust cap is in place. If air escapes when the cap is removed the valve could be loose in its core – a simple tool that is cheaply available and sometimes incorporated in the cap is needed to tighten the valve. Check the condition of the valve.
- If tyre damage is apparent, or unexplained loss of pressure is experienced, seek the advice of a tyre fitting specialist without delay.

Tyre tread depth:
- At the time of writing, UK law requires that tread depth must be at least 1 mm over 3/4 of the tread breadth all the way around the tyre, with no bald patches. Many riders, however, consider 2 mm tread depth minimum to be a safer limit. Honda recommend a minimum of 1.5 mm on the front and 2 mm on the rear, but note that German law requires a minimum of 1.6 mm for each tyre.
- Many tyres now incorporate wear indicators in the tread. Identify the location marking on the tyre sidewall to locate the indicator bar and replace the tyre if the tread has worn down to the bar.

1 Remove the dust cap from the valve. Do not forget to fit the cap after checking the pressure.

2 Check the tyre pressures when cold.

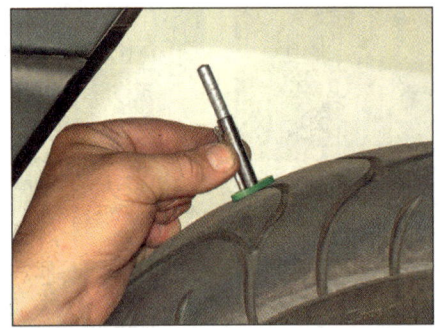

3 Measure tread depth at the centre of the tyre using a depth gauge.

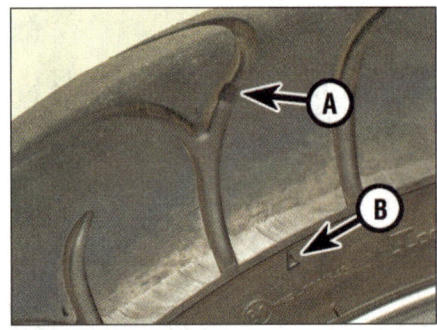

4 Tyre tread wear indicator (A) and its location marking (B) on the edge or sidewall (according to manufacturer).

Legal and safety

Lighting and signalling:
- Take a minute to check that the headlights, tail lights, brake lights, licence plate light, instrument lights and turn signals all work correctly.
- Check that the horn sounds when the button is pressed.
- A working speedometer, graduated in mph, is a statutory requirement in the UK.

Safety:
- Check that the throttle grip rotates smoothly when opened and snaps shut when released, in all steering positions. Also check for the correct amount of freeplay (see Chapter 1).
- Check that the brake lever and pedal, clutch lever and gearchange lever operate smoothly. Lubricate them at the specified intervals or when necessary (see Chapter 1).
- Check that the engine shuts off when the kill switch is operated. Check the starter interlock circuit (see Chapter 1).
- Check that sidestand return springs hold the stand up securely when retracted.

Fuel:
- This may seem obvious, but check that you have enough fuel to complete your journey. If you smell petrol (gasoline) or notice signs of fuel leakage, rectify the cause immediately.
- Ensure you use the correct grade fuel – see Chapter 4 Specifications.

Chapter 1
Routine maintenance and servicing

Contents

	Section
Air filter	18
Battery	21
Brake fluid level check	see *Pre-ride checks*
Brake system	2
Centrestand, sidestand, and starter interlock circuit	12
Clutch	3
Clutch fluid level check	see *Pre-ride checks*
Coolant level check	see *Pre-ride checks*
Cooling system	9
Engine oil and filter	7
Engine oil level check	see *Pre-ride checks*
Engine wear assessment	see Chapter 2
EVAP system (California models)	19

	Section
Final drive gear oil	8
Fuel system	4
Idle speed	1
Headlight aim	11
Nuts and bolts	17
PAIR system	10
Spark plugs	6
Stand, lever pivot and cable lubrication	16
Steering head bearings	14
Suspension	13
Throttle cables	5
Valve clearances	20
Wheels, wheel bearings and tyres	15

Degrees of difficulty

| Easy, suitable for novice with little experience 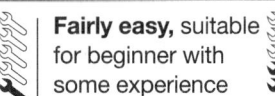 | Fairly easy, suitable for beginner with some experience | Fairly difficult, suitable for competent DIY mechanic | Difficult, suitable for experienced DIY mechanic | Very difficult, suitable for expert DIY or professional 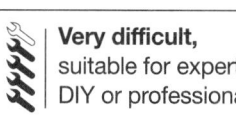 |

1•2 Specifications

Engine

Cylinder numbering	No. 1 – front left; No. 2 – front right; No. 3 – rear left; No. 4 – rear right
Spark plug type	
Standard	NGK CR7EH-9 or Nippondenso U22FER9
For extended high speed riding	NGK CR8EH-9 or Nippondenso U24FER9
Spark plug electrode gap	0.8 to 0.9 mm
Engine idle speed	1000 ± 100 rpm
Valve clearances (COLD engine)	
Intake valves	0.16 ± 0.03 mm
Exhaust valves	0.25 ± 0.03 mm

Cycle parts

Throttle cable freeplay	2 to 6 mm
Tyre pressures (cold)	42 psi (2.9 Bar) front and rear
Steering head bearing pre-load (see text)	9.5 to 14.2 N (0.97 to 1.45 kgf; 2.14 to 3.20 lbf)

Lubricants and fluids

Engine oil type	see *Pre-ride checks*
Engine oil capacity	
Oil change	3.6 litres
Oil and filter change	3.9 litres
Following engine overhaul – dry engine, new filter	4.7 litres
Final drive oil type	SAE 80 Hypoid gear oil
Final drive oil capacity	
Oil change	0.155 litre
Following overhaul	0.175 litre
Coolant type	50% distilled water, 50% corrosion inhibited ethylene glycol anti-freeze
Coolant capacity	
Radiator and engine	2.66 litres
Reservoir	0.86 litre
Brake and clutch fluid	DOT 4
Steering head bearings	Urea based multi-purpose grease with EP2 rating
Swingarm pivot bearings	Multi-purpose grease with EP2 rating
Shock absorber pivot bearings	Multi-purpose grease with EP2 rating
Gearchange lever/rear brake pedal/footrest pivots	Multi-purpose grease with EP2 rating
Gearchange linkage rod ball joints	Multi-purpose grease with EP2 rating
Stand pivots	Multi-purpose grease with EP2 rating
Bearing seal lips	Multi-purpose grease with EP2 rating
Windshield sliders	Multi-purpose grease with EP2 rating
Luggage locking plates	Multi-purpose grease with EP2 rating
Throttle twistgrip	Multi-purpose grease with EP2 rating
Front brake lever pivot and pushrod	Silicone grease
Clutch lever pivot and pushrod	Silicone grease
Brake caliper slider pins and boots	Silicone grease
Rear master cylinder pushrod and boot	Silicone grease
Secondary master cylinder pushrod and boot	Silicone grease
Throttle cables	Cable lubricant

Torque settings

Crankshaft end cap	12 Nm
Engine oil drain plug	29 Nm
Engine oil filter	26 Nm
Final drive oil drain plug	20 Nm
Final drive oil filler cap	12 Nm
Fork clamp bolts (top yoke)	26 Nm
Handlebar end-weight screw	10 Nm
Spark plugs	16 Nm
Steering head bearing adjuster nut	
Initial setting (see text)	25 Nm
Final setting (see text)	
2002 to 2007 models	15 Nm + 45°
2008-on models	29 Nm
Steering stem nut	103 Nm
Timing inspection cap	10 Nm

Maintenance schedule 1•3

Note: *The Pre-ride checks outlined in the owner's manual cover those items which should be inspected before every ride. Also perform the pre-ride inspection at every maintenance interval (in addition to the procedures listed).*

Pre-ride
☐ See 'Pre-ride checks' at the beginning of this manual

After the initial 600 miles (1000 km)
Note: *This check is usually performed by a Honda dealer after the first 600 miles (1000 km) from new. Thereafter, maintenance is carried out according to the following intervals of the schedule.*

Every 4000 miles (6000 km) or 6 months
☐ Check and adjust the engine idle speed (Section 1)
☐ Check the brake pads for wear (Section 2)

Every 8000 miles (12,000 km) or 12 months
Carry out all the items under the 4000 mile (6000 km) check, plus the following:
☐ Check the clutch (Section 3)
☐ Check the fuel system and hoses (Section 4)
☐ Check the throttle cables and adjust if necessary (Section 5)
☐ Check the spark plugs (Section 6)
☐ Change the engine oil and fit a new filter (Section 7)
☐ Check the final drive gear oil level (Section 8)
☐ Check the cooling system (Section 9)
☐ Check the pulse secondary air injection (PAIR) system (Section 10)
☐ Check the brake system and brake light switch operation (Section 2)
☐ Check the headlight beam aim (Section 11)
☐ Check the stands and starter interlock circuit (Section 12)
☐ Check the front and rear suspension (Section 13)
☐ Check the steering head bearings and adjust if necessary (Section 14)
☐ Check the condition of the wheels, wheel bearings and tyres (Section 15)
☐ Lubricate the clutch, gearchange and brake levers, brake pedal, stand pivots, and the throttle cables (Section 16)
☐ Check the tightness of all nuts, bolts and fasteners (Section 17)

Every 12,000 miles (18,000 km) or 18 months
Carry out all the items under the 4000 mile (6000 km) check, plus the following:
☐ Fit a new air filter element (Section 18)
☐ Check the EVAP (evaporative emission control) system (California models only) (Section 19)

Every 12,000 miles (18,000 km) or two years
Carry out all the items under the 4000 mile (6000 km) check, plus the following:
☐ Change the brake fluid and clutch fluid (Sections 2 and 3)

Every 16,000 miles (24,000 km) or two years
Carry out all the items under the 8000 mile (12,000 km) check, plus the following:
☐ Fit new spark plugs (Section 6)
☐ Check the valve clearances and adjust if necessary (Section 20)

Every 24,000 miles (36,000 km) or two years
Carry out all the items under the 12,000 mile (18,000 km) and 8000 mile (12,000 km) checks, plus the following:
☐ Change the coolant (Section 9)

Every 24,000 miles (36,000 km) or three years
Carry out all the items under the 12,000 mile (18,000 km) and 8000 mile (12,000 km) checks, plus the following:
☐ Change the final drive gear oil (Section 8)

Non-scheduled maintenance
☐ Check the battery (Section 21)
☐ Fit new brake and clutch master cylinder and caliper/release cylinder seals (Sections 2 and 3)
☐ Fit new brake and clutch hoses (Sections 2 and 3)
☐ Fit a new fuel filter and clean the strainer (Section 4)
☐ Fit new fuel system hoses (Section 4)
☐ Change the front fork oil (Section 13)
☐ Re-grease the swingarm and shock absorber bearings (Section 13)
☐ Re-grease the steering head bearings (Section 14)

1•4 Component locations

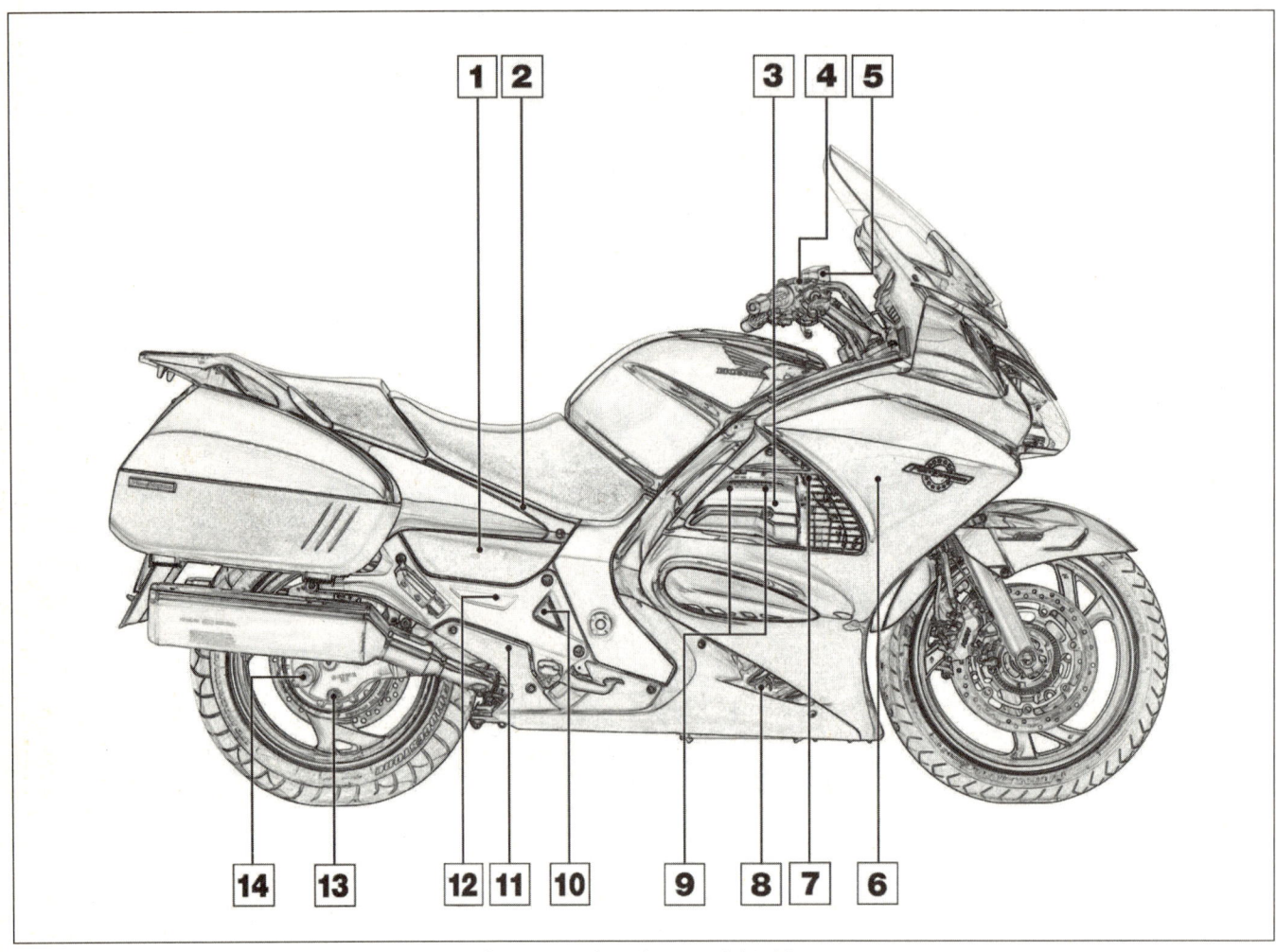

Component locations on right side

1 Battery
2 Rear brake fluid reservoir
3 Engine oil filler cap
4 Throttle cable upper adjuster
5 Front brake fluid reservoir
6 Radiator pressure cap
7 Idle speed adjuster
8 Engine oil level window
9 Spark plugs
10 Rear brake light switch
11 Rear brake pedal height adjuster
12 Rear shock rebound damping adjuster
13 Final drive oil drain bolt
14 Final drive oil filler cap

Component locations 1•5

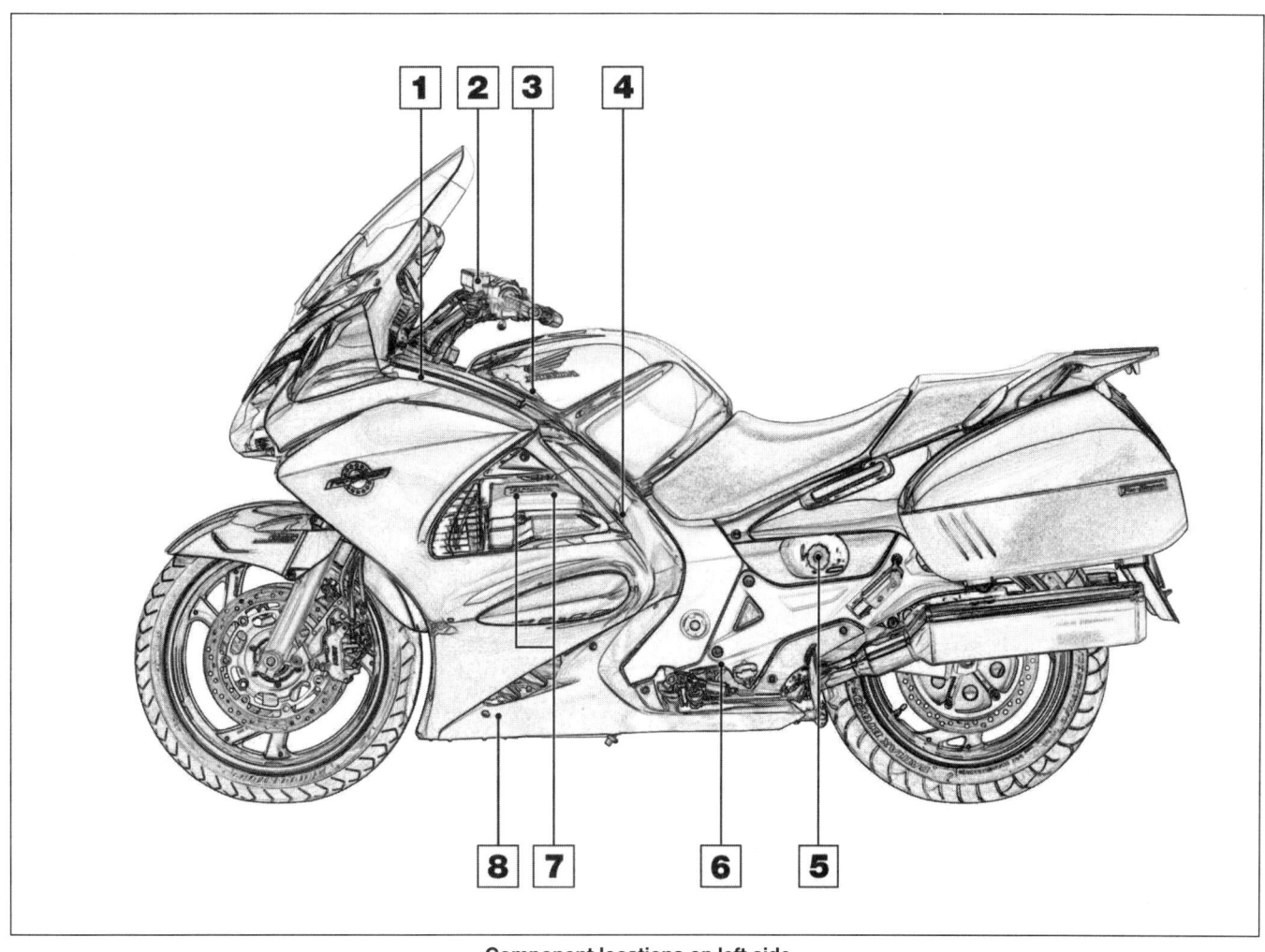

Component locations on left side

1 Steering head bearing adjuster
2 Clutch fluid reservoir
3 Air filter
4 Coolant reservoir
5 Rear shock preload adjuster
6 Engine oil filter
7 Spark plugs
8 Engine oil drain bolt

Introduction

1 This Chapter is designed to help the home mechanic maintain his/her motorcycle for safety, economy, long life and peak performance.

2 Deciding where to start or plug into the routine maintenance schedule depends on several factors. If your motorcycle has been maintained according to the warranty standards and has just come out of warranty, start routine maintenance as it coincides with the next mileage or calendar interval. If you have owned the machine for some time but have never performed any maintenance on it, start at the nearest interval and include some additional procedures to ensure that nothing important is overlooked. If you have just had a major engine overhaul, then start the maintenance routine from the beginning. If you have a used machine and have no knowledge of its history or maintenance record, combine all the checks into one large service initially and then settle into the specified maintenance schedule.

3 Before beginning any maintenance or repair, clean the machine thoroughly, especially around the oil filter, valve covers, body panels, suspension, wheels, etc. Cleaning will help ensure that dirt does not contaminate the engine and will allow you to detect wear and damage that could otherwise easily go unnoticed. If you use a pressure washer make sure you do not direct the jet at wheel bearing and suspension seals and at the steering head, or at any electrical/ignition components and connectors.

4 Certain maintenance information is sometimes printed on labels attached to the motorcycle. If the information on the labels differs from that included here, use the information on the label.

1 Idle speed

Note: *If other engine-related service items are to be carried out (i.e. spark plugs, air filter, valve clearances), do these before checking and adjusting the idle speed.*

1 The engine must be at normal operating temperature when the idle speed is checked. Take the machine for a 10 to 15 minute ride, then place it on its centrestand with the engine running and the transmission in neutral. Check the idle speed shown on the tachometer against the figure specified at the beginning of this Chapter.

2 If adjustment is required, locate the knurled idle speed adjuster knob on the right-hand side of the bike between the valve cover and the grille on the fairing side panel **(see illustration)**. Turn the knob until the engine idles at the speed specified – turn it clockwise to increase idle speed and anti-clockwise to decrease it.

3 Snap the throttle open and shut a few times, then recheck the idle speed and if necessary readjust it.

4 Turn the handlebars from side-to-side and check the idle speed does not change as you do. If it does, the throttle cables may not be adjusted or routed correctly, or may be worn out. This is a dangerous condition that can cause loss of control of the bike. Be sure to correct this problem before proceeding.

5 If a smooth, steady idle can't be achieved check the starter valves (see Chapter 4).

2 Brake system

Brake pad wear check

1 Each brake pad has wear indicators in the form of cut-outs in the friction material. The wear indicators should be plainly visible by looking from below each front caliper, and from behind the rear caliper, but note that an accumulation of road dirt and brake dust could make them difficult to see **(see illustrations)**.

2 If the indicators aren't visible, then the amount of friction material remaining should

1.2 Idle speed adjuster (arrowed)

2.1a Front brake pad wear indicator cut-outs (arrowed)

2.1b Rear brake pad wear indicator cut-out (arrowed)

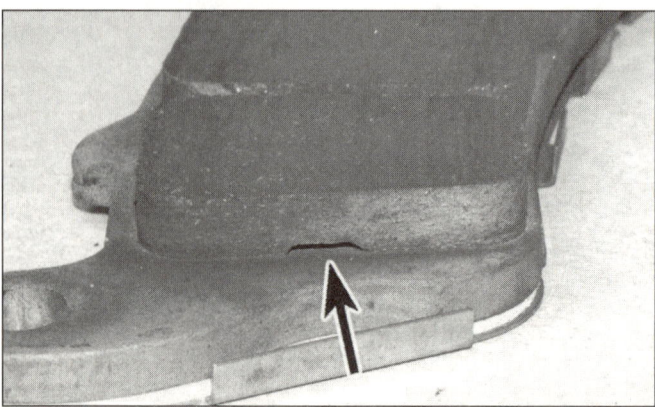

2.1c Close-up of pad wear indicator cut-out (arrowed)

Routine maintenance and servicing

be, and it will be obvious when the pads need replacing. Honda do not specify a minimum thickness for the friction material, but anything less than 1 mm should be considered excessively worn. **Note:** *Some after-market pads may use different indicators to those on the original equipment.* Also check for uneven wear in the front brake pads, which is indicative of a sticking or seized piston. If found, the calipers must be overhauled (see Chapter 6).

3 If the pads are worn to or beyond the beginning of the cut-out, or there is little friction material remaining, they must be replaced with new ones, though it is advisable to fit new pads before they become this worn.

4 If the pads are dirty or if you are in doubt as to the amount of friction material remaining, remove them for inspection (see Chapter 6). If the pads are excessively worn, also check the brake discs (see Chapter 6).

5 Refer to Chapter 6 for details of pad removal and installation.

Brake system check

6 A routine general check of the brake system will ensure that any problems are discovered and remedied before the rider's safety is jeopardised.

7 Check the brake pads for wear (see above) and make sure the fluid level in the reservoirs is correct (see *Pre-ride checks*).

8 Check the brake lever and pedal pivots for sloppy or rough action, excessive play, bends, and other damage. Replace any damaged parts with new ones (see Chapter 5). Clean and lubricate the lever and pedal pivots if their action is stiff or rough (see Section 16). If the lever or pedal is spongy, bleed the brakes (see Chapter 6).

9 Look for leaks at the hose and pipe connections and check for cracks in the hoses, pipes and unions **(see illustration)**. Make sure all brake hose and pipe fasteners are tight.

10 Make sure the brake light operates when the front brake lever is pulled in. The front brake light switch, mounted on the underside of the master cylinder, is not adjustable. If it fails to operate properly, check it (see Chapter 8).

11 Make sure the brake light is activated just before the rear brake takes effect. The rear brake light switch is mounted behind the rubber pad fitted in the right-hand footrest bracket. If adjustment is necessary, remove the rubber pad, then hold the switch body and turn the adjuster ring until the brake light is activated when required – do not turn the switch itself **(see illustrations)**. If the brake light comes on too late or not at all, turn the ring clockwise so the switch is drawn up out of its bracket. If the brake light comes on too soon or is permanently on, turn the ring anti-clockwise so the switch is drawn down into the bracket. If the switch doesn't operate the brake light, check it (see Chapter 8).

12 Place the motorcycle on its centrestand and make sure the transmission is in neutral. Check that the rear wheel is off the ground.

13 Push the top of the left-hand front brake caliper towards the fork so that the secondary master cylinder pushrod is activated **(see illustration)**. Keeping the caliper pushed, check that the rear wheel is locked by the brake. If the wheel can be turned, the linked brake system (known as dual combined brake system or DCBS) is faulty and must be checked (see Chapter 6). Also check that the linkage between the left-hand caliper and the secondary master cylinder pushrod moves smoothly and freely.

14 Raise the front wheel off the ground, either by having an assistant press down on the rear, or by placing a jack under the engine (use a piece of wood between the jack head and the engine to spread the weight, and make sure no contact is made with the lower fairing). Press the rear brake pedal down and check that the front wheel is locked by the brake. If the wheel can be turned, the DCBS system is faulty and must be checked (see Chapter 6).

15 The front brake lever has a span adjuster which alters the distance of the lever from the handlebar. Each setting is identified by a number on the adjuster which aligns with the

2.9 Check all hoses, pipes and unions for cracks and leaks

2.11a Remove the pad . . .

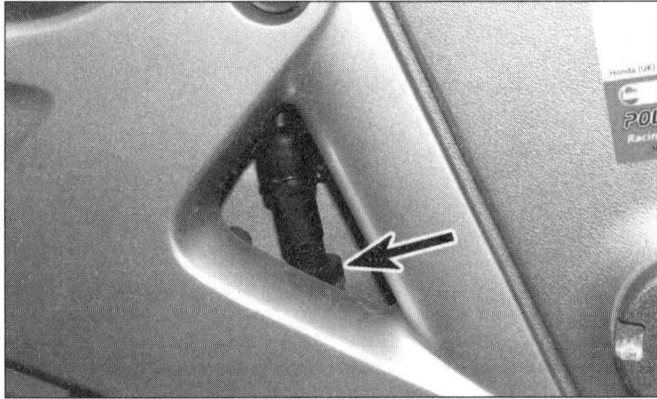

2.11b . . . then turn the adjuster ring (arrowed) as required

2.13 Push the caliper to activate the secondary master cylinder

Routine maintenance and servicing

triangular index mark on the lever. Push the lever away from the handlebar and turn the adjuster ring until the setting which best suits the rider is obtained, then release the lever **(see illustrations)**. Do not set the adjuster between the defined settings.

16 The height of the rear brake pedal can be adjusted to suit the rider's preference if required. Slacken the locknut on the master cylinder pushrod, then turn the pushrod using a spanner on the hex at the top of the rod until the pedal is at the desired height **(see illustration)**. On completion tighten the locknut. Note that Honda specify the distance between the centre of the clevis pin hole and the lower mounting bolt hole measured parallel to the pushrod should be 87 mm, but you need to displace the footrest bracket to do this – refer to Chapter 6, Section 10 if required. Adjust the rear brake light switch after adjusting the pedal height (see Step 11).

Brake fluid change

17 The brake fluid should be changed at the prescribed interval or whenever a master cylinder or caliper overhaul is carried out. Refer to Chapter 6, Section 12 for details. Ensure that all the old fluid is be pumped from the hydraulic system and that the level in the fluid reservoir is checked and the brakes tested before riding the motorcycle.

Brake hoses

18 The flexible hoses will deteriorate with age and should be replaced with new ones regardless of their apparent condition (see Chapter 6).
19 Always replace the banjo union sealing washers with new ones when fitting new hoses. Refill the system with new brake fluid and bleed the system as described in Chapter 6.

Brake caliper and master cylinder seals

20 Brake system seals will deteriorate over a period of time and lose their effectiveness, leading to sticky operation of the brake master cylinders or the pistons in the brake calipers, or fluid loss. Although seal replacement is not subject to a specific time or mileage interval, it is advised after a high mileage has been covered and particularly if fluid leakage or a sticking master cylinder or caliper action is apparent.
21 Replace all the seals in each caliper as a set – a seal kit for each piston in each caliper is available; master cylinder seals are supplied in a rebuild kit for each master cylinder (see Chapter 6).

3 Clutch

Clutch check

1 All models are fitted with an hydraulic clutch. Make sure the fluid level in the reservoir is correct (see *Pre-ride checks*).
2 Check the clutch lever pivot and pushrod for sloppy or rough action, excessive play, bends, and other damage. Replace any damaged parts with new ones (see Chapter 5). Clean and lubricate the lever pivot and pushrod components if its action is stiff or rough (see Section 16).
3 Check the operation of the clutch. If there is evidence of air in the system (spongy feel to the lever, difficulty in engaging gear, drag when in gear), bleed the clutch (see Chapter 2). If the lever feels stiff or sticky, overhaul the release mechanism (see Chapter 2).
4 Look for leaks at the hose connections and check for cracks in the hoses, pipe and their joints – a hose runs from the master cylinder and joins to a section of pipe that runs along the inside of the frame on the left-hand side then to a final short section of hose down to the release cylinder on the back of the engine.

Clutch fluid change

5 The clutch fluid should be changed at the prescribed interval or whenever a master cylinder or release cylinder overhaul is carried out. Refer to Chapter 2 for details. Ensure that all the old fluid is be pumped from the system and that the level in the fluid reservoir is checked and the clutch tested before riding the motorcycle.

Clutch hoses

6 The flexible hoses will deteriorate with age and the hose/pipe (which comes as one complete piece) should be replaced with a new one after a high mileage (see Chapter 2). Also check the bleed pipe and replace that with a new one if necessary.
7 Always replace the banjo union sealing washers with new ones when fitting the new hose. Refill the system with new fluid and bleed the system as described in Chapter 2.

Clutch master and release cylinder seals

8 Clutch release mechanism seals will deteriorate over a period of time and lose their effectiveness, leading to sticky operation of the master cylinder or the piston in the release cylinder, or fluid loss. Although seal replacement is not subject to a specific time or mileage interval, it is advised after a high mileage has been covered and particularly if fluid leakage or poor clutch action is apparent.

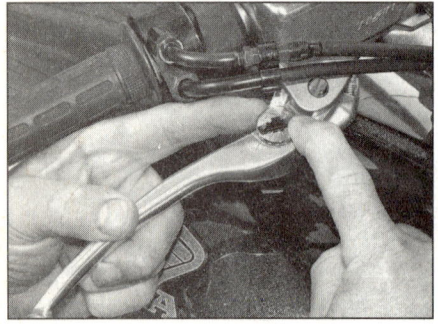

2.15a Pull the lever away and turn the adjuster . . .

2.15b . . . aligning the required setting with the index mark (arrowed)

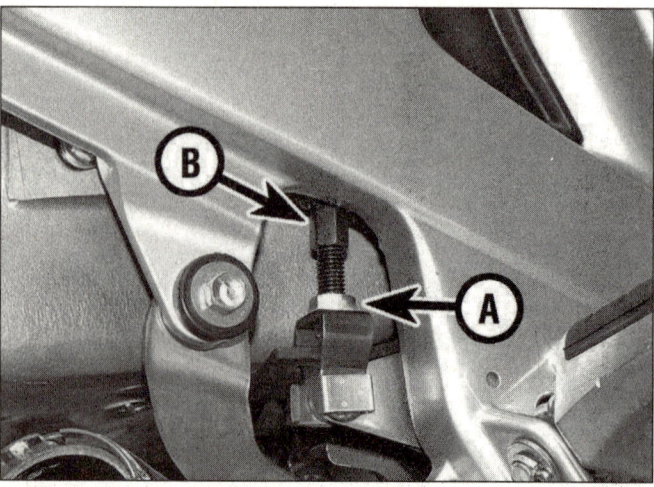

2.16 Slacken the locknut (A) and turn the pushrod using the hex (B) to adjust pedal height

Routine maintenance and servicing

4.2a Check the supply hose (A) and return hose (B) ...

4.2b ... the joint hose (arrowed) ...

9 A rebuild kit for the master cylinder is available; and new seals are available for the release cylinder along with a new piston and spring if necessary (see Chapter 2).

4 Fuel system

Warning: *Petrol (gasoline) is extremely flammable, so take extra precautions when you work on any part of the fuel system. Don't smoke or allow open flames or bare light bulbs near the work area, and don't work in a garage where a natural gas-type appliance is present. If you spill any fuel on your skin, rinse it off immediately with soap and water. When you perform any kind of work on the fuel system, wear safety glasses and have a fire extinguisher suitable for a Class B type fire (flammable liquids) on hand.*

Check fuel system hoses

1 Raise the main fuel tank (see Chapter 4).
2 Check each fuel tank, the fuel supply and return hoses, the joint hose between the tanks, the tank drain and breather hoses, the PAIR system hoses (see Section 10), and on California models the EVAP system hoses (see Section 19), for signs of leaks, deterioration or damage **(see illustrations)**. In particular check that there are no leaks from the fuel hoses or hose unions.
3 Check the joint between the fuel level sensor and the main tank **(see illustration 4.2c)**, and the fuel pump mounting plate and the secondary tank **(see illustration 4.2a)**. If there is evidence of fuel leakage, check the mounting nuts are tightened to the specified torque setting (see Chapter 4). If the leak persists, remove the level sensor or pump as required and fit a new seal (see Chapter 4).
4 Remove the air filter housing (see Chapter 4).
5 Check the fuel supply and return unions on

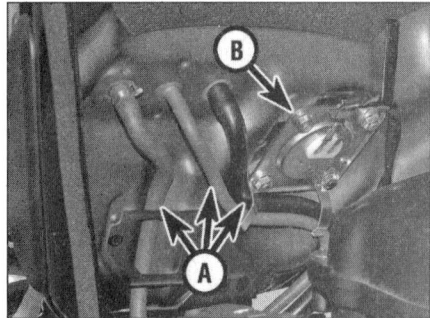

4.2c ... the drain and breather hoses (A) and level sensor joint (B)

the throttle bodies and check the throttle body vacuum hoses and joints and the crankcase breather hose **(see illustration)**. Replace any hose that is cracked or deteriorated with a new one (see Chapter 4).
6 Inspect the joints between the fuel rails, the injectors and the throttle bodies, and the fuel rail connecting pie **(see illustration)**. If there

4.5 Check the supply hose (A), return hose (B), vacuum hoses (C) and crankcase breather hose (D)

4.6 Check the fuel rail-to-injector joints (A) and the fuel rail joint pipe (B)

1•10 Routine maintenance and servicing

are any leaks, remove the fuel rail(s) and fit new seals and O-rings to the injectors and/or pipe as required (see Chapter 4).

Fuel strainer and filter

7 Replacement of the fuel filter and cleaning of the fuel strainer is advised after a particularly high mileage has been covered, although no interval is specified. It is also necessary if fuel starvation is suspected. Remove the pump from the secondary fuel tank to access the filter and strainer (see Chapter 4).

5 Throttle cables

1 Make sure the throttle grip rotates smoothly and freely from fully closed to fully open with the front wheel turned at various angles. The grip should return automatically from fully open to fully closed when released.
2 If the throttle sticks, this is probably due to a cable fault. Remove the cables (see Chapter 4) and lubricate them (see Section 16). Check that the inner cables slide freely and easily in the outer cables. If not, replace the cables with new ones.
3 With the cables removed, make sure the throttle twistgrip rotates freely on the handlebar – dirt combined with a lack of lubrication can cause the action to be stiff. If necessary, undo the handlebar end-weight screw and remove the end-weight, then slide the twistgrip off the handlebar **(see illustration)**. Clean any old grease from the bar and the inside of the tube. Smear some new grease of the specified type (see under Lubricants and fluids at the beginning of the Chapter) onto the bar, then refit the twistgrip. When fitting the end-weight, align the boss with the cut-out on the inner weight inside the handlebar. Clean the threads of the screw, then apply a suitable non-permanent thread locking compound and tighten it to the torque setting specified at the beginning of the Chapter. Install the cables, making sure they are correctly routed (see Chapter 4). If this fails to improve the operation of the throttle, the cables must be replaced with new ones. Note that in very rare cases the fault could lie in the throttle bodies. Remove the air filter housing (see Chapter 4) and check the action of the throttle pulley and linkage.
4 With the throttle operating smoothly, check for a small amount of freeplay in the cables, measured in terms of the amount of twistgrip rotation before the throttle opens, and compare the amount to that listed in this Chapter's Specifications **(see illustration)**. If it's incorrect, adjust the cables to correct it as follows.
5 Initially adjust freeplay using the adjuster in the throttle opening cable where it leaves the throttle pulley housing on the handlebar – first release the cable holder **(see illustration)**. Loosen the locknut and turn the adjuster in or out as required until the specified amount of freeplay is obtained (see this Chapter's Specifications), then retighten the locknut **(see illustration)**.
6 If the adjuster has reached its limit of adjustment, reset it to its start point by turning it fully in, so that freeplay is at a maximum, then remove the air filter housing (see Chapter 4) to access the adjuster at the throttle body end.
7 The adjuster is on the upper cable in the bracket. Slacken the adjuster locknut, then screw the adjuster in or out as required, making sure the captive nut remains held in the bracket, thereby threading itself along the adjuster as you turn it, until the specified amount of freeplay is obtained, then tighten the locknut **(see illustration)**. Subsequent adjustments can be made at the throttle end when required. If the cable cannot be adjusted as specified, replace it with a new one (see Chapter 4). Check that the throttle twistgrip operates smoothly and snaps shut quickly when released.

5.3 Undo the screw (arrowed) to free the end-weight and twistgrip

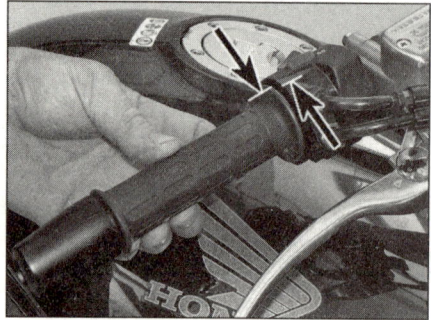

5.4 Throttle cable freeplay is measured in terms of twistgrip rotation

5.5a Release the holder from the adjuster . . .

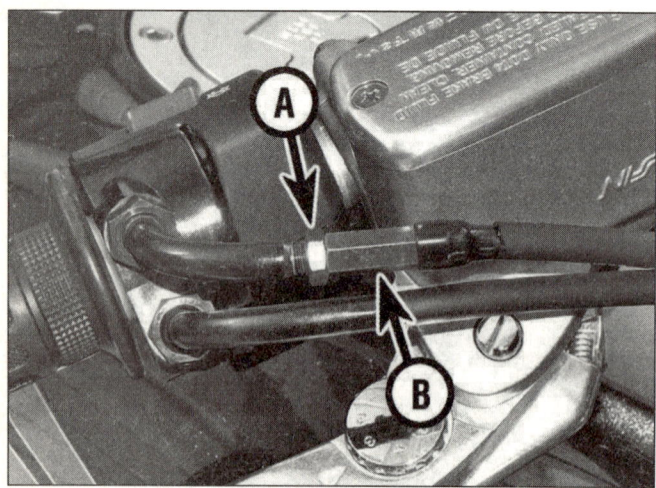

5.5b . . . then slacken the adjuster locknut (A) and turn the adjuster (B) as required

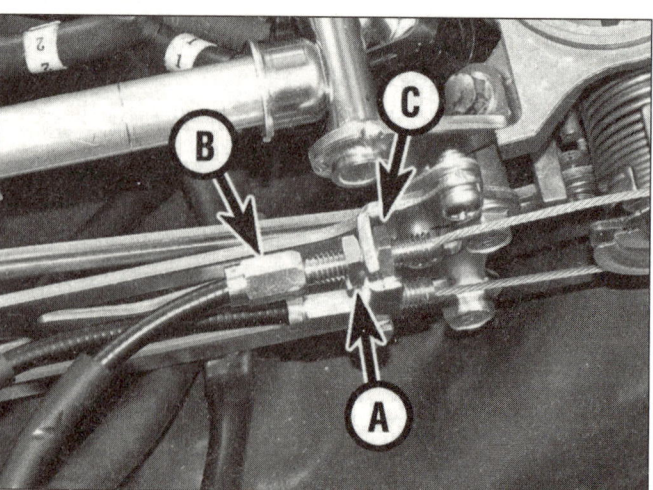

5.7 Throttle cable adjuster locknut (A), adjuster (B) and lower nut (C)

Routine maintenance and servicing

6.4 Pull the cap off the plug

6.5a Unscrew the plug . . .

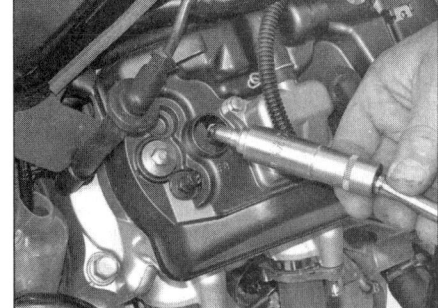

6.5b . . . and lift it out with the tool – the rubber insert should grip around the plug top

6 Spark plugs

Check

1 Make sure your spark plug socket is the correct size before attempting to remove the plugs – a suitable one is supplied in the motorcycle's tool kit which is stored under the passenger seat.

2 Remove the fairing side panels, then remove the trim cover from the top of the valve cover (see Chapter 7).

3 Clean the area around each spark plug cap to prevent any dirt falling into the spark plug channels.

4 Pull the cap off each spark plug **(see illustration)**.

5 Using either the plug removing tool supplied in the bike's toolkit or a deep spark plug socket and extension, unscrew and remove the plugs from the cylinder head **(see illustrations)**. Lay each plug out in relation to its cylinder; if any plug shows up a problem it will then be easy to identify the troublesome cylinder.

6 Before cleaning the plugs refer to the colour spark plug chart at the end of this manual and compare your plugs to those shown, identifying any abnormal condition and assessing its cause if necessary.

7 Clean the electrodes using a wire brush – if any deposits do not come off, replace the plugs with new ones. Cleaning spark plugs by sandblasting is fine as long as you clean the plugs with a high flash-point solvent afterwards. Also clean any deposits off the white ceramic body of the plug.

8 Check the condition of the cleaned electrodes. Both the centre and side electrodes should have square edges and the side electrodes should be of uniform thickness. Check for evidence of a cracked or chipped insulator around the centre electrode. Check the plug threads, the washer and the ceramic insulator body for cracks and other damage.

9 If in doubt concerning the condition of the plugs, replace them with new ones, as the expense is minimal.

10 If the plugs can be re-used check the gap between the electrodes with a wire type gauge or feeler gauge **(see illustration)**. The gap should be as given in the Specifications at the beginning of this chapter. If the electrodes have worn and the gap is wider than it should be, or for some reason the gap is narrower than it should be (if the plug has been dropped for instance) carefully bend the outer electrode as required to restore the correct gap **(see illustration)**.

11 Fit the plug into the end of the tool, then use the tool to insert the plug **(see illustration 6.5b)**. Alternatively there are dedicated plug insertion tools **(see illustration)**, or you can use some hose (see Haynes Hint). Thread the plugs as far as possible into the head turning the tool or hose by hand, making sure they do not cross-thread. Once the plugs are finger-tight, tighten them using a spanner on the tool supplied or a socket drive **(see illustration 6.5a)**. If a torque wrench can be applied, tighten the spark plugs to the torque setting specified at the beginning of the Chapter. Otherwise, if new plugs are being used tighten them by 1/2 a turn after the washer has seated, and if the old plugs are being reused tighten them by 1/8 to 1/4 turn after they have seated. Do not over-tighten them.

HAYNES HiNT

As the plugs are quite recessed, slip a short length of hose over the end of the plug to use as a tool to thread it into place. The hose will grip the plug well enough to turn it, but will start to slip if the plug begins to cross-thread in the hole – this will prevent damaged threads.

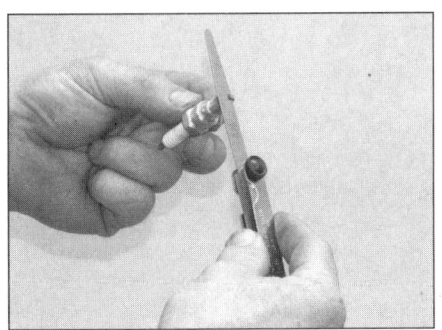

6.10a Using a feeler blade to measure the spark plug electrode gap

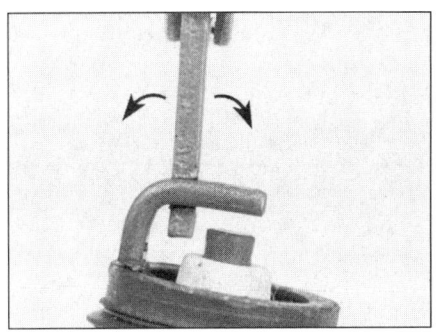

6.10b Adjusting the electrode gap

6.11 Using a proper tool to insert the spark plug

1•12 Routine maintenance and servicing

12 Fit the caps onto the plugs and push them down so they are fully seated (see illustration 6.4).
13 Fit the trim cover onto the valve cover and install the fairing side panels (see Chapter 7).

 Haynes Hint: *Stripped plug threads in the cylinder head can be repaired with a thread insert – see 'Tools and Workshop Tips' in the Reference section.*

Renewal

14 At the prescribed interval, whatever the condition of the existing spark plugs, remove the plugs as described above and install new ones.

7 Engine oil and filter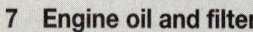

Special tool: *A filter removing tool is necessary for this job. Honda can supply one, either as a kit along with the oil filter or separately, or alternatively there are several after-market options.*

 Warning: *Be careful when draining the oil, as the exhaust pipes, the engine, and the oil itself can cause severe burns.*

1 Consistent routine oil and filter changes are the single most important maintenance procedure you can perform. The oil not only lubricates the internal parts of the engine, transmission and clutch, but it also acts as a coolant, a cleaner, a sealant, and a protector. Because of these demands, the oil takes a terrific amount of abuse and should be replaced often with new oil of the recommended grade and type. The oil filter should be changed with every oil change.

 **Haynes Hint:** *Saving a little money on the difference in cost between a good oil and a cheap oil won't pay off if the engine is damaged.*

7.4 Unscrew the oil filler cap to act as a vent

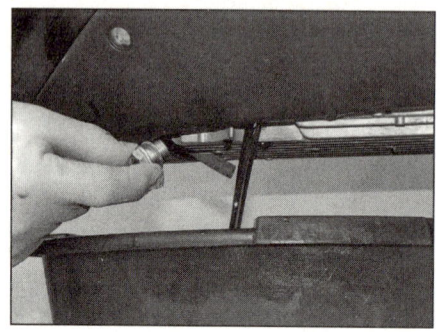
7.5b . . . and allow the oil to completely drain

2 Before changing the oil, warm up the engine so the oil will drain easily. Place the bike on its centrestand on level ground. If preferred (to avoid the possibility of damage) remove the lower fairing (see Chapter 7). The oil drain plug is in the bottom of the sump under the engine, and the filter is at the back of the engine on the left-hand side.
3 Remove the access panel from the right-hand fairing side panel and the trim cover from the top of the valve cover (see Chapter 7).
4 Unscrew the oil filler cap from the valve cover to vent the crankcase and to act as a reminder that there is no oil in the engine (see illustration).
5 Position a clean drain tray below the engine. Unscrew the oil drain plug and allow the oil to flow into the tray (see illustrations). Check the condition of the sealing washer and

7.5a Unscrew the oil drain plug (arrowed) . . .

7.5c Depending on the type the sealing washer may need to be cut off

replace it with a new one if necessary, though it is advisable to use a new one whatever its condition (see illustration).
6 When the oil has completely drained, fit the sealing washer onto the plug if removed, preferably using a new one, then fit the plug into the sump, and tighten it to the torque setting specified at the beginning of the Chapter (see illustration). Do not overtighten it as the threads in the sump are easily damaged.
7 Now place the drain tray below the oil filter. Unscrew the filter using a filter socket (one can be obtained with the new filter from Honda dealers under part No. 07HAA-PJ70101, or otherwise there are commercially available equivalents available), filter pliers, or a filter removing strap or a chain-wrench, and tip any residual oil into the drain tray (see illustrations). The filter socket is preferable

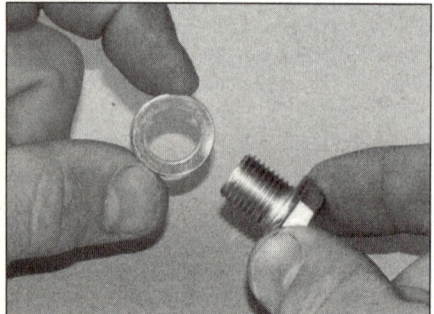
7.6 It is best to use a new sealing washer

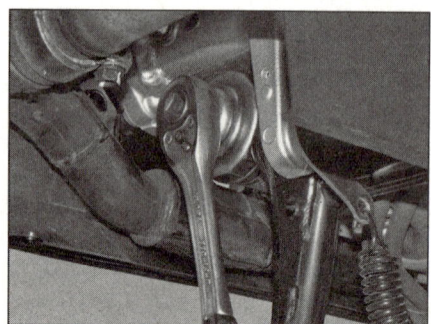
7.7a Unscrew the filter using a filter removing socket or strap . . .

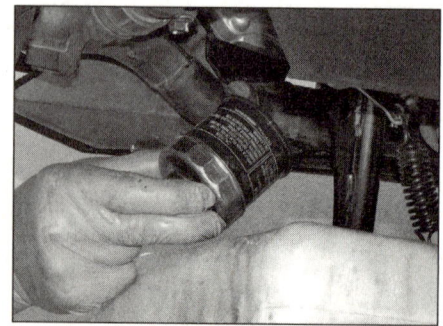
7.7b . . . and allow the oil to drain

Routine maintenance and servicing 1•13

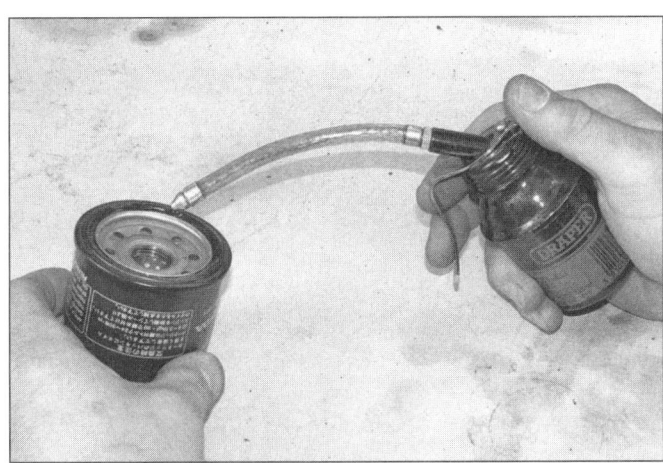

7.8a Smear clean oil onto the seal . . .

7.8b . . . then fit the filter and tighten it as described

because it provides a means of tightening the new filter to the correct torque.

8 Smear clean engine oil onto the rubber seal on the new filter and thread the filter onto the engine **(see illustrations)**. Tighten it to the specified torque setting using the filter socket if available, or tighten the filter as tight as possible by hand, or by the number of turns specified on the filter itself or its packaging. **Note:** *Do not use a strap or chain-type filter removing tool to tighten the filter as you will damage it.*

9 Refill the engine to the proper level using the recommended type and amount of oil (see Specifications) **(see illustration)**. With the motorcycle vertical, the oil level should lie between the upper and lower level lines on the inspection window **(see illustration)**. Check the condition of the O-ring on the filler cap and replace it with a new one if it is damaged or worn **(see illustration)**. Fit the filler cap.

10 Start the engine and let it run for two or three minutes (make sure that the oil pressure light extinguishes after a few seconds). Shut it off, wait a few minutes, then check the oil level again. If necessary, add more oil to bring the level close to the upper line, but do not go above it.

11 Check around the drain plug and the filter for leaks. If leaks are evident, and the plug and filter are correctly tightened using a new washer and a lubricated seal, there is another cause which must be investigated before riding the bike.

12 Fit the trim cover onto the valve cover and the access panel onto the fairing side panel, and the lower fairing if removed (see Chapter 7).

13 The old oil drained from the engine cannot be re-used and should be disposed of properly. Check with your local refuse disposal company, disposal facility or environmental agency to see whether they will accept the used oil for recycling. Don't pour used oil into drains or onto the ground.

> **HAYNES HiNT** *Check the old oil carefully – if it is very metallic coloured, then the engine is experiencing wear from break-in (new engine) or from insufficient lubrication. If there are flakes or chips of metal in the oil, then something is drastically wrong internally and the engine will have to be disassembled for inspection and repair. If there are pieces of fibre-like material in the oil, the clutch is experiencing excessive wear and should be checked.*

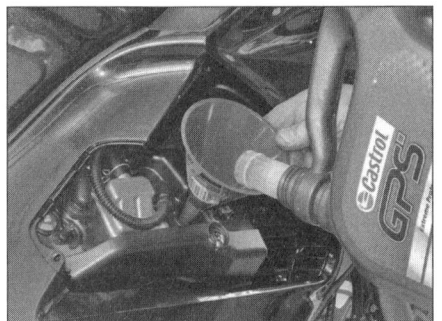

7.9a Add the specified type and amount of oil . . .

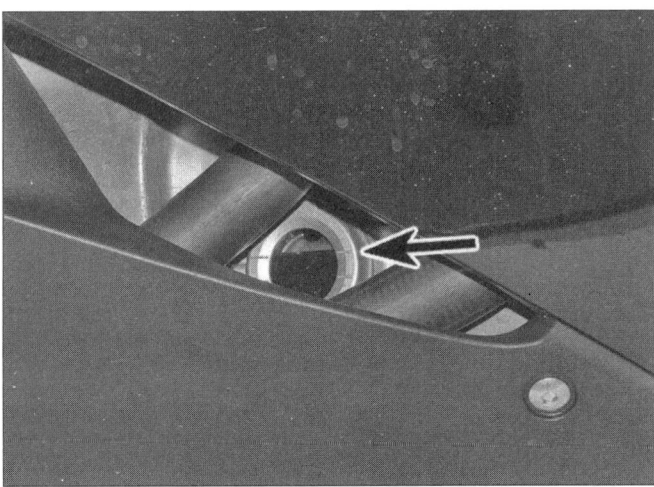

7.9b . . . so the level is almost up to the upper level line (arrowed)

7.9c Make sure the O-ring (arrowed) is in place and in good condition

1•14 Routine maintenance and servicing

8.2a Unscrew the filler cap (arrowed)

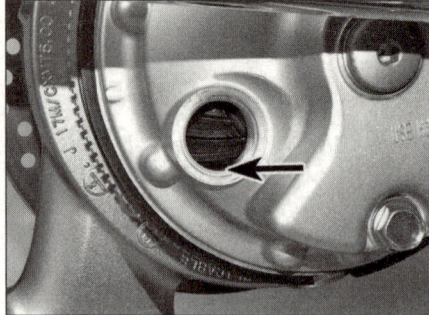

8.2b The oil should come up to the bottom edge (arrowed)

8.3 Fit a new O-ring (arrowed) and smear it with oil

8.5 Unscrew the drain plug and drain the oil

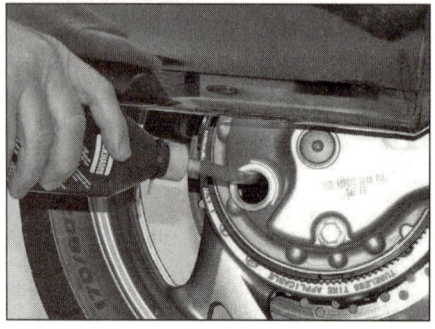

8.7 Add the specified oil up to the lower edge of the hole

7 Pour the gear oil specified at the beginning of the Chapter into the filler hole until it is up to the lower edge of the hole **(see illustration)**.
8 Fit the filler cap using a new O-ring smeared with clean oil, and tighten it to the specified torque setting **(see illustration 8.3)**.

9 Cooling system

Check

⚠️ *Warning: The engine must be cool before beginning this procedure.*

1 Check the coolant level in the reservoir (see *Pre-ride checks*).
2 Remove the fairing side panels (see Chapter 7). Check the entire cooling system for evidence of leaks. Examine each rubber coolant hose along its entire length. Look for cracks, abrasions and other damage. Squeeze each hose at various points to see whether they are dried out or hard **(see illustration)**. They should feel firm, yet pliable, and return to their original shape when released. If necessary, replace them with new ones (see Chapter 3).
3 Check for evidence of leaks at each cooling system hose connection, and around the pump on the front of the engine, at the outlet union on each cylinder head, at the thermostat housing between the cylinders, and around the oil cooler on the back of the engine. Tighten the hose clips carefully to prevent future leaks. If the pump is leaking around the cover, check that the bolts are tight. If they are, remove the cover and replace the O-ring with a new one (see Chapter 3).
4 To prevent leakage of coolant from the cooling system to the lubrication system and vice versa, two seals are fitted on the pump shaft. The coolant seal on the water pump side is of the mechanical type which bears on the rear face of the impeller. The oil seal, which is mounted behind the mechanical seal is of the normal feathered lip type. On the side of the pump housing there is a drain hole (2002 to 2007 models) or hose (2008-on models) **(see illustration)**. If either seal fails, the drain allows the coolant or oil to escape. If on inspection

8 Final drive gear oil

Level check

1 Place the motorcycle on its centrestand on level ground.
2 The check should be made after the machine has been standing for a few hours. Unscrew the oil filler cap and check that the oil is up to the lower edge of the filler hole **(see illustrations)**. If the level is below this, look for signs of leakage, such as oil staining on the underside of the casing. If leakage is evident, the problem must be rectified to avoid the possibility of damage to the final drive and oil contaminating the rear tyre (see Chapter 6).
3 Replenish the oil if necessary to the correct level using the type and grade specified at the beginning of the Chapter **(see illustration 8.7)**. Fit the filler cap using a new O-ring smeared with clean oil, and tighten it to the torque setting specified at the beginning of the Chapter **(see illustration)**.

Oil change

4 Place the motorcycle on its centrestand on level ground.
5 Place a drain tray under the drain plug in the final drive housing. Unscrew the filler cap **(see illustration 8.2a)**. Unscrew the drain plug and allow the oil to drain into the pan **(see illustration)**.
6 Check the condition of the drain plug sealing washer and replace it with a new one if necessary, though it is advisable to use a new one whatever its condition. Fit the plug and tighten it to the torque setting specified at the beginning of the Chapter **(see illustration 8.5)**.

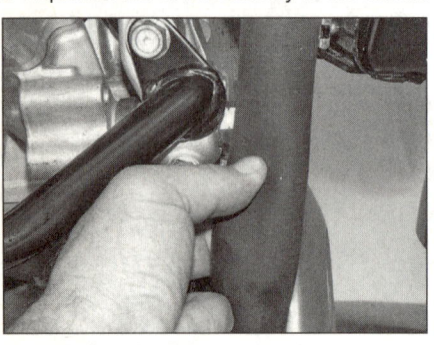

9.2 Check all the coolant hoses as described

9.4 Check the pump drain hole or hose (arrowed) for signs of leakage

Routine maintenance and servicing

the drain shows signs of leakage, remove the pump and replace the seals and bearing with new ones (see Chapter 3).

5 Check the radiator on the front of the engine for leaks and other damage **(see illustration)**. Leaks in the radiator leave tell-tale scale deposits or coolant stains on the outside of the core below the leak. If leaks are noted, remove the radiator (see Chapter 3) and have it repaired or replace it with a new one – do not use a liquid leak stopping compound to try to repair leaks.

6 Check the radiator fins for mud, dirt and insects, which may impede the flow of air through it. If the fins are dirty, remove the radiator (see Chapter 3) and clean it using water or low pressure compressed air directed through the fins from the inner side of the radiator. If the fins are bent or distorted, straighten them carefully with a screwdriver. If the air flow is restricted by bent or damaged fins over more than 20% of the radiator's surface area, replace the radiator with a new one.

 Warning: Do not remove the pressure cap when the engine is hot. It is good practice to cover the cap with a heavy cloth and turn the cap slowly anti-clockwise. If you hear a hissing sound (indicating that there is still pressure in the system), wait until it stops, then continue turning the cap until it can be removed.

7 Remove the pressure cap from the radiator filler neck by turning it anti-clockwise until it reaches the stop. Now press down on the cap and continue turning it until it can be removed **(see illustration)**.

8 Check the condition of the coolant in the system. If it is rust-coloured or if accumulations of scale are visible, drain, flush and refill the system with new coolant (see below). Check the antifreeze content of the coolant with an antifreeze hydrometer. The system must have the correct coolant mixture (see Specifications) – if the coolant is too weak (too little anti-freeze) there will not be adequate protection against freezing and corrosion, and if it is too strong the ability to cool the engine is reduced. If the hydrometer indicates an incorrect mixture, drain, flush and refill the system (see below).

9 Check the cap seal for cracks and other

9.5 Check the radiator and fins as described

damage. If in doubt about the pressure cap's condition, have it tested by a Honda dealer or fit a new one.

10 Fit the cap by turning it clockwise until it reaches the first stop then push down on it and continue turning until it can turn no further. Start the engine and let it reach normal operating temperature, then check for leaks again. As the coolant temperature increases, the electric fans (mounted on the back of the radiator) should come on automatically and the temperature should begin to drop. If they do not, refer to Chapter 3 and check the fans and fan circuit.

11 If the coolant level is consistently low, and no evidence of leaks can be found, have the entire system pressure checked by a Honda dealer.

12 Check the oil cooler on the back of the engine (between the oil filter and the crankcase) for any signs of oil leakage between it and the engine **(see illustration)**. If there is leakage remove the oil filter (see Section 7) and check the cooler bolt is tight. If the leakage persists you will have to fit a new O-ring between the cooler and the engine (see Chapter 2). Check that the coolant hoses are secure on the unions, and that there is no evidence of coolant leakage from the body of the cooler. If there is, the cooler is damaged and must be replaced with a new one.

Change the coolant

 Warning: Allow the engine to cool completely before performing this maintenance operation. Also,

9.7 Remove the pressure cap as described

don't allow anti-freeze to come into contact with your skin or the painted surfaces of the motorcycle. Rinse off spills immediately with plenty of water. Anti-freeze is highly toxic if ingested. Never leave anti-freeze lying around in an open container or in puddles on the floor; children and pets are attracted by its sweet smell and may drink it. Check with local authorities (councils) about disposing of anti-freeze. Many communities have collection centres which will see that anti-freeze is disposed of safely. Anti-freeze is also combustible, so don't store it near open flames.

Draining

13 Place the motorcycle on its centrestand on level ground. Remove the fairing side panels (see Chapter 7).

14 Remove the pressure cap from the top of the radiator by covering it with a heavy cloth and turning it anti-clockwise until it reaches a stop **(see illustration 9.7)**. If you hear a hissing sound (indicating there is still pressure in the system), wait until it stops. Now press down on the cap and continue turning the cap until it can be removed. Also remove the coolant reservoir cap.

15 Position a suitable container beneath the water pump on the right-hand side of the engine. Slacken the coolant inlet hose clamp, then pull the hose off its union and allow the coolant to completely drain **(see illustrations)**.

16 Reposition the container so it is below the right-hand cylinder block. Unscrew the

9.12 Check the oil cooler (arrowed) for leaks and damage

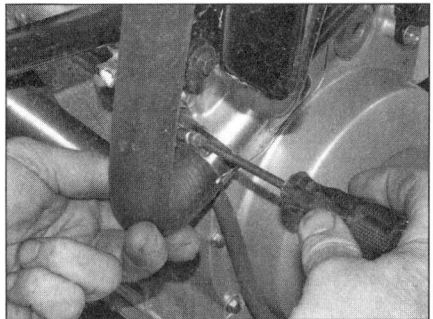

9.15a Slacken the clamp . . .

9.15b . . . then detach the hose and allow the coolant to drain

1•16 Routine maintenance and servicing

9.16a Unscrew the bolt (arrowed)...

9.16b ...and drain the block

cylinder drain bolt and allow the block to drain **(see illustrations)**. A new sealing washer is needed, but keep the old one for use during flushing if required.

17 Now place the container on the left-hand side of the engine and drain the left-hand cylinder block in the same way **(see illustration)**.

18 Finally place the tray below the reservoir. Disconnect the radiator overflow hose from the bottom of the reservoir and allow the reservoir to drain into the container **(see illustration)**.

Flushing

19 Flush the system with clean tap water by inserting a hose in the radiator filler neck. Allow the water to run through the system until it is clear and flows out cleanly. If the radiator is extremely corroded, remove it (see Chapter 3) and have it cleaned by a specialist. Also flush the reservoir, then fit the hose back onto its union.

20 Clean the drain hole in each cylinder block then fit the drain bolts using the old sealing washers. Reconnect the inlet hose to the pump and tighten the clamp.

21 Fill the cooling system via the radiator with clean water mixed with a flushing compound **(see illustration 9.27)**. Make sure the flushing compound is compatible with aluminium components, and follow the manufacturer's instructions carefully. Fit the radiator cap.

22 Start the engine and allow it to reach normal operating temperature. Let it run for about ten minutes.

23 Stop the engine. Let it cool for a while, then cover the pressure cap with a heavy rag and turn it anti-clockwise to the first stop, releasing any pressure that may be present in the system. Once the hissing stops, push down on the cap and remove it completely.

24 Drain the system once again.

25 Fill the system with clean water and repeat Steps 22 to 24.

Refilling

26 Fit the cylinder drain bolts using new sealing washers and tighten them. Reconnect the inlet hose to the pump and tighten the clamp **(see illustration 9.15a)**. Fit the reservoir hose back onto its union and seat the clamp **(see illustration 9.18)**.

27 Fill the system to the base of the radiator filler neck with the proper coolant mixture (see this Chapter's Specifications) **(see illustration)**. **Note:** *Pour the coolant in slowly to minimise the amount of air entering the system, and when full carefully waggle the bike from side to side to dislodge any trapped air.* Fill the reservoir to the UPPER level line (see *Pre-ride checks*).

28 Start the engine and allow it to idle for 2 to 3 minutes. Flick the throttle twistgrip part open 3 or 4 times, so that the engine speed rises to approximately 4000 to 5000 rpm, then stop the engine. Any air trapped in the system should bleed back to the radiator filler neck.

29 If necessary, top up the coolant level to the base of the radiator filler neck, then install the pressure cap. Also top up the coolant reservoir to the UPPER level line.

30 Start the engine and allow it to reach normal operating temperature, then shut it off. Let the engine cool then remove the pressure cap as described in Step 14. Check that the coolant level is still up to the base of the upper radiator filler neck. If it's low, add the specified mixture until it reaches the base of the filler neck. Refit the cap.

31 Check the coolant level in the reservoir and top up if necessary.

32 Check the system for leaks. Install the fairing panels (see Chapter 7).

33 Do not dispose of the old coolant by pouring it down the drain. Instead pour it into a heavy plastic container, cap it tightly and take it into an authorised disposal site or service station – see **Warning** on page 0•15.

Hose renewal

34 The hoses will deteriorate with age and should be replaced with new ones regardless of their apparent condition (see Chapter 3).

9.17 Left-hand cylinder drain bolt (arrowed)

9.18 Detach the hose (arrowed) and allow the reservoir to drain

9.27 Fill the system and bleed it as described

Routine maintenance and servicing 1•17

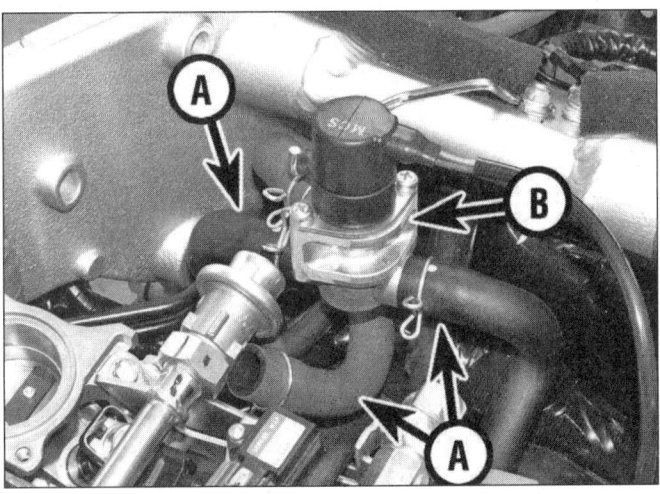

10.3 Check the PAIR system hoses (A) as described. PAIR control valve (B)

11.2 Vertical adjuster (arrowed) – both beam units

10 PAIR (Pulse secondary air supply) system

1 To reduce the amount of unburned hydrocarbons released in the exhaust gases, a pulse secondary air supply (PAIR) system is fitted. The system consists of the control valve (mounted behind the air filter housing), the reed valves (fitted in the valve cover) and the hoses linking them. The control valve is actuated electronically by the ECM.

2 Under normal operating conditions, the valve allows filtered air to be drawn through the reed valves and cylinder head passages and into the exhaust ports. The air mixes with the exhaust gases, causing any unburned particles of the fuel in the mixture to be burnt in the exhaust port/pipes. This process changes a considerable amount of hydrocarbons and carbon monoxide into relatively harmless carbon dioxide and water. The reed valves in the valve cover are fitted to prevent the flow of exhaust gases back up the cylinder head passages and into the air filter housing.

3 The system is not adjustable and requires little maintenance. Raise the main fuel tank (see Chapter 4). Check that the hoses are not kinked or pinched, are in good condition and are securely connected at each end (see illustration). Replace any hoses that are cracked, split or generally deteriorated with new ones.

4 Refer to Chapter 4 for further information on the system and for checks if it is believed to be faulty.

11 Headlight aim

Note: *An improperly adjusted headlight may cause problems for oncoming traffic or provide poor, unsafe illumination of the road ahead. Before adjusting the headlight aim, be sure to consult with local traffic laws and regulations – for UK models refer to MOT Test Checks in the Reference section.*

1 The headlight beam can adjusted both horizontally and vertically. Before making any adjustment, check that the tyre pressures are correct and the suspension is adjusted as required. Make any adjustments to the headlight aim with the machine on level ground, with the fuel tank half full and with an assistant sitting on the seat. If the bike is usually ridden with a passenger on the back, have a second assistant to do this.

2 Vertical adjustment is made by turning the adjuster knob on the left-hand side of the cockpit with the ignition on (see illustration). Turn it clockwise to move the beam up, and anti-clockwise to move it down. If the adjuster does not operate refer to Chapter 8 to check it.

3 Horizontal adjustment is made by turning the adjuster knob on the bottom outer corner of the relevant beam unit (see illustration).

12 Centrestand, sidestand and starter interlock circuit

1 Check the stand springs for damage and distortion (see illustrations). The springs must be capable of retracting the stand fully and holding it retracted when the motorcycle is in use. If a spring is sagged or broken it must be replaced with a new one.

2 Lubricate the stand pivots regularly (see Section 16).

3 Check the stand and its mount(s) for bends and cracks. Stands can often be repaired by welding.

4 Check the operation of the starter interlock circuit as follows:

● Make sure the transmission is in neutral, then retract the stand and start the engine.

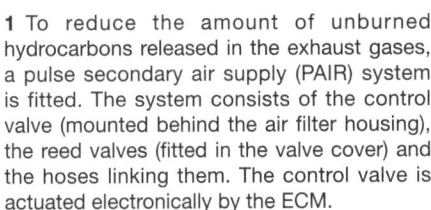

11.3 Horizontal adjuster (arrowed) – right-hand beam unit

12.1a Check the sidestand springs (arrowed) . . .

12.1b . . . and the centrestand springs (arrowed) as described

1•18 Routine maintenance and servicing

Pull in the clutch lever and select a gear. Keeping the clutch lever pulled in, extend the sidestand. The engine should stop as the sidestand is extended.
- Make sure the engine is in neutral and the sidestand is down, then start the engine. Pull the clutch lever in and select a gear. The engine should cut out.
- Check that when the sidestand is down the engine can only be started if the transmission is in neutral, and when the sidestand is up and the transmission is in gear the engine can only be started if the clutch lever is pulled in.

5 If the circuit does not operate as described, check the sidestand switch, neutral switch, clutch switch and diodes, and the circuit between them (see Chapter 8).

13 Suspension

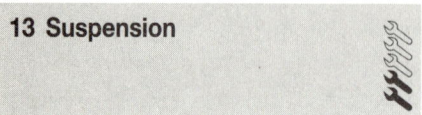

1 The suspension components must be maintained in top operating condition to ensure rider safety. Loose, worn or damaged suspension parts decrease the motorcycle's stability and control.

Front suspension check

2 While standing alongside the motorcycle, apply the front brake and push on the handlebars to compress the forks several times. See if they move up-and-down smoothly without binding **(see illustration)**. If binding is felt, the forks should be disassembled and inspected (see Chapter 5).
3 Inspect the length of each fork inner tube for scratches, corrosion and pitting, which will cause seal failure **(see illustration)** – if the damage is excessive, new inner tubes should be fitted (see Chapter 5).
4 Inspect the area above the dust seal for signs of oil leakage **(see illustration)**. Carefully lever the seal up using a flat-bladed screwdriver and inspect the area around the oil seal. If leakage is evident, the seals must be replaced with new ones (see Chapter 5). If there is evidence of corrosion between the oil seal retaining ring and its groove in the fork tube, spray the area with a penetrative lubricant, otherwise the ring will be difficult to remove if needed. Press the dust seal back into the top of the outer tube on completion.
5 Check the tightness of all suspension nuts and bolts to be sure none have worked loose, referring to the torque settings specified at the beginning of Chapter 5.

Rear suspension check

6 Inspect the rear shock absorber for fluid leakage. If leakage is found, the shock must be replaced with a new one (see Chapter 5).
7 With the aid of an assistant to support the bike, compress the rear suspension several times. It should move up-and-down freely without binding. If any binding is felt, the worn or faulty component must be identified and checked (see Chapter 5). The problem could be due to either the shock absorber, the shock mount bearing, or the swingarm pivots.
8 Place the motorcycle on its centrestand so that the rear wheel is off the ground. Grab the swingarm and final drive housing and rock the swingarm from side-to-side – there should be no discernible movement at the rear.
9 Next, grasp the top of the rear wheel and pull it upwards **(see illustration)** – there should be no discernible freeplay before the shock absorber begins to compress.

13.2 Compress the forks to check their action

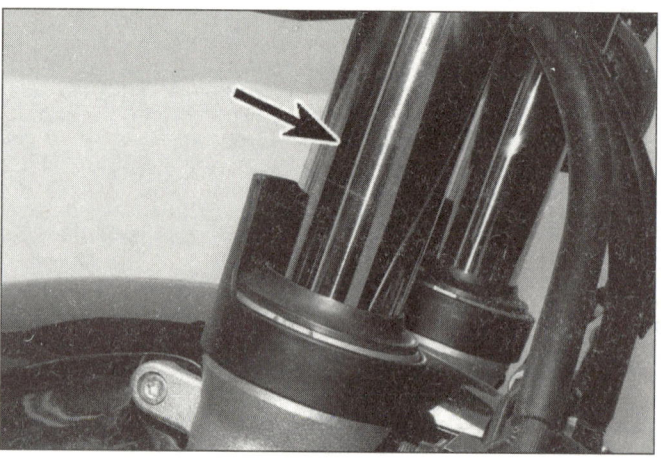

13.3 Check the fork inner tube surface (arrowed) for corrosion and pitting

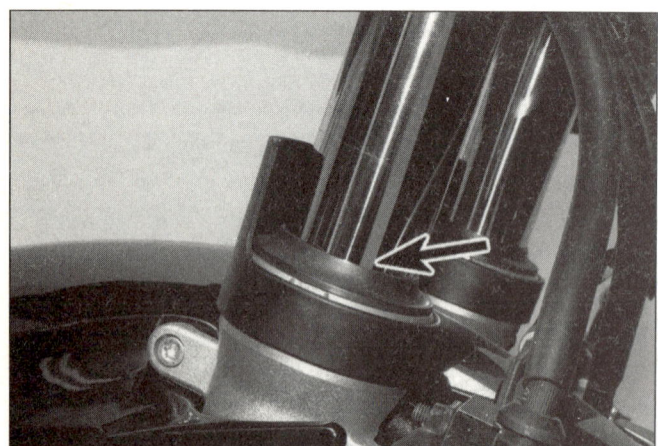

13.4 Check for leakage above the dust seal (arrowed), then lever it up and check for corrosion below

13.9 Checking for play in the rear shock mountings

Routine maintenance and servicing

10 If there's a little movement or a slight clicking can be heard, check the tightness of the swingarm pivots, referring to the procedure in Chapter 5, and re-check for movement. Also check the shock absorber mounting bolts/nuts. If there is still some noise or freeplay after everything has been correctly tightened then there is either a worn bush or bearing in the shock absorber mountings, or worn swingarm bearings. The worn components must be identified and replaced with new ones (see Chapter 5).

11 To make an accurate assessment of the swingarm bearings, remove the rear wheel (see Chapter 6) and the bolt securing the shock absorber to the swingarm (see Chapter 5). Grasp the rear of the swingarm with one hand and place your other hand at the junction of the swingarm and the frame. Try to move the rear of the swingarm from side-to-side. Any wear (play) in the bearings should be felt as movement between the swingarm and the frame at the front. If there is any play, the swingarm will be felt to move forward and backward at the front (not from side-to-side). Next, move the swingarm up and down through its full travel. It should move freely, without any binding or rough spots. If there is any play in the swingarm or if it does not move freely, remove the bearings for inspection (see Chapter 5).

Front fork oil change

12 Although there is no set interval for changing the fork oil, the oil will degrade over a period of time and lose its damping qualities. Refer to Chapter 5 for details of front fork removal, oil draining and refilling. The forks do not need to be completely disassembled to change the oil.

Rear suspension bearing lubrication

13 Although there is no set interval for re-greasing the suspension bearings, over a considerable mileage (or through incorrect use of jet washers) the seals may fail allowing the ingress of dirt and water and the grease in the bearings will be washed out or will harden.

14 The shock absorber and swingarm should be removed periodically and the bearings cleaned and re-greased as necessary (see Chapter 5).

14 Steering head bearings

Freeplay check and adjustment

1 Steering head bearings can become dented, rough or loose during normal use of the machine. In extreme cases, worn or loose steering head bearings can cause steering wobble – a condition that is potentially dangerous.

Check

2 Place the motorcycle on its centrestand on level ground. Raise the front wheel off the ground, either by having an assistant press down on the rear, or by placing a jack under the engine (use a piece of wood between the jack head and the engine to spread the weight, and make sure no contact is made with the lower fairing).

3 Point the front wheel straight-ahead and slowly move the handlebars from lock to lock. Any dents or roughness in the bearing races will be felt – if the bearings are too tight the bars will not move smoothly and freely. Again point the wheel straight-ahead, and tap the front of the wheel to one side. The wheel should 'fall' under its own weight to the limit of its lock, indicating that the bearings are not too tight (take into account the restriction that cables, hoses and wiring may have). Check for similar movement to the other side.

4 If available, attach one end of a spring balance (graduated zero to 30 N) to the fork tube between the top and bottom yokes. With the steering straight-ahead, pull on the balance and check the reading at which the handlebars start to turn **(see illustration)**. If the reading is below the minimum value specified in the pre-load range given in the Specifications at the beginning of the Chapter, the steering head is too loose, if the reading is above the maximum value specified the steering head is too tight. If the steering doesn't perform as described, and it's not due to the resistance of cables or hoses, then the bearings should be adjusted as described below.

5 Next, grasp the bottom of the forks and gently pull and push them forward and backward **(see illustration)**. Any looseness or freeplay in the

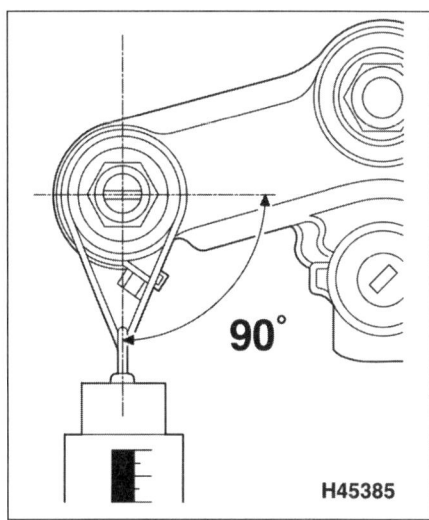

14.4 Checking steering head bearing pre-load using a spring balance

steering head bearings will be felt as front-to-rear movement of the forks. If play is felt, adjust the bearings as described below.

> **HAYNES HiNT** Make sure you are not mistaking any movement between the bike and stand, or between the stand and the ground, for freeplay in the bearings. Do not pull and push the forks too hard – a gentle movement is all that is needed. Freeplay between the fork tubes due to worn bushes can also be misinterpreted as steering head bearing play – do not confuse the two.

Adjustment

Special tool: A suitably sized C-spanner is useful for this procedure **(see illustration 14.10a)**.

6 As a precaution, remove the fairing (see Chapter 7), and raise or remove the main fuel tank (see Chapter 4). Though not actually essential, this will prevent the possibility of damage should a tool slip.

7 Slacken the fork clamp bolts in the top yoke **(see illustration)**. Unscrew the steering stem nut **(see illustration)**.

14.5 Checking for play in the steering head bearings

14.7a Slacken the fork clamp bolt (arrowed) on each side

14.7b Unscrew the steering stem nut . . .

Routine maintenance and servicing

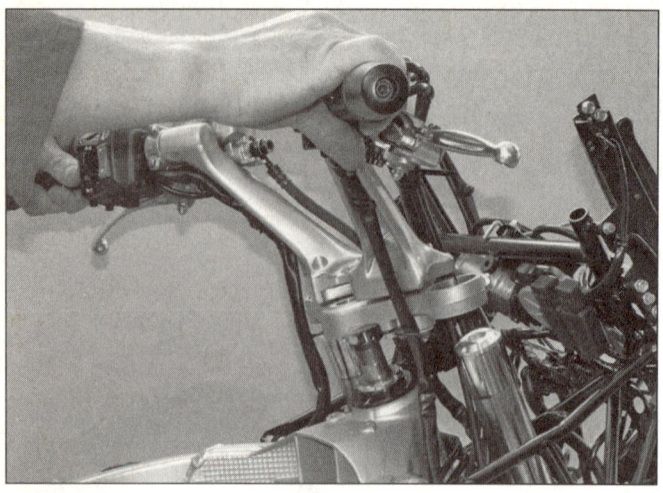

14.8a ... then gently ease the handlebar/yoke assembly up off the forks ...

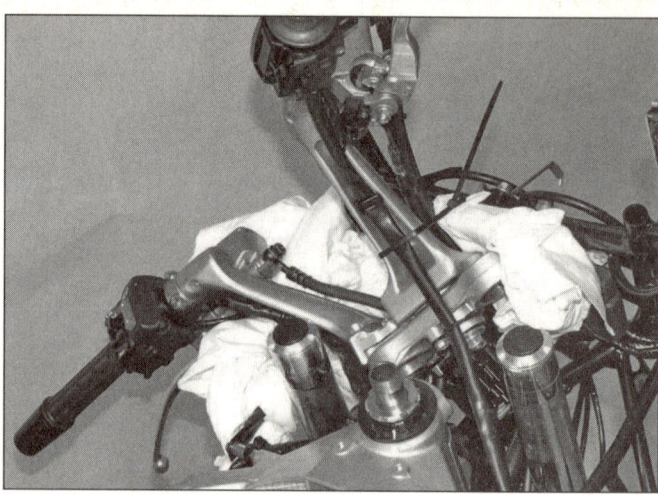

14.8b ... and rest them on some rag

8 Gently ease the top yoke and handlebar assembly up off the fork tubes and position it forwards clear of the head bearings, using a rag to protect other components **(see illustrations)**.

9 Bend the lockwasher tabs out of the notches in the locknut **(see illustration)**. Unscrew the locknut using either your fingers (it shouldn't be tight), a C-spanner or a suitable drift located in one of the notches **(see illustration)**. Remove the lockwasher **(see illustration)**. Inspect the tabs for cracks or signs of fatigue. If there is any sign of damage, discard the lockwasher and use a new one; otherwise the old one can be re-used, but note that Honda recommend using a new one as a matter of course.

10 Slacken the adjuster nut slightly until pressure is just released, then tighten it until all freeplay is removed, yet the steering is able to move freely **(see illustrations)**. The object is to set the adjuster nut so that the bearings are under a very light loading, just enough to remove any freeplay, but not so much that the steering is prevented from moving freely from side-to-side. If the Honda service tool (Pt. No. 07916-3710101 in Europe or 3710100 in the US) or a suitable peg spanner (which can be made by cutting castellations into an old socket) is available, tighten the adjuster nut to the initial torque setting specified at the beginning of the Chapter, then turn the steering from lock-to-lock five times, then slacken the nut **(see illustration)**. On 2002 to 2007 models now tighten the nut firstly to the final specified torque setting, and then through a further 45° (1/8 turn) – you can use the notches, which are 90° apart, as a guide, along with paint marks for alignment. On 2008-on models now tighten the nut to the final specified torque setting. On all models do not rely on the torque setting and angle method alone and assume the loading to be correct – check

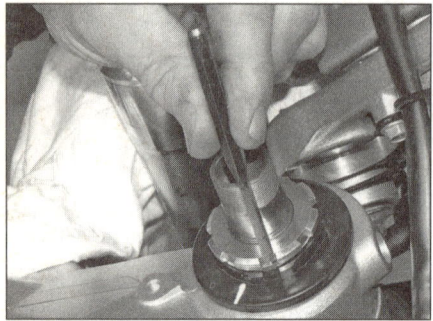

14.9a Bend down the tabs securing the locknut ...

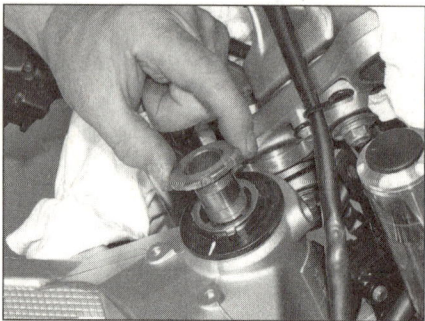

14.9b ... then unscrew the locknut ...

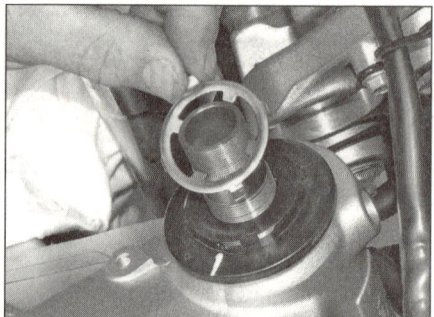

14.9c ... and remove the lockwasher

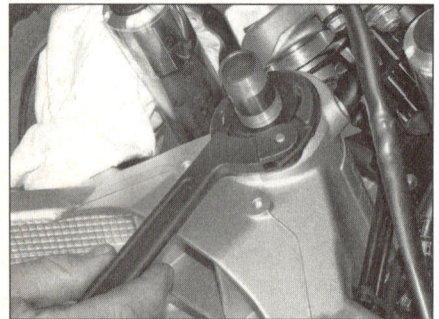

14.10a Adjust the bearings as described using either a C-spanner ...

14.10b ... or a drift

14.10c Use a home-made tool as shown or the Honda tool to apply the correct torque settings as described

Routine maintenance and servicing

14.13 Bend the tabs up into the notches in the locknut

the physical feel as described as well. If you have the spring balance (see Step 4), set the adjuster nut so that the steering starts to move at around the mid-point of the pre-load range given in the Specifications at the beginning of the Chapter.

Caution: Take great care not to apply excessive pressure because this will cause premature failure of the bearings.

11 If the bearings cannot be correctly adjusted, disassemble the steering head and check the bearings and races (see Chapter 5).
12 With the bearings correctly adjusted, fit the lockwasher, using a new one if the tabs are weakened or cracked, onto the adjuster nut and fit the two short tabs into the notches in the adjuster nut **(see illustration 14.9c)**.
13 Fit the locknut and tighten it finger-tight **(see illustration 14.9b)**. Tighten the locknut further (but no more than 90°) until its notches align with the remaining lockwasher tabs, making sure the adjuster nut does not turn as well (though that is unlikely). Secure the locknut in position by bending up the long lock washer tabs into its notches **(see illustration)**.
14 Fit the top yoke/handlebar assembly onto the steering stem **(see illustration 14.8a)**. Fit the steering stem nut and tighten it to the torque setting specified at the beginning of the Chapter **(see illustration 14.7b)**.
15 Tighten the fork clamp bolts to the specified torque **(see illustration 14.7a)**.
16 Check the bearing adjustment as described above and re-adjust if necessary.
17 Install the fuel tank (Chapter 4) and fairing (Chapter 7) as required.

Lubrication

18 Over a considerable time the grease in the bearings will be dispersed or will harden allowing the ingress of dirt and water.
19 The steering head should be disassembled periodically and the bearings cleaned and re-greased (see Chapter 5).

15 Wheels and tyres

Wheels

1 Cast wheels are virtually maintenance free, but they should be kept clean and checked periodically for cracks and other damage. Also check the wheel runout and alignment (see Chapter 6). Never attempt to repair damaged cast wheels; they must be renewed if damaged. Check that the wheel balance weights are fixed firmly to the wheel rim. If you suspect that a weight has fallen off, have the wheel rebalanced by a motorcycle tyre specialist.

Tyres

2 Check the tyre condition and tread depth thoroughly – see Pre-ride checks. Check the valve rubber for signs of damage or deterioration and have it replaced with a new one if necessary by a tyre fitting specialist. Also, make sure the valve stem cap is in place and tight **(see illustration)**.

Wheel bearings

3 Wheel bearings will wear over a considerable mileage and should be checked periodically to avoid handling problems.
4 Place the motorcycle on its centrestand. When checking the front wheel raise the wheel off the ground, either by having an assistant press down on the rear, or by placing a jack under the engine (use a piece of wood between the jack head and the engine to spread the weight, and make sure no contact is made with the lower fairing). Turn the handlebars to full lock on one side and hold the wheel against the lock.
5 Check for any play in the bearings by pushing and pulling the wheel against the hub **(see illustration)**. Also rotate the wheel and check that it turns smoothly and without any grating noises (bearing in mind that the brakes and final drive may make some noise – do not confuse them).
6 If any play is detected in the hub, or if the wheel does not rotate smoothly (and this is not due to brake or transmission drag), the wheel should be removed and the bearings inspected for wear or damage (see Chapter 6).

16 Stand, lever pivot and cable lubrication

Pivot points

1 Since the controls, cables and various other components of a motorcycle are exposed to the elements, they should be checked and lubricated periodically to ensure safe and trouble-free operation.
2 The footrest pivots, clutch and brake lever pivots, brake pedal and gearchange lever pivots and linkage, and stand pivots should be lubricated frequently. In order for the lubricant to be applied where it will do the most good,

15.2 Check each valve as described and make sure a cap is fitted

15.5 Checking for play in the wheel bearings

1•22 Routine maintenance and servicing

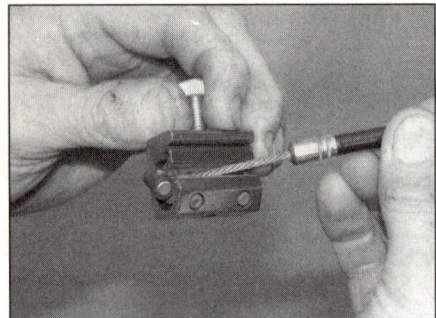

16.3a Fit the cable into the adapter . . .

16.3b . . . and tighten the screw to seal it in . . .

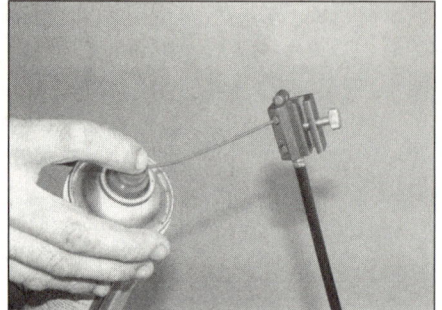

16.3c . . . then apply the lubricant using the nozzle provided inserted in the hole in the adapter

the component should be disassembled and cleaned (see Chapter 5). The lubricant recommended by Honda for each application is listed at the beginning of the Chapter. If aerosol chain or cable lubricant is being used, it can be applied to the pivot joint gaps and will usually work its way into the areas where friction occurs, so less disassembly of the component is needed (however it is always better to do so and clean off all corrosion, dirt and old lubricant first). If motor oil or light grease is being used, apply it sparingly as it may attract dirt (which could cause the controls to bind or wear at an accelerated rate). **Note:** *A good lubricant for the control lever pivots is a dry-film lubricant (available from many sources by different names).*

Cables

Special tool: *A cable lubricating adapter is necessary for this procedure (see illustration 16.3c).*

3 To lubricate the throttle cables, disconnect the relevant cable at its upper end, then lubricate it with a pressure adapter and aerosol lubricant **(see illustrations)**. See Chapter 4 for throttle cable removal procedures.

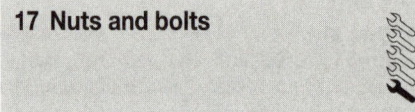

17 Nuts and bolts

1 Since vibration of the machine tends to loosen fasteners, all nuts, bolts, screws, etc. should be periodically checked for proper tightness.
2 Pay particular attention to the following, referring to the relevant Chapter:
● Spark plugs

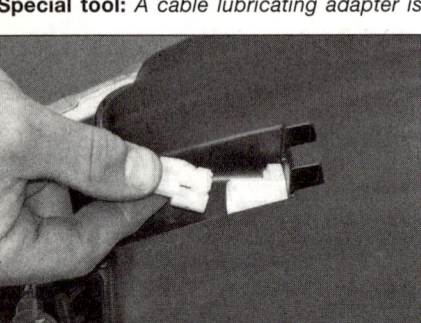

18.2 Disconnect the IAT sensor wiring connector

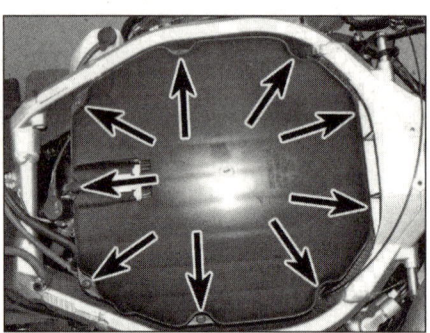

18.3 Undo the screws (arrowed) and remove the cover . . .

18.4 . . . then remove the filter element

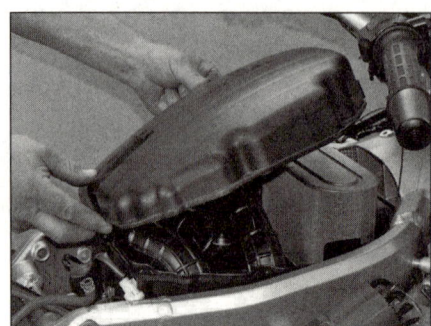

18.6 Fit the cover onto the housing

● Engine oil drain plug
● Final drive oil drain plug and filler cap
● Lever and pedal bolts
● Footrest and stand bolts
● Engine mounting bolts
● Shock absorber and swingarm pivot bolts
● Handlebar bolts
● Front fork clamp bolts (top and bottom yoke) and fork top bolts
● Steering stem nut
● Front wheel axle bolt and axle clamp bolts
● Rear wheel axle nut
● Brake caliper and master cylinder mounting bolts, brake caliper body bolts
● Brake hose banjo bolts, brake pipe nuts, and caliper bleed valves
● Brake disc bolts
● Exhaust system bolts/nuts

3 If a torque wrench is available, use it along with the torque settings given at the beginning of this and other Chapters.

18 Air filter

Caution: *If the machine is continually ridden in wet or dusty conditions, the filter should be replaced more frequently.*
1 Raise or remove the main fuel tank (see Chapter 4).
2 Disconnect the intake air temperature (IAT) sensor wiring connector **(see illustration)**.
3 Undo the air filter housing cover screws and lift the cover off **(see illustration)**.
4 Lift the filter element from the housing, and discard it **(see illustration)**.
5 Fit the new filter element into the housing, making sure it seats properly **(see illustration 18.4)**.
6 Make sure the perimeter seal is seated in its groove in the housing. Fit the cover and tighten the screws **(see illustration)**.
7 Connect the IAT (intake air temperature) sensor wiring connector **(see illustration 18.2)**.
8 Install the fuel tank (see Chapter 4).
9 To clean the filter between renewal intervals, tap it on a hard surface to dislodge any dirt and use compressed air to clear the element, directing the air in the opposite way to normal

Routine maintenance and servicing 1•23

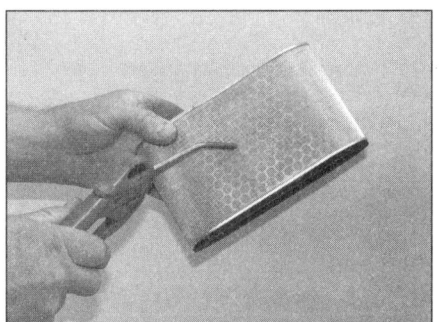

18.9 Direct the air in the opposite direction of normal flow

flow, i.e. from the outside **(see illustration)**. Do not use any solvents or cleaning agents on the element.

19 EVAP (Evaporative emission control) system (California models)

1 Remove the right-hand fairing side panel (see Chapter 7). Raise the fuel tank (see Chapter 4). Visually inspect all the system hoses between the fuel tank, the canister and the purge control solenoid valve, for kinks and splits and any other damage or deterioration. Make sure that the hoses are securely connected with a clamp on each end. Replace any hoses that are damaged or deteriorated.
2 Check the EVAP canister and the valve for cracks or other damage.
3 See Chapter 4 for further information and tests on the system. Note that there is an emission control system hose routing diagram on a label stuck to the top of the air filter housing, and an information label under the passenger seat.

20 Valve clearances

1 The engine must be completely cool for this maintenance procedure, so let the bike stand overnight before beginning.
2 Remove the spark plugs (see Section 6). Remove the valve covers (see Chapter 2).
3 Make a chart or sketch of all valve positions so that a note of each clearance can be made against the relevant valve. The cylinder numbering is as follows: No. 1 is the front left cylinder, No. 2 is the front right, No. 3 is the rear left, No. 4 is the rear right – the number is cast into the valve cover adjacent the plug hole. The intake valves are on the inner side of the cylinder head and the exhaust valves are on the outer side.
4 Unscrew the timing inspection cap and the crankshaft cap from the front of the engine **(see illustration)**. Check the condition of the O-rings and obtain new ones if necessary.
5 To check the valve clearances the engine must be turned so that the valve being checked is closed. The engine can be turned using a socket on the timing rotor bolt and turning it in an anti-clockwise direction only **(see illustration)**.
6 Turn the engine anti-clockwise until the line above to the T1 mark on the timing rotor aligns with the static timing mark, which is a pointer in the top of the inspection hole, and the L-IN and L-EX marks on the left-hand cylinder head intake and exhaust camshaft sprockets respectively are facing away from each other and are flush with the cylinder head top surface **(see illustrations)**. If the sprocket

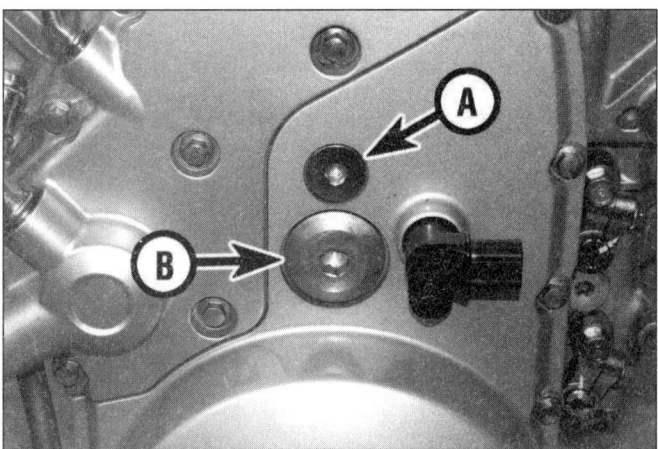

20.4 Unscrew the timing inspection cap (A) and the crankshaft cap (B)

20.5 Turn the engine anti-clockwise using a socket on the bolt . . .

20.6a . . . until the line next to the T1 mark aligns with the pointer (arrowed) . . .

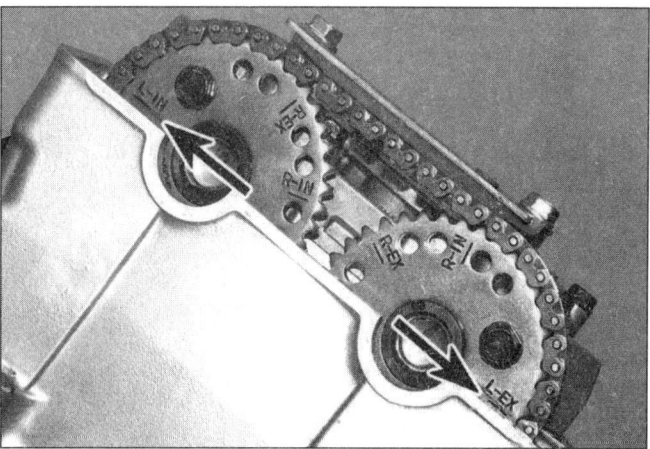

20.6b . . . and the camshaft sprocket L-IN and L-EX marks (arrowed) on the left-hand head are as shown

1•24 Routine maintenance and servicing

20.7 Insert the feeler gauge between the base of the cam lobe and the top of the follower as shown

using a feeler gauge, remembering there are two valves per cylinder. Select a feeler gauge blade of the same thickness as the correct valve clearance (see Specifications) and insert it between the camshaft lobe and the follower of each valve and check that it is a firm sliding fit – you should feel a slight drag when the you pull the gauge out **(see illustration)**. If not, use the feeler gauges to obtain the exact clearance. Record the measured clearance on the chart.

8 Now rotate the engine 90° anti-clockwise until the line above to the T2 mark on the timing rotor aligns with the static timing mark, and the R-IN and R-EX marks on the right-hand cylinder head intake and exhaust camshaft sprockets respectively are facing each other and are flush with the cylinder head top surface **(see illustrations)**. With the engine in this position, check the clearances on the No. 4 cylinder valves using the method described in Step 7.

9 Now rotate the engine 270° anti-clockwise until the line above the T1 mark on the timing rotor aligns with the static timing mark, and the L-IN and L-EX marks on the left-hand intake and exhaust camshaft sprockets respectively are facing each other and are flush with the cylinder head top surface **(see illustration)**. With the engine in this position, check the clearances on the No. 3 cylinder valves using the method described in Step 7.

10 Now rotate the engine 90° anti-clockwise until the line above the T2 mark on the timing rotor aligns with the static timing mark, and the R-IN and R-EX marks on the right-hand intake and exhaust camshaft sprockets respectively are facing away from each other and are flush with the cylinder head top surface **(see illustrations)**. With the engine in this position, check the clearances on the No. 2 cylinder valves using the method described in Step 7.

11 When all clearances have been measured and charted, identify whether the clearance on any valve falls outside the specified range. If any do, the shim must be replaced with one of a thickness which will restore the correct clearance.

marks are facing towards each other, rotate the engine anti-clockwise one full turn (360°) until the line next to the T1 mark again aligns with the static timing mark. The sprocket marks will now be facing away.

7 With the engine in this position, check the clearances on the No. 1 cylinder valves

20.8a Turn the engine 90° until the line next to the T2 mark aligns with the pointer (arrowed) . . .

20.8b . . . and the camshaft sprocket R-IN and R-EX marks (arrowed) on the right-hand head are as shown

20.9 Position the camshaft sprocket L-IN and L-EX marks (arrowed) on the left-hand head as shown

20.10 Position the camshaft sprocket R-IN and R-EX marks (arrowed) on the right-hand head as shown

Routine maintenance and servicing

12 Shim replacement requires removal of the camshafts (see Chapter 2). Place rags over the spark plug holes and the cam chain tunnel to prevent a shim from dropping into the engine on removal. Work on one valve at a time to prevent the possibility of mixing up the followers, which must be returned to their original location. If you want to remove more than one shim and follower at a time, store them in a marked container or bag, denoting which cylinder and which valve the shim and follower are from, so that they do not get mixed up.

13 With the camshaft removed, remove the cam follower of the valve in question using a magnet or the suction created by a valve lapping tool, but long nosed pliers can be used with care **(see illustration)**. Retrieve the shim either from the inside of the follower or pick it out of the top of the valve spring retainer using either a magnet, a screwdriver with a dab of grease on it (the shim will stick to the grease), or a very small screwdriver and a pair of pliers **(see illustrations)**. Do not allow the shim to fall into the engine.

14 A size mark should be stamped on one face of the shim – a shim marked 180 is 1.80 mm thick **(see illustration)**. If the mark is not visible measure the shim thickness using a micrometer **(see illustration)**. It is recommended that the shim is measured anyway to check whether it has worn.

15 Calculate the required replacement shim by using the formula $A = (B - C) + D$, where A is the required replacement shim size, B is the measured valve clearance, C is the specified valve clearance, and D is the existing shim thickness. For example:

The measured clearance of an intake valve is 0.22 mm, so $B = 0.22$

The specified clearance range for an intake valve is 0.13 to 0.19 mm, the mid-point being 0.16 mm, so $C = 0.16$

The thickness of the existing shim is 2.00 mm, so $D = 2.0$

Therefore, the required replacement shim $A = 0.22 - 0.16 + 2.0$ ($A = 2.06$ mm). The nearest available size to this is 2.05 mm see (Step 16).

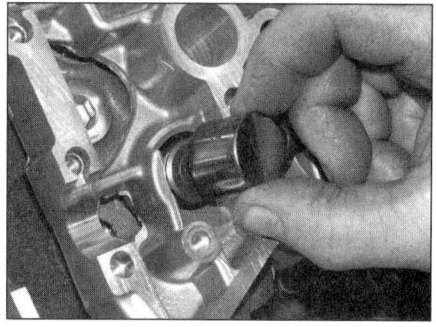

20.13a Carefully lift out the follower using grips, a lapping tool or a magnet . . .

Note: *If the required replacement shim is greater than 2.800 mm, the valve is probably not seating correctly due to a build-up of carbon deposits and should be checked and cleaned or resurfaced as required, and the clearance checked again, before fitting a new shim (see Chapter 2).*

16 Shims are available in 0.025 mm

20.13b . . . and retrieve the shim (arrowed) from inside it . . .

20.13c . . . or from the top of the valve

20.14a The shim size is marked on one face . . .

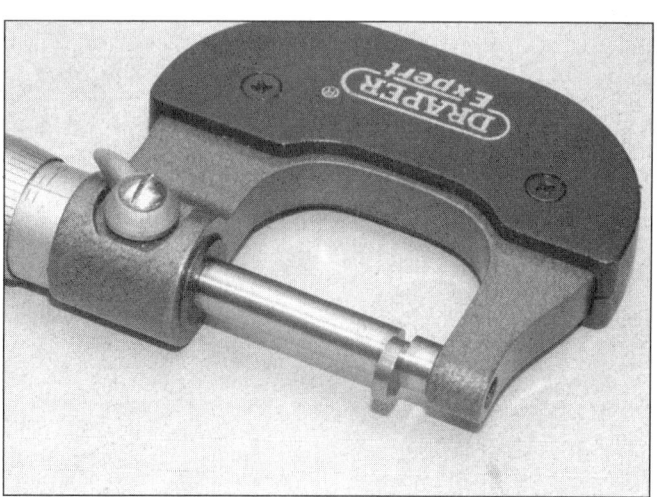

20.14b . . . but check the thickness of the shim using a micrometer

1•26 Routine maintenance and servicing

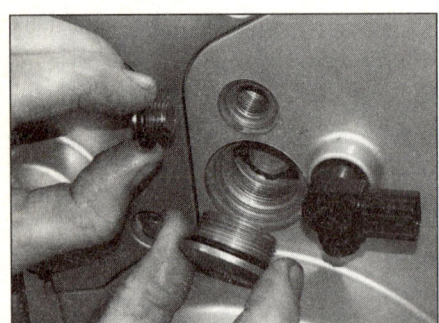

20.19 Smear the cap O-rings with grease, and use new ones if required

increments from 1.200 mm to 2.900 mm. Obtain the replacement shim, then lubricate it with molybdenum disulphide oil (a 50/50 mixture of molybdenum disulphide grease and engine oil) and fit it into the recess in the top of the valve spring retainer with the size mark facing up **(see illustration 20.13c)**.

17 Check that the shim is correctly seated, then lubricate the follower with molybdenum disulphide oil and fit it onto the valve, making sure it fits squarely in its bore **(see illustration 20.13a)**. Repeat the process for any other valves until the clearances are correct, then install the camshafts (see Chapter 2).

18 Rotate the crankshaft anti-clockwise several turns to seat the new shim(s), then check the clearances again. Install the valve covers (see Chapter 2).

19 Install all disturbed components in a reverse of the removal sequence. Install the timing inspection cap and crankshaft end cap using new O-rings if required, and smear the O-rings and the cap threads with grease **(see illustration)**. Tighten the caps to the torque settings specified at the beginning of the Chapter.

20 On completion, check and adjust the idle speed (see Section 1).

21 Battery

1 All models covered in this manual are fitted with a sealed MF (maintenance free) battery. **Note:** *Do not attempt to remove the battery caps to check the electrolyte level or battery specific gravity. Removal will damage the caps, resulting in electrolyte leakage and battery damage. All that should be done is to check that the terminals are clean and tight and that the casing is not damaged or leaking. See Chapter 8 for further details.*

2 If the machine is not in regular use, disconnect the battery and give it a refresher charge every month to six weeks (see Chapter 8).

Chapter 2
Engine, clutch and transmission

Contents

	Section		Section
Alternator/regulator/rectifier	see Chapter 8	Idle speed check and adjustment	see Chapter 1
Alternator drive, middle and driven gears	19	Neutral switch	see Chapter 8
Balancer shafts	34	Oil and filter change	see Chapter 1
Cam chain tensioners	8	Oil cooler	6
Camshaft position sensor	see Chapter 4	Oil level check	see Pre-ride checks
Camshafts and followers	9	Oil pressure switch	see Chapter 8
Cam chains, tensioner blades and guides	10	Oil pump and pressure relief valve	26
Clutch	13	Oil sump and strainers	25
Clutch check	see Chapter 1	Piston rings	33
Clutch release mechanism	14	Pistons	32
Component access	2	Primary damper shaft	16
Connecting rod and main bearing information	29	Primary drive gear	15
Connecting rods and bearings	31	Running-in procedure	35
Crankcase separation and reassembly	27	Selector drum and forks	22
Crankcases and cylinder bores	28	Spark plugs	see Chapter 1
Crankshaft and main bearings	30	Starter clutch and gears	18
Crankshaft position sensor	see Chapter 4	Starter motor	see Chapter 8
Cylinder head removal and installation	11	Thermostat and housing	see Chapter 3
Cylinder head and valve overhaul	12	Transmission assembly removal and installation	21
Engine wear assessment	3	Transmission shaft and bearing removal and installation	23
Engine overhaul information	5	Transmission shaft overhaul	24
Engine removal and installation	4	Valve clearance check and adjustment	see Chapter 1
Final output shaft and gears	17	Valve covers	7
Gearchange mechanism	20	Water pump	see Chapter 3
General information	1		

Degrees of difficulty

Easy, suitable for novice with little experience	Fairly easy, suitable for beginner with some experience	Fairly difficult, suitable for competent DIY mechanic	Difficult, suitable for experienced DIY mechanic	Very difficult, suitable for expert DIY or professional

Specifications

General
Type	Four-stroke 90° V-four
Capacity	1261 cc
Cylinder numbering	No. 1 – front left; No. 2 – front right; No. 3 – rear left; No. 4 – rear right
Firing order	1-4-3-2
Bore	78.0 mm
Stroke	66.0 mm
Compression ratio	10.8:1
Cooling system	Liquid cooled
Lubrication	Wet sump, trochoid pump
Clutch	Wet multi-plate
Transmission	Five-speed constant mesh
Final drive	Shaft

Camshafts and followers

Intake lobe height
    Standard .... 36.48 to 36.64 mm
    Service limit (min) .... 36.45 mm
Exhaust lobe height
    Standard .... 36.37 to 36.53 mm
    Service limit (min) .... 36.34 mm
Oil clearance
    Standard .... 0.020 to 0.062 mm
    Service limit (max) .... 0.10 mm
Runout (max) .... 0.05 mm
Camshaft follower diameter
    Standard .... 25.978 to 25.993 mm
    Service limit (min) .... 25.97 mm
Camshaft follower bore diameter
    Standard .... 26.010 to 26.026 mm
    Service limit (min) .... 26.04 mm

Cylinder head

Warpage (max) .... 0.10 mm

Valves, guides and springs

Valve clearances .... see Chapter 1
Stem diameter
    Intake valve
        Standard .... 4.975 to 4.990 mm
        Service limit (min) .... 4.965 mm
    Exhaust valve
        Standard .... 4.960 to 4.975 mm
        Service limit (min) .... 4.950 mm
Guide bore diameter – intake and exhaust valves
    Standard .... 5.000 to 5.012 mm
    Service limit (max) .... 5.040 mm
Stem-to-guide clearance
    Intake valve
        Standard .... 0.010 to 0.037 mm
        Service limit .... 0.075 mm
    Exhaust valve
        Standard .... 0.020 to 0.052 mm
        Service limit .... 0.090 mm
Seat width – intake and exhaust valves
    Standard .... 0.90 to 1.10 mm
    Service limit (max) .... 1.50 mm
Valve guide projection above cylinder head
    Intake valve .... 15.6 to 15.8 mm
    Exhaust valve .... 15.8 to 16.0 mm
Valve spring free length
    Standard .... 43.4 mm
    Service limit (min) .... 42.5 mm

Starter clutch

Starter driven gear hub OD
    Standard .... 51.699 to 51.718 mm
    Service limit (min) .... 51.59 mm

Clutch

Friction plates 8
Plain plates 7
Friction plate thickness
    Standard .... 3.72 to 3.88 mm
    Service limit (min) .... 3.5 mm
Plain plate warpage (max) .... 0.3 mm
Spring free length
    Standard .... 55.1 mm
    Service limit (min) .... 54.0 mm

Engine, clutch and transmission

Clutch (continued)

Clutch guide ID
- Standard.. 27.989 to 28.006 mm
- Service limit (max)..................................... 28.016 mm

Primary damper shaft OD at clutch guide
- Standard.. 27.974 to 27.987 mm
- Service limit (max)..................................... 27.964 mm

Clutch release mechanism

Clutch fluid... DOT 4

Master cylinder bore ID
- Standard.. 14.000 to 14.043 mm
- Service limit (max)..................................... 14.055 mm

Piston OD
- Standard.. 13.957 to 13.984 mm
- Service limit (max)..................................... 13.945 mm

Primary damper shaft

Primary damper shaft spring free length
- Standard.. 58.4 mm
- Service limit (min)..................................... 56.0 mm

Oil pump

Oil pressure (at oil pressure switch, with engine warm)...... 71 psi (4.9 Bar) @ 6000 rpm, oil @ 80°C

Inner rotor tip-to-outer rotor clearance
- Standard.. 0.15 mm
- Service limit (max)..................................... 0.20 mm

Outer rotor-to-body clearance
- Standard.. 0.15 to 0.22 mm
- Service limit (max)..................................... 0.35 mm

Rotor end-float
- Standard.. 0.02 to 0.09 mm
- Service limit (max)..................................... 0.10 mm

Selector drum and forks

Selector fork end thickness
- Standard.. 5.93 to 6.00 mm
- Service limit (min)..................................... 5.90 mm

Selector fork bore ID
- Standard.. 12.000 to 12.018 mm
- Service limit (max)..................................... 12.03 mm

Selector fork shaft OD
- Standard.. 11.957 to 11.968 mm
- Service limit (min)..................................... 11.95 mm

Transmission

Gear ratios (no. of teeth)
- Primary reduction...................................... 1.785 to 1 (75/42)
- Secondary reduction.................................. 0.925 to 1 (37/40)
- Final reduction.. 2.833 to 1 (34/12)
- 1st gear.. 2.571 to 1 (36/14)
- 2nd gear... 1.722 to 1 (31/18)
- 3rd gear.. 1.285 to 1 (27/21)
- 4th gear.. 1.041 to 1 (25/24)
- 5th gear.. 0.862 to 1 (25/29)

Input shaft 4th and 5th gears ID
- Standard.. 31.000 to 31.025 mm
- Service limit (max)..................................... 31.04 mm

Input shaft 4th and 5th gears bush OD
- Standard.. 30.950 to 30.975 mm
- Service limit (min)..................................... 30.93 mm

Input shaft 4th and 5th gears gear-to-bush clearance......... 0.025 to 0.075 mm

Input shaft 4th gear bush ID
- Standard.. 27.985 to 28.006 mm
- Service limit (max)..................................... 28.02 mm

Input shaft OD at 4th gear bush point
- Standard.. 27.967 to 27.980 mm
- Service limit (min)..................................... 27.96 mm

Transmission (continued)

Input shaft-to-bush clearance at 4th gear bush point	0.005 to 0.039 mm
Output shaft 1st gear ID	
Standard	26.000 to 26.021 mm
Service limit (max)	26.04 mm
Output shaft 2nd and 3rd gears ID	
Standard	33.000 to 33.025 mm
Service limit (max)	33.04 mm
Output shaft 2nd and 3rd gear bush OD	
Standard	32.955 to 32.980 mm
Service limit (min)	32.93 mm
Output shaft 2nd and 3rd gear gear-to-bush clearance	0.020 to 0.070 mm
Output shaft 2nd gear bush ID	
Standard	29.985 to 30.006 mm
Service limit (max)	30.02 mm
Output shaft OD at 2nd gear bush point	
Standard	29.967 to 29.980 mm
Service limit (min)	29.96 mm
Output shaft-to-bushing clearance at 2nd gear bush point	0.005 to 0.039 mm

Cylinder bores

Bore	
Standard	78.000 to 78.015 mm
Service limit (max)	78.100 mm
Warpage (max)	0.10 mm
Ovality (out-of-round) (max)	0.10 mm
Taper (max)	0.10 mm
Cylinder compression	142 to 178 psi (10 to 12.2 Bar) @ 300 rpm

Crankshaft and bearings

Main bearing oil clearance	
Standard	0.020 to 0.038 mm
Service limit (max)	0.05 mm
Runout (max)	0.05 mm

Connecting rods

Small-end internal diameter	
Standard	19.030 to 19.051 mm
Service limit (max)	19.06 mm
Small-end-to-piston pin clearance	
Standard	0.030 to 0.057 mm
Service limit	0.077 mm
Big-end side clearance	
Standard	0.10 to 0.30 mm
Service limit (max)	0.40 mm
Big-end oil clearance	
Standard	0.036 to 0.054 mm
Service limit (max)	0.074 mm

Pistons

Piston diameter (measured 8 mm up from skirt, at 90° to piston pin axis)	
Standard	77.965 to 77.985 mm
Service limit (min)	77.90 mm
Piston-to-bore clearance	
Standard	0.015 to 0.050 mm
Service limit (min)	0.10 mm*
Piston pin diameter	
Standard	18.994 to 19.000 mm
Service limit (min)	18.980 mm
Piston pin bore diameter in piston	
Standard	19.002 to 19.008 mm
Service limit (max)	19.020 mm
Piston pin-to-piston pin bore clearance	
Standard	0.002 to 0.014 mm
Service limit	0.04 mm

* If the piston-to-bore clearance exceeds the service limit, the cylinders can be rebored – Honda supply +0.25 and +0.50 oversize pistons and rings. Following rebore, the piston-to-bore clearance must be as standard for normal pistons

Piston rings
Ring-to-groove clearance
  Top ring
    Standard . . . . 0.030 to 0.065 mm
    Service limit (max) . . . . 0.11 mm
  Second ring
    Standard . . . . 0.020 to 0.055 mm
    Service limit (max) . . . . 0.10 mm
Ring end gap (installed)
  Top ring
    Standard . . . . 0.25 to 0.40 mm
    Service limit (max) . . . . 0.50 mm
  Second ring
    Standard . . . . 0.32 to 0.47 mm
    Service limit (max) . . . . 0.60 mm
  Oil ring side-rail
    Standard . . . . 0.20 to 0.70 mm
    Service limit (max) . . . . 0.9 mm

Torque settings

Engine mountings – early 2002 models, 2003 models
Lower front mounting bolts
  Initial setting . . . . 10 Nm
  Final setting (see Text) . . . . 64 Nm/45°
Lower rear mounting bolt, right-hand side
  Initial setting . . . . 10 Nm
  Final setting (see Text) . . . . 64 Nm/75°
Lower rear mounting bolt, left-hand side
  Initial setting . . . . 10 Nm
  Final setting (see Text) . . . . 64 Nm/20°
Upper rear mounting bolt nut
  Initial setting . . . . 10 Nm
  Final setting (see Text) . . . . 42 Nm/360°
Engine protection bar bolts/nut
  Front bolt . . . . 39 Nm
  Rear and lower bolt/nut . . . . 26 Nm
Side mounting bracket bolts
  Front bolt . . . . 39 Nm
  Rear bolt . . . . 26 Nm
Engine mount pinch-bolts . . . . 26 Nm
Front cross-plate and mounting bracket bolts/nuts . . . . 26 Nm

Engine mountings – late 2002 models
Upper rear mounting bolt nut
  Initial setting . . . . 10 Nm
  Final setting . . . . 270°
Lower rear mounting bolt, right-hand side
  Pre-load setting . . . . 103 Nm
  Second setting . . . . slacken 180°
  Initial torque setting . . . . 20 Nm
  Final setting (see Text) . . . . 65°
Lower rear mounting bolt, left-hand side
  Pre-load setting . . . . 103 Nm
  Second setting . . . . slacken 180°
  Initial torque setting . . . . 20 Nm
  Final setting (see Text) . . . . 65°
Lower front mounting bolts
  Initial setting . . . . 20 Nm
  Final setting (see Text) . . . . 42.5°
Engine protection bar bolts/nuts
  Front bolt . . . . 39 Nm
  Rear and lower bolts/nuts . . . . 26 Nm
Side mounting bracket bolts
  Front bolt . . . . 39 Nm
  Rear bolt . . . . 26 Nm
Engine mount pinch-bolts . . . . 27 Nm
Front cross-plate and mounting bracket bolts/nuts . . . . 27 Nm

Torque settings (continued)

Engine mountings – 2004-on models

Upper rear mounting bolt nut	
Initial setting	10 Nm
Final setting	270°
Lower rear mounting bolt, right-hand side	
Pre-load setting	103 Nm
Second setting	slacken 180°
Initial torque setting	20 Nm
Final setting (see Text)	65°
Lower rear mounting bolt, left-hand side	
Pre-load setting	103 Nm
Second setting	slacken 180°
Initial torque setting	20 Nm
Final setting (see Text)	65°
Lower front mounting bolts	
Initial setting	20 Nm
Final setting (see Text)	42.5°
Engine protection bar bolts/nuts	
Front bolt	39 Nm
Rear and lower bolts/nuts	26 Nm
Side mounting bracket bolts	
Front bolt	39 Nm
Rear bolt	26 Nm
Engine mount pinch-bolts	27 Nm
Front cross-plate and mounting bracket bolts/nuts	27 Nm

All other bolts/nuts

Alternator drive gear bolts	16 Nm
Alternator middle gear case bolts	57 Nm
Cam chain guide blade bolts	12 Nm
Cam chain tensioner blade pivot bolts	12 Nm
Camshaft holder bolts	12 Nm
Camshaft sprocket bolts	20 Nm
Clutch hose banjo bolts	34 Nm
Clutch master cylinder clamp bolts	12 Nm
Clutch nut	127 Nm
Clutch release mechanism bleed valve	9 Nm
Clutch spring bolts	12 Nm
Connecting rod nuts	35 Nm
Crankcase bolts	
Crankshaft journal 10 mm bolts	48 Nm
8 mm bolts	26 Nm
Crankshaft end cap	12 Nm
Cylinder head 10 mm bolts	69 Nm
Final output drive gear nut	186 Nm
Final output shaft nut	
Actual	186 Nm
Indicated (see Text)	163 Nm
Oil cooler bolt	75 Nm
Oil pump back plate bolt	12 Nm
Oil pump driven sprocket bolt	15 Nm
Oil sump bolts	12 Nm
Primary damper shaft bearing retainer plate bolts	12 Nm
Primary drive gear bolt	93 Nm
Selector drum bearing retainer bolts	12 Nm
Selector drum cam bolt	23 Nm
Starter clutch bolt	93 Nm
Stopper arm bolt	12 Nm
Timing inspection cap	10 Nm
Transmission cover bolts	30 Nm
Transmission output shaft bearing retainer bolts	12 Nm
Valve cover bolts	10 Nm

Engine, clutch and transmission 2•7

1 General information

The engine/transmission unit is a liquid-cooled 90°V-four. The valves are operated by double overhead camshafts driven by chain and sprockets. The engine/transmission assembly is constructed from aluminium alloy. The crankcase is divided horizontally.

The crankcase incorporates a wet sump, pressure-fed lubrication system which has a chain-driven, dual-rotor oil pump, an oil filter and by-pass valve assembly, a relief valve, oil pressure switch, and cooler.

Power from the crankshaft is routed to the transmission via the clutch and a damper shaft. The clutch is of the wet, multi-plate type and is gear-driven off the front of crankshaft. The transmission is a five-speed constant-mesh unit. Final drive to the rear wheel is by shaft.

The alternator is driven by a gear train off the back of the crankshaft.

2 Component access

Operations possible with the engine in the frame

The components and assemblies listed below can be removed without having to remove the engine from the frame.
- Valve covers
- Camshafts
- Clutch
- Primary drive gear/timing rotor
- Primary damper shaft
- Cam chains, tensioners and blades
- Alternator
- Oil filter and oil cooler
- Oil sump and oil strainers
- Starter motor
- Water pump

Operations requiring engine removal

To remove the components and assemblies listed below the engine must be removed from the frame.
- Cylinder heads
- Gearchange mechanism
- Clutch release cylinder
- Final output shaft and gears
- Alternator drive gears
- Selector drum and forks
- Transmission shafts
- Starter clutch and gears
- Oil pump and pressure relief valve
- Crankshaft and bearings
- Balancer shafts
- Connecting rods and bearings
- Pistons, piston rings and cylinder bores

3 Engine wear assessment

Cylinder compression check

Special tool: *A compression gauge is needed. It is best to use one with a threaded adaptor to fit the spark plug holes (use either the Honda gauge and adapter (pt. No. 07RMJ-MY50100) or an aftermarket version) to ensure a perfect seal. Depending on the outcome of the initial test, a squirt-type oil can may also be needed.*

1 Poor engine performance may be caused by leaking valves, incorrect valve clearances, a leaking head gasket, or worn pistons, piston rings or cylinder walls. A cylinder compression check will highlight these conditions and can also indicate the presence of excessive carbon deposits in the cylinder head, and a leakdown test (for which special equipment is needed – consult a Honda dealer) will pinpoint the actual cause(s) of the problem.

2 Start by making sure the valve clearances are correctly set (see Chapter 1). Also make sure the battery is well charged.

3 Run the engine until it is at normal operating temperature. Remove the spark plugs (see Chapter 1). Remove the left-hand side cover (see Chapter 7). Disconnect the fuel pump (3-pin black) wiring connector **(see illustration)**.

4 Fit the gauge into the No. 1 cylinder spark plug hole **(see illustration)** – make sure the threaded adapter has the same threads as the spark plugs (M10 x 1.0).

5 With the ignition switch ON, the kill switch set to RUN, and the throttle held fully open, turn the engine over on the starter motor until the gauge reading has built up and stabilised **(see illustration)**.

6 Compare the reading on the gauge to the cylinder compression figure specified at the beginning of the Chapter. Repeat for the remaining cylinders.

7 If a reading is low, it could be due to a worn cylinder bore, piston or rings, failure of the head gasket, or worn valve seats. To determine which is the cause, pour a small quantity of engine oil into the spark plug hole to seal the rings, then repeat the compression test. If the figures are noticeably higher the cause is worn cylinder, piston or rings. If there is no change the cause is a leaking head gasket or worn valve seats.

8 In the unlikely event of the reading being too high there could be a build-up of carbon deposits in the combustion chamber. Remove the cylinder head and scrape all deposits off the piston and the cylinder head, and on installation fit a new gasket.

Engine oil pressure check

Special tool: *An oil pressure gauge is required to perform this test.*

9 An oil pressure check can provide useful information about the condition of the engine and its lubrication system.

10 The oil pressure warning light should come on when the ignition switch is turned ON and extinguish a few seconds after the engine is started. If the oil pressure light comes on whilst the engine is running, low oil pressure is indicated – stop the engine immediately and carry out an oil level check (see *Pre-ride checks*). If the oil level is good next check the switch and its circuit (see Chapter 8). If that is good check the oil pressure as follows.

11 To check the oil pressure, a suitable gauge and adapter, along with a special attachment

3.3 Disconnect the fuel pump wiring connector

3.4 This is an aftermarket gauge with dual sized threaded adapter

3.5 Checking compression on the No. 1 cylinder

2•8 Engine, clutch and transmission

![Oil pressure check equipment]

3.11 Oil pressure check equipment
1 Oil filter   2 Honda attachment   3 O-ring

4.6 Disconnect the hoses at the joints (arrowed), not from the tank, and bring them away with the tank

piece that fits between the oil filter and the oil cooler, are needed **(see illustration)**. The attachment piece must come from Honda (Pt. No. 07RMK-MW40100), who can also provide a gauge and adapter (Pt. Nos. 07506-3000001 and 07406-0030001), or the gauge and adapter can be obtained from a tool supplier.

12 Drain the engine oil and remove the filter (see Chapter 1). Lubricate the attachment piece O-ring with oil then fit the attachment onto the oil cooler and tighten it. Screw the gauge adapter into the attachment. Connect the oil pressure gauge to the adapter. Fit the oil filter and replenish the engine oil. Check the oil level (see *Pre-ride checks*).

13 Warm the engine up to normal operating temperature.

14 Briefly increase the engine speed to 6000 rpm whilst watching the gauge reading. The oil pressure should be similar to that given in the Specifications.

15 If the pressure is too low, either the pressure relief valve is stuck open, the oil pump or its drive mechanism is faulty, the oil strainer is blocked, or there is other engine damage resulting in an internal leak. Also make sure the correct grade oil is being used. Begin diagnosis by checking the oil strainer and relief valve, then the oil pump (see Sections 25 and 26). If those items check out okay, chances are the bearing oil clearances are excessive and the engine needs to be overhauled.

16 If the pressure is too high, either the filter or an oil passage is clogged, the relief valve is stuck closed or the wrong grade of oil is being used.

17 Stop the engine. Drain the engine oil. Remove the gauge and adapter, followed by the filter and attachment piece. Fit a new filter then replenish the engine oil (see Chapter 1).

⚠ **Warning: Be careful when removing the pressure gauge adapter as the exhaust pipes, the engine and the oil itself can cause severe burns.**

4 Engine removal and installation

⚠ **Warning: The engine is very heavy and awkward to remove. Engine removal and installation should be carried out with the aid of at least two assistants; personal injury or damage could occur if the engine falls or is dropped.**

Note: *When removing the engine mounting hardware keep all related components, such as any washers, spacers, collars, nuts and brackets, together by sliding them back onto the bolts in the correct order and way round to avoid confusion on installation.*

Removal

1 Support the bike on its centrestand. Tie the front brake lever to the handlebar so the brake is on. Work can be made easier by raising the machine to a suitable working height on an hydraulic ramp or a suitable platform. Make sure the motorcycle is secure and will not topple over (also see *Tools and Workshop Tips* in the Reference section).

2 Remove the lower fairing and fairing side panels, and to avoid the possibility of damage the fairing (see Chapter 7).

3 If the engine is dirty, particularly around its mountings, wash it thoroughly. This will make work much easier and rule out the possibility of caked on lumps of dirt falling into some vital component.

4 Drain the engine oil and coolant (see Chapter 1). Remove the oil filter (see Chapter 1).

5 Disconnect the negative (–) lead from the battery (see Chapter 8).

6 Remove the main fuel tank along with the drain and breather hoses **(see illustration)**, releasing them from their tie(s) and guides and noting their routing (see Chapter 4). Remove the air filter housing and the throttle bodies (see Chapter 4). Plug the engine intake manifolds with clean rag.

7 Remove the trim cover from the top of each valve cover (see Chapter 7). Clean the area around each spark plug cap to prevent any dirt falling into the spark plug channels. Pull the cap off each spark plug **(see illustration)**.

8 Remove the radiator along with its hoses, noting their routing (see Chapter 3). Detach the hoses from the coolant reservoir and drain the reservoir via the bottom hose union (see Chapter 3).

9 Remove the exhaust system (see Chapter 4).

10 Unscrew the secondary fuel tank mounting bolts and move the tank as far back as possible, then wedge a piece of wood or plastic (the handle of a spark plug cleaning brush is shown in the photo) between the front of the tank and the frame cross-piece to hold it back **(see**

4.7 Pull the caps off the spark plugs

Engine, clutch and transmission 2•9

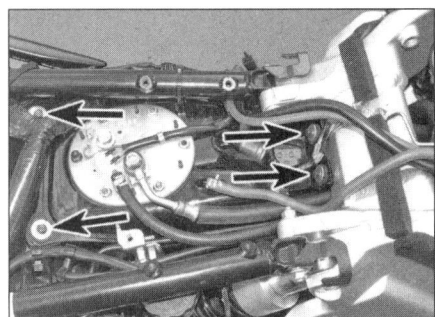

4.10a Unscrew the bolts . . .

4.10b . . . then wedge the tank away from the frame

4.13a Disconnect the sub-loom connector (arrowed) . . .

4.13b . . . the CKP sensor wiring connector . . .

4.13c . . . and the speed sensor wiring connector

4.14 Detach the hoses (arrowed) from the valve covers

illustrations) – only a small amount of movement is needed for the engine to clear the tank when lowering it out of the frame.
11 Remove the shock absorber and the swingarm (see Chapter 5).
12 Remove the starter motor (see Chapter 8).
13 Disconnect the alternator wiring connectors inside the boot behind the left-hand cylinder head. Disconnect the large grey sub-loom wiring connector behind the right-hand cylinder head for the ECT sensor, knock sensors, neutral switch and oil pressure switch **(see illustration)**. Disconnect the wiring connector from the CKP sensor **(see illustration)**. Disconnect the speed sensor (3-pin black) wiring connector **(see illustration)**.
14 Detach the PAIR system hoses and the crankcase breather hose from the valve covers, and remove the breather hose **(see illustration)**.
15 Make an alignment mark between the slit in the gearchange linkage arm and the shaft, then unscrew the pinch-bolt and slide the arm off the shaft **(see illustration)**.
16 At this point, position an hydraulic or mechanical jack under the engine with a block of wood between the jack head and sump **(see illustration)**. Make sure the jack is centrally positioned so the engine will not topple in any direction when the last mounting bolt is removed. Raise the jack to take the weight of the engine, but make sure it is not lifting the bike and taking the weight of that as well. The idea is to support the engine so that there is no pressure on any of the mounting bolts once they have been slackened, so they can be easily withdrawn. Note that it may be necessary to alter the position of the jack as some of the bolts are removed to relieve the stress transferred to the other bolts.
17 Unscrew the engine protection bar and side mounting bracket nut(s)/bolts and remove the bar and bracket from each side, noting whether there is a bolt or a nut securing the bottom mount on the left-hand engine bar, and on 2004-on models also removing the stiffening plates, noting how they fit, and noting the spacer between the left-hand bracket and the engine **(see illustration)**. Remove the left-hand bar with the coolant reservoir attached – there is no need to remove it.
18 Unscrew the clutch release cylinder bleed

4.15 Make an alignment mark then unscrew the pinch-bolt

4.16 Support the engine using a jack

4.17 Left-hand engine bar, stiffening plate and mounting bracket nut and bolts (arrowed) – later model shown

4.18a Unscrew the bleed pipe bolt bracket (arrowed) . . .

4.18b . . . and pipe and hose banjo bolt (arrowed)

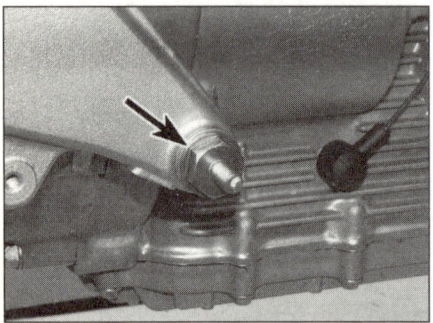

4.19 Right-hand lower rear mounting bolt (arrowed)

4.20 Upper rear mounting pinch-bolt (arrowed)

pipe bracket bolt **(see illustration)**. Unscrew the banjo bolt on the release cylinder on the back of the engine and detach the hose and pipe banjo unions, noting their alignment **(see illustration)**. Seal the banjo unions using plastic foodwrap. Remove the pipe, and secure the hose in an upright position to minimise fluid loss. Discard the sealing washers as new ones must be fitted on reassembly.

19 Unscrew the lower rear mounting bolt on the right-hand side and remove the washer, then remove the spacer from between the engine and frame **(see illustration)**. If the spacer is too tight to remove at this stage wait until the rest of the bolts are undone. Note that on late 2002 models and 2004-on models (i.e. all except early 2002 models and 2003 models – see installation sub-sections) a new spacer is required on installation.

20 Slacken the pinch-bolt for the upper rear mounting **(see illustration)**.

21 On models that have a bolt securing the bottom of the left-hand engine protection bar (early 2002 models and 2003 models), slacken the pinch-bolt for the lower rear mounting on the left-hand side, then unscrew the mounting bolt and remove the washer from between the engine and frame **(see illustration 4.22)**.

22 On models that have a nut securing the bottom of the left-hand engine protection bar (late 2002 models and 2004-on models), unscrew the lower rear mounting bolt on the left-hand side, then slacken the pinch-bolt and remove the collar from the frame and the spacer from between the engine and frame **(see illustration)**. A new spacer is required on installation.

23 Unscrew the front cross-plate and mounting bracket nuts/bolts and remove the plate and brackets, noting the spacer between the left-hand bracket and the engine **(see illustration)**. On 2004-on models note the difference in the head of the lower left-hand

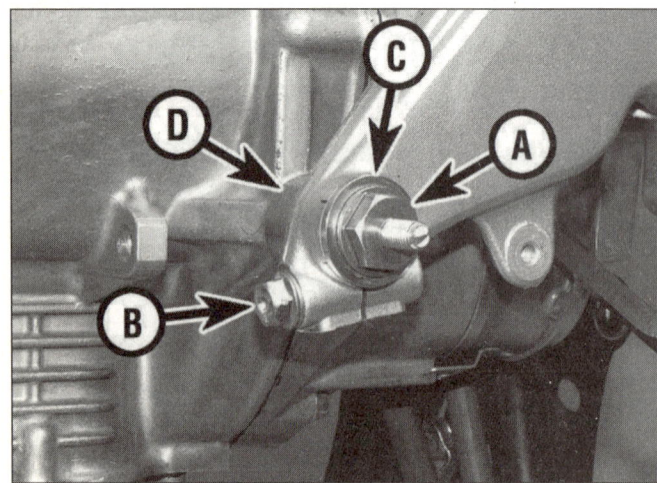

4.22 Right-hand lower rear mounting bolt (A), pinch-bolt (B), collar (C) and spacer (D)

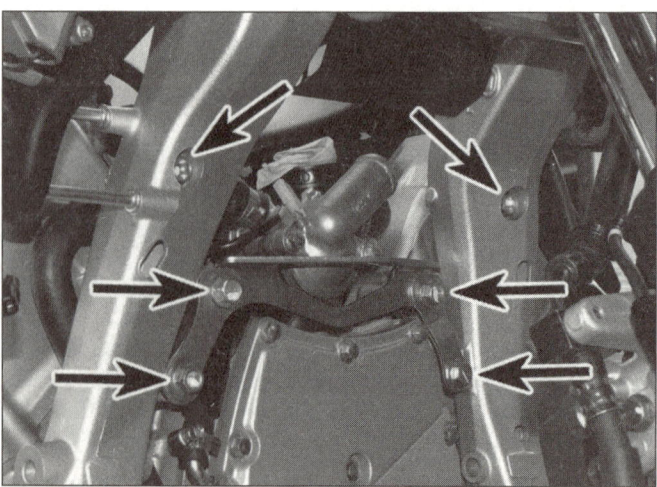

4.23 Front cross-plate and mounting bracket nuts/bolts – later model shown

Engine, clutch and transmission 2•11

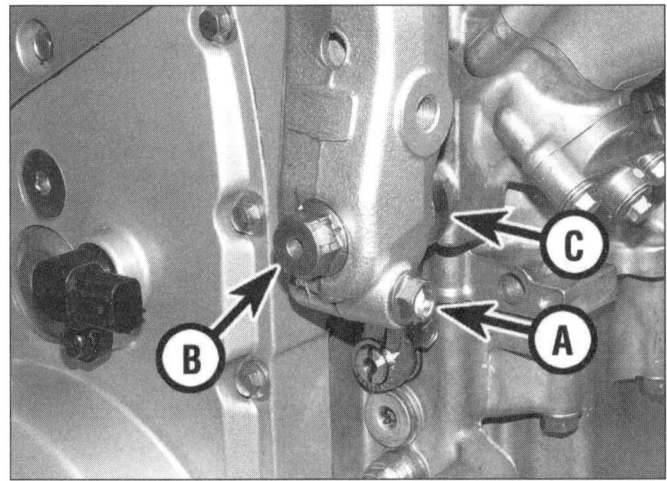

4.24a Left-hand lower front mounting pinch-bolt (A), mounting bolt (B) and spacer (C)

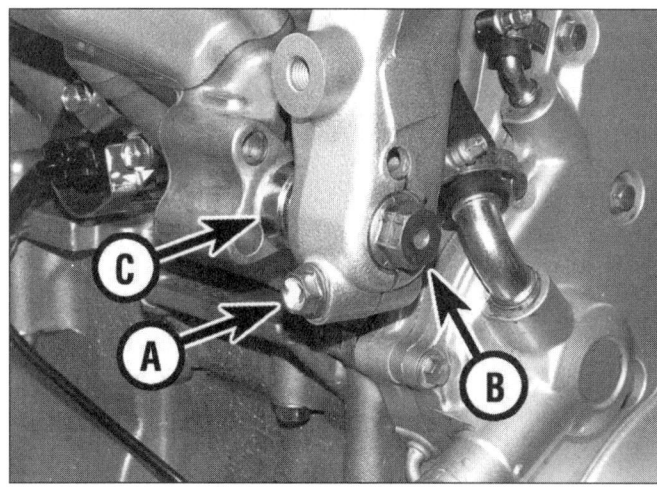

4.24b Right-hand lower front mounting pinch-bolt (A), mounting bolt (B) and spacer (C)

bolt for the cross-plate from the other three bolts.

24 Slacken the pinch-bolt for each lower front mounting (see illustrations). Unscrew each mounting bolt and remove the spacer from between the engine and frame.

25 Unscrew the nut on the right-hand end of the upper rear mounting bolt (see illustration).

26 Check that the engine is properly supported by the jack. Withdraw the upper rear mounting bolt from the left-hand side and remove the spacers (see illustrations 4.64a and b).

27 The engine can now be removed from the frame (see Warning at the start of this section). Make sure the front brake is tied on so the wheel is locked. Check that all wiring, cables and hoses are free and clear. Slowly and carefully fully lower the jack while moving the engine as required so it does not contact the frame – it is advisable to slip a piece of card between the engine and each frame section at the front. Next have two people lift the engine slightly while a third removes the jack from under the engine, then lower the engine to the ground. Now you need one person to raise the bike up off the engine by lifting the rear so the whole frame pivots round the front wheel, and with it raised the other two can manoeuvre the engine out to one side and remove it. Alternatively you can use a form of hoist or a purpose-built frame and some ratchet straps as shown (see illustration). Lower the bike's frame back to the ground, making sure the centrestand is still down to support it.

28 With the engine removed, and if required (for example for a full engine strip), you can now disconnect the ECT sensor wiring connector and its earth wire and remove the thermostat housing and all coolant hoses, detaching them from the coolant outlet union on each cylinder head and from the water pump cover on the front of the engine and the oil cooler on the back, noting which hose fits where and how they are routed (see illustration) – tagging the hose ends with masking tape and writing the location of the union the hose fits onto on the tape is a good way of not getting them muddled up later. You can also disconnect the wiring connectors from the alternator and remove the alternator sub-loom, and disconnect the wiring connectors from the knock sensors, the neutral switch and the oil pressure switch and detach the wiring guide remove their sub-loom, noting its routing (see illustration).

Installation

29 If removed fit the wiring sub-looms and the thermostat housing and coolant hoses (see Step 28). With the front wheel locked by the front brake, raise the frame as on removal and manoeuvre the engine into position under it. Carefully lower the frame over the engine, moving the engine as required so no contact is made with the frame, and making sure the centrestand is still down to support it. With the engine and frame correctly positioned have two people lift the engine while the third slides the jack into a central position under it, not forgetting the piece of wood between them (see illustration 4.16). Let the jack take the weight of the engine. Raise the engine using the jack to align all the mounting bolt holes,

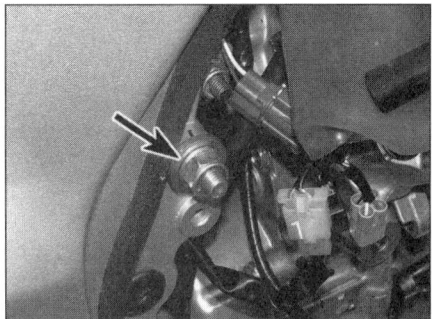

4.25 Upper rear mounting bolt nut (arrowed)

4.27 Using a frame and ratchet strap to raise and hold the back of the bike

4.28a If required remove the thermostat housing (arrowed) and the coolant hoses . . .

4.28b . . . and the wiring sub-loom (arrowed)

2•12 Engine, clutch and transmission

and making sure that all cables and wiring are correctly routed and do not get trapped – use card as on removal between the engine and frame sections at the front for protection. Note that during the installation process it may be necessary to adjust the jack as some of the bolts are installed and tightened to realign the other bolt holes.

Early 2002 and 2003 Europe, 2003 and 2004 US and Canada

Note: *For identification of the different models there is a bolt, not a nut, securing the bottom of the left-hand engine protection bar, and there are no stiffening plates between the engine bars and the side mounting plates.*

30 Smear some grease into the lower front mounting bolt holes in the frame.

31 Slide the upper rear mounting bolt through from the left-hand side, locating each spacer between the engine and frame **(see illustrations 4.64a and b)**. Smear some oil onto the threads and mating flange of the nut, then fit the nut with its washer and tighten it finger-tight **(see illustration 4.64c)**.

32 Fit the lower front mounting bolts, locating the spacers between the engine and frame, and thread them in loosely **(see illustrations 4.66a and b)**.

33 Fit the front mounting brackets and cross-plate, not forgetting the spacer between the left-hand bracket and the engine, and tighten the nuts and bolts finger-tight **(see illustrations 4.63a, b, c and d)**.

34 Fit the lower rear mounting bolts **(see illustrations 4.19 and 4.22)**, not forgetting the washer with the right-hand bolt, and locating the spacer (right-hand side) and washer (left-hand side) between the engine and frame, and tighten them finger-tight so the bolt flanges are seated. Make sure there is no freeplay in the spacer (right-hand side) and washer (left-hand side).

35 Tighten each lower front mounting bolt until the bolt flange seats, then check there is no freeplay in the spacer. Tighten the bolts to a torque setting of 10 Nm. Fix a degree disc to the torque wrench and set the pointer to 45°. Now tighten each bolt to 64 Nm, and if the bolt has not turned through 45° when the torque setting is reached, tighten it further to the 45° mark. If the bolt goes through 45° without reaching 64 Nm keep going until 64 Nm is reached.

36 Tighten the lower front mounting pinch-bolts to 26 Nm **(see illustrations 4.24a and b)**.

37 Tighten the lower rear mounting bolt on the right-hand side to a torque setting of 10 Nm. Fix a degree disc to the torque wrench and set the pointer to 75°. Now tighten the bolt to 64 Nm, and if the bolt has not turned through 75° when the torque setting is reached, tighten it further to the 75° mark. If the bolt goes through 75° without reaching 64 Nm keep going until 64 Nm is reached.

38 Fit the right-hand side mounting bracket and engine protection bar, and tighten the nut/bolts finger-tight.

39 Tighten the lower rear mounting bolt on the left-hand side to a torque setting of 10 Nm. Fix a degree disc to the torque wrench and set the pointer to 20°. Now tighten the bolt to 64 Nm, and if the bolt has not turned through 20° when the torque setting is reached, tighten it further to the 20° mark. If the bolt goes through 20° without reaching 64 Nm keep going until 64 Nm is reached.

40 Fit the left-hand side mounting bracket and engine protection bar, not forgetting the spacer between the bracket and the engine, and tighten the bolts finger-tight.

41 Tighten the upper rear mounting bolt nut to a torque setting of 10 Nm. Fix a degree disc to the torque wrench and set the pointer to 360°. Now tighten the bolt to 42 Nm, and if the bolt has not turned through 360° when the torque setting is reached, tighten it further to the 360° mark. If the bolt goes through 360° without reaching 42 Nm keep going until 42 Nm is reached.

42 Tighten the front bolt on the right-hand side mounting bracket to 39 Nm, then tighten the rear bolt to 26 Nm. Tighten the front bolt on the engine protection bar to 39 Nm, and tighten the rear bolt and the nut to 26 Nm.

43 Tighten the front bolt on the left-hand side mounting bracket to 39 Nm, then tighten the rear bolt to 26 Nm. Tighten the front bolt on the engine protection bar to 39 Nm, and tighten the rear and lower bolts to 26 Nm.

44 Tighten the front cross-plate bolts to 26 Nm. Tighten the front mounting bracket bolt nuts to 26 Nm.

45 Tighten the pinch-bolts for the upper and lower rear mountings on the left-hand side to 26 Nm.

Late 2002 Europe

Note 1: *For identification of different models there is a nut, not a bolt, securing the bottom of the left-hand engine protection bar, and there are no stiffening plates between the engine bars and the side mounting plates.*

Note 2: *A new spacer is required for the lower rear mounting bolt on each side.*

46 Fit the left-hand front mounting bracket with its upper and lower bolts, not forgetting the spacer between it and the engine, and tighten the nuts to 27 Nm **(see illustrations 4.63d and c)**.

47 Fit the right-hand front mounting bracket with its upper and lower bolts and tighten the nuts finger-tight **(see illustration 4.63a and b)**.

48 Slide the upper rear mounting bolt through from the left-hand side, locating each spacer between the engine and frame **(see illustrations 4.64a and b)**. Smear some grease onto the threads and mating flange of the nut, then fit the nut with its washer and tighten it finger-tight **(see illustration 4.64c)**.

49 Smear some grease into the lower front mounting bolt holes in the frame.

50 Fit the lower front mounting bolts, locating the spacers between the engine and frame, and thread them in loosely **(see illustrations 4.66a and b)**.

51 Fit a new spacer between the engine and frame for the lower rear mounting on the right-hand side – make sure the ridges on the new spacer do not sit in the indents made by the ridges on the old spacer, and use a suitable bar to carefully lever the frame away from the engine to get the clearance **(see illustrations 4.67a and b)**. Smear the threads of the lower rear mounting bolt with oil then fit the bolt with its washer and tighten it finger-tight **(see illustration 4.67c)**. Make sure there is no freeplay in the spacer.

52 Smear the threads of the left-hand lower rear mounting bolt with oil then fit the bolt with its collar (do not fit the spacer at this stage) and tighten it finger-tight **(see illustration 4.68)**.

53 Fit the front cross-plate and tighten the bolts finger-tight.

54 Tighten the upper rear mounting bolt nut to a torque setting of 10 Nm **(see illustration 4.25)**. Now tighten the bolt through 270° (3/4 turn) either using a degree disc, or by making a mark on the rim of the nut flange at 12 o'clock and a mark on the frame at 9 o'clock, then tightening the nut until the marks align.

55 Tighten the upper rear mounting pinch-bolt to 27 Nm **(see illustration 4.20)**.

56 Tighten the lower rear mounting bolt on the right-hand side to a torque setting of 103 Nm **(see illustration 4.19)**. Unscrew the bolt 180° (1/2 a turn). Now tighten the bolt to 20 Nm. Finally tighten the bolt through 65° either using a degree disc, or by marking the nut and frame as shown (the angle between two points of the bolt head is 60°) and tightening the nut from one mark to the other **(see illustration 4.71)**.

57 Remove the lower rear mounting bolt from the left-hand side **(see illustration 4.68)**. Fit a new spacer between the engine and frame **(see illustration 4.72)** – make sure the ridges on the new spacer do not sit in the indents made by the ridges on the old spacer, and use a suitable bar to carefully lever the frame away from the engine to get the clearance **(see illustrations 4.67a and b)**. Fit the mounting bolt and tighten it to a torque setting of 103 Nm. Unscrew the bolt 180° (1/2 a turn). Tighten the bolt again to 103 Nm, then unscrew it again 180° (1/2 a turn). Tighten the pinch-bolt to 27 Nm. Now tighten the mounting bolt to 20 Nm. Finally tighten the bolt through 65° using a degree disc, or by marking the nut and frame as shown (the angle between two points of the bolt head is 60°) and tightening the nut from one mark to the other **(see illustration 4.71)**.

58 Tighten each lower front mounting bolt until the bolt flange seats, then check there is no freeplay in the spacer **(see illustrations 4.24a and b)**. Tighten the bolts, right-hand first, then left-hand, to a torque setting of 20 Nm. Now tighten the bolts through 42.5° either using a degree disc or by making marks as before.

59 Tighten the right-hand front mounting

Engine, clutch and transmission 2•13

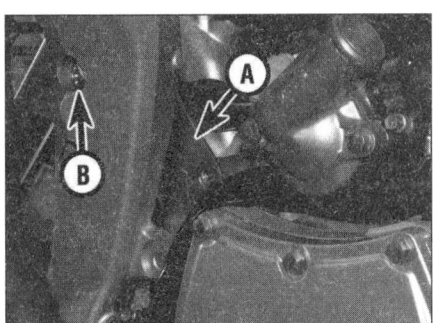
4.63a Fit the flat right-hand bracket (A) first, securing it with the upper bolt (B) . . .

4.63b . . . and the nut (arrowed)

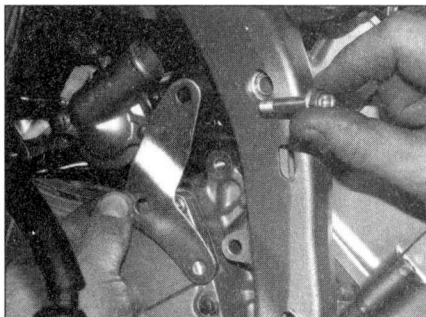
4.63c Fit the stepped bracket on the left . . .

4.63d . . . not forgetting the spacer (arrowed) between it and the frame

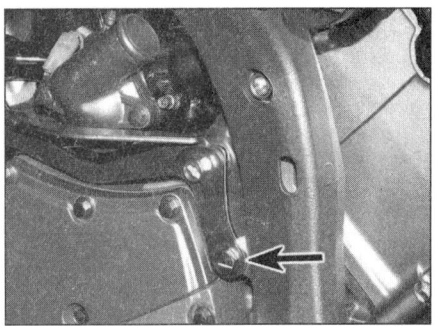
4.63e Next fit the cross-plate, with the odd bolt (arrowed) as shown . . .

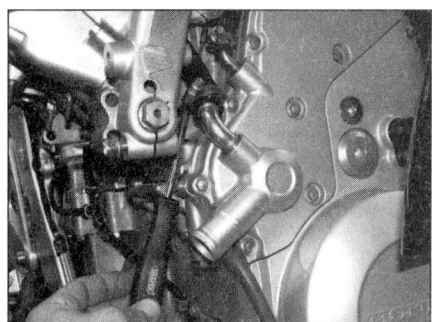
4.63f . . . the nut for the bottom right bolt is difficult to fit – we used a telescopic magnet to locate and hold it

bracket bolt nuts to 27 Nm. Tighten the front cross-plate bolts to 27 Nm.

60 Tighten the lower front mounting pinch-bolts to 27 Nm **(see illustrations 4.24a and b)**.

61 Fit the right-hand engine bracket and engine protection bar, and tighten the nut/bolts finger-tight. Tighten the front bolt on the mounting bracket to 39 Nm, then tighten the rear bolt to 26 Nm. Tighten the front bolt on the engine protection bar to 39 Nm, and tighten the rear bolt and the nut to 26 Nm.

62 Fit the left-hand engine bracket and engine protection bar, not forgetting the spacer between the bracket and the engine, and tighten the bolts finger-tight. Tighten the front bolt on the mounting bracket to 39 Nm, then tighten the rear bolt to 26 Nm. Tighten the front bolt on the engine protection bar to 39 Nm, and tighten the rear bolt and the nut to 26 Nm.

2004-on Europe, 2005-on US and Canada

Note 1: *For identification of different models there is a nut, not a bolt, securing the bottom of the left-hand engine protection bar, and there are stiffening plates between the engine bars and the side mounting plates.*

Note 2: *A new spacer is required for the lower rear mounting bolt on each side.*

63 Fit the front mounting brackets and cross-plate, not forgetting the spacer between the upper left mounting on the engine and the left-hand bracket, and tighten the nuts and bolts finger-tight **(see illustrations)** – make sure the cross-plate bolt with the different head is fitted in the lower left mount **(see illustration)**.

64 Slide the upper rear mounting bolt through from the left-hand side, locating each spacer between the engine and frame **(see illustrations)**. Smear some grease onto the threads and mating flange of the nut, then fit the nut with its washer and tighten it finger-tight **(see illustration)**.

65 Smear some grease into the lower front mounting bolt holes in the frame.

66 Fit the lower front mounting bolts, locating

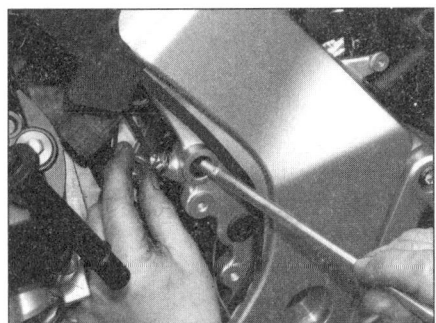
4.64a Fit the upper rear bolt and left-hand spacer . . .

4.64b . . . and the right-hand spacer . . .

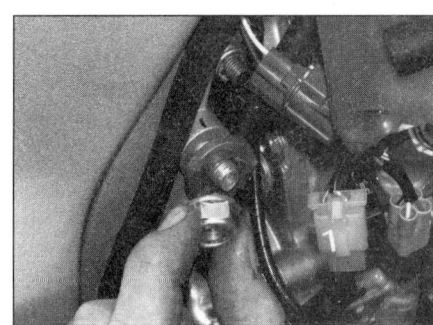
4.64c . . . then fit the greased washer and nut

2•14 Engine, clutch and transmission

4.66a Fit the left-hand lower front bolt and spacer ...

4.66b ... then fit the right-hand lower front bolt and spacer

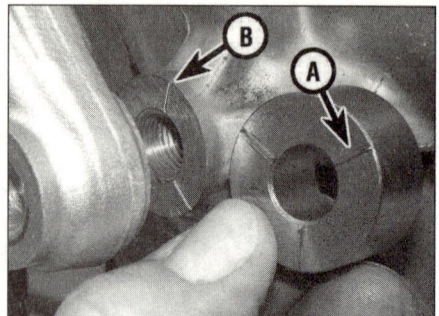

4.67a Offset the three ridges (A) on the new spacer from the indents (B) made by the old spacer ...

the spacers between the engine and frame, and thread them in loosely **(see illustrations)**.

67 Fit a new spacer between the engine and frame for the lower rear mounting on the right-hand side – make sure the ridges on the new spacer do not sit in the indents made by the ridges on the old spacer, and use a suitable bar to carefully lever the frame away from the engine to get the clearance **(see illustrations)**. Smear the threads of the lower rear mounting bolt with oil then fit the bolt with its washer and tighten it finger-tight **(see illustration)**. Make sure there is no freeplay in the spacer.

68 Smear the threads of the left-hand lower rear mounting bolt with oil then fit the bolt with its collar (do not fit the spacer at this stage) and tighten it finger-tight **(see illustration)**.

69 Tighten the upper rear mounting bolt nut to a torque setting of 10 Nm **(see illustration 4.25)**. Now tighten the nut through 270° (3/4 turn) either using a degree disc, or by making a mark on the rim of the nut flange at 12 o'clock and a mark on the frame at 9 o'clock, then tightening the nut until the marks align.

70 Tighten the upper rear mounting pinch-bolt to 27 Nm **(see illustration 4.20)**.

71 Tighten the lower rear mounting bolt on the right-hand side to a torque setting of 103 Nm **(see illustration 4.19)**. Unscrew the bolt 180° (1/2 a turn). Tighten the bolt again to 103 Nm, then unscrew it again 180° (1/2 a turn). Now tighten the bolt to 20 Nm. Finally tighten the bolt through 65° either using a degree disc, or by marking the nut and frame as shown (the angle between two points of the bolt head is 60°) and tightening the nut from one mark to the other **(see illustration)**.

72 Remove the lower rear mounting bolt from the left-hand side **(see illustration 4.68)**. Fit a new spacer between the engine and frame **(see illustration)** – make sure the ridges on the new spacer do not sit in the indents made by the ridges on the old spacer, and use a suitable bar to carefully lever the frame away from the engine to get the clearance **(see illustrations 4.67a and b)**. Fit the mounting bolt and tighten to a torque setting of 103 Nm. Unscrew the bolt 180° (1/2 a turn). Tighten the bolt again to 103 Nm, then unscrew it again 180° (1/2 a turn). Tighten the pinch-bolt to 27 Nm. Now tighten the mounting bolt to 20 Nm. Finally tighten the bolt through 65° using a degree disc, or by marking the nut and frame as shown (the angle between two points of the bolt head is 60°) and tightening the nut from one mark to the other **(see illustration 4.71)**.

73 Tighten each lower front mounting bolt until the bolt flange seats, then check there is no freeplay in the spacers **(see illustrations 4.24a and b)**. Tighten the bolts, right-hand first, then left-hand, to a torque setting of 20 Nm. Now tighten the bolts through 42.5° either using a degree disc or by making marks as before.

74 Tighten the front mounting bracket bolt nuts to 27 Nm **(see illustration 4.23)**. Tighten the front cross-plate bolts/nuts to 27 Nm.

75 Tighten the lower front mounting pinch-bolts to 27 Nm **(see illustrations 4.24a and b)**.

76 Fit the right-hand engine bracket, engine protection bar and stiffening plate in that

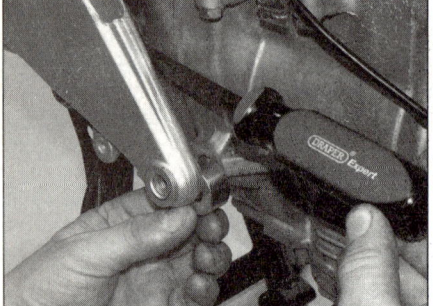

4.67b ... and use a lever to create clearance to fit the spacer ...

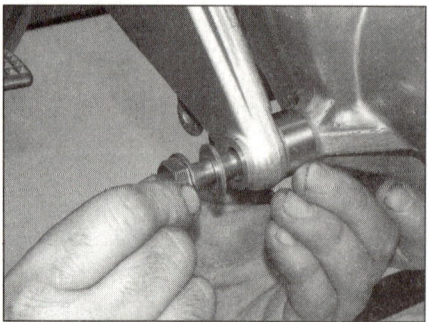

4.67c ... then fit the oiled right-hand lower rear bolt with its washer

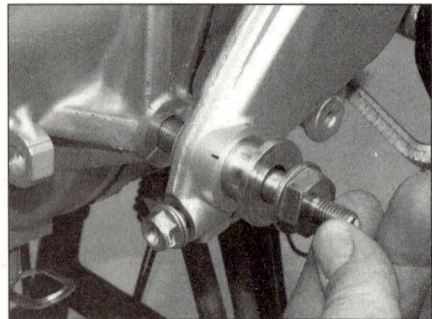

4.68 Fit the oiled left-hand lower rear bolt and collar

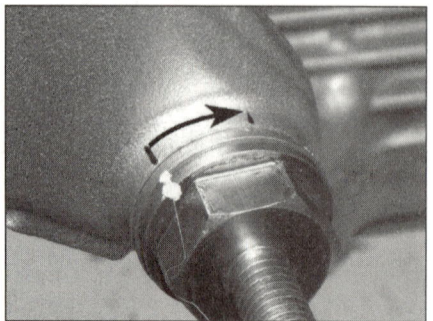

4.71 Mark the nut and frame as shown then tighten the nut from one frame mark to the other

4.72 Fit the spacer between the engine and frame, offsetting the ridges and old indents as before

Engine, clutch and transmission 2•15

4.76a Fit the bracket and the lower rear bolt . . .

4.76b . . . then fit the engine bar and its rear bolt . . .

4.76c . . . and front bolt . . .

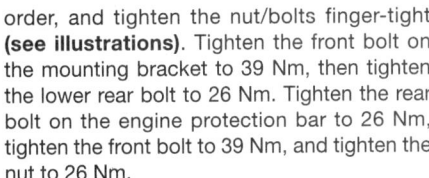
4.76d . . . then locate the stiffening plate and fit its upper bolt . . .

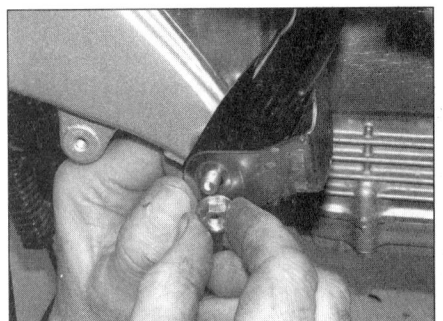
4.76e . . . and the lower nut

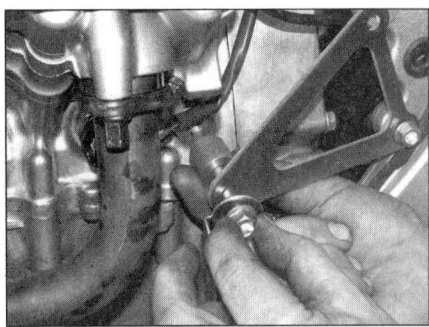
4.78 Fit the spacer between the front of the bracket and the frame

order, and tighten the nut/bolts finger-tight **(see illustrations)**. Tighten the front bolt on the mounting bracket to 39 Nm, then tighten the lower rear bolt to 26 Nm. Tighten the rear bolt on the engine protection bar to 26 Nm, tighten the front bolt to 39 Nm, and tighten the nut to 26 Nm.

77 Position a new sealing washer on each side of the clutch bleed pipe union and clutch hose union (three washers in all) and loosely fit the banjo bolt **(see illustration 4.18b)**. Fit the pipe bracket and tighten its bolt **(see illustration 4.18a)**. Ensure the hose is correctly positioned then tighten the banjo bolt to the torque setting specified at the beginning of the Chapter. Bleed the system (see Section 15).

78 Fit the left-hand engine bracket, engine protection bar and stiffening plate in that order and in the same way as the right-hand **(see illustration 4.17)**, but not forgetting the spacer between the bracket and the engine, and tighten the bolts finger-tight **(see illustration)**. Tighten the front bolt on the mounting bracket to 39 Nm, then tighten the rear bolt to 26 Nm. Tighten the rear bolt on the engine protection bar to 26 Nm, tighten the front bolt to 39 Nm, and tighten the nut to 26 Nm.

All models

79 The remainder of the installation procedure is the reverse of removal, referring to the relevant Chapters where directed, and noting the following points:
- Make sure all wires, cables and hoses are correctly routed and connected, and secured by any clips or ties.
- Use new gaskets on the exhaust pipe connections.
- Refill the engine with oil and coolant (see Chapter 1).
- Adjust the throttle cable freeplay.
- Start the engine and check that there are no oil or coolant leaks. Adjust the idle speed (see Chapter 1).

5 Engine overhaul information

1 Before beginning the engine overhaul, read through the related procedures to familiarise yourself with the scope and requirements of the job. Overhauling an engine is not all that difficult, but it is time-consuming. Check on the availability of parts and make sure that any necessary special tools are obtained in advance.

2 Most work can be done with a typical workshop hand tools, although a number of precision measuring tools are required for inspecting parts to determine if they are worn.

3 To ensure maximum life and minimum trouble from a rebuilt engine, everything must be assembled with care in a spotlessly clean environment.

Disassembly

4 Before disassembling the engine, thoroughly clean and degrease its external surfaces. This will prevent contamination of the engine internals, and will also make the job a lot easier and cleaner. A high flash-point solvent, such as paraffin (kerosene) can be used, or better still, a proprietary engine degreaser such as Gunk. Use old paintbrushes and toothbrushes to work the solvent into the various recesses of the casings. Take care to exclude solvent or water from the electrical components and intake and exhaust ports.

 Warning: The use of petrol (gasoline) as a cleaning agent should be avoided because of the risk of fire.

5 When clean and dry, position the engine on the workbench, leaving suitable clear area for working. Gather a selection of small containers, plastic bags and some labels so that parts can be grouped together in an easily identifiable manner. Also get some paper and a pen so that notes can be taken. You will also need a supply of clean rag, which should be as absorbent as possible.

6 Before commencing work, read through the appropriate section so that some idea of the necessary procedure can be gained. When removing components note that great force is seldom required, unless specified (checking the specified torque setting of the particular bolt being removed will indicate how tight it is, and therefore how much force should be needed). In many cases, a component's reluctance to be removed is indicative of an incorrect approach or removal method – if in any doubt, re check with the text.

7 When disassembling the engine, keep 'mated' parts together (including gears,

2•16 Engine, clutch and transmission

pistons, connecting rods, valves, etc, that have been in contact with each other during engine operation). These 'mated' parts must be reused or replaced as an assembly.

8 A complete engine disassembly should be done in the following general order with reference to the appropriate Sections.
- *Remove the valve covers*
- *Remove the camshafts*
- *Remove the cylinder heads*
- *Remove the clutch*
- *Remove the primary drive gear*
- *Remove the cam chain and blades*
- *Remove the primary damper shaft*
- *Remove the final output shaft and gears*
- *Remove the starter clutch and gears*
- *Remove the alternator gears*
- *Remove the alternator (see Chapter 8)*
- *Remove the gearchange mechanism*
- *Remove the transmission assembly*
- *Remove the oil sump*
- *Remove the oil pump*
- *Separate the crankcase halves*
- *Remove the balancer shafts*
- *Remove the crankshaft*
- *Remove the connecting rods and pistons*

Reassembly

9 Reassembly is accomplished by reversing the general disassembly sequence.

6 Oil cooler

Note: *The oil cooler can be removed with the engine in the frame. If the engine has been removed, ignore the steps which do not apply.*

Removal

1 The cooler is located on the back of the engine.
2 Drain the engine oil and remove the oil filter (see Chapter 1). Either drain the coolant (see Chapter 1), or fit hose clamps onto the hoses to the cooler **(see illustration 6.3)**.
3 Slacken the clamp securing each hose to the cooler and detach the hoses **(see illustration)** – be prepared with some rag to catch residual coolant.
4 Unscrew the centre bolt and remove the washer, noting which way round it fits **(see illustration)**. Remove the cooler, noting its

6.3 Slacken the clamps (arrowed) and detach the hoses

6.6a Fit a new O-ring into the groove

alignment. Discard the O-ring as a new one must be used.
5 Check the cooler body for cracks and dents and any evidence of coolant leakage and replace it with a new one if necessary. Also check the hoses for splits, cracks, hardening and deterioration and fit new ones if required.

Installation

6 Installation is the reverse of removal, noting the following:
- Ensure the mating surfaces of the crankcase and the cooler are clean and dry.
- Use a new O-ring on the cooler body and smear it with clean engine oil. Make sure it seats in its groove **(see illustration)**.
- Locate the tabs on the cooler on each side of the lug on the engine **(see illustration)**.
- Fit the cooler bolt washer with the punch mark facing in. Lubricate the cooler bolt threads and seating surface with oil.

7.5a Unscrew the bolts (arrowed) . . .

7.5b . . . and remove the cover

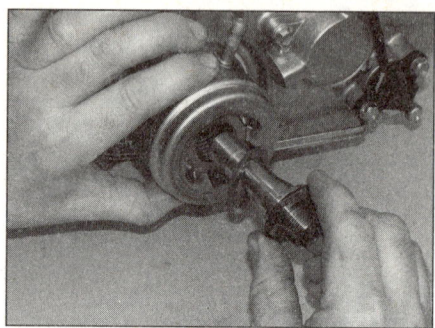

6.4 Unscrew the bolt and remove the cooler

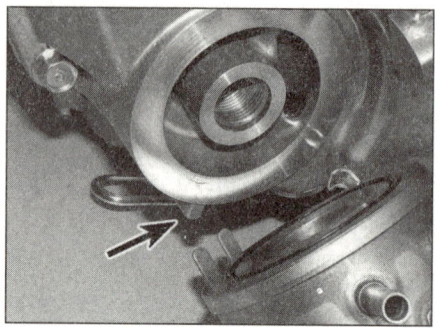

6.6b Locate the tabs around the lug (arrowed)

- Tighten the bolt to the torque setting specified at the beginning of the Chapter.
- Make sure the coolant hoses are pressed fully onto their unions and are secured by the clamps.
- Fit a new oil filter and refill the engine with the specified amount and type of oil (see Chapter 1).
- Refill the cooling system (see Chapter 1).

7 Valve covers

Note: *The valve covers can be removed with the engine in the frame. If the engine has been removed, ignore the steps which do not apply.*

Removal

1 Remove the fairing side panels (see Chapter 7).
2 Remove the trim cover from the top of the valve cover (see Chapter 7).
3 Clean the area around each spark plug cap to prevent any dirt falling into the spark plug channels. Pull the cap off each spark plug **(see illustration 4.7)**.
4 Detach the PAIR system hose from the cover, and detach the crankcase breather hose from the left-hand cover **(see illustration 4.14)**. When removing the left-hand cover release the wiring loom tie from the fairing side panel stud.
5 Unscrew the three valve cover bolts and lift the cover off the cylinder head **(see illustrations)**. If the cover is stuck, do not try

Engine, clutch and transmission 2•17

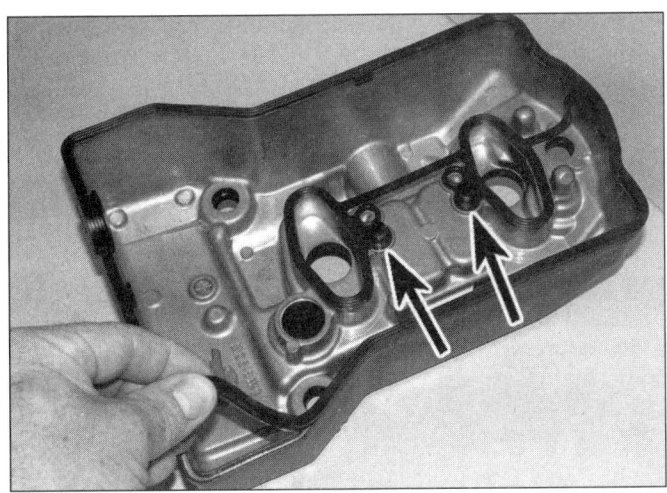

7.12a Make sure the gasket locates over the dowels (arrowed) and in the groove and stays there

7.12b Apply a sealant to the cutouts (arrowed) in the cylinder head

to lever it off with a screwdriver. Tap it gently around the sides with a rubber hammer or block of wood to dislodge it. Note the rubber washers for the bolts and remove them if they are loose **(see illustration 7.13a)**.

6 The rubber gasket is normally glued into the groove in the cover, and is best left there if it is reusable. If the gasket is in any way damaged, deformed or deteriorated, remove it **(see illustration 7.12a)**.

7 Note the two dowels that link the PAIR system air passages between the valve cover and cylinder head and remove them for safekeeping if they are loose **(see illustration 7.12a)**.

8 If required, remove the PAIR system reed valves (see Chapter 4).

Installation

9 Clean the engine breather hose union, then check the breather is not blocked by blowing through the hole.
10 If removed, install the PAIR system reed valves (see Chapter 4).
11 If removed, fit the PAIR system dowels into the valve cover **(see illustration 7.12a)**.
12 Examine the valve cover gasket for signs of damage or deterioration and fit a new one if necessary. If a new one is used, clean all traces of the old glue from the groove in the cover and clean it and the cylinder head

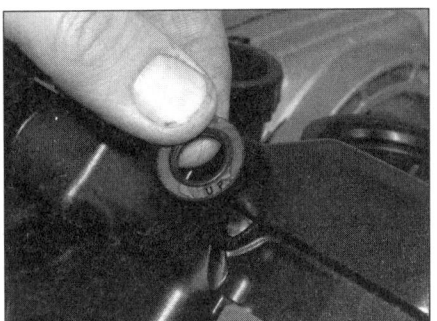

7.13a Make sure the UP marks on the washers face up

mating surface with solvent. Fit the new gasket into the grooves, using a suitable glue, sealant or grease to hold it in place **(see illustration)**. Also apply a suitable sealant to the cut-outs in the cylinder head **(see illustration)**.
13 Position the valve cover on the cylinder head, making sure the gasket stays in place **(see illustration 7.5b)** – make sure the cover with the oil filler cap is on the right-hand cylinder head. If removed, fit the rubber washers into the cover, using new ones if required, and making sure they are installed with the UP mark facing up **(see illustration)**. Install the cover bolts and tighten them to the specified torque setting **(see illustration)**.

7.13b Fit the bolts and tighten them to the specified torque

14 Connect the PAIR system hose to the cover, and connect the crankcase breather hose to the left-hand cover **(see illustration 4.14)**. When fitting the left-hand cover secure the wiring loom tie over the fairing side panel stud.
15 Fit the caps onto the plugs and push them down so they are fully seated **(see illustration 4.7)**.
16 Install the trim cover and fairing side panels (see Chapter 7).

8 Cam chain tensioners

Note: *The cam chain tensioners can be removed with the engine in the frame. If the engine has been removed, ignore the steps which do not apply.*

Removal

1 To access the right-hand tensioner remove the throttle bodies (see Chapter 4), and to access the left-hand tensioner remove the left-hand fairing side panel (see Chapter 7) **(see illustration)**.
2 Unscrew the tensioner cap bolt and remove the sealing washer **(see illustration)**. Slacken the tensioner mounting bolts slightly.

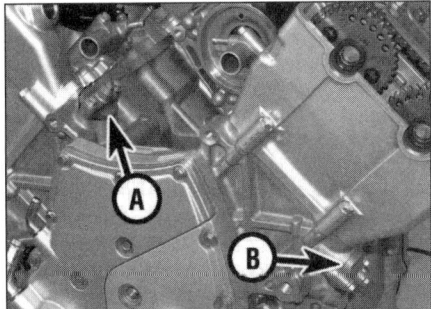

8.1 Right-hand tensioner (A), left-hand tensioner (B)

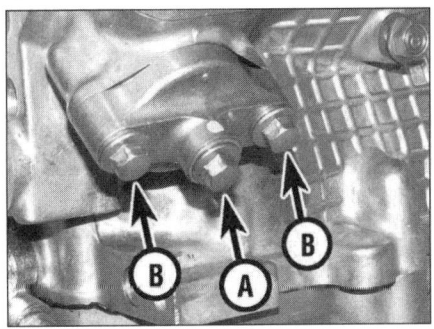

8.2 Unscrew the cap bolt (A) then slacken the mounting bolts (B)

2•18 Engine, clutch and transmission

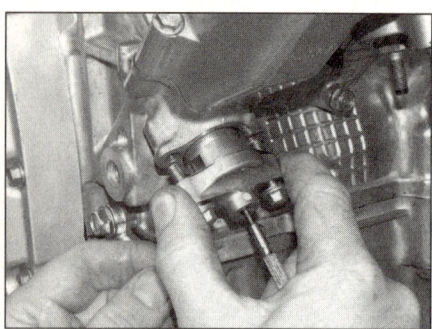

8.3 Insert the screwdriver and retract the plunger, then unscrew the bolts and remove the tensioner

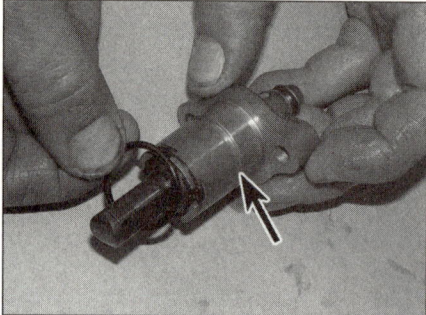

8.5 Fit a new O-ring into the groove (arrowed)

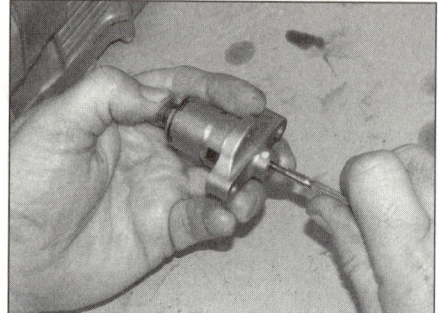

8.6a Insert the screwdriver and retract the plunger . . .

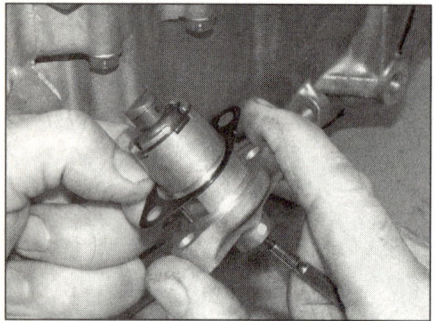

8.6b . . . then fit a new gasket

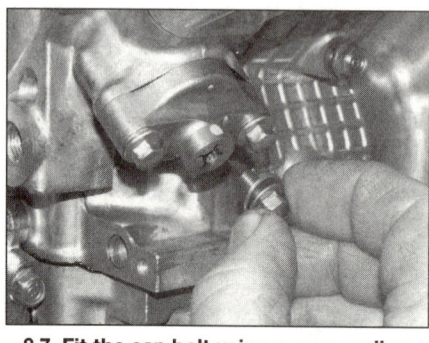

8.7 Fit the cap bolt using a new sealing washer

9 Camshafts and followers

Note: *The camshafts can be removed with the engine in the frame. Place clean rags in the spark plug holes and the cam chain tunnel to prevent any component from dropping into the engine.*

Removal

1 Remove the spark plugs (see Chapter 1). Remove the valve cover(s) (see Section 7).
2 Unscrew the timing inspection cap and the crankshaft cap from the front of the engine **(see illustration)**. Check the condition of the O-rings and obtain new ones if necessary.
3 The engine must be set so that when removing the left-hand cylinder camshafts the No. 1 piston is at TDC (top dead centre) on its compression stroke, and when removing the right-hand cylinder camshafts the No. 2 piston is at TDC (top dead centre) on its compression stroke. Turn the engine using a socket on the timing rotor bolt and turning it in an anti-clockwise direction only **(see illustration)**. **Note:** *If you know that you are going to fit one or more new camshaft(s) or sprocket(s), slacken the relevant sprocket bolts now, turning the engine anti-clockwise as required to access them, then counter-holding the engine using the timing rotor bolt to prevent it turning. Now set the engine in the correct position as described in Step 4 or 5, according to side. If possible work on one head at time, i.e. complete the installation of the camshafts to that head before removing the camshafts from the other head – this avoids having to turn the engine with one set of camshafts removed. If not keep the free cam chain held taut while turning the engine to prevent it dropping down and jamming.*
4 To remove the left-hand cylinder camshafts turn the engine anti-clockwise until the line above the T1 mark on the timing rotor aligns with the static timing mark, which is a pointer in the top of the inspection hole, and the L-IN and L-EX marks on the left-hand intake and exhaust camshaft sprockets respectively are facing away from each other and are flush with the

3 Insert a small flat-bladed screwdriver in the end of the tensioner so that it engages the slot in the plunger **(see illustration)**. Turn the screwdriver clockwise until the plunger is fully retracted and hold it in this position while unscrewing the tensioner mounting bolts. Remove the bolts, then withdraw the tensioner from the engine. Release the screwdriver – the plunger will spring back out.
4 Remove the O-ring from the right-hand tensioner **(see illustration 8.5)**. Discard the gaskets, sealing washers and O-ring – new ones must be used on installation. Do not attempt to dismantle the tensioner.

Installation

5 Check that the plunger moves smoothly when wound into the tensioner and springs back out freely when released **(see illustration 8.6a)**. Ensure the tensioner and cylinder block surfaces are clean and dry. When installing the right-hand tensioner fit a new O-ring into the groove **(see illustration)**.
6 Insert a small flat-bladed screwdriver in the end of the tensioner so that it engages the slotted plunger **(see illustration)**. Turn the screwdriver clockwise until the plunger is fully retracted and hold it in this position whilst the tensioner is installed. Fit a new gasket onto the tensioner body **(see illustration)**.
7 Install the tensioner with its mounting bolts and washers and tighten them **(see illustration 8.3)**. Release the screwdriver – as you release it should turn as the plunger extends. Remove the screwdriver, then fit the tensioner cap bolt with a new sealing washer and tighten it **(see illustration)**.
8 Install the throttle bodies (see Chapter 4) and the fairing side panel (see Chapter 7).

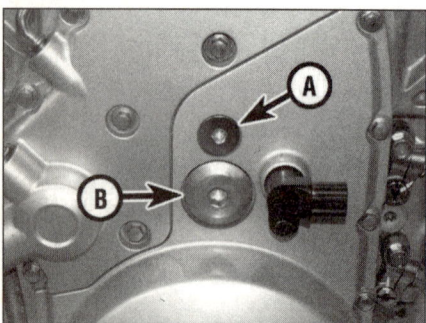

9.2 Unscrew the timing inspection cap (A) and the crankshaft cap (B)

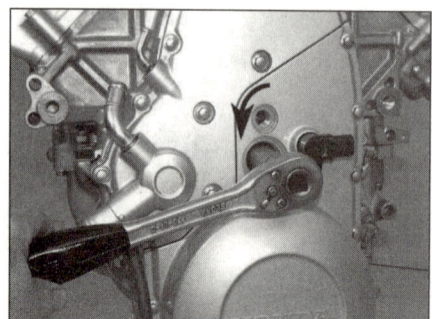

9.3 Turn the engine anti-clockwise using a socket on the bolt

Engine, clutch and transmission 2•19

9.4a For the left-hand camshafts turn the engine until the line next to the T1 mark aligns with the pointer (arrowed) . . .

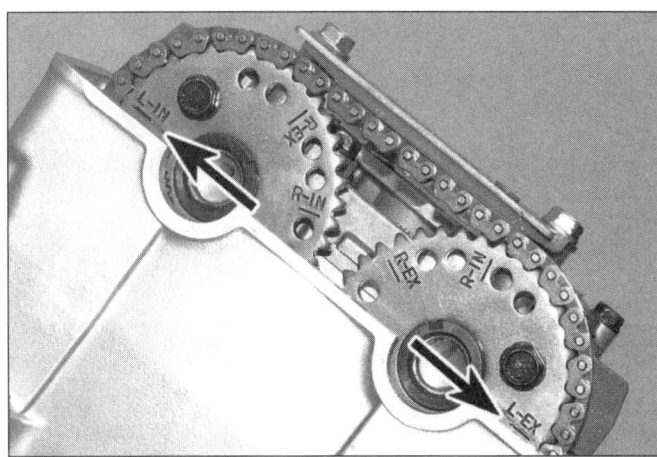

9.4b . . . and the camshaft sprocket L-IN and L-EX marks (arrowed) on the left-hand head are as shown

9.5a For the right-hand camshafts turn the engine until the line next to the T2 mark aligns with the pointer (arrowed) . . .

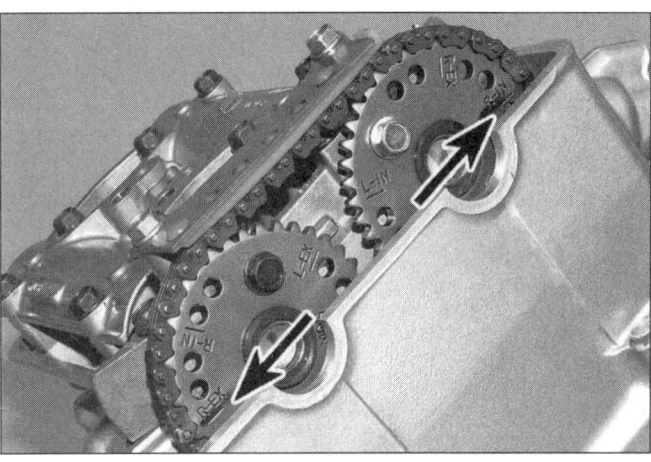

9.5b . . . and the camshaft sprocket R-IN and R-EX marks (arrowed) on the right-hand head are as shown

cylinder head top surface **(see illustrations)**. If the sprocket marks are facing towards each other, rotate the engine anti-clockwise one full turn (360°) until the line next to the T1 mark again aligns with the static timing mark. The sprocket marks will now be facing away.

5 To remove the right-hand cylinder camshafts turn the engine anti-clockwise until the line above the T2 mark on the timing rotor aligns with the static timing mark, which is a notch in the inspection hole rim, and the R-IN and R-EX marks on the right-hand intake and exhaust camshaft sprockets respectively are facing away from each other and are flush with the cylinder head top surface **(see illustrations)**. If the sprocket marks are facing towards each other, rotate the engine anti-clockwise one full turn (360°) until the line next to the T2 mark again aligns with the static timing mark. The sprocket marks will now be facing away.

6 Remove the relevant cam chain tensioner (see Section 8).

7 Unscrew the bolts securing the cam chain top guide and remove it **(see illustration)**.

8 There are two camshaft holders on each head, each bridging both camshafts. The main holder is marked IN which faces the intake side of the head – also mark the holder L or R according to which side of the engine you are working on to avoid confusion on reassembly **(see illustration)**. The front holder is marked L or R according to side **(see illustration)**.

9.7 Unscrew the bolts (arrowed) and remove the guide

9.8a The intake side of the main holder is marked IN – also mark it L or R according to side

9.8b The front holder is marked L or R according to side

9.9 Front holder bolts (A), main holder bolts (B)

9.11 Each camshaft is marked so they can't be muddled up

9 Unscrew the front camshaft holder bolts, slackening them evenly and a little at a time, then remove the bolts, and lift off the holder **(see illustration)**. Do not remove the dowels unless they are loose and liable to drop out.

10 Unscrew the main camshaft holder bolts, slackening them evenly and a little at a time in a criss-cross pattern starting from the outside **(see illustration 9.9)**. Remove the bolts, noting the sealing washers fitted with the four bolts around the spark plug bores. Lift off the holder. Remove the sealing rings from their grooves around the spark plug holes, noting how they also locate around the PAIR system air passage dowels **(see illustration 9.35a)**. Discard sealing rings and washers as new ones must be used. Do not remove the dowels unless they are loose and liable to drop out.

Caution: Make sure the holders lift up squarely and evenly and do not stick on a dowel or distort from some of the bolts being slackened more than the others as they or a camshaft could easily break.

11 The camshafts are marked for identification – on the left-hand cylinder head the intake camshaft is marked LH-IN and the exhaust camshaft is marked LH-EX **(see illustration)**. On the right-hand head the intake camshaft is marked RH-IN and the exhaust camshaft is marked RH-EX. If the marks aren't clear make your own as the camshafts must be installed in their original location.

12 When working on the left-hand head remove the exhaust camshaft first, then the intake **(see illustrations 9.33d and a)**. When working on the right-hand head remove the intake camshaft first, then the exhaust **(see illustrations 9.34c and a)**. Carefully lift each camshaft in turn off the head and disengage the sprocket from the chain. If you are only working on one head tie the chain up or secure it using a rod of some sort to prevent it from dropping. While the camshafts are out do not rotate the crankshaft. If you are now going to remove the camshafts from the other head make sure the chain is held up while turning the engine.

13 If the followers and shims are being removed from the cylinder head, obtain a container which is divided into eight compartments, and label each compartment with the location of a valve, i.e. left or right cylinder head, front or rear cylinder, intake or exhaust camshaft, front or rear valve. If a container is not available, use labelled plastic bags (egg cartons also do very well!). Remove the cam follower of the valve in question using a magnet or the suction created by a valve lapping tool if required, or long nosed pliers can be used with care **(see illustration)**. Retrieve the shim either from the inside of the follower or pick it out of the top of the valve spring retainer using either a magnet, a screwdriver with a dab of grease on it (the shim will stick to the grease), or a very small screwdriver and a pair of pliers **(see illustrations)**. Do not allow the shim to fall into the engine.

14 If required unscrew the sprocket bolts and take the sprockets off the camshafts, noting the alignment and fitting of the camshaft position (CMP) sensor rotor on the right-hand cylinder intake camshaft **(see illustration)**. All sprockets are identical and are therefore interchangeable, but mark them according to their camshaft so they can be installed in their original position. Also make alignment marks

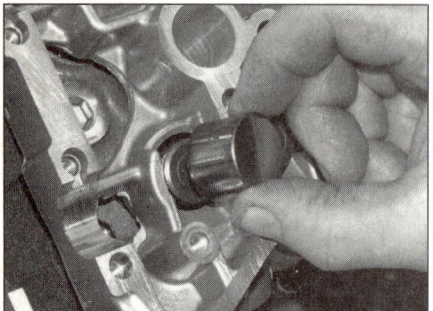

9.13a Carefully lift out the follower . . .

9.13b . . . and retrieve the shim (arrowed) from inside it . . .

9.13c . . . or from the top of the valve

9.14 Camshaft sprocket bolts (arrowed)

between the sprocket and the camshaft so that the sprocket can be easily installed the correct way round to avoid confusion when setting up the timing.

Inspection

15 Inspect the bearing surfaces of the camshaft holders and cylinder head and the corresponding journals on the camshafts. Look for score marks, deep scratches and evidence of spalling (a pitted appearance). Check the oil passages for clogging.

16 Check the camshaft lobes for heat discoloration (blue appearance), score marks, chipped areas, flat spots and spalling. Measure the height of each lobe with a micrometer **(see illustration)** and compare the results to the minimum height listed in this Chapter's Specifications. If damage is noted or wear is excessive, the camshaft must be replaced with a new one.

17 Check the amount of camshaft runout by supporting each end on V-blocks, and measuring any runout using a dial gauge. If the runout exceeds the specified limit the camshaft must be replaced with a new one.

 *Refer to Tools and Workshop Tips in the Reference section for details of how to read a micrometer and dial gauge.*

18 Next, check the camshaft journal oil clearances – this is done using a product called Plastigauge, available direct from the manufacturer or from good automotive suppliers. Follow the manufacturer's instructions. Clean the camshafts and the bearing surfaces in the cylinder head and camshaft holder with a clean lint-free cloth, then lay each camshaft in its correct location in the cylinder head (see Step 11), with the lobes positioned so they are not contacting the followers.

19 Cut some strips of Plastigauge and lay one piece on each journal, parallel with the camshaft centreline. Make sure the camshaft holder dowels are fitted **(see illustration 9.35a)**. Make sure the holders are fitted in their correct place (see Step 8). Fit the holders squarely onto the dowels and tighten the bolts evenly and a little at a time in a criss-cross sequence to the torque setting specified at the beginning of the Chapter. While doing this, don't let the camshafts rotate, or the Plastigauge will be disturbed and you will have to start again.

20 Now unscrew the camshaft holder bolts evenly and a little at a time in a criss-cross sequence, and lift off the holders.

21 To determine the oil clearance, compare the crushed Plastigauge (at its widest point) on each journal to the scale printed on or contained in the Plastigauge container. Compare the results to this Chapter's Specifications. If the oil clearance is greater than specified, replace the camshaft with a new one and recheck the clearance. If the clearance is still too great, also replace the cylinder head and holder with new ones.

 *Before replacing the camshafts, cylinder head or holders because of damage, check with motorcycle cylinder head specialists to see whether worn components can be renewed. Due to the cost of new components it is recommended that all options be explored.*

22 Except in cases of oil starvation, the cam chains should wear very little. If a chain has stretched excessively, which makes it difficult to maintain proper tension, or if it is stiff or the links are binding or kinking, replace it with a new one. Refer to Section 10 for replacement.

23 Check the sprockets for wear, cracks and other damage, and replace them with new ones if necessary (see Steps 14 and 26). If the sprockets are worn, the cam chains are also worn, and so probably are the sprockets on the crankshaft. If severe wear is apparent, the entire engine should be disassembled for inspection.

24 Inspect the cam chain guides and tensioner blade (see Section 10).

25 Inspect the outer surface of each cam follower for evidence of scoring or other damage **(see illustration 9.13a)**. If a follower is in poor condition, it is probable that the bore in the cylinder head in which it works is also damaged. Fit the follower and check for clearance between it and its bore. If necessary measure the outer diameter of each follower and the inner diameter of its bore (but note this is tricky with the valves installed, but to remove them means removing the head, which means removing the engine), and compare the results to the Specifications **(see illustration)**. If any follower is worn beyond its service limit replace it with a new one. If any bore is worn beyond its limit, is seriously out-of-round or tapered, replace the cylinder head with a new one.

Installation

26 If separated, fit the sprockets onto the camshafts, not forgetting the camshaft position (CMP) sensor rotor on the right-hand cylinder intake camshaft. Make sure they are installed the correct way round and in their original location as identified by the marks made on removal (Step 14). Apply a suitable non-permanent thread locking compound to the sprocket bolts and tighten them to the torque setting specified at the beginning of the Chapter.

27 If removed, lubricate each shim and its follower with molybdenum disulphide oil (a 50/50 mixture of molybdenum disulphide grease and engine oil). Fit each shim into its recess in the top of the valve spring retainer with the size mark facing up, making sure it is correctly seated **(see illustration 9.13c)**. **Note:** *It is most important that the shims and followers are returned to their original valves otherwise the valve clearances will be inaccurate.* Install each follower, making sure it fits squarely in its bore **(see illustration 9.13a)**.

28 When turning the engine in any of the following three steps, make sure that the cam chain(s) is/are held taut to prevent it/them dropping and jamming.

29 If the camshafts from both cylinder heads have been removed, turn the engine anti-clockwise until the line above the T1 mark on the timing rotor aligns with the static timing mark, which is a pointer in the top of the inspection hole **(see illustration 9.4a)**, so that the No. 1 piston is at TDC, and install the left-hand cylinder camshafts as described in Step 32 onwards. Then turn the engine anti-clockwise 450° (1¼ turns) so that the line above the T2 mark on the timing rotor aligns with the static timing mark **(see illustration 9.5a)** and the No. 2 piston is at TDC, and install the right-hand cylinder camshafts in the same way.

30 If only the camshafts from the left-hand cylinder head have been removed, and the engine has been turned since removing them (or if you are any doubt as to the position of the engine), remove the right-hand valve cover (see Section 7), then turn the engine to position it as in Step 5. From there turn the engine anti-clockwise 270° (¾ turn) so that the line above

9.16 Measure the height of the camshaft lobes with a micrometer

9.25 Measure the external diameter of each follower and the internal diameter of each bore

2•22 Engine, clutch and transmission

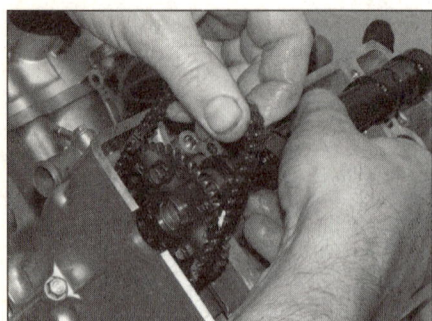

9.33a Install the intake camshaft as described . . .

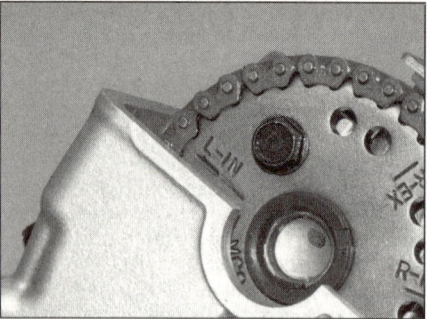

9.33b . . . so the L-IN mark is as shown

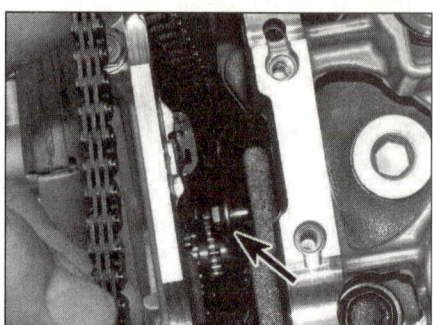

9.33c Make sure the chain does not get caught under the bolt (arrowed)

the T1 mark on the timing rotor aligns with the static timing mark **(see illustration 9.4a)** and the No. 1 piston is at TDC, and install the left-hand cylinder camshafts as described in Steps 32 onward.

31 If only the camshafts from the right-hand cylinder head have been removed, and the engine has been turned since removing them (or if you are any doubt as to the position of the engine), remove the left-hand valve cover (see Section 7), then turn the engine to position it as in Step 4. From there turn the engine anti-clockwise 450° (1¼ turns) so that the line above the T2 mark on the timing rotor aligns with the static timing mark **(see illustration 9.5a)** and the No. 2 piston is at TDC, and install the right-hand cylinder camshafts as described in Step 32 onward.

32 Make sure the bearing surfaces on the camshafts, holders, and cylinder head are clean, then apply molybdenum disulphide oil (a 50/50 mixture of molybdenum disulphide grease and engine oil) to each of them. Also apply it to the camshaft lobes. Make sure that none gets on the mating surfaces between the holder and the head, or in the bolt holes.

33 When installing the left-cylinder camshafts lay the intake camshaft (marked LH-IN) onto the head first with the L-IN mark on the sprocket facing out and parallel with the cylinder head top mating surface **(see illustrations)**. Fit the cam chain around the sprocket as you install the camshaft, pulling up on the chain to remove all slack in the inner run between the crankshaft and the camshaft, and making sure the chain does not get caught under the head of the tensioner blade pivot bolt **(see illustration)**. Lay the exhaust camshaft (marked LH-EX) onto the head with the L-EX mark on the sprocket facing out and parallel with the cylinder head top mating surface **(see illustrations)**. Fit the cam chain around the sprocket as you install the camshaft, pulling on it to remove all slack from between the two camshaft sprockets. Any slack in the chain must lie in the outer run of the chain between the exhaust camshaft and the crankshaft so that it is later taken up by the tensioner.

34 When installing the right-cylinder camshafts lay the exhaust camshaft (marked RH-EX) onto the head with the R-EX mark on the sprocket facing out and parallel with the cylinder head top mating surface **(see illustrations)**. Fit the cam chain around the sprocket as you install the camshaft, pulling up on the chain to remove all slack in the outer run between the crankshaft and the camshaft. Lay the intake camshaft (marked RH-IN) onto the head with the R-IN mark on the sprocket facing out and parallel with the cylinder head top mating surface **(see illustrations)**. Fit the cam chain around the sprocket as you install the camshaft, pulling

9.33d Install the exhaust camshaft as described . . .

9.33e . . . so the L-EX mark is positioned as shown

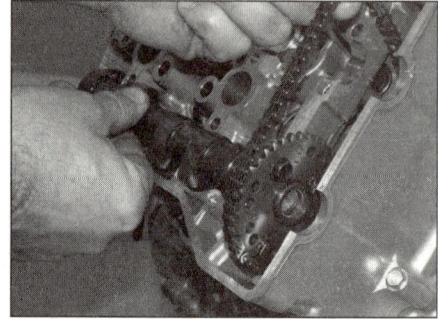

9.34a Install the exhaust camshaft as described . . .

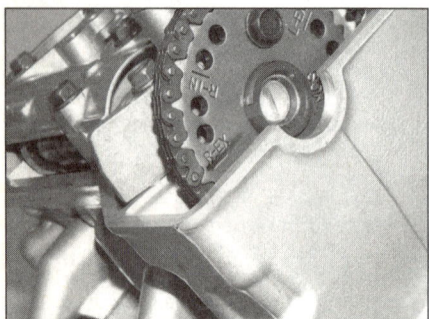

9.34b . . . so the R-EX mark is positioned as shown

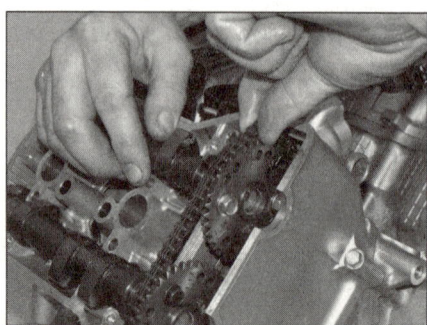

9.34c Install the intake camshaft as described . . .

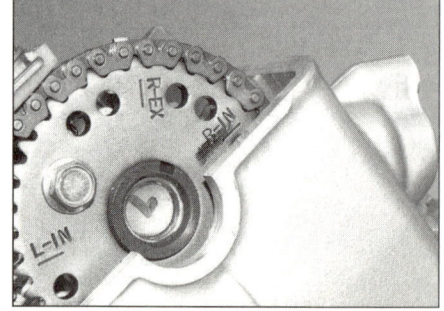

9.34d . . . so the R-IN mark is as shown

Engine, clutch and transmission 2•23

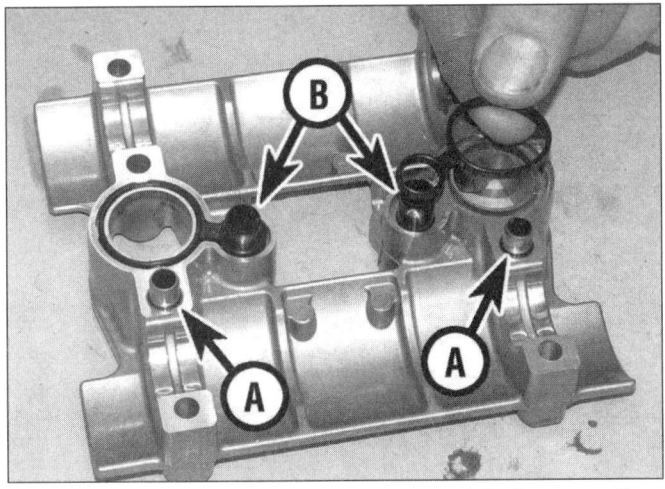

9.35a Main camshaft holder locating dowels (A). Fit new sealing rings over the air passage dowels (B) and into the grooves around the plug holes

9.35b Fit the main holder as described . . .

on it to remove all slack from between the two camshaft sprockets. Any slack in the chain must lie in the inner run of the chain between the intake camshaft and the crankshaft so that it is later taken up by the tensioner.

35 Make sure the locating dowels and PAIR system air passage dowels are installed in the main camshaft holder **(see illustration)**. Fit new sealing rings into the grooves around the spark plug holes on the underside of the main holder, making sure they also locate around the PAIR system air passage dowels. Lay the main holder in the head making sure it is correctly positioned (see Step 8) **(see illustration)**. Apply clean engine oil to the threads and under the heads of the holder bolts. Fit the bolts, using new sealing washers with the four bolts around the spark plug bores, and fitting the longer bolts into the outer holes, and tighten them finger-tight **(see illustration)**. Fit the front holder locating dowels if removed, then fit the holder **(see illustration)** – make sure the cut-out channels fit over the ribs on the camshafts to ensure correct axial alignment of the shafts, and that the holder marked L is on the left cylinder head, and that marked R is on the right **(see illustration 9.8b)**. Now gradually and evenly tighten the bolts fitted in the dowelled holes until the dowels are in their bores. Now tighten all the bolts evenly and a little at a time in a criss-cross sequence until the holder seats on the head, again making sure it is being pulled down squarely. When both holders are seated, tighten the main holder bolts evenly and a little at a time in a criss-cross sequence to the torque setting specified at the beginning of the Chapter, then tighten the front holder bolts to the specified torque.

Caution: Whilst tightening the bolts, make sure the holders are being pulled evenly and squarely down and are not binding on the dowels or tilting to one side – if they do, adjust the relevant bolts until the holders are again square to the head. A holder or camshaft is likely to break if they are not tightened down evenly and squarely.

36 Press on the back of the cam chain tensioner blade via the tensioner bore in the cylinder block to ensure that any slack in the cam chain is taken up and transferred to the rear run of the chain (where it will later be taken up by the tensioner. At this point check that all the timing marks are still in exact alignment as described in Step 4 or 5 **(see illustrations 9.4a and b or 9.5a and b)**. Note that it is easy to be slightly out (one tooth on the sprocket) without the marks appearing drastically out of alignment. If the marks are out, verify which sprocket is misaligned, then turn the crankshaft slightly as required to get all the slack in the chain next to the sprocket that is out, then feed the chain round the sprocket to transfer the slack to between the sprockets, then move the camshaft round to transfer the slack back. Do this as many times as is necessary, and in both camshafts if necessary, until the marks are correctly aligned.

Caution: If the marks are not aligned exactly as described, the valve timing will

9.35c . . . using new sealing washers on the inner bolts

9.35d Front holder dowels (A). Locate the channels over the ribs (B)

2•24 Engine, clutch and transmission

9.37 Fit the top guide

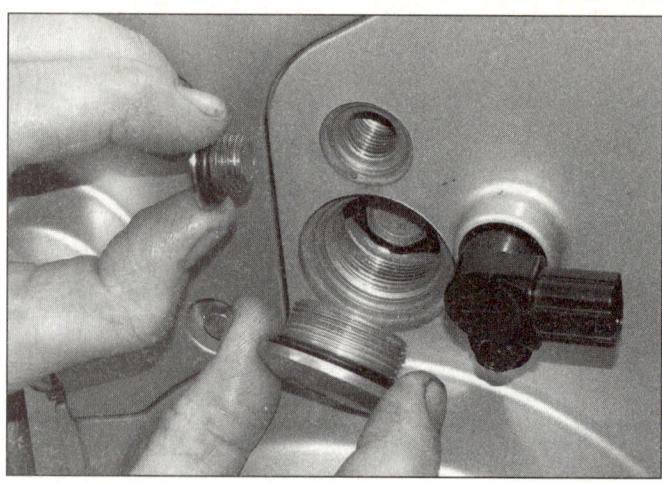

9.39 Smear the cap O-rings with grease, and use new ones if required

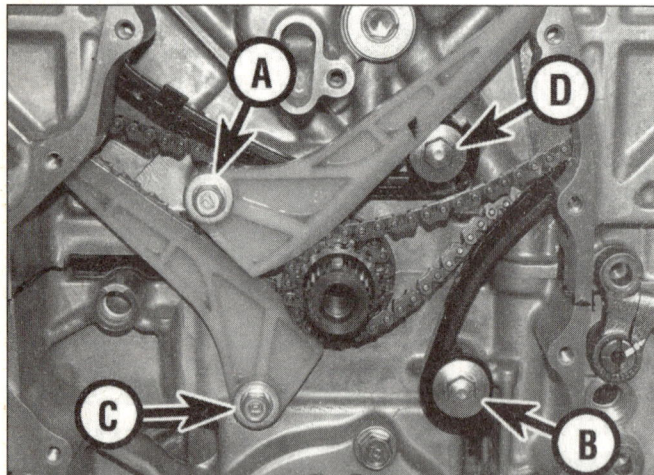

10.3 Left cylinder guide blade bolt (A) and tensioner blade bolt (B). Right cylinder guide blade bolt (C) and tensioner blade bolt (D)

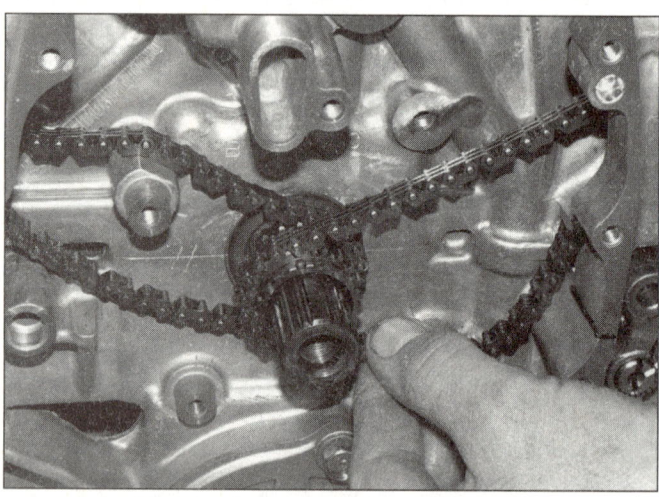

10.5a Remove the cam chains . . .

be incorrect and the valves may strike the pistons, causing extensive damage to the engine.

37 Fit the cam chain top guide and tighten its bolts **(see illustration)**. Install the cam chain tensioner (see Section 8).

38 When all camshafts and both top guides and tensioners have been installed, turn the engine anti-clockwise through two full turns

10.5b . . . and slide the sprocket off the shaft

and check again that all the timing marks on both sides align correctly (see Steps 4 and 5) **(see illustrations 9.4a and b or 9.5a and b)**. Check the valve clearances and adjust them if necessary (see Chapter 1).

39 Install the timing inspection cap and crankshaft end cap using new O-rings if required, and smear the O-rings and the cap threads with grease **(see illustration)**. Tighten the caps to the torque settings specified at the beginning of the Chapter.

40 Install the valve covers (see Section 7). Install the spark plugs (see Chapter 1).

10 Cam chains, tensioner blades and guides

Note: *The cam chain and its blades can be removed with the engine in the frame. If the engine has been removed, ignore the steps which do not apply. Keep the left cylinder components together and separate from the right cylinder components*

Removal

1 Remove the camshafts – this procedure involves removing the top guide blade (see Section 9).

2 Remove the primary drive gear (see Section 15).

3 Unscrew the left-hand cylinder guide blade bolt and remove the blade. Unscrew the left cylinder tensioner blade pivot bolt and remove the blade **(see illustration)**.

4 Unscrew the right-hand cylinder guide blade bolt and remove the blade. Unscrew the right cylinder tensioner blade pivot bolt and remove the blade.

5 Mark the outer face of one link on each chain so they can be fitted, and therefore run, the same way round. Also mark the outer rim of the sprocket piece to ensure correct installation. Disengage the cam chains from the sprockets and draw them out of the engine **(see illustration)**. Slide the sprocket piece off the end of the crankshaft, noting the wide splines that mean it can only be installed in one position **(see illustration)**.

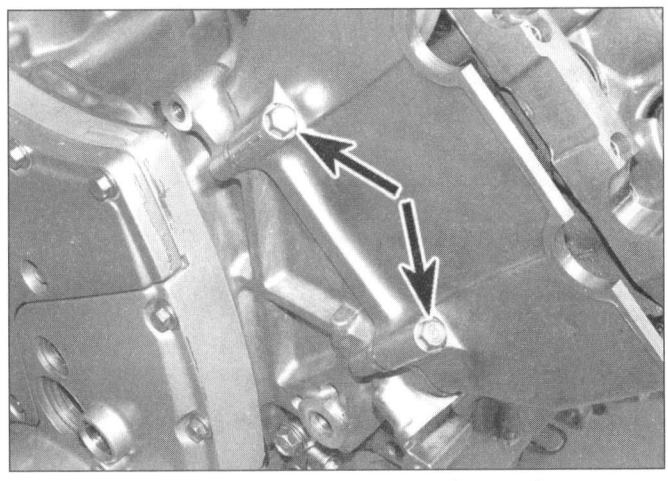

11.4a Cylinder head 6 mm bolts (arrowed)

11.4b Cylinder head 10 mm bolts (arrowed)

Inspection

Cam chain and sprockets

6 Check the chains for binding, kinks and any obvious damage and replace them with new ones if necessary. Check the camshaft and crankshaft sprocket teeth for wear and replace the cam chain, camshaft sprockets and crankshaft sprocket piece with a new set if necessary.

Tensioner and guide blades

7 Check the sliding surface and edges of the blades for excessive wear, deep grooves, cracking and other obvious damage, and replace them with new ones if necessary.

Installation

8 Installation of the sprocket, chain and blades is the reverse of removal, noting the following:
- When fitting the sprocket piece onto the crankshaft align the wide splines and fit it with the marked face outermost **(see illustration 10.5b)**.
- The chain for the right-hand head runs on the inner sprocket. Fit the right-hand cylinder blades first.
- Tighten the guide blade and tensioner blade pivot bolts to the torque settings specified at the beginning of the Chapter.

11 Cylinder head removal and installation

Note: *To remove the cylinder heads the engine must be removed from the frame.*

Removal

1 Remove the engine (see Section 4). Work on one head at a time and keep all related components together.
2 Remove the camshafts, followers and shims (see Section 9). If not already done, remove the cam chain tensioner (see Section 8).
3 Remove the camshaft position sensor from the right-hand head (see Chapter 4).
4 Each cylinder head is secured by two 6 mm bolts and six 10 mm bolts with fitted washers

(i.e. they can't be separated from the bolts) **(see illustrations)**. First unscrew and remove the 6 mm bolts. Now unscrew and remove the 10 mm bolts, slackening them evenly and a little at a time in a criss-cross pattern working from the outside to the middle until they are all loose.
5 Hold the cam chain up and pull the cylinder head up off the block, and pass the cam chain down through the tunnel **(see illustration)**. Do not let the chain fall into the crankcase – secure it with a piece of wire or metal bar to prevent it from doing so. If the head is stuck, tap around the joint faces with a soft-faced mallet. Do not attempt to free the head by inserting a screwdriver between the head and block mating surfaces – you'll damage them.
6 Remove the cylinder head gasket and discard it as a new one must be used. If they are loose, remove the dowels from the crankcase or the underside of the cylinder head **(see illustration 11.10b)**.
7 Check the cylinder head gasket and the mating surfaces on the cylinder head and crankcase for signs of leakage, which could indicate warpage. Refer to Section 12 and check the cylinder head gasket surface for warpage.

Installation

8 Clean all traces of old gasket material from the cylinder head and crankcase. If a scraper is used, take care not to scratch or gouge the

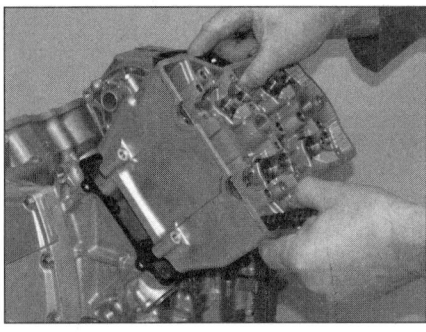

11.5 Carefully lift the head up off the block

soft aluminium. Be careful not to let any of the gasket material fall into the crankcase, the cylinder bore or the oil and coolant passages. Wipe over the mating surfaces with solvent.
9 Lubricate the cylinder bores with engine oil. If removed, fit the dowels into the crankcase **(see illustration 11.10b)**.
10 Ensure both cylinder head and block mating surfaces are clean. Check you have the correct gasket for the head being fitted – each gasket is marked either L or R according to side **(see illustration)**. Lay the new head gasket over the cam chain and blades and onto the block, locating it over the dowels and making sure all the holes are correctly aligned **(see illustration)**. Never reuse the old gasket.

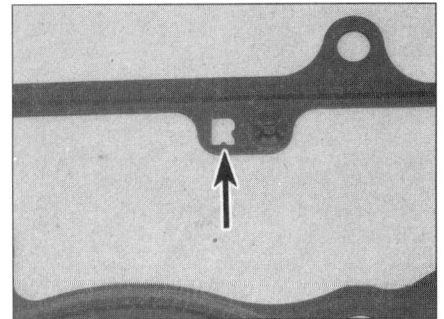

11.10a Each gasket is marked with a letter (arrowed) indicating its side

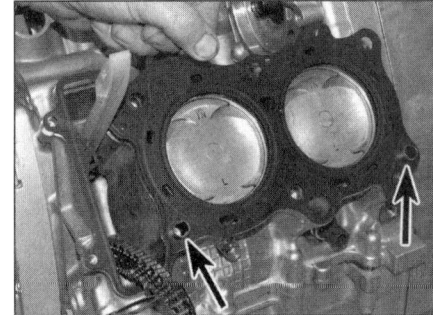

11.10b Fit the dowels (arrowed) then lay the new gasket on the block

2•26 Engine, clutch and transmission

11 Carefully fit the cylinder head onto the block, making sure it locates correctly onto the dowels **(see illustration 11.5)**. Feed the cam chain up through the tunnel as you install the head, then secure it in place with a piece of wire to prevent it from falling back down.

12 Smear some oil onto the threads, washers and under the heads of the 10 mm bolts. Note that if new bolts are being installed, first remove any anti-rust coating by cleaning them with solvent. Install the bolts and tighten them all finger-tight – the two shorter bolts fit into the holes at the back of the head **(see illustration)**. Fit the 6 mm bolts and tighten them finger-tight **(see illustration 11.4a)**.

13 Tighten the 10 mm bolts evenly and a little at a time in a criss-cross pattern working from the middle to the outside to the torque setting specified at the beginning of the Chapter. Now tighten the 6 mm bolts.

14 Install the remaining components in a reverse of their removal sequence, referring to the relevant Sections or Chapters.

12 Cylinder head and valve overhaul

1 Because of the complex nature of this job and the special tools and equipment required, most owners leave servicing of the valves, valve seats and valve guides to a professional. However, you can make an initial assessment of whether the valves are seating correctly, and therefore sealing, by pouring a small amount of solvent into each of the valve ports. If the solvent leaks past any valve into the combustion chamber area the valve is not seating correctly and sealing.

2 With the correct tools (a valve spring compressor is essential – make sure it is suitable for motorcycle work), you can also remove the valves and associated components from the cylinder head, clean them and check them for wear to assess the extent of the work needed, and, unless seat cutting or guide replacement is required, grind in the valves and reassemble them in the head.

3 A dealer service department or specialist can replace the guides and re-cut the valve seats.

11.12 Lubricate and install the bolts, fitting the shorter ones at the rear

4 After the valve service has been performed, be sure to clean the head very thoroughly before installation on the engine to remove any metal particles or abrasive grit that may still be present from the valve service operations. Use compressed air, if available, to blow out all the holes and passages.

Disassembly

5 Before proceeding, arrange to label and store the valves along with their related components in such a way that they can be returned to their original locations without getting mixed up **(see illustration)**. Either use the same container as the cam followers and shims are stored in (see Section 9), or obtain a separate container and label each compartment accordingly. Alternatively, labelled plastic bags will do just as well.

6 Compress the valve spring on the first valve with a spring compressor, making sure it is correctly located onto each end of the valve assembly **(see illustration)**. On the top of the valve the adaptor needs to be about the same size as the spring retainer – if it is too big it will contact the follower bore and mark it, and if it is too small it will be difficult to remove and install the collets **(see illustration)**. On the underside of the head make sure the compressor only contacts the valve and not the soft aluminium of the head **(see illustration)** – if the compressor has a plate that is too big for the valve, use a spacer between them. Do not compress the springs any more than is absolutely necessary.

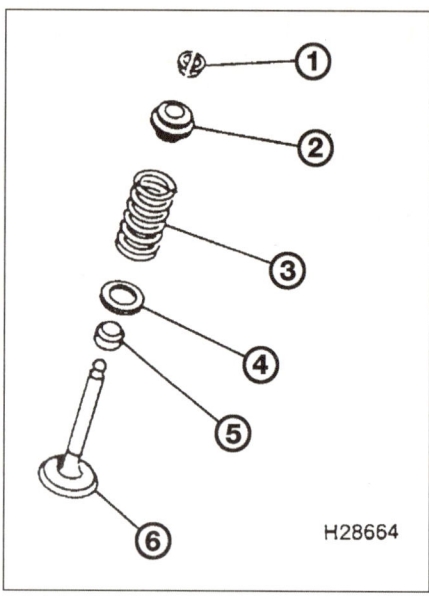
12.5 Valve components

1 Collets
2 Spring retainer
3 Valve spring
4 Spring seat
5 Valve stem oil seal
6 Valve

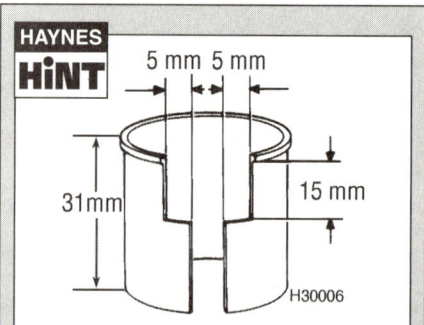
Protect the follower bore in the cylinder head from scratches by the valve spring compressor using either the Honda tool (Part No. 07HMG-MR70002) or by fabricating a shield from a 35 mm film canister or similar. Cut the canister to the dimensions shown.

12.6a Compressing the valve spring(s) using a valve spring compressor

12.6b Make sure the compressor locates correctly both on the top of the spring retainer . . .

12.6c . . . and on the bottom of the valve

Engine, clutch and transmission 2•27

12.7a Remove the collets ...

12.7b ... the spring retainer and spring ...

12.7c ... and the valve

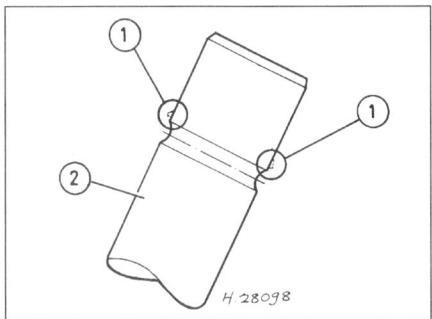

12.7d If the valve stem (2) won't pull through the guide, deburr the area (1) above the collet groove

12.8a Pull the seal off the valve stem ...

12.8b ... then remove the spring seat

Caution: Take great care not to mark the cam follower bore with the spring compressor.

7 Remove the collets, using a magnet or a screwdriver with a dab of grease on it **(see illustration)**. Carefully release the valve spring compressor and remove the spring retainer, noting which way up it fits, the spring and the valve **(see illustrations)**. If the valve binds in the guide and won't pull through, push it back into the head and deburr the area around the collet groove with a very fine file or whetstone **(see illustration)**.

8 Pull the valve stem seal off the top of the valve guide with pliers and discard it (the old seals should never be reused), then remove the spring seat noting which way up, it fits – using a magnet is the easiest way to remove the seat from the head **(see illustrations)**.

9 Repeat the procedure for the remaining valves. Remember to keep the parts for each valve together so they can be reinstalled in the same location.

10 Clean the cylinder head with solvent and dry it thoroughly. Compressed air will speed the drying process and ensure that all holes and recessed areas are clean. **Note:** *Do not use a wire brush mounted in a drill motor to clean the combustion chambers as the head material is soft and may be scratched or eroded away by the wire brush.*

11 Clean the valve springs, collets, retainers and spring seats with solvent and dry them thoroughly. Do the parts from one valve at a time so that no mixing of parts between valves occurs.

12 Scrape off any deposits that may have formed on the valve, then clean them with solvent. Again, make sure the valves do not get mixed up.

Inspection

13 Inspect the head very carefully for cracks and other damage. If cracks are found, a new head is required. Check the camshaft bearing surfaces for wear and evidence of seizure. Check the camshafts and holders for wear as well (see Section 9).

14 Using a precision straight-edge and a feeler gauge set to the warpage limit listed in the specifications at the beginning of the Chapter, check the head gasket mating surface for warpage. Refer to Tools and Workshop Tips in the Reference section for details of how to use the straight-edge. If the head is warped beyond the limit specified at the beginning of this Chapter, consult a Honda dealer or take it to a specialist repair shop for an opinion, though be prepared to buy a new one.

15 Examine the valve seats in the combustion chamber. If they are pitted, cracked or burned, the head will require work beyond the scope of the home mechanic. Measure the valve seat width and compare it to this Chapter's Specifications **(see illustration)**. If it exceeds the service limit, or if it varies around its circumference, overhaul is required. Similarly check the seat contact surface on the valve face.

16 Working on one valve and guide at a time, measure the valve stem diameter **(see illustration)**. Clean the valve's guide using a guide reamer to remove any carbon build-up – insert the reamer from the underside of the head and turn it clockwise only. Now measure

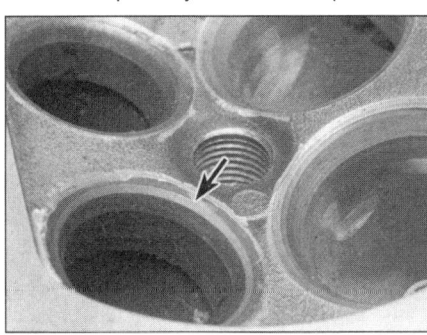

12.15 Measure the valve seat width

12.16a Measure the valve stem diameter with a micrometer

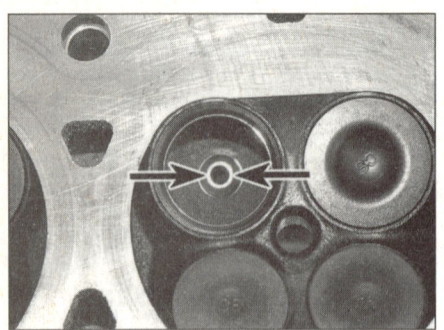

12.16b Measure the valve guide with a small bore gauge . . .

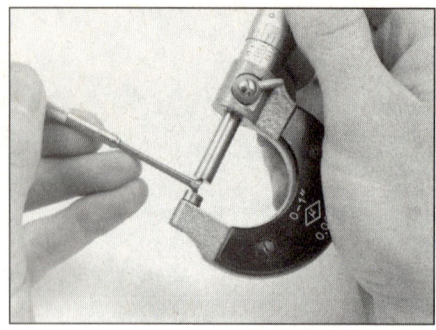

12.16c . . . then measure the bore gauge with a micrometer

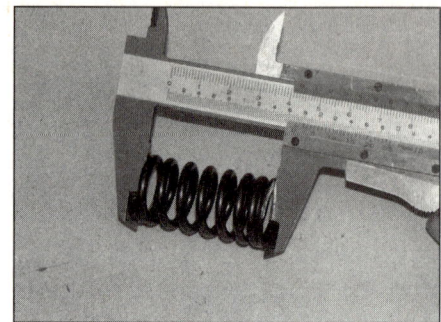

12.19a Measure the free length of the valve springs . . .

the inside diameter of the guide (at both ends and in the centre of the guide) with a small bore gauge, then measure the gauge with a micrometer **(see illustrations)**. Measure the guide at the ends and at the centre to determine if it is worn in a bell-mouth pattern (more wear at the ends). Subtract the stem diameter from the valve guide diameter to obtain the valve stem-to-guide clearance. If the stem-to-guide clearance is greater than listed in this Chapter's Specifications, replace whichever component is beyond its specification limits with a new one. If the valve guide is within specifications, but is worn unevenly, it should be replaced with a new one. Repeat for the other valves.

17 Carefully inspect each valve face, stem and collet groove area for cracks, pits and burned spots.

18 Rotate the valve and check for any obvious indication that it is bent, in which case it must be replaced with a new one. Check the end of the stem for pitting and excessive wear. The presence of any of the above conditions indicates the need for valve servicing.

19 Check the end of each valve spring for wear and pitting. Measure the spring free lengths and compare them to the specifications **(see illustration)**. If any spring is shorter than specified it has sagged and must be replaced with a new one. Also place the spring upright on a flat surface and check it for bend by placing a ruler against it, or alternatively lay it against a set square **(see illustration)**. If the bend in any spring is excessive, it must be replaced with a new one.

20 Check the spring seats, retainers and collets for obvious wear and cracks. Any questionable parts should not be reused, as extensive damage will occur in the event of failure during engine operation.

21 If the inspection indicates that no overhaul work is required, the valve components can be reinstalled in the head.

Reassembly

22 Unless a valve service has been performed, before installing the valves in the head they should be ground in (lapped) to ensure a positive seal between the valves and seats. This procedure requires coarse and fine valve grinding compound and a valve grinding tool (either hand-held or drill driven – note that some drill-driven tools specify using only a fine grinding compound). If a grinding tool is not available, a piece of rubber or plastic hose can be slipped over the valve stem (after the valve has been installed in the guide) and used to turn the valve.

23 Apply a small amount of coarse grinding compound to the valve face **(see illustration)**. Smear some molybdenum disulphide oil (a 50/50 mixture of molybdenum disulphide grease and engine oil) to the valve stem, then slip the valve into the guide **(see illustration 12.28)**. Note: *Make sure each valve is installed in its correct guide and be careful not to get any grinding compound on the valve stem.*

24 Attach the grinding tool to the valve and rotate the tool between the palms of your hands. Use a back-and-forth motion (as though rubbing your hands together) rather than a circular motion (i.e. so that the valve rotates alternately clockwise and anti-clockwise rather than in one direction only) **(see illustration)**. If a motorised tool is being used, take note of the correct drive speed for it – if your drill runs too fast and is not variable, use a hand tool instead. Lift the valve off the seat and turn it at regular intervals to distribute the grinding compound properly. Continue the grinding procedure until the valve face and seat contact area is of uniform width, and unbroken around the entire circumference.

25 Carefully remove the valve and wipe off all traces of grinding compound, making sure none gets in the guide. Use solvent to clean the valve and wipe the seat area thoroughly with a solvent soaked cloth.

26 Repeat the procedure with fine valve grinding compound, then use solvent to clean the valve and flush the guide, and wipe the seat area thoroughly with a solvent soaked cloth. Repeat the entire procedure for the remaining valves. On completion thoroughly clean the entire head again, then blow through all passages with compressed air. Make sure all traces of the grinding compound have been removed before assembling the head.

27 Working on one valve at a time, lay the spring seat in place in the cylinder head with its shouldered side facing up **(see illustration)**.

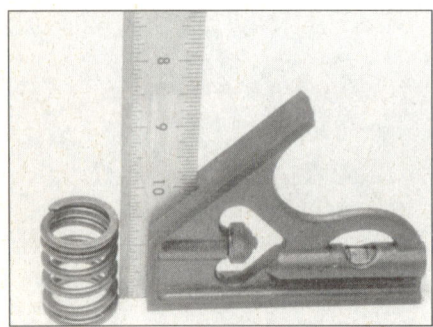

12.19b . . . and check them for bend

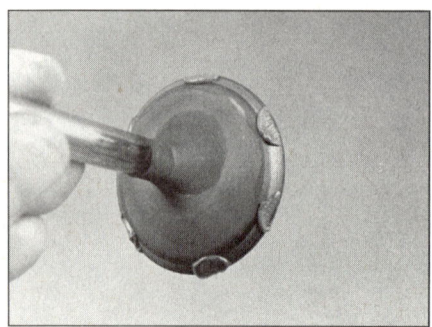

12.23 Apply dabs of paste round the valve face

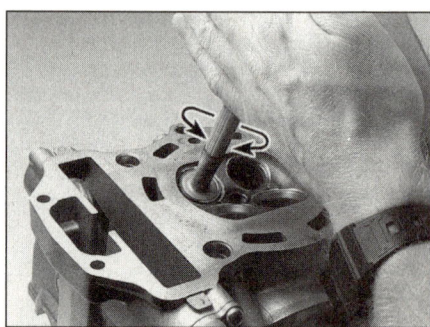

12.24 Rotate the valve grinding tool back and forth between the palms of your hands

12.27 Fit the spring seat using a rod to guide it if necessary

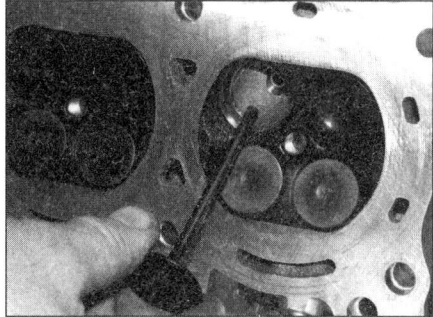

12.28 Lubricate the stem and slide the valve into its correct location

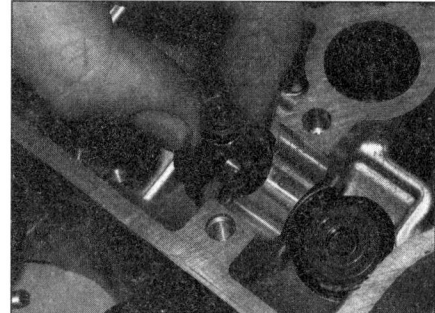

12.29a Fit a new seal over the valve stem . . .

As it is easy to cock the seat on the top of the valve guide, and then tricky to get it to sit properly, install it using a rod as a guide for it to slide down.

28 Coat the valve stem with molybdenum disulphide oil (a 50/50 mixture of molybdenum disulphide grease and engine oil), then slide it into its guide **(see illustration)**. Check that the valve moves up-and-down freely in the guide.

29 Fit a new seal over the valve stem and onto the guide, using finger pressure, a stem seal fitting tool or an appropriate size deep socket, to push the seal squarely onto the end of the valve guide until it is felt to clip into place **(see illustrations)**. Make sure the seal does not get cocked sideways as it could be damaged – using a rod as a guide as for the seat helps.

30 Fit the spring with the closer-wound coils facing down into the cylinder head **(see illustration)**. Fit the spring retainer, with its shouldered side facing down so that it fits into the top of the spring **(see illustration)**.

31 Apply a small amount of grease to the collets to help hold them in place. Compress the valve spring with a spring compressor, making sure it is correctly located onto each end of the valve assembly (see Step 6) **(see illustrations 12.6a, 12.6b and 12.6c)**. Do not compress the spring any more than is necessary to slip the collets into place. Locate each collet in turn into the groove in the valve

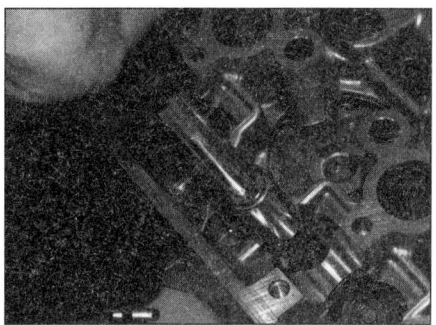

12.29b . . . and press it squarely onto the guide

stem using a screwdriver with a dab of grease on it **(see illustration)**. Carefully release the compressor, making sure the collets seat and lock in the retaining groove.

32 Repeat the procedure for the remaining valves. Remember to keep the parts for each valve together and separate from the other valves so they can be reinstalled in the same location.

33 Support the cylinder head on blocks so the valves can't contact the work surface, then tap the end of each valve stem lightly to seat the collets in their grooves **(see illustration)**.

34 After the cylinder head and camshafts have been installed, check the valve clearances and adjust as required (see Chapter 1).

12.30a Fit the valve spring . . .

13 Clutch

Note 1: *The clutch can be removed with the engine in the frame.*
Note 2: *The clutch nut must be discarded and a new one used on installation – it is best to obtain the new nut in advance.*

Removal

1 Refer to Chapter 3, Section 6, and remove the front crankcase cover – there is no need to remove the water pump from the cover.
2 Working in a criss-cross pattern, gradually slacken the clutch spring bolts until pressure

12.30b . . . then fit the spring retainer

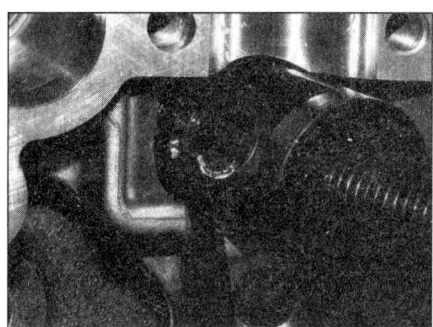

12.31 Locate each collet in its groove in the top of the valve stem

12.33 Seat the collets as described

2•30 Engine, clutch and transmission

13.2a Unscrew the bolts (arrowed) and remove the springs . . .

13.2b . . . then remove the pressure plate

13.2c Remove the lifter piece . . .

is released **(see illustration)**. To prevent the assembly from turning, cover it with a rag and hold it securely – the bolts are not very tight (if available, have an assistant hold it). Remove the bolts and springs, then remove the pressure plate **(see illustration)**. Remove the lifter from either the back of the pressure plate or the end of the shaft **(see illustration)**. If required withdraw the pushrod from the shaft **(see illustration)**.

3 Remove the clutch friction and plain plates, hooking the inner ones out if necessary, noting how they fit and keeping them in order **(see illustration)**. Note how the tabs on the outer friction plate (one of which is marked green) locate in the shallow slots in the housing, while the rest (of which one on each plate is marked black) sit in the deep slots. The inner friction plate is different to the rest – it has a larger internal diameter so it seats around the anti-judder spring and spring seat.

4 Remove the anti-judder spring and spring seat, noting which way round they fit **(see illustrations 13.24b and a)**.

5 The clutch nut rim is staked against the input shaft. Unstake the nut using a hammer and punch – take care not to damage the threads on the end of the shaft **(see illustration)**. To remove the clutch nut, the primary damper shaft must be locked. This can be done in several ways. If the engine is in the frame, engage 6th gear and have an assistant hold the rear brake on hard with the rear tyre in firm contact with the ground. Alternatively, the Honda service tool (Pt. No. 07724-0050002), or a similar commercially available tool, can be used to hold the clutch centre whilst the nut is slackened **(see illustration)**. Unscrew the nut and remove the washer. Discard the nut as a new one must be used on installation.

6 Remove the clutch centre and the thrust washer from the shaft **(see illustrations 13.22b and a)**.

7 Lock the teeth of the sprung sub-gear on the primary drive gear in alignment with those of the main gear by threading a 6 mm Allen bolt (a hex bolt's head is too large) into the threaded hole and tightening it securely (you may need to turn the gear if the hole is obscured by the clutch housing) **(see illustration)** – this prevents the gears springing out of alignment when the clutch housing is removed, so making its installation a lot easier. Remove the clutch housing **(see illustration)**. Note how the holes in the back

13.2d . . . then withdraw the pushrod if required

13.3 Withdraw the plates from the housing

13.5a Unstake the nut . . .

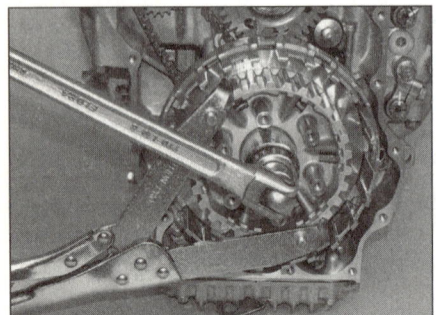

13.5b . . . then unscrew it as described and remove the washer

13.7a Thread a 6 mm Allen bolt into the hole and tighten it securely

13.7b Draw the housing off the shaft

Engine, clutch and transmission 2•31

13.8a Remove the water pump sprockets and chain . . .

13.8b . . . then slide the clutch guide off the shaft

13.9 Measure clutch friction plate thickness

of the housing engage with the pins on the water pump drive sprocket.

8 Remove the water pump drive and driven sprockets and chain **(see illustration)**. Slide the clutch housing guide off the shaft **(see illustration)**.

Inspection

9 After an extended period of service the clutch friction plates will wear and promote clutch slip. Measure the thickness of each friction plate using a Vernier caliper **(see illustration)**. If any plate has worn to or beyond the service limits given in the Specifications at the beginning of the Chapter, or if any of the plates smell burnt or are glazed, the friction plates must be replaced with a new set.

10 The plain plates should not show any signs of excess heating (bluing). Check for warpage using a flat surface and feeler gauges **(see illustration)**. If any plate exceeds the maximum permissible amount of warpage, or shows signs of bluing, all plain plates must be replaced with a new set.

11 Measure the free length of each clutch spring using a Vernier caliper **(see illustration)**. Place each spring upright on a flat surface and check it for bend by placing a ruler against it, or alternatively lay it against a set square **(see illustration 12.19b)**. If any spring is below the minimum free length specified or if the bend in any spring is excessive, replace all the springs as a set. Also check the anti-judder spring and spring seat for damage or distortion and replace them with new ones if necessary.

12 Inspect the friction plates and the clutch housing for burrs and indentations on the edges of the protruding tabs on the plates and/or the slots in the housing **(see illustration)**. Similarly check for wear between the inner teeth of the plain plates and the slots in the clutch centre **(see illustration)**. Wear of this nature will cause clutch drag and slow disengagement during gear changes as the plates will snag when the pressure plate is lifted. With care a small amount of wear can be corrected by dressing with a fine file, but if this is excessive the worn components should be replaced with new ones.

13 Inspect the needle roller bearing in the clutch housing and the bearing surfaces on the clutch guide **(see illustration and 13.8b)**. If there are any signs of wear, pitting or other damage the affected parts must be replaced with new ones – the needle bearing is part of the clutch housing and not available separately.

14 Using a Vernier caliper, measure the internal diameter of the clutch guide and the external diameter of the shaft where the guide sits **(see illustration 13.8b)**. Compare the measurements to the specifications at the beginning of the Chapter and replace any part that is worn beyond its service limit with a new one. Also check the water pump drive sprocket surface where it seats on the guide.

15 Check the pressure plate and its bearing for signs of wear or damage and roughness

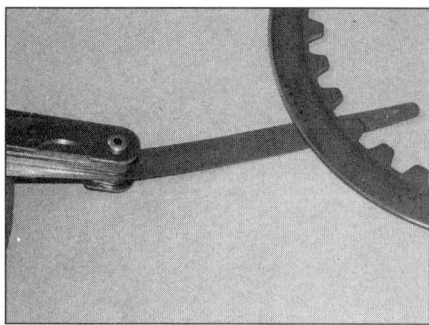

13.10 Check the plain plates for warpage

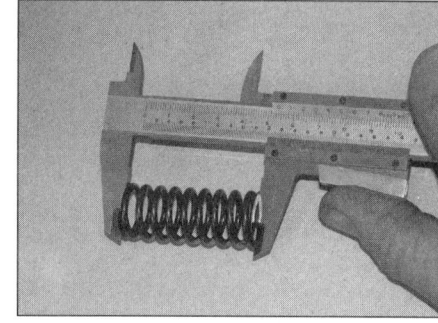

13.11 Measure the free length of the clutch springs

13.12a Check the friction plate tabs and housing slots . . .

13.12b . . . and the plain plate teeth and centre slots as described

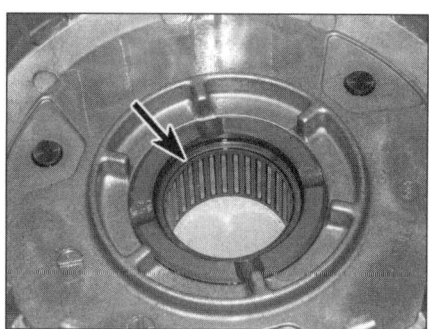

13.13 Check the bearing in the housing and the bearing surfaces on the guide

2•32 Engine, clutch and transmission

13.15 Check the bearing in the pressure plate

13.21 Slide the housing onto the shaft, engaging the gears and locating it on the sprocket pins

13.22a Fit the thrust washer . . .

(see illustration). Check that the bearing outer race is a good fit in the centre, and that the inner race rotates freely without any rough spots.

16 Check the pushrod is not bent by rolling it on a flat surface. Check the lifter for signs of wear or damage. Replace any parts necessary with new ones. The hydraulic release mechanism is covered in Section 14.

17 Check the teeth of the primary driven gear on the back of the clutch housing and the corresponding teeth of the primary drive gear on the crankshaft. Replace the clutch housing and/or crankshaft with a new one if worn or chipped teeth are discovered.

Installation

18 Remove all traces of old sealant from the crankcase and front cover surfaces. Note that if removed the primary drive gear must be installed now as it cannot be fitted once the clutch is in place – see Section 15.

19 Smear the inside and outside of the clutch guide with molybdenum disulphide oil (a 50/50 mixture of molybdenum disulphide grease and engine oil). Slide it onto the shaft with the lipped end innermost (see illustration 13.8b).

20 Fit the water pump drive and driven sprockets into the chain, making sure that when installed the driven sprocket pins will face out and the driven sprocket shaft will face in. As an assembly slide the drive sprocket onto the shaft and fit the driven sprocket shaft into its hole (see illustration 13.8a).

21 Check the teeth of the sprung sub-gear on the primary drive gear are still aligned with those of the main gear with the springs compressed – if the holding bolt was not tight enough and the springs have forced the gear around, in which case the teeth could either be mis-aligned (if the gear has only moved a bit) or the gear will feel loose even though the teeth may appear aligned (if the gear has moved all the way), remove the primary drive gear (see Section 15) and align them as described in Step 7 before refitting the gear. Smear the clutch housing needle bearing with molybdenum disulphide oil (see illustration 13.13). Slide the clutch housing onto the shaft (see illustration 13.7b) – you will need to jiggle the water pump driven sprocket until the drive sprocket pins are felt to locate in the holes in the clutch housing and the housing moves in a bit further (see illustration). Double-check by making sure the chain and sprockets can't turn independently of the housing. After fitting the housing remove the bolt from the primary drive gear (see illustration 13.7a).

22 Slide the thrust washer onto the shaft (see illustration). Slide the clutch centre onto the shaft splines (see illustration).

23 Fit the washer with its larger chamfered side facing out (see illustration). Smear the *new* clutch nut threads and seating face with oil, then thread it onto the input shaft. Using the method employed on removal to lock the shaft (see Step 5), tighten the nut to the torque setting specified at the beginning of the Chapter (see illustrations). Stake the rim of the nut into the indent on the end of the shaft (see illustration).

24 Fit the anti-judder spring seat into the

13.22b . . . and the clutch centre

13.23a Fit the thrust washer . . .

13.23b . . . and a new clutch nut . . .

13.23c . . . and tighten it to the specified torque

13.23d Stake the nut against the detent in the shaft end

Engine, clutch and transmission 2•33

13.24a Fit the anti-judder spring seat . . .

13.24b . . . and spring . . .

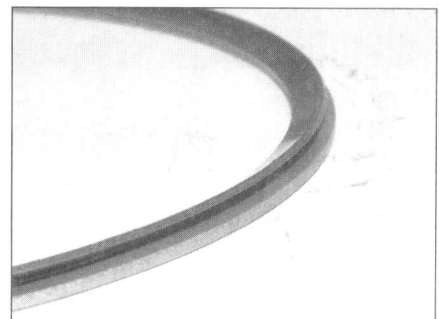

13.24c . . . so the spring's outer edge is raised off the seat

clutch centre, then fit the spring so that its outer edge is raised off the seat and facing outwards **(see illustrations)**.

25 Coat each clutch plate with engine oil prior to installation, then build up the plates as follows: fit the friction plate with the larger internal diameter over the spring and spring seat **(see illustration)**, then fit a plain plate, then alternate friction plates with the black tab and plain plates until all are installed except the outermost friction plate with the green tab, then fit that, locating the tabs in the shallow slots in the housing **(see illustrations)**.

26 Lubricate the bearing in the pressure plate, the lifter and the pushrod with oil. If removed slide the pushrod into the shaft and push it all the way in **(see illustration 13.2d)**. Fit the lifter over the pushrod and into the shaft **(see illustration 13.2c)**. Fit the pressure plate onto the clutch, engaging the protrusions on its inner rim in the slots in the clutch centre – you may have to push the plate so the pushrod pushes the release cylinder piston in if it has crept out **(see illustration)**. Fit the springs and the bolts and tighten them evenly and a little at a time in a criss-cross sequence to the specified torque setting **(see illustration)**. Counter-hold the clutch housing to prevent it turning when tightening the spring bolts.

27 Refer to Chapter 3, Section 6, and install the front crankcase cover.

14 Clutch release mechanism

> **Warning:** *If the master or release cylinder is in need of an overhaul all old fluid should be flushed from the system (see Step 58). Overhaul must be done in a spotlessly clean work area to avoid contamination and possible failure of the hydraulic system components. Do not, under any circumstances, use petroleum-based solvents to clean the parts – use DOT 4 brake/clutch fluid or denatured alcohol. To prevent damage from spilled fluid, always cover paintwork when working on the system.*

13.25a Fit the friction plate with the larger internal diameter first, locating it over the anti-judder assembly . . .

13.25b . . . then fit a plain plate . . .

13.25c . . . then a friction plate with a black tab (arrowed) and so on . . .

13.25d . . . fitting the friction plate with the green tab (arrowed) last and locating the tabs in the shallow slots in the housing

13.26a Fit the pressure plate, making sure it locates in the slots . . .

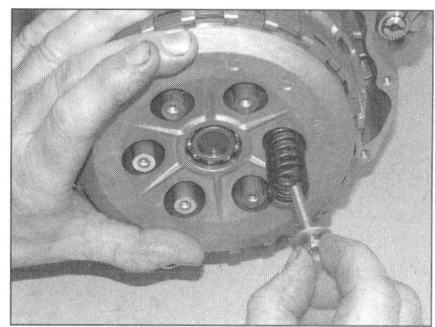

13.26b . . . then fit the springs and bolts and tighten them as described

2•34 Engine, clutch and transmission

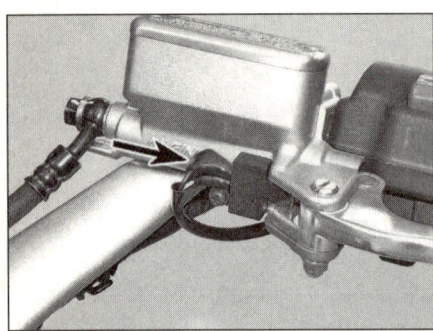

14.1 Disconnect the wiring connectors (arrowed)

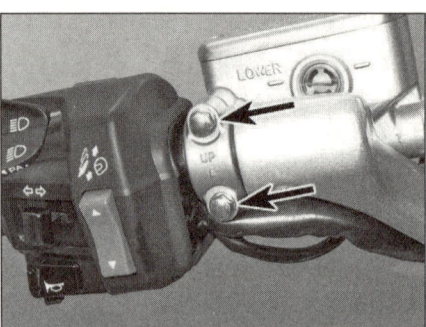

14.2 Clutch master cylinder clamp bolts (arrowed)

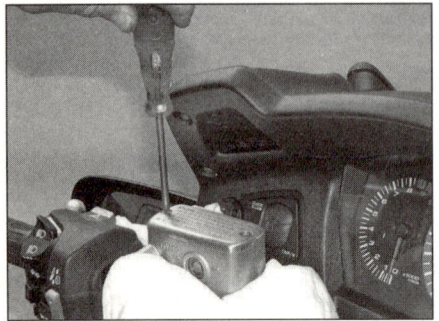

14.4 Slacken the cover screws

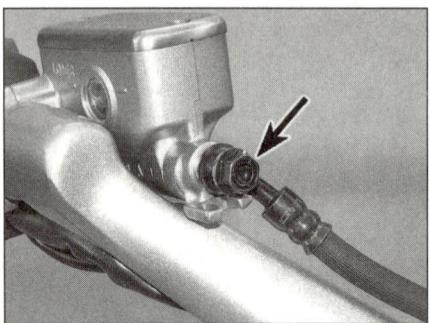

14.5 Clutch hose banjo bolt (arrowed)

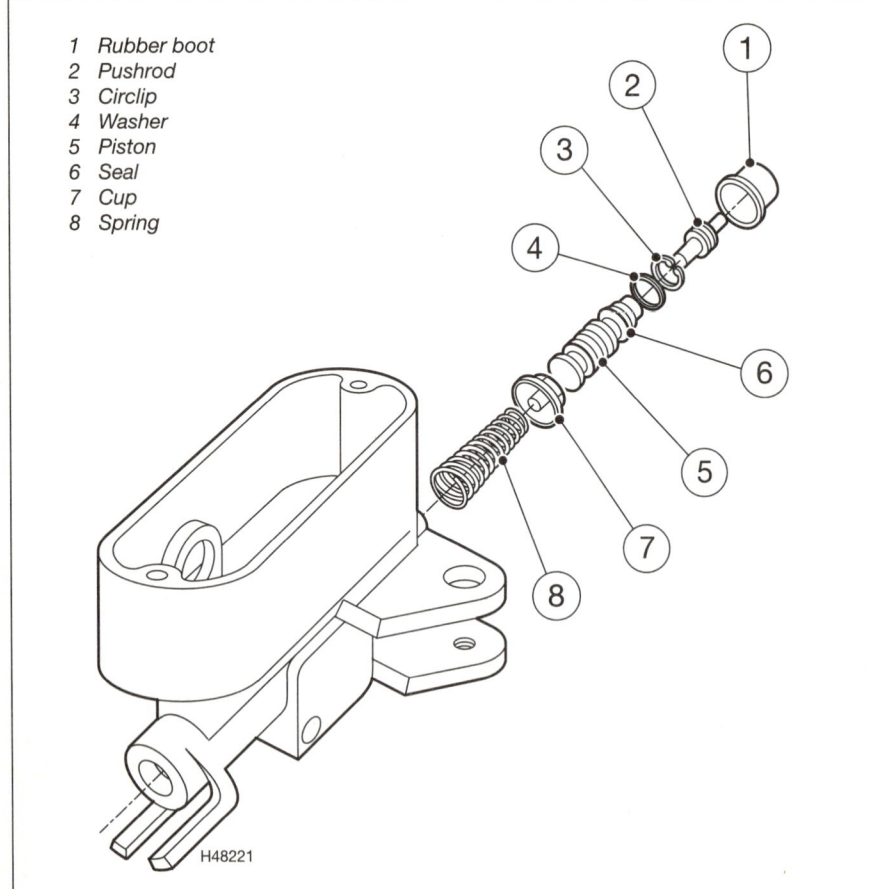

1 Rubber boot
2 Pushrod
3 Circlip
4 Washer
5 Piston
6 Seal
7 Cup
8 Spring

14.9 Clutch master cylinder components

Master cylinder

Note: *If the master cylinder is being overhauled (usually due to sticking or poor action, or fluid leaks) read through the entire procedure first and make sure that you have obtained all the new parts required, including some new DOT 4 brake/clutch fluid – a rebuild kit is available that includes the rubber boot, circlip, washer, piston, seal, cup and spring – do not reassemble the master cylinder without the rebuild kit – a new seal and cup must be used.*

Removal

1 Disconnect the wiring connectors from the clutch switch **(see illustration)**.
2 If the master cylinder is just being displaced, unscrew the master cylinder clamp bolts and remove the back of the clamp, noting how it fits, then position the master cylinder assembly clear of the handlebar **(see illustration)**. Ensure no strain is placed on the hydraulic hose. Keep the reservoir upright to prevent air entering the system.
3 If the master cylinder is being overhauled remove the clutch lever (see Chapter 5).
4 Slacken the reservoir cover screws **(see illustration)**.
5 Unscrew the clutch hose banjo bolt and detach the banjo union, noting its alignment with the master cylinder, and catching any residual fluid in a rag **(see illustration)**. Use plastic foodwrap to seal the banjo union and secure the hose in an upright position to minimise fluid loss if the system hasn't been drained. Discard the sealing washers as new ones must be fitted on reassembly.
6 Unscrew the master cylinder clamp bolts and remove the back of the clamp, noting how it fits, then lift the master cylinder and reservoir away from the handlebar **(see illustration 14.2)**.
7 Remove the reservoir cover, diaphragm plate and diaphragm. Drain the brake fluid from the master cylinder and reservoir into a suitable container. Wipe any remaining fluid out of the reservoir with a clean rag.
8 If required, undo the screw securing the clutch switch and remove the switch.

Overhaul

9 Carefully remove the pushrod and rubber boot from the master cylinder **(see illustration)**.
10 Depress the piston and use circlip pliers to remove the circlip, then slide out the washer, piston assembly and spring, noting how they fit. If they are difficult to remove, apply low pressure compressed air to the fluid outlet. Lay the parts out in the proper order to prevent confusion during reassembly.
11 Clean the master cylinder and reservoir with clean brake/clutch fluid. If compressed air is available, blow it through the fluid galleries to ensure they are clear (make sure the air is filtered and unlubricated).

Caution: *Do not, under any circumstances, use a petroleum-based solvent to clean brake parts.*

Engine, clutch and transmission 2•35

14.19 Align the clamp joint with the punch mark (arrowed)

14.26 Release cylinder bolts (arrowed)

12 Check the master cylinder bore for corrosion, scratches, nicks and score marks. If the necessary measuring equipment is available, compare the dimensions of the bore to those given in the Specifications at the beginning of this Chapter. If damage or wear is evident, the master cylinder must be replaced with a new one. If the master cylinder is in poor condition, then the release cylinder should be checked as well.

13 The boot, circlip, washer, piston, seal, cup and spring are all included in the master cylinder rebuild kit. Use all of the new parts, regardless of the apparent condition of the old ones. Lubricate the master cylinder bore with new brake fluid.

14 Smear the cup and seal with new brake fluid. Fit the cup onto the narrow end of the spring, locating the peg in the hole. Fit the seal into its groove in the piston so the flared end will fit into the master cylinder first.

15 Lubricate the spring and cup with clean brake fluid. Fit the spring wide end first into the master cylinder, and push the cup in, making sure its lip does not turn inside out.

16 Lubricate the piston and seal with clean brake fluid. Slide the piston into the master cylinder and up against the cup and spring. Make sure the lips on the seal do not turn inside out. Push the piston in to compress the spring, then fit the washer and the new circlip, making sure it locates in the groove. Smear the pushrod and rubber boot with silicone grease.

17 Lubricate the pushrod tips and inside the rubber boot with silicone grease. Fit the pushrod into the boot so the outer lip locates in the groove. Press the wide rim of the boot into place in the end of the cylinder.

Installation

18 If removed, fit the clutch switch onto the master cylinder.

19 Attach the master cylinder to the handlebar, aligning the clamp joint with the punch mark on the top of the handlebar, then fit the back of the clamp with its UP mark facing up **(see illustration)**. Tighten the upper bolt to the torque setting specified at the beginning of the Chapter, followed by the lower bolt **(see illustration 14.2)**.

20 Connect the clutch hose to the master cylinder, using new sealing washers on each side of the banjo fitting. Align the hose as noted on removal **(see illustration 14.5)**. Tighten the banjo bolt to the torque setting specified at the beginning of the Chapter.

21 Install the clutch lever (see Chapter 5).

22 Connect the clutch switch wiring **(see illustration 14.1)**.

23 Fill the fluid reservoir with new DOT 4 fluid (see *Pre-ride checks*). Refer to Step 44 and bleed the air from the system.

24 Check the operation of the clutch before riding the motorcycle.

Release cylinder

Note: *If the release cylinder is being overhauled (usually due to sticking or poor action, or fluid leaks) read through the entire procedure first and make sure that you have obtained all the new parts required, including some new DOT 4 brake/clutch fluid – do not reassemble the master cylinder using the old seal – a new one must be used. Note that there is a drain hole in the bottom of the release cylinder housing – if it is leaking hydraulic fluid the piston seal is leaking, and if it is leaking engine oil the pushrod seal is leaking.*

Removal

25 Remove the engine (see Section 4).

26 Unscrew the release cylinder bolts and remove the cylinder, taking care to catch residual fluid in a rag **(see illustration)**. Remove the dowels if they are loose **(see illustration 14.40)**. Remove the gasket and discard it as a new one must be used.

27 If required withdraw the pushrod **(see illustrations)**. If you do lever the oil seal out – a new one must be fitted.

Overhaul

28 Clean the exterior of the cylinder with denatured alcohol or brake system cleaner.

29 Withdraw the piston and spring from cylinder **(see illustration)**. If the piston cannot be withdrawn by hand, it can be pushed out

14.27a If required withdraw the pushrod . . .

14.27b . . . then lever the seal out

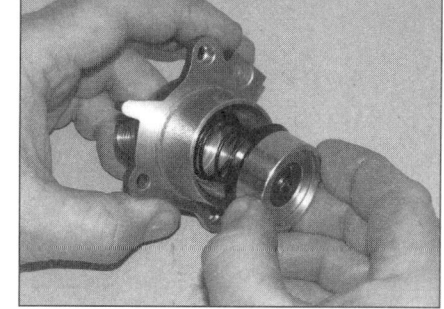

14.29 Remove the piston and spring

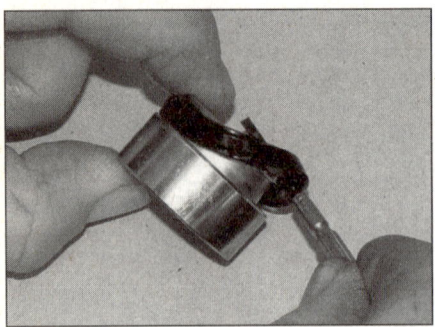

14.31a Remove the fluid seal . . .

14.31b . . . and the pushrod seal

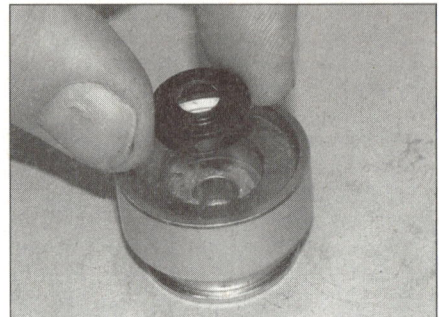

14.34 Push the new pushrod seal into place

by applying compressed air to the clutch hose union hole. Only low pressure should be required, such as is generated by a foot pump. Wrap the release cylinder in a wad of rag to prevent the piston being forcibly expelled.

30 Remove the spring from the piston, noting how it fits **(see illustration 14.36)**.

31 Carefully remove the fluid seal and pushrod seal from the piston, noting which way round they fit **(see illustrations)**. Discard the seals as new ones must be used.

32 Clean the piston and cylinder with clean brake fluid or denatured alcohol. If compressed air is available, use it to dry the parts thoroughly (make sure it's filtered and unlubricated).

Caution: Do not, under any circumstances, use a petroleum-based solvent to clean master cylinder parts.

33 Inspect the cylinder bore and piston for signs of corrosion, nicks and burrs and loss of plating. If surface defects are present, the cylinder assembly must be replaced with a new one. If it is in bad shape the master cylinder should also be checked. No specifications are given to check piston and bore wear.

34 Apply silicone grease to the pushrod socket in the piston. Fit the pushrod seal with its marked side facing out **(see illustration)**.

35 Lubricate the fluid seal with brake fluid. Fit the fluid seal onto the piston so its flared side will face into the cylinder **(see illustration)**.

36 Fit the narrow end of the spring over the boss on the inner end of the piston **(see illustration)**.

37 Lubricate the cylinder with clean brake fluid and fit the spring and piston into the bore **(see illustration 14.29)**. Make sure the spring remains

correctly positioned and make sure the fluid seal does not dislodge or turn inside out as you push it in. Using your thumbs, push the piston all the way in, making sure it enters the bore squarely.

Installation

38 Remove all traces of gasket from the cylinder and cover sealing surfaces.

39 If removed fit a new pushrod oil seal, flat side facing out **(see illustration)**. Make sure the pushrod is straight and clean and smear the shaft with oil, then slide it into place **(see illustration 14.27a)**.

40 Fit the dowels if removed. Fit a new gasket onto the dowels **(see illustration)**.

41 Apply a smear of silicone grease to the pushrod end. Fit the release cylinder, aligning it with the pushrod and locating dowels **(see illustration)**. Fit the bolts and tighten them.

42 Install the engine (see Section 4).

43 Fill the master cylinder to the correct level with new DOT4 hydraulic fluid (see *Pre-ride checks*) and bleed the hydraulic system (see Step 44). Check for leaks and thoroughly test the operation of the clutch before installing the fairing panels.

Clutch release mechanism bleeding

44 Bleeding the clutch is simply the process of removing air from the clutch fluid reservoir, the hose and the release cylinder. Bleeding is necessary whenever an hydraulic connection is loosened, after a component or hose is replaced with a new one, or when the release cylinder is overhauled. Leaks in the system

14.35 Fit the new fluid seal into the groove as shown

14.36 Fit the spring onto the piston

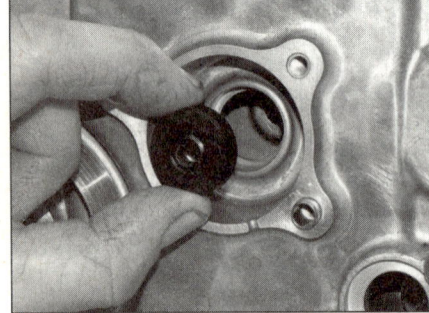

14.39 Push the new pushrod seal into place

14.40 Fit the new gasket onto the dowels (arrowed)

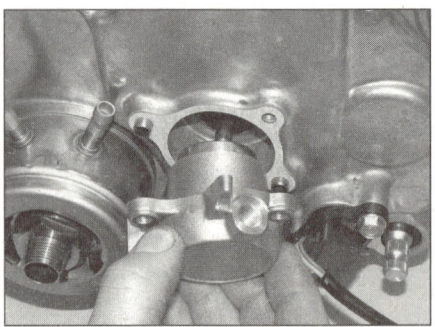

14.41 Fit the release cylinder over the pushrod and onto the dowels

Engine, clutch and transmission 2•37

14.48 Pull the cap off the bleed valve (arrowed)

may also allow air to enter, but leaking clutch fluid will reveal their presence and warn you of the need for repair.

45 To bleed the clutch, you will need some new DOT 4 brake/clutch fluid, a length of clear flexible hose, a small container partially filled with clutch fluid, some rags, a ring spanner to fit the release cylinder bleed valve, and to make the task simpler an assistant. Bleeding kits that include the hose, a one-way valve and a container are available relatively cheaply from a good auto store, and simplify the task as you don't need an assistant. Alternatively you can use a commercially available vacuum-type bleeding tool – follow the manufacturer's instructions

46 Remove the left-hand fairing side panel (see Chapter 7).

47 Remove the reservoir cover, diaphragm plate and diaphragm **(see illustration 14.4)**. Slowly pump the clutch lever a few times, until no air bubbles can be seen floating up from the holes in the bottom of the reservoir. This bleeds the air from the master cylinder end of the line. Temporarily refit the reservoir cover.

48 Pull the dust cap off the end of the bleed valve **(see illustration)**. Fit a ring spanner onto the valve, positioning it so it can turn a ¼ turn anti-clockwise without snagging. Attach one end of the clear vinyl or plastic hose to the bleed valve and submerge the other end in the clean clutch fluid in the container.

49 Check the fluid level in the reservoir. Do not allow the fluid level to drop below the lower mark during the procedure.

50 Carefully pump the clutch lever three or four times, then hold it in and open the bleed valve. When the valve is opened, clutch fluid will flow out of the bleed pipe and into the clear tubing, and the lever will move toward the handlebar. If there is air in the system there will be air bubbles in the fluid coming out of the pipe.

51 Tighten the bleed valve, then release the clutch lever gradually. Repeat the process until no air bubbles are visible in the fluid leaving the pipe, topping-up the reservoir as required. On completion, disconnect the hose, then tighten the bleed valve to the torque setting specified at the beginning of this Chapter and fit the dust cap.

52 Check the fluid level in the reservoir, then fit the diaphragm, diaphragm plate and cover (see *Pre-ride checks*). Wipe up any spilled clutch fluid. Check the entire system for fluid leaks.

Fluid change

53 Changing the clutch fluid is a similar process to bleeding the clutch and requires the same tools (see Step 45) plus a syringe for siphoning the fluid out of the reservoir (though if one isn't available it is no problem to displace the reservoir and tip the fluid out, or to soak up with some kitchen towel or similar). Make sure that the container is large enough to take all the old fluid when it is flushed out of the system.

54 Follow Steps 46 and 48, then remove the reservoir cover, diaphragm plate and diaphragm and siphon the old fluid out of the reservoir. Fill the reservoir with new clutch fluid, then carefully pump the clutch lever three or four times and hold it in while opening the bleed valve. When the valve is opened, clutch fluid will flow out of the release cylinder into the clear tubing.

55 Tighten the bleed valve, then release the clutch lever gradually. Repeat the process until new fluid can be seen emerging from the release cylinder bleed valve – keep the reservoir topped-up with new fluid to above the LOWER

level at all times or air may enter the system and greatly increase the length of the task.

 HAYNES HiNT *Old clutch fluid is invariably darker in colour than new fluid, making it easy to see when all old fluid has been expelled from the system.*

56 Disconnect the hose, then tighten the bleed valve to the specified torque setting and fit the dust cap.

57 Top-up the reservoir, then fit the diaphragm, diaphragm plate and cover (see *Pre-ride checks*). Wipe up any spilled clutch fluid. Check the entire system for fluid leaks.

Draining the system for overhaul

58 Draining the brake fluid is again a similar process to bleeding the brakes. Follow the procedure described above for changing the fluid, but quite simply do not put any new fluid into the reservoir – the system fills itself with air instead. An alternative is to use a commercially available vacuum-type brake bleeding tool as shown in Chapter 6.

15 Primary drive gear

Note: *The primary drive gear can be removed with the engine in the frame.*

Removal

1 Remove the clutch centre and the thrust washer, then leave the clutch housing on the shaft (see Section 13, Steps 1 to 6).

2 Lock the primary drive and driven gears using either the Honda special tool (Pt. No. 07724-0010100) or equivalent, a suitable piece of sheet aluminium (do not use steel), or a wad of thick rag, located between the teeth on the right-hand side **(see illustration)**.

3 With the gears locked slacken the bolt **(see illustration)**. Remove the locking tool. Refer to Section 13, Step 7, lock the sub- and main

15.2 Wedge the tool or a piece of aluminium or rag between the gears to jam them . . .

15.3 . . . while slackening the bolt

2•38 Engine, clutch and transmission

15.4a Remove the bolt and the timing rotor . . .

15.4b . . . and the primary drive gear

15.5a Lift the sub-gear off . . .

15.5b . . . and check the springs

15.6a Thread the bolt into the main gear . . .

15.6b . . . this will offset the sub and main gear teeth slightly

15.6c Slide the gear onto the shaft

gear teeth and remove the clutch housing, then if required follow Step 8 and remove the water pump drive and driven sprockets and clutch guide.

4 Remove the bolt with its washer, then remove the timing rotor (see illustration). Slide the gear off the shaft (see illustration).

Inspection

5 If required unscrew the locking bolt, then remove the sub-gear, noting the alignment of its various holes with those in the main gear, and check the springs (see illustrations). Also check the gear teeth and those on the primary driven gear on the back of the clutch housing. If necessary replace the primary drive gear assembly with a new one – individual components are not available. When fitting the sub gear back onto the main gear align the holes.

Installation

6 If the sub-gear was removed from the main gear, before fitting the gear the main and sub-gear teeth must be aligned with the springs compressed. To do this identify the threaded hole in the main gear and thread a 6 mm Allen bolt into it (see illustrations). Now slide the gear onto the shaft, aligning the wide splines and with the sub-gear on the outside (see illustration). Now the teeth must be aligned by inserting a screwdriver into the hole as shown and using it as a lever to turn the sub-gear, compressing the springs, and when the teeth are aligned tighten the Allen bolt to secure the sub-gear in position (see illustration).

7 Fit the timing rotor, aligning the wide splines (see illustration). Lubricate the bolt threads with oil, then fit the washer and tighten the bolt finger-tight. Refer to Section 13, Steps 19, 20 and 21 and fit the clutch guide and water pump drive and driven sprockets if removed, and the clutch housing. Lock the primary drive and driven gears as before, but locate the locking tool on the other side (see illustration). Tighten the bolt to the

15.6d Use a screwdriver in the hole shown to lever the sub-gear against the springs until the teeth align, then tighten the bolt securely

15.7a Slide the timing rotor onto the shaft then fit the bolt with its washer

15.7b Fit your locking tool as shown . . .

Engine, clutch and transmission 2•39

15.7c ... and tighten the bolt to the specified torque

16.2 Unscrew the bolts (arrowed)

16.3 Draw the shaft and housing out of the engine

torque setting specified at the beginning of the Chapter **(see illustration)**. Remove the locking tool. Remove the bolt from the primary drive gear – turn the gear if required for the bolt to clear the clutch housing **(see illustration 13.7a)**.

8 Install the remainder of the clutch (see Section 13, Step 22 onwards).

16 Primary damper shaft

Note: *The primary damper shaft can be removed with the engine in the frame.*

Removal

1 Remove the clutch (see Section 13).
2 Unscrew the damper shaft bearing housing bolts **(see illustration)**.
3 Grasp the end of the damper shaft and withdraw the shaft from the engine, bringing the bearing housing with it **(see illustration)**.

Inspection

4 To disassemble the shaft seat the flange on the front end of the shaft in an hydraulic press base and locate the press on the damper cam. Compress the spring by the minimum amount required to release the spring retainer halves from their groove in the shaft **(see illustration)**.
5 Slowly and carefully release the press and remove the washer, the damper cam, the lifter, the spring and the splined washer.
Caution: Do not compress the spring more than necessary.

⚠ **Warning: Take care when releasing the compressor or press.**

6 Check all components, in particular their contact surfaces and the engagement splines on each end of the shaft, for wear or damage. Measure the free length of the damper spring. If it is shorter than the service limit specified at the beginning of the Chapter replace the shaft with a new one – individual components are not available.
7 Check the condition of the front bearing in the housing and the rear bearing inside the crankcase, referring to *Tools and Workshop Tips* in the Reference Section – to remove the rear bearing, which also acts as the bearing for the front end of the transmission shaft, the transmission assembly must be removed – refer to Sections 21 and 23.
8 To replace the front bearing, undo the retainer plate bolts and remove the plate **(see illustration)**. Drive the bearing out from the outside using a suitable socket or bearing driver – heat the housing using a hot air gun to ease removal if necessary. If the bearing is very tight press it out using an hydraulic press. Fit the new bearing, driving or pressing it in until it seats, locating the driver on the outer race only – heat the housing and if required place the bearing in the freezer for a while to ease installation. Clean the threads of the retainer plate bolts and apply fresh threadlock. Fit the plate and tighten the bolts to the torque setting specified at the beginning of the Chapter.
9 Reassemble the components onto the shaft in a reverse of their removal order – align the punch mark on the inner face of the lifter with the hole in the shaft. Fit the retainer halves with the flat side facing into the groove, locating them above the washer, and make sure they locate correctly in the grooves **(see illustration 16.4)**. Slowly and carefully release the compressor or press and check the retainers are correctly seated.

Installation

10 Slide the shaft into the engine and over the front of the transmission input shaft,

16.8 Damper shaft bearing retainer bolts (arrowed)

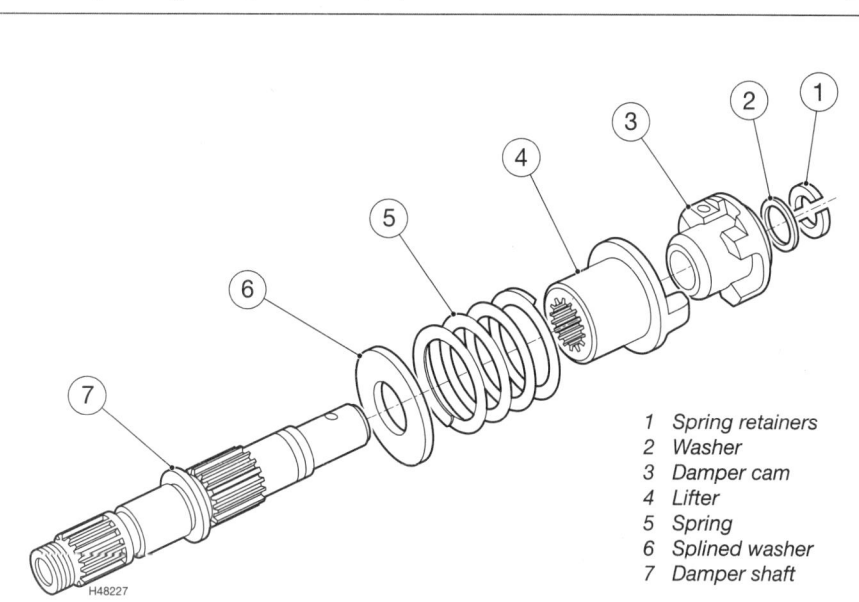

1 Spring retainers
2 Washer
3 Damper cam
4 Lifter
5 Spring
6 Splined washer
7 Damper shaft

16.4 Primary damper shaft components

2•40 Engine, clutch and transmission

16.10 Slide the shaft into place . . .

16.11 . . . then fit the bearing housing with the mark at the top

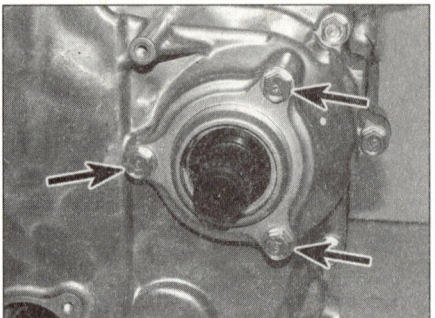

17.4 Unscrew the bolts (arrowed) and remove the cover

turning it as required to engage the splines **(see illustration)**.

11 Fit the bearing housing with the triangular mark at the top, aligning the bolts holes, then fit and tighten the bolts **(see illustration)**.

17 Final output shaft and gears

Note 1: *To remove the final output shaft the engine must be removed from the frame.*
Note 2: *The final output shaft and drive gear nuts should be discarded and new ones used on installation – it is best to obtain the new nuts in advance.*
Special Tools: *Two Honda special tools, a shaft spline holding tool and special socket with offset arm are required – see Steps 6 and 7. You will also need two long 1/2 inch drive bars, and an assistant.*

Removal

1 Remove the engine (see Section 4).
2 Remove the clutch release cylinder, withdraw the pushrod, and remove the oil seal (see Section 14).
3 If required remove the oil cooler (see Section 6) and the speed sensor (see Chapter 4).
4 Unscrew the final output shaft cover bolts and draw the cover off **(see illustration)**. Remove the O-ring and discard it – a new one must be used.
5 The final output shaft nut rim is staked into the cut-out in the shaft. Unstake the nut using a hammer and punch **(see illustration)**.
6 To hold the output shaft and prevent it from turning and to simultaneously unscrew the nut, which is very tight, two Honda special tools (Pt. Nos. 070MB-MCD0100 and 07916-MB00002) are needed **(see illustration)** – there is no alternative to these tools, because the nut is so tight you cannot hold the engine using the primary drive gear bolt or the clutch centre.
7 Fit the spline holder over the shaft, then fit the offset socket over the spline holder and onto the nut **(see illustrations)**. Fit long drive bars into the tools. Have an assistant hold the engine down, then counter-hold the shaft and unscrew the nut **(see illustration)**. Discard the nut – a new one should be used.
8 Unscrew the rear crankcase cover bolts, initially slackening them evenly in a criss-cross pattern **(see illustration)**. **Note:** *As each bolt is removed, store it in its relative position in a cardboard template of the crankcase halves*

17.5 Unstake the nut

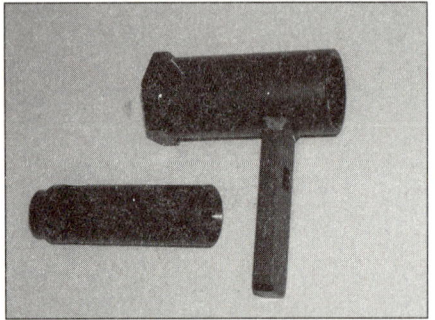

17.6 The Honda tools shown are essential for this procedure

17.7a Fit the spline holder over the shaft . . .

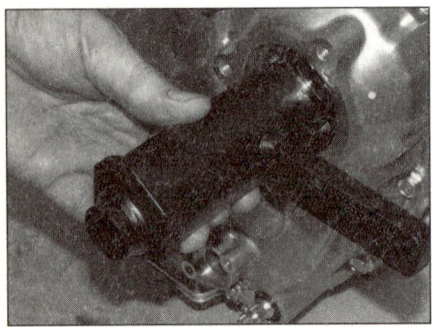

17.7b . . . then fit the socket onto the nut

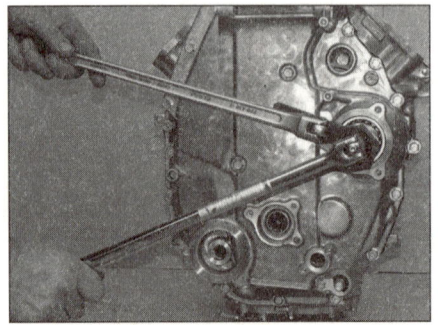

17.7c Counter-hold the shaft and unscrew the nut

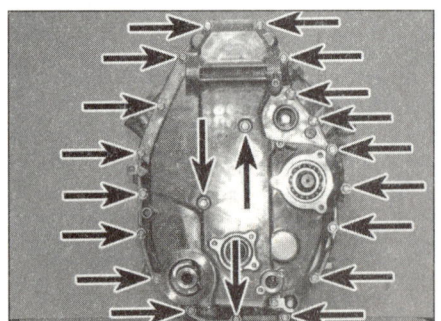

17.8a Rear crankcase cover bolts (arrowed)

Engine, clutch and transmission 2•41

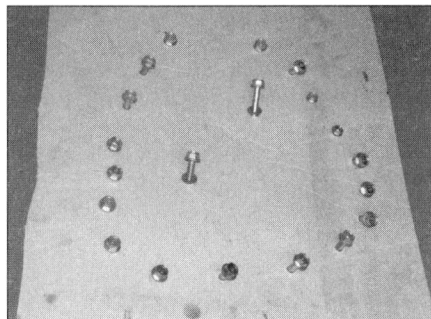

17.8b Store the bolts in a piece of card

17.8c Remove the two oil pipes – they are a push fit

17.9 Unstake the nut

(see illustration). *This will ensure all bolts are installed in the correct location on reassembly.* New sealing washers should be used on the centre bolts on installation. Remove the cover – note that there is a washer on the end of the gearchange shaft that could stick to the cover, in which case retrieve it and slide it back onto the shaft **(see illustration 20.3)**. Remove the two dowels if they are loose **(see illustrations 17.21a)**. Pull the oil pipes out and discard their seals **(see illustration)** – new ones must be used.

9 The final output drive gear nut rim is staked in two places into the cut-outs in the shaft. Unstake the nut using a hammer and punch – take care not to damage the threads on the end of the shaft **(see illustration)**.

10 Hold the final output shaft again using the spline holder and drive bar and slacken the drive gear nut **(see illustrations)** – it has left-hand threads and so must be undone by turning it clockwise. Note that as with the output shaft nut it is very tight and you will again need an assistant hold the engine – heat the nut using a hot air gun to ease its removal if required. Having slackened the nut remove the spline holder and the final output driven gear and shaft **(see illustration)**. Mark the outer face of the gear so it can be fitted the same way round and slide it off the shaft.

11 Remove the nut and washer and slide the final output drive gear off, noting which way round all three components fit **(see illustration)**. Discard the nut – a new one should be used.

Inspection

12 Check the teeth of the gears and the splines in the gears and on the shafts. Replace the gears and/or shafts if worn or chipped teeth or splines are discovered – refer to Sections 22 and 24 to remove and strip the transmission output shaft.

13 Check the condition of the rear bearing in the crankcase cover and the front bearing in the transmission cover, referring to *Tools and Workshop Tips* in the Reference Section.

14 To replace the rear bearing, drive it out from the inside using a suitable socket or bearing driver – heat the housing using a hot air gun to ease removal **(see illustration)**. If the bearing is very tight press it out using an hydraulic press. Fit the new bearing, driving or pressing it in until it seats, locating the driver or press on the outer race only **(see illustration)** – heat the housing and if required place the bearing in the freezer for a while to ease installation.

17.10a Fit the spline holder over the shaft . . .

17.10b . . . then counter-hold it while unscrewing the nut clockwise

17.10c Remove the final output shaft and driven gear

17.11 Unscrew the nut, remove the washer and slide the gear off

17.14a Drive the bearing out from the inside

17.14b Drive the new bearing in from the outside

2•42 Engine, clutch and transmission

17.17a Drive the shaft oil seal out of the cover

17.17b Unscrew the bolt (arrowed) and remove the retainer . . .

17.17c . . . then lever the gearchange shaft oil seal out

15 To replace the front bearing you need an internal expanding puller and slide hammer **(see illustrations 23.7a and b)**. Heat the bearing housing with a hot air gun to ease removal, then fit the tools and jar the bearing out. Fit the new bearing, driving it in until it seats, locating the driver on the outer race only – heat the housing and if required place the bearing in the freezer for a while to ease installation. If the tools are not available remove the transmission assembly from the crankcase, then remove the transmission shafts from the cover, and drive the bearing out from the inside of the cover – refer to Sections 21 to 23.

Installation

16 Clean all traces of old sealant from the crankcase and cover – if you use a scraper take care not to gouge the surface.

17 Drive the shaft oil seal out of the output shaft cover with a seal driver or socket, noting which way round it fits **(see illustration)**. Unscrew the gearchange shaft oil seal retainer bolt and remove the retainer, then lever the oil seal out of the rear crankcase cover **(see illustrations)**. Press or drive new seals squarely in using your fingers, a seal driver or suitable socket, making sure they are the correct way round **(see illustrations)**. Fit the gearchange shaft seal retainer.

18 Slide the drive gear onto its shaft **(see illustration 17.11)**. Fit the washer with the OUTSIDE mark facing out **(see illustration)**. Smear some oil onto the threads and seating surface of the new nut and thread it onto the shaft with its staking rim facing out and tighten it finger-tight **(see illustration)**. If removed slide the driven gear onto the shaft so its marked side will face out. Fit the shaft into the bearing in the transmission cover **(see illustration 17.10c)**.

19 Fit the spline holder over the shaft **(see illustration 17.10a)**. Counter-hold the spline holder and tighten the nut to the torque setting specified at the beginning of the Chapter **(see illustration)** – remember it has left-hand threads and so must be tightened anti-clockwise. Stake the rim of the nut into the indents on the end of the shaft **(see illustration)**.

20 Fit new seals into the grooves in the oil pipes and smear them with oil **(see illustration)** – the seals are shaped and must be fitted with the narrow side facing the end of the pipe. Fit the pipes into the oil gallery and pump, making sure the O-rings stay in place **(see illustration 17.8c)**.

17.17d Fit the new shaft seal with its marked side facing into the cover

17.17e Fit the gearchange shaft seal with the marked side facing out

17.18a Fit the washer . . .

17.18b . . . and the nut

17.19a Counter-hold the shaft and tighten the nut to the specified torque

17.19b Stake the nut in both places

Engine, clutch and transmission 2•43

21 Fit the dowels into the crankcase if removed **(see illustrations)**. Apply a suitable sealant (such as Three Bond 1207B or equivalent RTV sealant – ask your dealer) to the mating surface of the cover. Fit the cover, locating it over the dowels and making sure it seats correctly. Fit the bolts, using new sealing washers on the centre bolts, and tighten them evenly and in a criss-cross pattern **(see illustration)**.

22 Smear some oil onto the threads and seating surface of the new final output shaft nut and thread it onto the shaft with its staking rim facing out **(see illustration)**. Fit the spline holder over the shaft, then fit the offset socket over the spline holder and onto the nut **(see illustrations 17.7a and b)**. Fit a long drive bar into the holder and a large torque wrench with a ½ inch drive into the socket arm **(see illustration)**. Have an assistant hold the engine down, then counter-hold the shaft and tighten the nut to the indicated torque setting specified at the beginning of the Chapter – do not apply the actual torque setting given, as this would apply to a torque wrench located directly onto the nut, and the offset position of the special tools affects this (if 186 Nm is applied through the offset the nut will actually be tighter than it should, which could strip the threads, hence the lower value for the indicated setting). Note that the indicated torque setting is calculated using a torque wrench 450 mm long and given the 50 mm offset of the Honda special tool. If a longer or shorter torque wrench is used, or if you make up a tool with a different offset, you need to recalculate the indicated

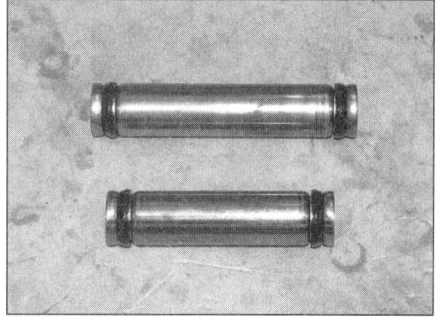

17.20 Fit a new seal onto each end of each pipe

17.21b ... and the lower dowel (arrowed) if removed

torque setting by using the facility provided at www.norbar.co.uk, entering the specific details in the required fields. Stake the rim of the nut into the indents on the end of the shaft **(see illustration)**.

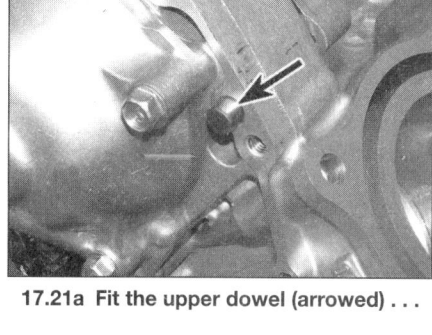

17.21a Fit the upper dowel (arrowed) ...

17.21c Apply sealant then fit the cover

23 Fit a new O-ring into the groove in the cover **(see illustration)**. Fit the cover and tighten the bolts **(see illustration)**.

24 Install the remaining components in reverse order (see Steps 3 to 1).

17.21d Use a new sealing washer on each of the centre bolts

17.22c Stake the nut into the indent

17.22a Thread the new nut onto the shaft ...

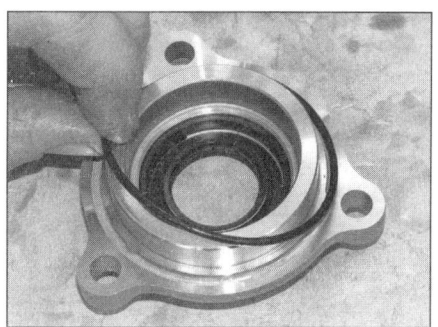

17.23a Fit a new O-ring into the groove ...

17.22b ... and tighten it to the specified torque

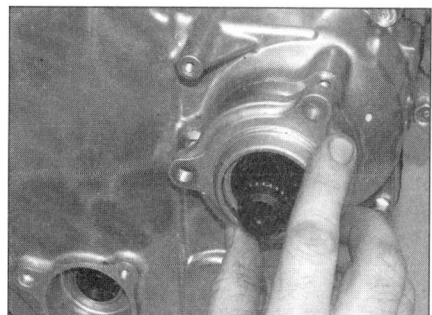

17.23b ... then fit the cover

2•44 Engine, clutch and transmission

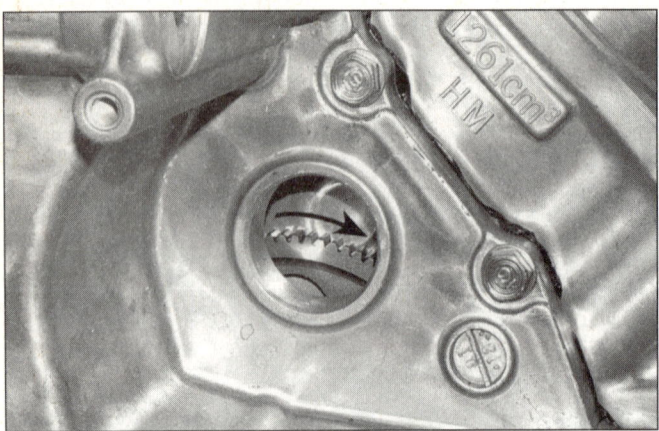

18.1 Check the operation of the clutch by turning the idle/reduction gear as described

18.3 Withdraw the shaft and remove the gear

18 Starter clutch and gears

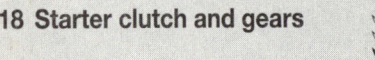

Note: *To remove the starter clutch and gears the engine must be removed from the frame.*

Check

1 The operation of the starter clutch can be checked while it is in situ. Remove the starter motor (see Chapter 8). Check that the reduction gear is able to rotate freely clockwise as you look at it via the starter motor aperture, but locks when rotated anti-clockwise **(see illustration)**. If not, the starter clutch is faulty and should be removed for inspection.

Removal

2 Remove the rear crankcase cover (see Section 17, Steps 1 to 8).
3 Withdraw the idle/reduction gear shaft and remove the gear **(see illustration)**.
4 Lock the alternator drive and middle gears using either the Honda special tool (Pt. No. 07724-0010100) or equivalent, a suitable piece of sheet aluminium (do not use steel), or a wad of thick rag, located between the teeth on the top **(see illustration)**.
5 With the gears locked slacken then remove the starter clutch bolt with its washer **(see illustration)**. Remove the locking tool.
6 Lock the oil pump driven sprocket to prevent it from turning using a pegged holding tool (such as the commercially and cheaply available one shown, known as a clutch holding tool but also with pegs on the reverse side of the clutch holders) or a pair of curved-end pliers in the sprocket holes as shown and unscrew the bolt **(see illustrations)**. Do not lock the oil pump using the same wedging tool as in Step 4 to avoid transmitting the tension through the chain. Remove the drive and driven sprockets and chain **(see illustration)**.
7 Remove the alternator middle gear case (see Section 19, Steps 4 and 7).
8 Slide the starter clutch assembly off the shaft **(see illustration)**.

Inspection

9 With the alternator drive gear face down on a workbench, check that the starter driven gear rotates freely clockwise and locks against

18.4 Wedge the tool or a piece of aluminium or rag between the gears to jam them . . .

18.5 . . . while slackening the bolt

18.6a Hold the sprocket using the pegged side of the clutch holding tool . . .

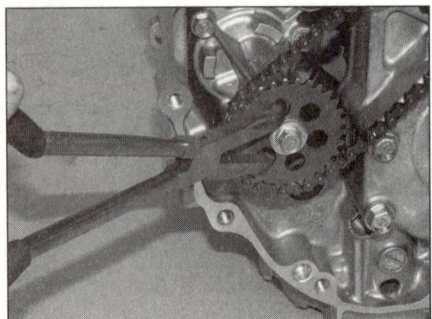

18.6b . . . or a pair of curved nosed pliers, while slackening the bolt

18.6c Slide the chain and sprockets off

18.8 Slide the starter clutch assembly off

Engine, clutch and transmission 2•45

18.9 Check the operation of the clutch as described

18.10 Withdraw the driven gear and remove the bearing

18.11 The sprag assembly is secured by a circlip (arrowed)

the rotor anti-clockwise **(see illustration)**. If it doesn't, the starter clutch should be dismantled for further investigation.

10 Withdraw the starter driven gear from the starter clutch **(see illustration)**. If the gear appears stuck, rotate it clockwise as you withdraw it to free it from the starter clutch. Remove the needle bearing.

11 Release the circlip then remove the sprag assembly from the housing by turning it anti-clockwise **(see illustration)**. Check the condition of the sprags and the cage – if they are damaged, marked or flattened at any point, or the sprags do not move freely, replace the sprag assembly with a new one. Lubricate the sprag assembly with oil and fit with its flanged side facing into the housing, turn it anti-clockwise as you do. Fit the circlip, locating it in the groove.

12 Check the external surface on the driven gear hub **(see illustration 18.10)**. Measure the outside diameter of the hub and check that it has not worn beyond the service limit specified. Check the needle roller bearing and the bearing surfaces on the starter driven gear hub and the starter clutch housing boss. If the bearing surfaces show signs of excessive wear or the bearing itself is worn or damaged, they should be replaced with new ones. If a new starter clutch housing is required remove the alternator drive gear first (see Section 19, Step 8).

13 Check the teeth of the idle/reduction gears and the corresponding teeth of the starter driven gear and starter motor drive shaft. Replace the gears and/or starter motor if worn or chipped teeth are discovered on related gears. Also check the idle/reduction gear shaft for damage, and check that the gear is not a loose fit on it. Check the reduction gear shaft ends and the bores they run in for wear.

Installation

14 Lubricate the needle roller bearing with clean engine oil and fit it over the starter clutch boss **(see illustration 18.10)**. Lubricate the outside of the starter driven gear hub with clean engine oil, then fit the gear into the clutch, rotating it clockwise as you do so to spread the sprags and allow the hub to enter.

15 Slide the starter clutch assembly onto the shaft **(see illustration 18.8)**.

16 Install the alternator middle gear case (see Section 19, Step 13).

17 Fit the oil pump drive and driven sprockets into the chain, making sure that when installed the driven sprocket OUT mark will face out. As an assembly slide the drive sprocket onto the shaft and locate the flats on the driven sprocket against those on the oil pump shaft **(see illustration 18.6c)**. Clean the threads of the driven sprocket bolt and apply fresh threadlock **(see illustration 26.24)**. Fit the bolt with its washer and tighten it to the torque setting specified at the beginning of the Chapter, holding the sprocket as on removal **(see illustration 18.6a or b)**.

18 Lubricate the threads and seating surface of the starter clutch bolt, then fit the bolt with its washer **(see illustration)**. Fit the locking tool used on removal between the teeth of the alternator drive and middle gears on the underside **(see illustration)**. Tighten the bolt to the specified torque setting. Remove the locking tool.

19 Lubricate the idle/reduction gear shaft with clean engine oil. Locate the gear as shown and slide the shaft into its bore in the crankcase **(see illustration 18.3)**.

20 Install the rear crankcase cover (see Section 17, Steps 16 and 17, then 20 to 24).

19 Alternator drive, middle and driven gears

Note: *To remove these components the engine must be removed from the frame.*

Removal

1 Remove the rear crankcase cover (see Section 17, Steps 1 to 8). If not already done remove the spark plugs (see Chapter 1).

18.18a Lubricate the bolt as described and fit it with its large washer

18.18b Fit the locking tool on the underside of the gears

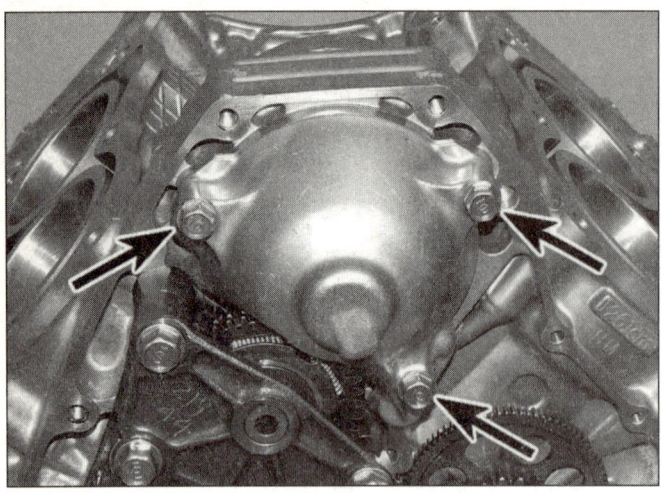

19.3a Unscrew the bolts (arrowed) and remove the cover

19.3b Remove the oil jet (arrowed) and its O-ring if required

2 Remove the alternator (see Chapter 8).

3 Unscrew the driven gear cover bolts and draw the cover off (see illustration). Remove the dowels if loose. If required withdraw the oil jet and remove its O-ring (see illustration). Discard the O-ring – a new one must be used.

4 Obtain two 6 mm bolts. Turn the engine using a socket on the starter clutch bolt until the threaded hole in the lower middle main gear aligns with the hole in the gear case, then thread one of the bolts into the hole (see illustration). The threaded hole in the upper middle main gear should also be exposed above the rim of the gear case at the top – thread the other bolt into the hole

(see illustration). The bolts keep the main and sprung sub-gear teeth aligned, making it much easier to remove and install the drive, middle and driven gears.

5 Withdraw the driven gear assembly (see illustration) – you may need to carefully lever it away to overcome the sealant. Remove the O-ring and discard it (see illustration 19.15a) – a new one must be used.

6 To remove the drive gear slacken the starter clutch bolt now (see Section 18, Steps 3 to 6).

7 Unscrew the alternator middle gear case bolts and remove the case (see illustration). Remove the dowels if loose (see illustration 19.13a).

8 Slide the starter clutch assembly off the shaft (see illustration 18.8). To remove the drive gear from the starter clutch housing mark its outer face so it can be fitted the same way round if being re-used, then unscrew the bolts securing it (see illustration) – use a rotor strap or similar to hold the gear. Note how it locates onto a pin – if required remove the pin for safekeeping if loose.

Inspection

9 Check the teeth of the alternator drive, middle, and driven gears. Replace the gears if worn or chipped teeth are discovered on related gears. Check the driven gear shaft bearings and damper assembly for wear and play.

10 The middle gears come as an assembly with the case, and no individual components are available for the driven gear assembly.

Installation

11 To fit the drive gear onto the starter clutch make sure the locating pin is in place. Fit the gear with the previously marked side facing out (unless a new one is being fitted), and locate it over the pin. Clean the threads of the bolts and apply fresh threadlock, then hold the gear and tighten the bolts to the torque setting specified at the beginning of the Chapter (see illustration 19.8).

19.4a Thread one 6 mm bolt into the threaded hole in the lower gear . . .

19.4b . . . and the other into the upper gear

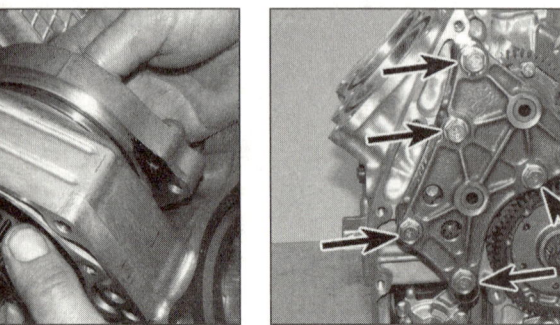

19.5 Withdraw the driven gear assembly

19.7 Unscrew the bolts (arrowed) and remove the gear case

19.8 Unscrew the perimeter bolts to separate the drive gear and starter clutch

Engine, clutch and transmission 2•47

19.13a Make sure dowels (arrowed) are in place . . .

19.13b . . . then fit the gear case

19.15a Fit a new O-ring into the groove . . .

19.15b . . . and apply sealant around the bolt holes (arrowed)

19.15c Align the line with the triangular mark on the crankcase

Remove the bolt from the upper middle gear **(see illustration 19.4b)**.

16 If removed fit the oil jet using a new O-ring smeared with oil **(see illustration 19.3b)**. Fit the driven gear cover dowels if removed **(see illustration)**. Fit the cover and tighten the bolts **(see illustration)**.

17 Install the rear crankcase cover (see Section 17, Steps 16 and 17, then 20 to 24). Install the spark plugs (see Chapter 1).

18 Install the alternator (see Chapter 8).

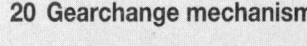 

20 Gearchange mechanism

Note: *To remove the gearchange mechanism the engine must be removed from the frame.*

Removal

1 Remove the rear crankcase cover and final output drive gear (see Section 17).

2 Note how the gearchange shaft centralising spring ends fit on each side of the locating pin in the casing, and how the pawls on the selector arm locate onto the pins on the end of the selector drum cam.

3 Grasp the end of the shaft and withdraw

12 Slide the starter clutch assembly onto the shaft **(see illustration 18.8)**.

13 Fit the middle gear case dowels **(see illustration)**. Make sure the gears are correctly aligned so the 6 mm locking bolts are exposed. Fit the gear case, making sure it seats over the dowels and the lower middle and drive gears engage **(see illustration)**. Tighten the bolts evenly in a criss-cross sequence to the torque setting specified at the beginning of the Chapter. Remove the bolt from the lower middle gear **(see illustration 19.4a)**.

14 Install the oil pump sprockets and chain

and starter clutch bolt (see Section 18, Steps 17 to 19).

15 Fit a new O-ring onto the driven gear assembly and smear it with oil **(see illustration)**. Apply a smear of suitable RTV sealant around each of the driven gear assembly bolt holes, not getting them muddled up with the alternator mounting bolt holes **(see illustration)**. Slide the assembly into place **(see illustration 19.5)**, aligning the bolt holes and the line on the top with the mark on the crankcase, and engaging the upper middle and driven gears **(see illustration)**.

19.16a Make sure dowels (arrowed) are in place . . .

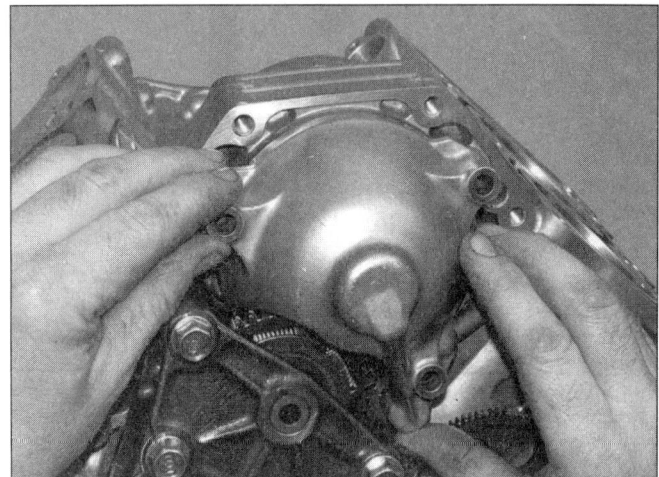

19.16b . . . then fit the cover

2•48 Engine, clutch and transmission

20.3 Withdraw the shaft/arm assembly, noting how it locates, and noting the washers (arrowed)

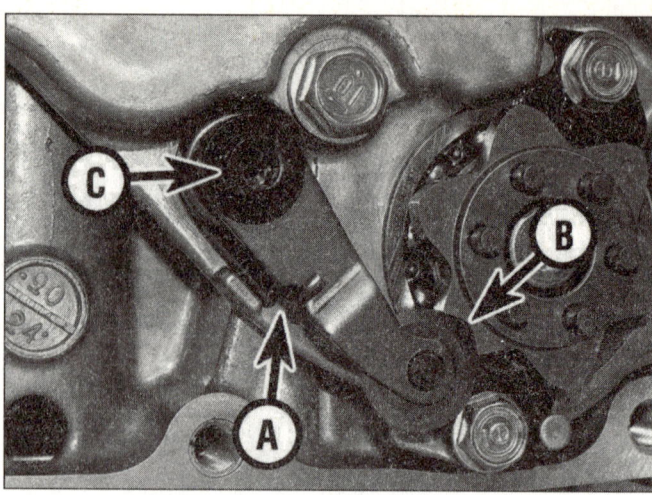

20.4 Note how the spring ends (A) locate, and how the roller sits in the neutral detent (B), then unscrew the bolt (C) and remove the arm

the shaft/arm assembly **(see illustration)**. Retrieve the washer from the transmission cover if it didn't come with the shaft.

4 Note how the stopper arm spring ends locate and how the roller on the arm locates in the neutral detent on the selector drum cam, then unscrew the stopper arm bolt and remove the arm, the washer and the spring, noting how they fit **(see illustration)**.

5 If required, remove the selector drum cam plate by counter-holding it using a large screwdriver blade under one of the pins and over an adjacent one and unscrewing the bolt in its centre **(see illustration 22.16c)**. Note the locating pin in the end of the drum and remove it for safekeeping if required **(see illustrations 22.16b and a)**.

Inspection

6 Check the selector arm for cracks, distortion and wear of its pawls, and check for any corresponding wear on the pins on the selector drum cam **(see illustration)**. Check the arm slides freely over its guide and returns under pressure from its spring **(see illustration)**. Check the shaft centralising spring and stopper arm spring for fatigue, wear or damage **(see illustration)**. To replace the shaft spring, slide the washer off the shaft, then remove the circlip and slide the spring off, noting how its ends locate **(see illustration)**. Fit the new spring, locating the ends on each side of the tab, and secure it with the circlip, making sure it locates in its groove. Slide the washer against the circlip.

7 Check the stopper arm roller and the surfaces of the selector drum cams for any

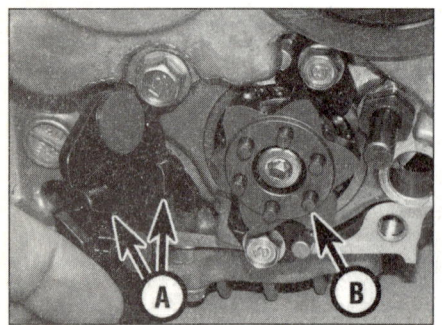

20.6a Check the selector arm pawls (A) and the pins (B) on the end of the drum

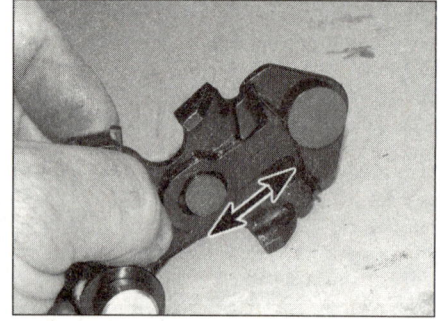

20.6b Check the movement of the arm and its spring

20.6c Check the springs (arrowed)

20.6d To remove the centralising spring slide the washer (A) off then release the circlip (B)

Engine, clutch and transmission 2•49

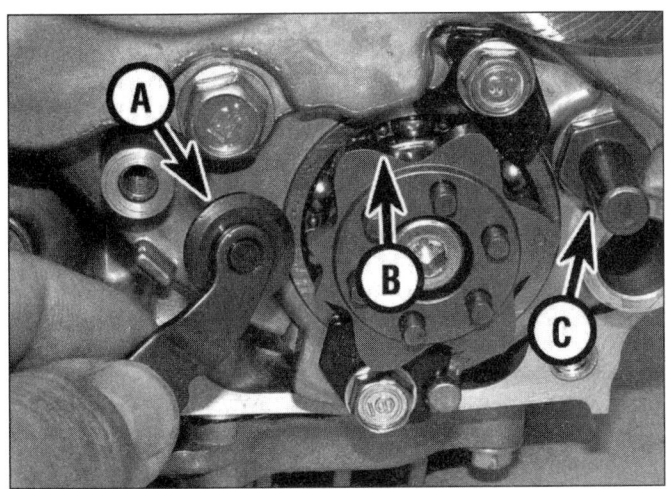

20.7 Check the roller (A) and the cams (B). Centralising spring locating pin (C)

20.10 Check the gearchange shaft bearing (arrowed)

wear or damage, and make sure the roller turns freely **(see illustration)**.

8 Check that the centralising spring locating pin in the crankcase is securely tightened **(see illustration 20.7)**. If it is loose, remove it and apply a non-permanent thread locking compound to its threads, then tighten it.

9 Check for wear and damage to the gearchange shaft splines and to the corresponding splines on the gearchange linkage arm. If necessary replace them with new ones.

10 Remove the gearchange shaft oil seal in the cover (see Section 17, Step 17). Check the condition of the needle bearing, and replace it with a new one if necessary **(see illustration)** – refer to *Tools and Workshop Tips* in the Reference Section for details and removing and fitting needle bearings.

Installation

11 If removed clean the threads of the selector drum cam plate bolt. Fit the locating pin into its hole then locate the plate on the end of the drum, aligning the large cut-out on its inner face with the locating pin **(see illustrations 22.16a**

and b). Apply a suitable non-permanent thread locking compound to the bolt and tighten it to the torque setting specified at the beginning of the Chapter, counter-holding the drum as before **(see illustration 22.16c)**.

12 Clean the threads of the stopper arm bolt and apply fresh threadlock. Fit the bolt through the stopper arm then fit the washer and spring, locating the curved end in the cut-out in the underside of the arm **(see illustration)**. Locate the assembly and thread the bolt in, locating the straight end of the spring against the lug and the roller onto the neutral detent on the cam plate **(see illustration 20.4)**. Tighten the bolt to the torque setting specified at the beginning of the Chapter. Check that the arm and spring ends are correctly positioned.

13 Check that the shaft centralising spring is properly positioned and slide the washer onto each end of the shaft if removed **(see illustration 20.6d)**. Slide the shaft into place **(see illustration 20.3)**, locating the selector arm pawls onto the pins on the selector drum and the centralising spring ends onto each

side of the locating pin in the crankcase.

14 Install the final output drive gear and rear crankcase cover (see Section 17).

21 Transmission assembly removal and installation

Note: *To remove the transmission shafts the engine must be removed from the frame.*

Removal

1 Remove the rear crankcase cover and final output drive and driven gears (see Section 17).

2 Remove the gearchange shaft assembly (see Section 20, Steps 2 and 3), and if you intend to remove the selector drum (or if otherwise required) also remove the stopper arm and selector drum cam (Steps 4 and 5).

3 Unscrew the transmission cover bolts evenly in a criss-cross sequence, noting the position of the shorter bolt **(see illustration)**.

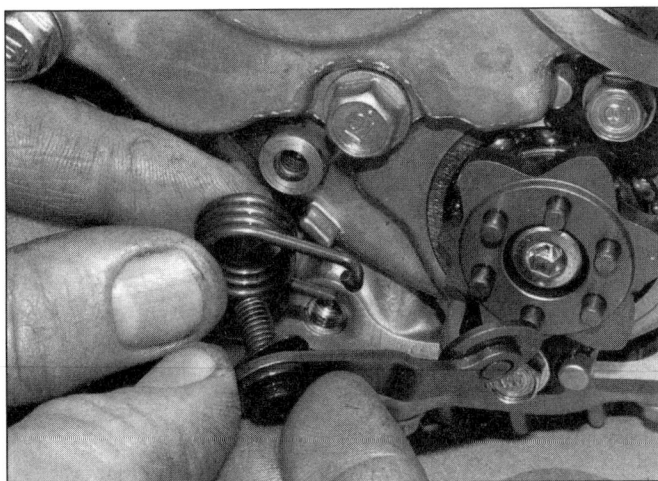

20.12 Fit the arm, washer and spring onto the bolt as shown, then fit the assembly

21.3a Unscrew the bolts (arrowed) . . .

2•50 Engine, clutch and transmission

21.3b ... and draw the transmission assembly out of the crankcase

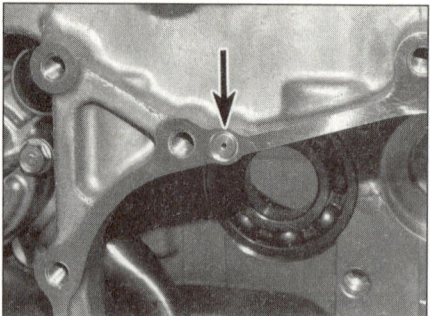

21.3c Note the oil jet (arrowed) and remove if required

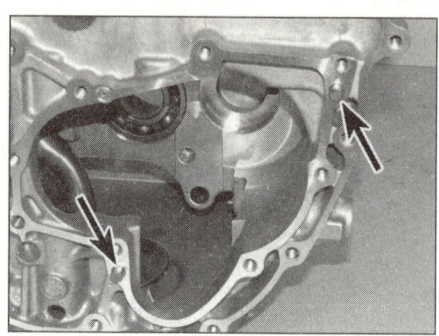

21.7 Make sure the dowels (arrowed) are fitted

Grasp the transmission output shaft and pull the assembly out of the crankcase (see illustration). Note that there is an oil jet in the crankcase which may come away with the cover and drop free – if not retrieve the jet from its bore for safekeeping if required, noting which way round it fits (see illustration). Remove the two dowels from either the cover or the crankcase if they are loose (see illustration 21.7).

4 Support the cover on blocks of wood with the transmission shafts pointing up. If required remove the selector drum and forks and the transmission shafts (see Sections 22 and 23). The drum and shaft bearings are covered in those Sections.

Installation

5 If removed fit the transmission shafts and the selector drum and forks into the cover (see Sections 22 and 23).

6 Make sure both transmission shafts are correctly seated and their related pinions and the selector forks are all correctly engaged. Position the gears in the neutral position and check the shafts are free to rotate easily and independently (i.e. the input shaft can turn whilst the output shaft is held stationary). Having done that now turn the selector drum to engage first gear so that when you turn the output shaft the input shaft turns – this is to allow easier engagement of the input shaft and primary damper shaft splines when installing of the assembly.

7 Clean the oil jet in solvent and blow it through with compressed air if available, then fit it into its bore in the crankcase with its smaller diameter end facing out (see illustration 21.3c). Fit the dowels if removed (see illustration).

8 Lubricate the transmission shafts, gears, selector drum tracks, selector forks and shaft with oil.

9 Fit the transmission assembly into the crankcase, engaging the splines on the inner end of the input shaft with those of the primary damper shaft by turning the end of the output shaft, and making sure the inner ends of the other shafts and the drum locate correctly (see illustration 21.3b). Push the cover fully against the crankcase making sure it locates onto the dowels. If the cover will not seat correctly refer to Section 23, Step 13, and check whether the tabbed and slotted washers have become disengaged.

10 Fit the bolts and tighten them evenly and a little at a time in a criss-cross pattern to the torque setting specified at the beginning of the Chapter (see illustration 21.3a).

11 Reposition the selector drum so the shafts are in neutral. Install the gearchange mechanism components as required according to removal (see Section 20).

12 Install the final output driven and drive gears and rear crankcase cover (see Section 17).

22 Selector drum and forks

Note: *To remove the selector drum and forks the engine must be removed from the frame.*

Removal

1 Remove the transmission assembly (see Section 21).

2 With the assembly on its side, counter-hold the selector drum using a bar through its centre and unscrew the bolt in the cam plate (see illustration). Remove the plate, noting how it locates on the pin, then remove the pin (see illustrations 22.16b and a). Remove the drum (see illustration).

3 Now support the cover on blocks of wood with the transmission shafts pointing up. Before removing the selector forks, note that they are marked R, C and F, for rear, centre and front (see illustration). On the engine

22.2 Counter-hold the drum and unscrew the cam plate bolt

22.3 Note the identification markings on the forks. After removal fit the forks back on the shaft the correct way round

Engine, clutch and transmission 2•51

22.4a Withdraw the shaft, then pivot the forks away from the drum . . .

22.4b . . . and remove the drum

22.6a Check the fit of each fork in its pinion . . .

photographed these letters all faced the transmission cover, but make a careful note of which way round the letters face on your engine. If necessary mark the forks yourself using a felt pen or paint, or a scratch mark to aid reassembly.

4 Withdraw the shaft then pivot the forks out of their tracks in the selector drum, noting how they locate **(see illustration)**. Remove the drum **(see illustration)**.

5 Remove the forks, noting how they fit **(see illustrations 22.11, 22.12 and 22.13)**. Once removed, slide the forks back onto the shaft in the correct order and way round **(see illustration 22.3)**.

Inspection

6 Inspect the selector forks for any signs of wear or damage, especially around the fork ends where they engage with the groove in the pinion. Check that each fork fits correctly in its pinion groove **(see illustration)**. Measure the thickness of the fork ends and compare the readings to the specifications **(see illustration)**. Check closely to see if the forks are bent. If the forks are in any way damaged or are worn beyond their specifications they must be replaced with new ones.

7 Check that the forks fit correctly on the shaft **(see illustration)**. They should move freely with a light fit but no appreciable freeplay. Measure the internal diameter of the fork bores and the corresponding diameter of the fork shaft. Replace the forks and/or shaft with new ones if they are worn beyond their

22.6b . . . and measure the thickness of the fork ends

specifications. Check that the shaft holes in the cover and crankcase are neither worn nor damaged.

8 Check the selector fork shaft is straight by rolling it along a flat surface. A bent shaft will cause difficulty in selecting gears and make the gearchange action heavy. Replace the shaft with a new one if it is bent.

9 Inspect the selector drum grooves and selector fork guide pins for signs of wear or damage **(see illustration)**. If either component shows signs of wear or damage the fork(s) and drum must be replaced with new ones.

10 Check that the selector drum bearing in the cover rotates freely and has no sign of freeplay between it and the housing **(see illustration)**. To fit a new bearing, remove the retainer plates. Remove the old bearing,

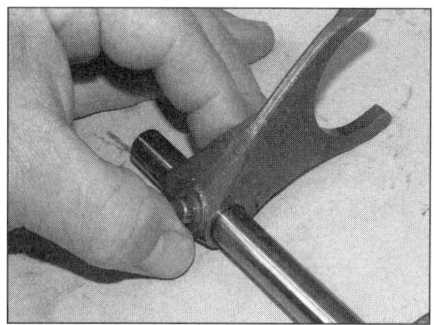
22.7 Check the fit of each fork on the shaft, then measure the fork bore ID and the fork shaft OD

driving it out from the inside and using heat to free it if necessary. Fit a new bearing, driving it in if necessary, making sure the driver or socket locates only on the outer race (see *Tools and Workshop Tips* in the Reference Section if necessary). Clean the retainer plate bolt threads and apply fresh threadlock. Fit the plates with the OUT marks facing out and tighten the bolts to the torque setting specified at the beginning of the chapter.

Installation

11 Lubricate the selector fork ends with clean engine oil as you fit them. Fit the fork marked R into its pinion groove in the output shaft with the R mark facing as noted on removal (see Step 3) **(see illustration)**.

12 Fit the fork marked C into its pinion groove

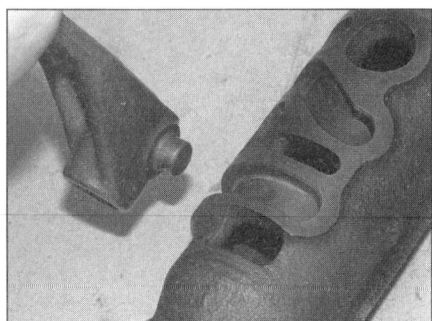
22.9 Check the guide pins and their grooves in the drum

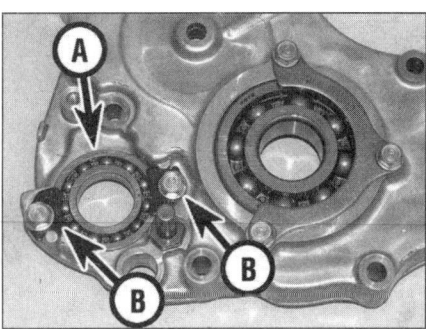
22.10 Selector drum bearing (A) and its retainer plates (B)

22.11 Fit the R fork . . .

2•52 Engine, clutch and transmission

22.12 ... the C fork ...

22.13 ... and the F fork

in the input shaft with the C mark facing the cover **(see illustration)**.

13 Fit the fork marked F into its pinion groove in the output shaft with the F mark facing the cover **(see illustration)**.

14 Fit the selector drum into its bearing in the cover **(see illustration 22.4b)**. Locate each fork's guide pin in its groove in the selector drum, lifting the gear slightly to align it if required.

15 Lubricate the fork shaft with clean engine oil. Slide the shaft through each fork and into its bore in the plate **(see illustration 22.4a)**.

16 Clean the threads of the selector drum cam plate bolt. With the assembly on its side, fit the locating pin into its hole then locate the plate on the end of the drum, aligning the large cut-out on its inner face with the locating pin **(see illustrations)**. Apply a suitable non-permanent thread locking compound to the bolt **(see illustration)**. Counter-hold the drum as before and tighten the bolt to the torque setting specified at the beginning of the Chapter, **(see illustration 22.2)**.

17 Install the transmission assembly (see Section 21).

23 Transmission shaft and bearing removal and installation

Shaft removal

1 Remove the transmission assembly (see Section 21).
2 Support the cover on blocks of wood with the transmission shafts pointing up.
3 Remove the selector drum and forks (Section 22).
4 Grasp both transmission shafts together and lift them out of the cover **(see illustration)**.
5 If required, disassemble and inspect the transmission shafts (see Section 24).

Bearing removal and installation

6 Check the condition of the transmission shaft bearings, referring to *Tools and Workshop Tips* in the Reference Section.
7 To replace the input shaft bearing in the cover you need an internal expanding puller and slide-hammer. Heat the bearing housing with a hot air gun to ease removal, then fit the tools and jar the bearing out **(see illustrations)**. Pull the clutch pushrod oil seal out using a hooked tool and replace it with a

22.16a Fit the locating pin ...

22.16b ... then locate the larger cut-out (arrowed) in the cam plate over it

22.16c Apply threadlock to the bolt

23.4 Grasp both shafts and lift them out of the cover

23.7a Fit the puller behind the inner race and expand it to lock it ...

Engine, clutch and transmission 2•53

23.7b ... then fit the slide-hammer attachment and jar the bearing out

23.7c Hook the oil seal out ...

23.7d ... and drive a new one in

new one **(see illustration)**. Drive the new seal into place using a socket **(see illustration)**. Fit the new bearing, driving it in until it seats, locating the driver on the outer race only – heat the housing and if required place the bearing in the freezer for a while to ease installation.

8 On the engine photographed the input shaft bearing in the crankcase was not a tight fit and could be pulled out with fingers, but if it is tight try heating the housing around it first **(see illustration)**. Otherwise you will have to remove the primary damper shaft (see Section 16), then heat the bearing housing with a hot air gun to ease removal, support the crankcase rib and drive the bearing out. Fit the new bearing, driving it in until it seats, locating the driver on the outer race only and supporting the crankcase as before – heat the housing and if required place the bearing in the freezer for a while to ease installation.

9 To replace the output shaft bearing in the cover first remove the retainer **(see illustration)**. Heat the housing using a hot air gun to ease removal then drive the bearing out from the inside using a suitable socket or bearing driver **(see illustration)**. If the bearing is very tight press it out using an hydraulic press. Fit the new bearing, driving or pressing it in until it seats, locating the driver or press on the outer race only – heat the housing and if required place the bearing in the freezer for a while to ease installation. Clean the retainer plate bolt threads and apply fresh threadlock. Fit the plate with the OUTSIDE mark facing out and tighten the bolts to the

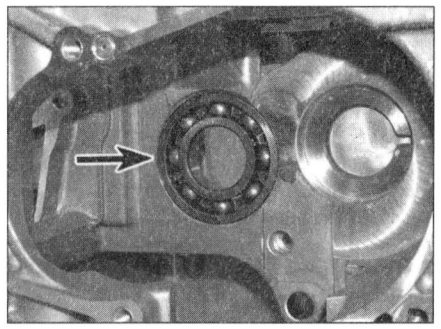

23.8 Remove the crankcase bearing (arrowed) as described

torque setting specified at the beginning of the chapter.

10 To replace the output shaft bearing on the shaft remove the circlip, then slide the bearing off **(see illustrations)** – if it is tight use a puller. With the bearing removed make sure the thrust washer does not come off. Drive the new bearing on using a socket that bears on the inner race. Make sure the circlip locates in the groove.

Shaft installation

11 Position both transmission shafts together so their related pinions engage.
12 Grasp the shafts and locate them in the cover, making sure they seat correctly **(see illustration 23.4)**.
13 Make sure both transmission shafts are correctly seated and their related pinions are correctly engaged. If the exposed end pinions

23.9a Remove the retainer plate (arrowed) ...

are not flush with each other check that the tabbed lockwasher on each shaft is correctly located in the slots of the slotted washer – if not align and seat them correctly (see Section 24, Steps 18 and 32), then the shafts should seat correctly.
14 Install the selector drum and forks (see Section 22).
15 Install the transmission assembly (see Section 21).

24 Transmission shaft overhaul

1 Remove the transmission shafts from the cover (see Section 23). Always disassemble the transmission shafts separately to avoid mixing up the components.

23.9b ... then drive the bearing out from the inside

23.10a Release the circlip ...

23.10b ... and remove the bearing

2•54 Engine, clutch and transmission

Keep all components in order on a rod to avoid getting them mixed up.

Input shaft

Disassembly

2 The 2nd gear pinion on the plain end of the shaft looks identical on each side – mark the outer face with a dab of paint or a scratch to ensure it is fitted the same way round **(see illustration 24.19)**.

3 The thrust washer on the rear end of the shaft has a slightly out-of round section on its inner rim so it is tight on the shaft – this prevents the washer and 2nd gear pinion sliding off when removing and installing the shaft. To remove the washer slip one or two flat-bladed screwdrivers behind the 2nd gear pinion and lever the pinion and washer towards and off the end of the shaft **(see illustration)**.

4 Slide the tabbed lockwasher off the shaft, then turn the slotted splined washer to offset the splines and slide it off the shaft, noting how they fit together **(see illustrations 24.18c, b and a)**. Slide the 5th gear pinion and its splined bush off the shaft, followed by the splined washer **(see illustrations 24.17c, b and a)**.

5 Remove the circlip securing the 3rd gear pinion, then slide the pinion off the shaft **(see illustrations 24.16b and a)**.

6 Remove the circlip securing the 4th gear pinion, then slide the splined washer, the pinion and its bush, and the thrust washer off the shaft **(see illustrations 24.15e, d, c, b and a)**. The 1st gear pinion is integral with the shaft **(see illustration)**.

24.11 Measure the diameters of the specified pinions, bushes and shaft to assess wear

24.3 Carefully lever behind the 2nd gear pinion to get the washer off the shaft

Inspection

7 Wash all of the components in clean solvent and dry them off.

8 Check the gear teeth for cracking, chipping, pitting and other obvious wear or damage. Any pinion that is damaged as such must be replaced with a new one.

9 Inspect the dogs and the dog holes in the gears for cracks, chips, and excessive wear especially in the form of rounded edges. Make sure mating gears engage properly. Replace the paired gears as a set if necessary.

10 Check for signs of scoring or bluing on the pinions, bushes and shaft. This could be caused by overheating due to inadequate lubrication. Check that all the oil holes and passages are clear. Replace any damaged pinions or bushes.

11 Check that each pinion moves freely on the shaft or its bush but without undue freeplay. Check that each bush moves freely

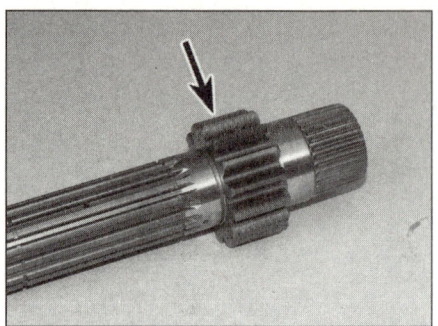

24.6 1st gear pinion (arrowed) is part of the shaft

on the shaft but without undue freeplay. If the necessary equipment is available the individual components for which dimensions are given in the Specifications at the beginning of this Chapter can be measured to assess the extent of wear **(see illustration)**.

12 The shaft is unlikely to sustain damage unless the engine has seized, placing an unusually high loading on the transmission, or the machine has covered a very high mileage. Check the surface of the shaft, especially where a pinion turns on it, and replace the shaft if it has scored or picked up, or if there are any cracks. Damage of any kind can only be cured by replacement.

13 Check the washers and circlips and replace any that are bent or appear weakened or worn. Use new ones if in any doubt. Note that it is good practice to renew all circlips when overhauling gearshafts.

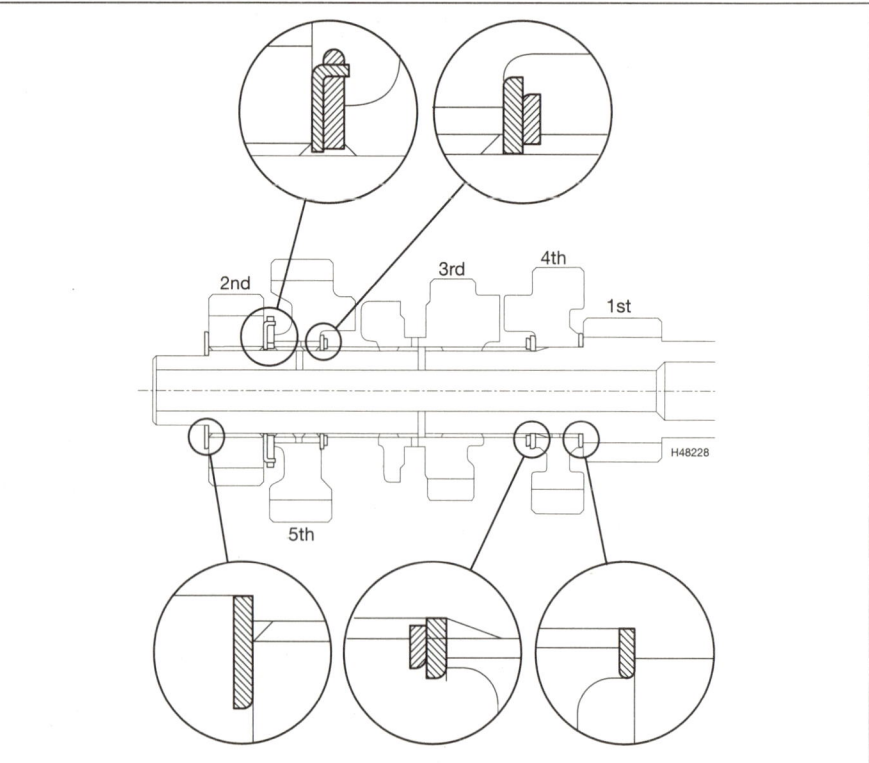

24.14 Input shaft washer and circlip positions

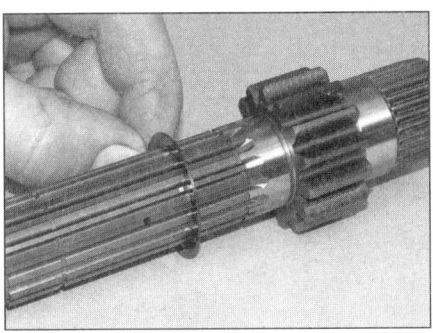
24.15a Slide the thrust washer . . .

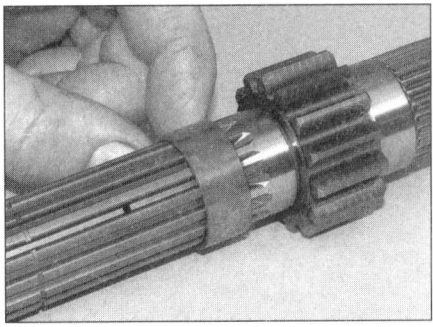
24.15b . . . the 4th gear pinion bush . . .

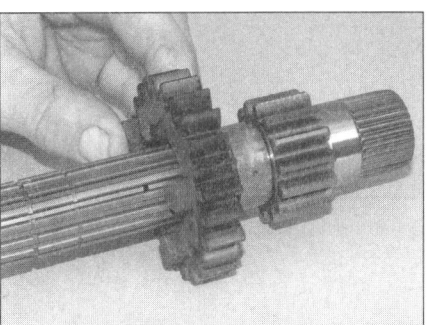
24.15c . . . the 4th gear pinion . . .

24.15d . . . and the splined washer onto the shaft . . .

24.15e . . . and secure them with the circlip . . .

24.15f . . . making sure it locates properly in its groove

Reassembly

14 During reassembly, apply molybdenum disulphide oil (a 50/50 mixture of molybdenum disulphide grease and clean engine oil) to the mating surfaces of the shaft, pinions and bushes. Fit the circlips with their chamfered side facing the pinion it secures **(see illustration)**. When installing the circlips, do not expand their ends any further than is necessary, and locate the ends so the gap between them aligns with a spline groove as shown.

15 Slide the thrust washer onto the left-hand end of the shaft, followed by the 4th gear pinion bush **(see illustrations)**. Fit the 4th gear pinion onto the bush with its dogs facing away from the integral 1st gear **(see illustration)**. Slide the splined washer onto the shaft, then fit the circlip, making sure that it locates correctly in the groove in the shaft **(see illustrations)**.

16 Slide the 3rd gear pinion onto the shaft with the selector fork groove away from the 4th gear pinion **(see illustration)**. Fit the circlip, making sure it is locates correctly in its groove in the shaft **(see illustrations)**.

17 Slide the splined washer onto the shaft, followed by the 5th gear pinion splined bush, aligning the oil hole in the bush with the hole

24.16a Slide the 3rd gear pinion onto the shaft . . .

24.16b . . . and secure it with the circlip . . .

24.16c . . . making sure it locates properly in its groove

2•56 Engine, clutch and transmission

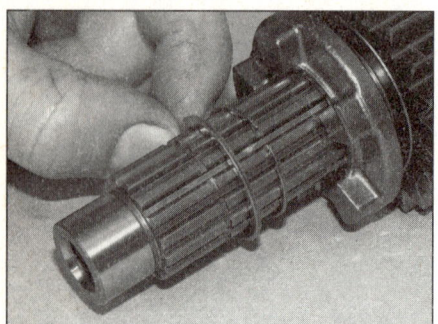

24.17a Slide the splined washer . . .

24.17b . . . the 5th gear pinion splined bush . . .

24.17c . . . and the 5th gear pinion onto the shaft

in the shaft. Slide the 5th gear pinion onto the bush, making sure its dogs face the 3rd gear pinion **(see illustrations)**.

18 Slide the slotted splined washer onto the shaft and locate it in its groove, then turn it in the groove so that the splines on the washer align with the splines on the shaft and secure the washer in the groove **(see illustrations)**. Slide the tabbed lockwasher onto the shaft and locate the tabs in the slots in the outer rim of the splined washer **(see illustration)**.

19 Slide the 2nd gear pinion onto the end of the shaft with the marked side facing out **(see illustration)**.

20 Fit the special thrust washer onto the end of the shaft and drive it down all the way onto its seat using a suitable socket **(see illustrations)**.

21 Check that all components have been correctly installed **(see illustration)**.

Output shaft

Disassembly

22 Remove the bearing from the front end of the shaft (see Section 23, Step 10).

23 Slide the thrust washer off the shaft, followed by the 1st gear pinion and its needle roller bearing, the thrust washer and the 4th gear pinion **(see illustrations 24.35c, b and a, and 24.34b and a)**.

24 Remove the circlip securing the 3rd gear pinion, then slide the splined washer, the pinion and its splined bush off the shaft **(see illustrations 24.33d, c, b and a)**.

25 Slide the tabbed lockwasher off the shaft, then turn the slotted splined washer to offset the splines and slide it off the shaft, noting how they fit together **(see illustrations 24.32c, b and a)**.

24.18a Slide on the slotted splined washer . . .

24.18b . . . and locate it as shown . . .

24.18c . . . then slide on the tabbed lockwasher and locate it the tabs in the slots

24.19 Slide the 2nd gear pinion onto the shaft

24.20a Fit the special washer onto the shaft . . .

24.20b . . . and drive it down until it seats

24.21 The complete input shaft assembly should be as shown

Engine, clutch and transmission 2•57

26 Slide the 5th gear pinion off the shaft **(see illustration 24.31)**.

27 Remove the circlip securing the 2nd gear pinion, then slide the splined washer, the pinion and its bush off the shaft **(see illustrations 24.30d, c, b and a)**.

Inspection

28 Refer to Steps 7 to 13 above.

Reassembly

29 During reassembly, apply molybdenum disulphide oil (a 50/50 mixture of molybdenum disulphide grease and clean engine oil) to the mating surfaces of the shaft, pinions and bushes. Fit the circlips with their chamfered side facing the pinion it secures **(see illustration)**. When installing the circlips, do not expand their ends any further than is necessary, and locate the ends so the gap between then aligns with a spline groove as shown.

30 Slide the 2nd gear pinion bush onto the shaft, then slide the 2nd gear pinion onto the bush with its dog holes facing away from the collar, followed by the splined washer **(see illustrations)**. Fit the circlip, making sure it is locates correctly in its groove in the shaft **(see illustrations)**.

31 Slide the 5th gear pinion onto shaft with its selector fork groove facing away from the 2nd gear pinion **(see illustration)**.

32 Slide the slotted splined washer onto the shaft and locate it in its groove, then turn it in the groove so that the splines on the washer align with the splines on the shaft and secure

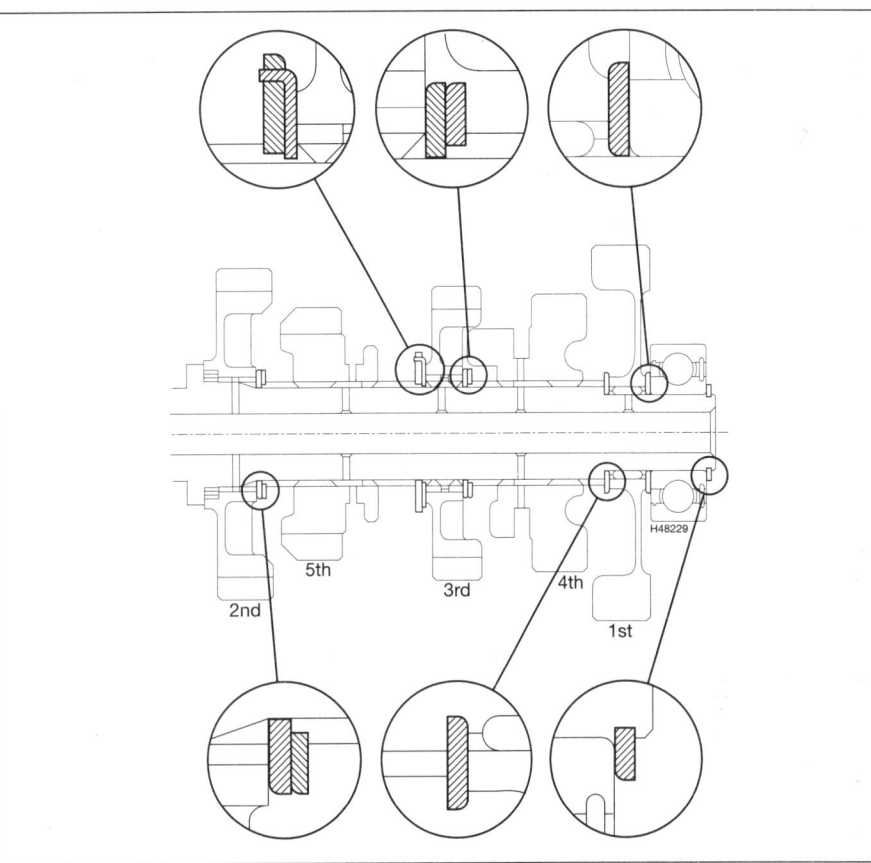

24.29 Output shaft washer and circlip positions

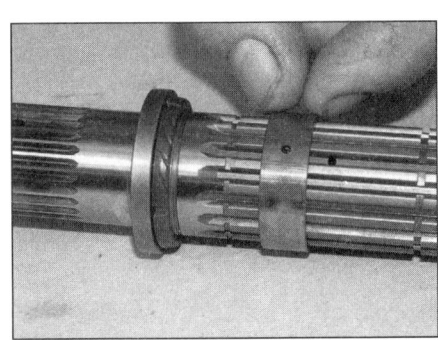

24.30a Slide the 2nd gear pinion bush . . .

24.30b . . . the 2nd gear pinion . . .

24.30c . . . and the splined washer onto the shaft . . .

24.30d . . . and secure them with the circlip . . .

24.30e . . . making sure it locates in the groove

24.31 Slide the 5th gear pinion onto the shaft

2•58 Engine, clutch and transmission

24.32a Slide the slotted splined washer onto the shaft . . .

24.32b . . . and locate it as shown

24.32c Slide the lockwasher onto the shaft and engage it with the slotted washer

24.33a Slide the 3rd gear pinion splined bush . . .

24.33b . . . the 3rd gear pinion . . .

24.33c . . . and the splined washer onto the shaft . . .

24.33d . . . and secure them with the circlip . . .

24.33e . . . making sure it locates in the groove

the washer in the groove **(see illustrations)**. Slide the tabbed lockwasher onto the shaft and locate the tabs in the slots in the outer rim of the splined washer **(see illustration)**.

33 Slide the 3rd gear pinion splined bush onto the shaft, making sure the oil hole in the bush aligns with the hole in the shaft **(see illustration)**. Slide the 3rd gear pinion onto its bush with its dog holes face away from the 5th gear pinion **(see illustration)**. Slide the splined washer on, then fit the circlip, making sure it is locates correctly in its groove in the shaft **(see illustrations)**.

34 Slide the 4th gear pinion onto the shaft with its selector fork groove facing the 3rd gear pinion, followed by the thrust washer **(see illustrations)**.

24.34a Slide the 4th gear pinion . . .

24.34b . . . and the thrust washer onto the shaft

Engine, clutch and transmission 2•59

24.35a Slide the needle bearing ...

24.35b ... the 1st gear pinion ...

24.35c ... and the thrust washer onto the shaft

35 Slide the 1st gear pinion needle roller bearing onto the shaft, then slide the 1st gear pinion onto the bearing with its dog holes facing the 4th gear pinion **(see illustrations)**. Fit the thrust washer **(see illustration)**.
36 Fit the bearing onto the front end of the shaft (see Section 23, Step 10).
37 Check that all components have been correctly installed **(see illustration)**.

25 Oil sump and strainers

Note: *The oil sump and strainer can be removed with the engine in the frame. If the engine has been removed, ignore the steps which don't apply.*

Removal

1 Remove the lower fairing (see Chapter 7). Drain the engine oil (see Chapter 1).
2 Release the fuel tank drain and breather hoses from the tie and guide at the back of the sump, and where fitted release the water pump drain hose from its guide at the front of the sump **(see illustration)**. Unscrew the bolt and remove the guide from the back **(see illustration)**.
3 Unscrew the sump bolts evenly in a criss-cross sequence, noting the position of the water pump hose guide where fitted, and remove the sump **(see illustration)**.
4 Pull the main strainer out of the oil pump, noting how it locates **(see illustration)**. Remove the rubber seal and discard it as a new one must be used.
5 To remove the small strainer at the front refer to Chapter 3, Section 6, and remove the front crankcase cover – there is no need to remove

24.37 The assembled output shaft should be as shown

the water pump from the cover. Unscrew the bolt securing the pipe **(see illustration)**. Pull the top of the pipe out of the crankcase and remove it. Remove the seal and discard it – a new one must be used **(see illustration)**.

25.2a Release the hoses from the guide(s) as required according to model

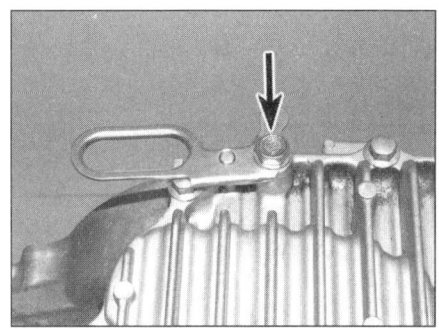

25.2b Unscrew the bolt (arrowed) and remove the guide

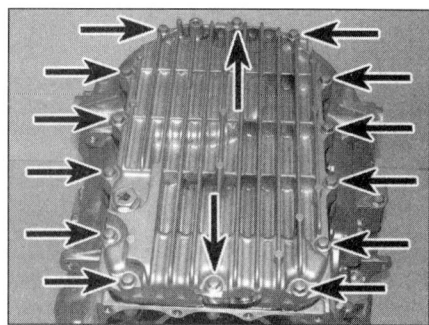

25.3 Unscrew the bolts (arrowed) and remove the sump

25.4 Remove the strainer, noting how the tab locates in the groove

25.5a Unscrew the bolt (arrowed) and remove the strainer ...

25.5b ... then hook the seal out

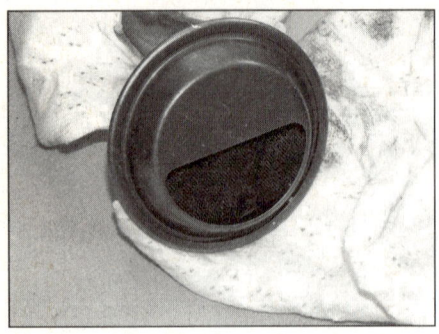
25.7a Clean and check the main strainer gauze...

25.7b ...and the small strainer gauze

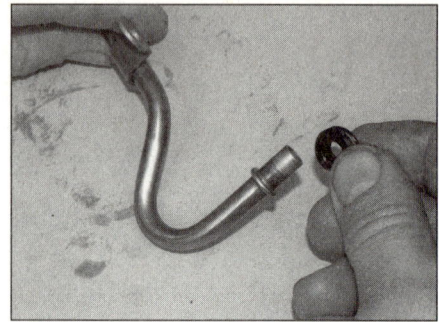
25.8a Fit a new seal onto the pipe...

25.8b ...the fit the pipe, pushing the seal into the bore

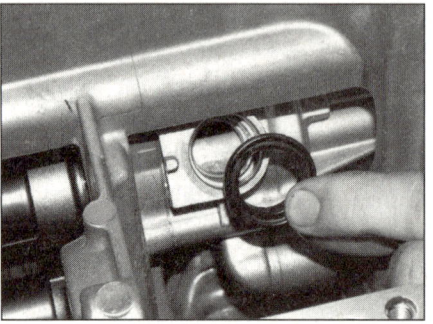
25.9a Lubricate the rubber seal and fit it into the pump

25.9b Locate the tabs around the lug (arrowed)

Inspection

6 Remove all traces of sealant from the sump and crankcase mating surfaces, and clean the inside of the sump with solvent. Blow the sump dry with compressed air if available.

7 Clean the oil strainers in solvent and remove any debris caught in the mesh (see illustrations). If the strainer gauze is damaged, replace the strainer with a new one.

Installation

8 If removed fit a new seal onto the front strainer pipe and smear it with clean oil, then manoeuvre the pipe into position and push it in (see illustrations). Fit the bolt (see illustration 25.5a). Refer to Chapter 3, Section 6, and install the front crankcase cover.

9 Fit a new rubber seal smeared with clean oil into the strainer socket in the pump (see illustration). Do not fit it onto the strainer as it will distort when the strainer is fitted. Fit the strainer, locating the tabs on each side of the lug (see illustration).

10 Clean the mating surfaces of the sump and crankcase with solvent. Apply a suitable sealant (such as Three Bond 1207B or equivalent RTV sealant – ask your dealer) to the sump mating surface. Position the sump onto the crankcase and fit the bolts finger-tight, not forgetting the water pump hose guide where fitted (see illustrations). Tighten the bolts evenly and a little at a time in a criss-cross pattern to the torque setting specified at the beginning of the Chapter (see illustration 25.3).

11 Fit the fuel tank drain and breather hose guide (see illustration 25.2b). Fit the hoses into the guide(s) and tie.

12 Fill the engine with the correct type and quantity of oil as described in Chapter 1. Start the engine and check that there are no leaks around the sump.

13 Install the lower fairing (see Chapter 7).

26 Oil pump and pressure relief valve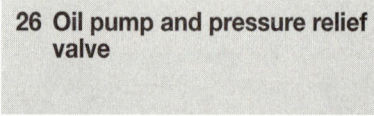

Note: *To remove the oil pump and pressure relief valve the engine must be removed from the frame.*

Removal

1 Remove the rear crankcase cover (see Section 17, Steps 1 to 8).

2 Remove the sump and main strainer (see Section 25).

3 Pull the pressure relief valve out of its socket in the cover – it is a push-fit (see illustration). Discard the O-ring as a new one must be used.

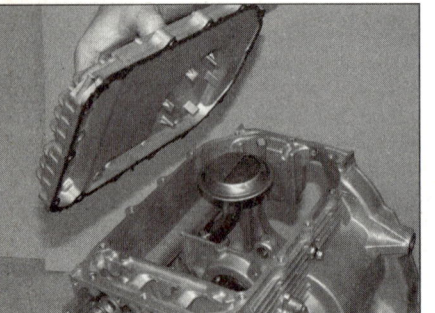
25.10a Apply the sealant then fit the sump

25.10b Fit the water pump hose guide (arrowed) with the front centre bolt where applicable

26.3 Pull the relief valve out of its socket

Engine, clutch and transmission 2•61

26.5 Unscrew the bolts (arrowed) and remove the pump

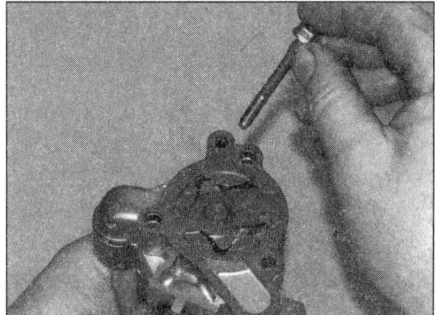

26.6a Unscrew the bolt . . .

26.6b . . . and remove the plate . . .

4 Lock the oil pump driven sprocket to prevent it from turning using a proper holding tool or a pair of curved-end pliers in the sprocket holes as shown and unscrew the bolt **(see illustrations 18.6a and b)**. Draw the sprocket off the shaft and out of the chain.
5 Unscrew the three bolts securing the pump to the crankcase, then remove the pump, noting how it fits **(see illustration)**. Remove the dowels from either the crankcase or the pump if they are loose **(see illustration 26.23a)**.

Inspection

6 Unscrew the bolt securing the plate to the back of the pump and remove the plate **(see illustrations)**. Remove the thrust washer **(see illustration)**.
7 Draw the main pump housing off the shaft and remove the main rotors **(see illustration)**. Remove the dowels if loose. Remove the drive pin and thrust washer from the shaft **(see illustrations)**.
8 Push the shaft through the sub pump and remove the drive pin and the inner and outer rotors from the sub pump, noting which way round they fit **(see illustration)**. Draw the shaft out **(see illustration)**.
9 Clean all the components in solvent.
10 Inspect the pump housings, shaft and rotors for scoring and wear. If any damage, scoring or uneven or excessive wear is evident, replace the pump with a new one (individual components are not available).
11 Fit the sub pump inner and outer rotors

26.6c . . . and the thrust washer

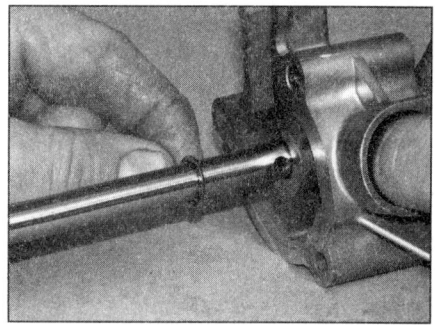

26.7a Draw the main housing off and remove the rotors

26.7b Remove the drive pin . . .

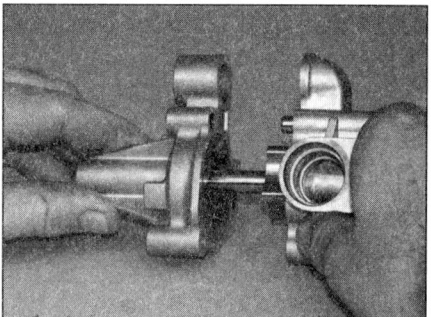

26.7c . . . and the washer . . .

into the pump body **(see illustrations 26.17a and b)**, then slide the shaft through **(see illustration 26.8b)**. Align the rotors as shown and measure the clearance between the inner

rotor tip and the outer rotor with a feeler gauge and compare it to the service limit listed in the specifications at the beginning of the Chapter **(see illustration)**. If the clearance measured is

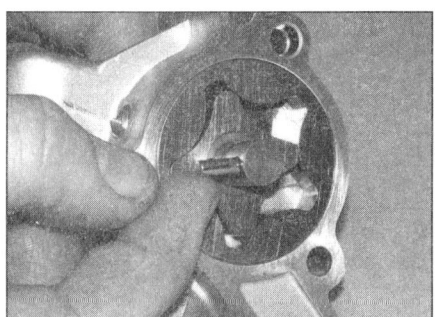

26.8a . . . then push the shaft through and remove the other drive pin and the sub pump rotors . . .

26.8b . . . and withdraw the shaft

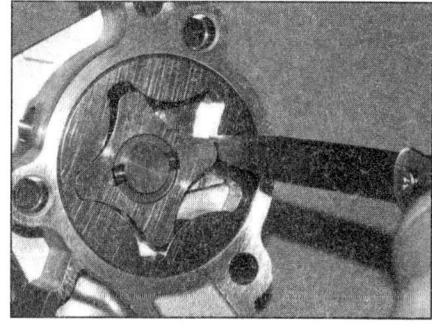

26.11 Measure the inner rotor tip-to-outer rotor clearance as shown (shaft shown removed for clarity)

2•62 Engine, clutch and transmission

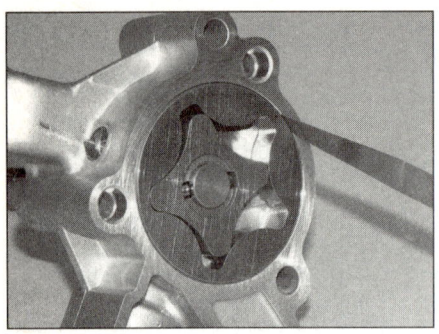

26.12 Measure the outer rotor-to-body clearance as shown

26.13 Measure rotor end-float as shown

greater than the maximum listed, replace the pump with a new one.

12 Measure the clearance between the outer rotor and the pump body with a feeler gauge and compare it to the maximum clearance listed in the specifications at the beginning of the Chapter **(see illustration)**. If the clearance measured is greater than the maximum listed, replace the pump with a new one.

13 Lay a straight-edge across the rotors and the pump body and, using a feeler gauge, measure the rotor end-float (the gap between the rotors and the straight-edge) **(see illustration)**. If the clearance measured is greater than the maximum listed, replace the pump with a new one.

14 Repeat Steps 11 to 13 for the main pump.

15 Check the pump drive chain and sprockets for wear or damage, and replace them with a new set if necessary – refer to Section 18 to remove the drive sprocket.

16 If the pump is good, make sure all the components are clean, and lubricate them with new engine oil as you fit them, reassembling the pump as follows:

17 Fit the sub pump outer rotor into the body **(see illustration)**. Fit the inner rotor into the outer rotor with the cut-outs in the inner rotor facing out **(see illustration)**. Slide the plain end of the shaft through the rotors from the back **(see illustration 26.8b)**. Fit the drive pin in the end hole and seat it in the inner rotor **(see illustration 26.8a)**.

18 Slide the thrust washer onto the shaft then fit the drive pin into its hole in the shaft **(see illustrations 26.7b and a)**.

19 Fit the main pump outer rotor into the body **(see illustration)**. Fit the inner rotor onto the shaft with the cut-outs in the inner rotor facing and seating over the drive pin **(see illustration)**. Fit the dowels if removed **(see illustration)**. Slide the main pump onto the shaft so the inner rotor locates in the outer and the body locates onto the dowels **(see illustration 26.7a)**.

20 Fit the thrust washer and the back plate and tighten the bolt to the torque setting specified at the beginning of the Chapter **(see illustrations 26.6c, b and a)**.

21 Rotate the pump shaft by hand and check it turns the rotors smoothly and freely.

22 Push the relief valve plunger into the valve body and check that it moves smoothly and freely against spring pressure **(see illustration)**. If not, remove the circlip, noting that it is under spring pressure, then remove the washer, spring and plunger. Clean all components in solvent, then check the plunger and the valve body for evidence of scoring, wear and any other damage. If any is found, replace the relief valve with a new one – individual components are not available. Otherwise, coat the plunger with oil and fit it closed end first back into the valve and recheck the movement. If it is good, install the spring and washer and secure them with the circlip.

Installation

23 Fit the pump locating dowels if removed

26.17a Fit the outer rotor . . .

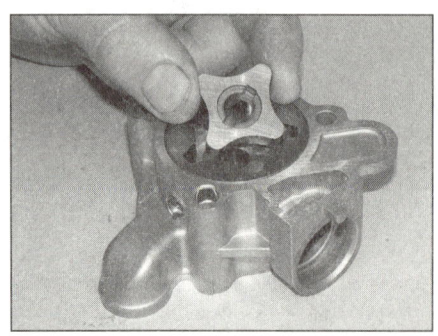

26.17b . . . and the inner rotor

26.19a Fit the outer rotor into the body . . .

26.19b . . . and the inner rotor onto the shaft, seating it over the drive pin

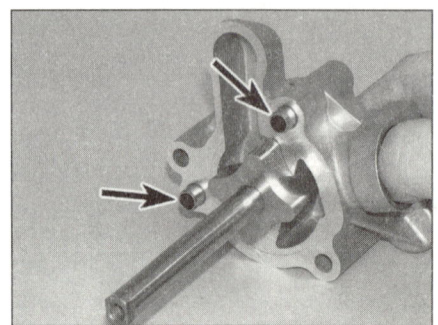

26.19c Fit the dowels (arrowed)

26.22 Push the plunger into the body and check that it moves smoothly

Engine, clutch and transmission 2•63

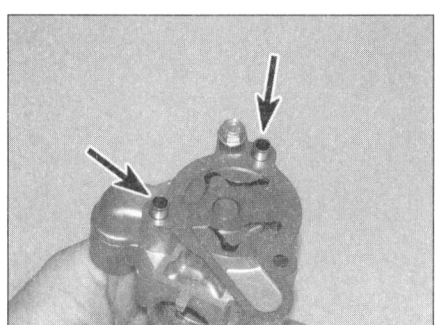

26.23a Fit the dowels (arrowed) ...

26.23b ... then install the pump

26.24 Align the flats when fitting the sprocket and apply threadlock to the bolt

(see illustration). Fit the pump, making sure the dowels locate correctly, then fit the bolts and tighten them (see illustration).

24 Fit the oil pump driven sprocket into the chain with the OUT mark facing out. Slide the sprocket onto the pump shaft, aligning the flats (see illustration). Clean the threads of the sprocket bolt and apply fresh threadlock. Fit the bolt with its washer and tighten it to the torque setting specified at the beginning of the Chapter, holding the sprocket as before (see illustrations 18.6a and b).

25 Fit a new O-ring smeared with oil onto the pressure relief valve and push it into its socket in the cover (see illustration 26.3).

26 Install the main strainer and sump (see Section 25).

27 Install the rear crankcase cover (see Section 17, Steps 16 and 17, then 20 to 24).

27 Crankcase separation and reassembly

Note: To separate the crankcase halves, the engine must be removed from the frame.

Separation

1 To access the pistons, connecting rods, crankshaft, balancer shafts and the main and big-end bearings, the crankcase must be split into its two halves.

2 Before the crankcases can be separated the following components must be removed – remove any other components not listed as required according to the extent of engine strip required, referring to Section 5 and thereafter to the relevant Sections:

- Valve covers (Section 7).
- Camshafts (Section 9) – see Note 3.
- Cylinder heads (Section 11) – see Note 3.
- Primary drive gear (Section 15).
- Cam chains and blades (Section 10) – see Note 3.
- Clutch, water pump drive chain and sprocket (Section 13).
- Primary damper shaft (Section 16).
- Final output shaft (Section 17).
- Starter clutch and gears (Section 18).
- Alternator drive and middle gears (Section 19).
- Transmission assembly (Section 21).
- Starter motor (Chapter 8).
- Oil sump and strainer (Section 25).

Note 3: If the crankcases are being separated to inspect the crankshaft without removing it, the camshafts and chains and cylinder heads can remain in situ, but the cam chain blades, and so the primary drive gear, must be removed. To remove the crankshaft without removing the connecting rods and pistons, the camshafts and chains must be removed but the heads can stay in place. However, if removal of the connecting rod assemblies is intended, full disassembly of the top-end is necessary.

3 If required remove the oil pressure switch and neutral switch (see Chapter 8), and the knock sensors (see Chapter 4). If not already done remove the engine sub-harness, freeing it from its guides and noting its routing.

27.4 Unscrew the bolt (arrowed)

27.6b ... along each side

4 Unscrew the upper balancer shaft holder mounting bolt (see illustration).

5 Turn the engine upside down – if you are working on a hard or rough surface rest the engine blocks of wood or some card.

6 Unscrew the ten 8 mm crankcase bolts evenly, a little at a time and in a criss-cross sequence until they are finger-tight, then remove them, noting the positions of the two longer bolts (see illustrations). **Note:** As each bolt is removed, store it in its relative position in a cardboard template of the crankcase halves (see illustration 17.8b). This will ensure all bolts are installed in the correct location on reassembly.

7 Now unscrew the six 10 mm crankshaft journal bolts evenly, a little at a time and in a criss-cross sequence until they are finger-tight, then remove them (see illustration).

8 Carefully lift the lower crankcase half off

27.6a Unscrew the 8 mm bolts (arrowed) ...

27.7 Crankshaft journal bolts (arrowed)

2•64 Engine, clutch and transmission

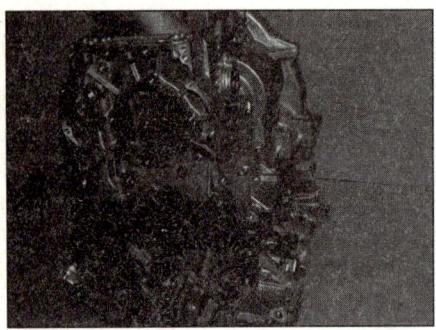

27.8 Carefully separate the crankcase halves

27.9a Remove the oil passage collars and O-rings (arrowed) . . .

27.9b . . . and the oil orifice (arrowed)

the upper half, using a soft-faced hammer to tap around the joint to initially separate the halves if necessary **(see illustration)**. **Note:** *If the halves do not separate easily, make sure all fasteners have been removed. Do not try and separate the halves by levering against the crankcase mating surfaces as they are easily scored and may leak oil in the future if damaged.* The lower crankcase half will come away with the balancer shafts, leaving the crankshaft in the upper crankcase half.

9 Remove the three locating dowels from the crankcase if they are loose (they could be in either crankcase half) **(see illustration 27.14)**. Remove the two oil passage collars and their

27.14 Make sure the dowels (arrowed) are fitted

O-rings – discard the O-rings, new ones must be used **(see illustration)**. Remove the oil orifice, noting which way round it fits **(see illustration)**.

10 Refer to Sections 28 to 34 for the removal, inspection and installation of the components housed within the crankcases.

Reassembly

Note: *It is best to highlight all alignment punch marks and lines on the balancer shaft gears and on the drive gear on the crankshaft with a dab of white paint – the punch marks are small and the paint makes them much easier to see, making installation and alignment much easier.*

11 Remove all traces of sealant from the crankcase mating surfaces.

12 Make sure the crankshaft, connecting rods and pistons and the balancer shafts and all bearings are in place in the upper and lower crankcase halves, and double check that the balancer shafts are correctly aligned with each other (see Section 34).

13 Generously lubricate the crankshaft and balancer shaft, particularly around the bearings, with clean engine oil. Using a rag soaked in high flash-point solvent wipe over the mating surfaces of both crankcase halves to remove all traces of oil.

14 Fit the two oil passage collars using new O-rings **(see illustration 27.9a)**. Fit the oil orifice in the upper crankcase half with the smaller end of the hole facing out **(see illustration 27.9b)**. If removed, fit the three locating dowels **(see illustration)**.

15 Now both the upper balancer shaft and the crankshaft must be correctly positioned. First set the timing marks on the upper balancer driven gear flush with the lower crankcase mating surface **(see illustration)** – if the balancer shafts are already positioned with their punch marks aligned as on installation these timing marks should already be correct. Position the crankshaft so the crankpins face directly up, setting the timing mark on the drive gear flush with the upper crankcase mating surface **(see illustration)**. Identify the punch mark on the inner face of the balancer drive gear on the crankshaft – this must align with the corresponding punch mark on the upper balancer driven gear when the crankcases are joined. Getting the drive and driven gears to engage aligned as you lower the crankcase is tricky as the gears are side-by-side – it is best to have an assistant to check they engage correctly and nothing turns as you fit the lower crankcase.

16 Apply a small amount of suitable sealant (Three-Bond 1207B or equivalent RTV sealant – ask your dealer) to the outer mating surfaces

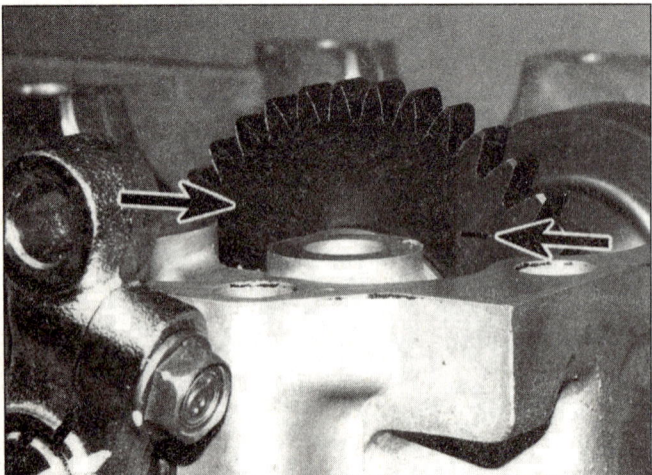

27.15a Set the upper balancer gear marks (arrowed) flush . . .

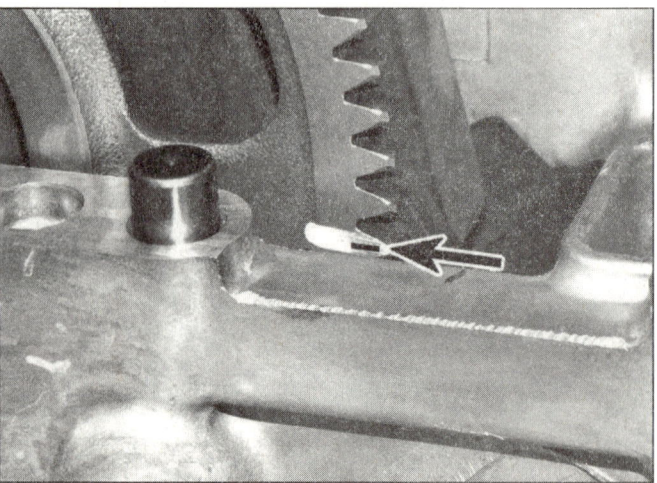

27.15b . . . and the balancer drive gear mark (arrowed) on the crankshaft flush

Engine, clutch and transmission 2•65

27.16 Apply the sealant to the mating surface

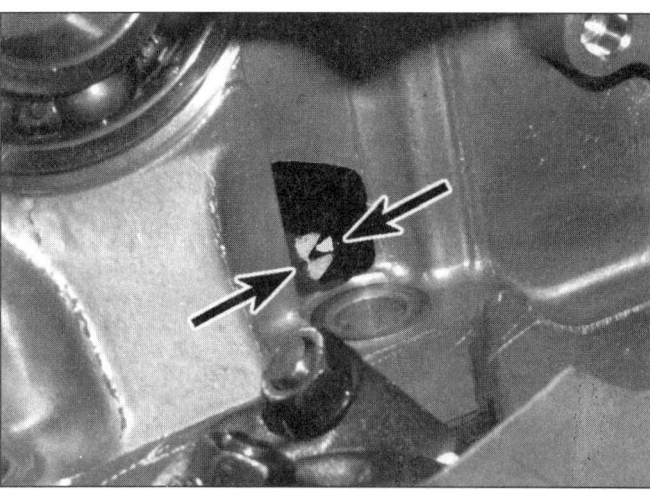

27.17 You can see the alignment marks (arrowed) on the teeth via the hole in the crankcase

of the lower crankcase half as shown **(see illustration)**.
Caution: Apply the sealant only to the shaded areas. Do not apply an excessive amount as it will ooze out when the case halves are assembled and may obstruct oil passages. Do not apply the sealant close to any of the bearing shells or surfaces, or oil passages.

17 Check again that all components are in position, and that the bearing shells are still correctly located in the lower crankcase half. Carefully fit the lower crankcase half down onto the upper crankcase half, making sure the dowels and oil passage collars locate correctly **(see illustration 27.8)**. As the balancer shaft and crankshaft gears engage, have your assistant make sure the punch marks align by looking through the aperture in the crankcase wall **(see illustration)**. Check that the lower crankcase half is correctly seated.
Caution: The crankcase halves should fit together without being forced. If the casings are not correctly seated, remove the lower crankcase half and investigate the problem. Do not attempt to pull them together using the crankcase bolts as the casing will crack and be ruined.

18 To double check correct alignment of the crankshaft and balancer shafts, unscrew the plug from the lower crankcase **(see illustration)** – discard the sealing washer, a new one should be used. Check the three timing marks are visible in the three holes as shown **(see illustration)**. If the marks do not align, or if you are not sure, remove the lower crankcase and start again, noting that you will have to clean and re-seal the mating surfaces. If all is good fit the plug using a new sealing washer.

19 Smear some oil onto the threads and under the heads of the six 10 mm crankshaft journal bolts. Fit the bolts and tighten them finger-tight **(see illustration 27.7)**. Fit the 8 mm bolts, making sure the longer ones are at the front, with the longest in the left-hand corner **(see illustrations 27.6a and b)**.

20 First tighten the 10 mm journal bolts evenly and a little at a time in a criss-cross sequence starting from the middle and working out to the torque setting specified at the beginning of the Chapter **(see illustration 27.7)**.

21 Now tighten the 8 mm bolts evenly and a little at a time in a criss-cross sequence starting from the middle and working out to the specified torque setting **(see illustrations 27.6a and b)**.

22 With all crankcase fasteners tightened, check that the crankshaft and balancer shaft rotate smoothly and easily, but at this stage do not worry about any noise from the gear teeth. Refer to Section 34 and adjust the backlash

following the static adjustment procedure.

23 If removed install the oil pressure switch and neutral switch (see Chapter 8), and the knock sensors (see Chapter 4). If required now, connect the engine sub-loom wiring, making sure it is correctly routed, or alternatively do it later (before installing the engine – see Section 4) **(see illustration 4.28b)**.

24 Fit the upper balancer shaft holder bolt **(see illustration 27.4)**. Carry out the static backlash adjustment procedure if required (see Section 34).

25 Install all other removed assemblies in a reverse of the sequence given in Step 2.

27.18a Remove the plug . . .

27.18b . . . and check the crankshaft mark . . .

27.18c . . . the upper balancer mark . . .

27.18d . . . and the lower balancer mark are all simultaneously aligned as shown

28.2 Unscrew the bolts (arrowed) and remove the window, noting the wiring clamp

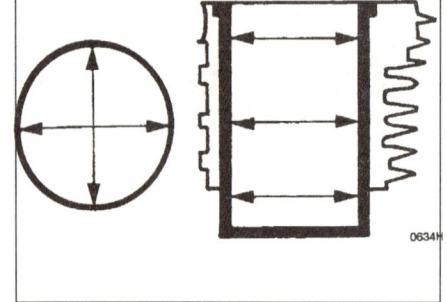

28.12a Measure the cylinder bore in the directions shown . . .

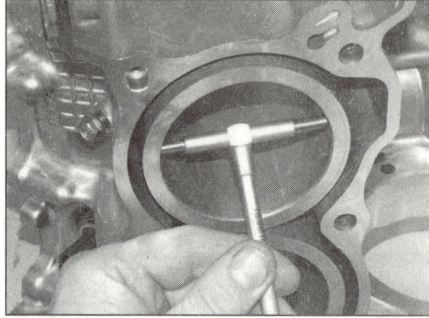

28.12b . . . using a telescoping gauge, then measure the gauge with a micrometer

28 Crankcases and cylinder bores

Crankcases

1 After the crankcases have been separated, remove the crankshaft and its bearing shells, the connecting rods and pistons, the balancer shafts, and any other components or assemblies not yet removed, referring to the relevant Sections of this Chapter and other Chapters as required.

2 If required remove the oil level inspection window, noting the guide secured by the upper bolt **(see illustration)**. Discard the O-ring – a new one must be used.

3 Clean the crankcases thoroughly with new solvent and dry them with compressed air. Blow out all oil passages with compressed air. Clean the inside of the oil level inspection window.

4 Remove all traces of old gasket sealant from the mating surfaces. Clean up minor damage to the surfaces with a fine sharpening stone or grindstone.

Caution: Be very careful not to nick or gouge the crankcase mating surfaces or oil leaks may result. Check both crankcase halves very carefully for cracks and other damage.

5 Small cracks or holes in aluminium castings can be repaired with an epoxy resin adhesive as a temporary measure, as they are not in a load-bearing place such as a bearing or shaft housing. Permanent repairs can be done by argon-arc welding (only a specialist in this process should carry out this work), or alternatively small repairs can be made using one of the low temperature welding kits. If any damage is found that can't be repaired, or shouldn't be repaired because of its location, replace the crankcase halves as a set.

6 Damaged threads can be economically reclaimed using a diamond section wire insert, for example of the Heli-Coil type (though there are other makes), which are easily fitted after drilling and re-tapping the affected thread.

7 Sheared studs or screws can usually be removed with extractors, which consist of a tapered, left-hand thread screw of very hard steel. These are inserted into a pre-drilled hole in the stud, and usually succeed in dislodging the most stubborn stud or screw. If a stud has sheared above its bore line, it can be removed using a conventional stud extractor which avoids the need for drilling.

> **HAYNES HiNT** *Refer to Tools and Workshop Tips for details of installing a thread insert and using screw extractors.*

8 If removed fit a new O-ring smeared with oil into the groove on the inside of the oil level inspection window. Fit the window, not forgetting the wiring guide and tighten the bolts **(see illustration 28.2)**.

9 Install the connecting rods and pistons, crankshaft and balancer shafts and all related bearings, referring to the relevant Sections of this Chapter, before reassembling the crankcase halves.

Cylinder bores

Note: *Do not attempt to separate the cylinder liners from the cylinder block and great care must be taken not to scratch or gouge them.*

10 Check the cylinder walls carefully for scratches and score marks.

11 Using a precision straight-edge and a feeler gauge set to the warpage limit listed in the specifications at the beginning of the Chapter, check the block mating surfaces for warpage. Refer to *Tools and Workshop Tips* in the Reference section for details of how to use the straight-edge. If warpage is excessive the crankcases must be replaced with new ones.

12 Using telescoping gauges and a micrometer (see *Tools and Workshop Tips*), check the dimensions of each cylinder to assess the amount of wear, taper and ovality. Measure near the top (but below the level of the top piston ring at TDC), centre and bottom (but above the level of the oil ring at BDC) of the bore, both parallel to and across the crankshaft axis **(see illustrations)**. Compare the results to the specifications at the beginning of the Chapter. If the cylinders are worn, oval or tapered beyond the service limit they can be re-bored – oversize (+ 0.25 and + 0.50) sets of pistons and rings and available. Note that the engineer carrying out the re-bore must be aware of the piston-to-bore clearance for the oversize pistons and rings (see Specifications).

13 If the precision measuring tools are not available, take the upper crankcase to a Honda dealer or specialist motorcycle repair shop for assessment and advice.

29 Connecting rod and main bearing information

1 Even though new main and connecting rod bearings are generally fitted during engine overhaul, the old bearings should be retained for close examination as they often reveal valuable information about the condition of the engine.

2 Bearing failure occurs mainly because of lack of lubrication, the presence of dirt or other foreign particles, overloading the engine and/or corrosion. Regardless of the cause of bearing failure, it must be corrected before the engine is reassembled to prevent it from happening again.

3 When examining the bearings, lay them out on a clean surface in the same general position as their location on the crankshaft journals. This will enable you to match any noted bearing problems with the corresponding crankshaft journal.

4 Dirt and other foreign particles get into the engine in a variety of ways. They may be left in the engine during assembly or they may pass through filters or breathers, then get into the oil and from there into the bearings. Metal chips from machining operations and normal engine wear are often present. Abrasives are sometimes left in engine components after reconditioning operations, especially when parts are not thoroughly cleaned using the proper cleaning methods. Whatever the source, foreign objects often end up imbedded in the soft bearing material and are easily recognised. Large particles will not imbed in the bearing and will score or gouge the bearing and journal. The best prevention for this cause of bearing failure is to clean all parts thoroughly and keep everything

Engine, clutch and transmission 2•67

spotlessly clean during engine reassembly. Regular scheduled oil and filter changes are essential.

5 Lack of lubrication or lubrication breakdown has a number of interrelated causes. Excessive heat (which thins the oil), overloading (which squeezes the oil from the bearing face) and oil leakage or throw off (from excessive bearing clearances, or high engine speeds) all contribute to lubrication breakdown, as does a lack of pressure due to a worn oil pump or other causes. Blocked oil passages will starve a bearing of lubrication and destroy it. When lack of lubrication is the cause of bearing failure, the bearing material is wiped or extruded from the steel backing of the bearing. Temperatures may increase to the point where the steel backing and the journal turn blue from overheating.

 *Refer to Tools and Workshop Tips for bearing fault finding.*

6 Riding habits can have a definite effect on bearing life. Full throttle low, speed operation, or labouring the engine, puts very high loads on bearings, which tend to squeeze out the oil film. These loads cause the bearings to flex, which produces fine cracks in the bearing face (fatigue failure). Eventually the bearing material will loosen in pieces and tear away from the steel backing. Short trip riding leads to corrosion of bearings, as insufficient engine heat is produced to drive off the condensed water and corrosive gases produced. These products collect in the engine oil, forming acid and sludge. As the oil is carried to the engine bearings, the acid attacks and corrodes the bearing material.

7 Incorrect bearing installation during engine assembly will lead to bearing failure as well. Tight fitting bearings which leave insufficient bearing oil clearances result in oil starvation.

Dirt or foreign particles trapped behind a bearing insert result in high spots on the bearing which lead to failure.

8 To avoid bearing problems, clean all parts thoroughly before reassembly, double check all bearing clearance measurements and lubricate the new bearings with clean engine oil during installation.

30 Crankshaft and main bearings

Note: *To remove the crankshaft the engine must be removed from the frame and the crankcase halves separated.*

Removal

1 Remove the engine from the frame (see Section 4) and separate the crankcase halves (see Section 27).

2 Refer to Section 31 and detach the connecting rods from the crankpins. Push the rods and pistons up to the tops of the bores so that the bottom ends are clear of the crankshaft, taking care to keep the rods clear of the cylinder walls **(see illustration 31.4c)**.
Note: *If no work is to be carried out on the piston/connecting rod assemblies there is no need to remove them from the bores. If you do need to remove them, continue to refer to Section 31.*

3 Lift the crankshaft out of the upper crankcase half, taking care not to dislodge the main bearing shells **(see illustration)**. Wrap some rag around each connecting rod to protect the cylinder walls.

4 If necessary remove the main bearing shells from the crankcase halves, but make sure you keep them in order **(see illustration)**. If they are being reused they must be returned to their original location – note that the centre main bearing shells have smaller holes.

Inspection

5 Clean the crankshaft with solvent, squirting it under pressure through all the oil passages. If available, blow the crank dry with compressed air, and also blow through the oil passages. Check the balancer drive gear and the splines on each end of the shaft for wear or damage. If any of the gear teeth or splines are excessively worn, or are chipped or broken, the crankshaft must be replaced with a new one. If wear or damage is found, also inspect the balancer driven gears (see Section 34), and the related splines on the primary drive gear (see Section 15) and the starter clutch/alternator drive gear (see Sections 18 and 19).

6 Refer to Section 29 and examine the main bearing shells. If they are scored, badly scuffed or appear to have been seized, new bearings must be installed. Always replace the main bearings as a set selected as described in Steps 20 and 21. If they are badly damaged, check the corresponding crankshaft journals. Evidence of extreme heat, such as discolouration, indicates that lubrication failure has occurred. Be sure to thoroughly check the oil pump and pressure relief valve as well as all oil holes and passages before reassembling the engine.

7 Give the crankshaft journals a close visual examination, paying particular attention where damaged bearings have been discovered. If the journals are scored or pitted in any way a new crankshaft will be required. Note that undersizes are not available, precluding the option of regrinding the crankshaft.

8 Place the crankshaft on V-blocks and check the runout at the centre main bearing journal using a dial gauge. Compare the reading to the maximum specified at the beginning of the Chapter. If the runout exceeds the limit, the crankshaft must be replaced with a new one.

Oil clearance check

9 Whether new bearing shells are being fitted or the original ones are being reused, the main

30.3 Lift the crankshaft out of the crankcase

30.4 Remove the shells from their housings

30.13 Place a strip of Plastigauge on each bearing journal

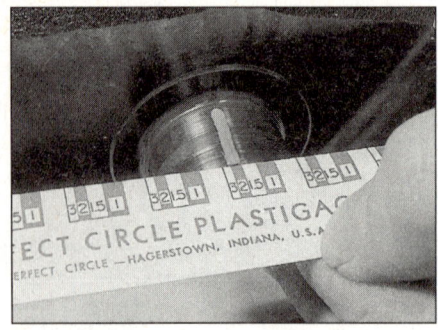

30.16 Measure the crushed Plastigauge using the scale on the pack

30.20a Main bearing journal size numbers

bearing oil clearance should be checked before the engine is reassembled. Main bearing oil clearance is measured with a product known as Plastigauge. If not already done remove the upper balancer shaft from the lower crankcase (see Section 34) – this is to prevent any possible rotation of the crankshaft, which will disturb the Plastigauge, as the crankcases are joined and then separated.

10 Remove the shells if not already done **(see illustration 30.4)**. Clean the shells and the bearing housings in both crankcase halves.

11 Press the bearing shells into their housings, ensuring that the tab on each shell engages in the notch **(see illustration 30.23b)**. Make sure the bearings are fitted in the correct locations and take care not to touch any shell's bearing surface with your fingers.

12 Ensure the shells and crankshaft are clean and dry. Lay the crankshaft in position in the upper crankcase **(see illustration 30.3)**. Install the three crankcase dowels if removed **(see illustration 27.14)**.

13 Cut three lengths of the appropriate size Plastigauge (they should be slightly shorter than the width of the crankshaft journals). Place a strand of Plastigauge on each (cleaned) journal, avoiding the oil hole **(see illustration)**. During the procedure make sure the crankshaft is not rotated at all as this will disturb the Plastigauge and give false readings, in which case you must start again.

14 Carefully fit the lower crankcase half onto the upper half **(see illustration 27.8)**. Check that the lower half is correctly seated. Smear some oil onto the threads and under the heads of the six 10 mm crankshaft journal bolts. Fit the bolts and tighten them finger-tight at first, then tighten them evenly and a little at a time in a criss-cross sequence to the torque setting specified at the beginning of the Chapter **(see illustration 27.7)**.

15 Slacken each bolt evenly and a little at a time until they are all finger-tight, then remove the bolts. Carefully lift off the lower crankcase half, making sure the Plastigauge is not disturbed.

16 Compare the width of the crushed Plastigauge on each crankshaft journal to the

30.20b Main bearing housing size letters

scale printed on the Plastigauge envelope to obtain the main bearing oil clearance **(see illustration)**. Compare the reading to the specifications at the beginning of the Chapter.

17 On completion carefully scrape away all traces of the Plastigauge material from the crankshaft journal and bearing shells; use a fingernail or other object which is unlikely to score them.

18 If the clearance is within the range listed in this Chapter's Specifications and the bearings are in perfect condition, they can be reused.

19 If the clearance is beyond the service limit, replace the bearing shells with new ones according to the size codes (see Steps 20 and 21). Check the oil clearance once again – if the clearances are still excessive replace the crankshaft with a new one, then again select new shells according to the size code of the new crankshaft if necessary. Always replace all of the shells as a set at the same time.

Main bearing shell selection

20 Replacement bearing shells for the main

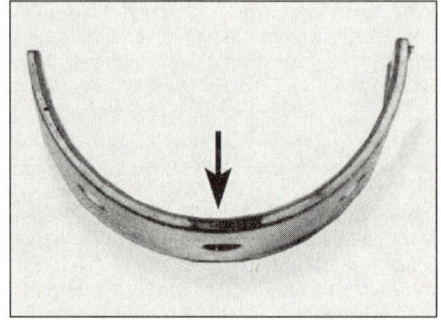

30.21 The colour code is marked on the side of the shell (arrowed)

bearings are supplied on a selected fit basis. Code numbers and letters stamped on the crankshaft and crankcase are used to identify the correct replacement bearings. Each crankshaft main bearing journal size number is stamped on the adjacent crankshaft web and is either a 1, 2 or 3 **(see illustration)**. The corresponding main bearing housing size letters are stamped into the front of the upper crankcase half and are either an A, B or C **(see illustration)**. The left-hand letter corresponds to the front journal, middle to middle, right-hand to rear.

21 A range of bearing shells is available. To select the correct bearing for a particular journal, use the table below and cross-refer the main bearing journal size number with the main bearing housing size letter to determine the letter/colour code of the bearing required. For example, if the journal code is 3, and the housing code is A, then the bearing required is C-Brown. The colour is marked on the side of the shell **(see illustration)** – the letter is not marked but is referred to in the parts listing. A-Blue is the thickest shell, E-Yellow the thinnest.

	Main bearing housing size		
Main bearing journal size	A	B	C
1 (42.010 to 42.016 mm)	E-Yellow	D-Green	C-Brown
2 (42.004 to 42.010 mm)	D-Green	C-Brown	B-Black
3 (41.998 to 42.004 mm)	C-Brown	B-Black	A-Blue

Engine, clutch and transmission 2•69

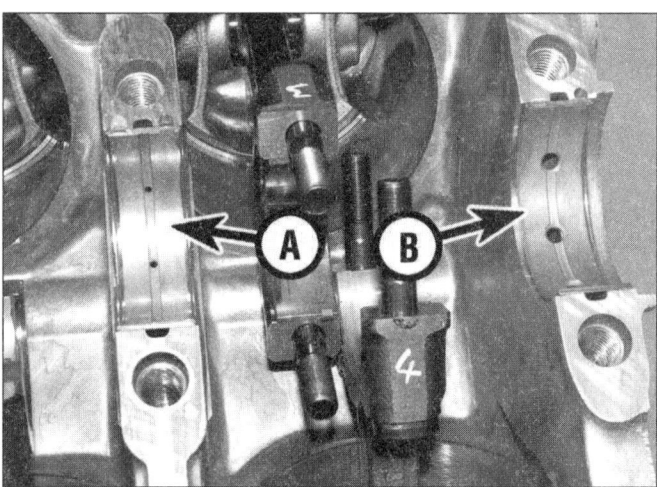

30.23a The centre shells (A) have smaller holes than the outer ones (B)

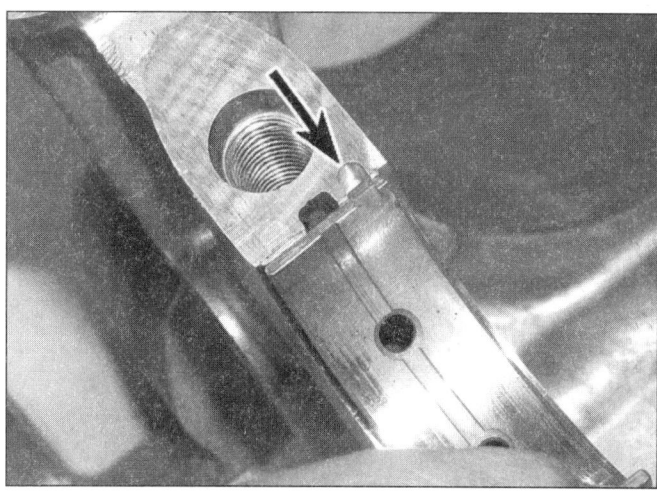

30.23b Fit the shells, locating the tabs in the notches (arrowed)

Installation

22 Clean the backs of the bearing shells and the bearing housings in both crankcase halves and dry them with a lint-free cloth. If new shells are being fitted clean off any protective grease using paraffin (kerosene). Make sure all the oil passages and holes are clear, and blow them through with compressed air if it is available.

23 If the original shells are being re-used make sure they are returned to their original housing. If new shells are being used note that the ones for the centre main bearing have smaller holes (see illustration). Press the bearing shells into their housings, making sure the tab on each shell engages in the notch (see illustration). Take care not to touch any shell's bearing surface with your fingers. Lubricate each shell with molybdenum disulphide oil (a 50/50 mixture of molybdenum disulphide grease and clean engine oil).

24 Lower the crankshaft into the upper crankcase, making sure all bearings remain in place (see illustration 30.3).

25 Refer to Section 31 and fit the connecting rods and caps onto the crankshaft.

26 Reassemble the crankcase halves (see Section 27).

31 Connecting rods and bearings

Note: *To remove the connecting rods the engine must be removed from the frame and the crankcases separated.*
Special tool: *A piston ring compressor is necessary for the installation procedure (see illustration 31.25b).*

Removal

1 Remove the engine from the frame (see Section 4) and separate the crankcase halves (see Section 27).

2 Before detaching the rods from the crankshaft, measure the side clearance (the gap between the connecting rod big-end and the crankshaft web) with a feeler gauge (see illustration). If the clearance is greater than the service limit listed in this Chapter's Specifications, replace the rods with new ones. If the clearance is still excessive, replace the crankshaft with a new one.

3 Using paint or a felt marker pen, mark the relevant cylinder number (see Specifications at the beginning of the Chapter) on each connecting rod and cap (see illustration). Note that the number already across the rod and cap joint indicates rod size grade (see illustration 31.20b).

4 Unscrew the connecting rod cap nuts (see illustration). Separate the caps from the crankpin (see illustration). Push the rods and pistons up to the tops of the bores so that the bottom ends are clear of the crankshaft, taking care to keep the rods clear of the

31.2 Measure the big-end clearance using a feeler gauge

31.3 Mark the cylinder number on each rod and its cap

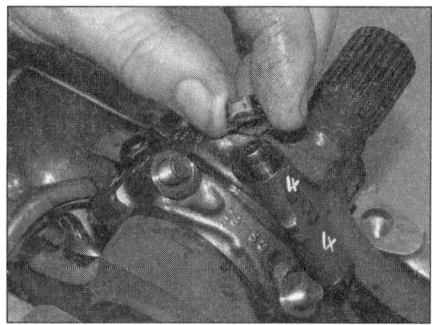

31.4a Unscrew the nuts ...

31.4b ... and remove the connecting rod caps

2•70 Engine, clutch and transmission

31.4c Push the rods off the crankpins and up the bores

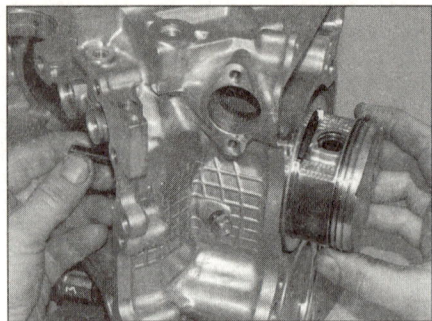

31.5 Carefully draw the piston and rod assembly out of the bore

Oil clearance check

12 Whether new bearing shells are being fitted or the original ones are being reused, the connecting rod bearing oil clearance should be checked prior to reassembly.

13 Remove the shells from the rods and caps (see illustration 31.10). Clean the backs of the bearing shells and the bearing housings in both the connecting rod and cap.

14 Press the bearing shells into their housings, making sure the tab on each shell engages the notch in the connecting rod/cap (see illustration 31.23). Make sure the bearings are fitted in the correct location and take care not to touch any shell's bearing surface with your fingers. Refer to Steps 24 and 25 and fit the rods and pistons into their bores. Turn the crankcase over and lay the crankshaft in the upper crankcase half (make sure the main bearing shells are installed), and position it so the crankpins are uppermost (see illustration 30.3). Pull the connecting rods onto the crankpins (see illustration 31.4c).

cylinder walls **(see illustration)**. Remove the crankshaft (see Section 30).

5 Sit the upper crankcase on one end. Push each piston/connecting rod assembly up its bore and remove it from the top making sure the connecting rod does not mark the cylinder walls **(see illustration)**. Mark the side of each piston with its cylinder number to ensure it is returned to the correct rod if separated, and then to the correct cylinder.

 To ease removal of the pistons, carefully remove any ridge of carbon built up on the top of each cylinder bore using a scraper, knife blade or scouring pad. If there is a pronounced wear ridge, remove it using a ridge reamer.

Caution: *Do not try to remove the piston/connecting rod from the bottom of the cylinder bore. The piston will not pass the crankcase main bearing webs. If the piston is pulled right to the bottom of the bore the oil control ring will expand and lock the piston in position. If this happens it is likely the ring will break.*

6 Keep the rod, cap, nuts, and the bearing shells (if they are to be reused) together in their correct positions to ensure correct installation – fit the caps back onto the rods and finger-tighten the nuts to make sure.

7 Remove the pistons from the connecting rods if required (see Section 32), but note that if you are doing a big-end oil clearance check they are best left in place as they will prevent the rod rotating on the crankpin and disturbing the Plastigauge.

Inspection

8 Check the connecting rods for cracks and other obvious damage.

9 Apply clean engine oil to the piston pin, insert it into the connecting rod small-end and check for any freeplay between the two **(see illustration)**. Measure the pin external diameter at its centre, and the small-end bore diameter, then calculate the difference to obtain the small-end-to-piston pin clearance **(see illustration)**. Compare the result to the specifications at the beginning of the Chapter. If the clearance is greater than specified, replace the components that are worn beyond their specified limits with new ones.

10 Refer to Section 29 and examine the connecting rod bearing shells. If they are scored, badly scuffed, corroded, or appear to have seized, new shells must be installed. Remove the shells from the rods and caps **(see illustration)**. Always replace the shells in the connecting rods as a set. If they are badly damaged, check the corresponding crankpin. Evidence of extreme heat, such as discoloration, indicates that lubrication failure has occurred. Be sure to thoroughly check the oil pump and pressure relief valve as well as all oil holes and passages before reassembling the engine.

11 Have the rods checked for twist and bend by a Honda dealer if you are in doubt they are straight.

15 Cut a length of the appropriate size Plastigauge (it should be slightly shorter than the width of the crankpin). Place a strand of Plastigauge on each crankpin journal, avoiding the oil holes (see illustration 30.13). Fit the caps onto the rods, making sure they are the correct way around so the markings align (see illustration 31.4b). Apply some clean oil to the threads and under the heads of the rod nuts (see illustration 31.4a). Fit the nuts and tighten them evenly and a little at a time to the torque setting specified at the beginning of the Chapter, making sure the crankshaft does not rotate.

16 Unscrew the nuts and remove the connecting rod caps. Compare the width of the crushed Plastigauge on the crankpin in two places (for each connecting rod) to the scale printed on the Plastigauge envelope to obtain the connecting rod bearing oil clearance (see illustration 30.16). Compare the readings to the specifications at the beginning of the Chapter.

17 On completion carefully scrape away all traces of the Plastigauge material from the crankpin and bearing shells using a fingernail or other object which is unlikely to score the shells.

18 If the clearance is within the range listed in this Chapter's Specifications and the bearings

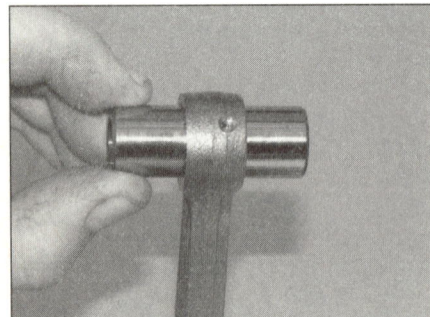

31.9a Check for freeplay between the rod and pin

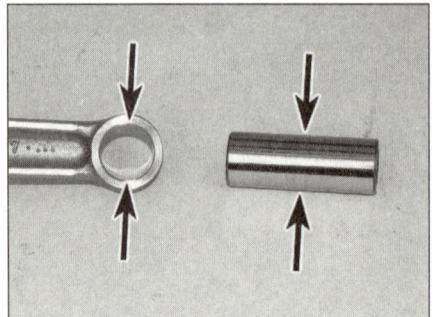

31.9b Measure the external diameter of the pin and the internal diameter of the rod small-end

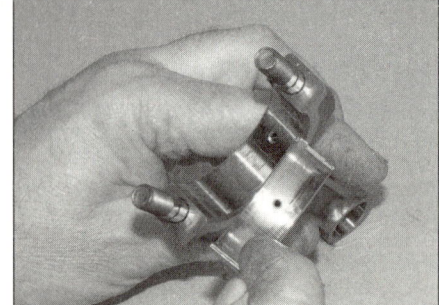

31.10 Remove the shells

Engine, clutch and transmission 2•71

31.20a Crankpin journal size letters

31.20b Connecting rod size number

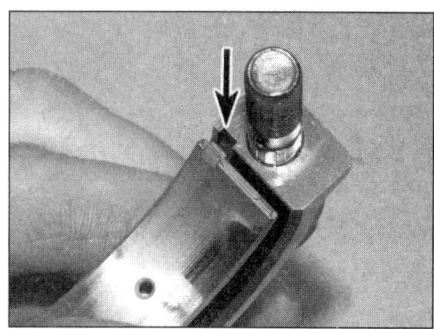

31.23 Fit the shells, locating the tabs in the notches (arrowed)

are in perfect condition, they can be reused.
19 If the clearance is beyond the service limit, replace the bearing shells with new ones according to the size codes (see Steps 20 and 21). Check the oil clearance once again – if the clearances are still excessive replace the crankshaft with a new one, and then again select new shells according to the size code of the new crankshaft if necessary. Always replace all of the shells as a set at the same time.

Bearing shell selection

20 Replacement bearing shells for the big-end bearings are supplied on a selected fit basis. Code letters and numbers stamped on the crankshaft and connecting rods are used to identify the correct replacement bearings. Each big-end journal size number is stamped on the adjacent crankshaft web and is either an A, B or C **(see illustration)**. The connecting rod size number is marked across the flat face of the connecting rod and cap and is either a 1, 2 or 3 **(see illustration)**.

21 A range of bearing shells is available. To select the correct bearing for a particular big-end, use the table below and cross-refer the big-end journal size letter with the connecting rod size number to determine the letter/colour code of the bearing required. For example, if the big-end code is A, and the connecting rod size is 1, then the bearing required is E-Yellow. The colour is marked on the side of the shell **(see illustration 30.21)** – the letter is not marked but is referred to in the parts listing. A-Blue is the thickest shell, E-Yellow the thinnest.

	Connecting rod size		
Big-end size	1	2	3
A (42.000 to 42.006 mm)	E-Yellow	D-Green	C-Brown
B (42.006 to 42.012 mm)	D-Green	C-Brown	B-Black
C (42.012 to 42.018 mm)	C-Brown	B-Black	A-Blue

Installation

22 Fit the pistons onto the connecting rods (see Section 32).
23 Clean the backs of the bearing shells and the bearing housings in both cap and rod. If new shells are being fitted, clean off any protective grease using paraffin (kerosene). Wipe the shells, cap and rod dry with a clean lint free cloth. Fit the bearing shells in the connecting rods and caps, making sure the tab on each shell engages the notch in the connecting rod/cap **(see illustration)**. Lubricate the shells with molybdenum disulphide oil (a 50/50 mixture of molybdenum disulphide grease and clean engine oil).
24 Position the crankcase the correct way up. Lubricate each piston, its rings and cylinder bore with clean engine oil as you fit it. Wrap some rag round the bottom of the connecting rod. Make sure each piston is fitted into the bore with the IN mark facing the intake side, and with each going to its correct cylinder number according to the marks made on removal.
25 Each piston must be fitted with the IN mark on the intake side of the bore **(see illustration)**. Fit a piston ring compressor around the first piston being installed and tighten it to compress the rings – a compressor is required because there is very little lead-in for the rings to be easily fed in by hand **(see illustration)**. Locate the piston/connecting assembly on the top of the bore with the IN mark on the piston crown on the intake side **(see illustration)** and tap the top of the piston using a wooden or plastic tool (such as the handle end of a hammer) until the piston is completely in the bore **(see illustration)**. If resistance is felt a ring may be catching the rim – do not try to force it in as rings are easily broken. Tighten the compressor a bit more to squash the ring. Install the other pistons/rods in the same way.

31.25a Make sure the IN mark is on the intake side

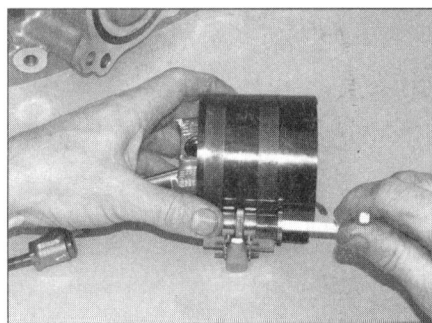

31.25b Fit the compressor over the piston and rings and compress the rings by tightening the bands on the compressor using an Allen key

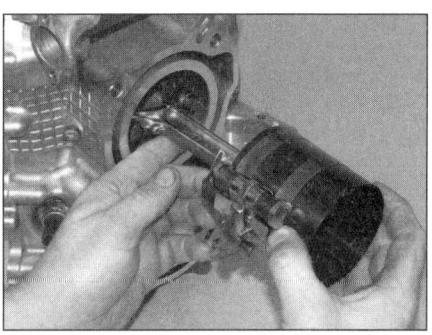

31.25c Fit the rod into the bore and rest the compressor on the crankcase . . .

31.25d . . . then tap the top of the piston with a soft tool so that it enters

26 Carefully turn the crankcase upside down. Install the crankshaft (see Section 30).
27 Lubricate the crankpins with molybdenum disulphide oil (a 50/50 mixture of molybdenum disulphide grease and clean engine oil). Remove the rag and carefully pull the each connecting rod onto its crankpin, taking care not to mark the cylinders **(see illustration 31.4c)**. Fit the caps onto the rods, making sure the markings align (see Step 3) **(see illustration 31.4b)**.
28 Apply some clean oil to the threads and under the heads of the connecting rod nuts. Fit the nuts and tighten them evenly and a little at a time to the torque setting specified at the beginning of the Chapter **(see illustration 31.4a)**.
29 Turn the crankshaft and check it and the pistons rotate and move smoothly and as freely as they should. If there are any signs of roughness or tightness, the problem must be investigated before further assembly of the engine – sometimes tapping the bottom of the connecting rod cap will relieve tightness, but if in doubt, remove the caps and recheck the clearances.
30 Reassemble the crankcase halves (see Section 27).

32 Pistons

Note: To remove the pistons the engine must be removed from the frame and the crankcase halves separated.

Removal

1 Remove the connecting rods (see Section 31).
2 Before removing the piston from the connecting rod, mark the cylinder number (see Specifications at the beginning of the Chapter) on the side of each piston or on the inside of the skirt using paint or a marker pen. Note the following: each piston crown is marked with the letters L-IN or R-IN (though they may be invisible until the piston is cleaned) and these letters face the intake side of the cylinder, with the L or R denoting which side of the engine **(see illustration 31.25a)**. Each connecting rod is also marked L or R according to its side. On the right-hand piston/rod assemblies the marks on the piston face the same way as the

32.2 Note the orientation of the IN mark on the piston with the oil hole (arrowed) in the big-end according to side

oil hole in the big-end of the connecting rod, while on the left-hand assemblies the marks on the piston face the opposite way to the oil hole **(see illustration)**.
3 Carefully prise out the circlip on one side of the piston using needle-nose pliers or a small flat-bladed screwdriver inserted into the notch **(see illustration)**. Push the piston pin out from the other side to free the piston from the connecting rod **(see illustration)**. Remove the other circlip and discard them as new ones must be used. When the piston has been removed, slide its pin back into its bore so that related parts do not get mixed up.

 *If a piston pin is a tight fit in the piston bosses, use a heat gun to heat the piston – this will expand the alloy piston sufficiently to release its grip on the pin. If the piston pin is particularly stubborn, extract it using a drawbolt tool, but be careful to protect the piston's working surfaces.*

4 Using your thumbs or a piston ring removal and installation tool, carefully remove the rings from the pistons **(see illustrations 33.10, 33.9a and b, 33.7c, b and a)**. Do not nick or gouge the pistons in the process. Carefully note which way up each ring fits and in which groove as they must be installed in their original positions if being reused. The upper surface of the top ring should be marked with the letter R at one end, and the second (middle) ring marked RN

(see illustration 33.9a). The top and middle rings can also be identified by the fact that the top ring is narrower and thinner than the second (middle) ring, and their cross-section profiles are different.
5 Scrape all traces of carbon from the tops of the pistons. A hand-held wire brush or a piece of fine emery cloth can be used once most of the deposits have been scraped away. Do not, under any circumstances, use a wire brush mounted in a drill motor to remove deposits from the pistons; the piston material is soft and will be eroded away by the wire brush.
6 Use a piston ring groove cleaning tool to remove any carbon deposits from the ring grooves. If a tool is not available, a piece broken off an old ring will do the job. Be very careful to remove only the carbon deposits. Do not remove any metal and do not nick or gouge the sides of the ring grooves.
7 Once the deposits have been removed, clean the pistons with solvent and dry them thoroughly. If the cylinder identification mark previously made on the piston is cleaned off, be sure to re-mark it with the correct identity. Make sure the oil return holes below the oil ring groove are clear.

Inspection

8 Carefully inspect each piston for cracks around the skirt, at the pin bosses and at the ring lands. Normal piston wear appears as even, vertical wear on the thrust surfaces of the piston. If the skirt is scored or scuffed, the engine may have been suffering from overheating and/or abnormal combustion, which causes excessively high operating temperatures. Also check that the circlip grooves are not damaged.
9 A hole in the top of the piston, in one extreme, or burned areas around the edge of the piston crown, indicate that pre-ignition or knocking under load have occurred. If you find evidence of any problems the cause must be corrected or the damage will occur again (see Fault Finding in the *Reference* section).
10 Measure the piston ring-to-groove clearance by laying each piston ring in its groove and slipping a feeler gauge in beside it **(see illustration)**. Make sure you have the correct ring for the groove. Check the clearance at three or four locations around

32.3a Prise out the circlip using a suitable tool in the notch . . .

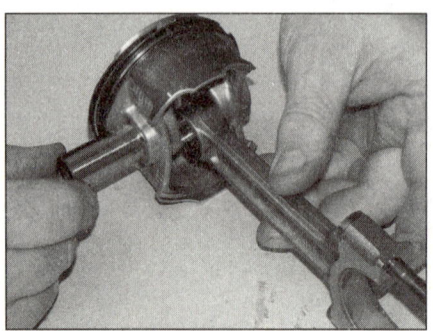

32.3b . . . then push out the pin and separate the piston from the rod

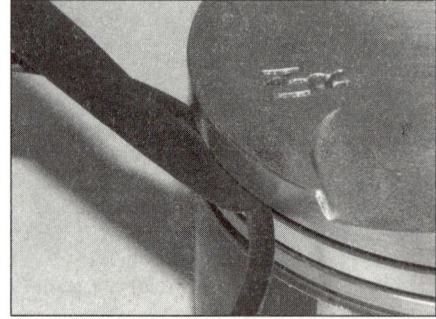

32.10 Measure the piston ring-to-groove clearance with a feeler gauge

Engine, clutch and transmission 2•73

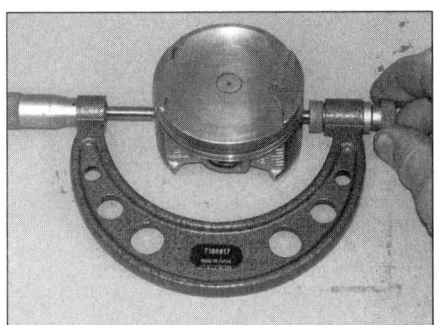

32.11 Measure the piston diameter with a micrometer at the specified distance from the bottom of the skirt

32.12a Check for freeplay between the rod and piston

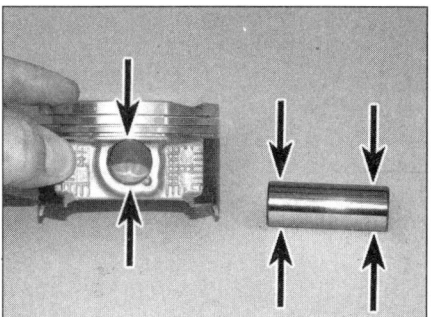

32.12b Measure the external diameter of the pin near each end and the internal diameter of the bore in the piston

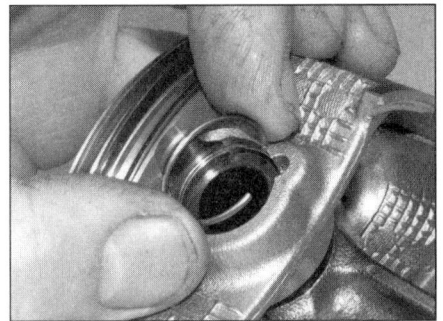

32.16 Secure the pin with new circlips

the groove. If the clearance is greater than specified, replace both the piston and rings as a set. If new rings are being used, measure the clearance using the new rings. If the clearance is greater than that specified, the piston is worn and must be replaced with a new one.

11 Check the piston-to-bore clearance by measuring the bore (see Section 28), then measure the piston 8 mm up from the bottom of the skirt and at 90° to the piston pin axis **(see illustration)**. Make sure each piston is matched to its correct cylinder. Refer to the Specifications at the beginning of the Chapter and subtract the piston diameter from the bore diameter to obtain the clearance. If it is greater than the specified figure, the piston must be replaced with a new one (assuming the bore itself is within limits).

12 Apply clean engine oil to the piston pin, insert it into the piston and check for any freeplay between the two **(see illustration)**. Measure the pin external diameter near each end, and the pin bores in the piston **(see illustration)**. Calculate the difference to obtain the piston pin-to-piston pin bore clearance. Compare the result to the specifications at the beginning of the Chapter. If the clearance is greater than specified, replace the components that are worn beyond their specified limits. If not already done, repeat the measurements between the pin and the connecting rod small-end (see Section 31).

Installation

13 Inspect and install the piston rings (see Section 33).
14 Lubricate the piston pin, the piston pin bore and the connecting rod small-end bore with molybdenum disulphide oil (a 50/50 mixture of molybdenum disulphide grease and clean engine oil).
15 When fitting the Nos. 1 and 3 (left-hand) pistons onto their connecting rods (marked L) make sure the L-IN on the piston crown is on the opposite side to the oil hole in the big-end of the connecting rod **(see illustration 32.2)**. When fitting the Nos. 2 and 3 (right-hand) pistons onto their connecting rods (marked R) make sure the R-IN on the piston crown is on the same side as the oil hole in the big-end of the connecting rod **(see illustration 32.2)**.
16 Fit a *new* circlip into one side of the piston (do not reuse old circlips). Line up the piston on its correct connecting rod, and insert the piston pin from the other side **(see illustration 32.3b)**. Secure the pin with the other *new* circlip **(see illustration)**. When fitting the circlips, compress them only just enough to fit them in the piston, and make sure they are properly seated in their grooves with the open end away from the removal notch.
17 Install the connecting rods (see Section 31) and reassemble the crankcase halves (see Section 27).

33 Piston rings

Inspection

1 It is good practice to replace the piston rings with new ones when an engine is being overhauled. Before installing the new rings, check their end gaps with the rings installed in the bore, as follows.
2 Lay out each piston with its ring set and keep them together so the rings will be matched with the same piston and bore during the end gap measurement procedure and engine assembly. If the old rings are being reused, make sure they are matched with their correct piston and cylinder.
3 To measure the installed ring end gap, fit the first ring into the top of its bore and square it up with the bore walls by pushing it down with the top of the piston **(see illustrations)**. The ring should be about 20 mm above the bottom of the bore. Slip a feeler gauge between the ends of the ring and compare the measurement to the specifications at the beginning of the Chapter **(see illustration)**.

33.3a Fit the ring in its bore . . .

33.3b . . . and square it up using the piston . . .

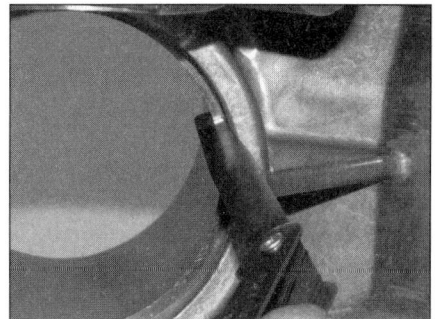

33.3c . . . then measure the end gap using a feeler gauge

2•74 Engine, clutch and transmission

33.7a Fit the oil ring expander in its groove . . .

33.7b . . . then fit the lower side rail . . .

33.7c . . . and the upper side rail on each side of it

33.9a Note the marking on each ring and make sure it faces up

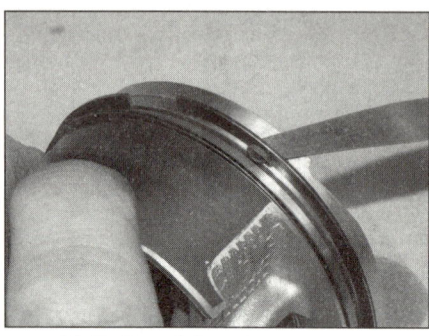
33.9b Install the middle ring . . .

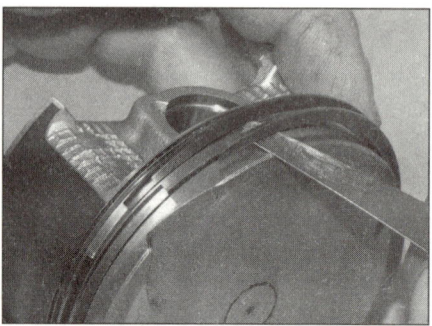
33.10 . . . and the top ring as described

4 Repeat the procedure for the middle ring and the oil control ring side-rails, but not the expander ring. Remember to keep the rings, pistons and bores matched up.
5 If the end gap exceeds the service limit check the bore for wear (see Section 28). If

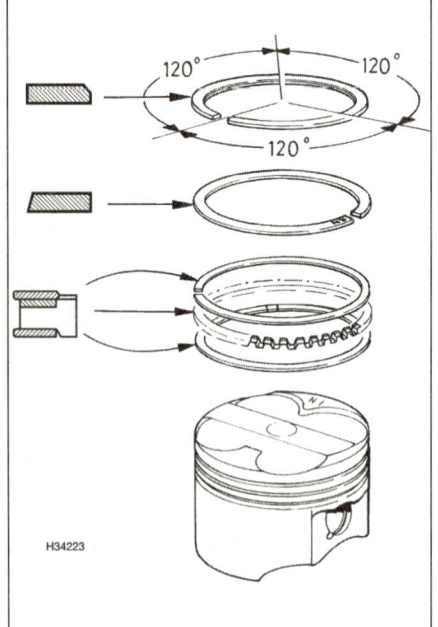
33.11 Piston ring installation details – stagger the ring end gaps as shown

the bore is within limits replace the rings with a new set. If the bore is worn it can be re-bored and oversize pistons and rings can be fitted (see Section 28).
6 If the gap is too small, the ring ends may come in contact with each other during engine operation, which can cause serious damage.

Installation

7 Fit the oil control ring (lowest on the piston) first. It is composed of three separate components, namely the expander and the upper and lower side-rails. Slip the expander into the groove, making sure the ends don't overlap, then fit the lower side-rail **(see illustrations)**. Do not use a piston ring installation tool on the side-rails as they may be damaged. Instead, place one end of the side-rail into the groove between the expander and the ring land. Hold it firmly in place and slide a finger around the piston while pushing the rail into the groove. Next, fit the upper side-rail in the same manner **(see illustration)**. Check that the ends of the expander have not overlapped.
8 After the three oil ring components have been installed, check to make sure that both the upper and lower side-rails can be turned smoothly in the ring groove.
9 Install the second (middle) ring next – it should be marked with the letters RN at one end, and it can also be identified by its cross-section profile **(see illustration)**. Make sure that the ring is installed with the identification letter facing up. Fit the ring

into the middle groove in the piston **(see illustration)**. Do not expand the ring any more than is necessary to slide it into place. To avoid breaking the ring, use a piston ring installation tool.
10 Finally, install the top ring, marked with the letter R, in the same manner into the top groove in the piston **(see illustration)**. Make sure the identification letter near the end gap is facing up.
11 Once the rings are correctly installed, check they move freely without snagging and stagger their end gaps as shown **(see illustration)**.

34 Balancer shafts
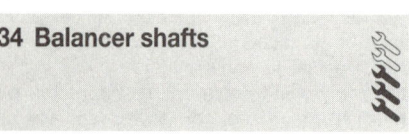

Note: *To remove the balancer shafts the engine must be removed from the frame and the crankcase halves separated.*

Removal

1 Separate the crankcase halves (see Section 27) – the balancer shafts are in the lower half. Sit the crankcase on the sump mating surface.
2 If you intend to separate the shaft holders from the shafts (there is no need unless you are fitting new parts), make an alignment mark across each holder and shaft – this will give a good indication as to the starting point for resetting the backlash adjustment

Engine, clutch and transmission 2•75

34.2a Upper balancer shaft holder mounting bolt (A) and pinch-bolt (B), lower balancer shaft holder mounting bolt (C) and pinch-bolt (D)

34.2b Make an alignment mark between each shaft and holder

when the crankcases are reassembled (see illustrations).

3 Support the upper balancer gear/weight assembly, then withdraw the shaft and remove the gear/weight (see illustration 34.14b) – you may need to either rotate the shaft as you withdraw it or lift the gear/weight assembly to ease removal against the offset of the shaft.

4 Support the lower balancer gear/weight assembly, then withdraw the shaft and remove the gear/weight in the same way (see illustration 34.13).

5 Remove the O-ring from each shaft and discard it as a new one must be used (see illustration 34.7). If required slacken the holder pinch-bolt and slide the holder off the shaft.

Inspection

6 Inspect the teeth on each gear for signs of wear or damage, and replace it with a new one if necessary. If damage is found, check the teeth on the drive gear on the crankshaft. The gear/weight can be disassembled if required – all components are available individually.

7 Remove the washer from each end of the gear/weight, noting which fits where (see illustration). Slide the shaft back into the gear/weight and check that it runs freely and smoothly in the bearings. If there is any evidence of wear on the shaft, or it is a sloppy fit in the bearings, and the bearings are good, replace the shaft with a new one. If the bearings do not run smoothly and freely, or if there is any wear or damage evident, replace them with new ones. Note that all components are matched by size and should be replaced either as a set, or by matching them using the coded markings (see Steps 9 and 10).

Withdraw the shaft and remove the bearings and spacer. Clean them with solvent.

8 Separate the weight from the gear (see illustration). Check the condition of the rubber dampers in the gear for damage, deformation and deterioration, and replace them with new ones if necessary.

Bearing selection

9 Replacement bearings for the balancer are supplied on a selected fit basis according to the internal diameter (ID) of the end it runs in and the external diameter of the shaft. Code letters stamped on the weight web and colours on the shaft are used to identify the correct replacement bearings, which themselves are letter and colour-coded. The balancer gear/weight size code letters (the right-hand one for the gear end and the left-hand one for

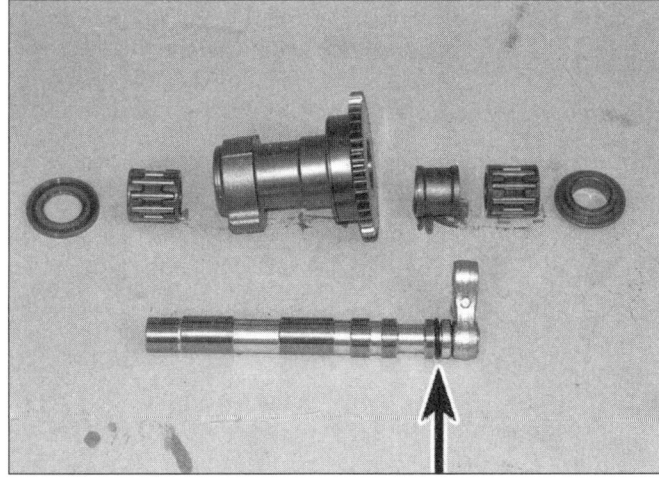

34.7 Balancer gear/weight assembly components – the O-ring (arrowed) on the shaft must be replaced with a new one

34.8 Draw the gear off the weight and check the rubber dampers

2•76 Engine, clutch and transmission

34.9 Balancer weight size code letters

34.11 Align the cut-outs (arrowed) when assembling the gear and weight

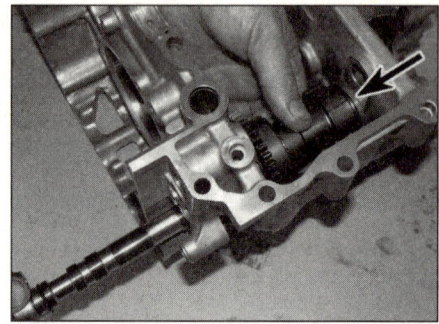

34.13 Position the lower gear/weight with the index line (arrowed) at the top and insert the shaft

the weight end) are either an A, B or C **(see illustration)**. The colour marks on the shaft, located on the plain section between the bearing surfaces, are either blue, black or red, with each mark adjacent to its corresponding bearing surface.

10 Measure the internal diameter of each end of the balancer and the external diameter of each bearing surface on the shaft and check it according to its letter or colour against the specifications given in the table below to check the weight or shaft bearing surface has not worn. If it has worn beyond its specification replace the balancer or shaft with a new one and select new bearings according to the numbers/colours on the new one. If the balancer and/or shaft have not worn, select new bearings according to the letters and colours. A range of bearings is available. To select the correct bearing use the table below and cross-refer the marks. For example, if the gear end size is B, and the shaft colour next to the gear bearing surface is black, then the bearing required for the gear end of the shaft is C-white. The colour is marked on the bearing – the letter is not marked but is referred to in the parts listing.

Installation

Note: *It is best to highlight all alignment punch marks and lines on the balancer shaft gears and on the drive gear on the crankshaft with a dab of white paint – the punch marks are small and the paint makes them much easier to see, making installation and alignment much easier.*

11 Smear the dampers with oil, then fit them onto the gear **(see illustration 34.8)**. Fit the gear onto the balancer, aligning the cut-out on the inner rim with the cut-out on the balancer, and making sure the dampers locate correctly **(see illustration)**. Lubricate the bearings and spacer with clean oil and slide them into the balancer, making sure they are correctly located according to the codes (see Steps 9 and 10) **(see illustration 34.7)**. Fit the shouldered washer onto the gear end and the dished washer onto the weight end.

12 Fit a new O-ring onto each shaft and smear it and the shaft with clean oil **(see illustration 34.7)**. If removed fit each holder onto the end of its shaft, aligning the marks made on removal and tighten its pinch-bolt **(see illustration 34.2b)**.

13 Position the lower balancer gear/weight assembly in the crankcase with the gear at the front and the weight facing the bottom, then slide the shaft in with – if the shaft is difficult to insert rotate it until it enters. Set the lower balancer so the index line above the weight is at the top **(see illustration)**.

14 Position the upper balancer gear/weight assembly in the crankcase with the gear at the front and the weight at the top, aligning the punch mark on the gear with that on the lower balancer gear **(see illustration)**, at which point the timing lines will be parallel with the crankcase mating surface (see illustration 27.15a), then slide the shaft in – if the shaft is difficult to insert rotate it until it enters **(see illustration)**. Check to make sure the punch marks on the gears are in exact alignment **(see illustration)**.

15 Reassemble the crankcase halves (see Section 27).

16 Carry out the static backlash adjustment procedure (see below).

17 Turn the engine clockwise through 360° (one full turn) and check that the crankshaft and balancer marks still align (see Section 27). Finish rebuilding the engine and install it (see Section 4).

18 Carry out the dynamic backlash adjustment procedure (see below).

Backlash adjustment

Note: *A backlash adjustment is provided so that the gears mesh at their optimum point for*

Balancer gear/weight size	Shaft size		
	Blue (17.996 to 18.000 mm)	Black (17.991 to 17.996 mm)	Red (17.987 to 17.991 mm)
A (26.996 to 27.000 mm)	C-White	B-Blue	A-Red
B (26.991 to 26.996 mm)	D-Green	C-White	B-Blue
C (26.987 to 26.991 mm)	E-Yellow	D-Green	C-White

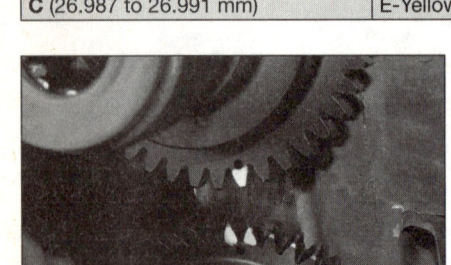

34.14a Align the gears so the punch marks align . . .

34.14b . . . then insert the shaft

34.14c Double-check the alignment of the marks on the gears

quiet running with minimal wear. If the amount of backlash is too great, the shafts will clatter. If the gears are running tight, they will whine, and wear very quickly. At the optimum point the gears will run very quietly – it is easy to tell the difference with the engine running. Adjustment is possible due to the offset on each shaft which allows eccentric movement of the balancer gear in relation to its drive gear when the shaft is turned. The static adjustment procedure allows the backlash to be set up in roughly the optimum position, but the dynamic procedure should always be carried out as well to fine tune the setting.

Static adjustment

Note: *This procedure must be carried out when the engine is cold.*
19 Slacken the balancer shaft holder pinch-bolts **(see illustrations 34.2a and b)**.
20 Turn the upper balancer shaft slightly anti-clockwise using a screwdriver in the slotted end until resistance is felt – at this point backlash between the gears has been eliminated. Now turn the shaft clockwise so the slot or index mark moves one graduation as marked on the holder, then temporarily tighten the pinch-bolt.
21 Turn the lower balancer shaft slightly clockwise using a screwdriver in the slotted end until resistance is felt – at this point backlash between the gears has been eliminated. Now turn the shaft anti-clockwise so the slot or index mark moves one graduation as marked on the holder, then temporarily tighten the pinch-bolt.
22 Now carry out the dynamic adjustment procedure (see below).

Dynamic adjustment

Note: *This procedure must be carried out when the engine is warm.*
23 Remove the left-hand fairing side panel (see Chapter 7). Start the engine and allow it to warm up, then let it idle.
24 Slacken the balancer shaft holder pinch-bolts **(see illustrations 34.2a and b)**.
25 Turn the upper balancer shaft slightly one way then the other to find the point at which the gears run at their quietest. Too far anti-clockwise and the gears will whine (no backlash), too far clockwise and they will clatter (excessive backlash).
26 Turn the lower balancer shaft slightly one way then the other to find the point at which the gears run at their quietest. Too far clockwise and the gears will whine (no backlash), too far anti-clockwise and they will clatter (excessive backlash).
27 Rev the engine and check that there is no unwanted noise at varying speeds.
28 On completion, tighten the shaft pinch-bolts. Install the left-hand fairing side panel (see Chapter 7).

35 Running-in procedure

1 Make sure the engine oil and coolant levels are correct (see *Pre-ride checks*). Make sure there is fuel in the tank.
2 Turn the engine kill switch to the ON position and shift the gearbox into neutral. Turn the ignition ON.
3 Start the engine and allow it to run at a moderately fast idle until it reaches operating temperature.

 Warning: *If the oil pressure warning light doesn't go off, or it comes on while the engine is running, stop the engine immediately.*

4 If a lubrication failure is suspected, stop the engine immediately and try to find the cause. If an engine is run without oil, even for a short period of time, severe damage will occur.
5 Check carefully for oil and coolant leaks and make sure the transmission and controls, especially the brakes, function properly before road testing the machine.
6 Treat the machine gently for the first few miles to make sure oil has circulated throughout the engine and any new parts installed have started to seat.
7 Even greater care is necessary if new pistons/rings or a new crankcase/bores have been fitted, and the bike will have to be run in as when new. This means greater use of the transmission and a restraining hand on the throttle until at least 300 miles (500 km) have been covered. There's no point in keeping to any set speed limit – the main idea is to keep from labouring the engine and to gradually increase performance up to the 300 miles (500 km) mark. Experience is the best guide, since it's easy to tell when an engine is running freely.
8 Upon completion of the road test, and after the engine has cooled down completely, recheck the valve clearances (see Chapter 1) and check the engine oil and coolant levels (see *Pre-ride checks*).

Notes

Chapter 3
Cooling system

Contents

	Section		Section
Coolant change	see Chapter 1	General information	1
Coolant hoses and unions	8	Oil cooler	see Chapter 2
Coolant level check	see Pre-ride checks	Radiator	5
Coolant reservoir	7	Temperature display and ECT sensor	3
Cooling fans and fan relay	2	Thermostat and housing	4
Cooling system checks	see Chapter 1	Water pump	6

Degrees of difficulty

| Easy, suitable for novice with little experience | Fairly easy, suitable for beginner with some experience 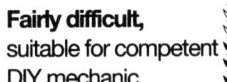 | Fairly difficult, suitable for competent DIY mechanic 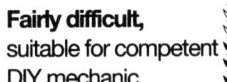 | Difficult, suitable for experienced DIY mechanic  | Very difficult, suitable for expert DIY or professional 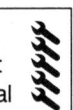 |

Specifications

Coolant
Mixture type and capacity .... see Chapter 1

ECT sensor
Resistance @ 80°C .... 2.1 to 2.6 K-ohms

Thermostat
Opening temperature .... 80 to 84°C
Fully open .... 95°C
Valve lift .... 8 mm (min)

Radiator
Cap valve opening pressure .... 16 to 20 psi (1.1 to 1.4 Bar)

Torque settings
Cooling fan blade nut .... 3 Nm
Cooling fan motor nuts .... 5 Nm
ECT sensor .... 23 Nm
Thermostat cover bolts .... 13 Nm

1 General information

The cooling system uses a water/anti-freeze coolant to carry away excess heat from the engine and maintain as constant a temperature as possible. The cylinders are surrounded by a water jacket from which the heated coolant is circulated by thermo-syphonic action in conjunction with a water pump, which is driven by chain and sprockets off the back of the clutch. The hot coolant passes upwards to the thermostat and through to the radiator. The coolant then flows across the core of the radiator, then to the water pump and back to the engine. Coolant is also circulated around the oil cooler, and around the heating system hoses in the throttle bodies.

A thermostat is fitted in the system to prevent the coolant flowing through the radiator when the engine is cold, therefore accelerating the speed at which the engine reaches normal operating temperature. A dual circuit sensor (containing the temperature gauge sensor and the ECT (engine coolant temperature) sensor) mounted in the thermostat housing transmits information to the temperature display on the instrument panel, and to the ECM (electronic control module). Two cooling fans fitted to the back of the radiator aid cooling in extreme conditions by drawing extra air through. The fan motor is controlled by a relay which receives a signal from the ECM which in turn receives information from the ECT sensor.

The complete cooling system is partially sealed and pressurised, the pressure being controlled by a valve contained in the spring-loaded radiator cap. By pressurising the coolant the boiling point is raised, preventing premature boiling in adverse conditions. The overflow pipe from the system is connected to a reservoir into which excess coolant is expelled under pressure. The discharged coolant automatically returns to the radiator by the vacuum created when the engine cools.

3•2 Cooling system

⚠️ **Warning:** Do not remove the pressure cap from the radiator when the engine is hot. Scalding hot coolant and steam may be blown out under pressure, which could cause serious injury. When the engine has cooled, place a thick rag, like a towel, over the pressure cap; slowly rotate the cap anti-clockwise to the first stop. This procedure allows any residual pressure to escape. When the steam has stopped escaping, press down on the cap while turning it anti-clockwise and remove it.

Caution: Do not allow anti-freeze to come in contact with your skin or painted surfaces of the motorcycle. Rinse off any spills immediately with plenty of water. Anti-freeze is highly toxic if ingested. Never leave anti-freeze lying around in an open container or in puddles on the floor; children and pets are attracted by its sweet smell and may drink it. Check with the local authorities about disposing of used anti-freeze. Many communities will have collection centres which will see that anti-freeze is disposed of safely.

Caution: At all times use the specified type of anti-freeze, and always mix it with distilled water in the correct proportion. The anti-freeze contains corrosion inhibitors which are essential to avoid damage to the cooling system. A lack of these inhibitors could lead to a build-up of corrosion which would block the coolant passages, resulting in overheating and severe engine damage. Distilled water must be used as opposed to tap water to avoid a build-up of scale which would also block the passages.

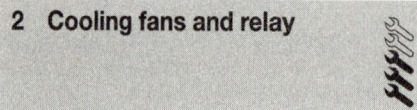

2 Cooling fans and relay

Cooling fan

Check

1 There are two cooling fans, one on each side of the radiator. If the engine is overheating and neither cooling fan is coming on, check the fan motor fuse (see Chapter 8). If the fuse is good, check the relay (see Steps 9 to 13).

2 If one fan is working but not the other, or otherwise to test a cooling fan motor, remove the relevant fairing side panel (see Chapter 7). Disconnect the fan wiring connector (see illustrations) - when disconnecting the right-hand connector free the connector from the bracket for clearance to disconnect it. Using a 12 volt battery and two jumper wires with suitable connectors, connect the battery positive (+) lead to the black/blue wire terminal on the fan side of the wiring connector, and the battery negative (–) lead to the green wire terminal on the connector. Once connected the fan should operate. If it does not, and the connector and wiring between it and the motor is good, then the fan motor is faulty.

Removal and installation

⚠️ **Warning:** The engine must be completely cool before carrying out this procedure.

3 Remove the radiator (see Section 5).
4 Free the fan wiring connector from the clip. Undo the screws and remove the fan (see illustration).
5 If required unscrew the fan blade nut and remove the blade. Undo the three nuts on the front of the fan motor and separate the motor from its bracket.
6 Installation is the reverse of removal. Tighten the fan motor nuts to the torque setting specified at the beginning of the Chapter. Apply a suitable non-permanent thread locking compound to the fan blade nut and tighten it to the specified torque.
7 Install the radiator (see Section 5).

Cooling fan relay

8 There are two cooling fans, one on each side of the radiator. If the engine is overheating and neither cooling fan is coming on, first check the fan motor fuse (see Chapter 8).
9 If the fuse is good, remove the left-hand side cover (see Chapter 7). Displace the relay and disconnect its wiring connector (see illustration).
10 Set a multimeter to the ohms x 1 scale and connect it across the relay's A and B (black/blue and adjacent black/pink wire)

2.2a Right-hand cooling fan wiring connector (arrowed)

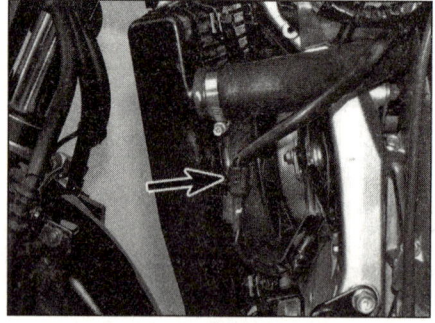

2.2b Left-hand cooling fan wiring connector (arrowed)

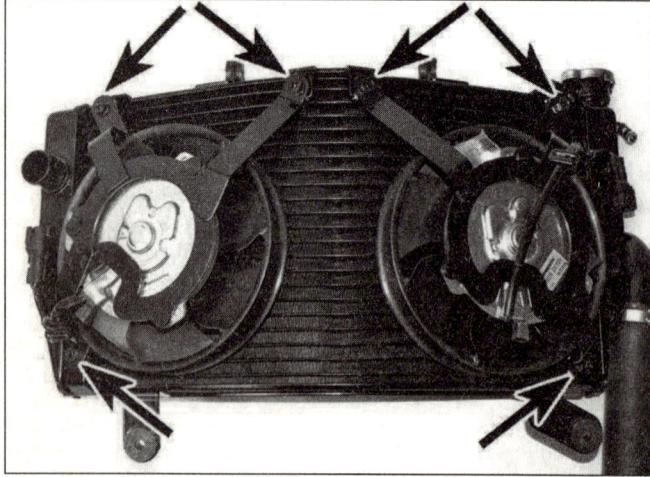

2.4 Fan assembly mounting screws (arrowed)

2.9 Cooling fan relay (arrowed)

Cooling system 3•3

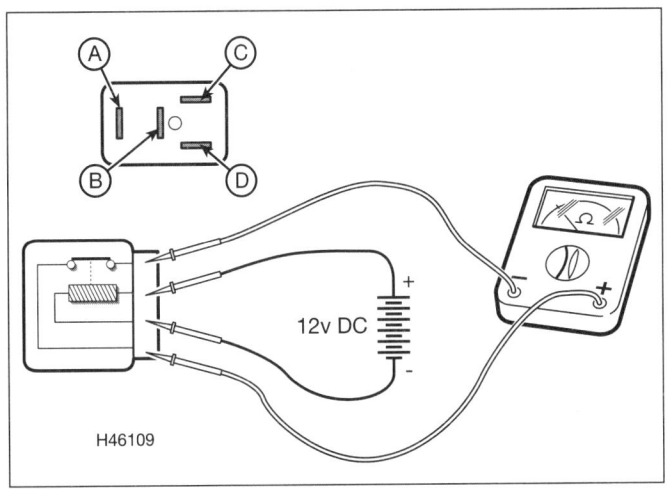

2.10 Fan relay test set-up

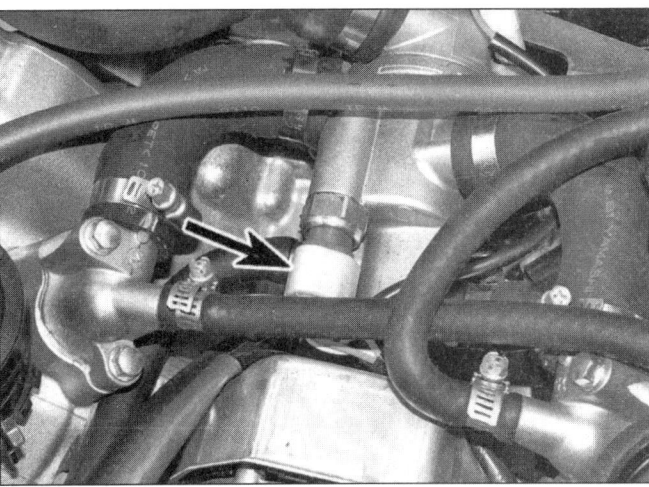

3.2 ECT sensor wiring connector (arrowed)

terminals **(see illustration)**. There should be no continuity (infinite resistance). Using a fully-charged 12 volt battery and two insulated jumper wires, connect the positive (+) terminal of the battery to the C (black/pink wire) terminal on the relay, and the negative (–) terminal to the D (brown wire) terminal on the relay. At this point the relay should be heard to click and the multimeter read 0 ohms (continuity). If this is the case the relay is proved good. If the relay does not click when battery voltage is applied and still indicates no continuity (infinite resistance) across its terminals, it is faulty and must be replaced with a new one.

11 If the relay is good, check for battery voltage at each black/pink wire in the wiring connector with the ignition switch ON. If there is no voltage, check the wiring between the relay and the fusebox for continuity, referring to the relevant wiring diagram at the end of Chapter 8. If voltage is present, check that there is continuity to earth in the black/blue wire with the ignition switch OFF. If there is no continuity, check the wiring between the relay, each fan wiring connector, the fans, then back to the connectors and then in each green wire to earth. If all is good check the brown wire between the relay and the ECM (electronic control module). There should be continuity in all wires.

12 If the fan is on the whole time, pull the relay off its connector. The fan should stop.

3.3 Pull the boot back to access the instrument wiring connectors

If it does, the relay is defective and must be replaced with a new one.

13 If the fan works but is suspected of cutting in at the wrong temperature, check the ECT sensor (see Section 3).

3 Temperature display and ECT sensor

Temperature display

1 The circuit consists of the ECT sensor mounted in the thermostat housing and the digital display which is part of the instrument cluster LCD unit. When the ignition is first switched on all the digital display segments and modes should come on temporarily – this serves as an indication that the LCD is functioning correctly (if not, refer to Chap-

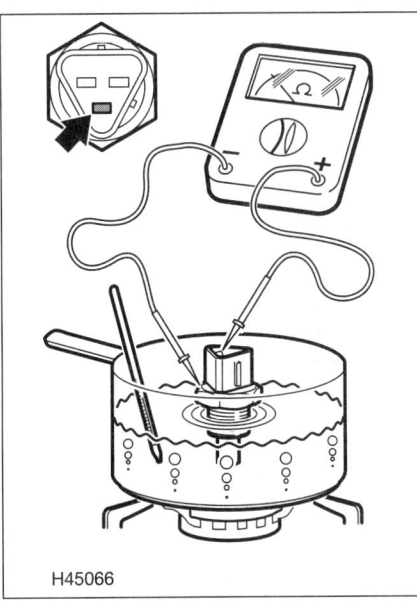

3.8 ECT sensor test set-up

ter 8). Under normal operating conditions, when the engine is up to temperature the display segments will lie between the C and H. Should coolant temperature get too high the H segment will start to flash. If this occurs stop the engine and check the coolant level in the reservoir (see *Pre-ride checks*).

2 If the LCD display as a whole works but the temperature display doesn't, remove the throttle bodies and rubber heat shield (see Chapter 4). Disconnect the ECT sensor wiring connector **(see illustration)**. Using a jump wire connect the green/blue wire terminal in the connector to earth. Turn the ignition ON – all the temperature gauge segments should come on.

3 If no segments come on remove the windshield and the inner screen cowl (see Chapter 7). Disconnect the instrument cluster 16-pin wiring connector **(see illustration)**. Check the green/blue wire for continuity between the ECT sensor and instrument cluster wiring connectors. If the wiring is good the instrument cluster could be faulty – refer to Chapter 8.

4 If the segments come on check the ECT sensor (see below).

5 If the temperature display works but is thought to be inaccurate, check the ECT sensor (see below).

ECT sensor

6 Drain the cooling system (see Chapter 1). Remove the throttle bodies and rubber heat shield (see Chapter 4). The sensor is mounted in the thermostat housing.

7 Disconnect the sensor wiring connector **(see illustration 3.2)**. Unscrew and remove the sensor, and discard the sealing washer.

8 Fill a small heatproof container with the specified coolant mix and place it on a stove. Using an ohmmeter, connect the positive (+) probe of the meter to the green/blue wire terminal on the sensor **(see illustration)**, and the negative (–) probe to the body of the sensor. Using some wire or other support suspend the sensor in the coolant so that just the sensing head up to the threads is submerged, and with the head a minimum of 40 mm above the bottom of the container. Also place a thermometer in the coolant so that its bulb is close to the sensor. **Note:** *None of the components should be allowed to directly touch the container.*

 Warning: This must be done very carefully to avoid the risk of personal injury.

9 Begin to heat the coolant, stirring it gently. When the temperature reaches around 80°C, turn the heat down and maintain the temperature steady for three minutes. The meter reading should be as specified at the beginning of the Chapter. Turn the heat on again. When the coolant reaches boiling point (around 102°C), again turn the heat down and maintain for three minutes. The resistance reading should have decreased to around 700 ohms if the sensor is functioning correctly.

Removal and installation

 Warning: The engine must be completely cool before carrying out this procedure.

10 Fit a new sealing washer onto the sensor. Fit the sensor and tighten it to the torque setting specified at the beginning of the Chapter. Connect the wiring.

11 Fit the rubber heat shield and install the throttle bodies (see Chapter 4). Refill the cooling system (see Chapter 1) and check the coolant level (see *Pre-ride checks*).

4 Thermostat and housing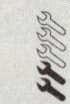

1 The thermostat is automatic in operation and should give many year's service without requiring attention. In the event of a failure, the valve will probably jam open, in which case the engine will take much longer than normal to warm up. Conversely, if the valve jams shut, the coolant will be unable to circulate and the engine will overheat. Neither condition is acceptable, and the fault must be investigated promptly.

Thermostat
Removal

 Warning: The engine must be completely cool before carrying out this procedure.

2 Drain the cooling system (see Chapter 1). Remove the radiator (see Section 5). The thermostat housing is on top of the engine at the front.

3 Unscrew the cover bolts and detach it from the housing, noting the earth wire terminal **(see illustration)**.

4 Withdraw the thermostat, noting how it fits **(see illustration)**.

5 Remove the O-ring from the cover and discard it – a new one must be used.

Check

6 Examine the thermostat visually before carrying out the test. If it remains in the open position at room temperature, it should be replaced with a new one.

7 Suspend the thermostat by a piece of wire in a container of cold water. Place a thermometer capable of reading temperatures up to 110°C in the water so that the bulb is close to the thermostat **(see illustration)**. Heat the water, noting the temperature when the thermostat opens, and compare the result with the specifications given at the beginning of the Chapter. Also check the amount the valve opens (lift) after it has been heated for a few minutes and compare the measurement to the specifications. If the readings obtained differ from those given, the thermostat is faulty and must be replaced with a new one.

8 In the event of thermostat failure, if the thermostat is permanently closed, as an emergency measure only it can be removed and the machine used without it (this is better than leaving it in as the engine will overheat). If it is permanently open you are better to leave it in. In both cases take care when starting the engine from cold as it will take much longer than usual to warm up. Ensure that a new unit is installed as soon as possible.

Installation

9 Fit the thermostat into the housing with the jiggle pin at the top and locating the rib in the groove **(see illustration)**.

10 Fit a new O-ring into the groove in the cover **(see illustration)**. Fit the cover and tighten the bolts, not forgetting the earth wire terminal **(see illustration)**.

11 Install the radiator (see Section 5). Refill the cooling system (see Chapter 1) and check the coolant level (see *Pre-ride checks*).

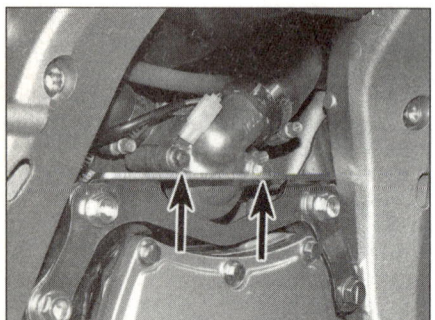

4.3 Unscrew the bolts (arrowed) and detach the cover . . .

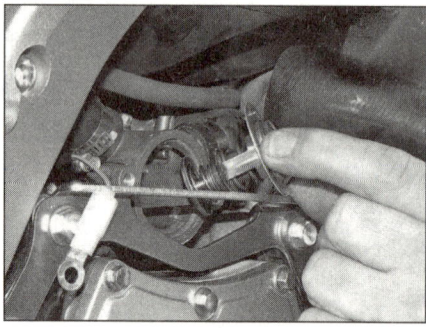

4.4 . . . then withdraw the thermostat from the housing

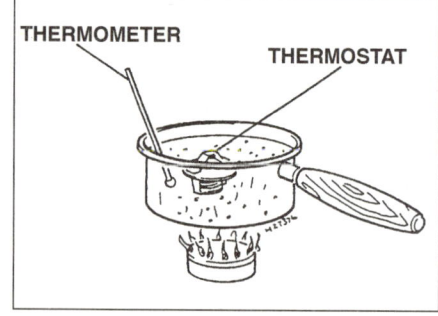

4.7 Thermostat testing set-up

4.9 Make sure the jiggle pin (arrowed) is at the top

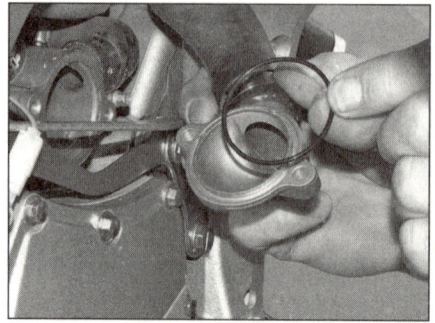

4.10a Fit a new O-ring into the groove . . .

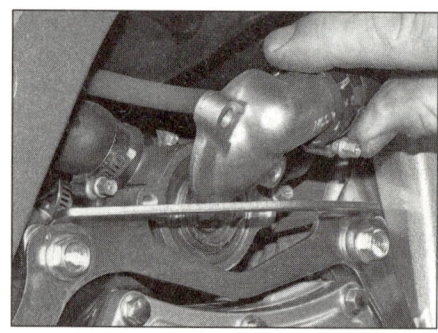

4.10b . . . then fit the cover

Cooling system 3•5

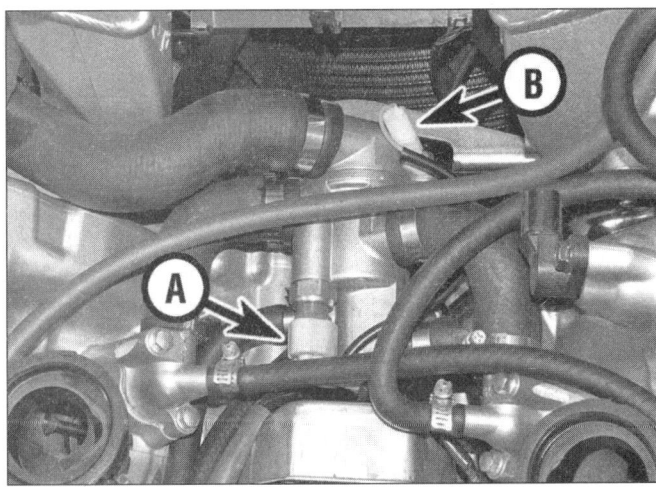

4.13 Disconnect the ECT sensor connector (A) and the earth connector (B)

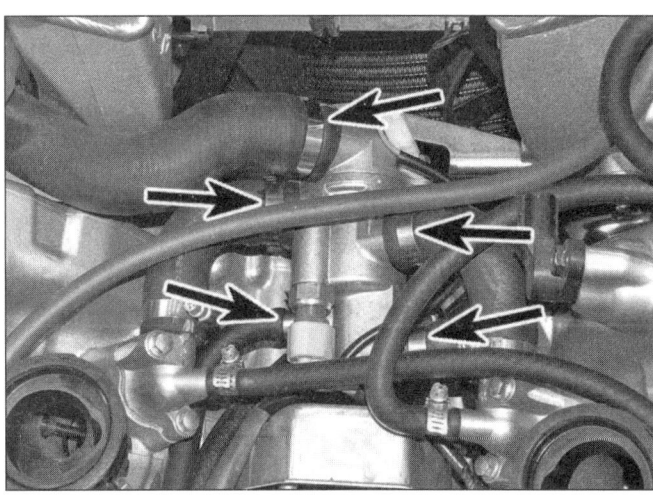

4.14 Slacken the clamps (arrowed) and detach the hoses then remove the housing

5.3a Detach the hoses (arrowed) from the right-hand side of the radiator . . .

5.3b . . . and from the left-hand side

Thermostat housing

Removal

 Warning: The engine must be completely cool before carrying out this procedure.

12 Drain the cooling system (see Chapter 1). Remove the throttle bodies and rubber heat shield (see Chapter 4). The thermostat housing is on top of the engine at the front.

13 Disconnect the ECT sensor and earth wiring connectors **(see illustration)**.

14 Slacken the clamps securing the hoses to the housing and detach them, noting which fits where **(see illustration)**. If you can't access a clamp screw lift or tilt the housing as required, and remember that you can use a spanner on the screw hex instead of a screwdriver. Alternatively detach the hose at its other end and remove the housing along with its hoses. Remove the housing.

Installation

15 Connect the hoses to their unions and tighten the clamps **(see illustration 4.14)**.

16 Connect the earth wire and ECT sensor wiring **(see illustration 4.13)**.

17 Fit the rubber heat shield and install the throttle bodies (see Chapter 4). Refill the cooling system (see Chapter 1) and check the coolant level (see Pre-ride checks).

5 Radiator

Note: If the radiator is being removed as part of the engine removal procedure, detach the hoses from their unions on the engine rather than on the radiator and remove the radiator complete with its hoses. Note the routing of the hoses.

Removal

 Warning: The engine must be completely cool before carrying out this procedure.

1 Drain the cooling system (see Chapter 1). Remove the fairing side panels (see Chapter 7).

2 Disconnect the fan wiring connectors **(see illustrations 2.2a and b)**.

3 Slacken the clamps securing the hoses to the radiator and detach them **(see illustrations)**.

4 Unscrew and remove the radiator lower mounting bolts with their washers **(see illustration)**. Unscrew the radiator upper mounting bolt. Ease the radiator out to the right to free the mounting lug from its grommet,

5.4a Unscrew the bolts (arrowed) . . .

3•6 Cooling system

5.4b ... then draw the radiator to the right to free the grommet from the lug (arrowed)

5.5 Check the condition of the grommets

6.3 Slacken the clamps (arrowed) and detach the hoses

then remove the radiator taking care not to catch the fins on anything **(see illustration)**.

5 Note the arrangement of the collars and rubber grommets in the radiator mounts **(see illustration)**. Replace the grommets with new ones if they are damaged, deformed or deteriorated.

6 Check the radiator for signs of damage and clear any dirt or debris that might obstruct air flow and inhibit cooling. If the radiator fins are badly damaged or broken the radiator must be replaced with a new one. To enable full examination and cleaning, remove the cooling fans from the radiator (see Section 2).

Installation

7 Installation is the reverse of removal, noting the following.

- Ensure the coolant hoses are in good condition (see Chapter 1), and are securely retained by their clamps, using new ones if necessary.
- Make sure the rubber grommets are in place.
- Make sure the collars are correctly fitted in the grommets **(see illustration 5.5)**.
- Make sure that the fan wiring is correctly connected.
- On completion refill the cooling system

as described in Chapter 1 and check the coolant level (see Pre-ride checks).

Pressure cap check

8 If problems such as overheating or loss of coolant occur, check the entire system as described in Chapter 1. The radiator cap opening pressure should be checked by a Honda dealer with the special tester required to do the job. If the cap is defective, replace it with a new one.

6 Water pump

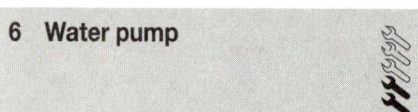

Check

1 Refer to Chapter 1, Section 9.

Removal

2 Drain the engine oil and coolant (see Chapter 1). Remove the radiator (see Section 5).

3 Slacken the clamps securing the coolant hoses to the unions on the pump cover and detach the hoses, noting which fits where **(see illustration)**.

4 Unscrew the pump cover bolts and

remove the cover **(see illustration)**. Remove the O-ring and discard it – a new one must be used. Remove the dowels if loose **(see illustration 6.15b)**.

5 Wiggle the water pump impeller back-and-forth and in-and-out **(see illustration)**. If there is excessive movement replace the seals and bearing with new ones (Steps 7 to 13).

6 On 2008-on models detach the drain hose from its union. On all models, unscrew the front crankcase cover bolts and remove the cover – draw it off square so the pump shaft comes out of the driven sprocket, rather than bringing the sprocket with it as it is engaged with the chain **(see illustration)**. Remove the coolant passage dowels and O-rings – discard the O-rings, new ones must be used **(see illustration 6.15a)**. Remove the locating dowels if loose **(see illustration 6.15c and d)**. Remove the gasket – a new one must be used.

Seal and bearing replacement

Note: *Honda specify the use of an hydraulic press for the removal of the pump shaft and the installation of all pump components – if an hydraulic press is not used there is a danger of damaging the front crankcase cover and bending the pump shaft. If you don't have*

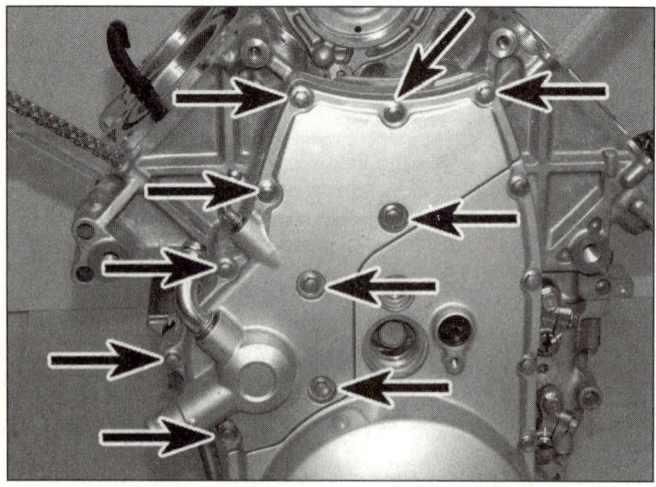

6.4 Unscrew the bolts (arrowed) and remove the cover

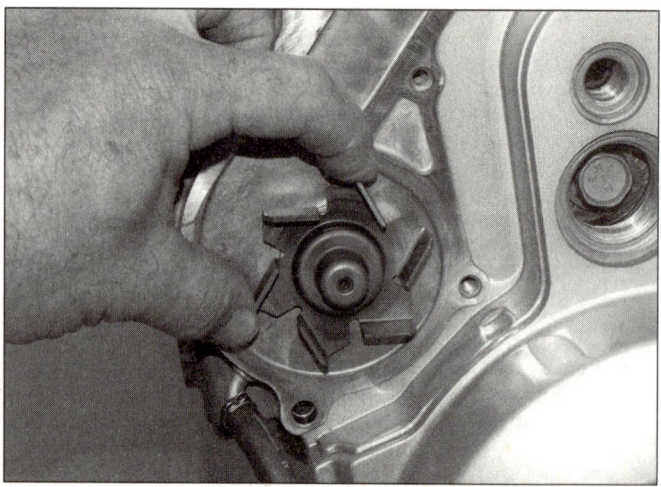

6.5 Check the pump impeller as described

Cooling system 3•7

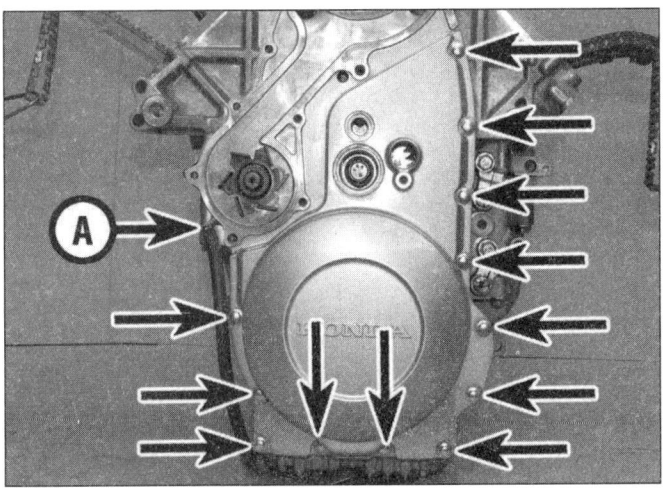

6.6 Crankcase cover bolts (arrowed) – on 2008-on models detach the hose from its union (A)

6.7 The pump shaft is a press-fit in the bearing

access to a press take the cover to a dealer and have them do it.

7 Press the water pump shaft/impeller out of the cover from the back using the hydraulic press **(see illustration)** – make sure the cover is supported around the pump housing with enough room below it.

8 Remove the bearing using an internal expanding puller with slide-hammer attachment.

9 Lever or drive the oil seal and the mechanical seal out.

10 Press the new mechanical seal in until it seats – make sure you press only on the outer seating rim of the seal.

11 Fit the new oil seal with its marked side facing out, and press it in until it seats.

12 Press the new bearing in until it seats – make sure you press only on the outer race of the bearing.

13 Support the bearing on its inner race and press the shaft and impeller in until there is exactly 24 mm of shaft protruding from the bearing – make sure you press only on the centre of the impeller or the blades could bend or break.

Installation

14 Clean all traces of old gasket off the crankcase and front cover mating surfaces –

if using a scraper take care not to gouge the surface. Clean any traces of glue or sealant from the O-ring groove in the pump cover.

15 Fit the coolant passage dowels and new O-rings **(see illustration)**. Fit the crankcase cover and pump cover locating dowels if removed **(see illustrations)**. Fit a new O-ring into the groove in the pump cover **(see illustration)**. Smear some sealant (Three Bond 1207B or equivalent RTV sealant – ask your dealer) over the crankcase joints **(see illustration)**. Fit a new gasket over the dowels **(see illustration)**.

16 Fit the front crankcase cover and the pump cover, making sure they locate correctly

6.15a Fit the dowels using new O-rings

6.15b Fit the crankcase cover upper dowel (arrowed) . . .

6.15c . . . and lower dowel (arrowed)

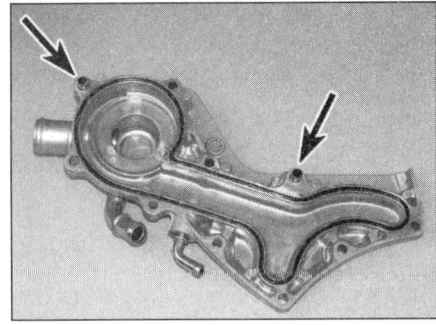

6.15d Fit the pump cover dowels (arrowed) and new O-ring

6.15e Smear some sealant over the crankcase joints (arrowed) . . .

6.15f . . . then fit the new gasket

3•8 Cooling system

6.16a Fit the crankcase cover . . .

6.16b . . . then fit the pump cover

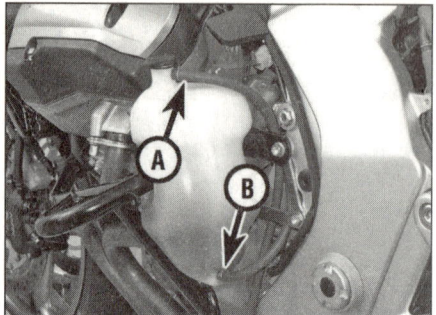

7.2a Detach the overflow hose (A) if required. Reservoir feed hose (B)

onto the dowels, and tighten the bolts evenly and a little at a time in a criss-cross sequence **(see illustrations)**.

17 Fit the coolant hoses onto the pump cover and secure them with their clamps **(see illustration 6.3)**. On 2008-on models fit the drain hose onto its union **(see illustration 6.4)**.

18 Install the radiator (see Section 5). Refill the cooling system and replenish the engine oil (see Chapter 1).

7 Coolant reservoir

Removal

1 The coolant reservoir is located on the left-hand side. Remove the left-hand fairing side panel (see Chapter 7). Get a suitable container to tip the coolant into.

2 If required disconnect the overflow hose from the top of the reservoir, otherwise note its routing and draw it out with the reservoir **(see illustration)**. Unscrew the reservoir mounting bolt and free the locating peg from the engine bar **(see illustrations)**.

3 Remove the reservoir filler cap and tip the coolant into the container. Disconnect the feed hose from the bottom of the reservoir **(see illustration 7.2a)**.

Installation

4 Installation is the reverse of removal. Make sure the peg on the bottom of the reservoir locates in its hole in the engine bar **(see illustration 7.2c)**. On completion refill the reservoir to the UPPER level line with the specified coolant mixture (see *Pre-ride checks*).

8 Coolant hoses and unions

Removal

1 Before removing a hose, drain the coolant (see Chapter 1).

2 Use a screwdriver to slacken the larger-bore hose clamps, then slide them back along the hose and clear of the union spigot. The smaller-bore hoses are secured by spring clamps which can be expanded by squeezing their ears together with pliers.

Caution: The radiator unions are fragile. Do not use excessive force when attempting to remove the hoses.

3 If a hose proves stubborn, release it by rotating it on its union before working it off. If all else fails, cut the hose with a sharp knife. Whilst this means replacing the hose with a new one – it is preferable to buying a new radiator.

4 The outlet unions from the engine are on the inner side of each cylinder head and can be removed by unscrewing their bolts **(see illustration)**. Note that they are marked L and R according to side. If the union is removed, the O-ring must be replaced with a new one.

Installation

5 Slide the clamps onto the hose and then work the hose on to its union as far as the spigot where present.

> **HAYNES HiNT**
> If the hose is difficult to push on its union, soften it by soaking it in very hot water, or alternatively a little soapy water on the union can be used as a lubricant.

6 Rotate the hose on its unions to settle it in position before sliding the clamps into place and tightening them securely.

7 If the outlet unions from the cylinder heads have been removed, fit a new O-ring into the groove in each union, using a dab of grease to hold it in place if necessary. Fit the union and tighten the bolts – make sure the union marked L is fitted on the left-hand head, and the one marked R is on the right.

8 Refill the cooling system with fresh coolant (see Chapter 1) and check the coolant level (see *Pre-ride checks*).

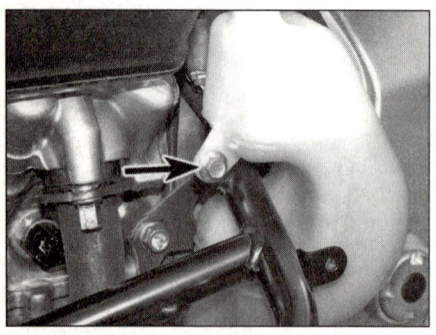

7.2b Unscrew the bolt (arrowed) . . .

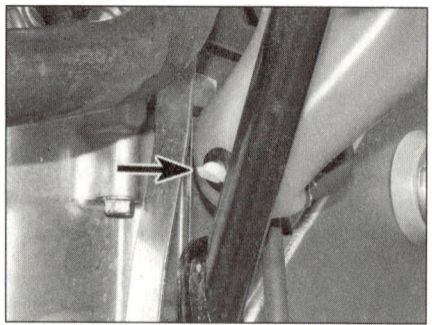

7.2c . . . and free the peg (arrowed)

8.4 Coolant outlet union bolts (arrowed)

Chapter 4
Engine management system

Contents

	Section		Section
Air filter	see Chapter 1	Fuel gauge and level sensor	13
Air filter housing	3	General information and precautions	1
Catalytic converters	19	Idle speed check	see Chapter 1
Clutch switch	see Chapter 8	Ignition coils	21
Evaporative emission control (EVAP) system	18	Ignition switch	see Chapter 8
Exhaust system	15	Ignition system check	20
Fast idle system wax unit	9	Ignition timing	22
Fuel injection system description	4	Immobiliser system	23
Fuel injection system fault diagnosis	5	Neutral switch	see Chapter 8
Fuel injection system components	6	Pulse secondary air (PAIR) system	17
Fuel pump and filter	12	Sidestand switch	see Chapter 8
Fuel pressure check	10	Spark plugs	see Chapter 1
Fuel pressure regulator	11	Starter valves	8
Fuel system check	see Chapter 1	Throttle bodies	7
Fuel system hoses	16	Throttle cable check and adjustment	see Chapter 1
Fuel tanks	2	Throttle cables	14

Degrees of difficulty

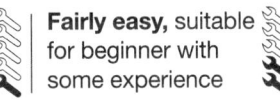

| **Easy,** suitable for novice with little experience | **Fairly easy,** suitable for beginner with some experience | **Fairly difficult,** suitable for competent DIY mechanic | **Difficult,** suitable for experienced DIY mechanic | **Very difficult,** suitable for expert DIY or professional |

Specifications

General information
Cylinder numbering .... No. 1 – front left; No. 2 – front right; No. 3 – rear left; No. 4 – rear right
Firing order 1-4-3-2
Spark plugs .... see Chapter 1

Fuel
Grade .... Unleaded. Minimum 95 RON (Research Octane Number) for Europe. Minimum pump octane number 91 for US

Fuel tank
  Capacity (including reserve) .... 29 litres
  Reserve volume .... approx. 5 litres

Fuel injection system
Idle speed .... 1000 ± 100 rpm
Starter valve synchronisation – max. difference between bodies ..... 20 mm Hg
Manifold absolute pressure at idle .... 200 to 250 mm Hg
Fuel pressure at specified idle speed* .... 50 psi (3.5 Bar)
Minimum fuel flow rate .... 180 cc every 10 seconds

*Fuel pressure regulator vacuum hose disconnected and plugged

Fuel injection system test data

Camshaft position (CMP) sensor
    Resistance . . . . 480 to 510 ohms @ 20°C
    Minimum peak voltage output . . . . 0.7 volts
Crankshaft position (CKP) sensor
    Resistance . . . . 480 to 510 ohms @ 20°C
    Minimum peak voltage output . . . . 0.7 volts
Engine coolant temperature (ECT) sensor resistance . . . . 2.1 to 2.6 K-ohms @ 20°C
Fuel injector resistance. . . . . 11.1 to 12.3 ohms @ 20°C
Intake air temperature (IAT) sensor resistance . . . . 1 to 4 K-ohms @ 20 to 30°C
Oxygen sensor heater resistance. . . . . 10 to 40 ohms @ 20°C

Fuel level sensor

Resistance
    FULL position. . . . . 1 to 6 ohms
    Empty position . . . . 213 to 219 ohms

Emission control systems

PAIR system control valve resistance . . . . 20 to 24 ohms @ 20°C
EVAP system control valve resistance . . . . 30 to 34 ohms @ 20°C

Ignition HT coils

Primary winding resistance . . . . approximately 2.8 ohms @ 20°C
Secondary winding resistance
    With plug caps . . . . approximately 32 K-ohms @ 20°C
    Without plug caps . . . . approximately 22 K-ohms @ 20°C
Plug cap resistance . . . . approximately 5 K-ohms
Initial voltage (see text). . . . . Battery voltage (approximately 12 volts)
Minimum peak voltage (see text) . . . . 100 volts

Torque settings

Crankshaft position (CKP) sensor bolts . . . . 12 Nm
Exhaust header pipe nuts. . . . . 17 Nm
Silencer clamp bolts
    2002 to 2007 models . . . . 22 Nm
    2008-on models . . . . 18 Nm
Fast idle system wax unit mounting screws. . . . . 5 Nm
Fuel pressure regulator nut. . . . . 27 Nm
Fuel pump assembly mounting plate nuts . . . . 12 Nm
Fuel rail bolts . . . . 10 Nm
Fuel hose
    Banjo bolt-to-secondary fuel tank . . . . 22 Nm
    Banjo union nut-to-fuel rail . . . . 22 Nm
Knock sensors . . . . 31 Nm
Oxygen sensors . . . . 25 Nm
Rear sub-frame
    Upper mounting bolt nuts. . . . . 39 Nm
    Lower mounting bolts. . . . . 42 Nm
Starter valve base nuts. . . . . 2 Nm
Timing inspection cap . . . . 10 Nm

1 General information and precautions

General information

Fuel system

The fuel supply system consists of the main and secondary fuel tanks, the fuel pump with integral filter, the fuel hoses, the fuel rails, the pressure regulator, the fuel injectors, the throttle bodies, and the throttle cables. The fuel pump is housed inside the secondary fuel tank. The fuel pump is switched on and off via a relay. The engine management system, known as PGM-FI, supplies fuel and air to the engine via 36 mm throttle bodies. The injectors are mounted in the throttle bodies below the throttle valve. The injectors are operated by the Engine Control Module (ECM) using the information obtained from the various sensors it monitors (refer to Section 4 for more information on the operation of the fuel injection system).

All models have a digital fuel gauge incorporated in the instrument cluster LCD, actuated by a level sensor inside the main fuel tank. When the ignition is first switched on all the digital display segments and modes should come on temporarily – this serves as an indication that the LCD is functioning correctly (if not, refer to Chapter 8). There is also a low fuel warning switch incorporated in the fuel pump assembly in the secondary tank that makes the E segment on the gauge flash when there is approximately 1 Imp gallon (1.3 US gallons) or 5 litres of fuel left.

Ignition system

The transistorised electronic ignition system is combined with the fuel injection system, both being controlled by the ECM (engine control module). The ignition system comprises a crankshaft position sensor (CKP sensor), knock sensors, the engine control module (ECM), the ignition coils and the spark plugs. There are two conventional coils, one for each cylinder pair, operating on the 'wasted spark' principal.

Engine management system 4•3

The triggers on the timing rotor (mounted on the front end of the crankshaft) generate a signal in the CKP sensor as the crankshaft rotates. The CKP sensor sends that signal to the ECM which, in conjunction with information received from the throttle position sensor, engine coolant temperature sensor and knock sensors, calculates the ignition timing and supplies the ignition coils with the power necessary to produce a spark at the plugs. There is no provision for checking or adjusting the ignition timing.

The system incorporates a safety interlock circuit which will cut the ignition if the sidestand is extended whilst the engine is running and in gear, or if a gear is selected whilst the engine is running and the sidestand is down. It also prevents the engine from being started if the sidestand is down and the engine is in gear. The engine can be started with the sidestand up when it is in gear as long as the clutch lever is pulled in.

All models are fitted with an immobiliser system (HISS – Honda Ignition Security System) which will not allow the engine to be started unless the correct key is used. The immobiliser system has its own fault diagnosis function.

Note that there is no provision for adjusting the ignition timing on these models.

Note: *Individual engine management system components can be checked but not repaired. If system troubles occur, and the faulty component can be isolated, the only cure for the problem in most cases is to replace the part with a new one. Keep in mind that most electronic parts, once purchased, cannot be returned. To avoid unnecessary expense, make very sure the faulty component has been positively identified before buying a new part.*

Precautions

Warning: Petrol (gasoline) is extremely flammable, so take extra precautions when you work on any part of the fuel system. Always remove the battery (see Chapter 8). Don't smoke or allow open flames or bare light bulbs near the work area, and don't work in a garage where a natural gas-type appliance is present. If you spill any fuel on your skin, rinse it off immediately with soap and water. When you perform any kind of work on the fuel system, wear safety glasses and have a fire extinguisher suitable for a class B type fire (flammable liquids) on hand.

It is vital that no dirt or debris is allowed to enter the fuel tank or the fuel rail assembly whilst the fuel hoses are disconnected. Any foreign matter in the fuel system components could result in injector damage or malfunction. Ensure the ignition is switched OFF before disconnecting or reconnecting any fuel injection system wiring connector. If a connector is disconnected or reconnected with the ignition switched ON, the engine control module (ECM) may be damaged.

Always perform service procedures in a well-ventilated area to prevent a build-up of fumes.

Never work in a building containing a gas appliance with a pilot light, or any other form of naked flame. Ensure that there are no naked light bulbs or any sources of flame or sparks nearby.

Do not smoke (or allow anyone else to smoke) while in the vicinity of petrol (gasoline) or of components containing it. Remember the possible presence of vapour from these sources and move well clear before smoking.

Check all electrical equipment belonging to the house, garage or workshop where work is being undertaken (see the Safety first! section of this manual). Remember that certain electrical appliances such as drills, cutters etc, create sparks in the normal course of operation and must not be used near petrol (gasoline) or any component containing it. Again, remember the possible presence of fumes before using electrical equipment.

Always mop up any spilt fuel and safely dispose of the rag used.

Any stored fuel that is drained off during servicing work must be kept in sealed containers that are suitable for holding petrol (gasoline), and clearly marked as such; the containers themselves should be kept in a safe place. Note that this last point applies equally to the fuel tank if it is removed from the machine; also remember to keep its filler cap closed at all times.

Read the *Safety first!* section of this manual carefully before starting work.

2 Fuel tanks

Warning: Refer to the precautions given in Section 1 before starting work.

Main fuel tank

Raise

1 Make sure the fuel cap is secure. Remove the rider's seat (see Chapter 7). Set the seat height adjuster to its rear position **(see illustration)**.
2 Disconnect the battery negative (–) lead (see Chapter 8).
3 Slacken the nut on the tank pivot bolt **(see illustration)**. Unscrew the tank front mounting bolts, noting the washers **(see illustration)**. Pull the tank back so the pivot bolt is at the rear of its track in the bracket **(see illustration)**.
4 Remove the blanking cap from one of the handlebar bolts **(see illustration)**. Remove the

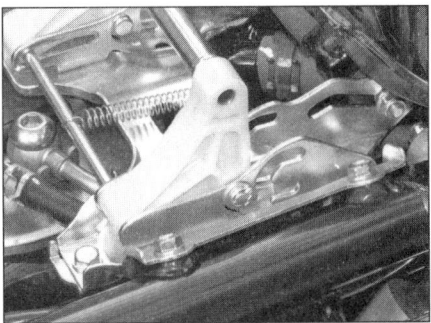

2.1 Slide the adjuster back to its rear position

2.3a Slacken the nut (arrowed) . . .

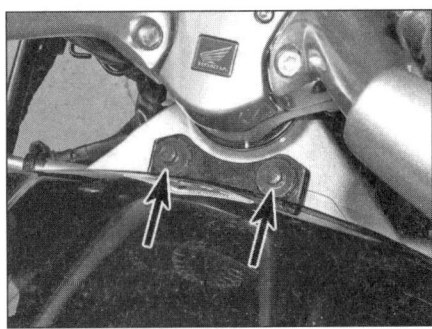

2.3b . . . then unscrew the bolts (arrowed) . . .

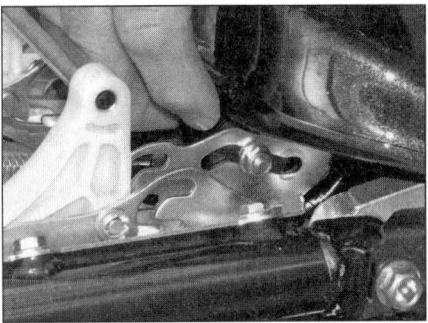

2.3c . . . and pull the tank back to its rearmost position in the bracket

2.4a Remove one of the blanking caps

4•4 Engine management system

2.4b Remove the tank prop (arrowed) . . .

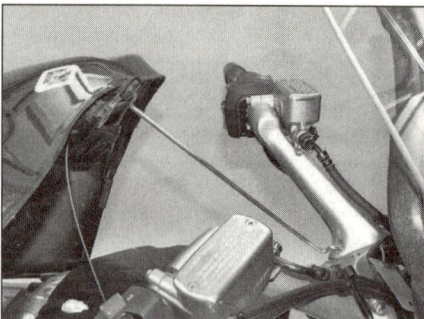

2.4c . . . and support the tank as described

2.5 Using a pump to empty the main tank

tank prop from its clips **(see illustration)**. Lift the front of the tank and place the bottom end of the support in the handlebar bolt head and the top in one of the tank bolt holes **(see illustration)** – take care that the front mounting rubber collars do not drop out as they fit from the underside.

2.7 Unscrew the nut (arrowed) and detach the cable

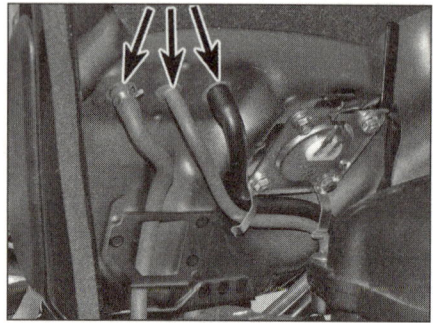

2.8 Detach the hoses (arrowed) and free them from the guides

Removal

Note: *Before removing the tank it must have **all** the fuel pumped or siphoned from it – this is because of the joint hose between the main and secondary tank. Alternatively make sure the tank is only removed when the last digital segment on the fuel gauge is flashing – at this point the main tank will be empty.*

5 To empty the main tank, pump the fuel from it using a commercially available fuel pump suitable for petrol (gasoline) and store it in a suitable container **(see illustration)**.

6 Raise the tank as described above. Remove the left-hand side cover (see Chapter 7).

7 Unscrew the nut securing the retaining cable to the tank and detach the cable **(see illustration)**.

8 Detach the overflow and breather hoses **(see illustration)**. Release the air vent hose clamp and detach the hose. Free all hoses from their guides.

9 Disconnect the level sensor wiring connector **(see illustration)**.

10 Remove the support and lower the tank. Remove the rear bolt **(see illustration)**. Unscrew the seat height adjuster bracket bolts and remove the adjuster/bracket assembly **(see illustration)**.

11 Release the fuel joint hose clamp and detach the hose from the union on the secondary tank, being prepared with some rag to catch any remaining fuel **(see illustration)**.

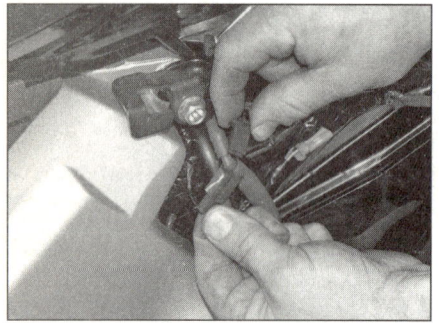

2.9 Disconnect the wiring connector

2.10a Withdraw the rear bolt . . .

2.10b . . . then unscrew the bolts (arrowed) and remove the bracket

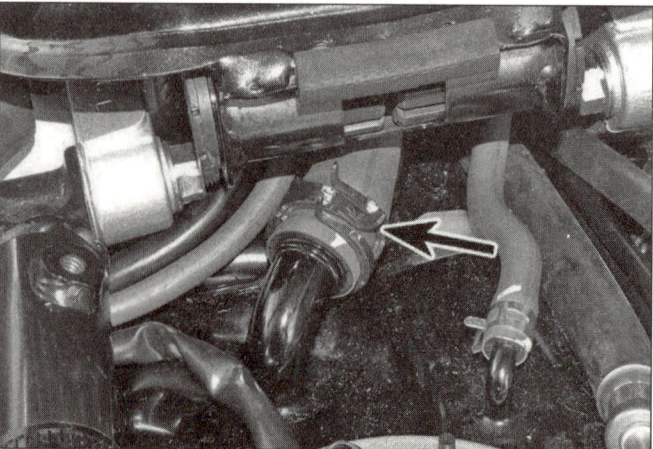

2.11 Release the clamp (arrowed) and detach the hose

Engine management system

2.12a Carefully remove the tank

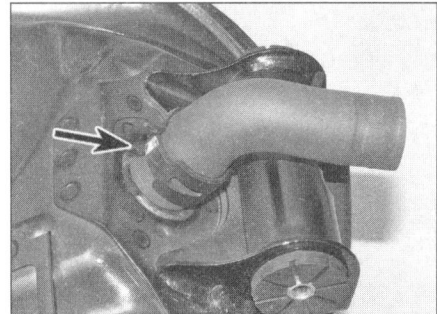

2.12b Release the clamp (arrowed) and detach the hose

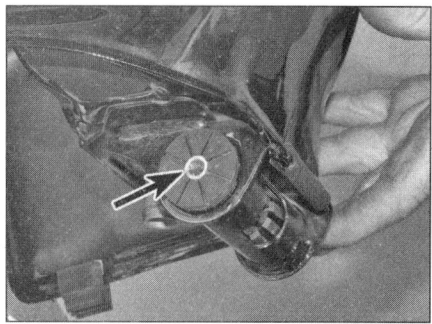

2.13 Note the sleeve (arrowed) for the bolt in the rear rubbers

Note that Honda specify that a new fuel joint hose and clamps should be fitted every time the hose is disconnected.

12 Carefully lift the tank off the frame and remove it **(see illustration)**. Release the fuel joint hose clamp and detach the hose from the union on the tank **(see illustration)**.

13 Check all the tank rubbers and hoses for signs of damage or deterioration and replace them with new ones if necessary. Note the collars for the front mounting rubbers **(see illustration 2.7)**, and the sleeve in the rear rubbers **(see illustration)**.

Installation

14 Make sure all support and mounting rubbers and their collars and sleeve are fitted **(see illustration 2.7 and 2.13)**.

15 Slide new clamps onto the new fuel joint hose – note that on 2002 to 2008 models the hose is wider at one end and this end fits onto the main tank union and is secured by the larger of the two clamps. On later models the shorter section of the L-shaped hose fits onto the main tank union **(see illustration 2.12b)**. The clamps come pre-expanded with a clip over the clamp ends – once the hose and clamp are correctly in position pull the clip off and the clamp will contract to secure the hose. Fit the new fuel joint hose onto its union on the main tank and secure it with a new clamp as described. Position the tank on the frame and connect the joint hose to the secondary tank using a new clamp **(see illustrations)**.

16 Fit the seat height adjuster/bracket and tighten the bolts **(see illustration)**. Insert the pivot bolt and tighten the nut finger-tight **(see illustration 2.10a)**. Raise and support the tank as before.

17 Connect the fuel level sensor wiring connector **(see illustration 2.9)**.

18 Route the air vent hose through its guide, then connect it and secure it with the clamp **(see illustration 2.8)**. Connect the overflow and breather hoses and secure them with the tie. Make sure all the hoses are secure.

19 Fit the retainer cable **(see illustration 2.7)**. Remove the prop and pivot the tank down onto the frame, making sure the hoses do not get squashed or kinked and are correctly positioned

2.15a Seat the tank and fit the hose onto its union . . .

2.15b . . . then remove the clip from the clamp

in relation to the level sensor wiring connector **(see illustration)**. Make sure the front mounting rubbers and collars are in place. Fit bolts and washers **(see illustration 2.3b)**. Tighten the rear pivot bolt nut **(see illustration 2.3a)**. Fit the blanking cap into the handlebar bolt **(see illustration 2.4a)**.

20 Start the engine and check that there is no sign of fuel leakage.

Secondary fuel tank

Removal

Note: *Refer to the Note above for the main tank. The secondary tank can be siphoned via the fuel hose union as long as the tube on your pump fits in and is flexible.*

2.16 Fit the seat adjuster/bracket

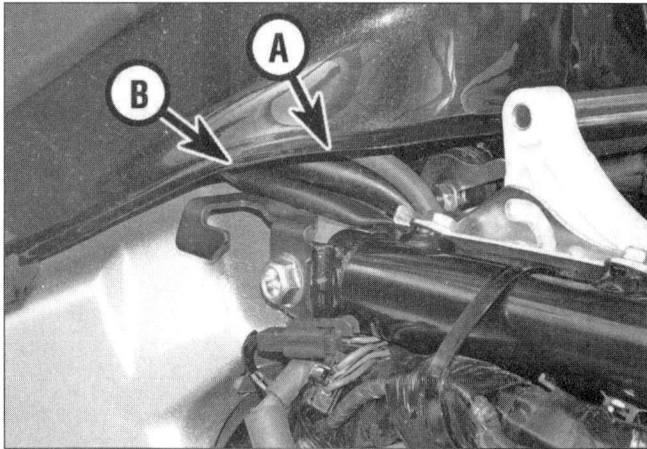

2.19 Make sure the hose (A) and wiring (B) are correctly routed

4•6 Engine management system

2.21a Fuel cut-off relay (arrowed)

2.21b Connect across the two larger terminal sockets in the connector using a jumper wire as shown

2.25 Displace the relays from their mounts

21 Remove the main tank (see Steps 5 to 12). Drain the secondary tank using a pump inserted in the fuel joint hose union. Alternatively, make sure the ignition is OFF, then remove the left-hand side cover (see Chapter 7), displace the fuel cut-off relay and disconnect the wiring connector **(see illustration)**. Prepare a short jumper wire with suitable spade terminals to fit into the connector terminals **(see illustration)**. Detach the fuel return hose from the pump and place the end into a suitable container – be prepared with some rag to catch any residual fuel. Turn the ignition switch ON – the pump will run and fuel will flow from the hose into the container.

22 Remove the rear wheel (see Chapter 6).
23 Remove the battery (see Chapter 8).
24 Remove the panniers and their holders, the rear mudguard, and the rear cowl (see Chapter 7).
25 Displace the relays from the upper rear mudguard **(see illustration)**.
26 Unscrew the bolt in the battery tray and manoeuvre the mudguard out **(see illustration)**.
27 Disconnect the sidestand switch (2-pin green) and fuel pump (3-pin black) wiring connectors **(see illustration)**. Release all wiring ties from the rear sub-frame.
28 Unscrew the rear shock absorber reservoir bracket bolt **(see illustration)**.
29 Displace the starter relay from the rear sub-frame **(see illustration)**.
30 On models with ABS unscrew the rear modulator bolts **(see illustration)** – support the modulator so no strain is placed on the pipes.
31 Unscrew the secondary fuel tank rear mounting bolts **(see illustration)** – note the collars in the grommets and remove them for safekeeping if loose.
32 Unscrew the rear sub-frame lower mounting bolts **(see illustration)**.

2.26 Unscrew the bolt (arrowed)

2.27 Disconnect the wiring connectors (arrowed)

2.28 Unscrew the bolt (arrowed)

2.29 Displace the relay from its mount

2.30 Unscrew the ABS modulator bolts (arrowed)

2.31 Unscrew the tank rear bolts (arrowed)

2.32 Unscrew the sub-frame bolts (arrowed) on each side

Engine management system

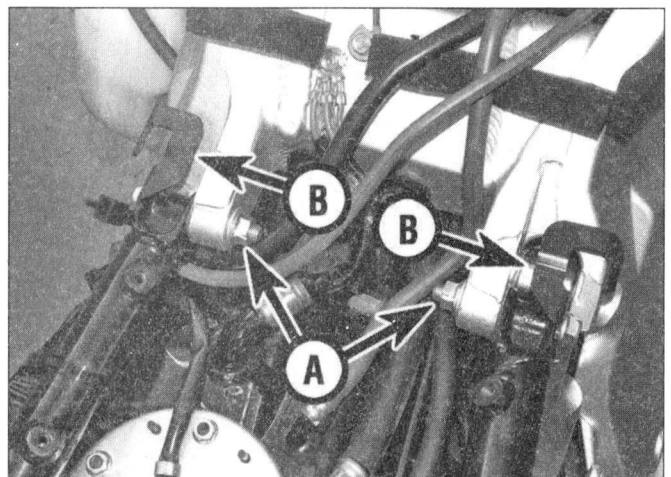

2.33 Unscrew the nuts (A), then withdraw the bolts and remove the seat plates (B) and sub-frame

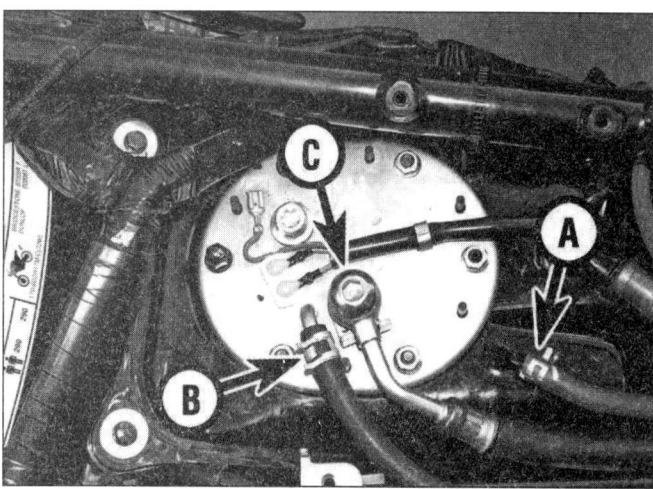

2.34 Detach the air vent hose (A) and fuel return hose (B). Fuel supply hose (C)

33 Unscrew the nuts on the upper mounting bolts **(see illustration)**. Withdraw the bolts and remove the seat plates, noting how they fit, then remove the rear sub-frame.

34 Release the air vent hose clamp, and if not already done to drain the tank the fuel return hose clamp, and detach the hose(s) **(see illustration)**.

35 Place a wad of rag for catching the residual fuel under the fuel supply hose union on the top of the pump, then slacken the banjo bolt **(see illustration 2.34)**. At this point some fuel will come out, so be ready with the rag to catch it. Unscrew the bolt and detach the hose, noting its alignment. Discard the sealing washers as new ones must be used.

36 Support the tank, then unscrew the front mounting bolts, noting the washers, and carefully lift the tank away **(see illustration)** – note the collars in the grommets and remove them for safekeeping if loose.

37 Check the tank rubbers for signs of damage or deterioration and replace them with new ones if necessary.

Installation

38 Installation is the reverse of removal, noting the following:

- Make sure the collars are fitted in the tank mounting rubbers – the front mounting collars fit in from the front, the rear collars from the top.
- Fit the fuel supply hose elbow between the lugs on the fuel pump mounting plate **(see illustration 2.34)**. Fit a new sealing washer on each side of the union and tighten the banjo bolt at the beginning of the Chapter.
- Tighten the rear sub-frame bolts to the specified torque settings – make sure the seat plates are correctly fitted with the upper bolts **(see illustration 2.33)**.
- Make sure the air vent and fuel return hoses are securely connected and held by their clamps.
- Make sure the fuel pump and sidestand switch wiring connectors are securely connected **(see illustration 2.27)**.
- Start the engine and check that there is no sign of fuel leakage.

Fuel tank repair

39 Any repair to either fuel tank should be carried out by a professional who has experience in this critical and potentially dangerous work. Even after cleaning and flushing of the fuel system, explosive fumes can remain and ignite during repair of the tank.

40 If the fuel tank is removed from the bike, it should not be placed in an area where sparks or open flames could ignite the fumes coming out of the tank. Be especially careful inside garages where a natural gas-type appliance is located, because the pilot light could cause an explosion.

3 Air filter housing

Removal

1 Raise or remove the main fuel tank as required (see Section 2).

2 Remove the air filter (see Chapter 1).

3 Bend the air funnel retaining plate tabs up, then undo the screws and remove the funnels, noting their alignment and which fits where **(see illustrations)**. Note that Honda specify to use new retaining plates, but as long as the tabs are not fractured you can re-use them.

2.36 Unscrew the front bolts (arrowed) and remove the tank

3.3a Bend the tabs up . . .

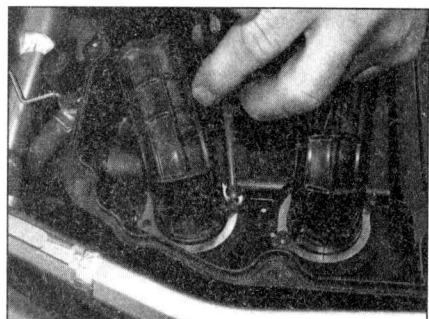

3.3b . . . then undo the screws and remove the funnels

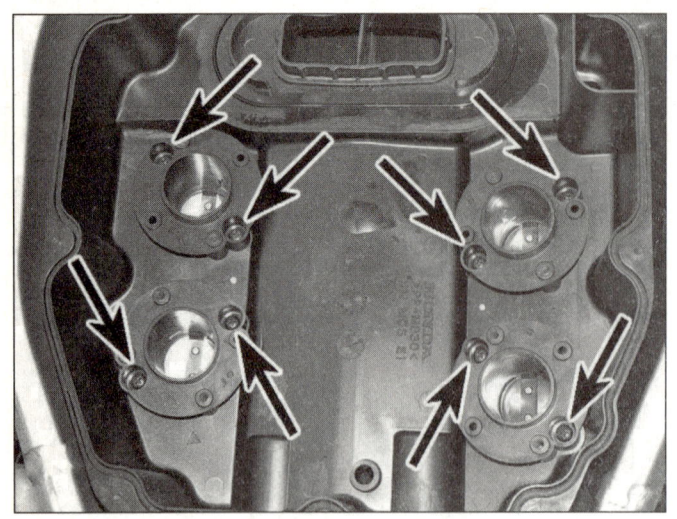
3.4a Undo the screws (arrowed) . . .

3.4b . . . and remove the funnel bases

3.5a Lift the housing and detach the PAIR hose . . .

3.5b . . . and the crankcase breather hose (arrowed)

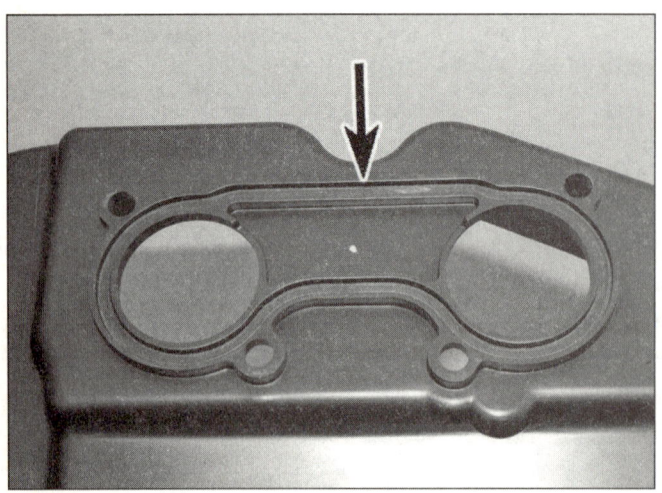
3.6a Check the throttle body seals

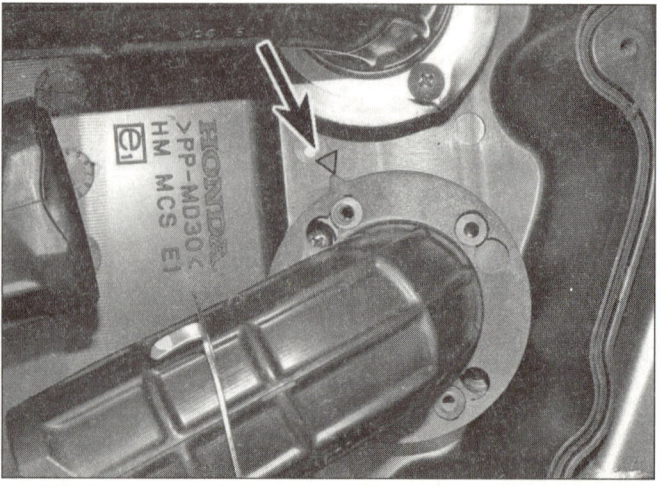
3.6b Make sure the funnels align with reference mark (arrowed) and seat correctly

Engine management system 4•9

4 Undo the funnel base screws and remove the bases **(see illustrations)**.

5 Lift the housing up off the throttle bodies and disconnect the PAIR system supply hose and crankcase breather hose, and release the breather hose from its guide **(see illustrations)**. Remove the air filter housing. Cover the throttle bodies with a clean rag.

Installation

6 Installation is the reverse of removal, noting the following:
- Check the condition of the throttle body seals in the underside of the housing and make sure they are in their groove **(see illustration)** – they are not listed as available separately from the housing.
- Check the condition of the PAIR and crankcase breather hoses and their clamps and use new ones if they are in any way damaged or deteriorated.
- Align the pointer on each funnel flange with the triangular mark on the housing, and make sure the holes locate correctly over the posts on the base allowing the flange to seat **(see illustration)**. Bend the tabs down over the screws.

4 Fuel injection system description

1 All models are equipped with Honda's programmed fuel injection (PGM-FI) system. It is controlled by a management system with an engine control module (ECM) that operates both the injection and ignition systems.

2 The engine control module (ECM) monitors signals from the following sensors.
- Throttle position (TP) sensor – informs the ECM of the throttle position, and the rate of throttle opening or closing.
- Engine coolant temperature (ECT) sensor – informs the ECM of engine temperature. It also actuates the temperature display (see Chapter 3).
- Manifold absolute pressure (MAP) sensor – informs the ECM of the engine load by monitoring the pressure in the throttle body intake tracts.
- Intake air temperature (IAT) sensor – informs the ECM of the temperature of the air entering the throttle body.
- Camshaft position (CMP) sensor – informs the ECM of engine speed and camshaft position.
- Crankshaft position (CKP) sensor – informs the ECM of engine speed and crankshaft position.
- Speed sensor – informs the ECM of the motorcycle's road speed (see Chapter 8).
- Oxygen sensors – informs the ECM of the oxygen content of the exhaust gases in each downpipe assembly.
- Knock sensors – detects and informs the ECM of detonation in each cylinder pair.
- Lean angle sensor – cuts the ignition and fuel pump if the bike falls over.

3 All the information from the sensors is analysed by the ECM, and from that it determines the appropriate ignition and fuelling requirements of the engine. The ECM controls each fuel injector by varying its pulse width – the length of time the injector is held open – to provide more or less fuel, as appropriate for cold starting, warm up, idle, cruising, and acceleration. The injection system is fully sequential, with each injector receiving its own signal from the ECM. The injectors are mounted in the throttle bodies below the throttle valve.

4 Cold starting and warm up idle speeds are controlled by an 'automatic fast idle system', which basically takes the place of a manual choke lever. A heat sensitive wax-filled unit that has engine coolant circulating around it actuates the starter valve arrangement in the throttle body assembly via a linkage rod. When the coolant is cold the wax unit is contracted and the starter valves are open. As the coolant heats up the wax expands, closing the starter valves. The starter valves allow additional air to bypass the throttle valves when the throttle is closed, and this increases the engine idle speed.

5 If there is an abnormality in any of the readings obtained from any sensor, the ECM enters its back-up mode. In this event, the ECM ignores the abnormal sensor signal, and assumes a pre-programmed value which will allow the engine to continue running (albeit at reduced efficiency). If the ECM enters this back-up mode, or when any faults occur, the fuel injection system (FI) warning light in the instrument cluster will come on or flash (depending on circumstances), and the relevant fault code will be stored in the ECM memory. The fault can be identified using the fault codes which can be accessed using the self-diagnosis function (see Section 5). However if there are certain faults detected in the injectors or the cam or crankshaft position sensors, the back-up mode becomes ineffective and the ECM will not allow the engine to run at all.

6 All models have an immobiliser system (HISS – Honda Ignition Security System) which will not allow the engine to be started unless the correct key is used. A fault in this system should not be confused with a fuel injection system fault. The immobiliser system has its own warning light and fault diagnosis function (see Section 23).

5 Fuel injection system fault diagnosis

1 If the fuel injection system (FI) warning light on the instrument cluster illuminates when the motorcycle is running, a fault has occurred in the fuel injection/ignition system. The engine control module (ECM) will store the relevant fault code in its memory and this code can be read as follows using the self-diagnostic mode of the ECM. While the engine is running above 5000 rpm and the motorcycle is being ridden, the lights will come on and stay on. When the motorcycle is on its sidestand and the engine

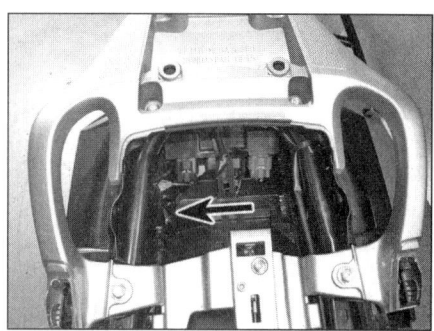

5.4 Data link connector (arrowed)

is running below 5000 rpm, the light will flash, the pattern of the flashes indicating the code for the fault the ECM has identified.

2 If the engine can be started, place the motorcycle on its sidestand then start the engine and allow it to idle. Whilst the engine is idling, observe the FI warning light on the instrument cluster.

3 If the engine cannot be started, place the motorcycle on its sidestand. With the kill switch in the run position turn the engine over on the starter motor for more than ten seconds and observe the FI warning light on the instrument cluster.

4 Alternatively, and to check for any stored fault codes even though the warning lights have not illuminated, remove the passenger seat (see Chapter 7) to gain access to the fuel injection system data link connector (DLC), which is a 4-pin connector coming out of the wiring loom **(see illustration)**. Ensure the ignition is switched OFF. On European models connect between the brown and green/pink wire terminals in the connector using a short jumper wire. On US and Canada models fit the Honda SCS service connector (Part No. 070PZ-ZY30100, available at reasonable cost from your dealer), following the instructions supplied with it, or seeking advice from your dealer as to its connection. With the terminals connected, make sure the kill switch is in the RUN position then turn the ignition ON and observe the FI warning light. If there are no stored fault codes, the light will come on and stay on. If there are stored fault codes, the light will flash.

5 The warning light emits long (1.3 second) and short (0.5 second) flashes to give out the fault code. A long flash is used to indicate the first digit of a double digit fault code (i.e. 10 and above). If a single digit fault code is being displayed (i.e. 0 – 9), there will be a number of short flashes equivalent to the code being displayed. For example, two long (1.3 sec) flashes followed by five short (0.5 sec) flashes indicates the fault code number 25. If there is more than one fault code, there will be a gap before the other codes are revealed (the codes will be revealed in order, starting with the lowest and finishing with the highest). Once all codes have been revealed, the ECM will continuously run through the code(s) stored in its memory, revealing each one in turn with a short gap between them. The fault codes are shown in the table overleaf.

4•10 Engine management system

Fault code (No. of flashes)	Symptoms	Possible causes
0 – no code; warning light off	Engine does not start	Blown fuse (PGM-FI 30A fuse or Starter/ignition 10A fuse)
		Faulty power supply to or from electronic control module (ECM)
		Faulty engine stop relay or wiring
		Faulty engine stop switch or wiring
		Faulty ignition switch
		Faulty lean angle sensor or wiring
		Faulty electronic control module (ECM)
0 – no code; warning light off	Engine runs normally	Open or short circuit in FI warning light wiring / Faulty electronic control module (ECM)
0 – no code; warning light constantly on	Engine runs normally	Short circuit in data link connector or wiring / Faulty electronic control module (ECM)
1	Engine runs normally	Faulty manifold absolute pressure (MAP) sensor or wiring
2	Engine runs normally	Faulty manifold absolute pressure (MAP) sensor or vacuum hose disconnected/broken
7	Engine difficult to start at low temperatures	Faulty engine coolant temperature (ECT) sensor or wiring
8	Poor throttle response	Faulty throttle position (TP) sensor or wiring
9	Engine runs normally	Faulty intake air temperature (IAT) sensor or wiring
11	Engine runs normally	Faulty speed sensor or wiring
12	Engine does not start	Faulty No. 1 injector or wiring
13	Engine does not start	Faulty No. 2 injector or wiring
14	Engine does not start	Faulty No. 3 injector or wiring
15	Engine does not start	Faulty No. 4 injector or wiring
18	Engine does not start	Faulty camshaft position (CMP) sensor or wiring
19	Engine does not start	Faulty crankshaft position (CKP) sensor or wiring
21	Engine operates normally	Faulty oxygen sensor or wiring for cylinders 1 and 3 exhaust
22	Engine operates normally	Faulty oxygen sensor or wiring for cylinders 2 and 4 exhaust
23	Engine operates normally	Faulty oxygen sensor heating element for cylinders 1 and 3 exhaust
24	Engine operates normally	Faulty oxygen sensor heating element for cylinders 2 and 4 exhaust
25	Engine operates normally	Faulty left cylinder knock sensor or wiring
26	Engine does not start	Faulty right cylinder knock sensor or wiring
33 (2002 to 2007 models)	Engine operates normally / No fault codes stored	Faulty ECM EPROM

Once all the codes have been revealed, switch off the ignition and (where necessary) remove the auxiliary wire or SCS connector from the data link connector. Identify the fault using the table above, then refer below for checking procedures.

6 Once the fault has been identified and corrected, it will be necessary to reset the system by removing the fault code from the ECM memory. To do this, ensure the ignition is switched OFF, then on Europe models bridge the brown and green/pink wire terminals of the data link connector (DLC) and on US and Canada models fit the Honda SCS service connector or (see Step 4). Make sure the kill switch is in the RUN position, then turn the ignition switch ON. Disconnect the auxiliary wire or tool from the DLC. When the wire is disconnected the warning light should come on for about five seconds, during which time the auxiliary wire must be reconnected. The light should start to flash when it is reconnected, indicating that all fault codes have been erased. However if the light flashes twenty times the memory has not been erased and the procedure must be repeated. Turn off the ignition then remove the auxiliary wire. Check the FI warning light (in some cases it may be necessary to repeat the erasing procedure more than once).

7 If a fault appears, use the diagnostic function and fault code system described above to work out which component is faulty. First ensure that the relevant system wiring connectors are securely connected and free of corrosion – poor connections are the cause of the majority of problems. Also check the wiring itself for any obvious faults or breaks, and use a continuity tester to check the wiring between the component, its connectors and the ECM, referring to the wiring diagrams at the end of Chapter 8. Next refer to Section 6 to see if there are any other specific checks that can be made on that particular component using home equipment. If this fails to reveal the cause of the problem, the motorcycle should be taken to a Honda dealer for testing. They will have the special tools which should locate the fault quickly and simply.

8 Also ensure that the fault is not due to poor maintenance – i.e. check that the air filter element is clean, that the spark plugs are in good condition, that the valve clearances are correctly adjusted, the cylinder compression pressures are correct, and the ignition timing is correct (refer to Chapters 1 and 2, and to Section 22). It is also worth removing the sensor(s) in question (see Section 6) and checking that the sensing tip or head is clean and not obstructed by anything. Where there is a vacuum hose to a sensor, make sure it is securely connected at both ends and has no cracks or splits.

6 Fuel injection system components

Caution: Ensure the ignition is switched OFF before disconnecting/reconnecting any fuel injection system wiring connector. If a connector is disconnected/reconnected with the ignition switched ON the engine control module (ECM) could be damaged.

Engine management system 4•11

6.3 Disconnect the wiring connector . . .

6.4 . . . and check the resistance between the terminals

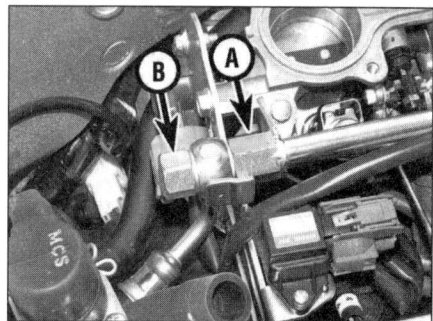

6.8 Counter-hold the hex (A) while unscrewing the nut (B)

Fuel rails and injectors

⚠ **Warning:** *Refer to the precautions given in Section 1 before starting work.*

Check

1 Raise the fuel tank (see Section 2).
2 If the engine runs, start it and allow it to idle. Check the operation of each primary injector in the throttle bodies using a stethoscope or sounding rod held against it; an injector will emit a 'clicking' noise when functioning. If any injector is silent, either the injector or its wiring harness is faulty.
3 If the engine does not run, remove the air filter housing (see Section 3). Disconnect the wiring connector from the injector **(see illustration)** – displace the MAP sensor for better access to the adjacent injectors if required **(see illustration 6.9)**.
4 Connect an ohmmeter between the injector terminals and measure the resistance **(see illustration)**. Compare the reading for the injector to that given in the Specifications. If the resistance differs greatly replace the injector with a new one.
5 Check that there is no continuity to earth on the black/white wire terminal on the injector. If there is, replace the injector with a new one.
6 Check for battery voltage at the black/white wire terminal in the wiring connector with the ignition ON. If there is no voltage, check the wiring between the injector and the lean angle sensor, then check the sensor. Check for continuity in the other wire to the ECM connector.

Removal

7 Remove the air filter housing (see Section 3). If required, remove the throttle bodies (see Section 7) – this is not essential, but will improve access.
8 If the throttle bodies have not been removed, counter-hold the hex on the fuel supply hose joint and unscrew the banjo union nut, noting the alignment of the hose and being prepared to catch any residual fuel with a rag **(see illustration)**. Detach the hose and discard the sealing washers – new ones must be used. Also release the fuel return hose clamp and detach the hose from the pressure regulator **(see illustration 11.2)**.
9 Detach the vacuum hose from the pressure regulator **(see illustration 11.2)**. Undo the MAP sensor screw and displace the sensor **(see illustration)**.

10 Make a note of which connector fits onto which injector – they are numbered according to the cylinder they feed for identification. Disconnect the wiring connector from each injector **(see illustration 6.3)**.
11 Unscrew the fuel rail bolts **(see illustration)**. Carefully lift off the fuel rail assembly and injectors, separating the rails at one end of the joint pipe to ease removal **(see illustration)**. Detach the joint pipe from the other rail if required. Remove the O-rings from the injector nozzles and joint pipe **(see illustration 6.13)**. Discard them as new ones must be used.
12 If required remove the injector retaining plates and pull the injectors from the fuel rail **(see illustrations)**. Remove the O-rings and discard them – new ones must be used.

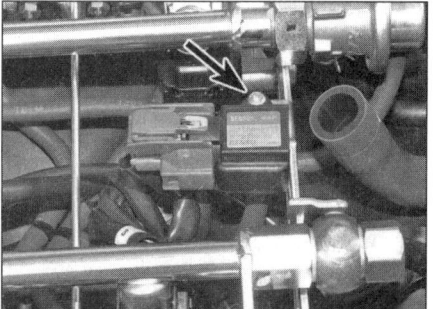

6.9 Undo the screw (arrowed) and displace the MAP sensor

6.11a Unscrew the bolts (arrowed) . . .

6.11b . . . then lift and separate the rails

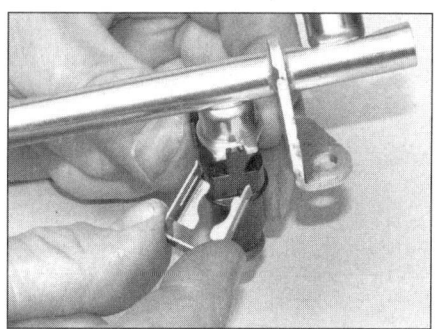

6.12a Slide the retaining plate out . . .

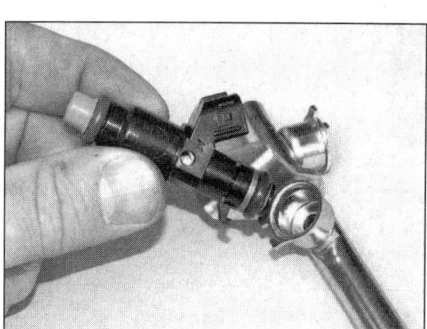

6.12b . . . and remove the injector

4•12 Engine management system

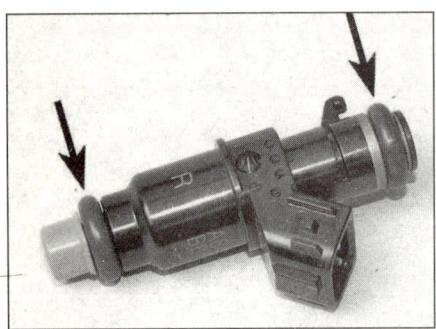

6.13 Replace the injector O-rings (arrowed) with new ones

6.19a Fit the inner sealing washer (arrowed) and the banjo union . . .

6.19b . . . followed by the outer sealing washer (arrowed) and the nut . . .

Installation

13 If the injectors have been removed from their rail, fit a new O-ring lubricated with clean engine oil into the groove in the top of each injector **(see illustration)**. Fit a new O-ring lubricated with clean engine oil into the groove above each injector nozzle. Note that the O-rings are slightly different in size and are identified by their colour – the black O-ring goes into the top of the injector and the brown ring goes next to the nozzle.

14 Align the injector so the tab will seat between the lugs and ease it into the rail, taking care not to damage the O-rings **(see illustration 6.12b)**. Fit the retaining plate **(see illustration 6.12a)**.

15 Fit new O-rings lubricated with clean engine oil onto the joint pipe and ease one end into one rail only at this stage **(see illustration 6.11b)**.

16 Fit the fuel rail assembly, joining the rail with the joint pipe, making sure each injector enters its seat and the O-rings stay in place and locate correctly **(see illustration 6.11b)**. Fit the fuel rail bolts and tighten them to the torque setting specified at the beginning of the Chapter **(see illustration 6.11a)**.

17 Reconnect the injector wiring connectors – make sure they are correctly connected according to the cylinder numbers noted on removal **(see illustration 6.3)**.

18 Fit the MAP sensor **(see illustration 6.9)**. Connect the vacuum hose to the pressure regulator **(see illustration 11.2)**.

19 If the throttle bodies have not been removed, fit a new fuel hose banjo union sealing washer onto the rail, then fit the hose, then the second new sealing washer, then fit the nut and tighten it to the specified torque setting, making sure you counter-hold the hex on the fuel rail, and butt the fuel hose elbow against the stopper **(see illustrations)**. Connect the fuel return hose to the pressure regulator and secure it with the clamp **(see illustration 11.2)**.

20 Install the throttle bodies if removed (see Section 7). Install the air filter housing (see Section 3). Run the engine and check that the fuel system is working correctly before taking the machine out on the road.

Throttle position (TP) sensor

Check

21 Raise the fuel tank (see Section 2). Disconnect the wiring connector from the sensor **(see illustration)**. Connect the positive (+) lead of a voltmeter to the yellow/red terminal of the sensor wiring connector, then connect the negative (–) lead to a good earth. Turn the ignition switch ON and check that a voltage of 4.75 to 5.25 volts is present. If it isn't, there is a fault in the yellow/red wire or the ECM. If voltage was present, now connect the negative lead to the green/orange wire terminal of the connector and check that the same voltage is present. If it isn't, there is a fault in the green/orange wire or the ECM. If there is voltage, check for continuity to the ECM in the light green wire. If all the wiring is good have the sensor output voltage checked by a Honda dealer. If that is good, then the ECM is faulty.

Removal and installation

22 The throttle sensor is an integral part of the throttle body assembly and is not available separately **(see illustration)**. If the sensor is faulty, a complete new throttle body assembly will have to be installed, though it is worth checking with your Honda parts specialist whether anything can be done to avoid this.

Engine coolant temperature (ECT) sensor

Note: *The sensor also operates the coolant temperature display – refer to Chapter 3 to check this aspect of its function.*

Check

23 Remove the throttle bodies and rubber heat shield (See Section 7). The sensor is mounted in the thermostat housing on the top of the engine **(see illustration)**.

6.19c . . . then hold the hex and tighten the nut to the specified torque

6.21 Disconnect the throttle position sensor wiring connector (arrowed)

6.22 The TP sensor (arrowed) is an integral part of the throttle body assembly

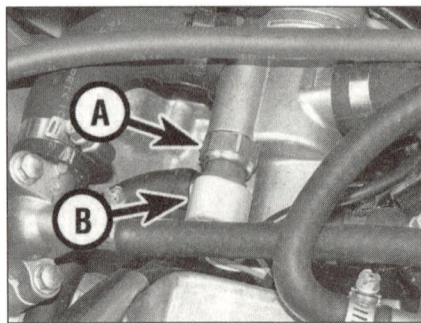

6.23 ECT sensor (A) and its wiring connector (B)

Engine management system 4•13

6.27 MAP sensor vacuum hose arrangement (arrowed) viewed from the underside

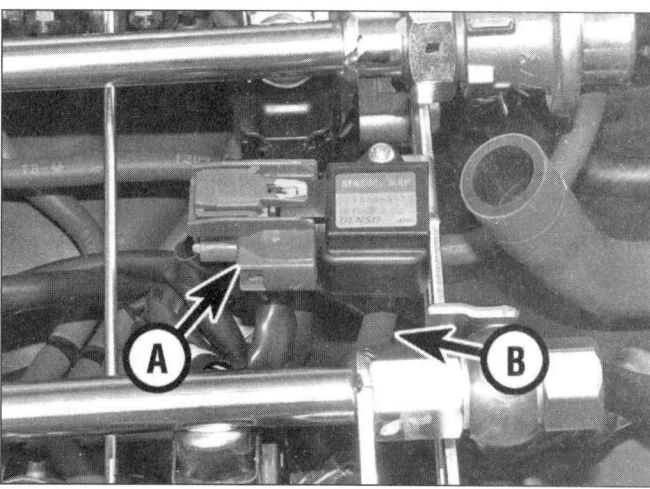

6.30 MAP sensor wiring connector (A) and vacuum hose (B)

24 Disconnect the wiring connector from the sensor. With the engine cold, connect an ohmmeter between the yellow/blue and green/orange wire terminals on the sensor and measure its resistance. Compare the reading obtained to that given in the Specifications, noting that the specified value is valid at 20°C (68°F); the sensor resistance will increase at lower temperatures and decrease at higher temperatures. If the resistance reading differs greatly from that specified, the sensor is probably faulty.

25 If the sensor appears to be functioning correctly, check its power supply. Connect the positive (+) lead of a voltmeter to the yellow/blue wire terminal in the sensor wiring connector, then connect the negative (–) lead to a good earth. Turn the ignition switch ON and check that a voltage of 4.75 to 5.25 volts is present. If it isn't, there is a fault in the yellow/blue wire or the ECM. If voltage was present, now connect the negative lead to the green/orange terminal of the connector and check that the same voltage is present. If it isn't, there is a fault in the green/orange wire or the ECM. If there is voltage, the ECM is probably faulty.

Removal and installation

 Warning: The engine must be completely cool before carrying out this procedure.

26 see Chapter 3, Section 3.

Manifold absolute pressure (MAP) sensor

Check

27 The MAP sensor is mounted on the throttle bodies **(see illustration 6.30)**. Remove the air filter housing (see Section 3). Make sure that the vacuum hoses to it are securely fixed at both ends, and have no cracks or splits **(see illustration)**. If the necessary equipment is available, connect a vacuum gauge into the hose between the throttle bodies and the MAP sensor using an auxiliary three-way joint and some rubber hose, and with the engine idling check that the manifold absolute pressure is as specified at the beginning of the Chapter. If not, replace all the vacuum hoses with new ones. If the pressure is out of specification with new or good hoses, check for leaks between the air filter housing, the throttle bodies and the cylinder head.

28 Connect the positive (+) lead of a voltmeter to the yellow/red terminal of the sensor wiring connector **(see illustration 6.30)**, then connect the negative (–) lead to a good earth. Turn the ignition switch ON and set the kill switch to RUN and check that a voltage of 4.75 to 5.25 volts is present. If it isn't, there is a fault in the yellow/red wire or the ECM. Similarly check for the same voltage between the yellow/red and green/orange wire terminals of the connector. If there is voltage, check for continuity to the ECM in the light green/white wire. If there is, trace the fault in the wire and repair it. If all the wiring is good have the sensor output voltage checked by a Honda dealer. If that is good, then the ECM is faulty.

Removal and installation

29 Remove the air filter housing (see Section 3).

30 Disconnect the wiring connector and detach the vacuum hose from the sensor **(see**

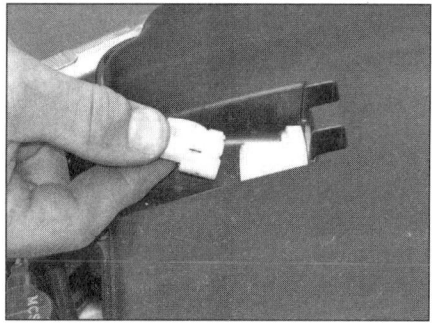

6.32 Disconnect the IAT sensor wiring connector

illustration). Undo the screw and remove the sensor **(see illustration 6.9)**.

31 Installation is the reverse of removal.

Intake air temperature (IAT) sensor

Check

32 Raise the fuel tank (see Section 2). The sensor is mounted in the top of the air filter housing cover. Disconnect its wiring connector **(see illustration)**.

33 With the sensor cold, connect an ohmmeter across the sensor terminals and measure its resistance. Compare the reading obtained to that given in the Specifications noting that the specified value is valid between 20 to 30°C (68 to 86°F); the sensor resistance will increase at lower temperatures and decrease at higher temperatures. If the resistance reading differs greatly from that specified, the sensor is probably faulty.

34 If the sensor appears to be functioning correctly, check its power supply. Connect the positive (+) lead of a voltmeter to the grey/blue terminal of the sensor wiring connector, then connect the negative (–) lead to a good earth. Turn the ignition switch ON and check that a voltage of 4.75 to 5.25 volts is present. If it isn't, there is a fault in the grey/blue wire or the ECM. If voltage was present, now connect

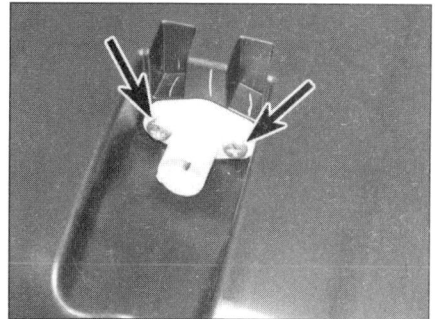

6.37 IAT sensor screws (arrowed)

4•14 Engine management system

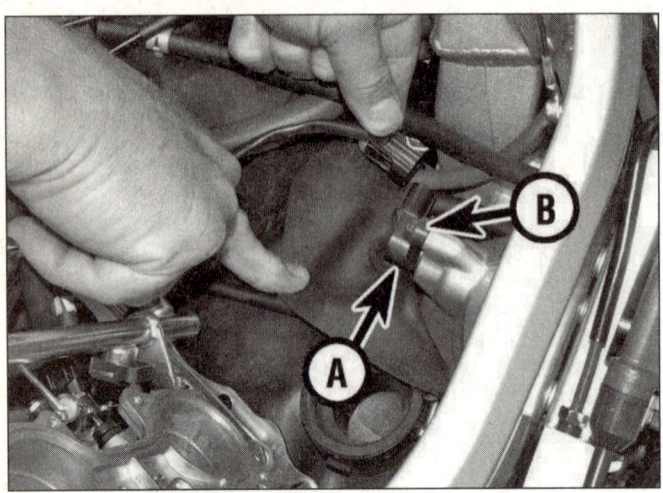

6.40 Lift the heat shield to access the sensor (A) and disconnect its wiring connector. Sensor mounting bolt (B)

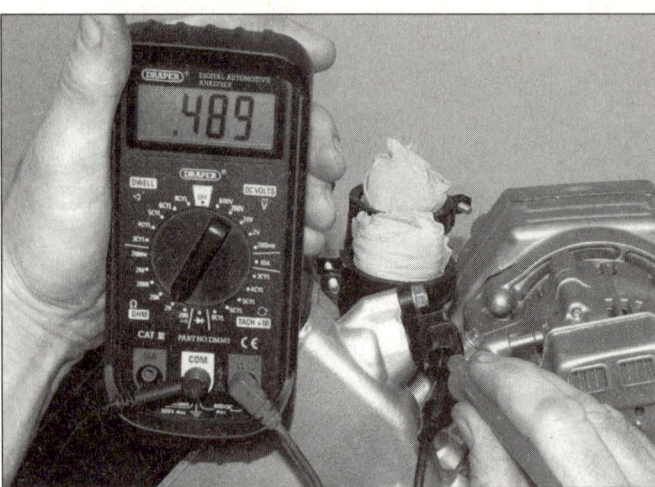

6.41 Checking CMP sensor resistance

the negative lead to the green/orange terminal of the connector and check that the same voltage is present. If it isn't, there is a fault in the green/orange wire or the ECM. If all the wiring is good have the sensor output voltage checked by a Honda dealer. If that is good, then the ECM is faulty.

Removal and installation

35 Raise the fuel tank (see Section 2). The sensor is mounted in the top of the air filter housing cover.
36 Disconnect the sensor wiring connector **(see illustration 6.32)**.
37 Undo the screws securing the sensor and remove it **(see illustration)**.
38 Installation is the reverse of removal.

Camshaft position (CMP) sensor

Check

39 Remove the air filter housing (see Section 3).
40 The sensor is on the right-hand cylinder head at the front. Lift the front right-hand corner of the rubber heat shield and disconnect the sensor wiring connector. **(see illustration)**. Perform the following check(s).
41 Using an ohmmeter check for continuity between the white/yellow wire terminal on the sensor and earth (ground). If there is continuity the sensor is faulty. Measure the resistance of the sensor by connecting the meter, set to the ohms x 100 scale, to the terminals and compare the reading to that specified at the beginning of the chapter **(see illustration)**. If the value obtained differs greatly or is zero or infinity the sensor is faulty.
42 Connect the positive (+) lead of a voltmeter and peak voltage adapter arrangement* to the grey wire terminal on the sensor and the negative (–) lead to the white/yellow wire terminal. Turn the engine over on the starter motor and note the voltage reading obtained. If this reading is below the specified minimum, the sensor is faulty.
*Note: *Honda specify their own peak voltage adapter (Pt. No. 07HGJ-0020100) with an aftermarket digital multimeter having an impedance of 10 M-ohm/DCV minimum for this test.*
43 If the sensor functions correctly check both wires to the ECM for continuity. If the wiring is good the ECM could be faulty.

Removal and installation

44 Remove the air filter housing (see Section 3).
45 The sensor is on the right-hand cylinder head at the front. Lift the front right-hand corner of the rubber heat shield and disconnect the sensor wiring connector **(see illustration 6.40)**.
46 Unscrew the bolt securing the sensor and draw it out of the head. Discard the O-ring.
47 Clean the sensor tip and fit a new O-ring smeared with oil into the groove in the sensor body **(see illustration)**. Fit the sensor into the cylinder head and tighten the bolt.
48 Reconnect the wiring connector. Install the air filter housing (see Section 3).

Crankshaft position (CKP) sensor

Check

49 Remove the centre section of the fairing side panels (see Chapter 7).
50 The sensor is on the front of the engine. Disconnect the wiring connector **(see illustration)**. Perform the following check(s).
51 Using an ohmmeter check for continuity between the white/yellow wire terminal on the sensor and earth (ground). If there is continuity the sensor is faulty. Measure the resistance of the sensor by connecting the meter, set to the ohms x 100 scale, to the terminals and compare the reading to that specified at the beginning of the chapter **(see illustration)**. If the value obtained differs greatly or is zero or infinity the sensor is faulty.
52 Connect the positive (+) lead of a voltmeter and peak voltage adapter arrangement* to

6.47 Fit a new O-ring into the groove (arrowed)

6.50 Disconnect the CKP sensor wiring connector

6.51 Checking CKP sensor resistance

Engine management system 4•15

6.56 Unscrew the bolt (arrowed) and remove the CKP sensor

6.61 Lean angle sensor wiring connector (arrowed)

6.65 Fit the sensor (arrowed) the correct way up and round

the yellow wire terminal on the sensor and the negative (–) lead to the white/yellow wire terminal. Turn the engine over on the starter motor and note the voltage reading obtained. If this reading is below the specified minimum, the sensor is faulty.

Note: Honda specify their own peak voltage adapter (Pt. No. 07HGJ-0020100) with an aftermarket digital multimeter having an impedance of 10 M-ohm/DCV minimum for this test.

53 If the sensor functions correctly check both wires to the ECM for continuity, noting that there is a 2-pin connector in the loom running along the right-hand side of the rear sub-frame – if there is no continuity in either of the wires check the connector for loose or broken wires or terminals. If the wiring is good the ECM could be faulty.

Removal and installation

54 Remove the centre section of the fairing side panels (see Chapter 7).
55 The sensor is on the front of the engine. Disconnect the wiring connector **(see illustration 6.50)**.
56 Unscrew the bolt securing the sensor and draw it out of the head **(see illustration)**. Discard the O-ring.
57 Clean the sensor tip and fit a new O-ring smeared with oil into the groove in the sensor body **(see illustration 6.47)**. Fit the sensor into the cylinder head and tighten the bolt.

58 Reconnect the wiring connector. Install the fairing panels (see Chapter 7).

Speed sensor

59 See Chapter 8, Section 16.

Lean angle sensor

Check

60 Position the motorcycle on an auxiliary stand so it is level. Remove the fairing (see Chapter 7) – the procedure involves displacing the lean angle sensor from it **(see illustration 6.65)**.
61 With the ignition switch ON and the kill switch set to run, connect the negative (–) lead of a voltmeter to the green wire terminal of the lean angle sensor connector (with the connector still connected) **(see illustration)**. Connect the voltmeter positive (+) lead first to the white/black wire terminal and check that battery voltage (approximately 12 volts) is present, then connect it to the red/orange wire terminal and check that between 0 to 1 volt is present.
62 Hold the sensor horizontal and switch the ignition ON; the engine stop relay (behind the left-hand side cover – see illustration 6.67) should click, indicating the power supply is closed (on). Slowly tilt the sensor to the left whilst listening to the engine stop relay; once the sensor reaches an angle of approximately 60° the relay should be heard to click,

indicating the power supply is open (off). Switch the ignition OFF and return the sensor to the horizontal, then switch the ignition back ON again (engine stop relay should click again) and tilt the sensor to the right. The engine stop relay should be heard to click again once the sensor reaches an angle of around 60°.
63 If the voltage readings and/or relay performance are not as given, then it is likely the lean angle sensor is faulty.

Removal and installation

64 Remove the fairing – the procedure involves displacing the lean angle sensor from it. Disconnect the wiring connector and remove the sensor.
65 Installation is the reverse of removal. Make sure the sensor is fitted with its UP mark facing upwards and with the wiring facing back **(see illustration)**.

Engine stop relay

66 Remove the left-hand side cover (see Chapter 7).
67 Displace the relay and disconnect the wiring connector **(see illustration)**.
68 Set a multimeter to the ohms x 1 scale and connect it across the relay's A and B (black/pink and black/white wire) terminals **(see illustration)**. There should be no continuity (infinite resistance). Using a fully-charged 12 volt battery and two insulated jumper wires, connect the positive (+) terminal of the battery

6.67 Engine stop relay (arrowed)

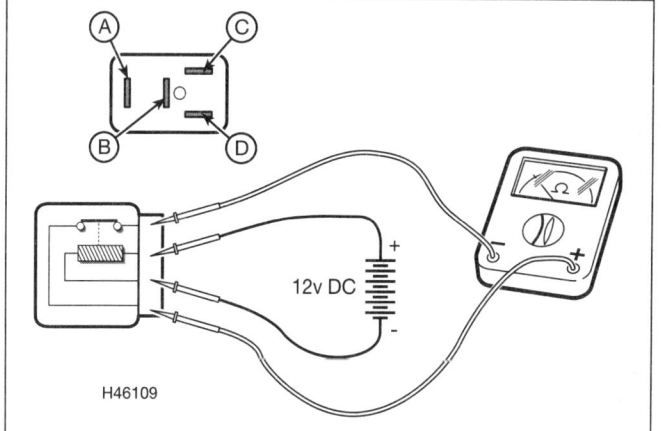

6.68 Engine stop relay terminal identification and test set-up

6.71 Fuel cut-off relay (arrowed)

6.76 ECM (arrowed)

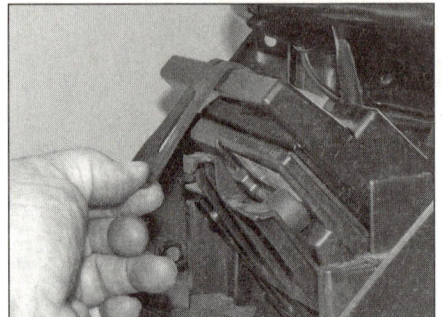

6.77a Release the strap . . .

to the C (black wire) terminal on the relay, and the negative (–) terminal to the D (red/orange wire) terminal on the relay. At this point the relay should be heard to click and the multimeter read 0 ohms (continuity). If this is the case the relay is proved good. If the relay does not click when battery voltage is applied and still indicates no continuity (infinite resistance) across its terminals, it is faulty and must be replaced with a new one.

69 Installation is the reverse of removal.

Fuel cut-off relay

70 Remove the left-hand side cover (see Chapter 7).
71 Displace the relay and disconnect the wiring connector **(see illustration)**.
72 Set a multimeter to the ohms x 1 scale and connect it across the relay's A and B (brown and adjacent black/white wire) terminals **(see illustration 6.68)**. There should be no continuity (infinite resistance). Using a fully-charged 12 volt battery and two insulated jumper wires, connect the positive (+) terminal of the battery to the C (black/white wire) terminal on the relay, and the negative (–) terminal to the D (brown/black wire) terminal on the relay. At this point the relay should be heard to click and the multimeter read 0 ohms (continuity). If this is the case the relay is proved good. If the relay does not click when battery voltage is applied and still indicates no continuity (infinite resistance) across its terminals, it is faulty and must be replaced with a new one.
73 Installation is the reverse of removal.

Engine control module (ECM)

Check

74 The engine control module (ECM) itself cannot be checked, but a process of elimination of other possible faulty components can point to it being faulty. The only other thing you can do is to disconnect the ECM wiring connectors (see Steps 75 to 77) and check for loose or broken terminal pins in the connectors or ECM sockets, then check for continuity in each wire to/from the ECM and to its related component or connector, or to earth (ground) as appropriate, according to the wiring diagram for you model at the end of Chapter 8, and referring to Electrical System Fault Finding at the beginning of Chapter 8 – start with the wires to/from the engine stop relay, fuel cut-off relay and lean angle sensor, and the green/pink, green/blue, and green/orange (where fitted, and not confusing it with the same colour wire to the knock and ECT sensors) wires to earth (ground). If any wire does not shown continuity check the connectors and terminals in the circuit before assuming there is a break in the wire.

Removal and installation

75 Make sure the ignition is OFF.
76 Remove the rear cowl (see Chapter 7). On models with ABS the ECM is the rear of the two control modules **(see illustration)**.
77 Release the rubber strap **(see illustration)**. Lift the ECM and disconnect the wiring connectors **(see illustration)**.
78 Installation is the reverse of removal.

Oxygen sensors

Check

79 There is a sensor for each pair of cylinders and their exhaust system. Apart from the wiring checks that are outlined in Section 5, the operation of the oxygen sensor can only be checked using the Honda diagnostic test pin box.
80 To check the sensor heater, remove the fairing side panel for the sensor being checked (see Chapter 7). Disconnect the sensor 4-pin wiring connector, which is in a boot behind the cylinder head (on 2002 to 2007 models the left-hand sensor connector is white and the right-hand is black, and on 2008-on models the left is green and right is grey) **(see illustrations)** – unscrew the coolant reservoir bolt and move the reservoir aside to improve access to the left-hand connector **(see illustration)**. Connect an ohmmeter between the white wire terminals

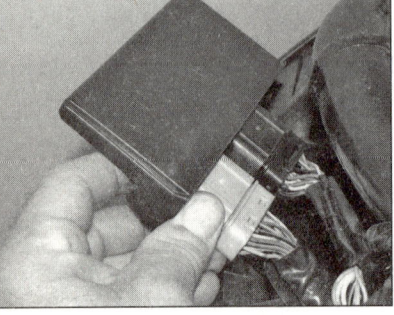

6.77b . . . then lift the ECM out and disconnect the wiring connectors

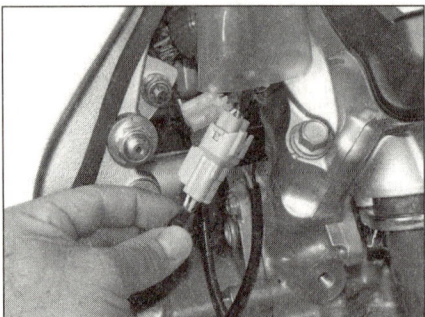

6.80a Right-hand oxygen sensor wiring connector

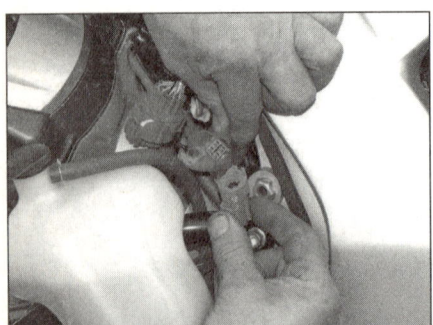

6.80b Left-hand oxygen sensor wiring connector . . .

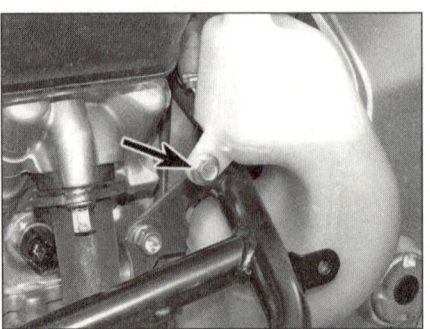

6.80c . . . unscrew the bolt (arrowed) and move the reservoir for access

on the sensor side of the connector and check that the resistance is between 10 and 40 ohms. Also check that there is no continuity to earth (ground) in the white wire. If the resistance is not as specified or if there is continuity to earth, replace the sensor with a new one. Otherwise check for battery voltage between the black/white (+) wire terminal and earth with the ignition ON. If there is no voltage, check the wiring, using the wiring diagrams at the end of Chapter 8. Otherwise have the sensor and its circuit tested by a Honda dealer equipped with the diagnostic tester.

Removal and installation

Note: *The oxygen sensors are delicate and will not work if dropped or knocked, or if any cleaning materials are used on them. Ensure the exhaust system is cold before proceeding. To tighten the sensor to the correct torque setting either a special socket to accommodate the sensor wiring (you can get one from Honda (part No. 07LAA-PT50101 in Europe or YA8875 in the US) or source a commercially available equivalent), or a crows-foot socket, is required.*

81 Remove the exhaust system (see Section 15).
82 Unscrew the oxygen sensor and remove it from the exhaust system **(see illustration)**.
83 Installation is the reverse of removal. Tighten the sensor to the torque setting specified at the beginning of the Chapter **(see illustration)**.

Knock sensors

Check

84 There is a sensor for each pair of cylinders, mounted on the outside of the cylinder head. Fist remove the fairing side panel and check the wiring connector.
85 Start the engine and run it at more than 3900 rpm for ten seconds. If the fuel injection system warning light is no longer blinking the indicated fault was a temporary glitch. Turn the ignition OFF.
86 If the fuel injection system warning light is still blinking disconnect the wiring connector and check the wire first for continuity to earth, and then for continuity to the ECM wiring connector (see Steps 75 to 77). If the wiring is good the sensor is faulty.

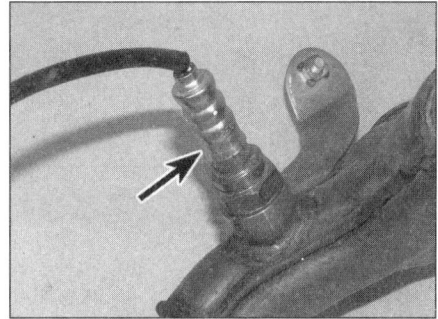

6.82 Oxygen sensor (arrowed)

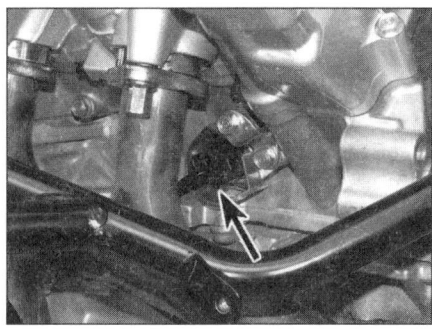

6.88a Right-hand knock sensor (arrowed)

Removal and installation

87 Remove the fairing side panel (see Chapter 7).
88 Disconnect the wiring connector **(see illustrations)**. If removing the right-hand knock sensor first remove the guard plate and guard, secured by two bolts.
89 Unscrew and remove the knock sensor.
90 Installation is the reverse of removal. Tighten the sensor to the torque setting specified at the beginning of the Chapter.

7 Throttle bodies

⚠️ *Warning: Refer to the precautions given in Section 1 before starting work.*

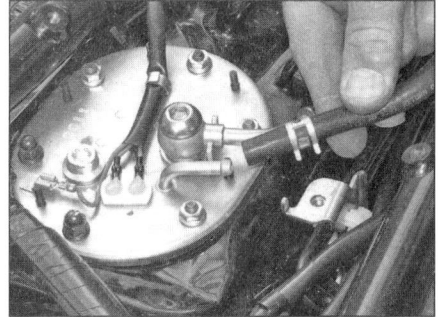

7.4 Release the clamp and detach the return hose

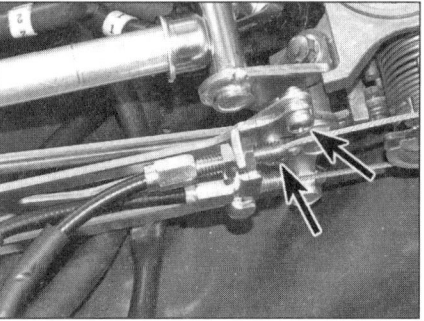

7.5a Undo the screws (arrowed) and displace the bracket . . .

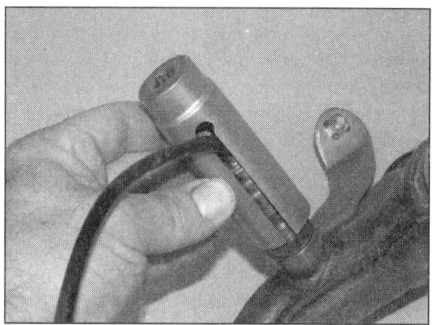

6.83 Purpose made oxygen sensor socket means the wiring does not interfere with the use of a torque wrench

6.88b Left-hand knock sensor (arrowed)

Removal

1 Remove the main fuel tank (see Section 2). Remove the air filter housing (Section 3).
2 Either drain the coolant (see Chapter 1), or prepare some hose clamps or blanking plugs for the fast idle system wax unit heating system hoses – there are two of them.
3 Counter-hold the hex on the fuel supply hose joint and unscrew the banjo union nut, noting the alignment of the hose and being prepared to catch any residual fuel with a rag **(see illustration 6.8)**. Detach the hose and discard the sealing washers – new ones must be used.
4 Release the clamp securing the fuel return hose to the union on the pump and detach the hose **(see illustration)**.
5 Undo the two throttle cable bracket screws, then detach the bracket and free the cable ends from the cam **(see illustrations)**.

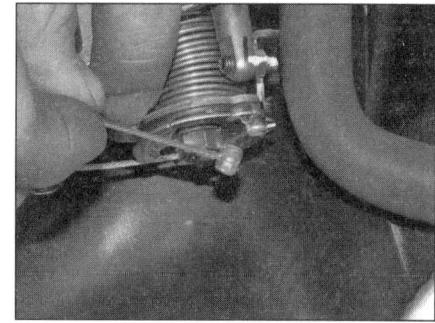

7.5b . . . then detach the cable ends

4•18 Engine management system

7.6 Disconnect the sub-loom wiring connector

7.7 Release the idle speed adjuster (arrowed) from its holder

7.9a Slacken the clamp screws (arrowed) . . .

Caution: Do not snap the throttle cam/valves from fully open to fully closed once the cables have been disconnected because this can lead to engine idle speed problems.

6 Disconnect the throttle body sub-loom wiring connector **(see illustration)**.

7 Release the idle speed adjuster from its clip and feed it through to the base of the throttle body assembly **(see illustration)**.

8 On California models, disconnect the EVAP system solenoid valve vacuum hose from the solenoid.

9 Fully slacken the clamps on the cylinder head intake manifold rubbers using a long screwdriver, noting their orientation **(see illustration)**. Ease the throttle body assembly up out of the rubbers, noting that it may be quite a tight fit – do not use the fuel rails as handles **(see illustration)**.

10 Rest the assembly on its left-hand side and slacken the clamps securing the coolant hoses to the fast idle system wax unit **(see illustration)**. Detach the hoses, and if the coolant wasn't drained, clamp or plug the ends. Lift the front right-hand corner of the rubber heat shield and disconnect the CMP sensor wiring connector **(see illustration 6.40)**.

11 Remove the throttle body assembly, drawing the fuel return hose through from the pump, noting its routing under the frame cross-member **(see illustration)**.

12 If required (for access to the alternator and thermostat housing) remove the rubber heat shield, noting how it fits **(see illustrations)**.

13 If the intake adapters on the cylinder head show signs of cracking or deterioration new ones must be fitted. Note the orientation of the adapters and their clamps before slackening them and removing the adapters **(see illustration)**.

Caution: Tape over or stuff clean rag into each cylinder head intake after removing the throttle body assembly to prevent anything from falling in.

14 Check the throttle body vacuum hoses for signs of damage or deterioration and replace any suspect hoses with new ones **(see illustration 6.27)**.

Caution: The throttle body assembly must be treated as a sealed unit. With the exception of the fast idle system wax unit screws, NEVER loosen any of the white-painted nuts/bolts/screws on the assembly as these are pre-set at the factory to ensure correct synchronisation of the throttle valves. The only components on the assembly which are serviceable are the starter valves (see Section 8) and the various vacuum hoses.

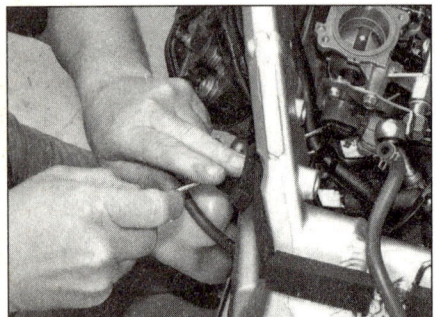

7.9b . . . using a long screwdriver

7.10 Release the clamps and detach the hoses

7.11 Remove the throttle bodies, drawing the fuel return hose (arrowed) out

7.12a Release the shield from its clips (arrowed) . . .

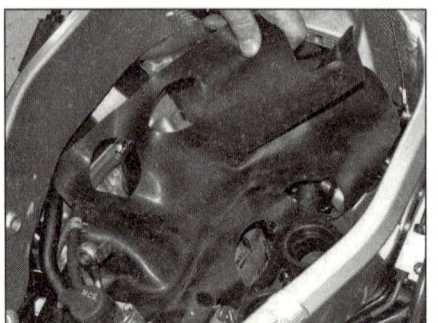

7.12b . . . and remove it

7.13 Note the orientation of the intake adapter clamps and how the adapters locates

Engine management system 4•19

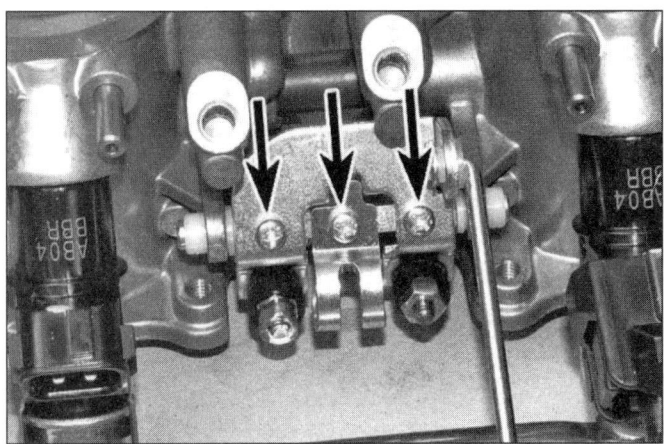

8.3a Undo the screws (arrowed) and remove the arm and plate, noting how they locate

8.3b Undo the screws (arrowed) and remove the plates, noting how they locate

Caution: NEVER use a solvent-based cleaner to clean the throttle body components. The throttle bores are covered with a molybdenum coating which could be removed by the cleaner.

Installation

15 If removed fit the intake adapters onto the heads making sure they and the clamps are correctly orientated **(see illustration 7.13)**. Tighten the lower clamps so that the gap between their ends is 9 to 11 mm. Make sure the upper clamp screws are correctly orientated as noted on removal **(see illustration 7.9a)**. Lubricate the inside of the rubbers with a light smear of engine oil to aid installation.
16 Fit the rubber heat shield if removed **(see illustrations 7.12b and a)**.
17 Remove the tape/plugs from the intakes.
18 Position the throttle body assembly in the engine bay on its left-hand side, feeding the fuel return hose under the frame section to the fuel pump. Connect the CMP sensor wiring connector **(see illustration 6.40)**. Fit the coolant hoses onto the wax unit, removing any plugs if used, and seat the clamps **(see illustration 7.10)**. If hose clamps were used to prevent coolant loss, release them.
19 Position the throttle bodies over the intakes and push them down until they are fully engaged – do not use the fuel rails as handles **(see illustration 7.11)**. Tighten the clamps so that the gap between their ends is 6 to 8 mm **(see illustration 7.9a)**.
20 On California models, connect the EVAP system solenoid valve vacuum hose to the five-way hose joint.
21 Fit the idle speed adjuster into its clip **(see illustration 7.7)**.
22 Connect the throttle body sub-loom wiring connector **(see illustration 7.6)**.
23 Connect the throttle cable ends to the pulley **(see illustration 7.5b)**. Locate the bracket and tighten the screws **(see illustration 7.5a)**. Check cable freeplay at the twistgrip and adjust if necessary (see Chapter 1).
24 Connect the fuel return hose to the pump and seat the clamp **(see illustration 7.4)**.

25 Use new sealing washers on the fuel supply hose banjo union and tighten the nut to the specified torque setting, making sure you counter-hold the hex on the hose joint or the fuel rail could distort or break **(see illustrations 6.19a, b and c)**.
26 If the cooling system was drained, do not forget to refill it (see Chapter 1). Otherwise, just check the level and top up if necessary (see *Pre-ride checks*).
27 Install the air filter housing and the main fuel tank (Sections 3 and 2).

8 Starter valves

⚠ *Warning: Refer to the precautions given in Section 1 before starting work.*

Note: If the starter valves are removed they will have to be synchronized using vacuum gauges after installation to ensure accurate set-up.

Removal

1 Remove the throttle bodies (see Section 7).
2 Remove the fast idle system wax unit (see Section 9). With the wax unit removed check the action of the starter valves and their linkage by moving the arm so the valves move in and out.

3 Undo the screw securing the arm for the wax unit and remove the arm, noting how it fits **(see illustration)**. Undo the screws securing the plate for the Nos. 1 and 3 starter valves and displace the plate, noting how the arms locate on the valves. Undo the screw securing the linkage arm plate between the Nos. 2 and 4 starter valves and remove the linkage arm/plate assembly **(see illustration)**. Undo the screws securing the plate for the Nos. 2 and 4 starter valves and remove the plate, noting how the arms locate on the valves. **Note:** *With the arms removed do not alter the setting of the synchronisation nuts to ensure minimal adjustment on installation – note that the No. 1 valve is the base valve, and the nut is pre-set and locked at the factory and must not be disturbed.*
4 Mark the cylinder number on each starter valve. Unscrew the starter valve base nut using a ring spanner or a deep socket and remove each valve from the throttle bodies **(see illustration)**.
5 If required draw the plate shafts out and remove the collars that the shafts run in. Remove the split pins and washers securing the linkage arm to its plates, noting how they fit. New split pins will be needed on reassembly.
6 Check all components for wear and damage and replace with new ones as necessary. Make sure the starter valve plungers move smoothly and freely **(see illustration)**.

8.4 Unscrewing a starter valve using a deep socket

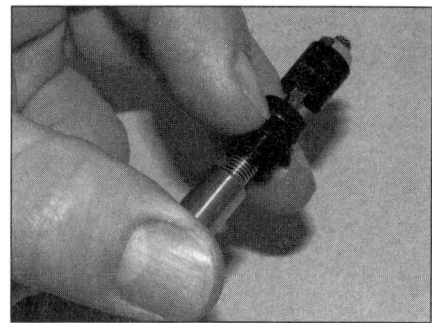

8.6 Check the action of the starter valve plungers

4•20 Engine management system

8.9 Fit the starter valves and tighten to the correct torque

8.10 Make sure the arm ends locate correctly against the flats

Installation

7 Clean the starter valves and throttle body passages using compressed air only. Do not use a throttle body/injector cleaner or any other solvent.

Caution: NEVER use a solvent-based cleaner to clean the throttle body components. The throttle bores are covered with a molybdenum coating which could be removed by the cleaner.

8 If removed, fit the collars into the shaft bores, making sure they are the correct way round. Slide the shafts in, making sure the collars stay in place. If separated reassemble the linkage arm and plates using new split pins, making sure everything is the correct way round.

9 Fit each starter valve into its original location and tighten the valve base nuts to the torque setting specified at the beginning of the Chapter **(see illustration)**. Check that each valve moves smoothly and easily in its bore by pulling on the valve end, and that it closes fully under spring pressure. Make sure the flats on each valve for the arm ends are vertical so they will locate correctly – if not turn the plunger so they are vertical.

10 Locate the plate for the Nos. 2 and 4 starter valves on the shaft and under the valve ends and secure it with the screws **(see illustration 8.3b)**. Make sure the arm ends engage correctly with the flat sides on the valves **(see illustration)**.

11 Locate the linkage arm and the plate for the Nos. 1 and 3 starter valves on the shafts tighten the screws **(see illustration 8.3a)**. Make sure the arm ends engage correctly with the flat sides on the valves. Finally fit the arm for the wax unit and secure it with the screw.

12 Check the operation of the starter valves by moving the linkage arm; the shafts should move smoothly and easily, drawing all the valves out simultaneously, and return to the fully closed position under pressure of the return springs. If any of the valves are obviously out of synchronisation with the No. 1 (base) valve (i.e. they start to move before or after it) turn the adjuster nut as required to approximate the setting **(see illustration)**.

13 Install the fast idle system wax unit (see Section 9).

14 Install the throttle body assembly (Section 7). On completion check the starter valve synchronisation (see below).

Synchronisation

 Warning: Do not allow exhaust gases to build up in the work area; either perform the check outside or use an exhaust gas extraction system.

Note: *Honda do not specify this as a service item, advising that it need only be carried out if the starter valves have been removed from the throttle body assembly. The procedure does not alter the setting of the throttle valves themselves (these are pre-set at the factory and fixed), but only the starter valves, which control the idle speed when the engine is cold and warming up. However on high mileage machines the linkage could wear and produce uneven idling when cold and warming up. If this is the case, then the synchronisation procedure should be carried out.*

15 Starter valve synchronisation is simply the process of adjusting the valves so they pass the same amount of fuel/air mixture to each cylinder on cold start and warm-up. This is done by measuring the vacuum produced in each intake duct. Starter valves that are out of synchronisation will result in uneven idling when cold starting and warming the engine. Before synchronising the starter valves, make sure the valve clearances are properly set (see Chapter 1).

16 To synchronise the starter valves, you will need a manometer, such as the Morgan Carbtune Pro4, or a set of vacuum gauges, suitable for a four cylinder engine, with the necessary adapters and hoses to fit the take-off points **(see illustration)**. When using such equipment always read the instructions supplied with it. The hoses usually have some form of restrictor in them for damping the movement of the manometer rod or gauge needle – make sure these are fitted correctly if not already in place otherwise it will be difficult to get an accurate reading, and that in the case of the Carbtune the hoses are connected with the restrictors closest to the take-off points on the throttle bodies.

17 Start the engine and warm it up to normal temperature, then stop it. Raise the main fuel tank and remove the air filter housing (see Sections 2 and 3).

18 Detach the four vacuum hoses (one coming from each throttle body) from the

8.12 The base valve (A) cannot be adjusted – the other valves have an adjuster nut (B)

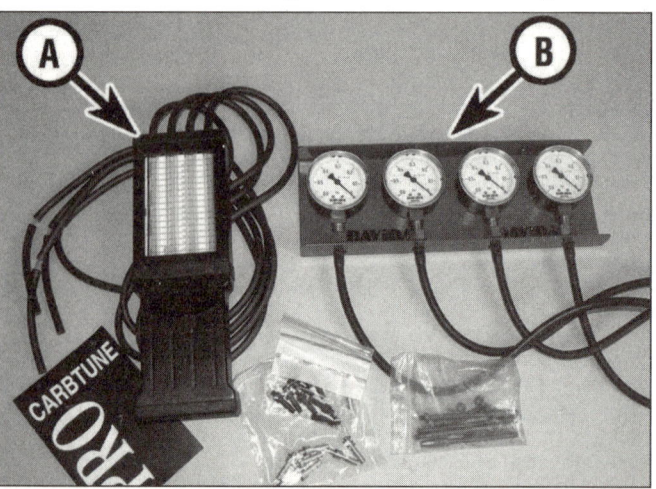

8.16 The Carbtune manometer (A) and a set of vacuum gauges (B), and the various adapters that come with them

Engine management system 4•21

five-way joint **(see illustration)**. Start the engine and run it above 2000 rpm for more than five seconds – this generates a MAP sensor failure code in the ECM.

19 Remove the access panel from each fairing side panel and the trim cover from the top of each valve cover (see Chapter 7). Detach the air hoses from the PAIR system reed valve cover unions on the valve cover and fit blanking caps in their place **(see illustration)**.

20 Connect the manometer or gauge hoses to the vacuum hoses previously detached from the five-way joint using suitable adapters, making sure the No. 1 manometer tube or gauge goes to the No. 1 throttle body and so on. Make sure everything is a good fit because any air leaks will result in false readings.

21 Start the engine and adjust the idle speed (see Chapter 1). If using vacuum gauges fitted with damping adjustment, set this so that the needle flutter is just eliminated but so that they can still respond to small changes in pressure. If using the Carbtune Pro4, and the rods are bouncing up and down, check that the restrictors in the hoses are nearer the throttle body end than the Carbtune end – this gives better damping. If they aren't, disconnect and reverse the hoses **(see illustration)**.

22 The vacuum readings for the Nos. 2, 3 and 4 cylinders should be the same as the No. 1 cylinder, or at least within the maximum difference specified at the beginning of the Chapter. The No. 1 cylinder starter valve is the base to which all the others are matched, and cannot itself be adjusted **(see illustration 8.12)**. If the vacuum readings vary, adjust the Nos. 2, 3 and 4 starter valves as required by turning the synchronisation nut on the end of the valve, until the readings are the same as No. 1 **(see illustration)**. **Note:** *Do not press hard on the nut whilst adjusting it, otherwise a false reading will be obtained.*

23 When the adjustment is complete, recheck the vacuum readings, then check and adjust the idle speed (see Chapter 1). Stop the engine.

24 Remove the manometer or vacuum gauges and the hose adapters. Fit the vacuum hoses on to the five-way joint **(see illustration 8.18)**. Fit the PAIR system hoses back onto the unions on the reed valve covers and secure

8.18 Detach the four hoses (arrowed) from the five-way joint

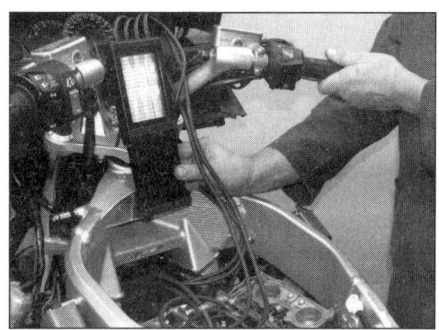

8.21 Starter valve synchronisation using the Carbtune Pro4

them with the clamps **(see illustration 8.19)**.

25 Install the air filter housing, and the main fuel tank (see Sections 3 and 2), and the trim covers and access panels (see Chapter 7).

26 Refer to Section 5, Step 6 and erase the MAP sensor fault code from the ECM.

9 Fast idle system wax unit

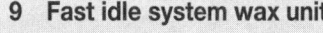 *Warning: Refer to the precautions given in Section 1 before starting work.*

Removal

1 Remove the throttle bodies (see Section 7).
2 Undo the two screws securing the wax unit **(see illustration)**.
3 Pivot the unit away from its mount and

9.2 Undo the screws . . .

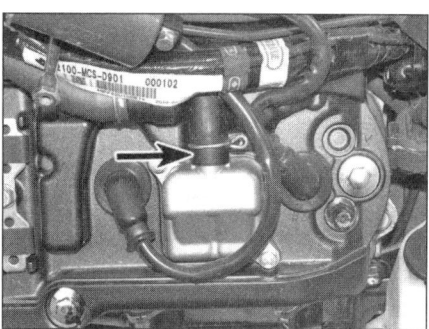

8.19 Detach the hose (arrowed) from the reed valve on each head

8.22 Nos. 2 and 4 starter valve synchronisation nuts (arrowed)

release the pushrod pivot piece from the link arm, easing it out with a small screwdriver if necessary, then remove the wax unit **(see illustration)**.

4 Do not attempt to dismantle the wax unit and do not adjust the position of the nut on the end of the pushrod **(see illustration)**.

Inspection

5 Visually inspect the unit for signs of damage.
6 If you suspect it is not working correctly, place it first in a cold place and check the position of the pushrod. Now gently heat it using a hairdryer or similar and check that the pushrod moves. If it doesn't it is faulty and must be replaced with a new one.

Installation

7 Fit the wax unit pushrod pivot piece into the link arm the pivot the wax unit onto its mount

9.3 . . . and pivot the wax unit upwards

9.4 Do not alter the position of the nut (arrowed)

4•22 Engine management system

(see illustration 9.3), fit the two screws and tighten them to the torque setting specified at the beginning of the Chapter (see illustration 9.2).

8 Install the throttle bodies (see Section 7).

10 Fuel pressure check

⚠️ **Warning: Refer to the precautions given in Section 1 before starting work.**

Note: *A pressure gauge is required for this check. Honda specify the gauge Pt. No. 07406-0040002 or 3 (or 07406-004000A or B in the US) along with a special banjo bolt and two sealing washers for the gauge to thread onto Pt. Nos. 90008-PP4-E02 (90008-PD6-010 in the US), 90428-PD6-003 and 90430-PD6-003. If a different gauge is used an adapter may be needed, either so it can thread onto the special banjo bolt, or that can be used in place of the special bolt. A gauge with a male end of the correct thread size and length could be used in place of the special bolt without an adapter. Two new sealing washers for the supply hose banjo bolt are also required.*

1 Remove the right-hand side cover and disconnect the battery negative (–) terminal (see Chapters 7 and 8).
2 Remove the main fuel tank and air filter housing (see Sections 2 and 3).
3 Detach the vacuum hose from the fuel pressure regulator, then plug or clamp the hose **(see illustration 11.2)**. Refit the air filter housing.
4 Place some rag around the fuel pump. Slacken the fuel supply hose banjo bolt until fuel comes out, but do not fully unscrew the bolt until all residual fuel pressure is released **(see illustration 12.9)**. Unscrew the bolt and remove the upper sealing washer, leaving the banjo union and lower sealing washer in place, and catch any remaining fuel.
5 Fit the special banjo bolt with the 12 mm sealing washer and tighten the bolt. Fit the gauge into the banjo bolt with the 6 mm sealing washer and tighten the gauge. Mop up any spilt fuel.
6 Connect the battery negative (–) lead. Start the engine and allow it to idle. Note the pressure present in the fuel system by reading the gauge, then turn the engine off. Compare the reading obtained to that given in the Specifications.
7 If the fuel pressure is higher than specified, first check for a pinched or blocked fuel return hose. If the hose is good fit a new pressure regulator (see Section 11), then check the fuel pressure again. If it is still too high the fuel pump is faulty and must be replaced with a new one.
8 If the fuel pressure is lower than specified, first check for a leak, which should be obvious from the smell of fuel. If there are no leaks remove the pump (see Section 12), clean the strainer and fit a new filter. Check the pressure again. If it is still low fit a new pressure regulator (see Section 11), then check the pressure again. If it is still too low the fuel pump is faulty and must be replaced with a new one.
9 On completion, disconnect the battery negative (–) lead again. Remove the fuel gauge assembly, being prepared to catch any residual fuel, then install the original bolt and two new sealing washers (one on each side of the hose banjo union), and tighten the bolt to the torque setting specified at the beginning of the Chapter **(see illustration 12.17)**.
10 Remove the air filter housing (see Section 3). Remove the plug or clamp from the vacuum hose, then connect the hose to the pressure regulator **(see illustration 11.2)**. Refit the air filter housing (see Section 3).
11 Reconnect the battery. Before fitting the seats start the engine and check that there is no sign of fuel leakage.

11 Fuel pressure regulator

⚠️ **Warning: Refer to the precautions given in Section 1 before starting work.**

Removal

1 Remove the main fuel tank and air filter housing (see Sections 2 and 3).
2 Detach the vacuum hose from the fuel pressure regulator **(see illustration)**.
3 Place some rag under the pressure regulator, then release the return hose clamp and detach the hose, catching any remaining fuel.
4 Counter-hold the fuel rail using the flats then unscrew the pressure regulator nut and remove the regulator **(see illustration)**. Remove the sealing washer and discard it.

Installation

5 Fit the regulator using a new sealing washer and tighten the nut to the torque setting specified at the beginning of the Chapter, counter-hold the fuel rail flats as before **(see illustration 11.4)**.
6 Connect the vacuum hose and fuel return hose to the fuel pressure regulator **(see illustration 11.2)** – make sure the return hose clamp is correctly seated.
7 Install the air filter housing and main fuel tank (see Sections 3 and 2).

12 Fuel pump and filter

⚠️ **Warning: Refer to the precautions given in Section 1 before starting work.**

Check

1 The fuel pump is located inside the secondary fuel tank. The fuel pump should

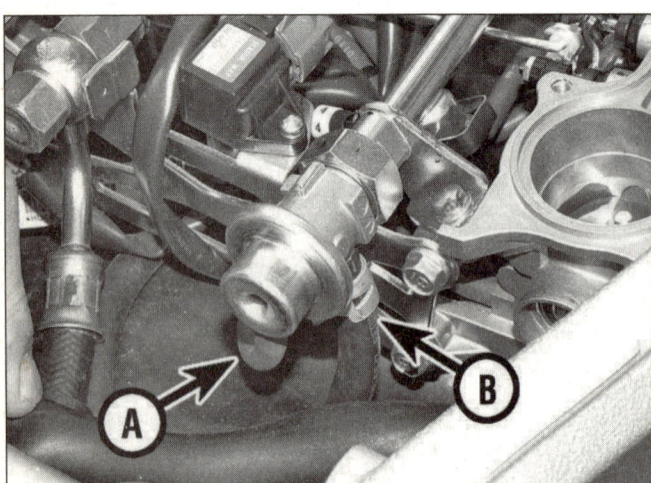

11.2 Fuel pressure regulator vacuum hose (A) and fuel return hose (B)

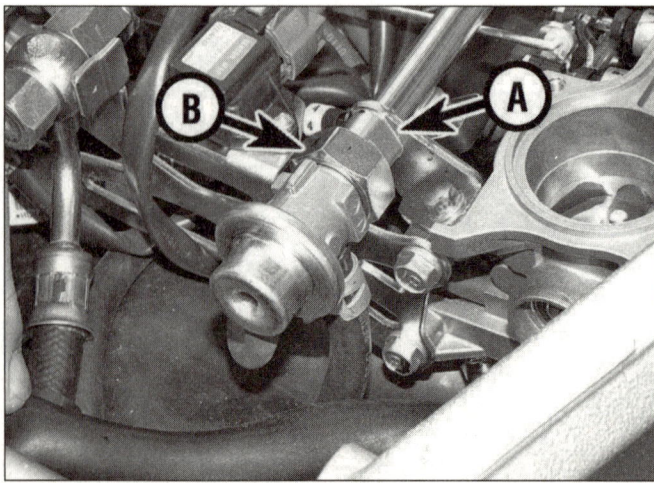

11.4 Counter-hold the rail on the flats (A) and unscrew the nut (B)

Engine management system 4•23

12.3 Disconnect the fuel pump wiring connector

12.9 Unscrew the banjo bolt (arrowed) and detach the supply hose

run for a few seconds when the ignition is switched ON to pressurise the fuel system, and then cut out until the engine is started. If the pump is thought to be faulty, first check the fuse (see Chapter 8). If all appears to be in good condition proceed as follows.

2 Remove the seats and the left-hand side cover (see Chapter 7).

3 Make sure the ignition is switched OFF then disconnect the fuel pump wiring connector **(see illustration)**. Connect the positive (+) lead of a voltmeter to the brown wire terminal on the loom side of the connector and the negative (–) lead to the green wire terminal. Switch the ignition ON whilst noting the reading obtained on the meter.

4 If battery voltage is present for a few seconds, the fuel pump circuit is operating correctly and the fuel pump itself is faulty and must be replaced with a new one.

5 If no reading is obtained, check the fuel pump circuit wiring for continuity and make sure all the connectors are free from corrosion and are securely connected. Repair/replace the wiring as necessary and clean the connectors using electrical contact cleaner. If this fails to reveal the fault, check the following components.

- Engine stop switch (see Chapter 8, Section 19).
- Fuel cut-off relay (see Section 6).
- Engine stop relay (see Section 6).
- Lean angle sensor (see Section 6).
- Engine control module (ECM) (see Section 6).

Removal

6 Remove the seats and the left-hand side cover (see Chapter 7).

7 Make sure the ignition is switched OFF then disconnect the fuel pump wiring connector **(see illustration 12.3)**.

8 Release the clamp securing the fuel return hose to the union on the pump and detach the hose **(see illustration 7.4)**.

9 Place some rag around the fuel pump. Slacken the fuel supply hose banjo bolt until fuel comes out, but do not fully unscrew the bolt until all residual fuel pressure is released **(see illustration)**. Unscrew the bolt and remove the upper sealing washer, detach the banjo union and remove the lower sealing washer, and catch any remaining fuel.

10 Unscrew the fuel pump mounting plate nuts, noting the positions of the two domed nuts **(see illustration)**. Carefully lift the pump assembly from the tank along with the mounting plate seal **(see illustration)**. Remove the seal, noting how it fits, and discard it **(see illustrations 12.14b and a)** – a new one must be used on installation.

11 Remove the rubber basket and fuel return

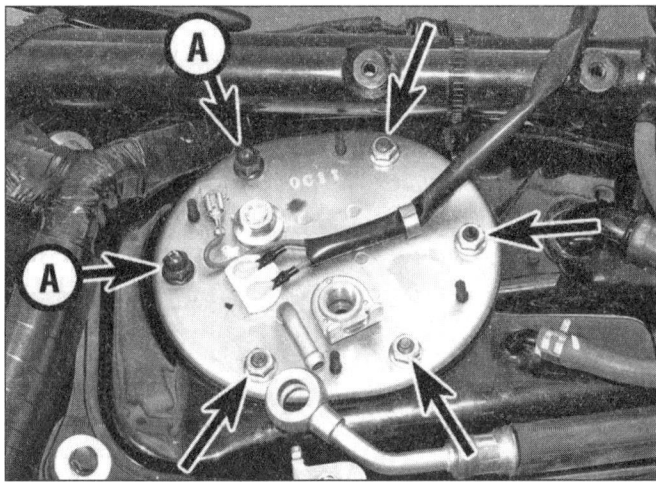

12.10a Unscrew the nuts (arrowed), noting the two domed ones (A) . . .

12.10b . . . then carefully draw the pump out of the tank

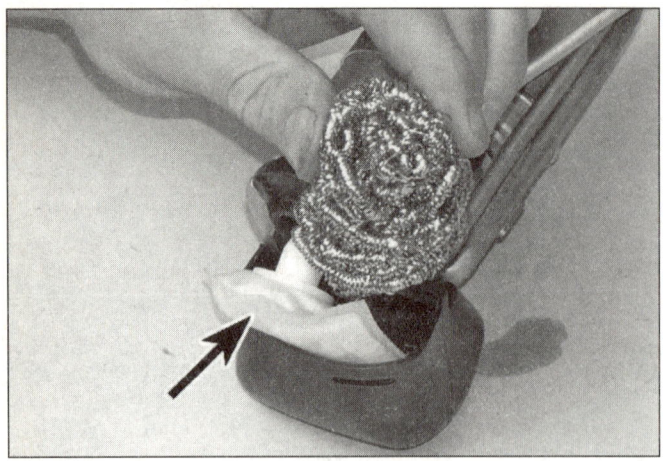

12.11 Remove the fuel return strainer and check the intake strainer (arrowed)

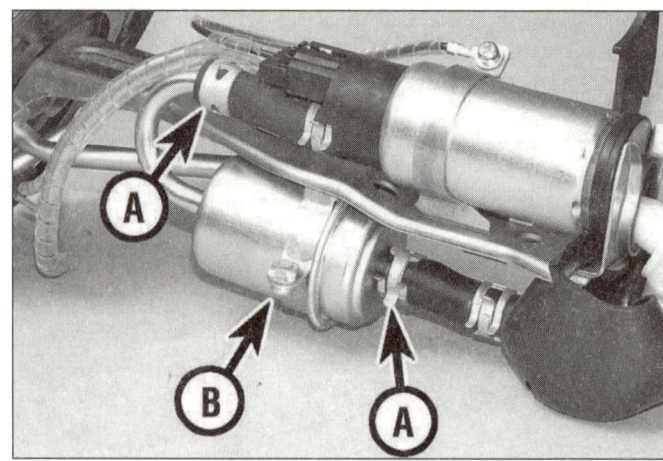

12.12 Release the clamps (A) then undo the screw (B) and remove the filter

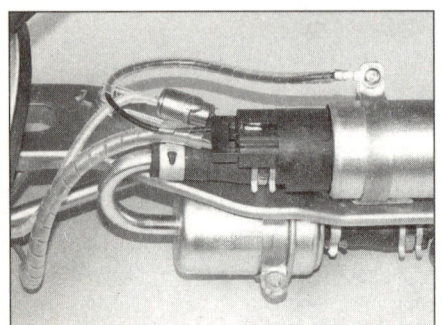

12.13 Make sure all connectors and terminals are secure

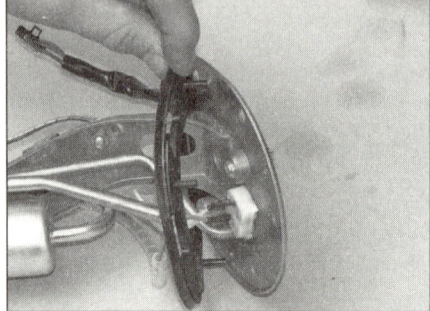

12.14a Fit the seal . . .

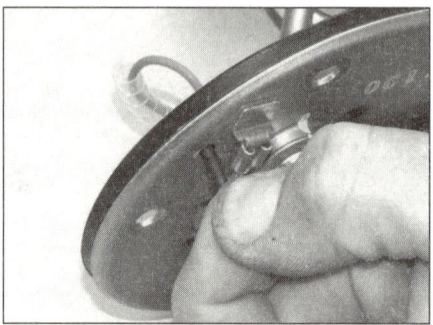

12.14b . . . and pull the pins through the holes

strainer **(see illustration)**. Check the intake strainer on the base of the pump for signs of dirt and clean it if necessary – note that the strainer is part of the fuel pump and is not available separately.

12 To remove the filter release and displace the hose clamps, then undo the filter holder screw and ease the filter out of the hoses **(see illustration)**. Fit the new filter and seat the clamps.

Installation

13 Make sure the wiring terminal screws, nuts and connectors are tight, both on the pump and the base **(see illustration)**.

14 Ensure the mounting plate and tank surfaces are clean and dry. Fit the new seal onto the plate – carefully pull the rubber locating legs through so the ribs are past the holes in the plate **(see illustrations)**.

15 Carefully manoeuvre the pump assembly into the tank, making sure it is positioned as shown, and seat the seal and plate over the studs **(see illustration 12.10b)**.

16 Fit the nuts, with the two domed ones positioned as shown, and tighten them finger-tight **(see illustration 12.10a)**. Now tighten them evenly and a little at a time in the numerical sequence shown for your model to the torque setting specified at the beginning of the Chapter **(see illustrations)**.

12.16a Fuel pump nut tightening sequence – 2002 and 2003 models

12.16b Fuel pump nut tightening sequence – 2004-on models

12.17 Fit the supply hose using a new sealing washer (arrowed) on each side of the union

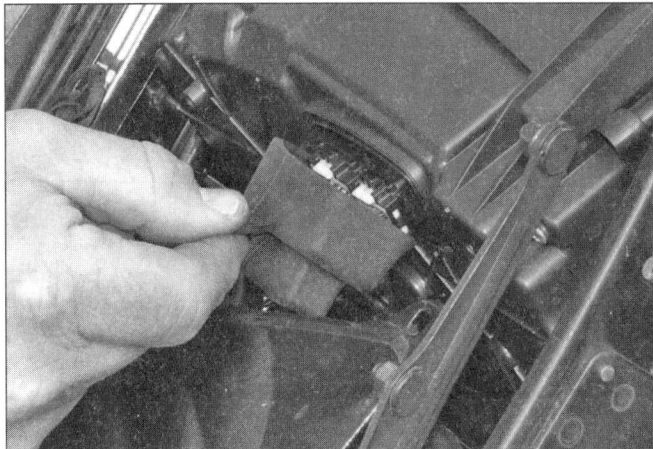

13.8 Pull the boot back to access the instrument wiring connectors

17 Connect the fuel supply hose using new sealing washers, one on each side of the banjo union, and tighten the bolt to the torque setting specified at the beginning of the Chapter (see illustration).
18 Connect the fuel return hose and seat the clamp (see illustration 7.4).
19 Connect the fuel pump wiring connector (see illustration 12.3).
20 Install the left-hand side cover and seats (see Chapter 7).

13 Fuel gauge and level sensor

Check

1 The circuit consists of the level sensor in the main fuel tank, the low fuel warning switch, which is an integral part of the fuel pump assembly in the secondary fuel tank, and the fuel gauge, which is part of the instrument cluster LED display. There is also the fuel consumption readout below the gauge that is a function of the ECM. Under normal circumstances with the main tank all segments of the gauge will show, when the main tank is empty there will be two segments lit, and when there are only about 5 litres left in the secondary tank the final segment will flash.
2 The system performs its own self diagnosis – if a fault occurs in the gauge/level sensor/low fuel warning circuit all segments of the gauge will flash, and the consumption readout will be replaced by two flashing bars. If there is a fault in the fuel consumption readout circuit the level gauge will be normal but the consumption readout will be replaced by two flashing bars.

Level sensor and low fuel warning switch

3 Refer to Section 2, Step 5 and drain the main fuel tank.
4 Remove the left-hand side cover (see Chapter 7).

5 If the gauge circuit is faulty disconnect the fuel level sensor wiring connector (see illustration 2.9). Connect an ohmmeter or multimeter set to the ohms scale to the terminals in the sensor side of the wiring connector. With the tank empty the reading should be as specified at the beginning of the Chapter. Disconnect the meter and reconnect the wiring connector. Turn the ignition ON. With the main tank empty there should be two segments of the gauge lit.
6 Disconnect the wiring connector and reconnect the meter. Now either fill the tank with fuel, or alternatively open the filler cap and raise the float to its full position using a suitable tool such as a piece of smooth wooden dowel, and check the resistance again. The reading should be as specified. Disconnect the meter and reconnect the wiring connector. Turn the ignition ON. With the float raised or main tank full all segments of the gauge should be lit.
7 If the resistance readings are not as specified remove the sensor (see Step 16). Check the internal wiring connections, and make sure the float is not full of fuel, and the arm is not bent. If they are good replace the level sensor with a new one.
8 If the resistance readings are good, but the gauge readout is not as described, remove the windshield and the inner screen cowl (see Chapter 7). Disconnect the instrument cluster 20-pin wiring connector (see illustration). Check the grey/black wire for continuity between the level sensor connector and instrument cluster connector. Also check for continuity to earth in the green/black wire. If the wiring is good the instrument cluster PCB could be faulty – refer to Chapter 8.
9 If the low fuel warning circuit is faulty disconnect the fuel pump wiring connector (see illustration 12.3). Using a piece of wire jump across the brown/black and green wire terminals in the loom side of the connector. Turn the ignition ON. If the last segment on the gauge flashes replace the fuel pump assembly with a new one. If it is still off, remove the

windshield and the inner screen cowl (see Chapter 7). Disconnect the instrument cluster wiring 20-pin connector (see illustration 13.8). Check the brown/black wire between the fuel pump connector and the instrument cluster connector for continuity. Also check the green wire for continuity to earth. If there is continuity, the instrument cluster PCB could be faulty – refer to Chapter 8; if there isn't check the wiring and connectors for a break or dirty contact.
10 If no faults are found, remove the pump (see Section 12) and check the internal wiring connectors (see illustration 12.13).

Fuel consumption readout

11 Remove the rear cowl, the windshield, and the inner screen cowl (see Chapter 7).
12 Disconnect the ECM and instrument cluster wiring connectors with the pink/orange wire, and check for continuity in the wire between the connectors (see illustrations 6.77a and b and 13.8). If there is no continuity check the wiring and connectors for a break or dirty contact.
13 If there is continuity remove the left-hand fairing side panel (see Chapter 7). Prepare a short jumper wire with suitable probes to connect between the pink/orange and green wires in the top of the large front loom wiring connector (see illustration). With the bike on its centrestand and the rear wheel off

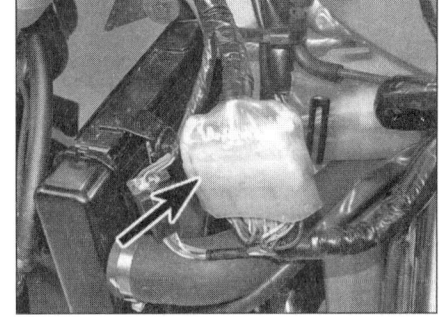

13.13 Front loom wiring connector (arrowed)

4•26 Engine management system

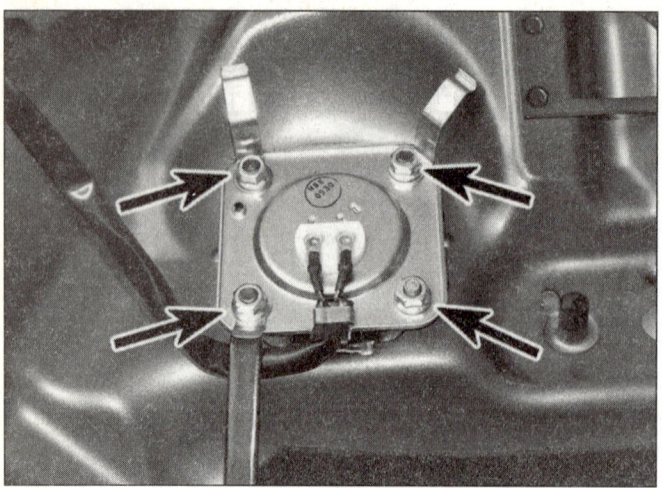

13.16a Unscrew the nuts (arrowed) and remove the guides . . .

13.16b . . . then draw the sensor out

the ground, start the engine and select first gear, then increase engine speed so that the speedometer reads more than 3 mph (5 km/h) for more than 15 seconds, then connect between the pink/orange and green wires in the connector momentarily while checking for a readout – if there is a readout the ECM is faulty (see Section 6); if there is no readout the instrument cluster PCB is faulty (see Chapter 8).

Removal and installation

14 If the gauge or consumption readout is faulty replace the instrument cluster PCB with a new one (see Chapter 8).

15 If the low fuel warning switch is faulty replace the fuel pump assembly with a new one (see Section 12) – the switch is not available separately.

16 To remove the sensor remove the main fuel tank (see Section 2). Unscrew the nuts and remove the wiring and hose guides, noting their positions (see illustration). Carefully lift the sensor out of the tank, taking care not to snag the float (see illustration). Remove the O-ring and discard it – a new one must be used.

17 Fit a new O-ring into the groove in the tank (see illustration). Manoeuvre the sensor float into the tank and seat the plate over the studs with the wiring to the front (see illustration 13.16a). Fit the nuts and wiring/hose guides, and tighten the nuts evenly and a little at a time in a criss-cross sequence. Install the tank and check for leakage around the sensor plate.

14 Throttle cables

> **Warning:** Refer to the precautions given in Section 1 before proceeding.

Removal

1 Remove the air filter housing (see Section 3). Mark each cable according to its location.

2 Slacken the locknut on the upper cable enough to free the captive nut, then release the cable from the bracket and detach the cable end from the cam (see illustrations). Unscrew the hex on the lower cable enough to free the captive nut, then release the cable from the bracket and detach the cable end from the cam (see illustration). Withdraw the cables from the frame noting their

13.17 Fit a new O-ring into the groove

14.2a Slacken the locknut (arrowed) . . .

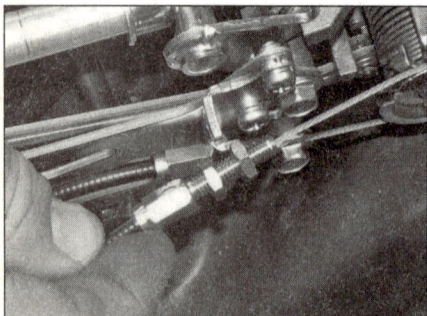

14.2b . . . then free the cable from the bracket . . .

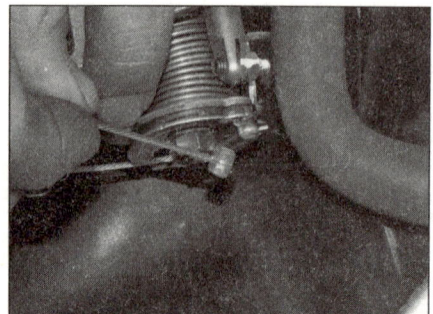

14.2c . . . and from the cam

14.2d Slacken the hex (arrowed) to free the lower cable

Engine management system 4•27

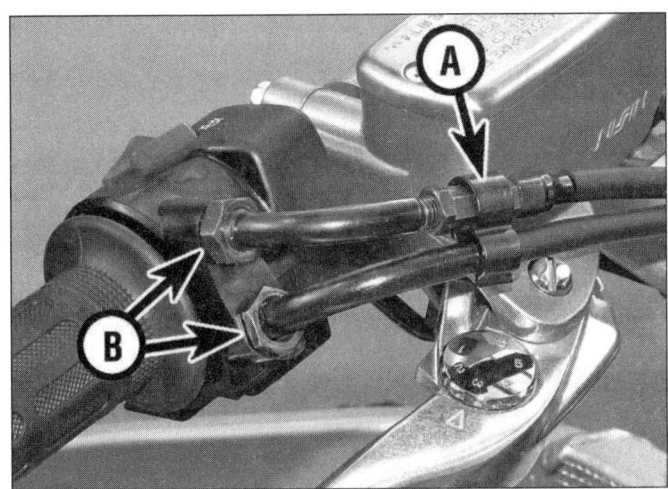

14.3a Remove the holder (A) then unscrew the nuts (B)

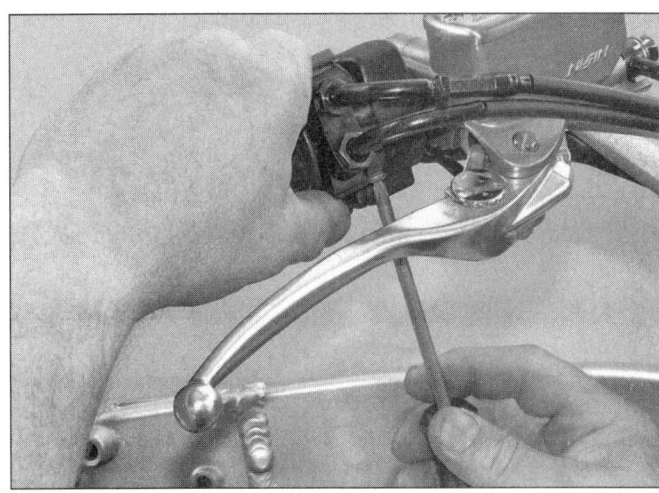

14.3b Undo the housing screws and separate the halves

correct routing, and freeing them from any guides.

3 Remove the holder from the cables, then unscrew the cable elbow nuts at the throttle pulley housing **(see illustration)**. Remove the housing screws and separate the halves **(see illustration)**. Detach the cable nipples from the pulley, then withdraw the throttle closing cable from the housing **(see illustrations)**. Thread the throttle opening cable elbow out of the housing and withdraw the cable **(see illustration)**. Mark each cable to ensure it is connected correctly on installation.

Installation

4 Fit the throttle opening cable elbow into the upper socket of the throttle pulley housing and thread the elbow into it without it becoming tight on the bottom of the threads **(see illustration 14.3e)** – the elbow must stay loose so that it aligns itself. Fit the closing cable into the lower socket **(see illustration 14.3d)**. Lubricate the cable nipples with multi-purpose grease and fit them into the throttle pulley **(see illustration 14.3c)**. Thread the lower cable nut into the housing and the upper cable nut onto the cable, leaving them both loose **(see illustrations)**. Assemble the housing onto the handlebar, making sure the pin locates in the hole, then fit the screws and tighten them **(see illustration)**.

5 Feed the cables through to the throttle bodies, making sure they are correctly routed through any guides. The cables must not interfere with any other component and should not be kinked or bent sharply. Fit the cable holder over the two cables **(see illustration 14.3a)**. Now tighten both cable elbow nuts on the housing.

6 Fit the lower cable end into the cam then

14.3c Detach the cables from the pulley . . .

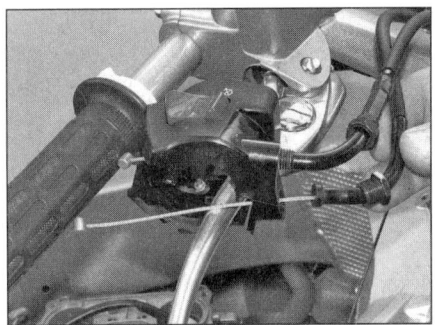

14.3d . . . then withdraw the closing cable . . .

14.3e . . . and thread the opening cable out

14.4a Thread the lower nut into the housing . . .

14.4b . . . and the upper nut onto the cable

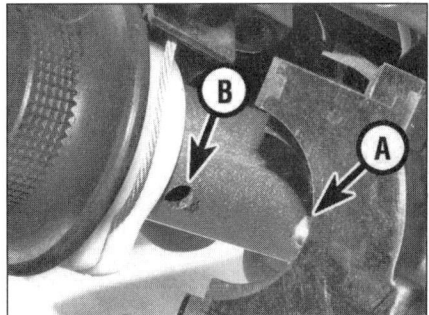

14.4c Locate the pin (A) in the hole (B)

4•28 Engine management system

14.6 Fit the lower cable and tighten the hex against the bracket

fit the cable into the bracket and fully tighten the hex **(see illustration)**. Fit the upper cable end into the cam then fit the cable into the bracket and lightly tighten the locknut **(see illustrations 14.2c, b and a)**.

7 Operate the throttle to check that it opens and closes freely.

8 Check and adjust the throttle cable freeplay (see Chapter 1). Turn the handlebars back-and-forth to make sure the cable doesn't cause the steering to bind.

9 Install the air filter housing (see Section 3).

10 Start the engine and check that the idle speed does not rise as the handlebars are turned. If it does, the throttle cable is routed incorrectly. Correct the problem before riding the motorcycle.

15 Exhaust system

⚠️ *Warning: If the engine has been running the exhaust system will be very hot. Allow the system to cool before carrying out any work.*

Removal

Silencers

> **HAYNES HiNT** *Exhaust system clamp bolts tend to become corroded and seized. It is advisable to spray them with WD40 or a similar product before attempting to slacken them.*

1 Remove the panniers (see Chapter 7).
2 Slacken the clamp bolts **(see illustration)**.
3 Unscrew the nuts on the silencer mounting bolts **(see illustration)**. Withdraw the bolts, noting the washers with the rear ones, and ease the silencer out of the downpipe assembly **(see illustration)**. On 2004-on models if required remove the shield from the left-hand silencer.
4 Check the condition of the sealing ring, either on the end of the silencer pipe or in the end of the downpipe and replace it with a new one if it is damaged or deformed or no longer sealing correctly **(see illustration)** – note that Honda specify to always use a new one, but use your judgement.
5 Check the condition of the nuts and bolts, washers, collars and rubbers and replace them with new ones if necessary.

Downpipe assembly

6 Remove the fairing side panels (see Chapter 7).
7 Remove the silencers (see above).
8 Disconnect the oxygen sensor 4-pin wiring connectors, one on each side in a boot behind the cylinder head (on 2002 to 2007 models the left-hand sensor connector is white and the right-hand is black, and on 2008-on models the left is green and right is grey) **(see illustrations 6.80a and b)** – unscrew the coolant reservoir bolt and move the reservoir aside to improve access to the left-hand connector **(see illustration 6.80c)**. Feed the wiring down to the sensor, noting its routing – on the left-hand side the wiring has a tight and awkward route, so it is best to tie some wire to the connector and draw the wire down with it, then release it from the connector and leave it there so it can then be used to pull the connector back through on installation **(see illustration)**.
9 Slacken the clamp bolt on the joining pipe **(see illustration)**. Note that the downpipe assembly must be detached from both sides of the engine and frame as an assembly and lowered to the ground as such, then separated at the joint pipe before manoeuvring each side out separately. It is useful to have an assistant

15.2 Slacken the clamp bolts (arrowed)

15.3a Silencer mounting bolts (arrowed)

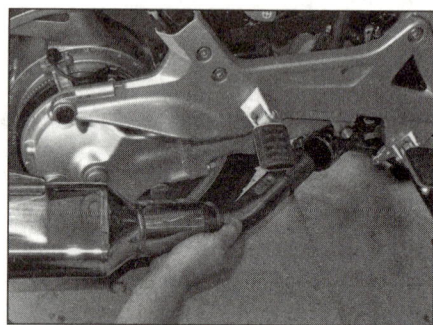

15.3b Ease the silencer out of the downpipe

15.4 Replace the sealing ring (arrowed) with a new one if necessary

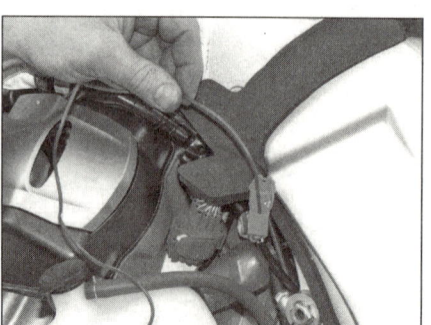

15.8 Tie some wire to the connector to make sure it is easily and correctly re-routed

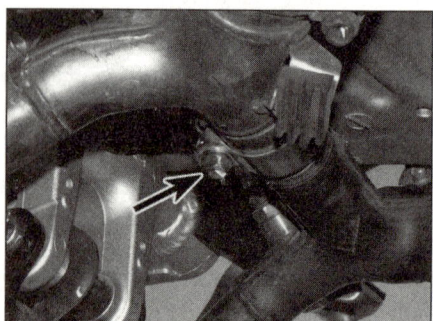

15.9 Slacken the clamp bolt (arrowed)

Engine management system 4•29

15.10a Unscrew the rear bolt (arrowed) on each side

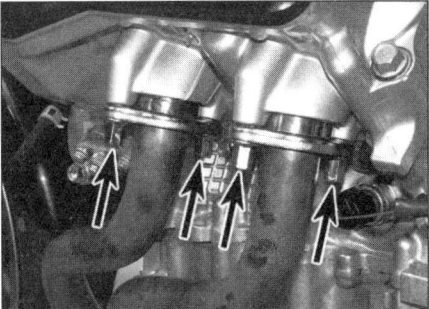

15.10b Unscrew the nuts (arrowed) on each side . . .

15.10c . . . then detach and lower the downpipe assembly

to support the assembly while the nuts and bolts are unscrewed from each side.

10 Unscrew the rear mounting bolt on each side **(see illustration)**. Unscrew the nuts securing the header pipes to the cylinder heads **(see illustration)**. Draw the flanges off the studs and manoeuvre the downpipe assembly out of the heads and lower it **(see illustration)**.

11 Separate the pipes at the joint and remove them from each side **(see illustration)**.

12 Remove the sealing ring from each port in the cylinder head and discard them as new ones must be used **(see illustration)**. Check the condition of the joint pipe sealing ring and replace it with a new one if it is damaged or deformed or no longer sealing correctly **(see illustration)** – note that Honda specify to always use a new one, but use your judgement.

13 Check the condition of the nuts and bolts, collars and rubbers and replace them with new ones if necessary.

Installation

14 Installation is the reverse of removal, noting the following:
- Replace any damaged, deformed or deteriorated mounting rubbers with new ones. Make sure the collars are fitted in the rubbers.
- Use a new sealing ring in each cylinder head port, and dab them with grease to stick them in place **(see illustration)**.
- Apply a smear of copper grease to all nuts and bolts to prevent them from seizing

up. Tighten the nuts/bolts to the torque settings specified at the beginning of the Chapter.
- Do not forget to reconnect the oxygen sensor wiring connectors **(see illustrations 6.80b and a)**. Make sure the wiring is correctly routed – on the left-hand side tie the wire used before to the connector then pull the wire through from the top, thereby pulling the connector through **(see illustration 15.8)**. Do not forget to remount the reservoir **(see illustration 6.80c)**.
- Run the engine and check the system for leaks.

16 Fuel system hoses

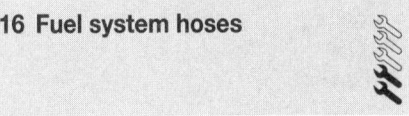

1 The fuel delivery, fuel return, vacuum and PAIR system hoses should be replaced with new ones at the first sign of deterioration. On California models, also replace the EVAP emission control system hoses. The fuel joint hose between the main and secondary tanks should be replaced with a new one each time it is detached, along with new clamps (see Section 2).

2 Remove the main fuel tank and the air filter housing (see Sections 2 and 3). To access the PAIR system hoses remove the access panel from each fairing side panel and the trim cover from the top of each valve cover (see Chapter 7). To access the EVAP system hoses remove the right-hand fairing side panel (see Chapter 7).

15.11 Separate the pipes at the joint

3 Before detaching a hose, note any clamp that secures it and its routing between the components.

4 Disconnect the vacuum hoses from the throttle bodies, MAP sensor and fuel pressure regulator, referring to the relevant Sections where necessary **(see illustration 6.27)** – if access is too restricted displace the throttle bodies to get to the underside (see Section 7).

5 Disconnect the PAIR system hoses from the control valve and reed valves, noting the routing of each one and how it is secured (see Section 17). On California models refer to Section 18 for the EVAP system. **Note:** *It is advisable to make a sketch of the hoses before removing them to ensure they are correctly installed.*

6 Make sure each new hose is correctly routed, not kinked or pinched, and fully pushed onto its union. Use new clamps if necessary, where fitted.

15.12a Remove and discard the sealing rings

15.12b Check the joint pipe sealing ring (arrowed)

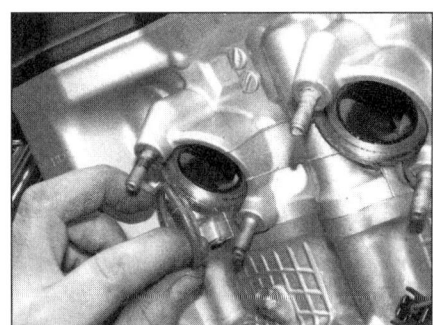

15.14 Fit a new sealing ring into each port

4•30 Engine management system

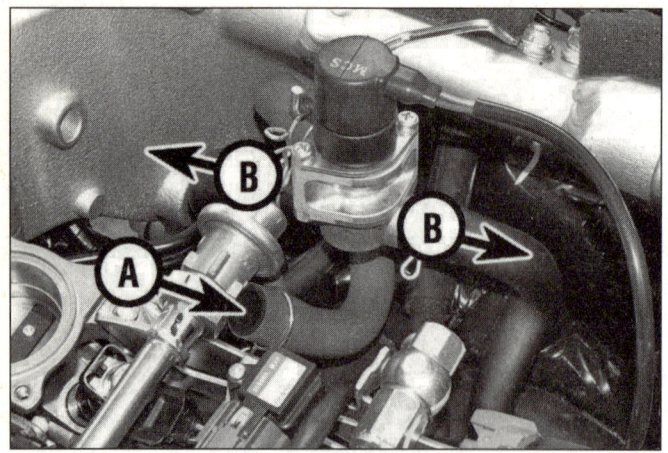

17.4a When blowing into hose (A) with no battery connected air should flow through hoses (B)

17.4b Disconnect the wiring connector (arrowed)

7 Detach the fuel supply hose from the throttle bodies and fuel pump as described in Sections 7 and 12, and detach the fuel return hose from the pressure regulator and pump as described in Sections 11 and 12. Refer to the same Sections for installing the new hoses, using new sealing washers on the supply hose and tightening the banjo union bolt and nut to the torque settings specified at the beginning of the Chapter.

8 Run the engine and check that the fuel system is working correctly, and in particular that there are no leaks, before taking the machine out on the road.

17 Pulse secondary air (PAIR) system

General information

1 To reduce the amount of unburned hydrocarbons released in the exhaust gases, a pulse secondary air (PAIR) system is fitted. The system consists of the control valve (mounted under the main fuel tank), the reed valves (fitted in the valve covers) and the hoses linking them. The control valve is actuated electronically by the ECM.

2 Under normal operating conditions the valve is open allowing filtered air to be drawn through the reed valves and cylinder head passages and into the exhaust ports. The air mixes with the exhaust gases, causing any unburned particles of the fuel in the mixture to be burnt in the exhaust port/pipes. This process changes a considerable amount of hydrocarbons and carbon monoxide into relatively harmless carbon dioxide and water. The reed valves in the valve cover are fitted to prevent the flow of exhaust gases back up the cylinder head passages and into the air filter housing.

Testing

3 Remove the air filter housing (see Section 3).
4 Check the operation of the system by blowing through the air filter housing hose union; air should flow freely through the control valve and reed valves **(see illustration)**. Disconnect the control valve wiring connector, then apply battery voltage (12 volts) across the valve terminals and repeat the check **(see illustration)**; no air should flow through the control valve. Disconnect the battery. If the valve does not behave as described check its resistance (Step 6).
5 Now suck on the air filter hose union; you should not be able to suck air back up the hose, indicating the reed valves are closing and sealing correctly. If you can suck air through, first identify which reed valve is faulty by blocking one hose, then the other.

Having identified the faulty valve remove it for cleaning, then test it again. Replace the valve with a new one if necessary.
6 Check the resistance of the control valve solenoid by connecting an ohmmeter between its connector terminals and compare the reading obtained to that given in the Specifications. Replace the valve with a new one if faulty.

Component renewal

Control valve

7 Remove the air filter housing (see Section 3).
8 Disconnect the control valve wiring connector **(see illustration 17.4b)**.
9 Displace the control valve from its mount then release the clamps and detach the hoses **(see illustration 17.4a)**.
10 Installation is the reverse of removal.

Reed valves

11 Remove the access panel from each fairing side panel and the trim cover from the top of each valve cover (see Chapter 7).
12 Release the clamp and detach the air hose from its union **(see illustration 8.19)**. Unscrew the bolts and remove the cover **(see illustration)**. Remove the reed valve and the base plate, noting which way around they fit **(see illustration)**.
13 Installation is the reverse of removal. Make sure the reed valve components and housings are clean and correctly fitted.

18 Evaporative emission control (EVAP) system

Note: *This system is fitted to California market models only.*

General information

1 The evaporative emission control system (EVAP) is fitted to minimise the escape of fuel vapour into the atmosphere **(see illustration)**. The fuel tank is sealed and a charcoal canister collects the fuel vapours generated when the

17.12a Unscrew the bolts (arrowed) and remove the cover . . .

17.12b . . . then remove the reed valves and the base plates (arrowed)

Engine management system 4•31

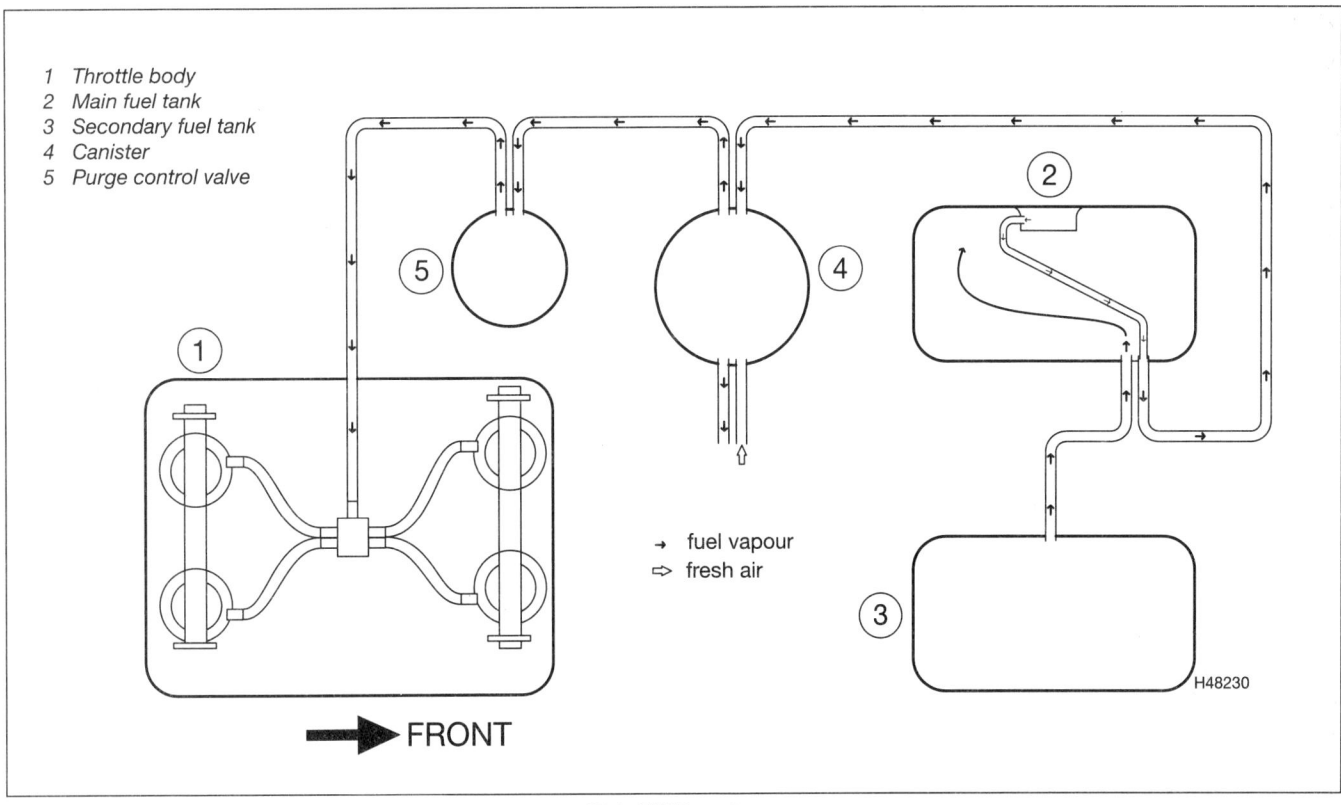

1 Throttle body
2 Main fuel tank
3 Secondary fuel tank
4 Canister
5 Purge control valve

→ fuel vapour
⇨ fresh air

18.1 EVAP system

motorcycle is parked and stores them until they can be cleared from the canister, via the control valve, into the throttle body intake tracts to be burned by the engine during normal combustion. The purge control valve for the fuel tank vapour is opened and closed by the engine control module (ECM).

2 The valve should be tested if there is a problem starting the engine when it is hot.

Testing

Purge control valve

3 Remove the valve from the motorcycle (see below).

4 Check the operation of the control valve by blowing through the intake (canister hose) union; air should not flow from the outlet hose union. Connect battery voltage (12 volts) across the valve terminals and repeat the check; air should flow from the outlet union if it is functioning correctly.

5 If an ohmmeter is available, check the resistance of the control valve windings by connecting an ohmmeter between its connector terminals and compare the reading obtained to that given in the Specifications. Replace the valve with a new one if the reading differs.

6 If the valve behaves as described, check for battery voltage using a multimeter across the terminals on the loom side of the valve wiring connector with the engine running. If no voltage is present check the wiring.

Charcoal canister

7 No testing of the canister is possible, if it is thought to be faulty a new one must be installed.

Component renewal

Purge control valve

8 Remove the right-hand fairing side panel (see Chapter 7).

9 Disconnect the wiring connector and hoses from the valve, noting which fits where, then unscrew the bolts and remove the valve.

10 Installation is the reverse of removal.

Charcoal canister

11 Remove the purge control valve (see above).

12 Disconnect the hoses, noting which fits where. Unscrew the canister mounting bolts and remove the canister.

13 Installation is the reverse of removal.

19 Catalytic converters

Note: *A catalytic converters is fitted in each silencer.*

General information

1 Catalytic converters are incorporated in the exhaust system to minimise the level of exhaust pollutants released into the atmosphere.

2 A catalytic converter consists of a canister containing a fine mesh impregnated with a catalyst material, over which the hot exhaust gases pass. The catalyst speeds up the oxidation of harmful carbon monoxide, unburned hydrocarbons and soot, effectively reducing the quantity of harmful products released into the atmosphere via the exhaust gases.

3 The catalytic converters are of the closed-loop type with exhaust gas oxygen content information being fed back to the engine control module (ECM) by the oxygen sensors.

4 The oxygen sensors contain a heating element which is controlled by the ECM. When the engine is cold, the ECM switches on the heating element which warms the exhaust gases as they pass over the sensor. This brings the catalytic converter quickly up to its normal operating temperature and decreases the level of exhaust pollutants emitted whilst the engine warms up. Once the engine is sufficiently warmed up, the ECM switches off the heating element.

5 Refer to Section 15 for exhaust system removal and installation, and Section 6 for oxygen sensor removal and installation information.

Precautions

6 A catalytic converter is a reliable and simple device which needs no maintenance in itself, but there are some facts of which an owner

4•32 Engine management system

20.3 Pull the cap off the spark plug

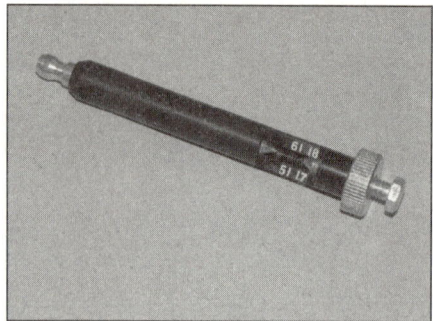

20.5 Typical ignition system spark gap testing tool

should be aware if the converter is to function properly for its full service life.
- DO NOT use leaded or lead replacement petrol (gasoline) – the additives will coat the precious metals, reducing their converting efficiency and will eventually destroy the catalytic converter.
- Always keep the ignition and fuel systems well-maintained in accordance with the manufacturer's schedule – if the fuel/air mixture is suspected of being incorrect have it checked on an exhaust gas analyser.
- If the engine develops a misfire, do not ride the bike at all (or at least as little as possible) until the fault is cured.
- DO NOT use fuel or engine oil additives – these may contain substances harmful to the catalytic converter.
- DO NOT continue to use the bike if the engine burns oil to the extent of leaving a visible trail of blue smoke.
- Remember that the catalytic converter and oxygen sensor are FRAGILE – do not strike them with tools during servicing work.

20 Ignition system check
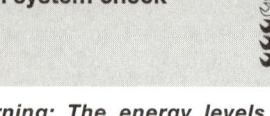

⚠ **Warning: The energy levels in electronic systems can be very high. On no account should the ignition be switched on whilst the plugs or caps are being held. Shocks from the HT circuit can be most unpleasant. Secondly, it is vital that the engine is not turned over or run with any of the plug caps removed, and that the plugs are soundly earthed (grounded) when the system is checked for sparking. The ignition system components can be seriously damaged if the HT circuit becomes isolated.**

1 As no means of adjustment is available, any failure of the system can be traced to failure of a system component or a simple wiring fault. Of the two possibilities, the latter is by far the most likely. In the event of failure, check the system in a logical fashion, as described below.
2 Remove the fairing side panels (see Chapter 7).

3 Make sure the ignition is OFF. Working on one cylinder at a time, pull the cap off the spark plug **(see illustration)**. Connect the cap to a spare spark plug (preferably use a new plug). Earth the plug either against one of the valve cover bolts or against the rear of the cylinder head – do not earth the plug against the valve cover itself. If necessary, hold the spark plug with an insulated tool.

⚠ **Warning: Do not remove any of the spark plugs from the engine to perform this check – atomised fuel being pumped out of the open spark plug hole could ignite, causing severe injury! Make sure the plugs are securely held against the engine – if they are not earthed when the engine is turned over, the ECM could be damaged.**

4 Having observed the above precautions, check that the kill switch is in the RUN position and the transmission is in neutral, then turn the ignition switch ON and turn the engine over on the starter motor. If the system is in good condition a regular, fat blue spark should be evident at the plug electrode. If the spark appears thin or yellowish, or is non-existent, further investigation is necessary. Turn the ignition OFF and repeat the check for each coil.
5 The ignition system must be able to produce a spark which is capable of jumping at least a 6 mm gap. Simple ignition spark gap testing tools are commercially available – follow the manufacturer's instructions **(see illustration)**.
6 If the test results are good the entire ignition system can be considered good. If the spark

appears thin or yellowish, or is non-existent, further investigation is necessary.
7 Ignition faults can be divided into two categories, namely those where the ignition system has failed completely, and those which are due to a partial failure. The likely faults are listed below, starting with the most probable source of failure. Work through the list systematically, referring to the subsequent sections for full details of the necessary checks and tests. **Note:** *Before checking the following items ensure that the battery is fully charged and that all fuses are in good condition.*
- Loose, corroded or damaged wiring connections, broken or shorted wiring between any of the component parts of the ignition system (see Chapter 8).
- Loose spark plug cap connection, faulty spark plug cap or HT lead, faulty spark plug, dirty, worn or corroded plug electrodes.
- Faulty neutral, clutch or sidestand switch (see Chapter 8).
- Faulty ignition coil(s) (Section 21).
- Faulty ignition switch or engine kill switch (see Chapter 8).
- Faulty crankshaft position (CKP) sensor (Section 6) or damaged triggers on timing rotor (Chapter 2).
- Faulty engine stop relay or lean angle sensor (Section 6).
- Faulty ECM (Section 6).

8 If the above checks don't reveal the cause of the problem, have the ignition system tested by a Honda dealer.

21 Ignition coils
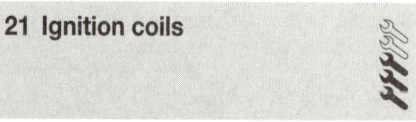

Check

1 Disconnect the battery negative (–) lead (see Chapter 8).
2 Remove the fairing side panels (see Chapter 7). A coil is mounted on each frame beam above the valve cover **(see illustrations)**.
3 Check each coil visually for loose or damaged connectors and terminals, cracks and other damage.

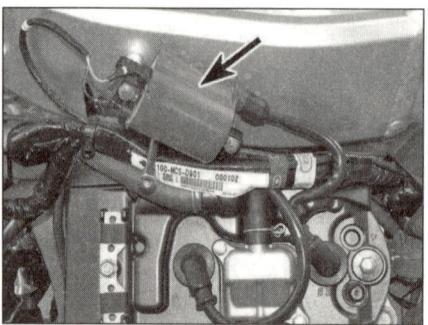

21.2a Ignition coil (arrowed) for cylinders 1 and 3

21.2b Ignition coil (arrowed) for cylinders 2 and 4

Engine management system 4•33

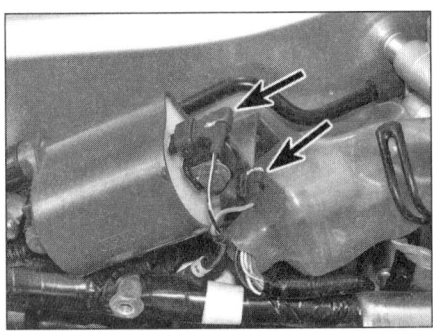

21.4 Disconnect the primary wiring connectors (arrowed)

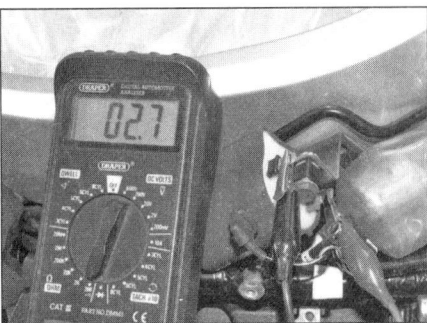

21.5 To test the coil primary resistance, connect the multimeter leads to the primary wiring terminals

21.6a To test the coil secondary resistance, connect the multimeter probes to the spark plug sockets

21.6b Unscrew the cap from the lead and the lead from the coil as required

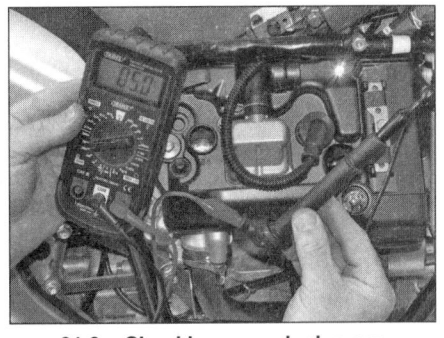

21.6c Checking a spark plug cap resistance

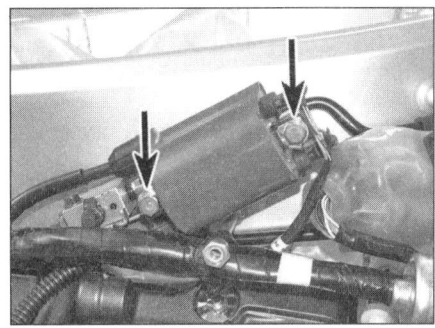

21.11 Coil mounting bolts (arrowed)

4 Disconnect the primary circuit wiring connectors from the coil (see illustration). Pull the caps off the spark plugs (see illustration 20.3).

5 To check the condition of the primary windings, set a multimeter to the ohms x 1 scale. Connect the meter probes to the primary terminals on the coil and measure the resistance (see illustration). If the reading obtained is not as given in the Specifications, it is likely that the coil is defective.

6 To check the resistance of the secondary windings, set the meter to the K-ohm scale. Connect the meter probes to the contacts in the spark plug caps and measure the resistance (see illustration). If the reading obtained is not as given in the Specifications, unscrew the plug caps and test the coil again, this time inserting the probes into the ends of the HT leads. If the reading obtained is not as given in the Specifications (resistance without caps) unscrew the leads from the coil and test the coil again, this time connecting the probes to the sockets in the coil (see illustration). If the reading obtained is not as given in the Specifications (resistance without caps) it is likely the coil is defective. If the reading is good check the resistance of each plug cap, and if that is as specified replace the HT leads with new ones, otherwise replace the plug cap with a new one (see illustration).

7 To confirm a coil is defective have it peak voltage tested by a Honda dealer.

Removal and installation

8 Disconnect the battery negative (–) lead (see Chapter 8).

9 Remove the fairing side panels (see Chapter 7). A coil is mounted on each frame beam above the valve cover (see illustrations 21.2a and b).

10 Disconnect the primary circuit wiring connectors from the coil (see illustration 21.4). Pull the caps off the spark plugs (see illustration 20.3).

11 Unscrew the coil mounting bolts and remove the coil, noting the spacers (see illustration).

12 Installation is the reverse of removal.

22 Ignition timing

General information

1 Since no provision exists for adjusting the ignition timing and since no component is subject to mechanical wear, there is no need for regular checks; only if investigating a fault such as a loss of power or a misfire should the ignition timing be checked.

2 The ignition timing is checked dynamically (engine running) using a stroboscopic lamp. The inexpensive neon lamps should be adequate in theory, but in practice may produce a pulse of such low intensity that the timing mark remains indistinct. If possible, one of the more precise xenon tube lamps should be used, powered by an external source of the appropriate voltage. Note: *Do not use the machine's own battery as an incorrect reading may result from stray impulses within the machine's electrical system.*

Check

3 Warm the engine up to normal operating temperature then stop it. Remove the centre section of the fairing side panels (see Chapter 7). Remove the access panel from the left-hand fairing side panel and the trim cover from the top of the valve cover (see Chapter 7).

4 Unscrew the timing inspection cap from the front crankcase cover (see illustration). Discard the O-ring as a new one must be used.

22.4 Unscrew the timing inspection cap (arrowed)

4•34 Engine management system

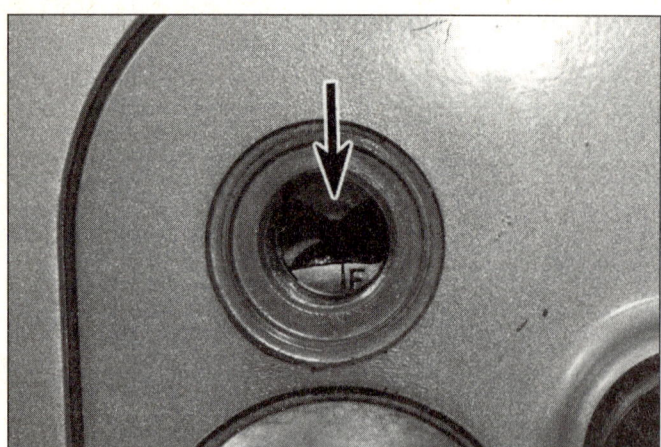

22.5 'F' mark and static timing mark (arrowed)

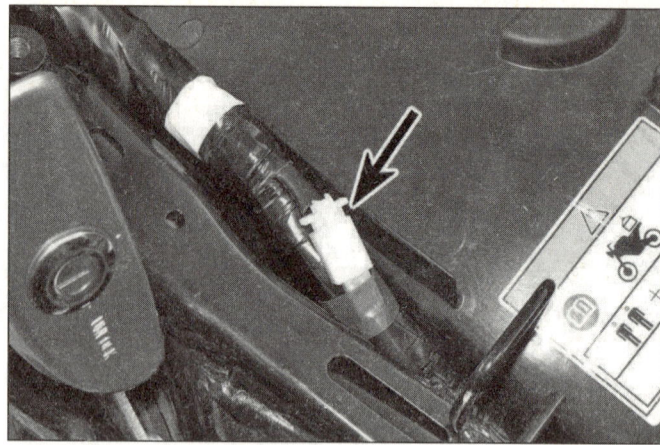

23.5 Disconnect the CKP wiring connector (arrowed) and fit the special tool as described

5 The dynamic timing mark on the rotor which indicates the firing point at idle speed for the No. 1 cylinder is the line next to the F mark **(see illustration)**. The static timing mark with which this should align is a pointer in the top of the inspection hole.

 *The timing marks can be highlighted with white paint to make them more visible under the stroboscope light.*

6 Connect the timing light to the No. 1 cylinder coil HT lead.
7 Start the engine and aim the light at the static timing mark.
8 With the machine idling, the timing mark should align with the notch (see Step 5). Now increase engine speed to approximately 2000 rpm. At this point the dynamic timing mark should move clockwise in relation to the static mark. This confirms the ignition is advancing.
9 As already stated, there is no means of adjustment of the ignition timing. If the ignition timing is incorrect, or suspected of being incorrect, one of the ignition system components is at fault, and the system must be tested as described in the preceding Sections of this Chapter.
10 When the check is complete, fit the timing inspection cap using a new O-ring, and smear it and the cap threads with grease. Tighten the cap to the torque setting specified at the beginning of the Chapter.

23 Immobiliser system

General information

1 An immobiliser system (known as HISS – Honda Ignition Security System) is fitted in certain markets as an anti-theft device. The system will only allow the machine to be started if the correct registered key is used to turn the ignition ON. The system consists of a transponder which is part of the ignition key, a receiver which is fitted around the ignition switch **(see illustration 23.52)**, and the electronic control module (ECM).
2 When the ignition is switched ON, the ECM sends power through the receiver to the transponder. The transponder sends a coded signal back through the receiver to the ECM. If the signal sent by the transponder matches the signal stored in the ECM memory, the HISS immobiliser indicator light in the instrument cluster comes on for two seconds, then goes out, and the ECM allows the engine to be started. If the key code signal is not recognised, or if there is a fault in the system, the indicator light stays on. If the light stays on, refer to the fault diagnosis and troubleshooting procedures below. Likewise if the light does not come on at all.
3 The ECM can store the codes for up to four registered keys. They keys should be kept separately (i.e. not on the same key-ring) as the proximity of another key to the one being used in the switch can lead to the signal from it being jammed, and the bike will not start. The key has a built in transponder which can be damaged if the key is dropped or knocked, gets too hot, is too close to a magnetic object, or is submerged in water for too long. If all the keys are lost, the ECM must be replaced with a new one, so always make sure you have at least one spare key. If a new key is obtained, it must be registered into the system before the bike can be started with the key.

Key registration procedure

With old ignition switch

Note: *The following procedures refer to the Honda special tools (Part Nos. 07XMZ-MBW0101 and 070MZ-MCS0100) which are wiring loom adapters to connect a battery into the loom side of the crankshaft position (CKP) sensor wiring connector.*
4 Obtain a new key from a Honda dealer, and have it cut to match the original key.
5 Remove the passenger seat (see Chapter 7). Disconnect the crankshaft position (CKP) sensor wiring connector **(see illustration)**. Connect the special tools together at the connector, then connect the wiring connector end to the loom side of the CKP sensor connector, and connect the red coloured clip of the tool to the battery positive (+) terminal and the black coloured clip to the battery negative (–) terminal.
6 Turn the ignition switch ON using your original key. The immobiliser indicator light should come on and stay on – if it starts to flash after ten seconds, then there is a fault in the system, which will have gone into fault diagnosis, and the pattern of the flashes it emits should be matched with the fault code (see table). Now disconnect the red clip from the battery positive terminal and leave it disconnected for at least two seconds, then reconnect it. The indicator should now come on for two seconds, then begin to flash repeatedly four times. This indicates that the system is in registration mode. At this point the registrations of all keys except the one in the switch will have been cancelled, so if you have another spare apart from the new one you want to register, this will also have to be registered.
7 Turn the ignition OFF and remove the original key, placing it well away from the receiver.
8 Insert the new key into the switch and turn it ON. The indicator should now come on for four seconds, then begin to flash repeatedly four times. This indicates that the system has registered the new key. Turn the ignition OFF and remove the key.
9 To register any other spare keys that will have been cancelled, repeat Step 8. Up to four keys can be registered.
10 On completion turn the ignition OFF, then remove the special tool and reconnect the crankshaft position (CKP) sensor wiring connector. Now turn the ignition ON using any of the registered keys to return the system to normal mode.

Engine management system

11 Check that all registered keys can start the motorcycle.

With a new ignition switch

12 Obtain a new switch and two (or more) new keys.

13 Remove the faulty switch (see Chapter 8), but retain the HISS receiver to fit with the new switch.

14 Remove the passenger seat (see Chapter 7). Disconnect the crankshaft position (CKP) sensor wiring connector **(see illustration 23.5)**. Connect the special tools together at the connector, then connect the wiring connector end to the loom side of the CKP sensor connector, and connect the red coloured clip of the tool to the battery positive (+) terminal and the black coloured clip to the battery negative (−) terminal.

15 Place one of the original registered keys for the faulty switch next to the receiver.

16 Connect the new ignition switch to its connector in the wiring loom, but keep it away from the receiver. Turn the new switch ON with one of the new keys. The immobiliser indicator light should come on and stay on, which means the ECM recognises the old key that is next to the receiver – if it starts to flash after ten seconds, then there is a fault in the system, which will have gone into fault diagnosis, and the pattern of the flashes it emits should be matched with the fault code (see table). Now disconnect the red clip from the battery positive terminal and leave it disconnected for at least two seconds, then reconnect it. The indicator should now come on for two seconds, then begin to flash repeatedly four times. This indicates that the system is in registration mode. At this point the registrations of all keys except the one near the receiver will have been cancelled.

17 Turn the ignition OFF and remove the new key.

18 Install the new ignition switch, then fit the receiver onto it (see Chapter 8).

19 Insert the new key into the switch and turn it ON. The indicator should now come on for four seconds, then begin to flash repeatedly four times. This indicates that the system has registered the new key. If the indicator starts to flash after ten seconds, then there is a fault in the system, which will have gone into fault diagnosis, and the pattern of the flashes it emits should be matched with the fault code (see table). Turn the ignition OFF and disconnect the red clip of the special tool from the battery positive terminal.

20 Turn the ignition ON using the newly registered key. The indicator light should come on for two seconds, then go off.

21 Turn the ignition OFF and reconnect the red clip to the battery positive terminal.

22 Turn the ignition ON using the newly registered key. The indicator light should come on and stay on. Now disconnect the red clip from the battery positive terminal and leave it disconnected for at least two seconds, then reconnect it. The indicator should now come on for two seconds, then begin to flash repeatedly four times. This indicates that the system is in registration mode. At this point the registrations of all old keys (for the faulty switch) are cancelled.

23 Turn the ignition OFF and remove the key, placing it well away from the receiver.

24 Insert the second new unregistered key and turn the ignition ON. The indicator should now come on for four seconds, then begin to flash repeatedly four times. This indicates that the system has registered the second new key. Turn the ignition OFF and remove the key.

25 To register any other new spare keys, repeat Step 24. Up to four keys can be registered.

26 On completion turn the ignition OFF, then remove the special tool and reconnect the CKP sensor wiring connector. Now turn the ignition ON using any of the registered keys to return the system to normal mode.

27 Check that all newly registered keys can start the motorcycle.

With a new ECM (electronic control module)

28 Obtain a new ECM along with two new keys. Install the new ECM (see Section 6). Have the keys cut to match the original key for your ignition switch.

29 Insert a new key into the switch and turn it ON. The indicator should now come on for two seconds, then begin to flash repeatedly four times. This indicates that the system has registered the new key. If the indicator stays on for ten seconds then starts to flash, then there is a fault in the system, which will have gone into fault diagnosis, and the pattern of the flashes it emits should be matched with the fault code (see table).

30 Turn the ignition OFF and remove the key.

31 Insert the second new key and turn the ignition ON. The indicator should now come on for two seconds, then begin to flash repeatedly four times. This indicates that the system has registered the second new key.

32 Turn the ignition OFF and remove the key.

33 The new ECM will only register two new keys at this stage. If you have a third key to register, refer to Steps 4 to 10 to register it, noting that you will need the special tool mentioned therein.

34 Check that both newly registered keys can start the motorcycle.

Fault diagnosis

35 There are two fault diagnosis modes, one for faults which occur during normal use, and one for a fault that occurs when registering a new key. Make sure you refer to the correct table below when matching the fault code pattern.

36 If the indicator light has come on and stayed on during normal use, remove the passenger seat (see Chapter 7). Disconnect the crankshaft position (CKP) sensor wiring connector **(see illustration 23.5)**. Connect the special tools together at the connector, then connect the wiring connector end to the loom side of the CKP sensor connector, and connect the red coloured clip of the tool to the battery positive (+) terminal and the black coloured clip to the battery negative (−) terminal.

37 Turn the ignition switch ON. The indicator light will come on for ten seconds, then start to flash. This means it has entered diagnostic mode, and the pattern of the flashes indicates the fault that has occurred. The pattern repeats continuously. Match the pattern with the fault codes below, making sure you refer to the relevant table. If the indicator stays on after ten seconds and does not flash, then there is no fault logged in the system.

If fault is indicated during normal use

Flash pattern	Fault	Solution
Two short, one long, one short	Faulty ECM	Install new ECM
Two short, two long	Faulty receiver or wiring	Follow Troubleshooting procedure below
One long, three short	Signal jammed by other key	Place other key well away from receiver
One long, two short, one long	Signal jammed by other key	Place other key well away from receiver

If fault is indicated during key registration

Flash pattern	Fault	Solution
One short, one long, one short, one long	Key already registered	Use a new or cancelled key
Two short, two long	Faulty receiver or wiring	Follow Troubleshooting procedure below
One short, one long, two short	Key already registered on old ECM	Use a new key

Troubleshooting procedure

Indicator light does not come on when ignition switched ON

38 Check the fuses (see Chapter 8).

39 If the fuses are good, make sure the engine is in neutral then turn the ignition ON and check whether the neutral and oil pressure warning lights have come on.

40 If the lights have not come on, remove the windshield and the inner screen cowl (see Chapter 7). Pull back the rubber boot on the instrument cluster wiring connectors **(see illustration 13.8)**. Using a voltmeter, connect the positive (+) probe to the black/brown wire terminal in the 20-pin connector (connectors still connected) and the negative (–) probe to the green wire terminal in the 16-pin connector. With the ignition ON there should be battery voltage. If voltage is present, the instrument cluster is faulty (see Chapter 8). If there is no voltage, check for continuity in the wiring, referring to the wiring diagrams at the end of Chapter 8. The green wire goes to earth (ground).

41 If the lights have come on, refer to Section 6 to access the ECM and disconnect the ECM black wiring connector **(see illustration 6.77b)**. Using a voltmeter, connect the positive (+) probe to the white/red wire terminal on the loom side of the ECM connector and the negative (–) probe to earth (ground). Turn the ignition ON – there should be battery voltage.

42 If there was no voltage, using a voltmeter, connect the positive (+) probe to the white/red wire terminal in the instrument cluster 20-pin connector and the negative (–) probe to earth. Turn the ignition ON – there should be no voltage for two seconds, then there should be battery voltage. If there is no voltage after two seconds, check for continuity in the white/red wire, and also in the green wire from the 16-pin connector to earth, referring to the wiring diagrams at the end of Chapter 8. If voltage is present, the instrument cluster is faulty (see Chapter 8).

43 If there is voltage in Step 41, using a voltmeter, connect the positive (+) probe to the black/white (ECM) wire terminal on the loom side of the ECM's grey connector and the negative (–) probe to earth (ground). Turn the ignition ON – there should be battery voltage. If there is no voltage, check for continuity in the black/white wire. If voltage is present, check for continuity to earth (ground) in the green wire. If the wiring is good, check the ECM connector for loose, damaged or corroded terminals. If the connector is good,

23.48 HISS receiver wiring connector (arrowed)

then the ECM could be faulty, and should be checked by a Honda dealer.

Indicator light stays on when ignition switched ON

44 Check that none of the other registered keys are close to the receiver. If they are, remove them and try the ignition again.

45 Turn the ignition ON with a spare key and check the indicator light, which should come on for two seconds, then go out. If it does, the first key is faulty. If it doesn't, perform the fault diagnosis procedure described above. If a fault code is displayed, use the appropriate table to determine the fault and the solution.

46 If no fault code is displayed, or the system does not go into fault diagnosis mode, refer to Section 6 to access the ECM and disconnect the ECM black wiring connector **(see illustration 6.77b)**. Using a voltmeter, connect the positive (+) probe to the white/red wire terminal on the loom side of the connector and the negative (–) probe to earth (ground). Turn the ignition ON – there should be battery voltage. If there is no voltage, check for continuity in the white/red wire between the ECM and the instrument cluster connector.

47 If there is voltage, check for continuity in the yellow and white/yellow wires between the ECM and the crankshaft position (CKP) sensor, referring to the wiring diagrams at the end of Chapter 8. If there is no continuity, trace the fault and repair or replace the wiring as necessary. If there is continuity, the ECM could be faulty and should be taken to a Honda dealer for assessment.

Fault code indicated by flash pattern

48 If the 'two short, two long' flash pattern has been indicated during the fault diagnosis procedure, remove the right-hand fairing side panel (see Chapter 7). Trace the wiring from the receiver on the ignition switch and disconnect it at the 4-pin connector **(see illustration)**.

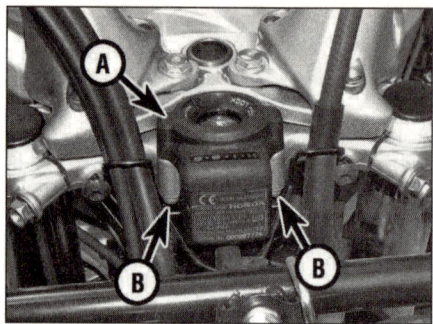

23.52 HISS receiver (A). Undo the screw (B) on each side

Using a voltmeter, connect the positive (+) probe to the yellow/red wire terminal on the loom side of the receiver connector and the negative (–) probe to earth (ground). Turn the ignition ON – there should be approximately 5 volts present. If there is no voltage, check for continuity in the yellow/red wire between the ECM and the receiver, and repair or replace the wiring if there is no continuity.

49 If there is 5 volts present, check for continuity to earth (ground) in the green/orange wire on the loom side of the connector, and repair or replace the wiring if there is no continuity.

50 If the wiring is good, using a voltmeter, connect the positive (+) probe to the pink wire terminal on the loom side of the receiver connector and the negative (–) probe to earth (ground). Turn the ignition ON – there should be approximately 5 volts present. If there is, the receiver is faulty.

51 If there is no voltage, check for continuity in the orange/blue and pink wires between the ECM and the receiver, and repair or replace the wiring if there is no continuity between the connectors, or if there is continuity in either to earth (ground). If the wiring is good, the receiver is faulty.

Replacement

52 To replace the receiver, remove the right-hand fairing side panel (see Chapter 7). Trace the wiring from the receiver on the ignition switch and disconnect it at the 4-pin connector **(see illustration 23.48)**. Feed the wiring back to the receiver, freeing it from any ties and noting its routing. Turn the handlebars to full right lock, then undo the screws and remove the receiver, noting how it fits **(see illustration)**. If you can't easily access the screws, removing the fairing and/or instrument cluster will help (see Chapter 7).

53 To replace the ECM see Section 6.

Chapter 5
Frame and suspension

Contents

Section		Section
Footrests, brake pedal and gearchange lever 3		Sidestand and centrestand 4
Fork overhaul. 8		Stand lubrication . . . . see Chapter 1
Fork oil change. 7		Sidestand switch . . . . see Chapter 8
Fork removal and installation 6		Steering head bearing check and adjustment . . . . see Chapter 1
Frame inspection and repair. 2		Steering head bearings 10
General information 1		Steering stem. 9
Handlebars and levers 5		Suspension adjustment 12
Handlebar switches . . . . see Chapter 8		Suspension check . . . . see Chapter 1
Rear shock absorber 11		Swingarm. 13

Degrees of difficulty

Easy, suitable for novice with little experience	Fairly easy, suitable for beginner with some experience	Fairly difficult, suitable for competent DIY mechanic	Difficult, suitable for experienced DIY mechanic	Very difficult, suitable for expert DIY or professional 

Specifications

Front forks
Fork oil type
    European models . . . . Honda Ultra Cushion 10W oil or equivalent 10W fork oil
    US models . . . . Pro-Honda SS-8 suspension fluid or equivalent 10W fork oil
Fork oil capacity. . . . . 638 ± 2.5 cc
Fork oil level* . . . . 62 mm
Fork spring free length (min)
    Standard. . . . . 249.6 mm
    Service limit . . . . 244.6 mm
Fork tube runout limit . . . . 0.2 mm
*Oil level is measured from the top of the tube with the fork spring removed and the leg fully compressed.

Steering head bearings
Bearing pre-load (see text) . . . . 9.5 to 14.2 N (0.97 to 1.45 kgf; 2.14 to 3.20 lbf)

5•2 Frame and suspension

Torque settings

Brake hose guide and delay valve bolts	12 Nm
Centrestand pivot holder bolt	12 Nm
Clutch master cylinder clamp bolts	12 Nm
Engine protection bar bolts/nuts	
Front bolt	39 Nm
Rear and lower bolts/nuts	26 Nm
Engine side mounting bracket bolts	
Front bolt	39 Nm
Rear bolt	26 Nm
Footrest bracket bolts	
Front bolts (to main frame)	64 Nm
Rear bolts (to sub-frame)	42 Nm
Fork damper cartridge bolt	20 Nm
Fork top bolt	23 Nm
Fork clamp bolts	26 Nm
Front brake master cylinder clamp bolts	12 Nm
Handlebar bolts	22 Nm
Handlebar end-weight screws	10 Nm
Rear brake master cylinder bolts	12 Nm
Shock absorber bolts/nuts	42 Nm
Sidestand bracket bolts	
2002 to 2007 models	44 Nm
2008-on models	54 Nm
Sidestand pivot bolt	10 Nm
Sidestand pivot bolt nut	29 Nm
Steering head bearing adjuster nut (see text)	
Initial setting	25 Nm
Final setting	
2002 to 2007 models	15 Nm + 45°
2008-on models	29 Nm
Steering stem nut	103 Nm
Swingarm	
Early 2002 and 2003 models	
Right-hand pivot bolt	108 Nm
Left-hand pivot bolt	
Initial torque	54 Nm
Final torque	41 Nm
Left-hand pivot bolt locknut	
Actual	108 Nm
Indicated (with special tool)	98 Nm
Late 2002 models	
Right-hand pivot bolt	108 Nm
Left-hand pivot bolt	
Initial torque	54 Nm
Final torque	41 Nm
Left-hand pivot centre bolt	44 Nm
2004-on models	
Right-hand pivot bolt	
Initial torque	20 Nm
Final torque	130 Nm
Left-hand pivot bolt – shimmed	130 Nm
Left-hand pivot bolt – re-shimming	
Initial torque	54 Nm
Final torque	34 Nm

1 General information

All models have a box-section twin-spar aluminium frame which uses the engine as a stressed member.

Front suspension is by a pair of oil-damped telescopic forks that have a cartridge damper. The forks are not adjustable.

At the rear, a box-section aluminium swingarm acts on a single shock absorber. The swingarm pivots through the frame. The shock absorber is adjustable for spring pre-load and rebound damping.

2 Frame inspection and repair

1 The frame should not require attention unless accident damage has occurred. In most cases, fitting a new frame is the only

Frame and suspension

satisfactory remedy for such damage. A few frame specialists have the jigs and other equipment necessary for straightening frames to the required standard of accuracy, but even then there is no simple way of assessing to what extent the frame may have been over stressed.

2 After a high mileage, the frame should be examined closely for signs of cracking or splitting at the welded joints. Loose engine mounting bolts can cause ovaling or fracturing of the mounting points. Minor damage can often be repaired by specialised welding, depending on the extent and nature of the damage.

3 Remember that a frame that is out of alignment will cause handling problems. If, as the result of an accident, misalignment is suspected, it will be necessary to strip the machine completely so the frame can be thoroughly checked.

3 Footrests, brake pedal and gearchange lever

Footrests

Removal

1 Remove the split pin and washer from the bottom of the footrest pivot pin, then withdraw the pivot pin and remove the footrest (see illustration). On the rider's footrests, note the

3.1 Remove the split pin (arrowed) and washer, then draw the pivot pin out the top

fitting of the return spring. On the passenger footrests, note the fitting of the detent plate, ball and spring, and take care not to let the ball and spring ping away when removing the footrest.

2 If necessary you can replace the footrest rubbers with new ones – unscrew the bolts on the underside to release the rubber, and note the setting plate fitted between the rubber and the footrest (see illustration).

Installation

3 Installation is the reverse of removal. Apply a small amount of copper-based grease to the pivot pin.

Brake pedal

Removal

4 Remove the battery (see Chapter 8).

3.2 Unscrew the bolts (arrowed) to release the rubber

Remove the right-hand silencer (see Chapter 4).

5 Unscrew the guard plate bolt and remove the plate (see illustration). Straighten the ends of the split pin and withdraw it from the master cylinder pushrod clevis pin (see illustration). Withdraw the clevis pin and detach the pushrod from the pedal (see illustration).

6 Unscrew the bolt securing the rear of the downpipe assembly (see illustration). Unscrew the bolt in the battery tray (see illustration).

7 Unscrew the footrest bracket bolts, then displace the assembly and turn it so the inside is accessible, supporting it so you don't strain the brake hoses or brake light switch wiring (see illustration).

8 Unhook the brake pedal return spring and

3.5a Unscrew the bolt (arrowed) and remove the plate

3.5b Remove the split pin . . .

3.5c . . . and withdraw the clevis pin

3.6a Unscrew the downpipe bolt . . .

3.6b . . . and the battery tray bolt (arrowed)

3.7 Unscrew the bolts (arrowed) and displace the footrest bracket

5•4 Frame and suspension

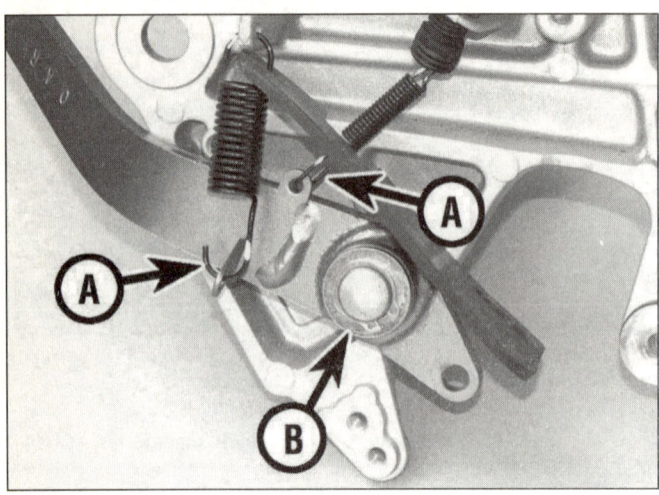

3.8 Unhook the springs (A), then release the circlip (B) and remove the washer and pedal

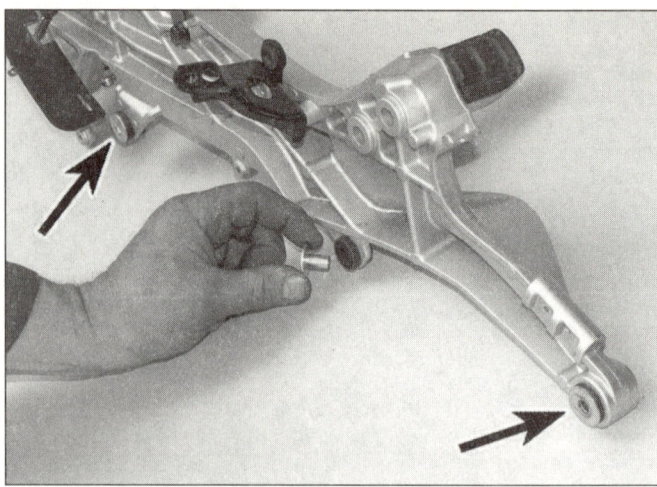

3.10 Make sure the three collars are fitted

the brake light switch spring from the pedal **(see illustration)**.

9 Release the circlip securing the brake pedal, then remove the washer **(see illustration 3.8)**. Slide the pedal off its pivot, and remove the wave washer.

Installation

10 Installation is the reverse of removal, noting the following:
- Clean any old grease off the pedal and pivot, then apply fresh grease.
- Slide the pedal onto the pivot, followed by the thrust washer. Make sure the circlip locates correctly in the groove, and use a new one if the old one deformed when removed **(see illustration 3.8)**. Connect the springs.
- Make sure none of the collars have fallen out of the exhaust mounting rubbers **(see illustration)**.
- Use a new split pin on the master cylinder pushrod clevis pin **(see illustration 3.5b)**.
- Tighten the footrest bracket bolts to the torque settings specified at the beginning of the Chapter.
- Check the operation of the rear brake light switch (see Chapter 1).

Gearchange lever and linkage

Removal

11 Remove the lower fairing (see Chapter 7). Remove the exhaust system (see Chapter 4).
12 Mark the alignment of the gearchange shaft with the slit in the linkage arm **(see illustration)**. Unscrew the linkage arm bolt and slide the arm off the shaft
13 Counter-hold the gearchange lever pivot bolt on the back of the frame cross-piece and unscrew the nut **(see illustration)**. Withdraw the pivot bolt far enough to allow the lever and linkage to be removed, then remove the washer that fits between the lever and the frame cross-piece **(see illustrations)**. Remove the bolt with its washer.
14 To separate the lever from the linkage rod note how far the rod is threaded into the lever and arm as this determines the height of the lever relative to the footrest. Slacken the linkage rod locknuts, then unscrew the rod and separate it from the lever and the arm – the rod is reverse-threaded on one end and will simultaneously unscrew from both lever

3.12 Mark the alignment of the arm with the shaft then unscrew the bolt (arrowed)

3.13a Unscrew the nut . . .

3.13b . . . withdraw the bolt . . .

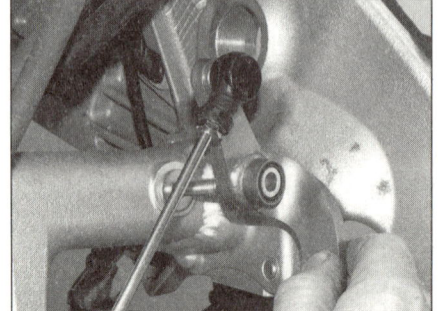

3.13c . . . and remove the linkage . . .

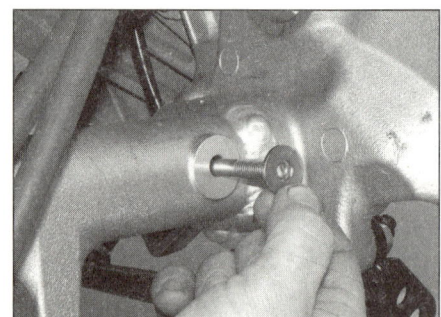

3.13d . . . and the washer

Frame and suspension 5•5

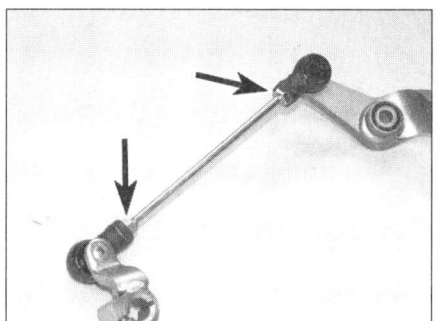

3.14 Linkage rod locknuts (arrowed)

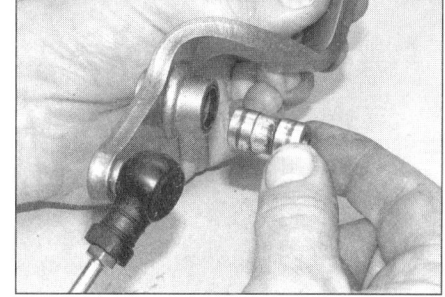

3.15a Withdraw the collar, clean and re-grease it

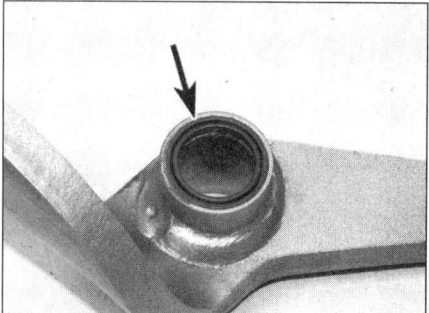

3.15b Fit a new seal (arrowed) on each side if required

and arm when turned in the one direction (see illustration).

Installation

15 Installation is the reverse of removal, noting the following:
- Withdraw the collar from the lever pivot (see illustration). Clean off all old grease and apply fresh grease. Fit new pivot seals if necessary (see illustration).
- Align the slit in the linkage arm clamp with the mark made on the gearchange shaft (see illustration 3.12).
- Adjust the gear lever height as required by screwing the linkage rod in or out of the lever and arm – to do this with the assembly in situ it is best to remove the oil filter (see Chapter 1) and sidestand assembly (see Section 4) to access the upper nut on the rod. Tighten the locknuts on completion.

4 Sidestand and centrestand

Sidestand

Removal

1 The sidestand is attached to a bracket that bolts onto the frame. Springs anchored between the stand and its bracket ensure the stand is held in the retracted or extended position. Support the bike on the centrestand. Remove the lower fairing (see Chapter 7).

2 To remove the sidestand without its bracket, first carefully unhook and remove the stand springs (see illustration). Unscrew the sidestand switch bolt and displace the switch – there is no need to disconnect its wiring connector or remove it completely, just let it hang from its wiring. Unscrew the nut from the pivot bolt (see illustration). Unscrew the pivot bolt and remove the stand.

3 To remove the complete sidestand assembly remove the left-hand side cover (see Chapter 7). Disconnect the sidestand switch wiring connector (see illustration). Feed the wiring down to the switch, noting its routing. Unscrew the sidestand bracket bolts and remove the stand assembly (see illustration).

Installation

4 If the stand was removed without its bracket, apply grease to the pivot bolt shank and tighten the bolt to the torque setting specified at the beginning of the Chapter. Fit the nut and tighten it to the specified torque (see illustration 4.2b). Fit the sidestand switch (see illustration 4.2a). Reconnect the springs and check that they hold the stand securely up when not in use – an accident is almost certain to occur if the stand extends while the machine is in motion (see illustration 4.2a).

5 If the complete sidestand assembly was removed, clean the threads of the bracket bolts and apply a suitable non-permanent thread locking compound. Fit the assembly and tighten the bolts to the torque setting specified at the beginning of the Chapter (see illustration 4.3b). Route the sidestand switch wiring up and connect it (see illustration 4.3a).

6 Check the operation of the stand and switch (see Chapter 1). Install the lower fairing, and the left-hand side cover if removed (see Chapter 7).

Centrestand

Removal

7 The centrestand pivots through the bottom of the frame. Springs anchored between the stand and the frame ensure the stand is held in the retracted or extended position. Support the bike on the sidestand and tie the front brake lever on. Remove the exhaust system (see Chapter 4).

4.2a Unhook the springs (A) then unscrew the sidestand switch bolt (B)

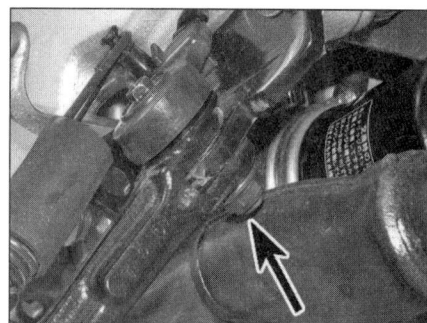

4.2b Unscrew the nut (arrowed), then unscrew the pivot bolt

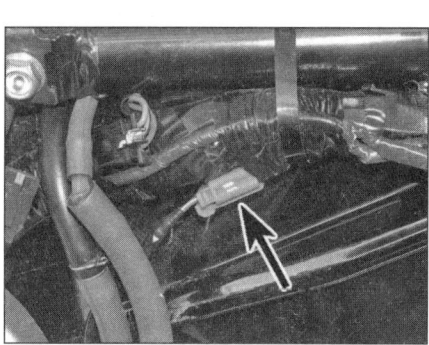

4.3a Sidestand switch wiring connector (arrowed)

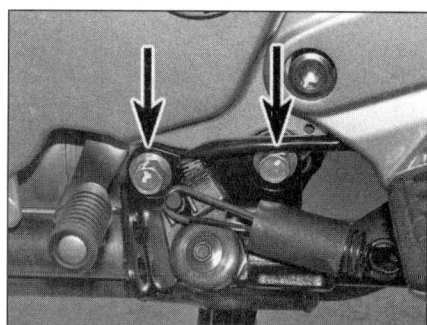

4.3b Sidestand bracket bolts (arrowed)

5•6 Frame and suspension

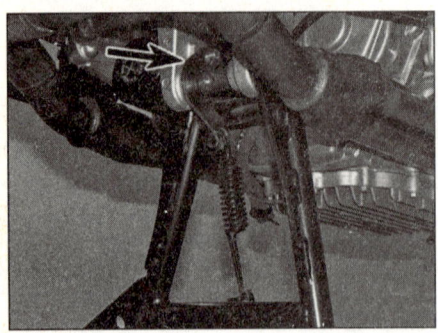

4.8 Carefully lever the arm (arrowed) off its post and remove the springs

4.9 Remove the split pin (arrowed) . . .

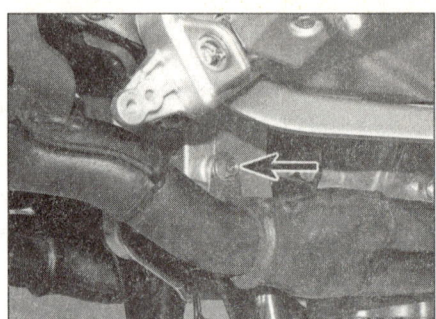

4.10 . . . then unscrew the bolt (arrowed) and withdraw the pivot

8 Unhook the spring arm from its post and remove the springs **(see illustration)**.

9 Straighten the ends of the split pin and withdraw it from the left-hand end of the pivot **(see illustration)** – discard it and use a new one on installation.

10 Unscrew the pivot holder bolt **(see illustration)**. Withdraw the pivot and remove the stand.

Installation

11 Apply grease to the pivoting surfaces on the stand. Tighten the pivot holder bolt to the torque setting specified at the beginning of the Chapter **(see illustration 4.10)**. Fit a new split pin and bend is ends round the pivot **(see illustration 4.9)**. Reconnect the springs and arm and check that they hold the stand securely up when not in use **(see illustration 4.8)** – an accident is almost certain to occur if the stand extends while the machine is in motion.

12 Check the operation of the stand (see Chapter 1). Install the exhaust system (see Chapter 4).

5 Handlebars and levers

Note: *The handlebars can be displaced from the top yoke without detaching any of the assemblies from them – follow Step 5 or 9.*

1 As a precaution, remove the fairing side panels and the fairing and instrument console (see Chapter 7), and raise the main fuel tank (see Chapter 4). Though not actually necessary, this will prevent the possibility of damage should a tool slip and improve access.

Right handlebar removal

2 Disconnect the wires from the brake light switch **(see illustration)**. Unscrew the two master cylinder assembly clamp bolts and position the assembly clear of the handlebar, making sure no strain is placed on the hydraulic hose **(see illustration)**. Keep the master cylinder reservoir upright to prevent possible fluid leakage.

3 Unscrew the two handlebar switch housing screws **(see illustration)**.

4 Undo the handlebar end-weight retaining screw and remove the weight from the end of the handlebar **(see illustration)**.

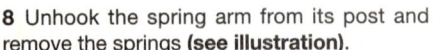

5.2a Disconnect the wiring connectors (arrowed)

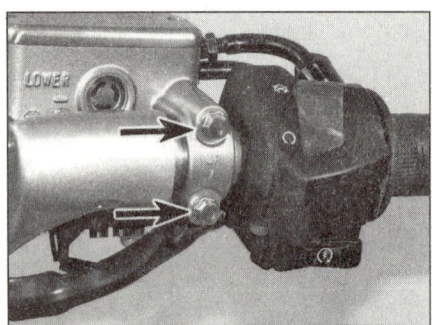

5.2b Unscrew the master cylinder clamp bolts (arrowed) and displace the assembly

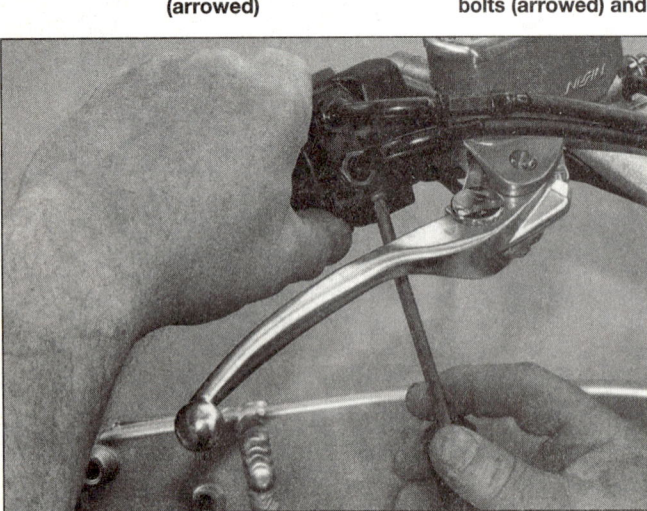

5.3 Undo the switch housing screws

5.4 Handlebar end-weight screw (arrowed)

Frame and suspension

5.5 Undo the screws (arrowed) and remove the cover

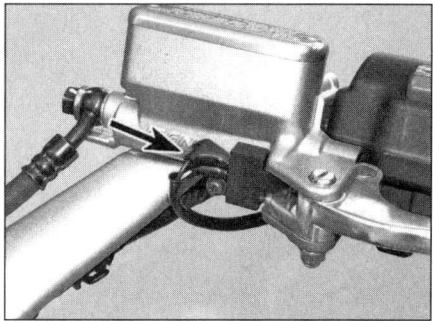

5.6a Disconnect the wiring connectors (arrowed)

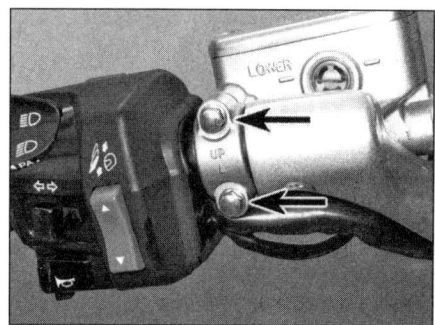

5.6b Unscrew the master cylinder clamp bolts (arrowed) and displace the assembly

5 Remove the handlebar centre cover (see illustration). Carefully prise the blanking caps out of the handlebar bolts (see illustration 5.9a). Unscrew the handlebar bolts, displace the handlebar and slide it out of the throttle twistgrip (see illustration 5.9b).

Left handlebar removal

6 Disconnect the wires from the clutch switch (see illustration). Unscrew the two master cylinder assembly clamp bolts and position the assembly clear of the handlebar, making sure no strain is placed on the hydraulic hose (see illustration). Keep the master cylinder reservoir upright to prevent possible fluid leakage.

7 Unscrew the two handlebar switch housing screws and detach the top half (see illustration). Undo the switch holder screw and detach the bottom half, noting how the holder fits.

8 If required, undo the handlebar end-weight retaining screw and remove the weight from the end of the handlebar (see illustration 5.4). Slide off the grip – if it has been glued on, you will probably have to slit it with a knife to remove it, which means replacing it with a new one.

9 Remove the handlebar centre cover (see illustration 5.5). Carefully prise the blanking caps out of the handlebar bolts (see illustration). Unscrew the handlebar bolts and remove the handlebar (see illustration).

Handlebar holder

10 To remove the handlebar holder from the top yoke, first displace or remove the handlebars. Counter-hold the bolt heads and unscrew the nuts on the underside of the yoke, noting the washers (see illustration). Withdraw the bolts and remove the handlebar holder. Check the condition of the rubber dampers and replace the holder with a new one if necessary.

Handlebar weights

11 If a new handlebar is being installed, you need to transfer the inner weight from the old bar to the new one – to do this, reinstall the end-weight and tighten its screw. Squirt some lubricant (such as WD40) into the inner weight retainer tab hole, then press down on the tab using a screwdriver, then twist and pull on the end-weight, drawing the inner weight assembly out. Remove the end-weight and discard the retainer as a new one should be used. Check the condition of the rubbers on the inner weight and fit new ones if they are damaged, deformed or deteriorated.

Installation

12 Installation is the reverse of removal, noting the following.
- To fit new grips onto the throttle twistgrip and left handlebar, apply a suitable glue (Pro Honda handgrip cement or equivalent) to each, making sure they are clean, then rotate the grip when in place to evenly distribute the glue. Align the groove on the inside of the inner end of the right-hand grip with the index line on the throttle twistgrip. Allow the glue to fully dry before riding the bike.

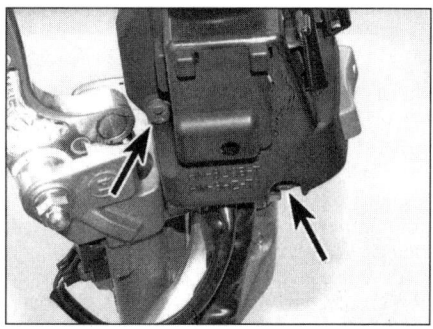

5.7 Undo the switch housing screws

5.9b Handlebar bolts (arrowed)

- When fitting the right handlebar, smear some grease onto throttle twistgrip sliding surface. Slide the throttle twistgrip and cable housing assembly onto the handlebar before fitting the handlebar onto the holder.
- Tighten the handlebar bolts to the torque setting specified at the beginning of the Chapter.
- When fitting the handlebar inner weights, locate the tab on the retainer in the hole in the handlebar.
- When fitting the handlebar end-weights, align the boss with the cut-out on the inner weight inside the handlebar. Tighten the screws to the specified torque setting.
- Make sure the front brake and clutch master cylinder clamps are installed with the UP mark facing up (see illustrations 5.2b and 5.6b), and with the clamp mating surfaces aligned with the punch mark on

5.9a Prise the blanking caps out

5.10 Handlebar holder bolt nut (arrowed)

5•8 Frame and suspension

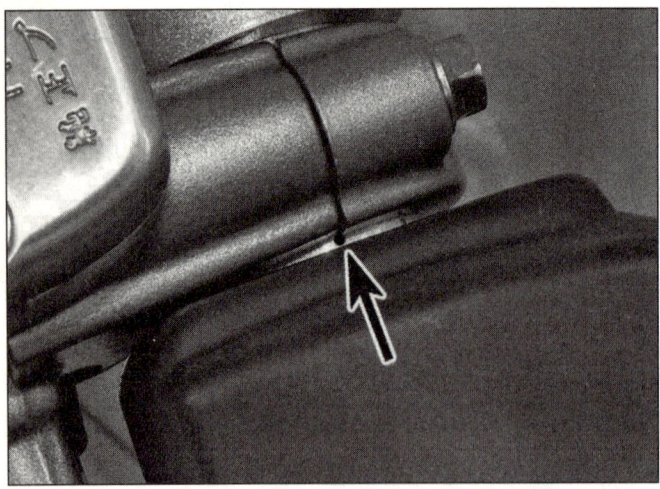

5.12a Align the clamp mating surfaces with the punch mark (arrowed)

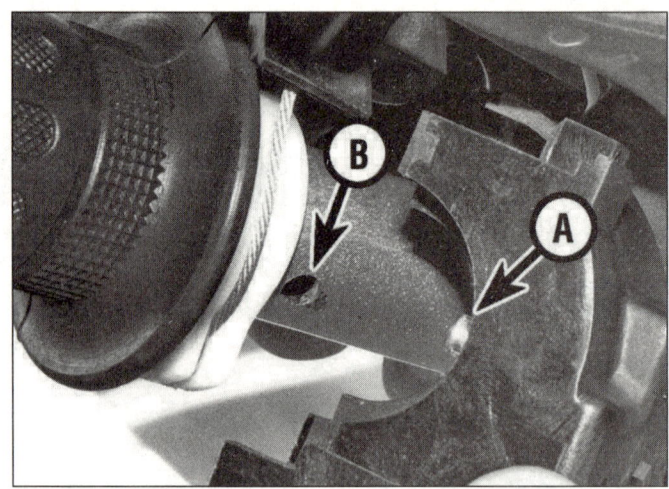

5.12b Locate the pin (A) in the hole (B)

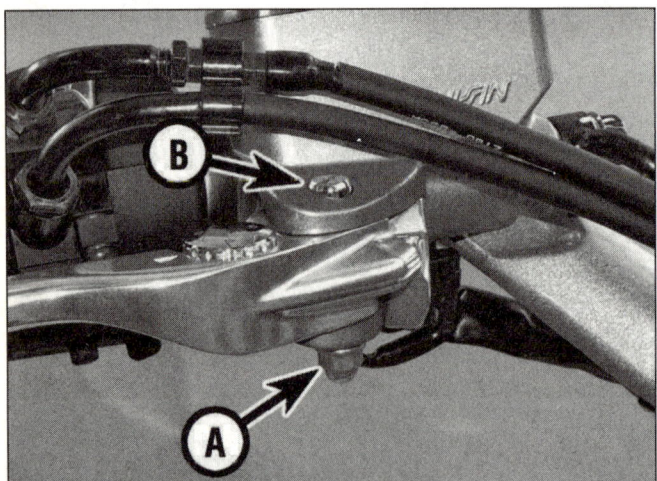

5.13a Front brake lever locknut (A) and pivot screw (B)

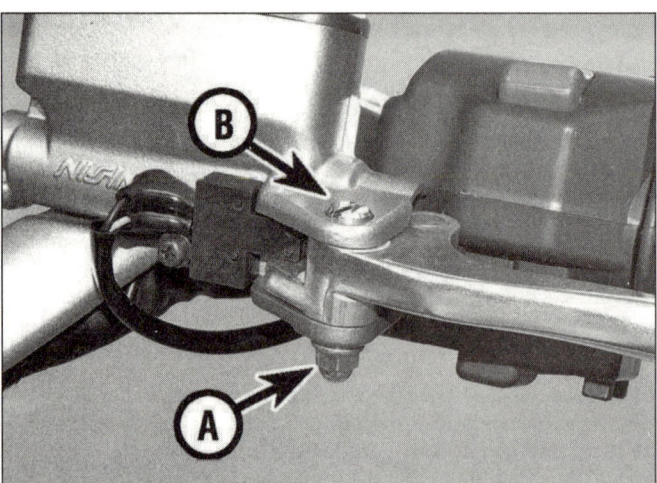

5.13b Clutch lever locknut (A) and pivot screw (B)

the top of the handlebar **(see illustration 5.12a)**. Tighten the master cylinder clamp bolts to the specified torque setting, tightening the top bolt first.
- Make sure the pin in the bottom half of each switch housing locates in its hole in the handlebar **(see illustration 5.12b)**. Do not forget to fit the holder for the bottom half of the left-hand housing. Tighten the front housing screw first, then the rear.
- Do not forget to reconnect the front brake light switch and clutch switch wiring connectors **(see illustrations 5.2a and 5.6a)**.

Levers

13 Undo the lever pivot screw locknut, then undo the pivot screw and remove the lever – there is a bush in the clutch lever that could drop out, so take care not to lose it **(see illustrations)**.
14 Installation is the reverse of removal.

Apply silicone grease to all sliding surfaces and contact points. Apply a spray lubricant such as WD40, or a dry-film Teflon lubricant to the brake lever span adjuster mechanism. Fit the bush into the clutch lever, and locate the pushrod tip into its hole. Tighten the pivot screw lightly, then counter-hold it and tighten the nut.

6 Fork removal and installation

Removal

1 Remove the fairing side panels (see Chapter 7). Remove the front mudguard (see Chapter 7). Remove the front wheel (see Chapter 6) – when displacing the calipers also displace the brake hose/delay valve assembly from the forks. Tie the front brake calipers and hoses back so that they are out of the way.

2 Note the routing of all cables, hoses and wiring around the forks.
3 Working on one fork at a time, slacken the fork clamp bolt in the top yoke **(see illustration)**.
4 If the fork is to be disassembled, or if the fork oil is being changed, remove the blanking

6.3 Slacken the fork clamp bolt (arrowed) in the top yoke

Frame and suspension 5•9

cap from the fork top bolt and slacken the bolt **(see illustration)**. Measure and note the amount of protrusion of the fork above the top yoke – as standard the top of the fork tube (not the top bolt) should be flush with the yoke surface **(see illustration 6.7)**.

5 Slacken the fork clamp bolts in the bottom yoke, and remove the fork by twisting it and pulling it downwards **(see illustrations)**.

  If the fork legs are seized in the yokes, spray the area with penetrating oil and allow time for it to soak in before trying again.

Installation

6 Remove all traces of corrosion from the fork tube and the yokes. Slide the fork up through the bottom yoke and into the top yoke, making sure all cables, hoses and wiring are routed on the correct side of the fork **(see illustration 6.5b)**.

7 Set the amount of protrusion of the fork tube above the top yoke as noted on removal – Honda specify that the top of the fork tube (not the top bolt) should be flush with the upper surface of the yoke **(see illustration)**.

8 Tighten the fork clamp bolts in the bottom yoke to the torque setting specified at the beginning of the Chapter **(see illustration 6.5a)**.

9 If the fork has been dismantled or if the fork oil was changed, tighten the fork top bolt to the specified torque setting, then fit the blanking cap **(see illustration 6.4)**.

10 Now tighten the fork clamp bolt in the top yoke to the specified torque **(see illustration 6.3)**.

11 Install the front wheel (see Chapter 6) and the front mudguard (see Chapter 7). Install the fairing side panels (see Chapter 7).

12 Check the operation of the front forks and brakes before taking the machine out on the road.

7 Fork oil change

1 After a high mileage the fork oil will deteriorate and its damping and lubrication qualities will be impaired. Always change the oil in both fork legs.

2 Remove the fork; ensure that the top bolt is loosened while the leg is still clamped in the bottom yoke (see Section 6).

3 Unscrew the fork top bolt from the top of the inner tube **(see illustration)** The bolt will remain on the damper rod, held by the locknut on its top.

4 Slide the inner tube down gently until it seats on the bottom. Hold the top bolt and

6.4 Remove the blanking cap and slacken the fork top bolt (arrowed) if the fork is to be disassembled

6.5b ... then draw the fork down and out of the yokes

push the spacer down against the spring to expose the locknut, and fit a spanner onto it. Counter-hold the locknut and unscrew the top bolt **(see illustration)**.

5 Remove the spacer, then hook the

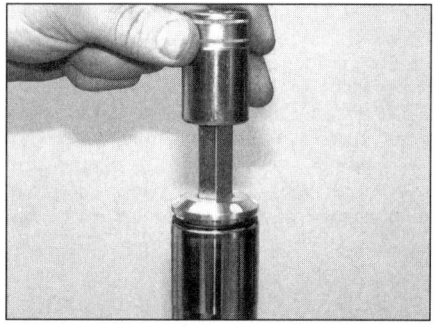

7.3 Thread the top bolt out of the tube

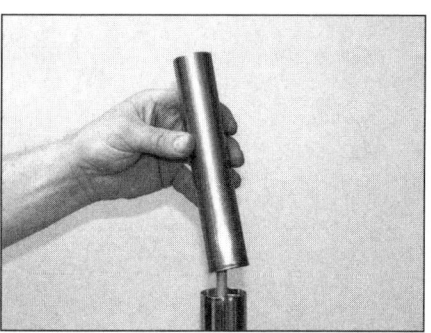

7.5a Remove the spacer ...

6.5a Slacken the fork clamp bolts (arrowed) in the bottom yoke ...

6.7 Set the fork in the top yoke as shown

spacer seat and spring out of the tube **(see illustrations)**.

6 Invert the fork leg over a suitable container and pump the fork and damper rod several times to expel as much fork oil as possible

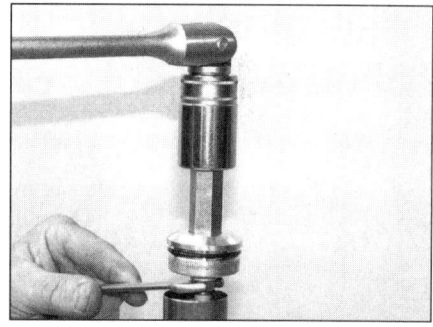

7.4 Hold the locknut and unscrew the top bolt

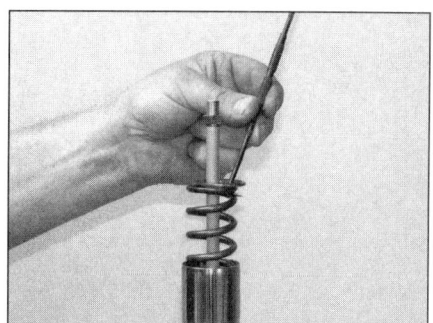

7.5b ... then hook the spacer seat and spring out

5•10 Frame and suspension

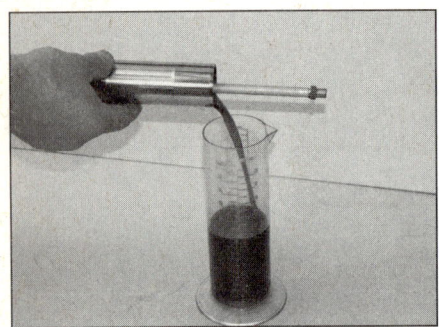

7.6 Drain the oil as described

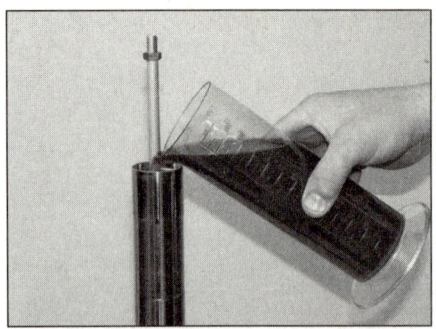

7.7a Pour the oil into the top of the tube and distribute and bleed it as described . . .

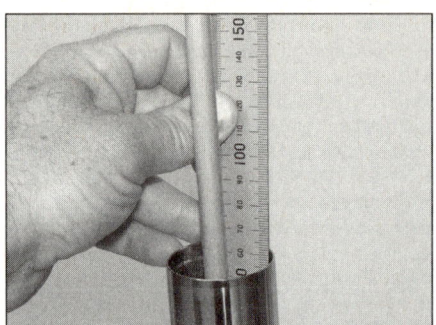

7.7b . . . then measure the level

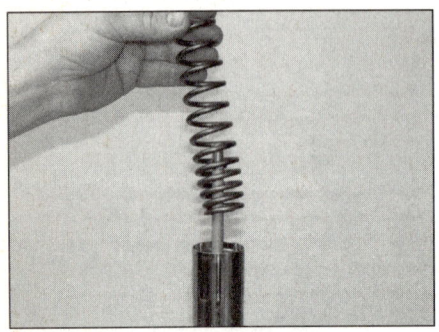

7.8a Fit the spring with its closer-wound coils at the bottom

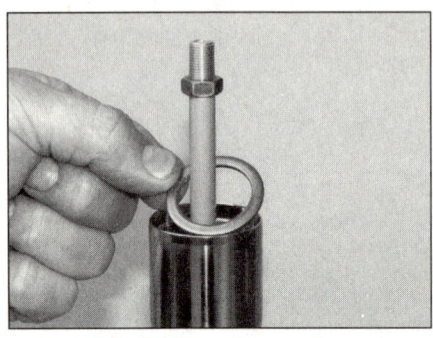

7.8b Fit the spacer seat . . .

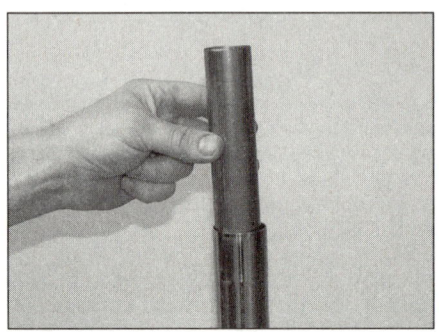

7.8c . . . and the spacer

(see illustration). Support the fork upside down in the container for a while to allow as much oil as possible to drain, then pump the fork and rod again. If the fork oil contains metal particles inspect the fork bushes for wear (see Section 8). Wipe any excess oil off the spring and spacer.

7 Stand the fork upright. Slowly pour in the specified quantity of the specified grade of fork oil **(see illustration)**. Now pump the fork and damper rod slowly at least ten times each to distribute the oil evenly and expel all air from the damper. Slide the inner tube down gently until it seats on the bottom. Measure the oil level from the top of the tube **(see illustration)**. Add or subtract oil until it is at the level specified at the beginning of this Chapter.

8 Make sure the locknut is at the bottom of its threads on the damper rod. Pull the damper rod and inner tube out as far as possible, then fit the spring with its closer-wound coils towards the bottom **(see illustration)**. Keeping the damper rod extended, fit the spacer seat and spacer **(see illustrations)**.

9 Keeping the damper rod extended push down on the spacer to compress the spring and thread the top bolt onto the damper rod **(see illustration)**. Counter-hold the locknut using a spanner as before and tighten the top bolt securely against it **(see illustration 7.4)**.

10 If the top bolt O-ring is damaged or deteriorated fit a new one. Smear some fork oil onto the O-ring. Extend the inner tube and thread the top bolt into it, making sure it does not cross-thread, and tighten it as much as possible holding the inner tube by hand **(see illustration)**. **Note:** *Tighten the top bolt to the specified torque setting when the fork has been installed in the bike and is held in the bottom yoke, but before the top yoke clamp bolt is tightened.*

11 Install the fork (see Section 6).

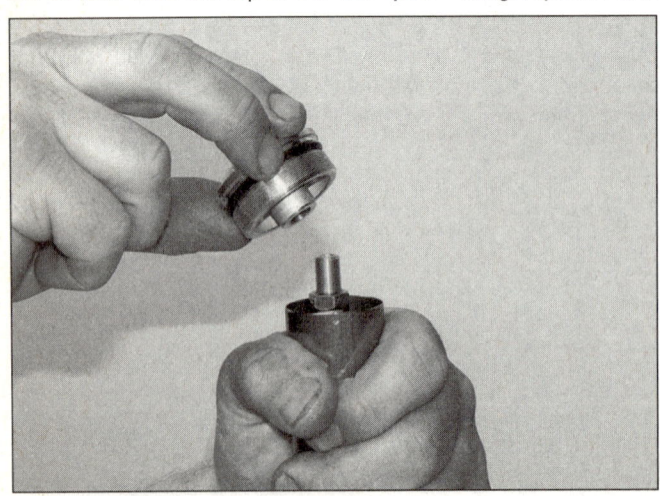

7.9 Compress the spring and thread the top bolt onto the rod

7.10 Thread the top bolt into the tube

Frame and suspension 5•11

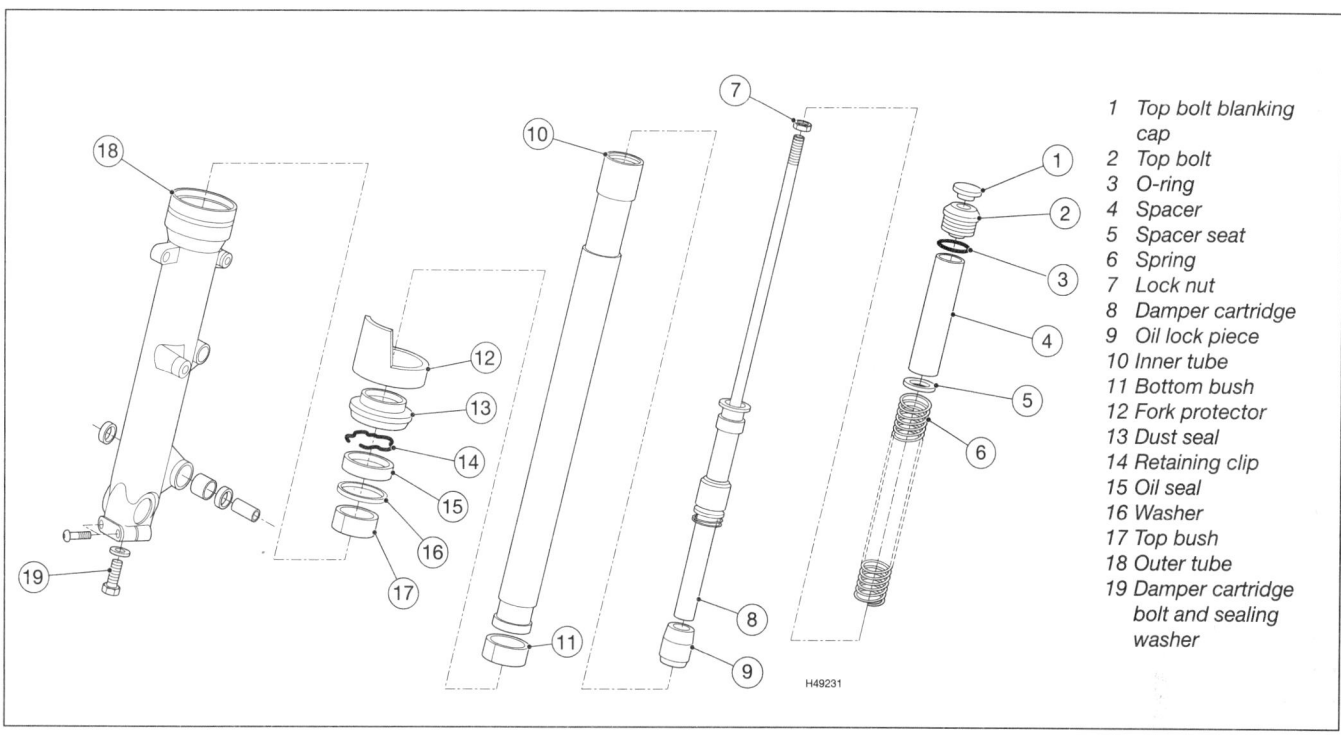

1 Top bolt blanking cap
2 Top bolt
3 O-ring
4 Spacer
5 Spacer seat
6 Spring
7 Lock nut
8 Damper cartridge
9 Oil lock piece
10 Inner tube
11 Bottom bush
12 Fork protector
13 Dust seal
14 Retaining clip
15 Oil seal
16 Washer
17 Top bush
18 Outer tube
19 Damper cartridge bolt and sealing washer

8.1 Front fork components

8 Fork overhaul

Disassembly

1 Remove the fork; ensure that the top bolt is loosened while the leg is still clamped in the bottom yoke (see Section 6). Always dismantle the fork legs separately to avoid interchanging parts and thus causing an accelerated rate of wear. Store all components in separate, clearly marked containers **(see illustration)**.
2 Remove the fork protector, noting how it locates **(see illustration)**.
3 Lay the fork flat on the bench with the caliper mounting lugs to the left, then hold the fork down and slacken the damper cartridge bolt in the base of the fork **(see illustration)**.
4 Refer to Section 7, Steps 3 to 6 and drain the oil from the fork.
5 Remove the damper cartridge bolt and its sealing washer from the bottom of the fork **(see illustration 8.24c)**. Discard the sealing washer as a new one must be used on reassembly. If the damper cartridge rotates inside the fork whilst attempting to unscrew the bolt, reinstall the fork spring, spacer and top bolt, and compress the fork so that the spring exerts pressure on the cartridge body whilst the bolt is unscrewed. Alternatively, if available use an air wrench.
6 Withdraw the damper cartridge from inside the fork tube **(see illustration)**. Remove the oil lock piece from the bottom of the damper **(see illustration)**.

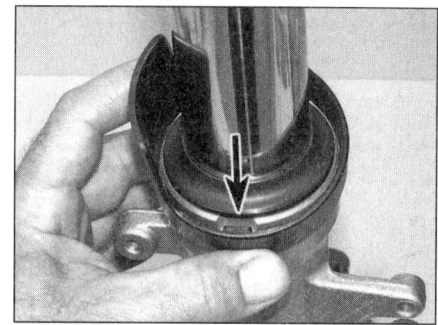

8.2 Remove the protector, noting how it locates in the cut-out (arrowed)

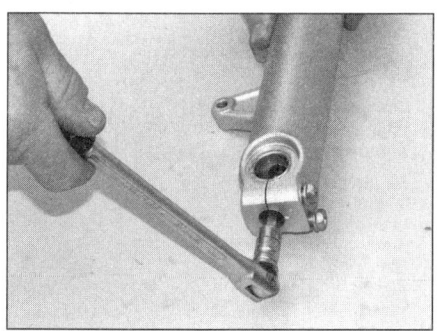

8.3 Slacken the damper cartridge bolt

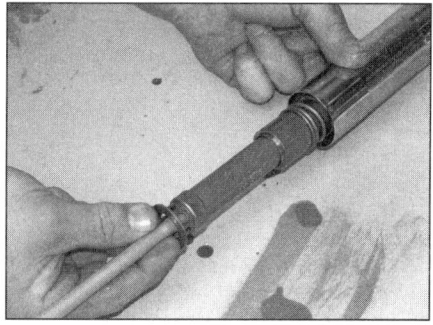

8.6a Withdraw the damper cartridge . . .

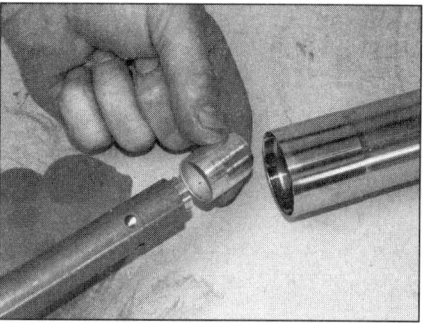

8.6b . . . and remove the oil lock piece

5•12 Frame and suspension

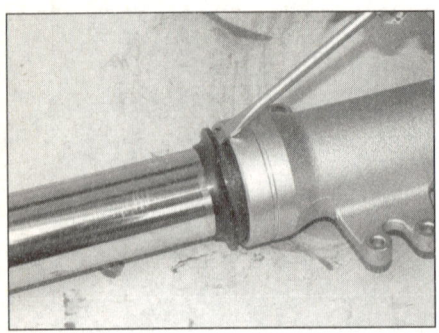

8.7 Prise out the dust seal using a flat-bladed screwdriver

8.8 Prise out the retaining clip using a flat-bladed screwdriver

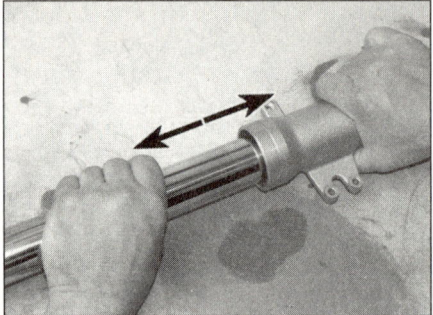

8.9a To separate the tubes pull them apart firmly several times . . .

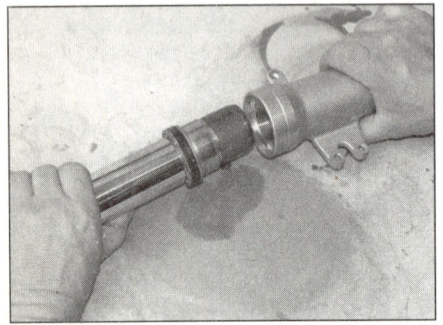

8.9b . . . the slide-hammer effect will displace the oil seal, washer and top bush

8.10 Carefully lever the bush ends apart to expand it

7 Carefully prise out the dust seal from the top of the outer tube **(see illustration)**.

8 Carefully prise out the oil seal retaining clip, taking care not to scratch the surface of the inner tube **(see illustration)**.

9 To separate the inner and outer tubes it is necessary to displace the top bush and oil seal from the top of the outer tube. The bottom bush on the inner tube will not pass through the top bush, and this can be used to good effect. Grasp the inner tube in one hand and the outer tube in the other and compress them slightly, then pull them apart so that the bottom bush strikes the top bush **(see illustration)**. Repeat this operation until the top bush and seal are tapped out **(see illustration)**.

10 Slide the oil seal, the oil seal washer and top bush off the inner tube, noting which way up they fit **(see illustration 8.9b)**. Discard the oil seal and the dust seal as new ones must be used. Do not remove the bottom bush from the inner tube unless it is being replaced with a new one – to remove it carefully lever its ends apart using a screwdriver and slide it out of its recess **(see illustration)**.

Inspection

11 Clean all parts in solvent and blow them dry with compressed air, if available.

12 Check the fork inner tube for score marks, dents, pitting, scratches, flaking of its surface and excessive or abnormal wear. Fit a new tube if any are found. Check the inner tube for runout using V-blocks and a dial gauge. If the amount of runout exceeds the service limit specified, a new tube should be fitted.

 Warning: If the inner tube is bent or exceeds the runout limit, it should not be straightened; replace it with a new one.

13 Check the fork outer tube for cracks. Check the fork seal seat and housing for nicks, gouges and scratches. If damage is evident, leaks will occur. Also check the oil seal washer for damage or distortion and fit a new one if necessary.

14 Check the spring for cracks and other damage. Measure the spring free length and compare the measurement to the specifications at the beginning of the Chapter **(see illustration)**. If it is defective or sagged below the service limit, replace the springs in both forks with new ones. Never renew only one spring.

15 Examine the working surfaces of the two bushes (i.e. the outer surface of the bottom bush and the inner surface of the top bush) **(see illustration)**; if the grey Teflon outer surface has been worn away to reveal the copper inner surface over more than 75% of the surface area, or if the bushes are scored or badly scuffed, they must be replaced with new ones.

16 Check the damper cartridge and rod, and the rebound spring fitted on it, for damage and wear **(see illustration)**. Hold the body of the cartridge and pump the rod in and out. If any wear or damage is found, or if the rod does not move smoothly in the damper, a new damper must be installed.

Reassembly

17 If removed fit the bottom bush into its recess in the bottom of the inner tube **(see illustration 8.10)**. Apply a smear of fork oil

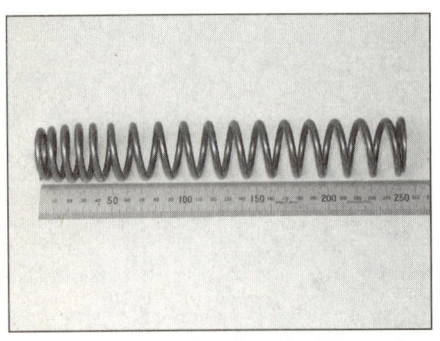

8.14 Measure the free length of the spring

8.15 Check the working surface (arrowed) of each bush for wear

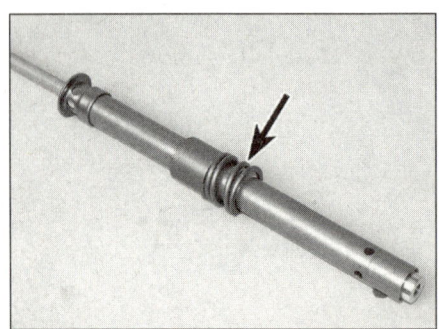

8.16 Check the damper and rebound spring (arrowed)

Frame and suspension 5•13

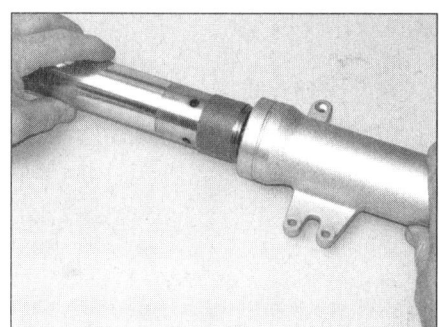

8.17 Slide the inner tube into the outer tube

8.18a Slide the top bush down and into the outer tube . . .

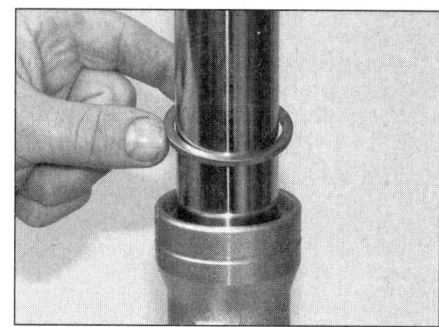

8.18b . . . then seat the washer on the bush . . .

to the bush. Slide the inner tube fully into the outer tube (see illustration).

18 Apply a smear of fork oil to the inner surface of the top bush. Slide the bush down the inner tube and seat it in the top of the outer tube (see illustration). Slide the oil seal washer onto the bush (see illustration).

19 Support the fork upright. Using either the special service tool (part No. 07KMD-KZ3010A in the US or 07KMD-KZ30100 in Europe) or a suitable drift, carefully drive the bottom bush fully into its recess – the oil seal washer prevents damaging the edges of the bush (see illustration). If using a drift, wrap tape around it to prevent scratching the chrome. Make sure the bush enters the recess squarely. It is best to make sure that the fork inner tube is withdrawn as much as possible from the outer tube so that any accidental scratching is confined to the area that does not affect the oil seal.

20 Lift the washer to check the bush is seated fully and squarely in its recess in the slider, then wipe the recess clean and re-seat the washer (see illustration).

21 Apply a smear of fork oil to the lips of the new oil seal. Slide the seal onto the tube with its marked side facing up (see illustration). Drive the seal into place as described in Step 19 until the retaining clip groove is visible (see illustrations).

22 Fit the retaining clip, making sure it is correctly located in its groove (see illustration).

8.19 . . . and drive the bush in and onto its seat

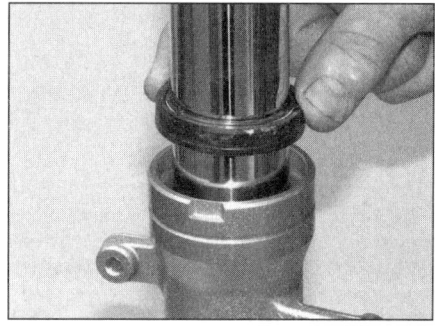

8.21a Slide the new oil seal down and into the outer tube . . .

23 Press the new dust seal into the top of the outer tube (see illustration).

24 Clean the threads of the damper cartridge

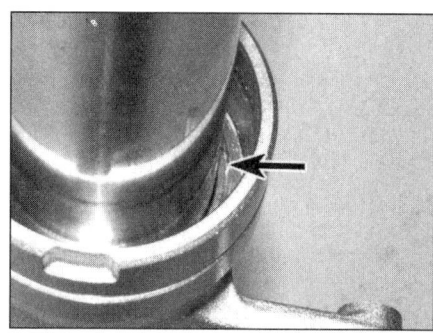

8.20 Make sure the bush (arrowed) is fully seated

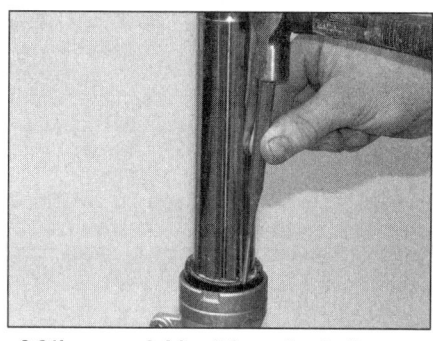

8.21b . . . and drive it in and onto its seat

bolt. Lay the fork flat on the bench with the caliper mounting lugs to the right. Fit the oil lock piece onto the bottom of the damper

8.21c Make sure the retaining clip groove (arrowed) is fully exposed

8.22 Fit the retaining clip in its groove . . .

8.23 . . . then press the new dust seal in

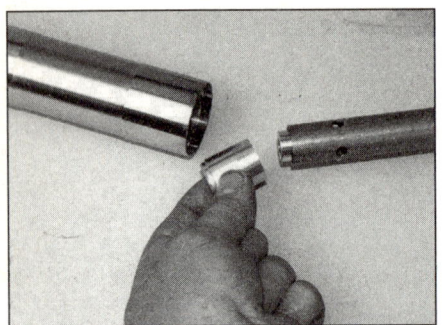

8.24a Fit the oil lock piece . . .

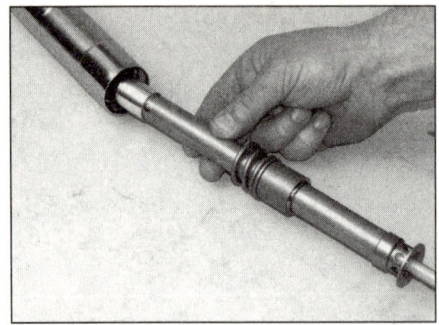

8.24b . . . then insert the damper

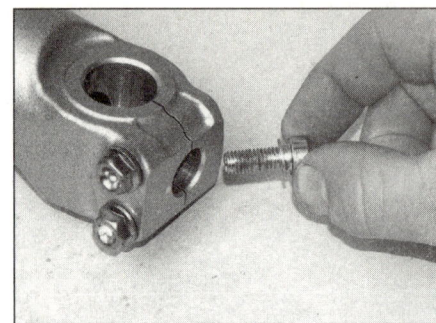

8.24c Fit a new sealing washer and apply threadlock . . .

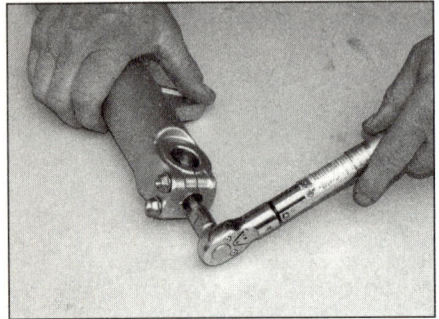

8.24d . . . and tighten the bolt to the specified torque

9.2 Unscrew the brake hose guide bolts (arrowed)

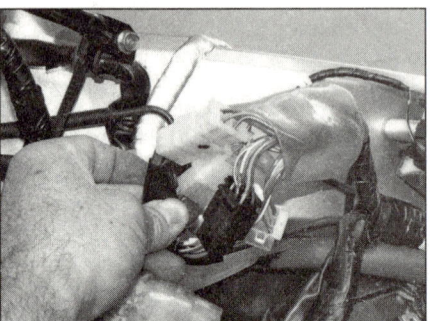

9.3a Disconnect the ignition switch wiring connector . . .

cartridge **(see illustration)**. Slide the cartridge fully into the fork tube **(see illustration)**. Fit a new sealing washer onto the cartridge bolt and apply a few drops of a suitable non-permanent thread locking compound **(see illustration)**. Fit the bolt into the bottom of the outer tube and thread it into the cartridge, tightening it to the torque setting specified at the beginning of the Chapter **(see illustration)**. If the damper cartridge rotates inside the tube as you tighten the bolt, wait until the fork is fully reassembled and tighten it then (the pressure of the spring on the cartridge will prevent it from turning).

25 Refer to Section 7, Steps 7 to 10 and fill the fork with the recommended amount and type of oil and finish reassembly.

26 If the damper cartridge bolt requires tightening (see Step 24), place the fork upside down on the floor, using a rag to protect it, then have an assistant compress the fork so that maximum spring pressure is placed on the damper cartridge head while tightening the bolt to the specified torque setting.

27 Install the fork (see Section 6).

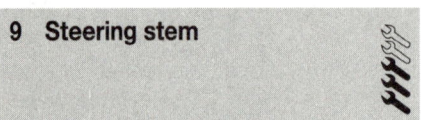

9 Steering stem

Special tool: *A peg spanner is required for tightening the head bearing adjuster nut (see Step 12). If the Honda tool is not available, and you are unable to fabricate your own, then a C-spanner will be required.*

Removal

1 Remove the front forks (see Section 6). As a precaution, remove the fairing (see Chapter 7), and raise the main fuel tank (see Chapter 4) – though not actually essential, this will prevent the possibility of damage should a tool slip.

2 Where fitted unscrew the bolts and remove the shield from the bottom yoke. Unscrew the bolts securing the front brake hose holder to the bottom yoke and displace it **(see illustration)**. Take care not to strain or knock the brake hoses when removing the steering stem.

3 You can remove the steering stem by just displacing the top yoke and handlebar assembly off the top, however to actually remove the top yoke, first displace the handlebars and their holder (see Section 5), then trace the wiring from the ignition switch, and where fitted the HISS receiver, and disconnect at the connector(s) **(see illustrations)**. Release the wiring from any clips or ties and feed it through to the yoke.

4 Unscrew the steering stem nut **(see illustration)**. Lift the top yoke, along with the handlebars, up off the steering stem and position it clear, using a rag to protect other components **(see illustration)**.

9.3b . . . and where fitted the HISS receiver wiring connector (arrowed)

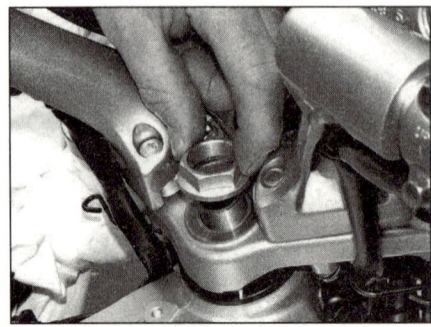

9.4a Unscrew the steering stem nut

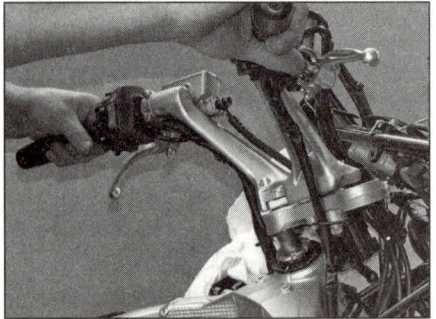

9.4b Displacing the handlebars and top yoke as an assembly

Frame and suspension 5•15

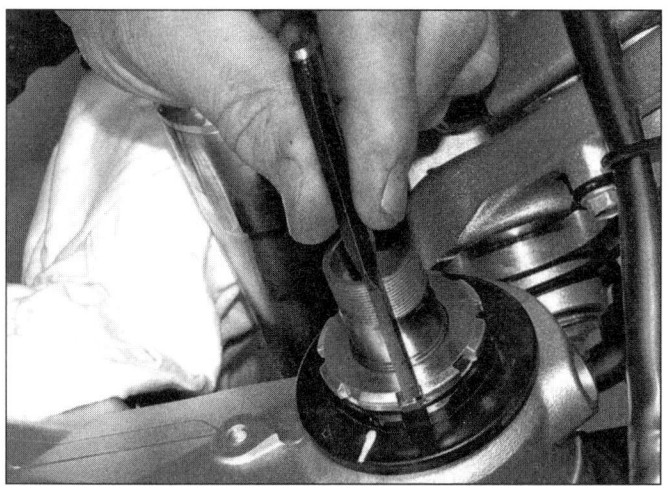

9.5a Bend down the lockwasher tabs . . .

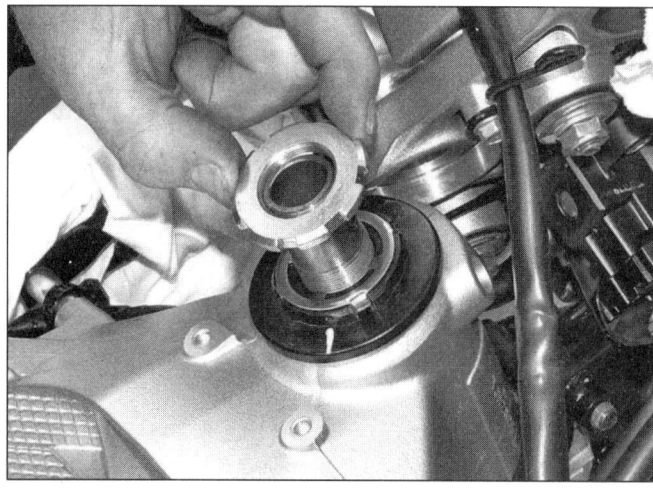

9.5b . . . then unscrew the locknut . . .

5 Bend the lockwasher tabs out of the notches in the locknut **(see illustration)**. Unscrew the locknut using either your fingers (it shouldn't be tight), a C-spanner or a suitable drift located in one of the notches **(see illustration)**. Remove the lockwasher **(see illustration)**. Inspect the tabs for cracks or signs of fatigue. If there is any sign of damage, discard the lockwasher and use a new one; otherwise the old one can be re-used, but note that Honda recommend using a new one as a matter of course.

6 If the peg spanner mentioned above is not available, make an alignment mark between the adjuster nut and the frame **(see illustration)** – this can serve as a rough guide for the tightness of the adjuster nut on installation. As you unscrew the nut count the number of turns.

7 Support the bottom yoke and unscrew the adjuster nut using a peg-spanner **(see illustration 9.12)** or socket, a C-spanner **(see illustration 9.13)**, or a drift located in one of the notches **(see illustrations)**. Gently lower the bottom yoke and steering stem out of the frame **(see illustration)**.

8 Remove the seal, inner race and bearing from the top of the steering head **(see illustration)**. Remove the bearing from the base of the steering stem **(see illustration 9.10)**.

9 Remove all traces of old grease from the bearings and races and check them for wear or damage as described in Section 10. **Note:** *Do not attempt to remove the races from the steering head or the steering stem unless they are to be replaced with new ones.*

Installation

10 Smear a liberal quantity of multi-purpose grease (Honda recommend a Urea-based grease with EP2 rating) onto the bearing races, and work some grease well into both the upper and lower bearings. Also smear the grease seal lip, using a new seal if necessary.

9.5c . . . and remove the lockwasher

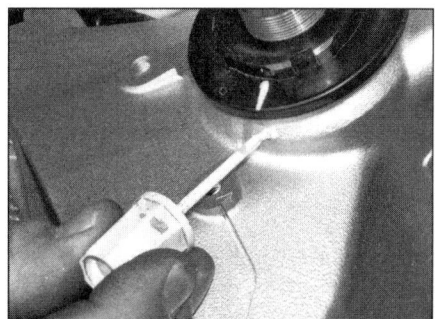

9.6 Make an alignment mark if required

9.7a Using a drift to initially slacken the adjuster nut

9.7b Unscrew the adjuster nut . . .

9.7c . . . and lower the steering stem out of the head

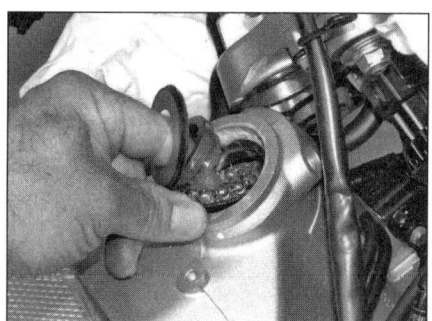

9.8 Remove the seal, inner race and upper bearing

5•16 Frame and suspension

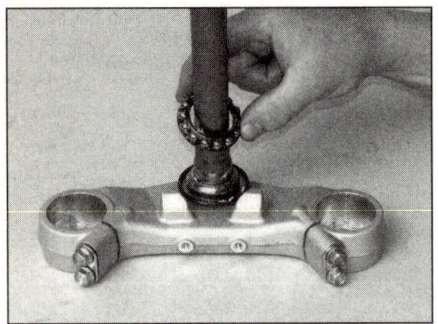

9.10 Fit the lower bearing onto the steering stem

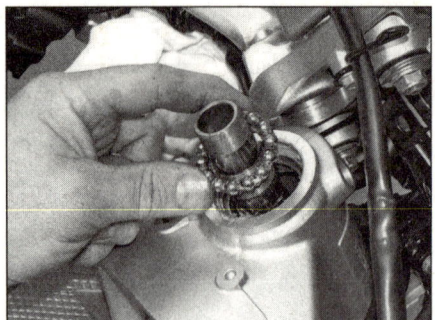

9.11a Fit the upper bearing . . .

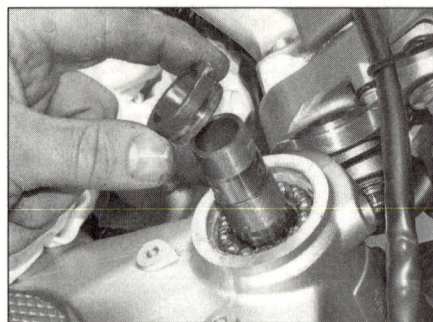

9.11b . . . the inner race . . .

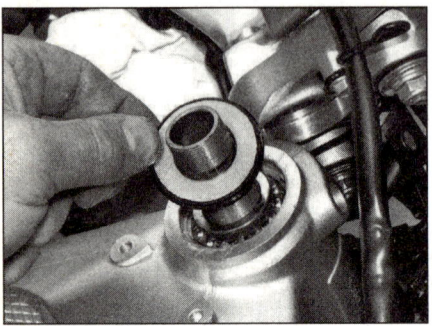

9.11c . . . and the seal

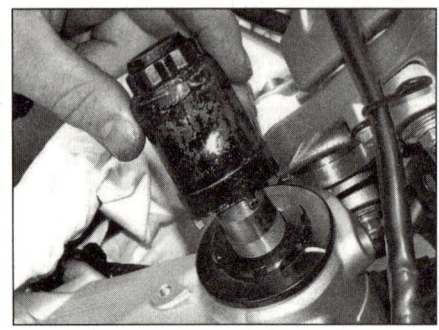

9.12 This is a home-made peg spanner to tighten the adjuster nut

Fit the lower bearing onto the steering stem **(see illustration)**.

11 Carefully lift the steering stem/bottom yoke up through the steering head and support it there **(see illustration 9.7c)**. Fit the upper bearing and its inner race into the top of the steering head **(see illustrations)**. Fit the seal **(see illustration)**. Apply oil to the adjuster nut threads and thread it onto the steering stem **(see illustration 9.7b)**.

12 Using the Honda service tool (Pt. No. 07916-3710101 or 3710100 according to country) or a suitable peg spanner, which can be made by cutting castellations into an old socket **(see illustration)**, tighten the adjuster nut to the initial torque setting specified at the beginning of the Chapter, then turn the steering from lock-to-lock five times, then slacken the nut and proceed according to model year:

On 2002 to 2007 models now tighten the nut firstly to the final specified torque setting, and then through a further 45° (1/8 turn) – you can use the notches, which are 90° apart, as a guide, along with paint marks for alignment.

On 2008-on models now tighten the nut to the final specified torque setting.

Ensure that the steering stem is able to move smoothly (though it may feel a bit tight, but this is normal as the weight of the forks and wheel is not influencing the feel) from lock-to-lock following adjustment – note that it is best to check and if necessary reset the bearing adjustment as described in Chapter 1 after the forks and front wheel and all other components have been installed.

13 If the correct tools are not available, tighten the nut the number of turns recorded on removal using a C-spanner or drift until the marks align **(see illustration)**. Turn the steering from lock-to-lock five times, then slacken the nut, and tighten it again until the marks align. Install the forks and wheel, then refer to the procedure in Chapter 1 and check the feel of the bearings as described, and adjust if necessary.

Caution: Take great care not to apply excessive pressure because this will cause premature failure of the bearings.

14 With the bearings correctly adjusted, fit the lockwasher, using a new one if the tabs are weakened or cracked, onto the adjuster nut and fit the two short tabs into the notches in the adjuster nut **(see illustration 9.5c)**.

15 Fit the locknut and tighten it finger-tight **(see illustration 9.5b)**. Tighten the locknut further (but no more than 90°) until its notches align with the remaining lockwasher tabs, making sure the adjuster nut does not turn as well (though that is unlikely). Secure the locknut in position by bending up the long lock washer tabs into its notches **(see illustration)**.

16 Fit the top yoke/handlebar assembly (if not detached) onto the steering stem **(see illustration 9.4b)**. Fit the steering stem nut and tighten it finger-tight **(see illustration 9.4a)**. Temporarily install one of the forks to align the top and bottom yokes, and secure it by tightening the bottom yoke clamp bolts only (see Section 6). Now tighten the steering stem nut to the torque setting specified at the beginning of the Chapter.

17 Install the remaining components in a reverse of the removal procedure, referring to the relevant Sections or Chapters, and to the torque settings specified at the beginning of the Chapter.

18 Carry out a final check of the steering head bearing freeplay as described in Chapter 1, and if necessary re-adjust.

10 Steering head bearings

Inspection

1 Remove the steering stem (see Section 9).
2 Remove all traces of old grease from the bearings and races and check them for wear or damage.
3 The outer races in the top and bottom of

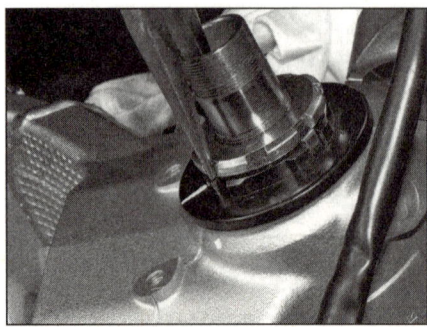

9.13 Using a C-spanner to tighten the adjuster nut

9.15 Bend the lockwasher tabs up into the notches in the lockwasher

Frame and suspension 5•17

10.3 Check the outer races in the top and bottom of the steering head

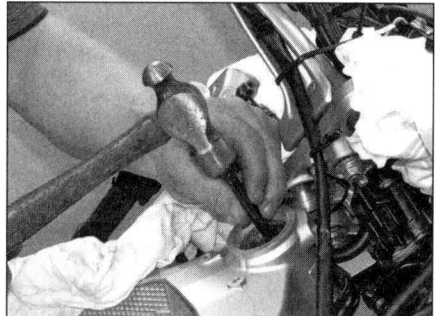

10.4a Drive the bearing races out with a brass drift . . .

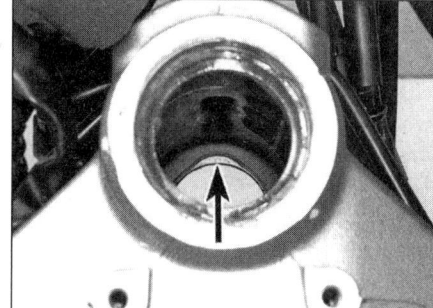

10.4b . . . locating it in the cut-outs (arrowed)

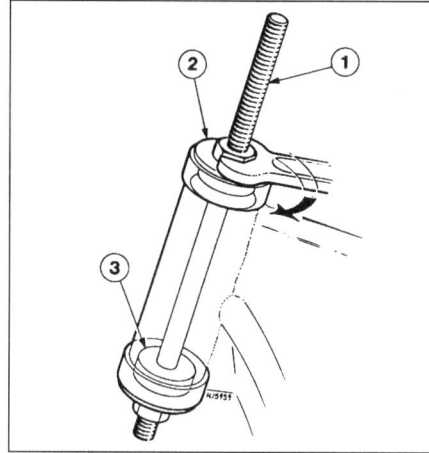

10.5 Drawbolt arrangement for fitting steering stem bearing races

1 Long bolt or threaded bar
2 Thick washer
3 Guide for lower race

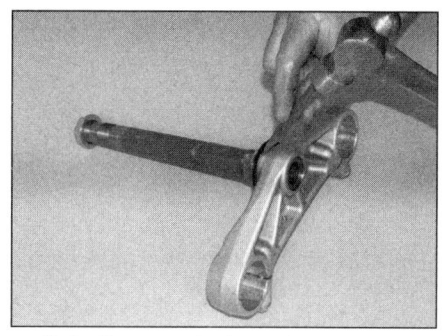

10.6a Remove the lower bearing race using a cold chisel . . .

10.6b . . . and/or screwdrivers . . .

the steering head should be polished and free from indentations **(see illustration)**. Inspect the bearing balls for signs of wear, damage or discoloration, and examine the ball retainer cage for signs of cracks or splits. If there are any signs of wear on any of the above components both upper and lower bearing assemblies must be renewed as a set. Only remove the outer races in the steering head and the lower bearing inner race on the steering stem if they need to be replaced with new ones – do not reuse them once they have been removed.

Replacement

4 The outer races are an interference fit in the steering head – tap them from position using a suitable drift located in the recesses provided in the steering head that expose the lip of the race **(see illustrations)**. Tap firmly and evenly between the recesses to ensure the race is driven out squarely. Curve the end of the drift slightly to improve access if necessary.
5 Press the new outer races into the head using a drawbolt arrangement **(see illustration)**, or drive them in using a large diameter tubular drift. Ensure that the drawbolt washer or drift (as applicable) bears only on the outer edge

of the race and does not contact the working surface. Alternatively, have the races installed by a Honda dealer equipped with the bearing race installation tools.

 *Installation of new bearing outer races is made much easier if the races are left overnight in the freezer. This causes them to contract slightly making them a looser fit. Alternatively, use a freeze spray.*

6 Only remove the lower bearing inner race from the steering stem if a new one is being fitted. To remove the race, first thread the steering stem nut onto the top then position the yoke on its front for stability – the nut will protect the threads from the transmitted

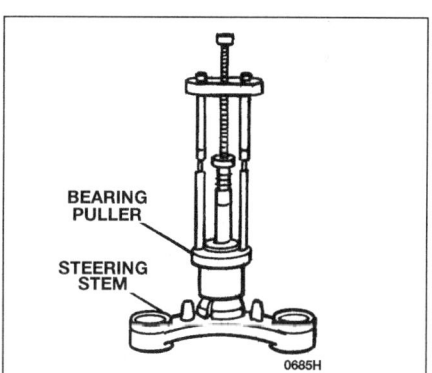

10.6c . . . or using a puller if necessary

force of the impact of the chisel. Tap under the race using a cold chisel to displace it, and if required use two screwdrivers placed on opposite sides to work it free, using blocks of wood to improve leverage and protect the yoke **(see illustrations)**. If the race is firmly in place it will be necessary to use a puller **(see illustration)**. Take the steering stem to a Honda dealer if required.
7 Remove the dust seal from the bottom of the stem and replace it with a new one. Smear the new one with grease.
8 Fit the new lower race onto the steering stem. Drive the new race into position using a length of tubing with an internal diameter slightly larger than the steering stem **(see illustration)** – heating the race and cooling the steering stem will make installation easier.
9 Install the steering stem (see Section 9).

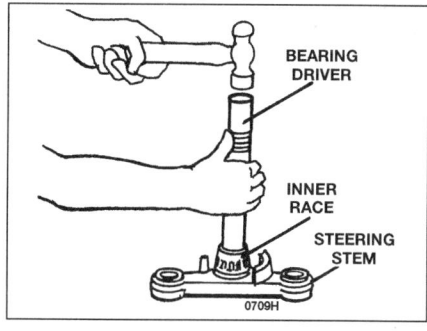

10.8 Drive the new inner race on using a suitable bearing driver or a length of tubing that bears only against the inner rim and not the bearing surface

5•18 Frame and suspension

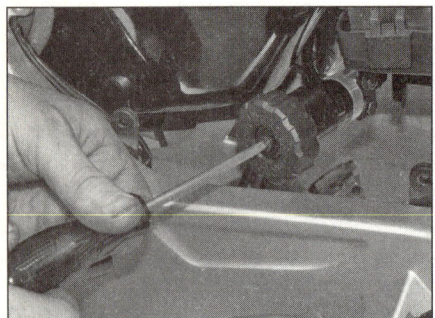

11.3a Undo the screw . . .

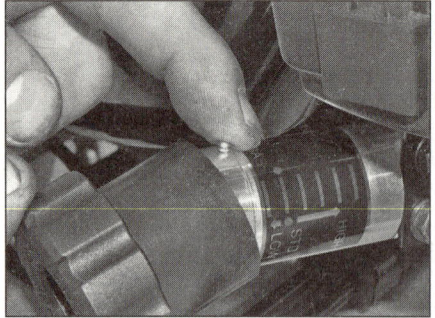

11.3b . . . then draw the knob off, taking care to retain the ball and spring

11.3c Remove the ball and the spring

11 Rear shock absorber

⚠️ **Warning:** *Do not attempt to disassemble the shock absorber in the home workshop. It is nitrogen-charged under high pressure. Improper disassembly could result in serious injury.*

Removal

1 Support the motorcycle on its centrestand. Tie the front brake lever to the handlebar so the bike can't roll forward. Position a support under the rear wheel, final drive housing or swingarm so that it does not drop when the shock absorber is removed, but also making sure that the weight of the machine is off the rear suspension so that the shock is not compressed.

11.3d Unscrew the bolts (arrowed) . . .

2 Referring to Chapter 6, Section 10, Steps 1, 2, 5, 6 and 7, displace the rear brake master cylinder from the right-hand footrest bracket.

3 Undo the screw securing the pre-load adjuster knob, then carefully draw the knob

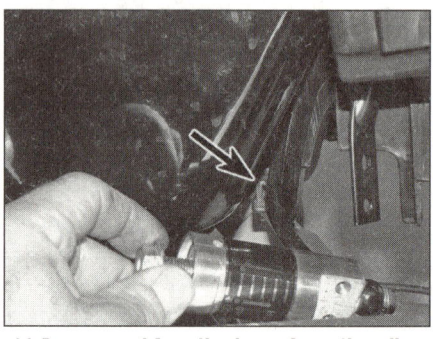

11.3e . . . and free the hose from the clips (arrowed)

off, keeping a finger against the rim on the top of the adjuster body to prevent the detent ball and spring pinging out **(see illustrations)**. Retrieve the ball and remove the spring **(see illustrations)**. Unscrew the adjuster bolts **(see illustration)**. Free the adjuster hose from its clips on the front of the mudguard and near the top of the shock **(see illustration)**.

4 Unscrew the nut and withdraw the bolt securing the bottom of the shock absorber **(see illustration)**.

5 Unscrew the nut on the bolt securing the top of the shock absorber **(see illustration)**. Support the shock from the bottom and withdraw the bolt, then remove the shock absorber, drawing the pre-load adjuster through and noting its routing **(see illustrations)**. Note that Honda specify to use a new upper mounting bolt – this is because it is pre-treated with a thread locking compound.

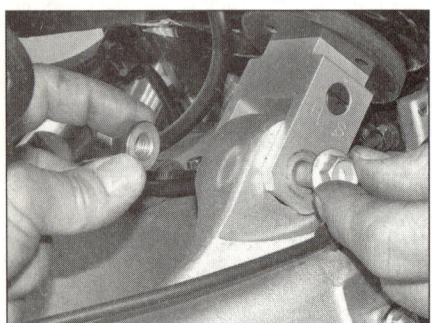

11.4 Unscrew the nut and withdraw the lower bolt

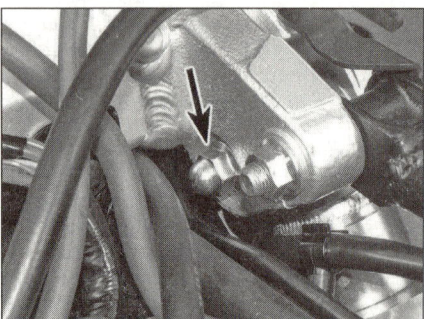

11.5a Unscrew the nut (arrowed) . . .

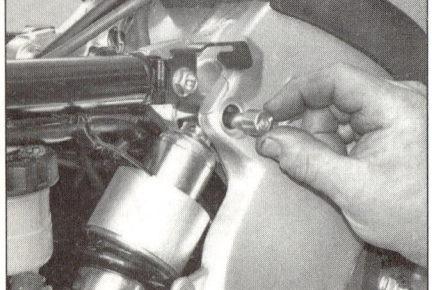

11.5b . . . then withdraw the upper bolt . . .

11.5c . . . and remove the shock . . .

11.5d . . . bringing the reservoir with it

Frame and suspension 5•19

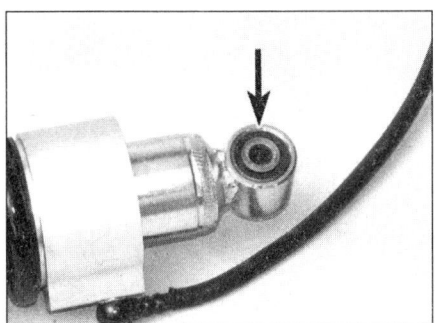

11.7 Check the bush (arrowed)

Inspection

6 Check the shock absorber, hose and pre-load adjuster for obvious physical damage and oil leakage, and the spring for looseness, cracks or signs of fatigue.

7 Check the bush in the top of the shock absorber for wear or damage (see illustration).

8 Parts are not available for the shock absorber itself. If it is worn or damaged, it must be replaced with a new one. Before disposing of an old shock absorber, you should release the nitrogen gas from the top. To do this, make a drill point 30 mm below the middle of the top mount using a centre punch. Mount the shock in a vice. Drill a hole using a sharp 2 or 3 mm drill bit to release the gas – it is best to cover the shock and drill and avert your face to prevent the possibility of injury, making sure the material used does not get caught in the chuck as it spins (see illustration).

⚠ **Warning:** *Wear protective eyewear and be very careful when releasing the gas pressure – it is possible for fine debris particles to be released with it, and as the pressure is high these could damage you eyes if done carelessly.*

9 Withdraw the spacer from the bottom mount on the swingarm (see illustration). Clean of old grease and dirt. Check the condition of the grease seals and bearing. If required lever out the grease seals (see illustration). Fit the

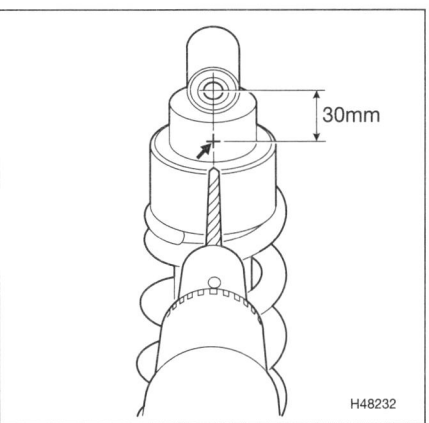

11.8 Release the gas as described before disposing of the shock absorber

spacer back in and check for play between it and the bearing. Refer to *Tools and Workshop Tips* (Section 5) in the Reference section for more information on bearings.

10 If the bearing is worn drive it out of the bore using a suitable driver or socket or draw it out using a drawbolt (one can be made up as described in *Tools and Workshop Tips* in the Reference section) – do not re-use the bearing after removing it. The new bearing should be pressed or drawn in, not driven in. When fitting the new bearing make sure it is central in the bore – the gap between the outer end and the rim of the bore should be 5.3 to 5.7 mm on each side.

11 Lubricate the bearing, spacer and new seals with a multi-purpose grease with EP2 rating. Press the new seals squarely into place (see illustration). Fit the spacer (see illustration 11.9a).

Installation

12 Installation is the reverse of removal, noting the following:
- Apply multi-purpose grease with EP2 rating to the shock absorber pivot points.
- Make sure the pre-load adjuster hose is correctly routed.

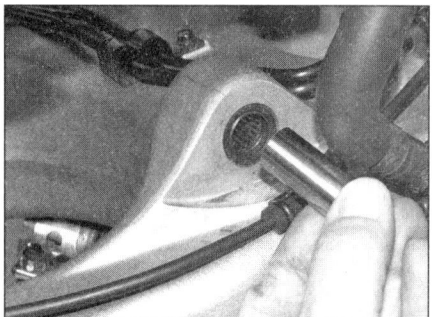

11.9a Withdraw the spacer and check the seals and bearing

11.9b If necessary lever the seals out using a screwdriver

- Install the shock absorber with the damping adjuster screw facing out.
- Use a new upper mounting bolt if available, or otherwise clean the threads of the old bolt and apply some fresh threadlock.
- Tighten the nuts/bolts to the torque setting specified at the beginning of the Chapter.
- When fitting the pre-load adjuster knob, align the channel on the inner side with the detent ball (see illustration). Keep a finger on the ball to prevent it becoming dislodged (see illustration 11.3b).
- Refer to Chapter 6 for installation of the master cylinder and footrest bracket.

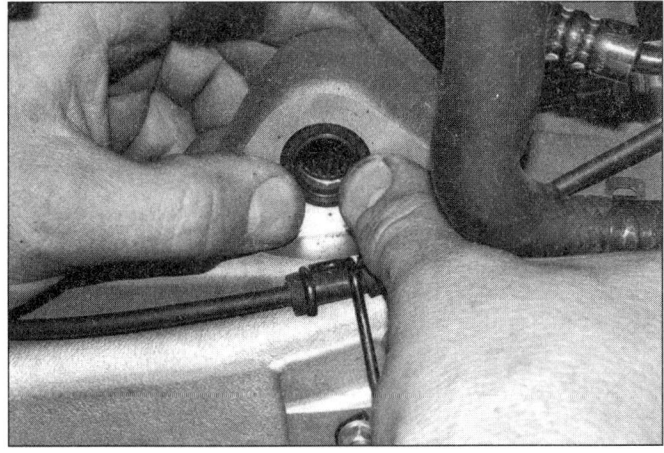

11.11 You can fit the seals using thumb pressure

11.12 Align the channel (A) with the ball (B)

5•20 Frame and suspension

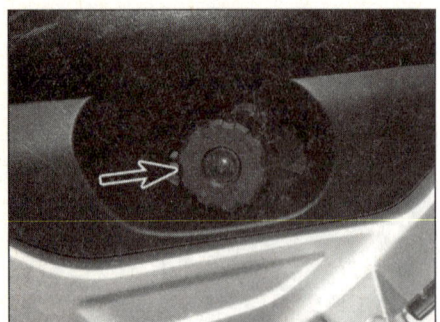

12.3 Spring pre-load adjuster (arrowed)

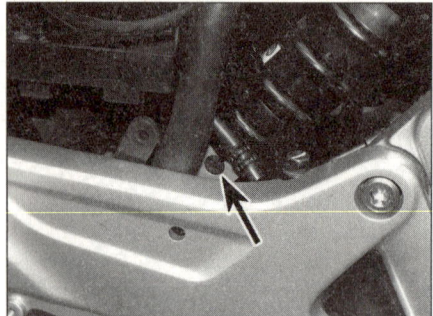

12.4a Rebound damping adjuster (arrowed) . . .

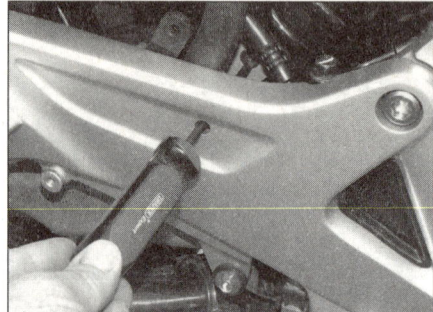

12.4b . . . turn it using a screwdriver inserted through the hole in the footrest bracket

12 Suspension adjustment

Front forks

1 The front forks are not adjustable.

Rear shock absorber

2 The shock absorber is adjustable for spring pre-load and rebound damping.
3 Spring pre-load is adjusted by turning the knob on the left-hand side of the bike **(see illustration)**. There are 35 to 40 preset positions, each indicated by a click (every half turn) as you turn the adjuster. To increase pre-load turn the adjuster clockwise, and to decrease turn the adjuster anti-clockwise. To set the standard position, turn the adjuster anti-clockwise until it stops, then turn it clockwise 7 clicks. Lines on the body of the adjuster give an indication as to the amount of pre-load set.
4 Rebound damping adjustment is made by turning the adjuster on the bottom of the shock absorber on the right-hand side using a flat-bladed screwdriver **(see illustrations)**. To increase the damping, turn the adjuster clockwise (in H direction). To decrease the damping, turn the adjuster anti-clockwise (in S direction). To set the standard position, turn the adjuster clockwise until it stops, then turn it anti clockwise 1 turn until the punch mark on the adjuster aligns with the index mark on the shock absorber.

13 Swingarm removal and installation

Special tool: A peg spanner is required to slacken and tighten the adjuster bolt or locknut or collar (according to model). If the Honda service tool applicable to your model (see text) is not available, where possible a suitable one will have to obtained commercially or fabricated out of a piece of steel tubing, or an old socket.

Removal

1 Remove the fairing side panels (see Chapter 7). Remove the silencers (see Chapter 4). Remove the rear wheel (see Chapter 6). Remove the final drive housing and driveshaft (see Chapter 6).
2 Refer to Chapter 6, Section 10, Steps 1, 2, 5, 6, 7, and displace the rear brake master cylinder from the right-hand footrest bracket. Refer to Section 11, Step 4, and remove the shock absorber lower mounting bolt.
3 On California models remove the EVAP canister (see Chapter 4).
4 Unscrew the brake hose/pipe bolts, and where fitted and if not already done the ABS sensor wire guide bolts **(see illustration)**. Tie the brake caliper and brake pipe assembly up out of the way and move the sensor wiring aside.
5 Disconnect the oxygen sensor 4-pin wiring connectors, one on each side in a boot behind the cylinder head (on 2002 to 2007 models the left-hand sensor connector is white and the right-hand is black, and on 2008-on models the left is green and right is grey) **(see illustrations)** – unscrew the coolant reservoir bolt and move the reservoir aside to improve access to the left-hand connector **(see illustration)**. Feed the wiring down though the swingarm, noting its routing – on the left-hand side the wiring has a tight and awkward route, so it is best to tie some wire to the connector and draw the wire down with it, then release it from the connector and leave it there so it

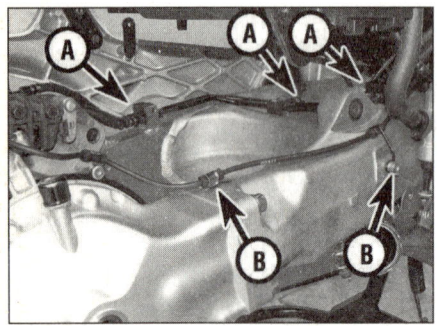

13.4 Displace the brake hose holders (A) and where fitted the ABS sensor wire holders (B)

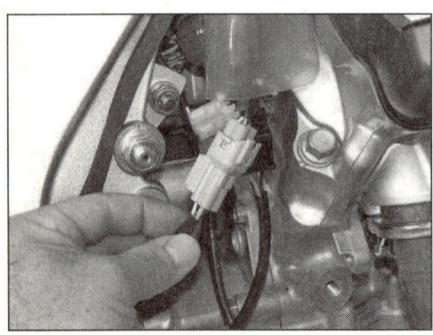

13.5a Right-hand oxygen sensor wiring connector

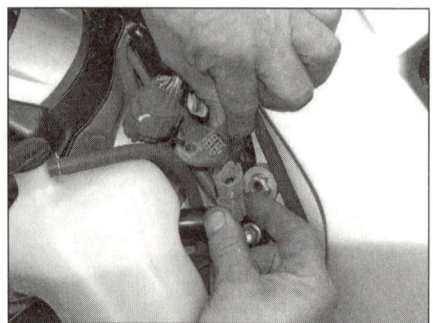

13.5b Left-hand sensor wiring connector (arrowed) . . .

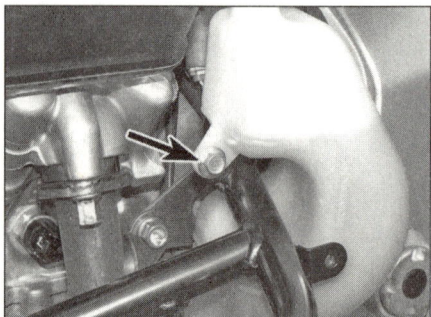

13.5c . . . unscrew the bolt (arrowed) and move the reservoir for access

Frame and suspension 5•21

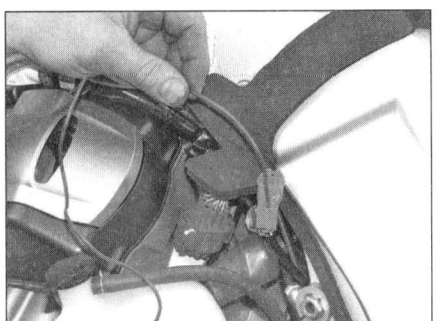

13.5d Tie some wire to the connector to make sure it is easily and correctly re-routed

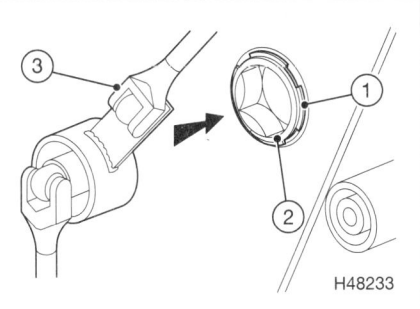

13.7 Left-hand pivot removal details – early 2002 and 2003 models

1 Locknut
2 Pivot bolt
3 Honda special tool

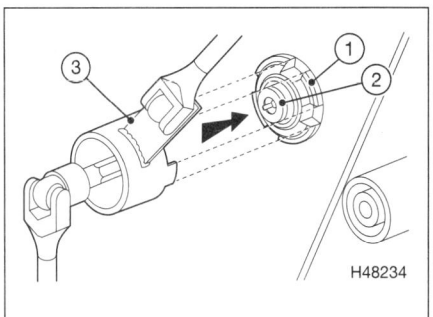

13.8 Left-hand pivot removal details – late 2002 models

1 Collar
2 Pivot bolt
3 Honda special tool

can then be used to pull the connector back through on installation **(see illustration)**.

6 Unscrew the right-hand engine protection bar and side mounting bracket nut/bolts and remove the bar and bracket, on 2004-on models also removing the stiffening plate, noting how it fits **(see illustrations 13.35e, d, c, b and a)**.

7 On early 2002 models and 2003 models unscrew the locknut on the left-hand pivot bolt using the Honda special tool (Part No. 07ZMA-MCA0100 in Europe or 07ZMA-MCAA101 in the US) or an equivalent peg spanner **(see illustration)**. Unscrew and remove the pivot bolt using a large hex bit. Unscrew and remove the right-hand pivot bolt.

8 On late 2002 models counter-hold the left-hand pivot bolt collar using the Honda special tool (Part No. 07ZMA-MCA0100 in Europe or 07ZMA-MCAA101 in the US) and unscrew the bolt in its centre **(see illustration)**. Remove the collar, then unscrew and remove the pivot bolt. Unscrew and remove the right-hand pivot bolt.

9 On 2004-on models remove the cover from the left-hand pivot **(see illustration)**. Unscrew the pivot bolt using the Honda special tool (Part No. 07916-KA50100) or equivalent and remove the shim(s) and the collar **(see illustration)**. Unscrew and remove the right-hand pivot bolt using the same tool.

10 Manoeuvre the swingarm back out of the frame **(see illustration)**.

11 Remove the universal joint rubber boot from the front of the swingarm, then draw the universal joint out **(see illustrations)**.

12 Remove the bearing from each side **(see illustration)**. Inspect all pivot components as described below.

Inspection

13 Thoroughly clean all pivot components, removing all traces of dirt, corrosion and grease.

14 Inspect the swingarm closely, looking for cracks or distortion due to accident damage.

15 Check the pivot bolts are a good fit in the bearing inner races. Check the bearing outer races in the swingarm for wear, pitting or cracks – if any are found, check with your dealer about the availability of parts.

16 Check the bearings themselves for roughness or distortion – refer to *Tools and Workshop Tips* (Section 5) in the Reference

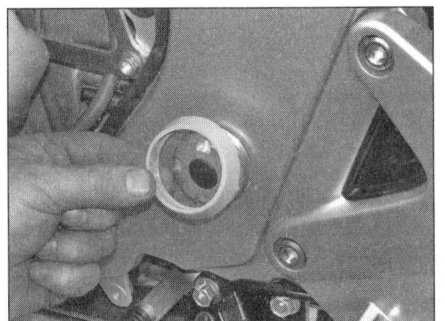

13.9a Remove the pivot cover

13.9b Unscrew the pivot bolt using the Honda tool or equivalent

13.10 Manoeuvre the swingarm out

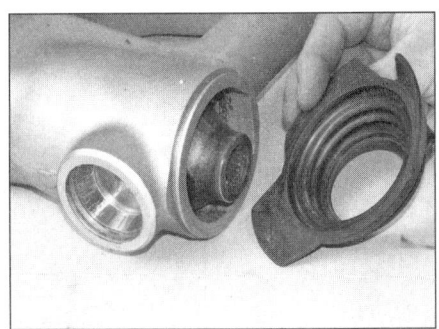

13.11a Remove the rubber boot . . .

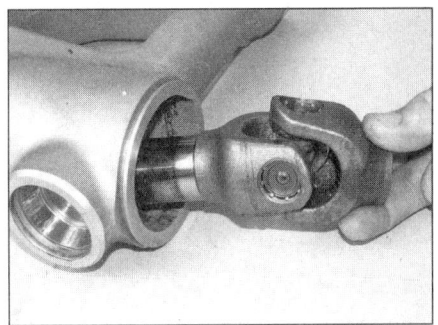

13.11b . . . and withdraw the universal joint from the front . . .

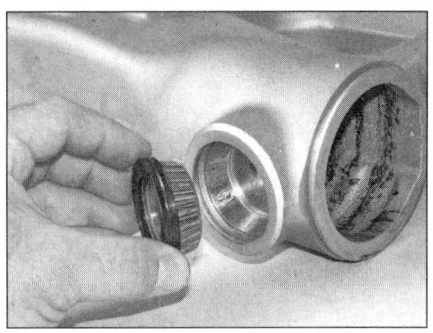

13.12 . . . and remove the bearing from each side

5•22 Frame and suspension

13.18a Fit the rubber boot onto the engine...

13.18b ...making sure it seats in the groove

13.18c Slide the UJ onto the output shaft

section for more information on bearings. Replace any worn or damaged components with new ones. On 2004-on models if any new components are fitted, the left-hand pivot must be re-shimmed (see Step 34).

17 Check the splines on the driveshaft, in each end of the universal joint and on the final output shaft on the engine for wear and damage. Check the joint itself – it should move smoothly and freely with no roughness or freeplay in the coupling. Replace any worn or damaged components with new ones – the output shaft is covered in Chapter 2.

Installation

18 Fit the rubber boot onto the back of the engine, making sure it seats in the groove **(see illustrations)**. Smear the drive shaft, universal joint and output shaft splines with molybdenum disulphide grease, then fit the universal joint onto the output shaft **(see illustration)**.

19 Generously lubricate the bearings and the seals with multi-purpose grease with an EP2 rating. Fit the bearings into the swingarm **(see illustration 13.12)**.

20 Make sure the pivot bolt threads are clean. On 2002 and 2003 models smear the threads with clean oil.

21 Offer up the swingarm and have an assistant hold it in place – make sure the bearings do not drop out **(see illustration)**. Fit the pivot bolts and tighten them finger-tight **(see illustration)** – on 2004-on models fit the shims and collar onto the bolt first **(see illustrations)**, but note that if any new components have been used the bolt will have to be removed later and re-shimmed (see Step 34).

22 Remove the driveshaft from the final drive housing (see Chapter 6). Slide the shaft into the swingarm and engage it with the universal joint **(see illustration)**. Push the shaft to make sure the UJ is fully engaged on the output shaft splines, and turn the shaft to confirm engagement. Leave the shaft in the swingarm.

Early 2002 models and 2003 models

23 Tighten the right-hand pivot bolt to the torque setting specified at the beginning of the Chapter.

24 Tighten the left-hand pivot bolt to the initial torque setting specified, then unscrew it ¼ turn (90°). Now tighten it to the final torque setting specified.

25 If removed thread the locknut onto the pivot bolt **(see illustration 13.7)**.

26 If using the Honda special tool with the offset arm, counter-hold the bolt and tighten the nut to the indicated torque setting specified using the special tool as on removal (see Step 7) – note that the actual torque setting given is the torque that would be applied using a direct tool rather than the offset one.

27 If the tool is not available and you are using a direct peg spanner, first make an alignment mark between the pivot bolt head and the frame so you can check whether the bolt turns when tightening the locknut. Now tighten the locknut to the actual torque setting specified. Check the alignment of the marks – if the bolt has turned you will have to repeat the tightening procedure, if necessary using the Honda tool so the pivot bolt can be counter-held and applying the indicated torque.

13.21a Fit the swingarm, guiding it over the universal joint

13.21b Fit the pivot bolts and tighten as described for your model...

13.21c ...on 2004-on models make sure the shim(s) and collar are in place...

13.21d ...before fitting the left-hand pivot bolt

13.22 Insert the shaft and engage it in the universal joint

Frame and suspension 5•23

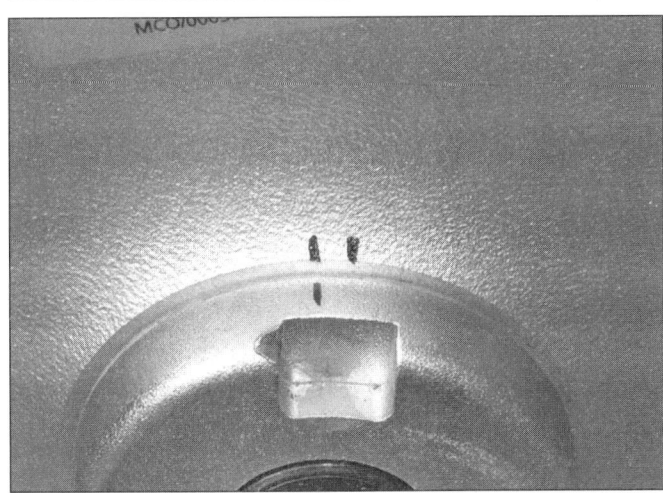

13.31a Make three marks as shown

13.31b After tightening, the line made on the bolt should be in line with or to the right of the right-hand mark on the frame

Late 2002 models

28 Tighten the right-hand pivot bolt to the torque setting specified at the beginning of the Chapter.
29 Tighten the left-hand pivot bolt to the initial torque setting specified, then unscrew it ¼ turn (90°). Now tighten it to the final torque setting specified.
30 Fit the collar onto the pivot bolt **(see illustration 13.8)**. Lubricate the threads and seating flange of the centre bolt, then counter-hold the collar using the Honda special tool (see Step 8) as on removal and tighten the bolt to the specified torque.

2004-on models

31 Tighten the right-hand pivot bolt to the initial torque setting specified at the beginning of the Chapter. Now make two marks on the frame 3.5 mm apart using a fine marker pen, then make a similar mark on the pivot bolt in line with the left-hand mark made on the frame **(see illustration)**. Alternatively stick a piece of 3.5 mm wide tape between the bolt and frame, then cut it across the bolt-frame joint. Now tighten the pivot bolt to the final torque setting specified. Check the alignment of the marks or tape – if the mark on the bolt is in line with or past the right-hand mark on the frame, or if there is no overlap of the two pieces of tape, no further tightening is required **(see illustration)**. If the mark on the bolt is to the left of the right-hand mark on the frame or if the pieces of tape overlap, tighten the bolt further until the marks align or the tapes no longer overlap. This ensures that the required extra tightening of 8.4° is achieved.
32 If no new swingarm components (i.e. bearings, pivot bolts or swingarm itself) have been installed, the original shims fitted with the left-hand pivot bolt can be re-used – follow Step 33. If any new components have been installed the left-hand pivot bolt must be re-shimmed – follow Step 34.
33 Tighten the left-hand pivot bolt to the torque setting specified at the beginning of the Chapter. Now unscrew it ¼ turn (90°). Tighten it again to the specified torque setting. Now check that the mark on the frame aligns within the top notch in the pivot bolt with the white paint mark **(see illustration)** – if it doesn't, re-shim the bolt (see Step 34). If it does align fit the pivot cover **(see illustration 13.9a)**. **Note:** *It is possible the shape and colour of marks made in the factory when building the bike differ from those shown here, though the principle described remains the same.*
34 Clean the threads of the left-hand pivot bolt and smear them with clean oil. Fit the collar onto the bolt – do not fit any shims. Fit the bolt and tighten it to the initial torque setting specified, then unscrew it 1/2 turn (180°). Now tighten it to the final torque setting specified. Make a mark on the frame in line with the right-hand edge of the top notch in the bolt, and also mark the notch. Measure the gap between the inner face of the pivot bolt and the outer face of the collar using either a set of feeler gauges, or using a selection of the available shims. Shims

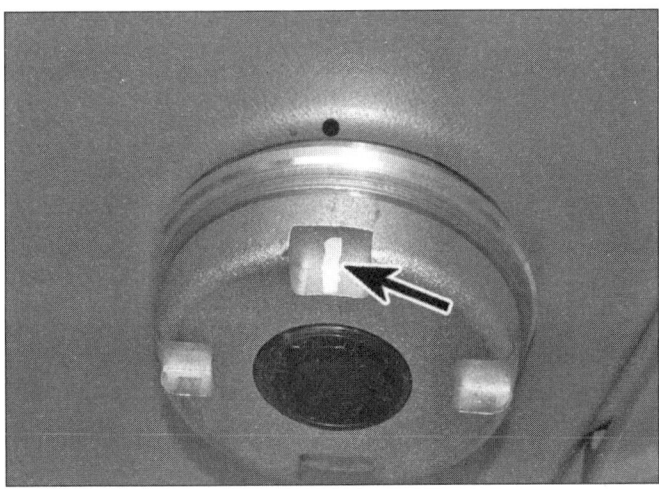

13.33 The mark on the frame should lie within the boundaries of the notch with the white paint mark

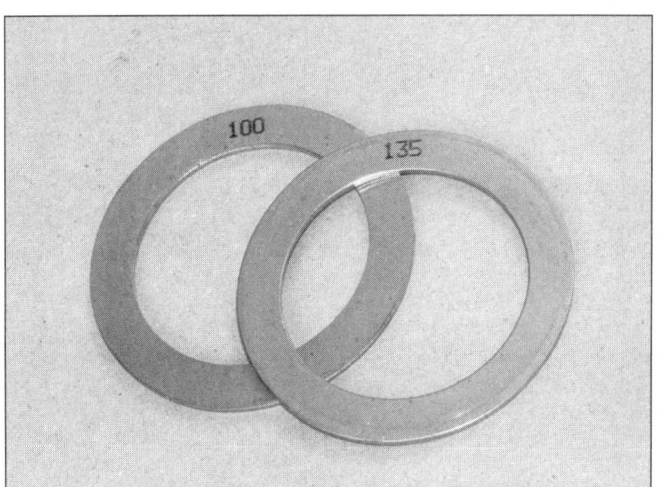

13.34 Shim size is marked on one face

5•24 Frame and suspension

13.35a Fit the bracket and the lower rear bolt . . .

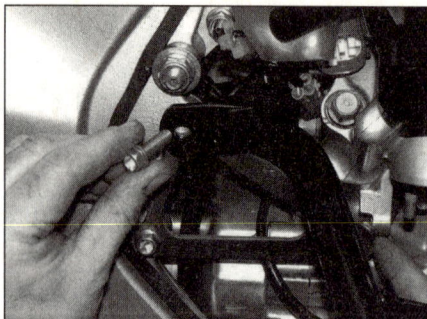

13.35b . . . then fit the engine bar and its rear bolt . . .

13.35c . . . and front bolt . . .

13.35d . . . then where fitted locate the stiffening plate and fit the bracket front bolt . . .

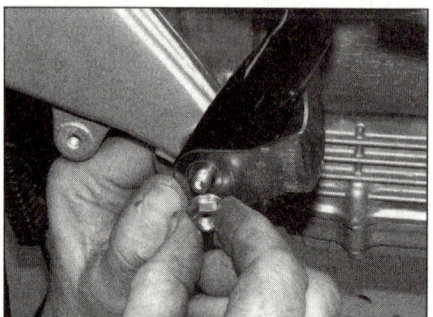

13.35e . . . and the engine bar lower nut

are available from 0.50 mm to 1.70 mm thick in increments of 0.05mm. The size of the shim is marked on one face **(see illustration)**. If the gap measured is greater than 1.70 mm use two shims. Remove the pivot bolt, then remove the collar from it, fit the shim(s) and refit the collar **(see illustration 13.21c)**, and tighten the bolt as in Step 33, using the marks you made on the frame and notch for the final alignment.

All models

35 Fit the right-hand engine bracket and engine protection bar, and on 2004-on models the stiffening plate, in that order, and tighten the nut/bolts finger-tight **(see illustrations)**. Tighten the front bolt on the mounting bracket to the torque setting specified at the beginning of the Chapter, then tighten the rear bolt to the specified torque. Tighten the rear bolt on the engine protection bar, then the front bolt, and finally the nut, again to the specified torques.

36 Reconnect the oxygen sensor wiring connectors **(see illustrations 13.5a and b)**. Make sure the wiring is correctly routed – on the left-hand side tie the wire used before to the connector then pull the wire through from the top, thereby pulling the connector through **(see illustration 13.5d)**. Fit the reservoir bolt **(see illustration 13.5c)**.

37 Locate the brake caliper and brake pipe assembly on the swingarm **(see illustration 13.4)**. Fit the brake hose/pipe bolts. On models with ABS fit the ABS sensor wire guide bolts.

38 On California models install the EVAP canister (see Chapter 4).

39 Install the shock absorber lower mounting bolt (see Section 11) and the right-hand footrest bracket (see Chapter 6).

40 Install the final drive housing (see Chapter 6). Install the rear wheel (see Chapter 6). Install the silencers (see Chapter 4). Install the fairing side panels (see Chapter 7).

41 Check the operation of the rear suspension and brake before taking the machine on the road.

Chapter 6
Brakes, wheels and final drive

Contents

	Section
ABS components	15
ABS fault diagnosis	14
ABS operation	13
Brake fluid level check	see Pre-ride checks
Brake hoses and fittings	11
Brake light switches	see Chapter 8
Brake pad wear check	see Chapter 1
Brake system bleeding and fluid change	12
Brake system check	see Chapter 1
Final drive housing and driveshaft	23
Final drive gear oil change	see Chapter 1
Final drive gear oil level check	see Chapter 1
Front brake calipers	3
Front brake discs	4
Front brake master cylinder	5
Front brake pads	2
Front wheel	18

	Section
General information	1
Rear brake caliper	8
Rear brake disc	9
Rear brake master cylinder	10
Rear brake pads	7
Rear wheel drive coupling	20
Rear wheel	19
Secondary master cylinder, delay valve and proportional control valve	6
Tyres	22
Tyre pressure, tread depth and condition	see Pre-ride checks
Wheel alignment check	17
Wheel bearing check	see Chapter 1
Wheel bearings	21
Wheel check	see Chapter 1
Wheel inspection and repair	16

Degrees of difficulty

| Easy, suitable for novice with little experience | Fairly easy, suitable for beginner with some experience | Fairly difficult, suitable for competent DIY mechanic | Difficult, suitable for experienced DIY mechanic | Very difficult, suitable for expert DIY or professional |

Specifications

Brake fluid
Brake fluid type .... DOT 4

Front brake calipers
Caliper bore ID
  Left caliper
    Standard .... 22.650 to 22.700 mm
    Service limit .... 22.712 mm
  Right caliper
    Upper and lower pistons
      Standard .... 27.000 to 27.050 mm
      Service limit .... 27.062 mm
    Centre piston
      Standard .... 22.650 to 22.700 mm
      Service limit .... 22.712 mm
Caliper piston OD
  Left caliper
    Standard .... 22.585 to 22.618 mm
    Service limit .... 22.573 mm
  Right caliper
    Upper and lower pistons
      Standard .... 26.935 to 26.968 mm
      Service limit .... 26.923 mm
    Centre piston
      Standard .... 22.585 to 22.618 mm
      Service limit .... 22.573 mm

Front brake master cylinder
Master cylinder bore ID
  2002 to 2007 models
    Standard.. 12.700 to 12.743 mm
    Service limit .... 12.755 mm
  2008-on models
    Standard.. 15.870 to 15.913 mm
    Service limit .... 15.925 mm
Master cylinder piston OD
  2002 to 2007 models
    Standard.. 12.657 to 12.684 mm
    Service limit .... 12.645 mm
  2008-on models
    Standard.. 15.827 to 15.854 mm
    Service limit .... 15.815 mm

Front brake discs
Disc thickness
  Standard... 5.0 mm
  Service limit .... 4.0 mm
Disc maximum runout .... 0.2 mm

Secondary master cylinder
Master cylinder bore ID
  Standard... 14.000 to 14.043 mm
  Service limit .... 14.055 mm
Master cylinder piston OD
  Standard... 13.957 to 13.984 mm
  Service limit .... 13.945 mm

Rear brake caliper
Caliper bore ID
  Outer pistons
    Standard.. 22.650 to 22.700 mm
    Service limit .... 22.712 mm
  Centre piston
    Standard.. 25.400 to 25.450 mm
    Service limit .... 25.462 mm
Caliper piston OD
  Outer pistons
    Standard.. 22.585 to 22.618 mm
    Service limit .... 22.560 mm
  Centre piston
    Standard.. 25.335 to 25.368 mm
    Service limit .... 25.323 mm

Rear brake master cylinder
Master cylinder bore ID
  Standard... 17.460 to 17.503 mm
  Service limit .... 17.515 mm
Master cylinder piston OD
  Standard... 17.417 to 17.444 mm
  Service limit .... 17.405 mm

Rear brake disc
Disc thickness
  Standard... 7.0 mm
  Service limit .... 6.0 mm
Disc maximum runout .... 0.3 mm

ABS system
Wheel speed sensor air gap
  Front .... 0.4 to 1.2 mm
  Rear .... 0.7 to 1.2 mm

Wheels
Maximum wheel runout (front and rear)
  Axial (side-to-side) .... 2.0 mm
  Radial (out-of-round) .... 2.0 mm
Maximum axle runout (front and rear) .... 0.2 mm

Tyres

Tyre pressures . . . . 42 psi (2.9 Bar) front and rear
Tyre sizes*
    Front 120/70-ZR18 (59W)
    Rear 170/60-ZR17 (72W)
*Refer to the owners handbook or a motorcycle tyre fitting specialist for approved tyre brands.

Torque settings

Brake caliper bleed valves	6 Nm
Brake disc bolts	
Front	20 Nm
Rear	42 Nm
Brake hose banjo bolts	34 Nm
Brake pipe nuts	
2002 to 2007 models	17 Nm
2008-on models	14 Nm
Delay valve bolts	12 Nm
Final drive housing nuts	44 Nm
Footrest bracket bolts	
Front bolts (to main frame)	64 Nm
Rear bolts (to sub-frame)	42 Nm
Front axle bolt	78 Nm
Front axle clamp bolts	22 Nm
Front brake caliper body joining bolts (2002 to 2007 models)	32 Nm
Front brake caliper mounting bolts	31 Nm
Front brake master cylinder clamp bolts	12 Nm
Front brake pad retaining pin	18 Nm
Front wheel ABS pulse ring bolts	8 Nm
Proportional control valve bolts	12 Nm
Rear axle nut	108 Nm
Rear brake caliper body joining bolts	32 Nm
Rear brake caliper bracket stopper bolt	69 Nm
Rear brake pad retaining pin	18 Nm
Rear master cylinder mounting bolts	12 Nm
Rear wheel ABS pulse ring bolts	8 Nm

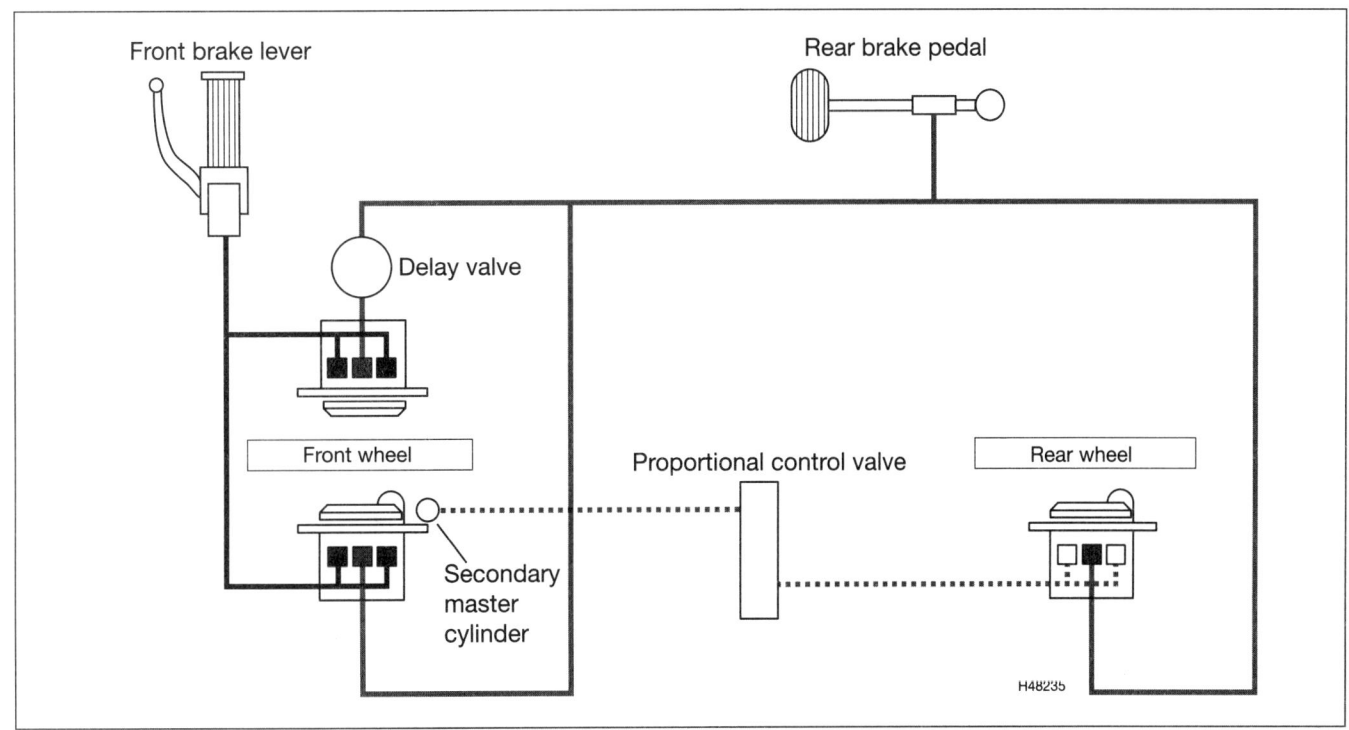

1.1 Dual combined brake system diagram

6•4 Brakes, wheels and final drive

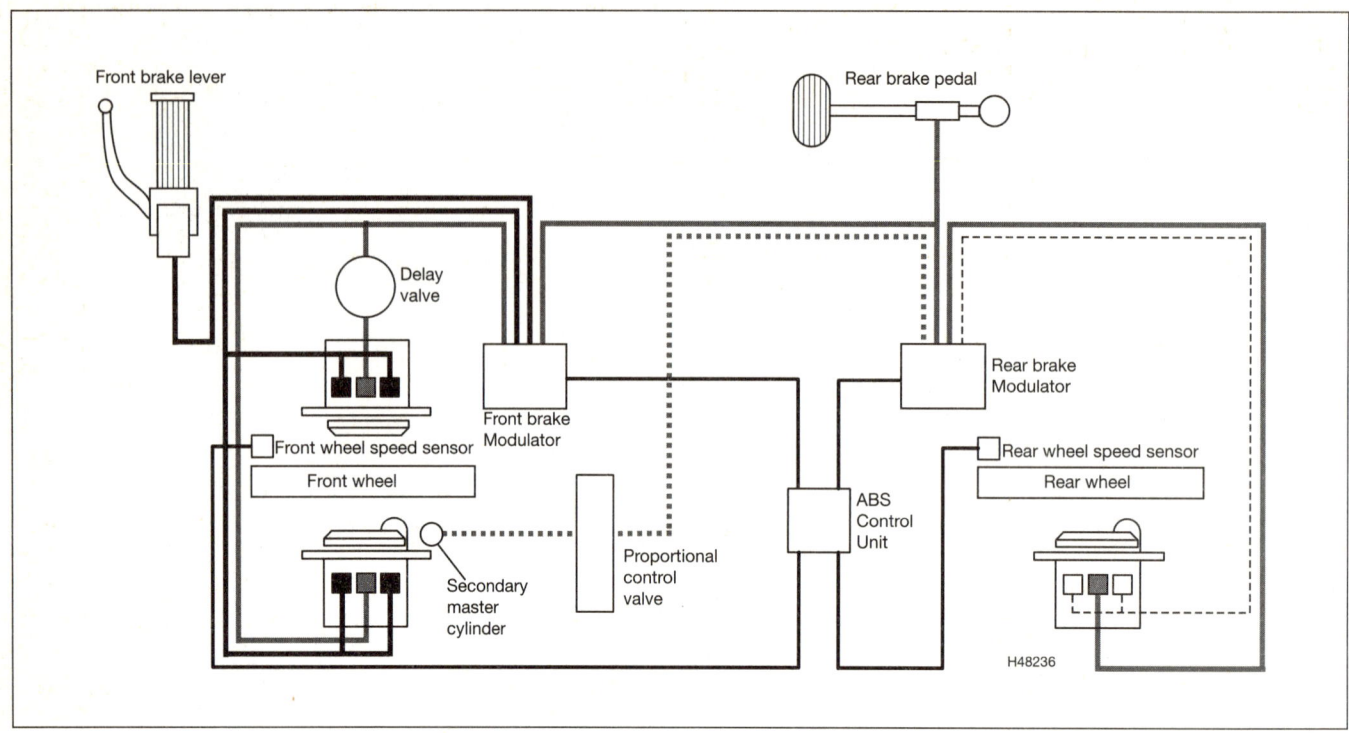

1.2 Dual combined anti-lock brake system diagram

1 General information

All models covered in this manual are fitted with cast alloy wheels designed for tubeless tyres only. Both front and rear brakes are hydraulically operated disc brakes. The machine is fitted with Honda's Dual Combined Braking System (DCBS) as standard **(see illustration on previous page)**. An anti-lock braking system (ABS) that prevents the wheels locking up under heavy braking is fitted on ST1300A models **(see illustration)**.

Each front brake is operated by a three-piston sliding caliper. The upper and lower piston of each caliper are hydraulically linked to the front master cylinder and the centre pistons are linked to the rear master cylinder. The right side caliper is fixed directly to the fork leg but the left side caliper is mounted onto a bracket which is allowed to pivot on the left fork leg. This mounting bracket incorporates the secondary master cylinder which is actuated by the torque action of the left caliper and is connected to the outer pistons of the rear brake caliper, via the proportional control valve.

The rear brake is also operated by a three-piston sliding caliper. The centre piston of the caliper is linked to the rear master cylinder and the outer pistons to the secondary master cylinder (via the proportional control valve). The rear master cylinder is also connected to the centre piston of each front brake caliper, via a delay valve. The system operates as follows:

DCBS

Front brake operation

When the front brake lever is applied, hydraulic pressure from the front master cylinder is applied to the upper and lower pistons of each front brake caliper (as in a conventional braking system). As the calipers grip the discs, the torque causes the left side caliper mounting bracket to pivot around its lower mounting. The forward motion of the mounting bracket transfers this force to the secondary master cylinder pushrod which then hydraulically applies the outer pistons of the rear brake caliper via a proportional control valve, which regulates the pressure to prevent the rear wheel locking under extreme braking.

Rear brake operation

When the rear brake pedal is applied, hydraulic pressure from the master cylinder is applied to the centre piston of the rear brake caliper (as in a conventional braking system) and also to the centre piston of each front brake caliper. The torque reaction of the front left caliper on the secondary master cylinder applies the outer pistons of the rear caliper, via the proportional control valve.

A delay valve is incorporated in the hydraulic supply to the front brake calipers. The valve allows hydraulic pressure to act immediately only on the left side caliper centre piston and isolates the right side caliper. Only when the pressure in the hydraulic system rises above a preset amount does the delay valve open and also apply the right side caliper centre piston. The action of the delay valve prevents the front forks 'diving' when the rear brake is applied hard and ensures a more natural feel to the braking system.

Models with ABS

On models fitted with ABS the DCBS operates in exactly the same way, but with the brake pressure to each caliper being monitored and controlled by wheel speed sensors, an electronic control unit and two modulators. The sensors read wheel speed, and if the ECU determines that a wheel is about to lock up the modulator for that wheel's caliper(s) will release then pulse brake pressure until the ECU determines there is no longer any danger of wheel lock.

Caution: Disc brake components rarely require disassembly. Do not disassemble components unless absolutely necessary. If an hydraulic brake hose is loosened or disconnected, the banjo union sealing washers must be replaced with new ones and the system must be bled upon reassembly. Do not use solvents on internal brake components. Solvents will cause the seals to swell and distort. Use only clean DOT 4 brake fluid for cleaning. Use care when working with brake fluid as it can injure your eyes and it will damage painted surfaces and plastic parts.

Brakes, wheels and final drive 6•5

2.1 Slacken the pad pin (arrowed)

2.2a Right-hand caliper mounting bolts (arrowed)

2.2b Left-hand caliper/secondary master cylinder assembly mounting bolts (arrowed)

2 Front brake pads

Note: *Honda recommend using new caliper mounting bolts. This is because the bolts are pre-treated with a locking compound. If they are not available it is possible, however, to clean up the old bolts and reinstall them using a suitable non-permanent thread locking compound that is commercially available.*

1 On 2002 to 2007 models remove the rubber plug from the pad pin. On all models slacken the pad retaining pin **(see illustration)**.

2 Unscrew the caliper mounting bolts and slide the caliper assembly off the disc **(see illustrations)**. **Note:** *Do not operate the brake lever while the pads are out of the caliper.*

3 Unscrew and remove the pad pin, then remove the pads, noting how they locate **(see illustrations)**. If required remove the shim from the back of each pad, noting how it fits **(see illustration 2.13a)** – note that new pads should come with new shims where applicable, but make sure they do, especially if fitting after-market pads, before discarding the old ones.

4 Slide the caliper and bracket apart **(see**

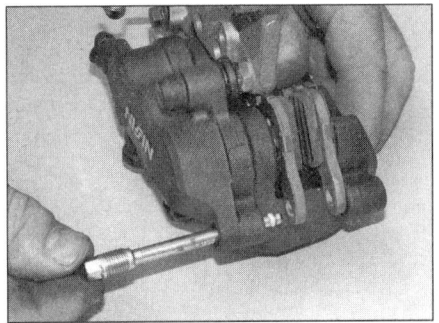

2.3a Unscrew the pin . . .

2.3b . . . and remove the pads

illustration). Remove the pad spring from the caliper if required **(see illustration 2.12a)**. Clean all old grease off the slider pins. Check the condition of the rubber boots and replace them with new ones if necessary **(see illustration)**.

5 Inspect the surface of each pad for contamination and check that the friction material has not worn beyond its service limit (see Chapter 1, Section 2). If any pad is worn down to, or beyond, the service limit wear indicator (i.e. the wear indicator is no longer visible), is fouled with oil or grease, or heavily scored or damaged, fit a complete set of new pads. Also check for even wear across the pad – uneven wear is indicative of a sticking or seized piston (see Steps 7 and 8). **Note:** *It is not possible to degrease the friction material; if the pads are contaminated in any way they must be replaced with new ones.*

6 If the pads are in good condition clean them carefully, using a fine wire brush which is completely free of oil and grease to remove all traces of road dirt and corrosion. Using a pointed instrument, dig out any embedded particles of foreign matter. If required, spray with a dedicated brake cleaner to remove any dust.

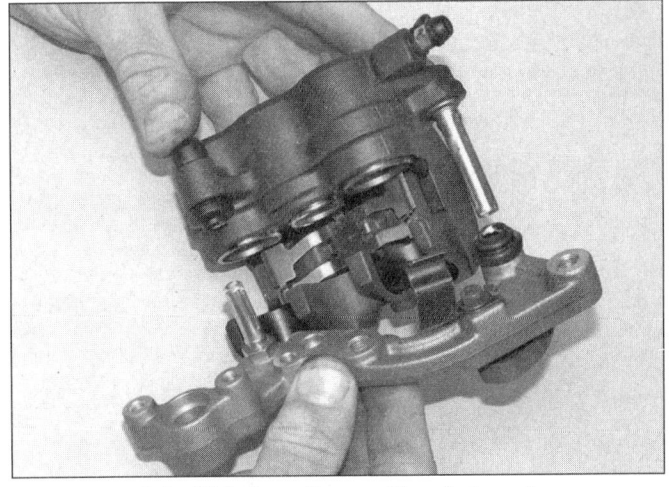

2.4a Slide the caliper and bracket apart

2.4b Check the condition of the boots (arrowed)

6•6 Brakes, wheels and final drive

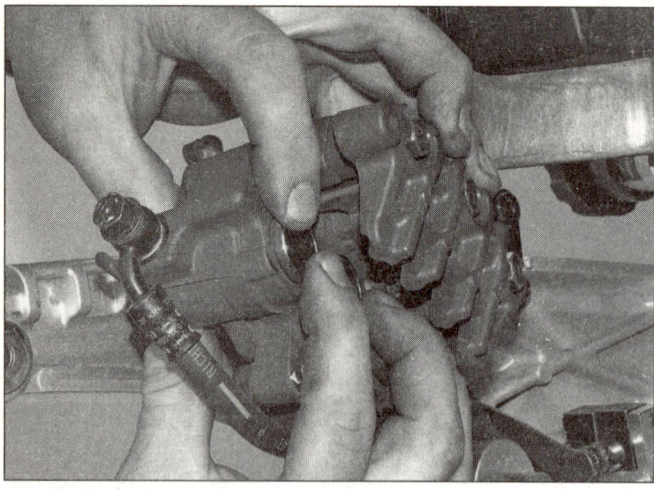

2.7a Press the pistons in as described to make clearance for new pads

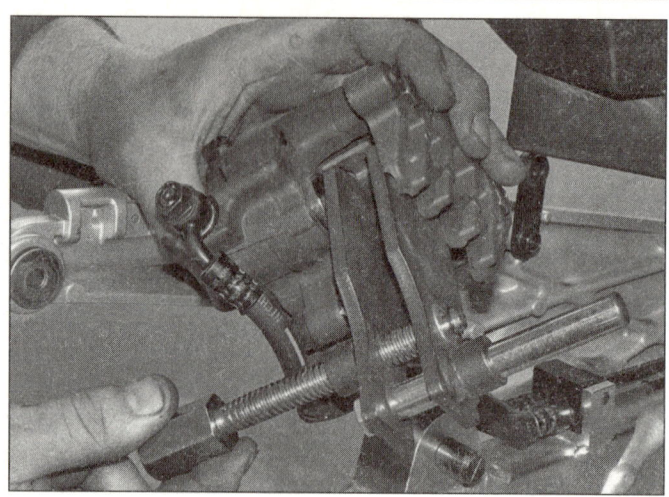

2.7b Using a commercially available piston pushing tool

7 Clean around the exposed section of each piston to remove any dirt or debris that could cause the seals to be damaged. If new pads are being fitted, now push the pistons all the way back into the caliper to create room for them; if the old pads are still serviceable push the pistons in a little way. To push the pistons back use finger pressure or a piece of wood as leverage, or place the old pads back in the caliper and use a metal bar or a screwdriver inserted between them (but take care not to damage the friction surface if the pads are being reused), or use grips and a piece of wood, with rag or card to protect the caliper body **(see illustration)**. Alternatively obtain a proper piston-pushing tool from a good tool supplier **(see illustration)**. It may be necessary to remove the master cylinder reservoir cover, plate and diaphragm and siphon out some fluid (see *Pre-ride checks*). If the pistons are difficult to push back, remove the bleed valve cap, then attach a length of clear hose to the bleed valve and place the open end in a suitable container, then open the valve and try again (see Section 12). Take great care not to draw any air into the system. If in doubt, bleed the brakes afterwards.

8 If any of the pistons appear seized, first block or hold the other pistons using wood or cable-ties, then apply the brake lever and check whether the piston in question moves at all. If it moves out but can't be pushed back in, the chances are there is some hidden corrosion stopping it. If it doesn't move at all, or to fully clean and inspect the pistons, disassemble the caliper and overhaul it (see Section 3).

9 Remove all traces of corrosion from the pad pin and check it for wear and damage. Check the condition of the stopper ring on the pin and replace it with a new one if it is damaged or deformed **(see illustration)**.

10 Check the condition of the brake discs (see Section 4).

11 Remove the spacer from the left-hand caliper bracket pivot in the bottom of the fork **(see illustration)**. Clean off all dirt, any corrosion and old grease and check the condition of the seals and bearing. If necessary lever the seals out and replace the bearing with a new one (see Tools and Workshop Tips in the Reference Section). Press new seals in. Lubricate the bearing, seal lips and spacer with fresh grease and insert the spacer.

12 If the pad spring was removed fit it into the caliper, making sure it locates correctly **(see illustration)**. Make sure the pad guide on the bracket is correctly fitted **(see illustration)**. Make sure the slider pins are tight. Smear the slider pins and inside the rubber boots with silicone grease, and apply a smear to the stopper ring on the pad pin. Slide the caliper and bracket together, making sure each boot lip locates correctly in the groove in the pin **(see illustration 2.4a)**.

13 If removed fit the shim onto the back of each pad, making sure it locates correctly

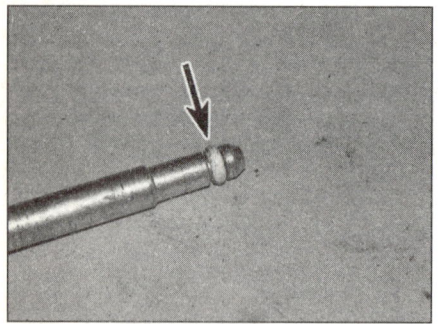

2.9 Make sure the stopper ring (arrowed) is fitted and in good condition

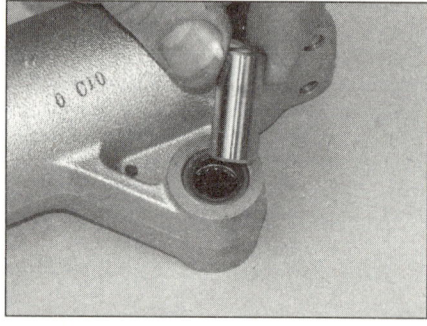

2.11 Withdraw the spacer and check the seals and bearing

2.12a Make sure the pad spring (arrowed) . . .

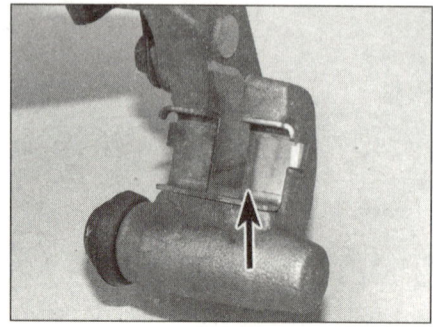

2.12b . . . and guide (arrowed) are correctly fitted

Brakes, wheels and final drive 6•7

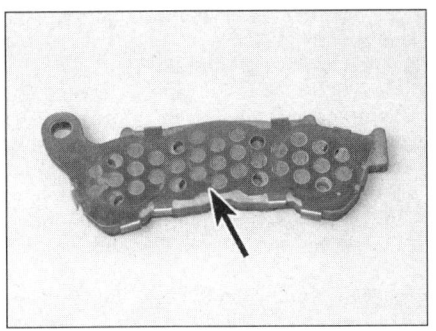

2.13a Make sure the shim (arrowed) is correctly in place

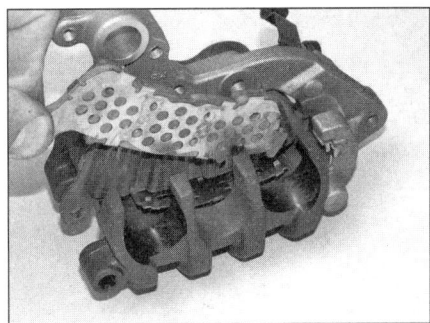

2.13b Fit the pads . . .

2.13c . . . making sure the shaped ends locate correctly in the pad guide

(see illustration). Fit the pads into the caliper so the friction material on each pad faces the other, and seat the pads in the guide on the bracket (see illustration). Press them up against the spring to align the holes, then insert the pad pin and tighten it finger-tight (see illustration 2.3a).

14 Slide the caliper assembly onto the disc making sure the pads locate correctly on each side (see illustrations). Either fit the new caliper mounting bolts, or clean the threads of the original bolts and apply fresh thread locking compound, then tighten them to the torque setting specified at the beginning of the Chapter.

15 Tighten the pad pin to the torque setting specified at the beginning of this Chapter (see illustration 2.1). On 2002 to 2007 models fit the rubber plug.

16 Operate the brake lever until the pads contact the disc – this pushes the outer pistons out. Now operate the brake pedal until the centre pistons contact the pads. Check the level of fluid in each reservoir and top-up if necessary (see Pre-ride checks).

17 Check the operation of the brakes before riding the motorcycle.

3 Front brake calipers

Warning: *If a caliper is in need of an overhaul it is best to drain all old brake fluid from the system, then fill with new fluid after the overhaul (see*

2.14a Fitting the right-hand caliper onto the disc

Section 12). Overhaul of the brake calipers must be done in a spotlessly clean work area to avoid contamination and possible failure of the brake hydraulic system components. Do not, under any circumstances, use petroleum-based solvents to clean brake parts. Use clean DOT 4 brake fluid, dedicated brake cleaner or denatured alcohol only, as described. To prevent damage from spilled brake fluid, always cover paintwork when working on the braking system.

Removal

Note 1: *If the caliper is being overhauled (usually due to sticking pistons or fluid leaks) read through the entire procedure first and make sure that you have obtained all the new parts required, including some new DOT 4 brake fluid.*

3.1a Unscrew the hose joint block bolt (arrowed) and displace the block . . .

2.14b Fitting the left-hand caliper/ secondary master cylinder assembly onto the disc

Note 2: *Honda recommend using new caliper mounting bolts, and on 2002 to 2007 new body joining bolts (if the calliper is being overhauled). This is because the bolts are pre-treated with a locking compound. If they are not available it is possible, however, to clean up the old bolts and reinstall them using a suitable non-permanent thread locking compound that is commercially available.*

1 If you just want to displace the calipers for front wheel removal, on the right-hand side detach the brake hose joint block from the delay valve, then displace the delay valve from the fork and mudguard, on ABS models noting the sensor wire guide (see illustrations). On the left-hand side displace the brake hose guide from the fork and mudguard (see illustration). Tie the front brake calipers and hoses back so that they are out of the

3.1b . . . then unscrew the delay valve bolts (arrowed)

3.1c Unscrew the brake hose guide bolts (arrowed), noting the wire guide on ABS models

3.2a Brake hose banjo bolts (arrowed)

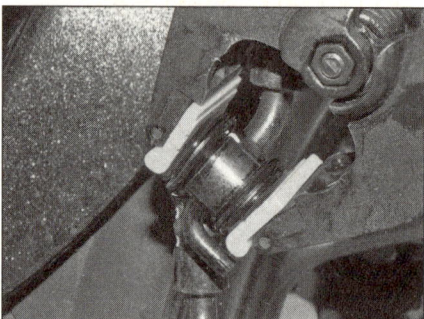

3.2b Seal each banjo union using pieces of rubber and a clamp

3.8a Use a block of wood to protect the pistons and caliper . . .

3.8b . . . then apply compressed air to force the pistons out

7 On 2002 to 2007 models unscrew the caliper body joining bolts and separate the body halves **(see illustration 8.2)**.

8 On 2002 to 2007 models position the caliper 'piston-side down' on a block of wood. On 2008-on models fit a block of wood between the pistons and the inner wall of the caliper **(see illustration)**. Apply compressed air gradually and progressively, starting with a fairly low pressure, to the fluid passage and allow the pistons to ease out of their bores **(see illustration)**, on 2002 to 2007 models controlling them with hand pressure on the caliper. Make sure the pistons are displaced evenly, using pressure to block one while the other moves if necessary.

9 If a piston is stuck in its bore due to corrosion the caliper should be replaced with a new one. Do not try to remove a piston by levering it out or by using pliers or other grips.

10 Mark each piston and the caliper body to ensure that the pistons can be matched to their original bores on reassembly. Note that two sizes of piston are used in each caliper (see Specifications at the beginning of this Chapter).

11 Remove the dust seals and the piston seals from the piston bores using a plastic tool to avoid scratching the bores **(see illustrations)**. Discard the seals as new ones must be fitted on reassembly.

12 Clean the pistons and bores with clean brake fluid. If compressed air is available, blow it through the fluid passages to ensure they are clear (make sure it is filtered and unlubricated).

Caution: Do not, under any circumstances, use a petroleum-based solvent to clean brake parts.

13 Inspect the caliper bores and pistons for signs of corrosion, nicks and burrs and loss of plating **(see illustration)**. If surface defects are present, the pistons and/or the caliper assembly must be replaced with new ones. If the necessary measuring equipment is available, compare the dimensions of the caliper bores and pistons to those specified at the beginning of this Chapter, and obtain new pistons or a new caliper if necessary. If one caliper is in poor condition, the other front caliper and the master cylinder should also be checked.

14 Lubricate the new piston seals with clean

way. Unscrew the caliper mounting bolts and slide the caliper assembly off the disc **(see illustrations 2.2a and b)**. **Note:** *Do not operate the brakes while the pads are out of the caliper.*

2 If the caliper is being completely removed or overhauled, unscrew the brake hose banjo bolts and detach the banjo unions, noting their alignment with the caliper **(see illustrations)**. If the brake fluid has not been drained seal the banjo unions – a good way of doing this is to place a piece of rubber over each side of the union (we used some rubber blanking caps), and clamp them in place using a spring clamp. Discard the sealing washers – new ones must be used.

3 On 2002 to 2007 models, if the caliper is being overhauled, loosen the caliper body joining bolts at this stage and retighten them lightly **(see illustration 8.2)** – the bolts are on the inner side of the caliper, so if you haven't got the necessary tools to access them you will have to slacken them with the caliper removed, in which case you may need an assistant to hold it, or use a vice with some protective card or a wad of rag.

4 Unscrew the caliper mounting bolts and slide the caliper assembly off the disc **(see illustrations 2.2a and b)**.

5 If the caliper is being overhauled, remove the brake pads (see Section 2, Steps 1, 3 and 4), slide the caliper and bracket apart **(see illustration 2.4a)** and remove the pad spring **(see illustration 2.12a)**. If you want to completely remove the left-hand caliper bracket/secondary master cylinder assembly refer to Section 6.

Overhaul

6 Clean the exterior of the caliper with denatured alcohol or brake system cleaner. Have some clean rag ready to catch any spilled brake fluid.

3.11a Remove the dust seal . . .

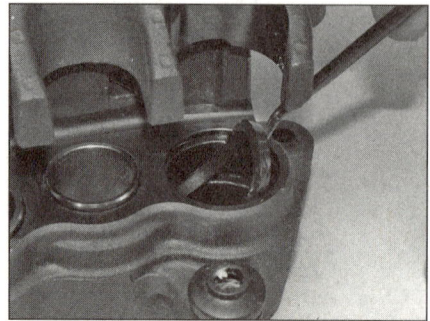

3.11b . . . and the piston seal

3.13 Check the surfaces of the pistons and bores

Brakes, wheels and final drive 6•9

3.14a Lubricate the new piston seals with brake fluid . . .

3.14b . . . then fit them into their grooves

3.15a Lubricate the new dust seals with silicone grease . . .

3.15b . . . then fit them into their grooves

3.16 Fit the pistons and push them all the way in

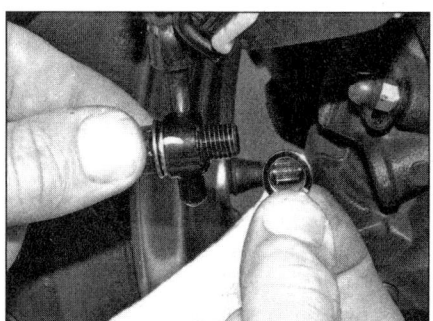

3.20 Use a new sealing washer on each side of the banjo union

brake fluid and fit them into their grooves in the caliper bores **(see illustrations)**. Note that there are two sizes of bore in each caliper and care must therefore be taken to ensure that the correct size seals are fitted to the correct bores (see Specifications). The same applies when fitting the new dust seals and pistons.

15 Lubricate the new dust seals with silicone grease and fit them into their grooves in the caliper bores **(see illustrations)**.

16 Lubricate the pistons with clean brake fluid and fit them, closed-end first, into the caliper bores, taking care not to displace the seals **(see illustration)**. Using your thumbs, push the pistons all the way in, making sure they enter the bore squarely.

17 On 2002 to 2007 models join the two halves of the caliper body together and fit the new bolts – if using the old bolts clean the threads and apply fresh thread locking compound. Tighten the bolts evenly to the torque setting specified at the beginning of the Chapter **(see illustration 8.2)**.

Installation

18 Refer to Section 2 and clean and check the pads, caliper slider pins and rubber boots, then fit the pad spring, join the caliper and bracket, and fit the brake pads, as required. If detached refer to Section 6 to fit the hoses to the left-hand caliper bracket/secondary master cylinder assembly.

19 Slide the caliper assembly onto the disc making sure the pads locate correctly on each side **(see illustrations 2.14a and b)**. Either fit the new caliper mounting bolts, or clean the threads of the original bolts and apply fresh thread locking compound, then tighten them to the torque setting specified at the beginning of the Chapter.

20 If removed, connect the brake hoses to the caliper, using new sealing washers on each side of the banjo fitting **(see illustration)**. Align the fittings as noted on removal. Tighten the banjo bolts to the specified torque setting.

21 Secure the brake hose/pipe assemblies on the front fork and mudguard **(see illustrations 3.1c, b and a)**.

22 Refer to Section 12 and fill and/or bleed the system as required. Check that there are no fluid leaks and test the operation of the brakes before riding the motorcycle.

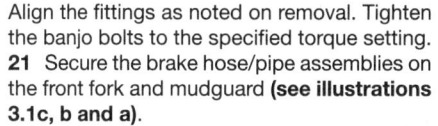

4 Front brake discs

Inspection

1 Inspect the surface of the disc for score marks and other damage. Light scratches are normal after use and won't affect brake operation, but deep grooves and heavy score marks will reduce braking efficiency and accelerate pad wear. If either disc is badly grooved replace both discs with a new ones.

2 The disc must not be allowed to wear down to a thickness less than the service limit listed in this Chapter's Specifications. The minimum thickness is also stamped on the disc **(see illustration)**. Check the thickness of the disc in the middle of the pad contact area using a micrometer – do not measure across the rim of the disc with a ruler. Replace the discs as a pair.

3 To check if the disc is warped, position the bike on an auxiliary stand with the front wheel raised off the ground. Mount a dial gauge to the fork leg, with the gauge plunger touching the surface of the disc about 10 mm from its outer edge **(see illustration)**.

4.2 The minimum thickness is marked on the disc

4.3 Checking disc runout with a dial gauge

4.5 The disc is secured by six bolts

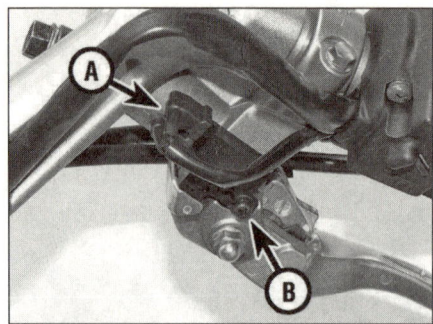

5.1 Disconnect the brake light switch wires (A). Switch mounting screw (B)

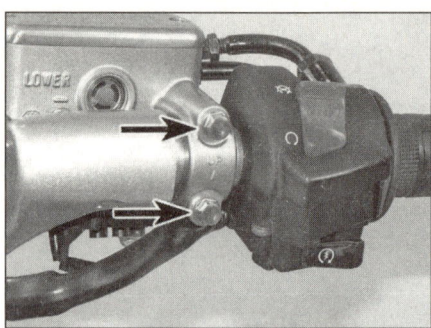

5.2 Unscrew the bolts (arrowed) and remove the master cylinder and its clamp

Rotate the wheel and watch the gauge needle, comparing the reading with the limit listed in the Specifications at the beginning of this Chapter. If the runout is greater than the service limit, check the wheel bearings for play (see Chapter 1). If the bearings are worn, install new ones (see Section 21) and repeat this check. If the disc runout is still excessive, remove the disc (Steps 4 and 5) and check for corrosion where it seats on the hub and clean it up if necessary. You can also try moving the disc around the wheel one bolt hole at a time and after each movement rechecking for runout. In most cases a new disc will have to be fitted.

Removal

Note: *Honda recommend using new disc mounting bolts. This is because the bolts are pre-treated with a locking compound. If they are not available it is possible, however, to clean up the old bolts and reinstall them using a suitable non-permanent thread locking compound that is commercially available.*

4 Remove the wheel (see Section 18). On models with ABS remove the pulse ring from the right-hand side of the wheel (see Section 15).

Caution: *Don't lay the wheel down and allow it to rest on either disc – the disc could become warped. Set the wheel on wood blocks so the wheel rim supports the weight of the wheel.*

5 If you are not replacing the disc with a new one, mark the relationship of the disc to the wheel, so it can be installed in the same position and on the same side as originally fitted. Unscrew the disc retaining bolts, loosening them evenly and a little at a time in a criss-cross pattern to avoid distorting the disc, then remove the disc **(see illustration)**.

Installation

6 Before installing the disc, make sure there is no dirt or corrosion where the disc seats on the hub. If the disc does not sit flat when it is bolted down, it will appear to be warped when checked or when the front brake is used.

7 Fit the disc on the wheel with its marked side facing out, aligning the previously applied matchmarks (if you're reinstalling the original disc), and making sure the arrow points in the direction of normal rotation.

8 Either fit the new bolts, or clean the threads of the original bolts and apply fresh thread locking compound, and tighten them evenly and a little at a time in a criss-cross pattern to the torque setting specified at the beginning of this Chapter. Clean the disc using acetone or brake system cleaner. If a new disc has been installed, remove any protective coating from its working surfaces and fit new brake pads.

9 On models with ABS fit the pulse ring onto the right-hand side of the wheel (see Section 15). Install the front wheel (see Section 18).

10 Operate the brake lever and pedal several times to push all pistons out and bring the pads into contact with the disc. Check the operation of the brakes before riding the motorcycle.

5 Front brake master cylinder

Warning: *If the brake master cylinder is in need of an overhaul it is best to drain all old brake fluid from the system, then fill with new fluid after the overhaul (see Section 12). Overhaul must be done in a spotlessly clean work area to avoid contamination and possible failure of the brake hydraulic system components. Do not, under any circumstances, use petroleum-based solvents to clean brake parts. Use clean DOT 4 brake fluid, dedicated brake cleaner or denatured alcohol only, as described. To prevent damage from spilled brake fluid, always cover paintwork when working on the braking system.*

Removal

Note: *If the master cylinder is being overhauled (usually due to sticking or poor action, or fluid leaks) read through the entire procedure first and make sure that you have obtained all the new parts required, including some new DOT 4 brake fluid.*

1 Disconnect the brake light switch wiring connectors **(see illustration)**.

2 If the master cylinder is just being displaced unscrew the clamp bolts and remove the back of the clamp, noting how it fits, then cover the master cylinder and reservoir in rag and position it clear of the handlebar **(see illustration)**. Ensure no strain is placed on the hydraulic hose. Keep the reservoir upright to prevent air entering the system.

3 If the master cylinder is being overhauled, remove the brake lever (see Chapter 5).

4 Slacken the reservoir cover screws **(see illustration)**.

5 Unscrew the brake hose banjo bolt and detach the banjo union, noting its alignment with the master cylinder **(see illustration)**. If the brake fluid has not been drained seal the banjo unions – a good way of doing this is to place a piece of rubber over each side of the union (we used some rubber blanking caps), and clamp them in place using a spring clamp **(see illustration 3.2b)**. Discard the sealing washers – new ones must be used.

6 Unscrew the master cylinder clamp bolts and remove the back of the clamp, noting

5.4 Slacken the cover screws

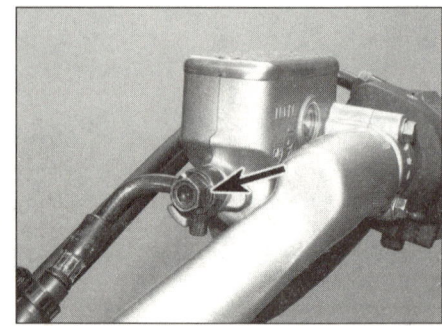

5.5 Brake hose banjo bolt (arrowed)

Brakes, wheels and final drive

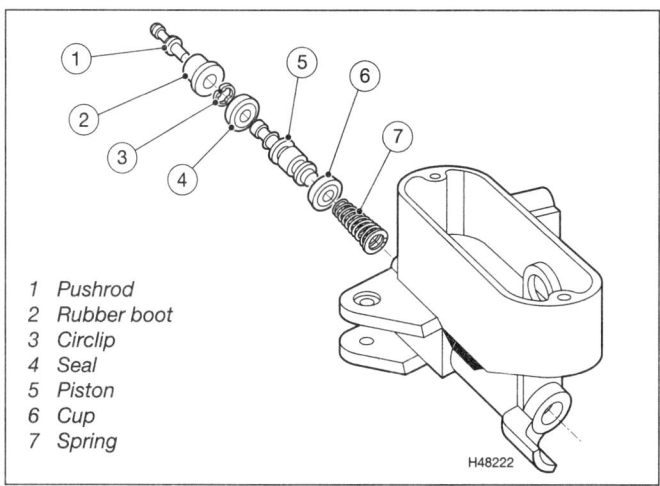

1 Pushrod
2 Rubber boot
3 Circlip
4 Seal
5 Piston
6 Cup
7 Spring

5.9 Front brake master cylinder – 2002 to 2007

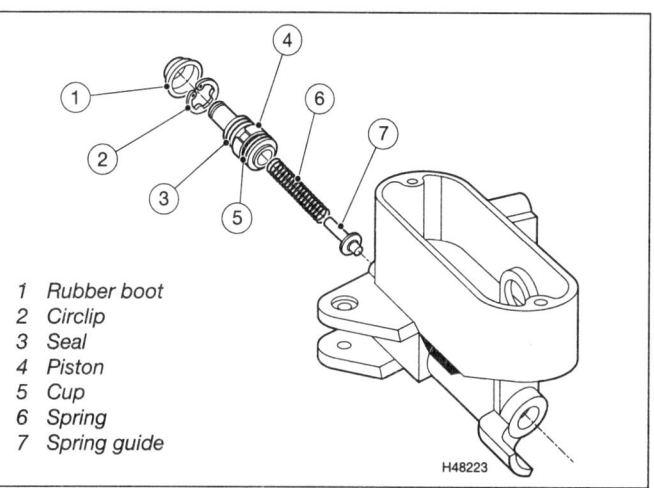

1 Rubber boot
2 Circlip
3 Seal
4 Piston
5 Cup
6 Spring
7 Spring guide

5.10a Front brake master cylinder – 2008-on

how it fits, then lift the master cylinder away from the handlebar **(see illustration 5.2)**.

7 Remove the reservoir cover, the diaphragm plate, the diaphragm, and where fitted the float. If the brake fluid wasn't drained tip the fluid from the master cylinder and reservoir into a suitable container. Wipe any remaining fluid out of the reservoir with a clean rag.

8 If required, undo the screw securing the brake light switch to the bottom of the master cylinder and remove the switch **(see illustration 5.1)**.

Overhaul

9 On 2002 to 2007 models remove the pushrod and the rubber boot from the master cylinder **(see illustration)**. Depress the piston and use circlip pliers to remove the circlip, then slide out the piston assembly and spring, noting how they fit. If they are difficult to remove, apply low pressure compressed air to the brake fluid outlet. Lay the parts out in the proper order to prevent confusion during reassembly.

10 On 2008-on models remove the rubber boot from the master cylinder **(see illustrations)**. Depress the piston and use circlip pliers to remove the circlip, then slide out the piston assembly, the spring and the spring guide, noting how they fit **(see illustration)**. If they are difficult to remove, apply low pressure compressed air to the brake fluid outlet. Lay the parts out in the proper order to prevent confusion during reassembly.

11 Clean the master cylinder with clean brake fluid. If compressed air is available, blow it through the fluid galleries to ensure they are clear (make sure the air is filtered and unlubricated).

Caution: Do not, under any circumstances, use a petroleum-based solvent to clean brake parts.

12 Check the master cylinder bore for corrosion, scratches, nicks and score marks. If the necessary measuring equipment is available, compare the dimensions of the piston and bore to those given in the Specifications at the beginning of this Chapter. If damage or wear is evident, the master cylinder must be replaced with a new one. If the master cylinder is in poor condition, then the calipers should be checked as well.

13 The dust boot, circlip, piston and its cup and seal, spring, and on 2008-on models the spring guide, are all included in a master cylinder rebuild kit, and all components except the piston, cup, seal, spring and spring guide are available individually. Use all of the new parts, regardless of the apparent condition of the old ones. Lubricate the master cylinder bore with new brake fluid. On 2002 to 2007 models remove the pushrod from the boot as this does not come in the kit.

14 Smear the cup and seal with new brake fluid and if not already in place fit them into their grooves in the piston so their wider ends will fit into the master cylinder first **(see illustration)**.

15 On 2002 to 2007 models fit the spring wide end first into the master cylinder **(see illustration 5.9)**. Lubricate the piston, cup and seal with clean brake fluid and slide it into the master cylinder and up against the spring. Make sure the lips on the cup and seal do not turn inside out. Push the piston in to compress the spring and fit the new circlip, making sure it locates in the groove. Smear the inner end of the pushrod with silicone grease. Fit the boot onto the pushrod so its narrow end lips locate in the groove. Locate the inner end of the pushrod in the end of the piston and carefully push the wide rim of the boot onto its seat in the master cylinder.

16 On 2008-on models fit the spring guide

5.10b Remove the boot from the end of the master cylinder piston . . .

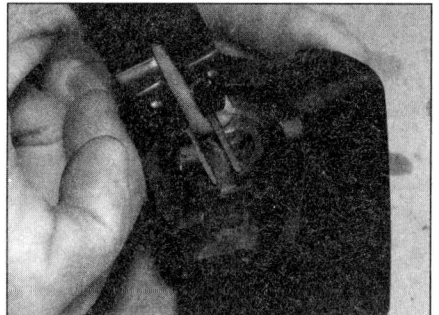

5.10c . . . then depress the piston, remove the circlip, and draw out the piston and spring

5.14 Make sure the cup and seal are correctly installed

6•12 Brakes, wheels and final drive

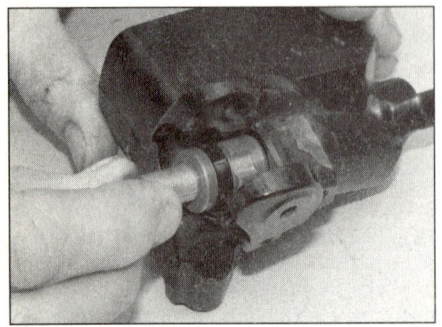

5.16a Fit the guide into the end of the spring ...

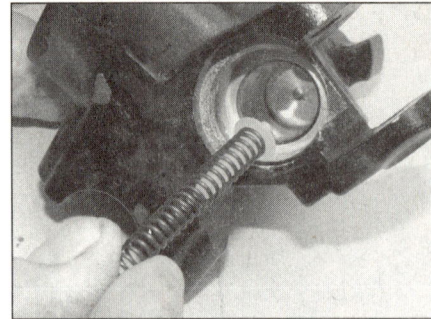

5.16b ... then fit the spring into the bore

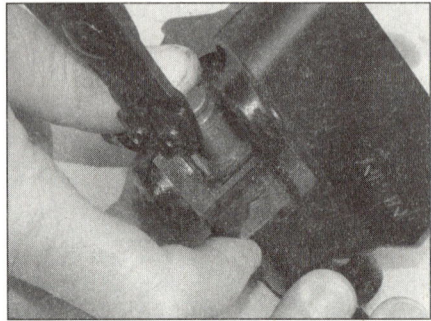

5.16c Push the piston into the bore ...

5.16d ... and hold it there while fitting the circlip

into the end of the spring **(see illustration)**. Fit the spring guide and spring into the master cylinder **(see illustration)**. Lubricate the piston, cup and seal with clean brake fluid and slide it into the master cylinder and up against the spring **(see illustration)**. Make sure the lips on the cup and seal do not turn inside out. Push the piston in to compress the spring and fit the new circlip, making sure it locates in the groove **(see illustrations)**. Smear the outer end of the pushrod with silicone grease. Carefully push the wide rim of the boot onto its seat in the master cylinder and locate the narrow end lips in the groove in the piston.

17 Inspect the reservoir diaphragm and fit a new one if it is damaged or deteriorated.

Installation

18 If removed, fit the brake light switch onto the bottom of the master cylinder, making sure the pin locates in the hole, and tighten the screw **(see illustration 5.1)**.

19 Attach the master cylinder to the handlebar, aligning the clamp joint with the punch mark on the top of the handlebar, then fit the back of the clamp with its UP mark facing up **(see illustration 5.2)**. Tighten the upper bolt to the torque setting specified at the beginning of this Chapter, followed by the lower bolt.

20 Connect the brake hose to the master cylinder, using new sealing washers on each side of the banjo fitting. Align the hose as noted on removal **(see illustration 5.5)**. Tighten the banjo bolt to the torque setting specified at the beginning of this Chapter.

21 Install the brake lever (see Chapter 5).

22 Connect the brake light switch wiring **(see illustration 5.1)**.

23 Refer to Section 12 and fill and/or bleed the system as required. Check that there are no fluid leaks and test the operation of the brakes before riding the motorcycle.

6 Secondary master cylinder, delay valve and proportional control valve

Warning: If the secondary master cylinder is in need of an overhaul, or if one of the valves is being removed, it is best to drain all old brake fluid from the system, then fill with new fluid after the overhaul (see Section 12). Overhaul must be done in a spotlessly clean work area to avoid contamination and possible failure of the brake hydraulic system components. Do not, under any circumstances, use petroleum-based solvents to clean brake parts. Use clean DOT 4 brake fluid, dedicated brake cleaner or denatured alcohol only, as described. To prevent damage from spilled brake fluid, always cover paintwork when working on the braking system.

Secondary master cylinder

Note: *If the master cylinder is being overhauled (usually due to sticking or poor action, or fluid leaks) read through the entire procedure first and make sure that you have obtained all the new parts required, including some new DOT 4 brake fluid.*

Removal

1 The master cylinder is incorporated in the left-hand caliper bracket. Remove the caliper from the bracket (see Section 3).

2 Unscrew the brake hose banjo bolts and detach the banjo unions, noting their alignment **(see illustration)**. If the brake fluid

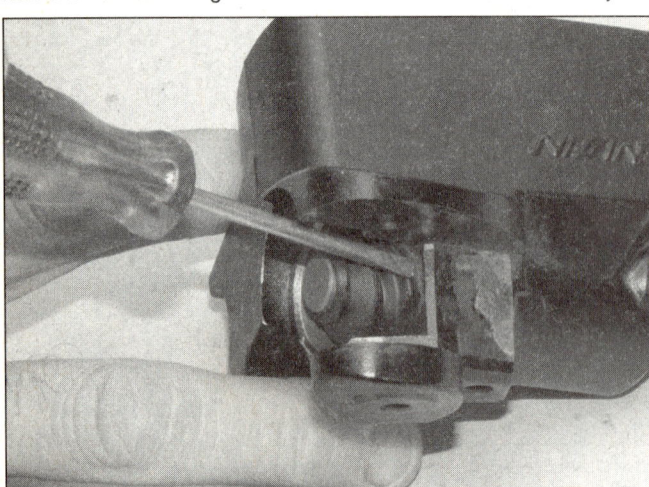

5.16e Feed the rim of the boot into the bore

6.2 Brake hose banjo bolts (arrowed)

Brakes, wheels and final drive 6•13

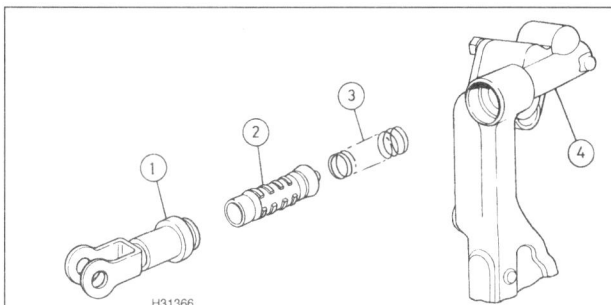

1 Pushrod
2 Piston assembly
3 Spring
4 Master cylinder body

6.3 Secondary master cylinder components

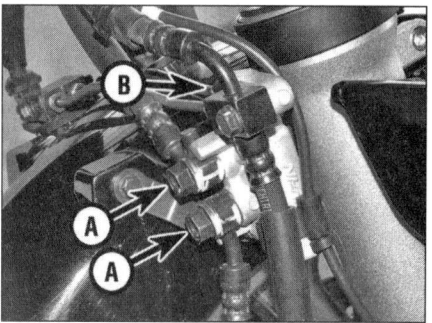

6.16a Brake hose banjo bolts (A) and brake pipe nut (B)

has not been drained seal the banjo unions – a good way of doing this is to place a piece of rubber over each side of the union (we used some rubber blanking caps), and clamp them in place using a spring clamp **(see illustration 3.2b)**. Discard the sealing washers – new ones must be used.

Overhaul

3 Dislodge the rubber dust boot from the master cylinder **(see illustration)**.
4 Depress the pushrod and, using circlip pliers, release the circlip. Slide out the pushrod, piston assembly and spring. If they are difficult to remove, apply low pressure compressed air to the fluid outlet. Lay the parts out in the proper order to prevent confusion during reassembly.
5 Clean the master cylinder with clean brake fluid or denatured alcohol.

Caution: Do not, under any circumstances, use a petroleum-based solvent to clean brake parts. If compressed air is available, use it to dry the parts thoroughly (make sure it's filtered and unlubricated).

6 Check the master cylinder bore for corrosion, scratches, nicks and score marks. If the necessary measuring equipment is available, compare the dimensions of the piston and bore to those given in the Specifications Section of this Chapter. If damage is evident, the master cylinder must be replaced with a new one.

7 The dust boot, circlip, piston assembly and spring are included in the rebuild kit. Use all of the new parts, regardless of the apparent condition of the old ones. If the cup and seal are not on the piston, fit them according to the layout of the old one.
8 Fit the spring wide end first into the master cylinder.
9 Lubricate the piston, cup and seal with clean brake fluid and slide it into the master cylinder and up against the spring. Make sure the lips on the cup and seal do not turn inside out.
10 Apply some silicone grease to the contact area between the pushrod and piston. Fit the pushrod and depress it, then secure it with the circlip, making sure it is properly seated in the groove.
11 Seat the rubber dust boot in the master cylinder, and make sure it is correctly located around the pushrod.
12 Refer to Section 2 Step 11 and check the pivot in the bottom of the fork.

Installation

13 Connect the brake hoses using new sealing washers on each side of the banjo union **(see illustration 3.20)**. Ensure that the hoses are positioned as noted on removal **(see illustration 6.2)**. Tighten the banjo bolts to the torque setting specified at the beginning of the Chapter.
14 Install the caliper (see Section 3).

15 Refer to Section 12 and fill and/or bleed the system as required. Check that there are no fluid leaks and test the operation of the brakes before riding the motorcycle.

Delay valve and proportional control valve

Removal

16 The delay valve is mounted on the right-hand fork. Unscrew the two brake hose banjo bolts, noting the alignment of the hoses on the valve and which fits where, and separate the hoses from the valve **(see illustration)**. If the brake fluid has not been drained seal the banjo unions – a good way of doing this is to place a piece of rubber over each side of the union (we used some rubber blanking caps), and clamp them in place using a spring clamp **(see illustration 3.2b)**. Discard the sealing washers – new ones must be used. Also unscrew the brake pipe joining nut and detach the pipe from the valve, again sealing the end of the pipe. Unscrew the bolt securing the brake hose/pipe joint to the right-hand fork and displace it to access the delay valve bolts **(see illustration 3.1a)**. Unscrew the delay valve mounting bolts and remove the valve **(see illustration)**.
17 The proportional control valve is mounted on the frame on the right-hand side **(see illustration)**. Remove the right-hand fairing

6.16b Delay valve mounting bolts (arrowed) – note the ABS sensor wire guide where fitted

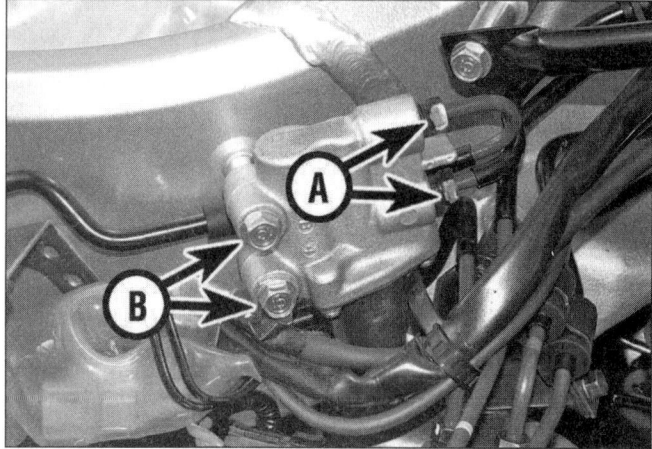

6.17 PCV pipe nuts (A) and mounting bolts (B)

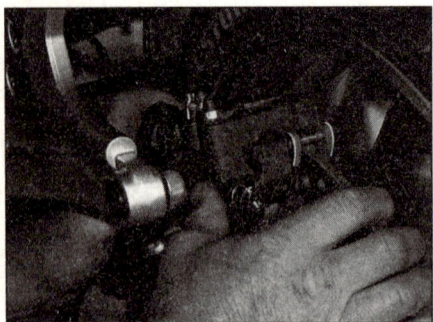
7.1 Push the caliper against the disc to force the pistons in

7.3a Remove the plug . . .

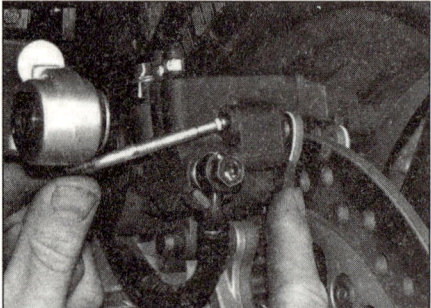
7.3b . . . unscrew and withdraw the pin . . .

7.3c . . . and remove the pads

7.9a Slide the pads into the caliper . . .

7.9b . . . then press them up against the spring and insert the pin

side panel for access (see Chapter 7). Unscrew the pipe joint nuts and detach the pipes from the valve. If the brake fluid hasn't been drained plug the ends or wrap something tightly around them to minimise fluid loss and prevent dirt entering the system. Unscrew the two bolts securing the valve and remove the valve.

Overhaul

18 Neither the delay valve nor the proportional control valve can be dismantled for overhaul, and no component parts are available. If either valve fails, it must be replaced with a new one.

Installation

19 Installation is the reverse of removal. Use new sealing washers on each side of the banjo bolt unions. Tighten the banjo bolts and the valve mounting bolts to the torque settings specified at the beginning of the Chapter.

20 Refer to Section 12 and fill and/or bleed the system as required. Check that there are no fluid leaks and test the operation of the brakes before riding the motorcycle.

7 Rear brake pads

1 Push the caliper against the disc, all the way across if new pads are being fitted so the pistons are pushed fully into the caliper to create room for them **(see illustration)**. It may be necessary to remove the master cylinder reservoir cover, plate and diaphragm and siphon out some fluid (see Pre-ride checks). If the pistons are difficult to push back, remove the bleed valve cap, then attach a length of clear hose to the bleed valve and place the open end in a suitable container, then open the valve and try again (see Section 12). Take great care not to draw any air into the system. If in doubt, bleed the brakes afterwards.

2 If the caliper is difficult to push in the chances are there is some hidden corrosion stopping it. If it doesn't move at all, or to fully clean and inspect the pistons, remove the caliper and overhaul it (see Section 8).

3 Remove the rubber plug from the pad pin, then unscrew the pin and remove the pads **(see illustrations)**. Note: *Do not operate the brakes while the pads are out of the caliper.* If required remove the shim from the back of each pad, noting how it fits **(see illustration 2.13a)** – note that new pads should come with new shims where applicable, but make sure they do, especially if fitting after-market pads, before discarding the old ones.

4 Inspect the surface of each pad for contamination and check that the friction material has not worn beyond its service limit (see Chapter 1, Section 2). If either pad is worn down to, or beyond, the service limit wear indicator (i.e. the wear indicator is no longer visible), is fouled with oil or grease, or heavily scored or damaged, fit a set of new pads. Also check for even wear across the pad – uneven wear is indicative of a sticking or seized piston, in which case remove the caliper for further inspection (see Section 8).

Note: *It is not possible to degrease the friction material; if the pads are contaminated in any way they must be replaced with new ones.*

5 If the pads are in good condition clean them carefully, using a fine wire brush which is completely free of oil and grease to remove all traces of road dirt and corrosion. Using a pointed instrument, dig out any embedded particles of foreign matter. If required, spray with a dedicated brake cleaner to remove any dust.

6 Remove all traces of corrosion from the pad pin and check it for wear and damage. Check the condition of the stopper ring on the pin and replace it with a new one if it is damaged or deformed **(see illustration 2.9)**.

7 Check the condition of the brake disc (see Section 9).

8 Where applicable fit the shim(s) onto the back of each pad **(see illustration 2.13a)**. Lightly smear the back of the pad backing material or shim and the edges of the backing material where it contacts the caliper body with copper-based grease, making sure that none gets on the friction material. Apply a smear of silicone grease to the stopper ring on the pad pin. Make sure the pad spring and guide are correctly fitted **(see illustration 8.4)**.

9 Fit the pads into the caliper so the friction material faces the disc, and seat the ends in the guide on the bracket **(see illustration)**. Press them up against the spring to align the holes, then insert the pad pin and tighten it to the torque setting specified at the beginning of this Chapter **(see illustration)**. Fit the rubber plug **(see illustration 7.3a)**.

Brakes, wheels and final drive 6•15

10 Operate the brake pedal until the pads contact the disc – this pushes the centre piston out. Now push up on the front left caliper so the secondary master cylinder pushes the outer pistons out and contact the pads. Check the level of fluid in each reservoir and top-up if necessary (see *Pre-ride checks*).

11 Check the operation of the brakes before riding the motorcycle.

8 Rear brake caliper

⚠️ **Warning:** *If the brake caliper is in need of an overhaul it is best to drain all old brake fluid from the system, then fill with new fluid after the overhaul (see Section 12). Overhaul must be done in a spotlessly clean work area to avoid contamination and possible failure of the brake hydraulic system components. Do not, under any circumstances, use petroleum-based solvents to clean brake parts. Use clean DOT 4 brake fluid, dedicated brake cleaner or denatured alcohol only, as described. To prevent damage from spilled brake fluid, always cover paintwork when working on the braking system.*

Removal

Note 1: *If the caliper is being overhauled (usually due to a sticking piston or fluid leak) read through the entire procedure first and make sure that you have obtained all the new parts required, including some new DOT 4 brake fluid.*

Note 2: *Honda recommend using new caliper body joining bolts (if caliper being overhauled). This is because the bolt threads are pre-treated with a locking compound. It is possible, however, to clean up the old bolts and reinstall them using a suitable non-permanent thread locking compound that is commercially available.*

1 If the caliper is being completely removed or overhauled, unscrew the brake hose banjo bolts and detach the banjo unions, noting their alignment with the caliper **(see illustration)**. If the brake fluid has not been drained seal the banjo unions – a good way of doing this is to place a piece of rubber over each side of the union (we used some rubber blanking caps), and clamp them in place using a spring clamp **(see illustration 3.2b)**. Discard the sealing washers – new ones must be used.

2 If the caliper is being overhauled, loosen the caliper body joining bolts at this stage and retighten them lightly **(see illustration)** – the bolts are on the inner side of the caliper, so if you haven't got the necessary tools to access them you will have to slacken them after removing the wheel, in which case refit the caliper bracket stopper bolt and the rear axle to secure the bracket/caliper.

3 Remove the brake pads (see Section 7). Remove the rear wheel (see Section 19).

4 Slide the caliper and bracket apart **(see illustration)**. Remove the pad spring from the caliper if required. Clean all old grease off the slider pins. Check the condition of the rubber boots and replace them with new ones if necessary.

Overhaul

5 Clean the exterior of the caliper with denatured alcohol or brake system cleaner. Have some clean rag ready to catch any spilled brake fluid.

6 Unscrew the caliper body joining bolts and separate the body halves **(see illustration 8.2)**.

7 Sit the caliper 'piston-side down' on a block of wood. Apply compressed air gradually and progressively, starting with a fairly low pressure, to the fluid passage and allow the pistons to ease out of their bores, controlling them with hand pressure on the caliper **(see illustration 3.8b)**. Make sure the pistons are displaced evenly, using pressure to block one while the other moves if necessary.

8.1 Brake hose banjo bolts (arrowed)

8 If a piston is stuck in its bore due to corrosion, the caliper should be replaced with a new one. Do not try to remove a piston by levering it out or by using pliers or other grips.

9 Mark each piston and the caliper body to ensure that the pistons can be matched to their original bores on reassembly. Note that two sizes of piston are used in each caliper (see Specifications at the beginning of this Chapter).

10 Remove the dust seals and the piston seals from the piston bores using a plastic tool to avoid scratching the bores **(see illustrations 3.11a and b)**. Discard the seals as new ones must be fitted on reassembly.

11 Clean the pistons and bores with clean brake fluid. If compressed air is available, blow it through the fluid passages to ensure they are clear (make sure it is filtered and unlubricated).

Caution: *Do not, under any circumstances, use a petroleum-based solvent to clean brake parts.*

12 Inspect the caliper bores and pistons for signs of corrosion, nicks and burrs and loss of plating **(see illustration 3.13)**. If surface defects are present, the pistons and/or the caliper assembly must be replaced with new ones. If the necessary measuring equipment is available, compare the dimensions of the caliper bores and pistons to those specified

8.2 Caliper body joining bolts (arrowed)

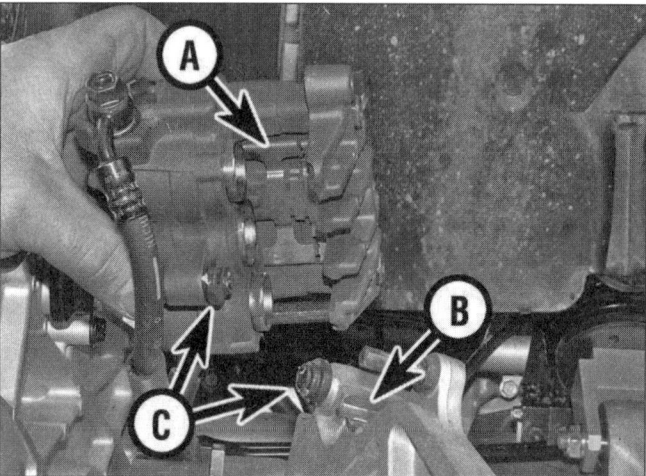

8.4 Slide the caliper and bracket apart. Note the pad spring (A), pad guide (B) and slider pin boots (C)

at the beginning of this Chapter, and obtain new pistons or a new caliper if necessary. If one caliper is in poor condition, the other front caliper and the master cylinder should also be checked.

13 Lubricate the new piston seals with clean brake fluid and fit them into their grooves in the caliper bores **(see illustrations 3.14a and b)**. Note that there are two sizes of bore in each caliper and care must therefore be taken to ensure that the correct size seals are fitted to the correct bores (see Specifications). The same applies when fitting the new dust seals and pistons.

14 Lubricate the new dust seals with silicone grease and fit them into their grooves in the caliper bores **(see illustrations 3.15a and b)**.

15 Lubricate the pistons with clean brake fluid and fit them, closed-end first, into the caliper bores, taking care not to displace the seals **(see illustration 3.16)**. Using your thumbs, push the pistons all the way in, making sure they enter the bore squarely.

16 Join the two halves of the caliper body together and fit the new bolts – if using the old bolts clean the threads and apply fresh thread locking compound. Tighten the bolts evenly to the torque setting specified at the beginning of the Chapter.

Installation

17 If the pad spring was removed fit it into the caliper, making sure it locates correctly **(see illustration 8.4)**. Make sure the pad guide on the bracket is correctly fitted. Make sure the slider pins are tight. Smear the slider pins and inside the rubber boots with silicone grease. Slide the caliper and bracket together, making sure each boot lip locates correctly in the groove in the pin.

18 Install the rear wheel (see Section 19). Install the brake pads (see Section 7).

19 If removed, connect the brake hoses to the caliper, using new sealing washers on each side of the banjo fitting **(see illustration 3.20)**. Align the fitting as noted on removal **(see illustration 8.1)**. Tighten the banjo bolts to the specified torque setting.

20 Refer to Section 12 and fill and/or bleed the system as required. Check that there are no fluid leaks and test the operation of the brakes before riding the motorcycle.

9 Rear brake disc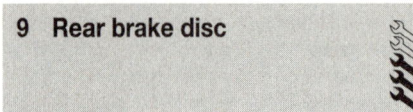

Inspection

1 Refer to Section 4 of this Chapter, noting that the dial gauge should be attached to the swingarm.

Removal

Note: *Honda recommend using new disc mounting bolts. This is because the bolts are pre-treated with a locking compound. It is possible, however, to clean up the old bolts and reinstall them using a suitable non-permanent thread locking compound that is commercially available.*

2 Remove the rear wheel (see Section 19).

Caution: *Don't lay the wheel down and allow it to rest on the disc – it could become warped.*

3 If you are not replacing the disc with a new one, mark the relationship of the disc to the wheel so it can be installed in the same position. Unscrew the disc retaining bolts, loosening them evenly and a little at a time in a criss-cross pattern to avoid distorting the disc, then remove the disc **(see illustration)**.

Installation

4 Before installing the disc, make sure there is no dirt or corrosion where the disc seats on the hub. If the disc does not sit flat when it is bolted down, it will appear to be warped when checked or when the rear brake is used.

5 Fit the disc on the wheel with its marked side facing out, aligning the previously applied matchmarks (if you're reinstalling the original disc).

6 Either fit the new bolts, or clean the threads of the original bolts and apply fresh thread locking compound, and tighten them evenly and a little at a time in a criss-cross pattern to the torque setting specified at the beginning of this Chapter. Clean the disc using acetone or brake system cleaner. If a new disc has been installed, remove any protective coating from its working surfaces and fit new brake pads.

7 Install the rear wheel (see Section 19).

8 Operate the brake lever and pedal several times to push all pistons out and bring the pads into contact with the disc. Check the operation of the brakes before riding the motorcycle.

10 Rear brake master cylinder

⚠️ **Warning:** *If the brake master cylinder is in need of an overhaul it is best to drain all old brake fluid from the system, then fill with new fluid after the overhaul (see Section 12). Overhaul must be done in a spotlessly clean work area to avoid contamination and possible failure of the brake hydraulic system components. Do not, under any circumstances, use petroleum-based solvents to clean brake parts. Use clean DOT 4 brake fluid, dedicated brake cleaner or denatured alcohol only, as described. To prevent damage from spilled brake fluid, always cover paintwork when working on the braking system.*

Removal

Note 1: *If the master cylinder is being overhauled (usually due to sticking or poor action, or fluid leaks) read through the entire procedure first and make sure that you have obtained all the new parts required, including some new DOT 4 brake fluid.*

Note 2: *Honda recommend using new master cylinder mounting bolts. This is because the bolts are pre-treated with a locking compound. It is possible, however, to clean up the old bolts and reinstall them using a suitable non-permanent thread locking compound that is commercially available.*

1 Remove the battery (see Chapter 8). Remove the right-hand silencer (see Chapter 4). Unscrew the bolt securing the rear of the downpipe assembly **(see illustration)**. Unscrew the bolt in the battery tray **(see illustration)**.

9.3 The disc is secured by six bolts

10.1a Unscrew the downpipe bolt . . .

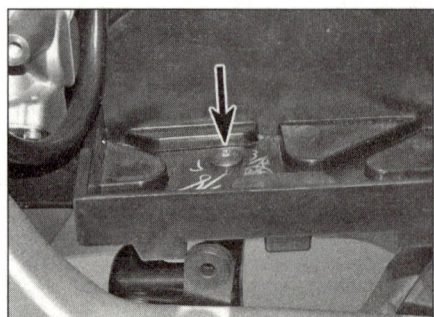

10.1b . . . and the battery tray bolt (arrowed)

Brakes, wheels and final drive 6•17

10.2 Unscrew the bolt (arrowed) and remove the plate

10.3 Unscrew the fluid reservoir bolt (arrowed)

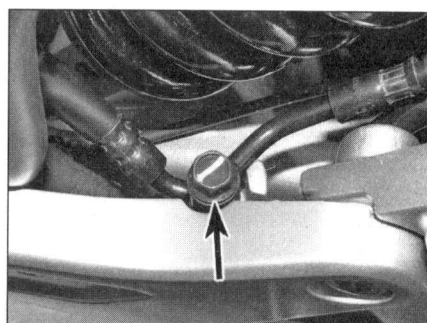

10.4 Brake hose banjo bolt (arrowed)

2 Unscrew the guard plate bolt and remove the plate (see illustration).
3 Unscrew the fluid reservoir bolt and displace the reservoir (see illustration).
4 Unscrew the brake hose banjo bolt and detach the banjo union, noting its alignment with the master cylinder (see illustration). If the brake fluid has not been drained seal the banjo unions – a good way of doing this is to place a piece of rubber over each side of the union (we used some rubber blanking caps), and clamp them in place using a spring clamp (see illustration 3.2b). Discard the sealing washers – new ones must be used.
5 Straighten the ends of the split pin and withdraw it from the master cylinder pushrod clevis pin (see illustration). Withdraw the clevis pin and detach the pushrod from the pedal (see illustration).
6 Unscrew the footrest bracket bolts, then displace the assembly and turn it so the inside is accessible, supporting it so you don't strain the brake light switch wiring (see illustration).
7 Unscrew the master cylinder bolts and remove it along with the reservoir, noting how the clevis locates in the rubber shield (see illustrations).

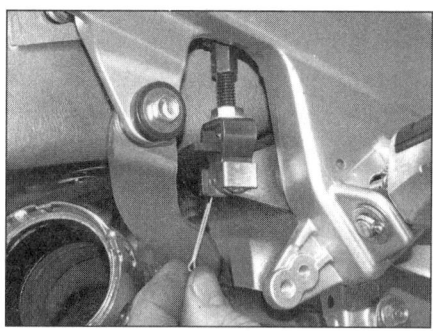

10.5a Remove the split pin . . .

10.5b . . . and withdraw the clevis pin

10.6 Unscrew the bolts (arrowed) and displace the footrest bracket

10.7a Unscrew the bolts (arrowed) and remove the master cylinder . . .

Overhaul

8 If the system wasn't drained undo the reservoir cap and tip the fluid out. Release the clip securing the reservoir hose to the union on the master cylinder and detach the hose,

being prepared to catch any residual fluid (see illustration).
9 If required, undo the reservoir hose union screw and detach it from the master cylinder (see illustration). Discard the O-ring as a new

one must be used. Inspect the reservoir hose for cracks or splits and replace it with a new one if necessary.
10 If required (doing so gives extra clearance for your circlip pliers in the next step), note how

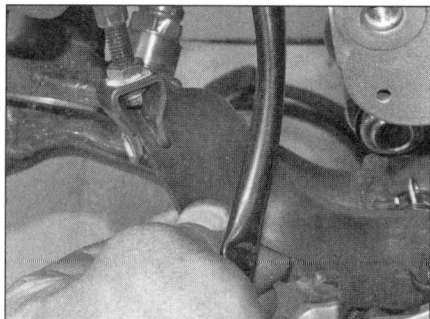

10.7b . . . noting how the clevis fits into the rubber shield

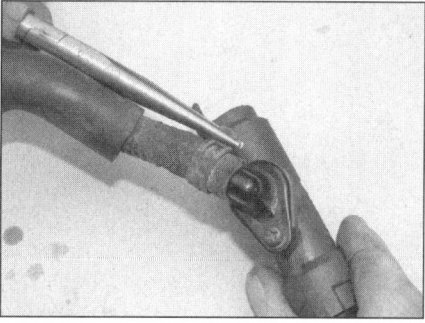

10.8 Release the clip and pull the hose off its union

10.9 Undo the screw and remove the union

6•18 Brakes, wheels and final drive

10.11a Remove the rubber boot . . .

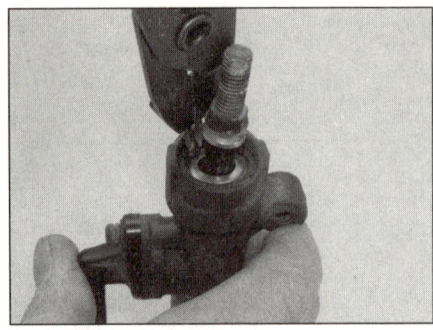

10.11b . . . then release the circlip . . .

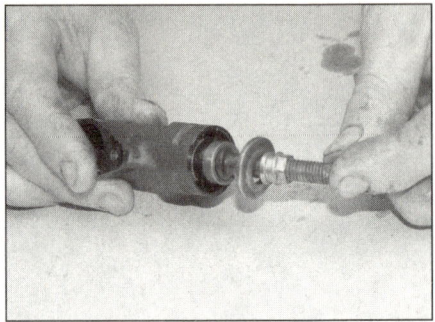

10.11c . . . and remove the pushrod, piston and spring

far the clevis is threaded up the pushrod, then slacken its locknut and thread it off, followed by the locknut **(see illustration 10.20)**.

11 Dislodge the rubber dust boot from the base of the master cylinder and from around the pushrod, noting how it locates **(see illustration)**. Push the pushrod in and, using circlip pliers, remove the circlip from its groove in the master cylinder and slide out the pushrod, piston and spring, noting how they fit **(see illustrations)**. Lay the parts out in order as you remove them to prevent confusion during reassembly.

12 Clean the master cylinder with clean brake fluid. If compressed air is available, blow it through the fluid galleries to ensure they are clear (make sure the air is filtered and unlubricated).

Caution: Do not, under any circumstances, use a petroleum-based solvent to clean brake parts.

13 Check the master cylinder bore for corrosion, scratches, nicks and score marks **(see illustration)**. If the necessary measuring equipment is available, compare the dimensions of the piston and bore to those given in the Specifications at the beginning of this Chapter. If damage or wear is evident, the master cylinder must be replaced with a new one. If the master cylinder is in poor condition, then the caliper should be checked as well.

14 The pushrod assembly (including the clevis, locknut, dust boot, circlip and washer), piston, seal, cup and spring are all included in the master cylinder rebuild kit. Use all of the new parts, regardless of the apparent condition of the old ones. If the pushrod components are not assembled, assemble them according to the layout of the old one.

15 Smear the cup and seal with new brake fluid. If the seal is not already on the piston, fit it into its groove so the wider end will fit into the master cylinder first **(see illustrations)**. Fit the cup onto the narrow end of the spring, locating the peg in the hole **(see illustration)**. Lubricate the master cylinder bore with new brake fluid.

16 Fit the spring wide-end first into the master cylinder and push the cup in, making sure its lips do not turn inside out **(see illustration)**.

17 Lubricate the piston with clean brake fluid and slide it into the master cylinder and up against the cup and spring **(see illustration)**. Make sure the lips on the seal do not turn inside out.

18 Smear some silicone grease onto the rounded end of the pushrod and around the

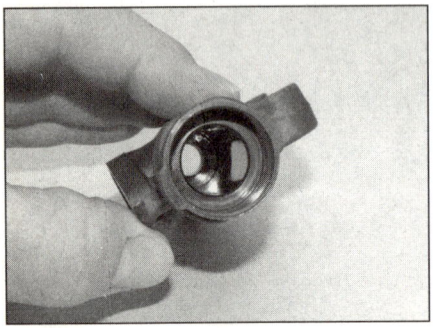

10.13 Check the cylinder for damage and wear

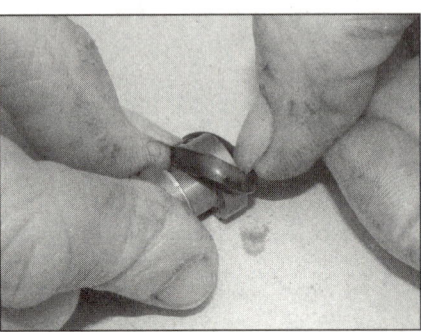

10.15a Fit the seal onto the piston . . .

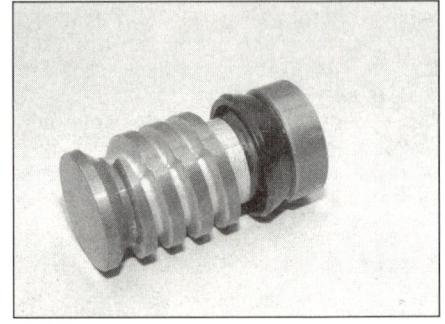

10.15b . . . as shown

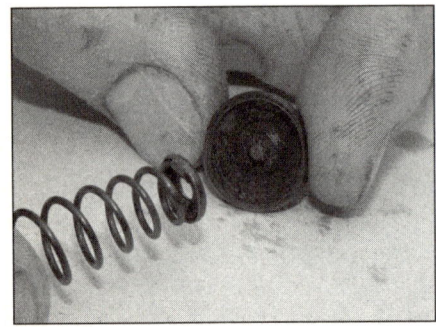

10.15c Fit the cup onto the end of the spring, locating the peg in the hole

10.16 Fit the spring making sure the cup locates correctly in the bore . . .

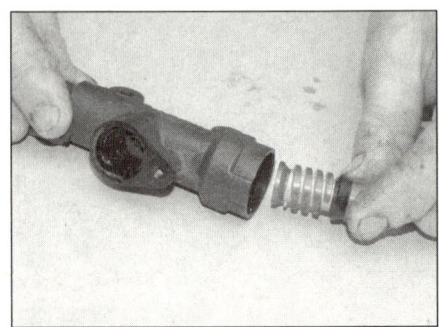

10.17 . . . then push the piston in

Brakes, wheels and final drive 6•19

10.18a Position the circlip on the washer . . .

10.18b . . . then depress the pushrod and fit the circlip into the groove

10.19a Fit the new boot . . .

lips of the boot. Fit the new washer and circlip onto the pushrod if not already in place **(see illustration)**. Push the piston in using the pushrod until the washer is beyond the circlip groove, then locate the circlip in the groove **(see illustration)**.

19 Fit the rubber boot, making sure the lips are seated correctly in the master cylinder and around the pushrod **(see illustrations)**.

20 If not already in place thread the locknut and clevis onto the pushrod, setting them as noted on removal – Honda specify the distance between the centre of the clevis pin hole and the lower mounting bolt hole measured parallel to the pushrod should be 87 mm **(see illustration)**. Tighten the locknut securely against the joint piece.

21 If removed fit a new fluid reservoir hose union O-ring smeared with brake fluid, then press the union into the master cylinder and secure it with the screw **(see illustrations)**.

22 Connect the hose to the union on the master cylinder and secure it with the clip **(see illustration)**. Check that the hose is secured with a clip at the reservoir end as well. If the clips have weakened, use new ones.

Installation

23 Either fit the master cylinder using new bolts, or clean the threads of the original bolts and apply fresh thread locking compound. Locate the master cylinder on the footrest bracket, fitting the rubber shield over the clevis, and tighten the bolts to the torque setting specified at the beginning of this Chapter **(see illustrations 10.7b and a)**.

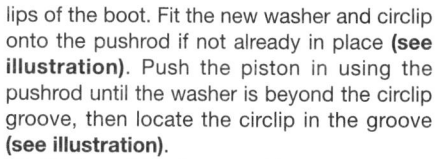

10.19b . . . then press it into the cylinder . . .

24 Make sure none of the collars have fallen out of the exhaust mounting rubbers **(see illustration)**. Locate the footrest bracket and tighten its bolts to the specified torque settings.

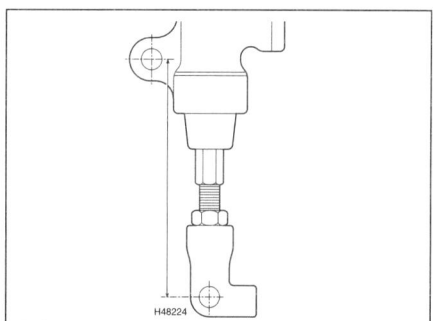

10.20 Set the clevis on the pushrod as shown

10.21b . . . then press the union into place

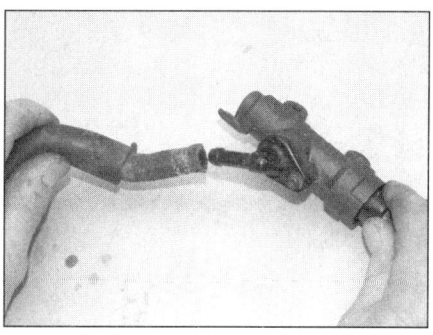

10.22 Fit the reservoir hose onto its union

10.19c . . . and make sure it is correctly located around the pushrod

25 Fit the fluid reservoir onto the frame, making sure the pin on the back locates in the hole **(see illustration 10.3)**.

26 Align the brake hose as noted on removal and connect the hose to the master cylinder,

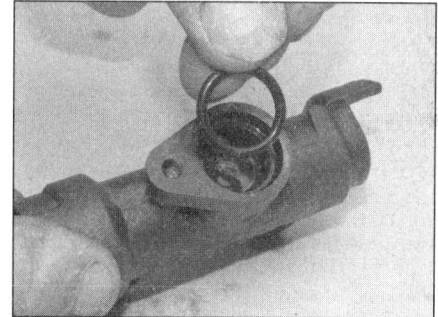

10.21a Fit a new O-ring . . .

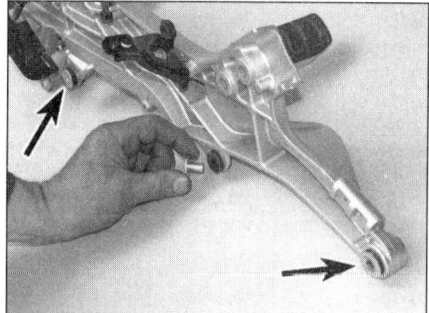

10.24 Make sure the three collars are fitted

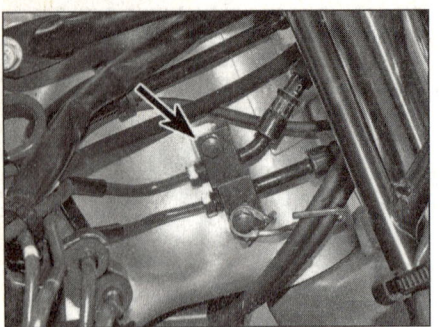

11.3a Do not omit checking the various hose/pipe joints (arrowed) . . .

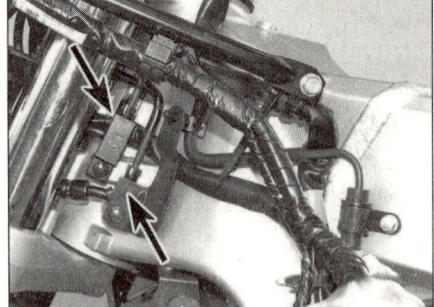

11.3b . . . along each side of the frame

12.2 Set-up for bleeding the brakes

using a new sealing washer on each side of the banjo fitting **(see illustration 10.4)**. Tighten the banjo bolt to the torque setting specified at the beginning of this Chapter.

27 Align the clevis with the brake pedal, then insert the pin and secure it with a new split pin **(see illustrations 10.5b and a)**. Bend the ends of the pin round to lock it.

28 Fit the guard plate, the battery tray bolt, and the exhaust downpipe bolt **(see illustrations 10.2 and 10.1b and a)**.

29 Install the right-hand silencer (see Chapter 4). Install the battery (see Chapter 8).

30 Refer to Section 12 and fill and/or bleed the system as required. Check that there are no fluid leaks and test the operation of the brakes before riding the motorcycle.

11 Brake hoses and fittings

Inspection

1 To fully inspect all the brake hoses and pipes remove the fairing side panels and the side covers (see Chapter 7).

2 Check brake hose condition regularly and replace the hoses with new ones at the specified interval (see Chapter 1). Twist and flex the hoses while looking for cracks, bulges and seeping hydraulic fluid. Check extra carefully around the areas where the hoses connect with the banjo fittings, as these are common areas for hose failure.

3 Also check the brake pipes, the hose and pipe joints, the proportional control and delay valves, and on models with ABS the modulators, referring to the relevant Sections of this Chapter, for signs of fluid leakage and for any dents or cracks in the pipes **(see illustrations)**.

4 Inspect the banjo fittings connected to the brake hoses and the pipe joints on ABS models. If the fittings are rusted, scratched or cracked, fit new ones.

Removal and installation

5 Drain all old brake fluid from the system (see Section 12).

6 The brake hoses have banjo fittings on each end. Cover the surrounding area with plenty of rags and unscrew the banjo bolt at each end of the hose, noting the alignment of the fitting with the master cylinder or brake caliper **(see illustrations 3.2a, 5.5, 6.2, 8.1, and 10.4)**. Free the hose from any clips or guides and remove it, noting its routing. Discard the sealing washers. **Note:** *Do not operate the brake lever or pedal while a brake hose is disconnected.*

7 Position the new hose, making sure it isn't twisted or otherwise strained, and ensure that it is correctly routed through any clips or guides and is clear of all moving components.

8 Check that the fittings align correctly, then install the banjo bolts, using new sealing washers on both sides of the fittings **(see illustration 3.2b)**. Tighten the banjo bolts to the torque setting specified at the beginning of this Chapter.

9 The brake pipes are held by nuts **(see illustrations 6.17, 15.21 and 15.28)**. There are no sealing washers. Unscrew the nuts and detach the pipes. Make sure the pipe is correctly positioned, fitted into any clips, and with any joint blocks secured, before tightening the nuts. If the correct tools are available tighten the nuts to the torque setting specified at the beginning of this Chapter for your model.

10 Refill the system with new DOT 4 brake fluid (see *Pre-ride checks*) and bleed the air from it (see Section 12).

11 Check the operation of the brakes before riding the motorcycle.

12 Brake system bleeding and fluid change

Note: *Honda recommend using a commercially available vacuum-type brake bleeding tool (see illustration 12.7). If bleeding the system using the conventional method does not work sufficiently well, it is advisable to obtain a bleeder and repeat the procedure detailed below, following the manufacturer's instructions for using the tool. If the tool is not available, take the machine to a Honda dealer.*

1 Bleeding the brakes is simply the process of removing any air bubbles from the system. Bleeding is necessary whenever a brake hose or pipe joint is loosened or disconnected. Leaks in the system may also allow air to enter, but leaking brake fluid will reveal their presence and warn you of the need for repair.

2 To bleed the brakes, you will need some new DOT 4 brake fluid, a length of clear flexible hose, a small container partially filled with clean brake fluid, some rags, a spanner to fit the caliper bleed valve, and help from an assistant **(see illustration)**. Due to the complexity of the system you may also need an assistant. Bleeding kits that include the hose, a one-way valve and a container are available relatively cheaply from a good auto store, and simplify the task, with the one-way valve negating the need of an assistant.

3 Cover painted components to prevent damage in the event that brake fluid is spilled. Remove the right-hand side cover to access the rear master cylinder reservoir and the right-hand fairing side panel to access the proportional control valve bleed valve (see Chapter 7).

4 Refer to *Pre-Ride checks* and remove the reservoir cover or cap, diaphragm plate and diaphragm and slowly pump the brake lever or pedal a few times, until no air bubbles can be seen floating up from the holes in the bottom of the reservoir. Doing this bleeds the air from the master cylinder end of the line. Loosely refit the reservoir cover.

5 The brake system should be bled in the following order, using the front brake lever or rear brake pedal as instructed:

  1 Left front caliper – upper bleed valve – front brake lever
  2 Right front caliper – upper bleed valve – front brake lever
  3 Proportional control valve (PCV) – secondary master cylinder (displaced and tilted so hose at top, and pumped by hand)
  4 Rear caliper – centre bleed valve – secondary master cylinder (displaced and tilted so hose at top, and pumped by hand)
  5 Right front caliper – lower bleed valve – rear brake pedal
  6 Left front caliper – lower bleed valve – rear brake pedal
  7 Rear caliper – rear bleed valve – rear brake pedal

Brakes, wheels and final drive 6•21

6 Pull the dust cap off the bleed valve **(see illustrations)**. If using a ring spanner fit it onto the valve. Attach one end of the hose to the bleed valve and, if not using a kit, submerge the other end in the clean brake fluid in the container **(see illustration 12.2)**. The hose must be an air-tight fit over the bleed valve.

 *To avoid damaging the bleed valve during the procedure, loosen it and then tighten it temporarily with a ring spanner before attaching the hose. With the hose attached, the valve can then be opened and closed either with an open-ended spanner, or by leaving the ring spanner located on the valve and fitting the hose above it.*

7 Do not allow the fluid level to drop below the lower mark during the bleeding process.

8 Carefully pump the brake lever or pedal, or the secondary master cylinder pushrod (as applicable), three or four times and hold it in or down while opening the bleed valve. When the valve is opened, brake fluid will flow out of the valve into the clear tubing and the lever, pedal or pushrod will move toward in or down.

9 Tighten the bleed valve, then release the lever, pedal or pushrod gradually. Repeat the process until no air bubbles are visible in the brake fluid leaving the bleed valve and the lever, pedal or pushrod is firm when applied. On completion, disconnect the bleeding equipment, then tighten the bleed valve to the torque setting specified at the beginning of the chapter and fit the dust cap.

10 Top-up the reservoir, then install the diaphragm, diaphragm plate, and cover or cap (see *Pre-ride checks*). Wipe up any spilled brake fluid. Check the entire system for fluid leaks.

11 Check the operation of the brakes before riding the motorcycle.

 If it's not possible to produce a firm feel to the lever or pedal the fluid may be aerated. Let the brake fluid in the system stabilise for a few hours and then repeat the procedure when the tiny bubbles in the system have settled out.

Fluid change

12 Changing the brake fluid is a similar process to bleeding the brakes and requires the same materials plus a suitable tool for siphoning the fluid out of the reservoirs. Also ensure that the container is large enough to take all the old fluid when it is flushed out of the system.

13 Follow Steps 3 and 6, then remove the reservoir cover or cap, diaphragm plate and diaphragm, and where fitted the front

12.6a Right-hand front brake caliper bleed valves (arrowed)

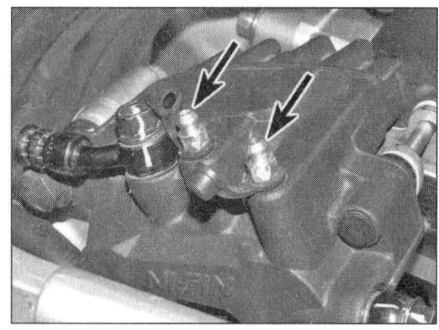

12.6c Rear brake caliper bleed valves (arrowed)

reservoir float, and siphon the old fluid out of the reservoirs. Fill the reservoirs with new brake fluid, then follow the bleeding procedure until new fluid can be seen emerging from the bleed valves. Keep the reservoirs topped-up with new fluid or air may enter the system and greatly increase the length of the task.

 *Old brake fluid is invariably much darker in colour than new fluid, making it easy to see when all old fluid has been expelled from the system.*

14 Disconnect the hose, then tighten the bleed valve to the specified torque setting and fit the dust cap.

15 Top-up the reservoir, then fit the float (where fitted), diaphragm, diaphragm plate, and cover or cap (see *Pre-ride checks*). Wipe up any spilled brake fluid. Check the entire system for fluid leaks.

16 Check the operation of the brakes before riding the motorcycle.

Draining the system for overhaul

17 Draining the brake fluid is again a similar process to bleeding the brakes. The quickest and easiest way is to use a commercially available vacuum-type brake bleeding tool **(see illustration)** – follow the manufacturer's instructions. Otherwise follow the procedure described above for changing the fluid, but

12.6b PCV bleed valve (arrowed)

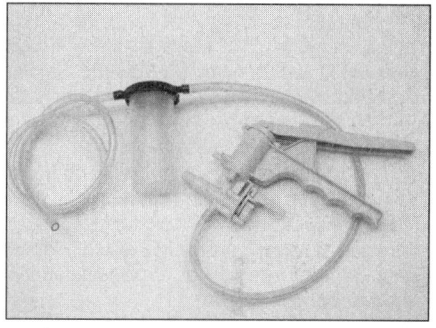

12.17 A commercial vacuum-operated bleeding tool

quite simply do not put any new fluid into the reservoir – the system fills itself with air instead.

13 ABS operation

1 The ABS prevents the wheels from locking up under hard braking or on uneven road surfaces. A sensor on each wheel transmits information about the speed of rotation to the ABS control unit; if the unit senses that a wheel is about to lock, it releases brake pressure to that wheel momentarily, preventing a skid.

2 The ABS is self-checking and is activated when the ignition switch is turned on – the ABS indicator light in the instrument cluster will come on and will remain on until road speed increases above 6 mph (10 kph) at which point, if the ABS is normal, the light will go off.

3 If the indicator light remains on, or starts flashing while the machine is being ridden, there is a fault in the system and the ABS function will be switched off – the brakes will still function but in normal mode.

4 If a fault is indicated, details will be stored in the control unit's memory. Access the fault code(s) as follows.

5 Remove the left-hand side cover (see Chapter 7).

6 Ensure the ignition switch is OFF. Open the lid of the rear fuse box and remove the two

6•22 Brakes, wheels and final drive

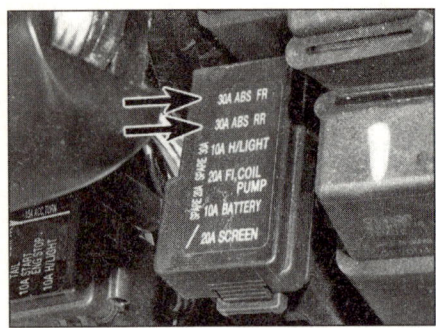

13.6 Open the lid and remove the two ABS modulator fuses (arrowed)

30A ABS modulator fuses **(see illustration)** – if either fuse has blown, perform the system checks relating to fault code 4 for the ABS FR fuse and fault code 5 for the ABS RR fuse (see Section 14). If the fuses are good, turn the ignition switch ON – the ABS indicator light should come on for 5 seconds, then go out. When the light goes out immediately (within 3 seconds) fit either of the two fuses – the indicator light will come on for 3 seconds, then give 0.25 second flashes at 0.25 second intervals, with the number of flashes denoting the fault code.

7 Two fault codes can be stored, and they are displayed most recent first, with a five second gap between them, during which the light comes on for 3 seconds. If the light gives 2.0 second flashes at 2.0 second intervals after fitting the fuse no fault code is stored. The code or codes are repeated until the ignition is switched OFF. If two fault codes are given correct the faults relating to the first given code first.

8 Turn the ignition switch OFF when the code or codes have been recorded.

9 To check the ABS components see Section 15.

10 Once the fault has been corrected, erase the fault code(s) as follows. Follow Step 6 to display the fault code(s), and while the light is flashing the code refit the other fuse. When the code(s) is/are erased the light will come on.

11 Turn the ignition switch OFF. Install the side cover (see Chapter 7). Check that the ABS is operating normally (see Step 2).

12 If necessary, repeat the reset procedure.

Note: *The ABS indicator may diagnose a fault if tyre sizes other than those specified by Honda are fitted, if the tyre pressures are incorrect, if the machine has been run continuously over bumpy roads, if the front wheel comes off the ground whilst riding (wheelie) or if the machine is on an auxiliary stand with the engine running and the rear wheel turning.*

14 ABS fault diagnosis

1 If a fault is indicated in the ABS, first check that the battery is fully charged, then check the ABS fuses (see Chapter 8).

2 Unless specified otherwise, carry-out all checks with the ignition switch OFF.

3 Refer to Chapter 8, Section 2, for general electrical fault finding procedures and equipment.

4 If, after a thorough check, the source of a fault has not been identified, have the ABS control unit tested by a Honda dealer.

Fault code/flashes	Faulty component or system	Possible causes
No code displayed, but light is on – problem not detected	No voltage at instrument cluster No voltage at control unit	Blown ABS control unit fuse Faulty wiring or wiring connector Faulty control unit Faulty ABS indicator light
2	Front wheel speed sensor Front wheel pulse ring	Faulty wiring or wiring connector Faulty sensor Damaged pulse ring
3	Rear wheel speed sensor Rear wheel pulse ring	Faulty wiring or wiring connector Faulty sensor Damaged pulse ring
4	Front modulator motor	Blown front modulator fuse Faulty front motor Faulty front crank angle sensor Faulty wiring or wiring connector
5	Rear modulator motor	Blown rear modulator fuse Faulty rear motor Faulty rear crank angle sensor Faulty wiring or wiring connector
6	Front crank angle sensor system	Faulty front crank angle sensor Faulty wiring or wiring connector
7	Rear crank angle sensor system	Faulty rear crank angle sensor Faulty wiring or wiring connector
8	ABS control unit – front control circuit	Blown front modulator fuse Faulty front motor Faulty front crank angle sensor Faulty wheel speed sensor Damaged pulse ring Faulty wiring or wiring connector Faulty control unit
9	ABS control unit – rear control circuit	Blown rear modulator fuse Faulty rear motor Faulty rear crank angle sensor Faulty wheel speed sensor Damaged pulse ring Faulty wiring or wiring connector Faulty control unit
10	ABS control unit – front relay circuit	Blown front modulator fuse Faulty front motor Faulty front crank angle sensor Faulty wiring or wiring connector Faulty control unit
11	ABS control unit – rear relay circuit	Blown rear modulator fuse Faulty rear motor Faulty rear crank angle sensor Faulty wiring or wiring connector Faulty control unit
12	ABS control unit – front motor driver circuit	Blown front modulator fuse Faulty front motor Faulty wiring or wiring connector Faulty control unit
13	ABS control unit – rear motor driver circuit	Blown rear modulator fuse Faulty rear motor Faulty wiring or wiring connector Faulty control unit
14	Power circuit	Damaged fuse Faulty wiring or wiring connector Faulty control unit

Brakes, wheels and final drive 6•23

14.5 Measuring front wheel sensor air gap

14.7a ABS control unit (arrowed). Release the strap ...

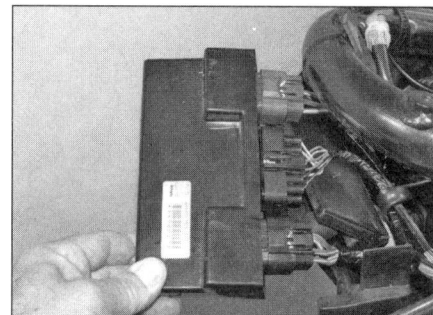

14.7b ... displace the control unit and disconnect the 12-pin black wiring connector

Fault codes 2 and 8

Note: *Before carrying out any of the checks, follow the procedure in Section 13 to reset the control unit memory, then activate the self-checking procedure. If the fault code is the result of unusual riding or conditions and the ABS is normal, the indicator light will go off. Otherwise perform the following checks.*

5 Measure the air gap between the front wheel speed sensor and the pulse ring with a feeler gauge, then compare the result with the Specification at the beginning of this Chapter **(see illustration)**. The gap is not adjustable – if it is outside the specification, check that the sensor and pulse ring fixings are tight, that the components are not damaged and that there is no dirt or anything else on the sensor tip or between the slots in the pulse ring. If any of the components are damaged they must be replaced with new ones.

6 Erase the fault code, but do not turn the ignition OFF afterwards (see Section 13). Raise the front wheel off the ground and spin the wheel in a forward direction – the ABS indicator light should start to flash. If it does, check the front wheel speed sensor wiring and connectors. If they are good it is possible the control unit has been disrupted by an extremely powerful radio wave.

7 If the light doesn't flash remove the rear cowl and right-hand fairing side panel (see Chapter 7). Disconnect the ABS control unit 12-pin black wiring connector **(see illustrations)**. Trace the wheel sensor wiring to the connector and disconnect it **(see illustration)**. Check for continuity first in the black/pink wire between the control unit wiring connector and the sensor wiring connector and then in the green/orange wire – there should be continuity in each wire. If not locate and repair the break.

8 If there is continuity in the wiring next check for continuity between each terminal on the sensor side of the connector and earth (ground). If there is continuity in either of the wires the sensor is faulty and must be replaced with a new one.

9 If all the checks have failed to identify the fault, replace the wheel sensor with a known good one. Connect all wiring connectors then follow the procedure in Section 13 to reset the control unit memory, then activate the self-checking procedure. If the indicator light is no longer flashing, the original sensor was faulty. If the fault code reappears have the ABS control unit checked by a Honda dealer.

Fault codes 3 and 9

Note: *Before carrying out any of the checks, follow the procedure in Section 13 to reset the control unit memory, then activate the self-checking procedure. If the fault code is the result of unusual riding or conditions and the ABS is normal, the indicator light will go off. Otherwise perform the following checks.*

10 Measure the air gap between the rear wheel speed sensor and the pulse ring with a feeler gauge, then compare the result with the Specification at the beginning of this Chapter **(see illustration)**. The gap is adjustable using a shim available from Honda – if it is outside the specification, first check that the sensor and pulse ring fixings are tight, that the components are not damaged and that there is no dirt or anything else on the sensor tip or between the slots in the pulse ring. If any of the components are damaged they must be replaced with new ones. If all is good and the gap was too small, and there is no shim fitted, fit one (se Section 15). If the gap was too big and there is a shim fitted, remove it.

11 Erase the fault code, but do not turn the ignition OFF afterwards (see Section 13). Raise the rear wheel off the ground and spin the wheel in a forward direction – the ABS indicator light should start to flash. If it does, check the rear wheel speed sensor wiring and connectors. If they are good it is possible the control unit has been disrupted by an extremely powerful radio wave.

12 If the light doesn't flash remove the rear cowl and right-hand fairing side panel (see Chapter 7). Disconnect the ABS control unit 12-pin black wiring connector **(see illustrations 14.7a and b)**. Trace the wheel sensor wiring to the connector and disconnect it **(see illustration)**. Check for continuity first in the black/orange wire between the control unit wiring connector and the sensor wiring connector and then in the blue/brown wire – there should be continuity in each wire. If not locate and repair the break.

13 If there is continuity in the wiring next check for continuity between each terminal on the sensor side of the connector and earth (ground). If there is continuity in either of the wires the sensor is faulty and must be replaced with a new one.

14.7c Disconnect the wheel sensor wiring connector (arrowed)

14.10 Measuring rear wheel sensor air gap

14.12 Disconnect the wheel sensor wiring connector (arrowed)

6•24 Brakes, wheels and final drive

14.19 Front modulator wiring connectors (arrowed)

14.25a Displace the relay and disconnect the wiring connectors (arrowed)

14.25b Disconnect the modulator wiring connector

14 If all the checks have failed to identify the fault, replace the wheel sensor with a known good one. Connect all wiring connectors then follow the procedure in Section 13 to reset the control unit memory, then activate the self-checking procedure. If the indicator light is no longer flashing, the original sensor was faulty. If the fault code reappears have the ABS control unit checked by a Honda dealer.

Fault code 4

15 Check the front modulator fuse (see Section 13, Steps 5 and 6). If the fuse has blown replace it with a new one.

16 Erase the fault code (see Section 13). Start the engine and go for a short ride so the ABS system performs its self-diagnosis. If the ABS indicator light stays off, check the front wheel speed sensor wiring and connectors. If they are OK it is possible there was a piece of fine foreign matter in the modulator or the control unit has been disrupted by an extremely powerful radio wave.

17 If the ABS indicator light flashes, remove the rear cowl (see Chapter 7). Disconnect the ABS control unit 5 pin black wiring connector **(see illustrations 14.7a and b)**. Check for battery voltage between the red/white wire terminal on the loom side of the connector and earth (ground) – there should be voltage at all times i.e. with the ignition OFF. If there is no voltage, check for a break in the red/white wire between the connector and the fusebox connector, and if that wire is good check the wire between the fusebox and the battery.

18 If there is voltage, check for continuity to earth in the green/yellow wire – there should be continuity. If not locate the break in the wire and repair it.

19 Remove the right-hand fairing side panel (see Chapter 7). Disconnect the front modulator 2-pin black wiring connector **(see illustration)**. Check for continuity first in the brown/yellow wire between the ABS and modulator wiring connectors (loom side) and then in the green/yellow wire. If continuity is not shown in either or both of the wires locate the break and repair it. Next check for continuity between each terminal in the modulator connector (modulator side) and earth (ground). If there is continuity in either of the wires either repair the wire or replace the modulator with a new one.

20 If all the wiring is good remove the both front and rear modulators and interchange them (see Section 15). Reconnect the control unit wiring connector. Erase the fault code (see Section 13). Start the engine and go for a short ride so the ABS system performs its self-diagnosis. If fault code 5 is now shown the front modulator (now fitted at the rear) is faulty. If fault code 4 is again shown the modulator is OK but the ABS control unit is faulty.

Fault code 5

21 Check the rear modulator fuse (see Section 13, Steps 5 and 6). If the fuse has blown replace it with a new one.

22 Erase the fault code (see Section 13). Start the engine and go for a short ride so the ABS system performs its self-diagnosis. If the ABS indicator light stays off, check the rear wheel speed sensor wiring and connectors. If they are OK it is possible there was a piece of fine foreign matter in the modulator or the control unit has been disrupted by an extremely powerful radio wave.

23 If the ABS indicator light flashes, remove the rear cowl (see Chapter 7). Disconnect the ABS control unit 5-pin brown wiring connector **(see illustrations 14.7a and b)**. Check for battery voltage between the black/blue wire terminal on the loom side of the connector and earth (ground) – there should be voltage at all times i.e. with the ignition OFF. If there is no voltage, check for a break in the black/blue wire between the connector and the fusebox connector, and if that wire is good check the wire between the fusebox and the battery.

24 If there is voltage, check for continuity to earth in the green/yellow wire – there should be continuity. If not locate the break in the wire and repair it.

25 Remove the right-hand side cover (see Chapter 7). Displace the starter relay and disconnect its red and white wiring connectors **(see illustration)**. Draw the rear modulator 5-pin brown wiring connector out and disconnect it **(see illustration)**. Check for continuity first in the brown/light green wire between the ABS and modulator wiring connectors (loom side) and then in the red/black wire. If continuity is not shown in either or both of the wires locate the break and repair it. Next check for continuity between each terminal in the connector (modulator side) and earth (ground). If there is continuity in either of the wires either repair the wire or replace the modulator with a new one.

26 If all the wiring is good remove the both front and rear modulators and interchange them. Reconnect the control unit wiring connector. Erase the fault code (see Section 13). Start the engine and go for a short ride so the ABS system performs its self-diagnosis. If fault code 4 is now shown the rear modulator (now fitted at the front) is faulty. If fault code 5 is again shown the modulator is OK but the ABS control unit is faulty.

Fault code 6

27 Erase the fault code (see Section 13). Start the engine and go for a short ride so the ABS system performs its self-diagnosis. If the ABS indicator light stays off, check the front wheel speed sensor wiring and connectors (see Section 15). If they are OK it is possible there was a piece of fine foreign matter in the modulator or the control unit has been disrupted by an extremely powerful radio wave.

28 If the ABS indicator light still flashes, remove the right-hand fairing side panel (see Chapter 7). Disconnect the front modulator 3-pin wiring connector **(see illustration 14.19)**. Check the voltage between the orange/green (+) wire terminal and the pink/blue (-) wire terminal on the loom side of the connector – there should be 4.5 to 5.5 volts with the ignition ON. If there is no voltage, remove the rear cowl (see Chapter 7). Disconnect the ABS control unit 12-pin black wiring connector **(see illustrations 14.7a and b)**. Check for continuity first in the orange/green wire between the ABS and modulator wiring connectors (loom side) and then in the pink/blue wire. If continuity is not shown in either or both of the wires locate the break and repair it.

29 If there is the correct voltage, remove the rear cowl (see Chapter 7). Disconnect the ABS control unit 12 pin black wiring connector **(see illustrations 14.7a and b)**. Check for continuity in the white/pink wire between the ABS and front modulator wiring connectors (loom side) – there should be continuity. If not locate the break in the wire and repair it.

30 Next check for continuity in the white/pink wire in the modulator connector (modulator side) to earth (ground). If there is continuity either repair the wire or replace the modulator with a new one.

31 If all the wiring is good remove the both front and rear modulators and interchange them. Reconnect the control unit wiring connector. Erase the fault code (see Section 13). Start the engine and go for a short ride so the ABS system performs its self-diagnosis. If fault code 7 is now shown the front modulator (now fitted at the rear) is faulty. If fault code 6 is again shown the modulator is OK but the ABS control unit is faulty.

Fault code 7

32 Erase the fault code (see Section 13). Start the engine and go for a short ride so the ABS system performs its self-diagnosis. If the ABS indicator light stays off, check the rear wheel speed sensor wiring and connectors (see Section 15). If they are OK it is possible there was a piece of fine foreign matter in the modulator or the control unit has been disrupted by an extremely powerful radio wave.

33 If the ABS indicator light still flashes, remove the right-hand side cover (see Chapter 7). Displace the starter relay and disconnect its white wiring connector **(see illustration 14.25a)**. Draw the rear modulator 5-pin wiring connector out and disconnect it **(see illustration 14.25b)**. Check the voltage between the orange/blue (+) wire terminal and the pink/white (-) wire terminal on the loom side of the connector – there should be 4.5 to 5.5 volts with the ignition ON. If there is no voltage, remove the rear cowl (see Chapter 7). Disconnect the ABS control unit 12-pin black wiring connector **(see illustrations 14.7a and b)**. Check for continuity first in the orange/blue wire between the ABS and modulator wiring connectors (loom side) and then in the pink/white wire. If continuity is not shown in either or both of the wires locate the break and repair it.

34 If there is the correct voltage, remove the rear cowl (see Chapter 7). Disconnect the ABS control unit 12 pin black wiring connector **(see illustrations 14.7a and b)**. Check for continuity in the white/pink wire between the ABS and rear modulator wiring connectors (loom side) – there should be continuity. If not locate the break in the wire and repair it.

35 Next check for continuity in the white/pink wire in the modulator connector (modulator side) to earth (ground). If there is continuity either repair the wire or replace the modulator with a new one.

36 If all the wiring is good remove the both front and rear modulators and interchange them. Reconnect the control unit wiring connector. Erase the fault code (see Section 13). Start the engine and go for a short ride so the ABS system performs its self-diagnosis. If fault code 6 is now shown the rear modulator (now fitted at the front) is faulty. If fault code 7 is again shown the modulator is OK but the ABS control unit is faulty.

Fault code 10

37 Erase the fault code (see Section 13). Start the engine and go for a short ride so the ABS system performs its self-diagnosis. If the ABS indicator light stays off, check the front wheel speed sensor wiring and connectors (see Section 15). If they are OK it is possible there was a piece of fine foreign matter in the modulator or the control unit has been disrupted by an extremely powerful radio wave.

38 If the ABS indicator light still flashes fault code 10, remove the both front and rear modulators and interchange them. Erase the fault code (see Section 13). Start the engine and go for a short ride so the ABS system performs its self-diagnosis. If fault code 11 is now shown the front modulator (now fitted at the rear) is faulty. If fault code 10 is again shown the modulator is OK but the ABS control unit is faulty.

39 If the ABS indicator light flashes a fault code other than 10 perform diagnosis relating to the latest code.

Fault code 11

40 Erase the fault code (see Section 13). Start the engine and go for a short ride so the ABS system performs its self-diagnosis. If the ABS indicator light stays off, check the rear wheel speed sensor wiring and connectors (see Section 15). If they are OK it is possible there was a piece of fine foreign matter in the modulator or the control unit has been disrupted by an extremely powerful radio wave.

41 If the ABS indicator light still flashes fault code 11, remove the both front and rear modulators and interchange them. Erase the fault code (see Section 13). Start the engine and go for a short ride so the ABS system performs its self-diagnosis. If fault code 10 is now shown the rear modulator (now fitted at the front) is faulty. If fault code 11 is again shown the modulator is OK but the ABS control unit is faulty.

42 If the ABS indicator light flashes a fault code other than 11 perform diagnosis relating to the latest code.

Fault codes 12 and 13

43 Erase the fault code (see Section 13). Start the engine and go for a short ride so the ABS system performs its self-diagnosis. If the ABS indicator light stays off, check the wheel speed sensor wiring and connectors (see Section 15). If they are OK it is possible there was a piece of fine foreign matter in the modulator or the control unit has been disrupted by an extremely powerful radio wave.

44 If the ABS indicator light still flashes fault code 12 or 13, the ABS control unit is faulty.

45 If the ABS indicator light flashes a fault code other than 12 or 13 perform diagnosis relating to the latest code.

Fault code 14

46 Check all the ABS fuses (see Chapter 8). If a fuse has blown replace it with a new one. If the fuse is good check the battery and the charging system (see Chapter 8). Also check the wiring and connectors between the fuse box and the ABS control unit **(see illustrations 14.7a and b)** – remove the rear cowl for access (see Chapter 8).

47 If all is good so far erase the fault code (see Section 13). Start the engine and go for a short ride so the ABS system performs its self-diagnosis. If the ABS indicator light stays off, check the wheel speed sensor wiring and connectors (see Section 15). If they are OK it is possible there was a piece of fine foreign matter in the modulator or the control unit has been disrupted by an extremely powerful radio wave.

48 If the light flashes fit a new battery, then erase the fault code (see Section 13). Start the engine and go for a short ride so the ABS system performs its self-diagnosis. If the ABS indicator light stays off, the battery was the problem. If the ABS indicator light still flashes fault code 14, the ABS control unit is faulty.

49 If the light comes on and stays on remove the rear cowl (see Chapter 7). Disconnect the ABS control unit 5-pin brown and 5-pin black wiring connectors **(see illustrations 14.7a and b)**. Check the voltage between the black/blue (+) wire terminal and the green/yellow (-) wire terminal on the loom side of the brown connector, and then between the red/white (+) and green/yellow (-) wire terminals in the black connector. Honda specifies a permanent voltage between 10 and 17 volts in each case. If there is no voltage, check for a break in a wire. If the voltage is below the specification, check the charging system (see Chapter 8). If there is voltage the ABS control unit is faulty.

No fault code detected

50 If no code is detected but the ABS indicator light stays on, check the ABS main fuse (see Chapter 8). If a fuse has blown replace it with a new one. If the fuse is good check the wiring and connectors between the fuse box and the ABS control unit **(see illustrations 14.7a and b)** – remove the rear cowl to access it (see Chapter 7).

51 If all is good so far disconnect the ABS control unit 5-pin brown wiring connector **(see illustrations 14.7a and b)**. Check the voltage between the red/brown (+) wire terminal and earth (ground) with the ignition ON. There should be battery voltage. If there is no voltage, check for a break in the wire.

52 If the voltage is good, reconnect the 5-pin brown wiring connector and disconnect the 5 pin black connector. Check the voltage between the blue/yellow (+) wire terminal and earth (ground) with the ignition ON. There should be 1 to 3 volts. If there is no voltage, check for a break in the wire between the ABS connector and the instrument cluster.

53 If the voltage is good, reconnect the 5-pin black wiring connector. Refer to Steps 7 and 12 and check the wiring between the control

15.2a Unscrew the bolts (arrowed) . . .

15.2b . . . and withdraw the sensor from the bracket

15.6 Front pulse ring screws (arrowed)

unit and each wheel speed sensor, then check for voltage at the black/pink wire terminal in the loom side of the front sensor connector and the black/orange wire in the rear sensor connector.

54 If the wiring is good erase the fault code (see Section 13). Start the engine and go for a short ride so the ABS system performs its self-diagnosis. If the ABS indicator light stays off, it is possible there was a piece of fine foreign matter in the modulator or the control unit has been disrupted by an extremely powerful radio wave.

55 If the ABS indicator light still flashes the ABS control unit is faulty.

15 ABS components

Front wheel sensor

1 Remove the right-hand fairing side panel (see Chapter 7). Trace the wheel sensor wiring to the connector and disconnect it **(see illustration 14.7c)**.

2 Undo the bolts securing the sensor wiring guides, and the sensor to the caliper bracket, and remove the sensor, releasing the wiring from any other clips or ties and noting its routing **(see illustrations)**.

3 Install the new sensor and tighten the mounting bolts. Feed the wiring up to the connector, routing and securing it as noted on removal.

4 Check the air gap (see Section 14, Step 5). Install the fairing side panel (see Chapter 7).

Front pulse ring

5 Remove the front wheel (see Section 18).

6 Undo the screws securing the ring and lift it off **(see illustration)**.

7 Ensure there is no dirt or corrosion where the ring seats on the hub – if the ring does not sit flat when it is installed the sensor air gap will be incorrect. Clean the threads of the bolts and apply a non-permanent thread locking compound (or alternatively use new bolts from Honda which come pre-treated) and tighten them to the torque setting specified at the beginning of the Chapter.

8 Install the front wheel (see Section 18). Check the speed sensor air gap (see Section 14, Step 5).

Rear wheel sensor

9 Remove the right-hand fairing side panel (see Chapter 7). Trace the wheel sensor wiring to the connector and disconnect it **(see illustration 14.12)**.

10 Undo the bolts securing the sensor wiring guides, and the sensor to the caliper bracket, and remove the sensor, releasing the wiring from any other clips or ties and noting its routing **(see illustration)**.

11 Install the new sensor and tighten the mounting bolts. Feed the wiring up to the connector, routing and securing it as noted on removal.

12 Check the air gap (see Section 14, Step 10). Install the right-hand fairing side panel (see Chapter 7).

Rear pulse ring

13 Remove the rear wheel (see Section 19).

14 Undo the screws securing the ring and lift it off **(see illustration)**.

15 Ensure there is no dirt or corrosion where the ring seats on the hub – if the ring does not sit flat when it is installed the sensor air gap will be incorrect. Clean the threads of the bolts and apply a non-permanent thread locking compound (or alternatively use new bolts from Honda which come pre-treated) and tighten them to the torque setting specified at the beginning of the Chapter.

16 Install the rear wheel (see Section 19). Check the speed sensor air gap (see Section 14, Step 10).

Front modulator

Note: *Before the modulator can be removed from the bike, the brake fluid must be drained from the hydraulic system (see Section 12).*

17 Remove the right-hand fairing side panel (see Chapter 7).

18 Drain the brake fluid (see Section 12).

19 Disconnect the two wiring connectors **(see illustration 14.19)**.

20 Cover the area around the modulator with clean rag to prevent damage to paintwork in the event that brake fluid is spilled.

21 Unscrew the four brake pipe nuts and detach the pipes **(see illustration)**.

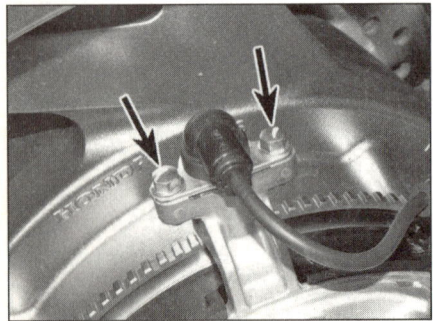

15.10 Unscrew the bolts (arrowed) and withdraw the sensor from the bracket

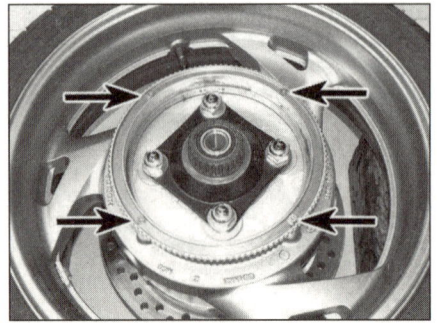

15.14 Rear pulse ring screws (arrowed)

15.21 Unscrew the nuts (arrowed) and detach the pipes

Brakes, wheels and final drive 6•27

15.22 Modulator mounting bolts (arrowed)

15.25a Displace the relay and disconnect the wiring connector (arrowed) . . .

15.25b . . . and free the wiring from the clip

22 Unscrew the modulator mounting bolts, noting the wiring clamp, and remove the modulator **(see illustration)**.
23 If required, unscrew the bracket bolts.
24 Installation is the reverse of removal, noting the following:
● Make sure the pipes are correctly connected. If the correct tools are available tighten the nuts to the torque setting specified at the beginning of the Chapter for your model.
● Ensure the wiring connectors are secure.
● Follow the procedure in Section 12 to refill and bleed the brake system.

Rear modulator

Note: *Before the modulator can be removed from the bike, the brake fluid must be drained from the hydraulic system (see Section 12).*

25 Remove the battery (see Chapter 8). Displace the starter relay, disconnect its wiring connector, and free the wiring from the clip on the modulator bracket **(see illustrations)**.
26 Drain the brake fluid (see Section 12).
27 Cover the area around the modulator with clean rag to prevent damage to paintwork in the event that brake fluid is spilled.
28 Unscrew the four brake pipe nuts and detach the pipes **(see illustration)**.
29 Unscrew the modulator mounting bolts, displace the modulator and disconnect the two wiring connectors **(see illustration)**.
30 If required, unscrew the bracket bolts.
31 Installation is the reverse of removal, noting the following:
● Make sure the pipes are correctly connected. If the correct tools are available tighten the nuts to the torque setting specified at the beginning of the Chapter for your model.
● Ensure the wiring connectors are secure.
● Follow the procedure in Section 12 to refill and bleed the brake system.

ABS control unit

32 Remove the rear cowl (see Chapter 8).
33 Release the control unit from its rubber strap then disconnect the three wiring connectors **(see illustrations 14.7a and b)**.
34 Installation is the reverse of removal. Make sure the wiring connectors are secure.

16 Wheel inspection and repair

1 In order to carry out a proper inspection of the wheels, support the bike on the centrestand. Clean the wheels thoroughly to remove mud and dirt that may interfere with the inspection procedure or mask defects. Make a general check of the wheels (see Chapter 1) and tyres (see *Pre-ride checks*).
2 Attach a dial gauge to the fork or the swingarm and position its tip against the side of the wheel rim. Spin the wheel slowly and check the axial (side-to-side) runout of the rim **(see illustration)**.
3 In order to accurately check radial (out of round) runout with the dial gauge, remove the wheel from the machine, and the tyre from the wheel. With the axle clamped in a vice and the dial gauge positioned on the top of the rim, the wheel can be rotated to check the runout **(see illustration 16.2)**.
4 An easier, though slightly less accurate, method is to attach a stiff wire pointer to the fork or the swingarm and position the end a fraction of an inch from the wheel rim where the wheel and tyre join. If the wheel is true, the distance from the pointer to the rim will be constant as the wheel is rotated. **Note:** *If wheel runout is excessive, check the wheel bearings very carefully before renewing the wheel.*
5 Inspect the wheels for cracks, flat spots on the rim and other damage. Look very closely for dents in the area where the tyre bead contacts the rim. Dents in this area may prevent complete sealing of the tyre against the rim, which leads to deflation of the tyre over a period of time. If damage is evident, or if runout in either direction is excessive, the wheel will have to be renewed. Never attempt to repair a damaged alloy wheel.

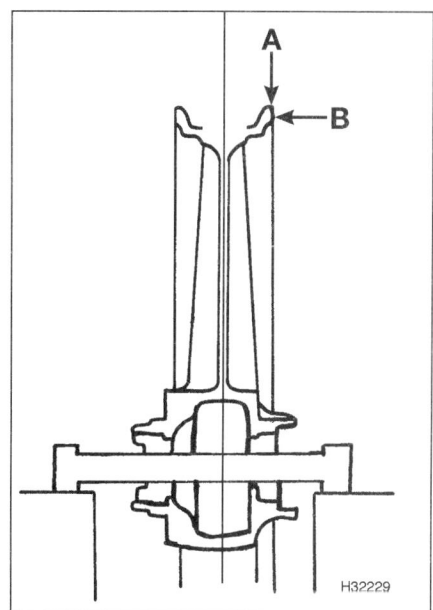

16.2 Check the wheel for radial (out-of-round) runout (A) and axial (side-to-side) runout (B)

15.28 Unscrew the nuts (arrowed) and detach the pipes

15.29 Modulator mounting bolts (arrowed)

6•28 Brakes, wheels and final drive

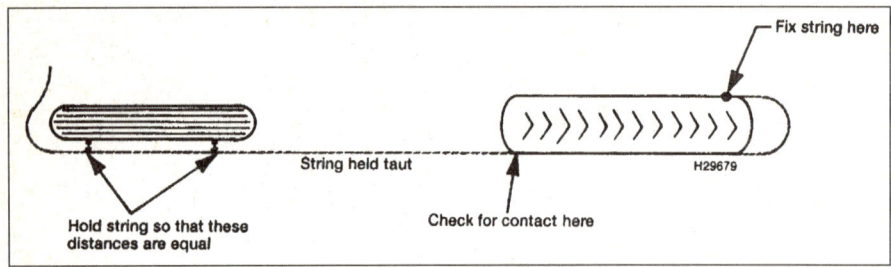

17.5 Wheel alignment check using string

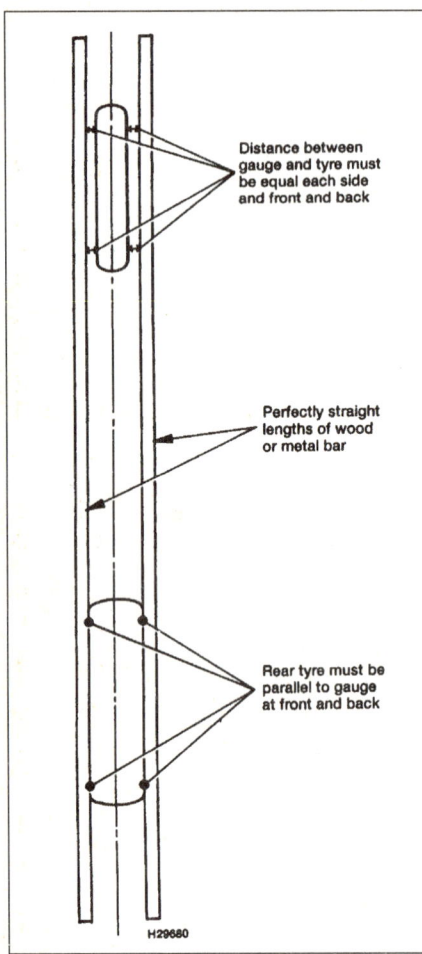

17.7 Wheel alignment check using a straight-edge

17 Wheel alignment check

1 Misalignment of the wheels due to a bent frame or forks can cause strange and possibly serious handling problems. If the frame or forks are at fault, repair by a frame specialist or renewal are the only options.

2 To check wheel alignment you will need an assistant, a length of string or a perfectly straight piece of wood and a ruler. A plumb bob or spirit level for checking that the wheels are vertical will also be required.

3 Support the bike on the centrestand. Measure the width of both tyres at their widest points. Subtract the smaller measurement from the larger measurement, then divide the difference by two. The result is the amount of offset that should exist between the front and rear tyres on both sides of the machine.

4 If the string method is used, have your assistant hold one end of it about halfway between the floor and the rear axle, with the string touching the back edge of the rear tyre sidewall.

5 Run the other end of the string forward and pull it tight so that it is roughly parallel to the floor (**see illustration**). Slowly bring the string into contact with the front edge of the rear tyre sidewall, then turn the front wheel until it is parallel with the string. Measure the distance from the front tyre sidewall to the string.

6 Repeat the procedure on the other side of the motorcycle. The distance from the front tyre sidewall to the string should be equal on both sides.

7 As previously mentioned, a perfectly straight length of wood or metal bar may be substituted for the string (**see illustration**).

8 If the distance between the string and tyre is greater on one side, or if the rear wheel appears to be out of alignment, have your machine checked by a Honda dealer or frame specialist.

9 If the front-to-back alignment is correct, the wheels still may be out of alignment vertically.

10 Using a plumb bob or spirit level, check the rear wheel to make sure it is vertical. To do this, hold the string of the plumb bob against the tyre upper sidewall and allow the weight to settle just off the floor. If the string touches both the upper and lower tyre sidewalls and is perfectly straight, the wheel is vertical. If it is not, adjust the stand until it is.

11 Once the rear wheel is vertical, check the front wheel in the same manner. If both wheels are not perfectly vertical, the frame and/or major suspension components are bent.

18 Front wheel

Removal

1 Position the motorcycle on the centrestand and support it so that the front wheel is off the ground. If a jack is being placed under the engine remove the lower fairing (see Chapter 7), and place a piece of wood between the jack head and the sump to spread the load. Always make sure the motorcycle is properly supported.

2 Displace the front brake calipers (see Section 3). Support the calipers with a cable-tie or a bungee cord so that no strain is placed on the hydraulic hoses. There is no need to disconnect the hoses from the calipers. **Note:** *Do not operate the brakes with the calipers removed.*

3 Remove the front mudguard (see Chapter 7).

4 Slacken the axle clamp bolts on the bottom of the right-hand fork, then unscrew the axle bolt most of the way out of the right-hand end of the axle (**see illustration**).

5 Slacken the axle clamp bolts on the bottom of the left-hand fork (**see illustration**). Take the weight of the wheel, then push the axle through from the right using the axle bolt, then remove the bolt and withdraw the axle from the left – there is a hole in the end of the axle that can be used to hook a tool in to ease withdrawal if required (**see illustration**). Carefully lower the wheel and draw it forwards.

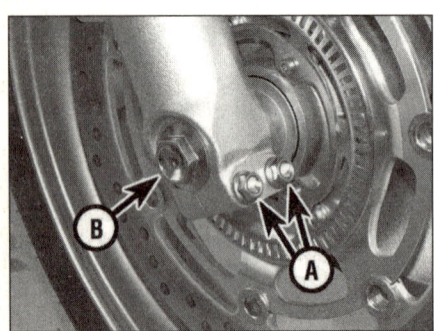

18.4 Slacken the axle clamp bolts (A), then unscrew the axle bolt (B)

18.5a Slacken the axle clamp bolts (arrowed) . . .

18.5b . . . then withdraw the axle and remove the wheel

18.6a Remove the long right-hand spacer . . .

18.6b . . . and the short left-hand spacer

18.12a Fit the axle bolt . . .

6 Remove the long spacer from the right-hand side of the wheel and the short spacer from the left-hand side **(see illustrations)**. Clean all old grease off the spacers, axle and seals.
Caution: Don't lay the wheel down and allow it to rest on a disc – the disc could become warped. Set the wheel on wood blocks so the disc doesn't support the weight of the wheel.

7 Check the axle is straight by rolling it on a flat surface such as a piece of plate glass (first wipe off all old grease and remove any corrosion using steel wool). If the equipment is available, place the axle in V-blocks and measure the runout using a dial gauge. If the axle is bent or the runout exceeds the limit specified, replace it with a new one.

8 Check the condition of the grease seals and wheel bearings (see Section 21).

Installation

9 Apply a smear of grease to the inside of the wheel spacers, and also to the outside where they fit into the seals. Fit the long spacer into the right-hand side of the wheel and the short spacer into the left-hand side **(see illustration 18.6a and b)**. Each side of the wheel can be identified using the directional arrow cast into one of the spokes, or by the pulse ring fitted on the right-hand side on ABS models. The arrow denotes the normal direction of wheel rotation.

10 Manoeuvre the wheel into position between the forks, making sure the directional arrows on the tyre, wheel and brake discs are all pointing the same way and in the direction of normal rotation. Apply a thin coat of grease to the axle.

11 Lift the wheel into place, making sure the spacers remain in position. Slide the axle all the way in from the left-hand side **(see illustration 18.5b)**.

12 Fit the axle bolt and tighten it to the torque setting specified at the beginning of the Chapter **(see illustrations)**. If the axle turns when tightening the bolt counter-hold it using a 17mm hex key, or a nut threaded tight against the head of the correct size bolt (fit the bolt head into the axle and counter-hold it using the nut). A deep nut can be used on its own with care, by half inserting it into the axle head and counter-holding the exposed half.

13 Tighten the axle clamp bolts on the bottom of the right-hand fork to the specified torque setting **(see illustration 18.4)**.

14 Lower the front wheel to the ground. Install the front mudguard (see Chapter 7). Install the brake calipers (see Section 3, and the Note therein regarding the caliper mounting bolts).

15 Apply the brake lever and pedal a few times to bring the pads back into contact with the discs, then with the front brake applied pump the front forks a few times to settle all components in position.

16 Tighten the axle clamp bolts on the bottom of the left-hand fork to the specified torque **(see illustration 18.5a)**. Check that the outer rim of the axle is flush with the surface of the fork.

17 Check that there is at least 0.7 mm clearance between each front brake disc and the caliper bracket – make the check using a feeler gauge. Clean the discs using brake system cleaner. Check for correct operation of the brakes before riding the motorcycle.

19 Rear wheel

Removal

Note: Honda recommend using a new caliper bracket stopper bolt. This is because the bolt threads are pre-treated with a locking compound. It is possible, however, to clean up the threads and fit the old bolt using a suitable non-permanent thread locking compound that is commercially available.

1 Position the motorcycle on the centrestand. Tie the front brake lever to the handlebar.

2 Remove the panniers and the rear mudguard (see Chapter 7).

3 Remove the right-hand silencer (see Chapter 4).

4 Remove the brake pads (see Section 7).

5 Unscrew the brake caliper bracket stopper bolt **(see illustration)**.

6 Unscrew the axle nut and remove the washer **(see illustration)**.

7 Take the weight of the wheel, then push the axle through from the left and withdraw it from

18.12b . . . and tighten it to the specified torque

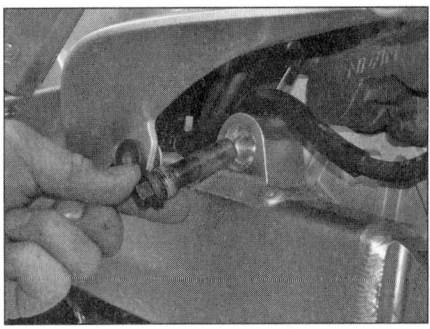

19.5 Unscrew the caliper bracket stopper bolt

19.6 Unscrew the axle nut and remove the washer

6•30 Brakes, wheels and final drive

19.7 Withdraw the axle, noting the washer

19.8 Draw the caliper bracket out . . .

19.9 . . . then remove the wheel

19.10a Remove the spacer from the wheel . . .

19.10b . . . and the final drive housing

the right, noting the washer under the head **(see illustration)**.

8 Remove the rear brake caliper/bracket and support it clear **(see illustration)**.

9 Draw the wheel to the left off the final drive housing, lower it to the ground and remove it **(see illustration)**.

Caution: Do not lay the wheel down and allow it to rest on the disc – it could become warped. Do not operate the brakes with the wheel removed.

10 Remove the spacer from the left-hand side of the wheel **(see illustration)**. Remove the spacer from inside the final drive housing

(see illustration). Clean all old grease of the spacers, axle and seals.

11 Check the axle is straight by rolling it on a flat surface such as a piece of plate glass (if the axle is corroded, first remove the corrosion with steel wool). If the equipment is available, place the axle in V-blocks and check the runout using a dial gauge. If the axle is bent or the runout exceeds the limit specified at the beginning of the Chapter, replace it with a new one.

12 Check the condition of the grease seals and wheel bearings (see Section 21). Check the condition of the drive coupling (see Section 20). Check the condition of the drive coupling O-ring and replace it with a new one if it is damaged or deformed **(see illustration)**.

Installation

13 Apply a smear of grease to the inside of the wheel spacers, and also to the outside where they fit into the seals. Fit the short spacer into the left-hand side of the wheel and the long spacer into the final drive housing, making sure it locates correctly **(see illustrations 19.10a and b)**. Apply a thin coat of grease to the axle. Make sure the drive coupling O-ring is in its groove **(see illustration 19.12)**. Apply some molybdenum disulphide paste or grease to the drive coupling splines and O-ring.

14 Manoeuvre the wheel into position between the ends of the swingarm, then lift it onto the final drive housing, engaging the splines and pushing it to the right **(see illustration)**.

15 Slide the brake caliper bracket between the wheel and the swingarm, making sure the spacer stays in place, and aligning the holes **(see illustration 19.8)**.

16 Make sure the washer is fitted against the axle head, then slide the axle in from the right **(see illustration 19.7)**. Check that everything is correctly aligned. Fit the washer and axle nut and tighten the nut to the torque setting

19.12 Check the O-ring (arrowed)

19.14 Lift the wheel onto the final drive housing and engage the splines

Brakes, wheels and final drive 6•31

specified at the beginning of the Chapter, counter-holding the axle head using a hex bit if required (see illustration 19.6).

17 Fit the new caliper bracket stopper bolt (see illustration 19.5) – if using the old bolt clean the threads and apply fresh thread locking compound. Tighten the bolt to the torque setting specified at the beginning of the Chapter.

18 Install the brake pads (see Section 7), the right-hand silencer (see Chapter 4), the rear mudguard and the panniers.

19 Clean the disc using brake system cleaner. Check the operation of the brakes carefully before riding the bike.

20 Rear wheel drive coupling

1 Remove the rear wheel (see Section 19). *Caution: Do not lay the wheel down on the disc as it could become warped. Lay the wheel on wooden blocks so that the disc is off the ground.*

2 Check the condition of the splines on the wheel coupling and those in the final drive housing for wear and damage **(see illustration and 19.12)**. Replace the coupling with a new one if necessary – it comes as an assembly (i.e. the spline plate is not available separately from the damper plate). If the splines in the final drive housing are worn or damaged refer to Section 23.

3 Check for play between the drive coupling and the wheel hub. Any play indicates worn rubber damper segments. If there is play release the circlip from the perimeter of the drive coupling, then lift the coupling out of the wheel **(see illustrations)**. Lift the rubber damper segments from the wheel and check them for cracks, hardening and general deterioration **(see illustration)**. Replace them with a new set if necessary. Check the condition of the O-ring on the wheel hub and replace it with a new one if it is damaged or deformed **(see illustration)**. Smear the O-ring with oil. Installation is the reverse of removal.

4 Checking and replacement procedures for the drive coupling bearings are in Section 21.

5 Check the condition of the drive coupling O-ring on the spline plate and replace it with a new one if it is damaged or deformed **(see illustration 19.12)**.

6 Clean the disc using brake system cleaner, then install the wheel (see Section 19).

21 Wheel bearings

Note: *Always renew the wheel bearings in sets, never individually. Avoid using a high pressure cleaner on the wheel bearing area.*

Front wheel bearings

1 Remove the wheel (see Section 18). Remove the discs (see Section 4) to prevent them being damaged or distorted during bearing removal. On ABS models remove the pulse ring (see Section 15).

2 Lever out the bearing seal from each side of the hub using a flat-bladed screwdriver or a seal hook **(see illustration)**. Take care not to damage the hub. Discard the seals as new ones must be fitted on reassembly.

3 Inspect the bearings – check that the inner race turns smoothly and that the outer race is a tight fit in the hub (see *Tools and Workshop Tips* (Section 5) in the Reference Section).
Note: *Do not remove the bearings unless they are going to be replaced with new ones.*

4 If the bearings are worn, remove them using an internal expanding puller with slide-hammer attachment, which can be obtained commercially – select the correct attachment and locate it behind the inner race of the bearing, then tighten the inner bolt to expand and lock the puller **(see illustration)**.

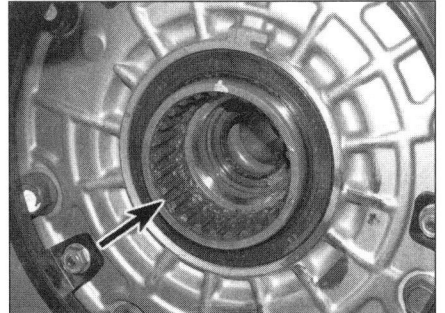
20.2 Check the splines (arrowed) in the final drive housing

20.3a Release the circlip . . .

20.3b . . . and lift the coupling out

20.3c Check the rubber damper segments . . .

20.3d . . . and the O-ring (arrowed)

21.2 Lever out the bearing seals

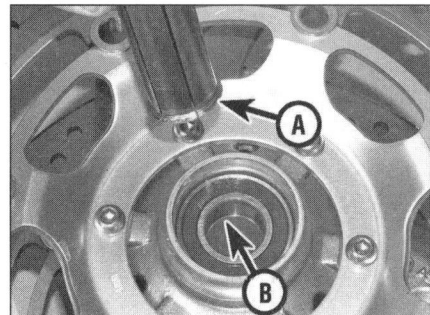
21.4a Locate the knife-edge of the attachment (A) in the gap (B)

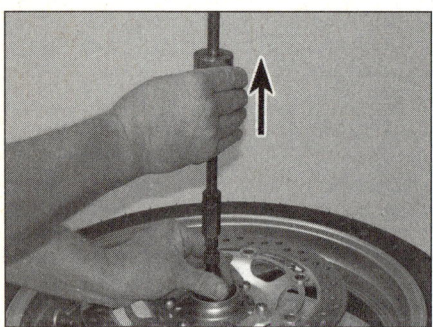

21.4b Jar the bearing out

21.7 Using a socket to drive the bearing in

21.9 Fit a new seal over the bearing

Attach the slide-hammer, hold the wheel firmly down and jar the bearing out **(see illustration)**. Having removed the first bearing remove the spacer which fits between the bearings.

5 Turn the wheel over and remove the other bearing using the same procedure.

6 Thoroughly clean the hub area of the wheel with a suitable solvent and inspect the bearing seats for scoring and wear. If the seats are damaged, consult a Honda dealer before reassembling the wheel.

7 Drive the new bearings into the hub using a bearing driver or suitable socket **(see illustration)**. Fit the right-hand bearing first, with its marked side facing outwards. Make sure that the driver or socket bears only on the outer race and the bearing fits squarely and all the way into its seat.

8 Turn the wheel over then fit the bearing spacer and the other new bearing.

9 Apply a smear of grease to the new seals, then drive them into the hub using a socket that seats around the raised inner lip of the seal, not on it **(see illustration)**.

10 Install the brake discs if removed (see Section 4). Clean the discs using brake system cleaner, then install the wheel (see Section 18).

Rear wheel bearings

11 Remove the wheel (see Section 19). Remove the disc (see Section 9) to prevent it being damaged or distorted during bearing removal. Remove the drive coupling and damper segments (see Section 20, Step 3). On ABS models remove the pulse ring (see Section 15).

12 Lever out the bearing seal from the left-hand side of the hub using a flat-bladed screwdriver or a seal hook **(see illustration 21.2)**. Take care not to damage the hub. Discard the seal as a new one should be fitted on reassembly.

13 Inspect the bearings in both sides of the hub – check that the inner race turns smoothly and that the outer race is a tight fit in the hub (see *Tools and Workshop Tips* (Section 5) in the Reference section). **Note:** *Do not remove the bearings unless they are going to be replaced with new ones.*

14 If the bearings are worn, remove the bearings using an internal expanding puller with slide-hammer attachment, which can be obtained commercially – select the correct attachment and locate it behind the inner race of the bearing, then tighten the inner bolt to expand and lock the puller **(see illustration 21.4a)**. Attach the slide-hammer, hold the wheel firmly down and jar the bearing out **(see illustration 21.4b)**. Having removed the first bearing remove the spacer which fits between the bearings.

15 Turn the wheel over and remove the other bearing using the same procedure.

16 Thoroughly clean the hub area of the wheel with a suitable solvent and inspect the bearing seats for scoring and wear. If the seats are damaged, consult a Honda dealer before reassembling the wheel.

17 Drive the new bearings into the hub using a bearing driver or suitable socket **(see illustration 21.7)**. Fit the left-hand bearing first, with its marked side facing outwards. Make sure that the driver or socket bears only on the outer race and the bearing fits squarely and all the way into its seat.

18 Turn the wheel over then install the bearing spacer and the other new bearing.

19 Apply a smear of grease to the new seal, then drive it into the left-hand side of the hub using a socket that seats around the raised inner lip of the seal, not on it **(see illustration 21.9)**.

20 Check the drive coupling and dampers (see Section 20). Fit the dampers and drive coupling to the wheel (see Section 20, Step 3). Install the brake disc if removed (see Section 9). Clean the disc using brake system cleaner, then install the wheel (see Section 19).

21.23 Drive the spacer out of the bearings from the outside

Rear wheel drive coupling bearings

21 Remove the rear wheel (see Section 19). Remove the drive coupling and damper segments (see Section 20, Step 3).

22 Inspect the bearings – check that the inner races turn smoothly and that the outer races are a tight fit in the coupling (see *Tools and Workshop Tips* (Section 5) in the Reference Section). **Note:** *Do not remove the bearings unless they are going to be replaced with new ones.*

23 If the bearings are worn, place the coupling on a work surface splined side up, and drive the bearing spacer out of the bearings using a suitably sized socket that only contacts the spacer and not the inner race of the bearing **(see illustration)**.

24 Turn the coupling over and support it on blocks of wood, and drive the bearings out from the inside.

25 Thoroughly clean the bearing seat with a suitable solvent and inspect the seat for scoring and wear. If the seat is damaged, consult a Honda dealer before reassembling the wheel.

26 Drive one bearing, marked side facing up, onto the spacer until it seats on the shoulder using a socket that bears on the inner race of the bearing.

27 Now drive the second bearing on using the same method until it seats against the first bearing.

28 Turn the coupling splined side up. Drive the new bearings and spacer as one into the hub using a bearing driver or suitable socket on the outer race of the outer bearing **(see illustration)**.

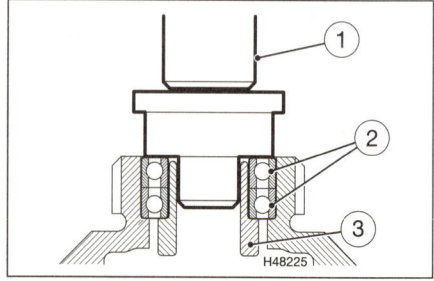

21.28 Drive the bearing and spacer assembly in as one

1 Bearing driver or socket
2 Bearings
3 Spacer

Ensure that the driver or socket bears only on the outer race. Ensure the bearings are fitted squarely and all the way into the seat.

29 Check the drive coupling and dampers (see Section 20). Fit the dampers and drive coupling into the wheel (see Section 20, Step 3). Clean the disc using brake system cleaner, then install the wheel (see Section 19).

22 Tyres

General information

1 The wheels are designed to take tubeless tyres only. Tyre sizes are given in the Specifications at the beginning of this chapter.

2 Refer to the *Pre-ride checks* listed at the beginning of this manual for tyre maintenance.

Fitting new tyres

3 When selecting new tyres, refer to the tyre information in the Owner's Handbook. Ensure that front and rear tyre types are compatible, the correct size and correct speed rating; if necessary seek advice from a Honda dealer or tyre fitting specialist **(see illustration)**.

4 It is recommended that tyres are fitted by a motorcycle tyre specialist rather than attempted in the home workshop. This is particularly relevant in the case of tubeless tyres because the force required to break the seal between the wheel rim and tyre bead is substantial, and is usually beyond the capabilities of an individual working with normal tyre levers. Additionally, the specialist will be able to balance the wheels after tyre fitting.

5 Note that punctured tubeless tyres can in some cases be repaired. Repairs must be carried out by a motorcycle tyre fitting specialist. Honda advise that a repaired tyre should not be used at speeds above 50 mph (80 kmh) for the first 24 hours, and not above 80 mph (130 kmh) thereafter. Refer to the advice given in the owner's manual provided with the machine and local laws regarding repairs to ZR rated tyres.

23 Final drive housing and driveshaft

Removal

1 If required drain the final drive gear oil (see Chapter 1) – note that oil will not leak out under normal circumstances, only if a seal has failed or if the housing is not supported upright, in which case it could come out of the breather.

2 On ABS models, free the wheel speed sensor wiring from its clip on the top of the final drive housing, then unscrew the mounting bolts and displace the sensor **(see illustration 15.10)**. Note any shim fitted between the sensor and the housing.

3 Remove the rear wheel (see Section 19).

4 Support the final drive housing and unscrew the four nuts securing it to the swingarm, and

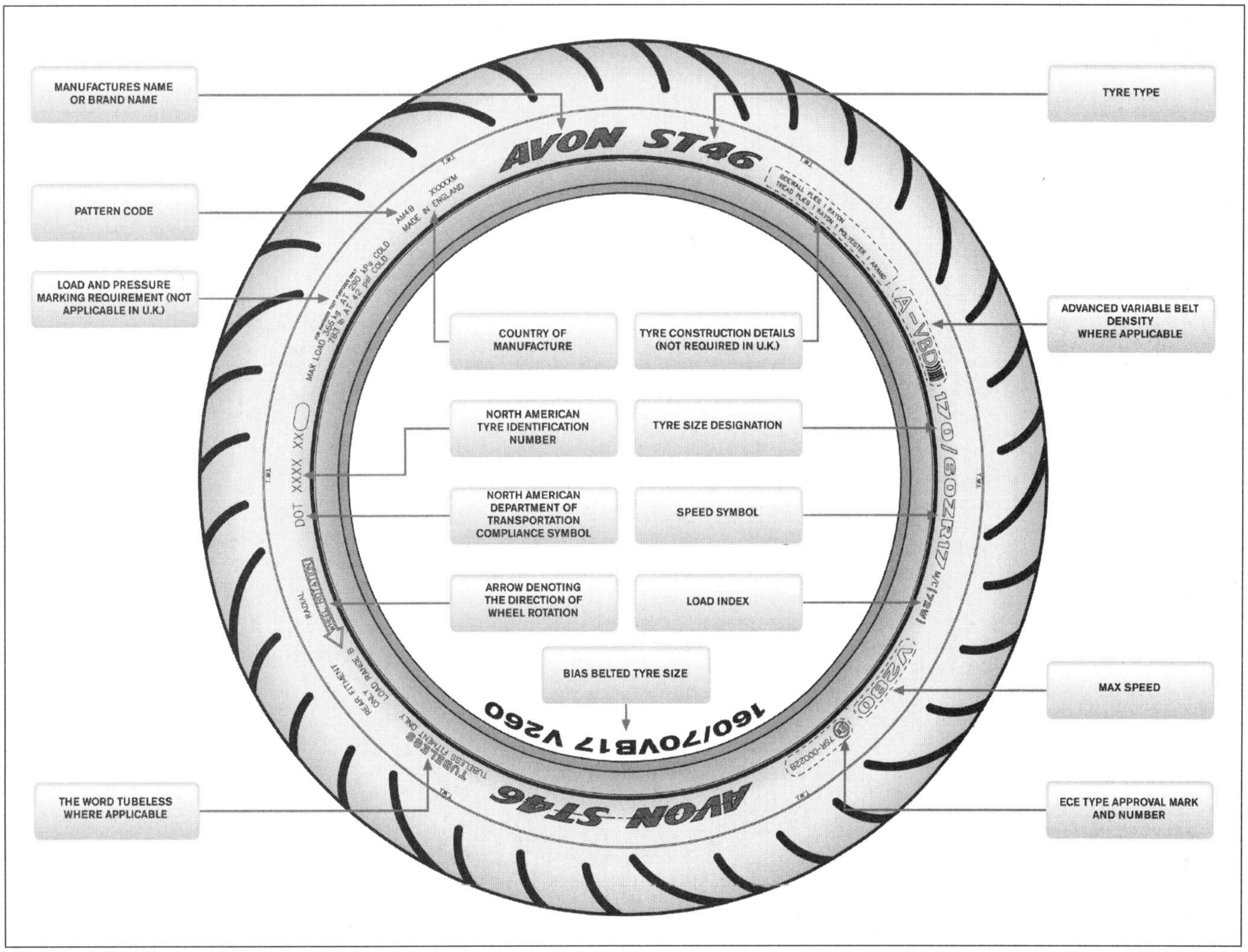

22.3 Common tyre sidewall markings

6•34 Brakes, wheels and final drive

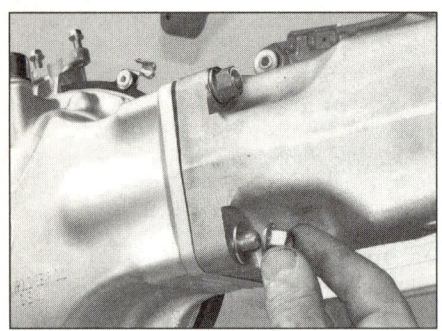

23.4a Unscrew the nuts and remove the washers . . .

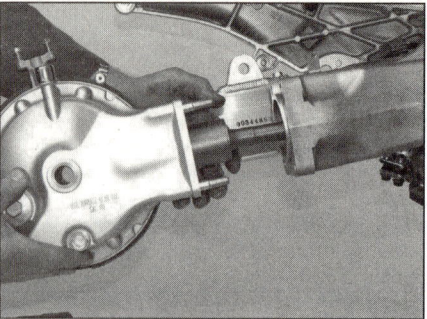

23.4b . . . then draw the housing off and the shaft out

23.5a Remove the spring . . .

remove the washers **(see illustration)**. Draw the housing off the swingarm – the driveshaft will come with it **(see illustration)**.

5 If required pull the driveshaft out of the final drive housing. Remove the spring from the rear end of the shaft **(see illustration)**. Remove the oil seal from the shaft and replace it with a new one **(see illustration)**. Remove the snap ring from its groove and replace it with a new one **(see illustration)**.

Inspection

6 Rotate the driveshaft joint in the front of the final drive housing – check it rotates smoothly and freely and that the power is transmitted correctly through the bevel gear assembly to the output boss. If there are any signs of roughness or notchiness or any evidence of wear or excessive backlash, the unit must be disassembled and examined further.

7 Check the housing for any evidence of oil leakage from the seals.

8 Check the splines on each end of the driveshaft and those in the final drive housing for wear and damage. If wear is evident on the front splines of the shaft remove the swingarm (see Chapter 5) and check the universal joint. Replace worn or damaged components with new ones.

9 If attention to the final drive housing is required, the complete unit should be taken to a Honda dealer or service agent who will have the necessary special tools and expertise to carry out the complicated inspection and overhaul procedure.

Installation

10 Smear the inner and outer lips of the new oil seal with molybdenum disulphide grease, then slide it onto the shaft with the marked side facing the front **(see illustration)**. Fit a new snap ring into its groove **(see illustration)**. Fit the spring into the rear end of the shaft **(see illustration 23.5a)**. Smear the driveshaft and final drive housing splines with molybdenum disulphide grease.

11 Slide the shaft into the swingarm and engage it with the universal joint **(see illustration)**. Push the shaft to make sure the UJ is fully engaged on the output shaft splines, and turn the shaft to confirm engagement. Leave the shaft in the swingarm.

12 Fit the final drive housing onto the swingarm, making sure the driveshaft joint engages correctly with the driveshaft and the snap ring locates in its groove – press the housing on until it mates flush with the swingarm **(see illustration)**. Fit the nuts with their washers and tighten them evenly in a criss-cross pattern to the torque setting specified at the beginning of the Chapter **(see illustration 23.4a)**.

13 Install the rear wheel (see Section 19). Go round the final drive housing nuts again, tightening them to the specified torque.

14 On ABS models, fit the wheel speed sensor with its shim where present and tighten the bolts **(see illustration 15.10)**. Secure the wiring in its clip on the housing.

15 If drained fill the final drive housing with the correct grade and quantity of oil (see Chapter 1).

23.5b . . . the oil seal . . .

23.5c . . . and the snap ring

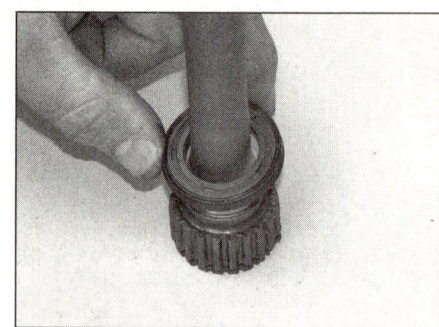

23.10a Fit a new oil seal . . .

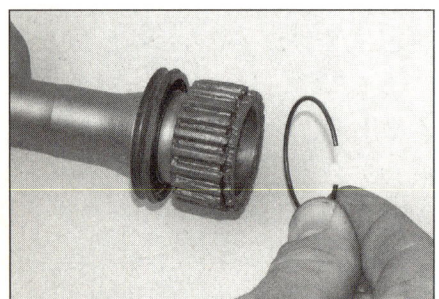

23.10b . . . and a new snap ring

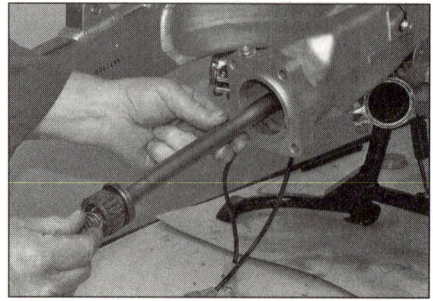

23.11 Insert the drive shaft and engage it in the universal joint

23.12 Fit the housing onto the swingarm and driveshaft

Chapter 7
Bodywork

Contents

	Section		Section
Access panels and trim covers	5	Mirrors covers and mirrors	9
Fairing	8	Rear cowl	12
Fairing side panels	7	Seats and panniers	3
Mudguards	11	Side covers	4
General information	1	Trim clips	2
Lower fairing	6	Windshield and inner cowl	10

Degrees of difficulty

Easy, suitable for novice with little experience	Fairly easy, suitable for beginner with some experience	Fairly difficult, suitable for competent DIY mechanic	Difficult, suitable for experienced DIY mechanic	Very difficult, suitable for expert DIY or professional

1 General information

This Chapter covers the procedures necessary to remove and install the bodywork. Since many service and repair operations on these motorcycles require the removal of the body panels, the procedures are grouped here and referred to from other Chapters.

In the case of damage to the bodywork, it is usually necessary to remove the broken component and replace it with a new (or used) one. Note that there are however some companies that specialise in 'plastic welding' and there are a number of bodywork repair kits now available for motorcycles.

When attempting to remove any body panel, first study it closely, noting any fasteners and associated fittings, to be sure of returning everything to its correct place on installation. In some cases the aid of an assistant will be required when removing panels, to help avoid the risk of damage to paintwork. Once the evident fasteners have been removed, try to withdraw the panel as described but DO NOT FORCE IT – if it will not release, check that all fasteners have been removed and try again.

When installing a body panel, first study it closely, noting any fasteners and associated fittings removed with it, to be sure of returning everything to its correct place. Check that all fasteners are in good condition, including the trim clips and damping/rubber mounts; replace any faulty fasteners with new ones before the panel is reassembled. Check also that all mounting brackets are straight and repair them or replace them with new ones if necessary before attempting to install the panel.

Tighten the fasteners securely, but be careful not to overtighten any of them or the panel may break (not always immediately) due to the uneven stress.

2 Trim clips

1 Three types of plastic trim clip are used, so carefully note which fits where when removing the fairing panels.
2 The first type has a centre pin which you push into the body of the clip to allow the clip to be drawn out of the panel **(see illustration)**. To install the clip, first expand the pawls of the clip body and push the centre pin back out **(see illustration)**. Now fit the clip body into its hole, then push the centre pin in so that it is

2.2a Push the centre pin (arrowed)...

2.2b ...into the body to release the clip

2.2c Push the centre pin out before installing the clip, then push it in when installed to lock it

7•2 Bodywork

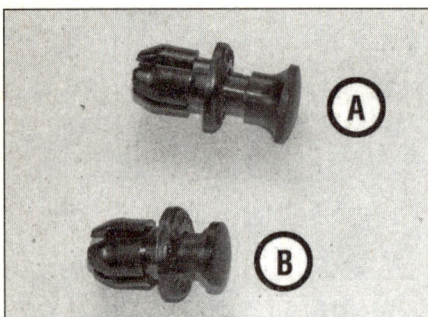

2.3 Pull the centre pin out to release the clip (A), and push it back in to lock it (B)

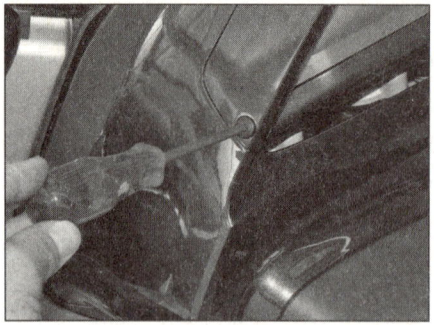

2.4a Undo the centre screw then pull the clip out

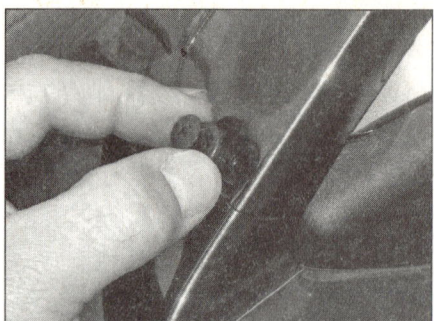

2.4b Fit the clip in the hole then push the centre in to lock it

flush with the clip head. The clip should now be locked in place.

3 The second type, of which there are two sizes, has a protruding centre pin which you pull out of the body of the clip to allow the clip to be drawn out of the panel **(see illustration)**. To install the clip, fit the clip body into its hole, then push the centre pin in. The clip should now be locked in place.

4 The third type of trim clip has a Phillips screw head. To release, unscrew the centre of the clip, then pull the body of the clip out of the panel **(see illustration)**. When installing, unscrew the centre of the clip and insert it in the panel then push the centre fully into the body **(see illustration)**. As they are made of plastic, the threads easily become worn in which case the centres may not unscrew. If this happens, lever the centre out of the body using a small screwdriver and replace the trim clip with a new one.

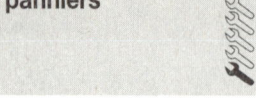

3 Seats and panniers

Removal

Passenger seat

1 Unlock and raise the left-hand pannier lever. Pull the seat release lever, then draw the seat up and back to remove it, noting how the tabs at the front locate **(see illustrations)** – note that removing the passenger seat may well dislodge the rider's seat due to the way the tab locates between the bar and the seat.

Rider's seat

2 Remove the passenger seat (see Step 1).
3 Draw the seat up and back, noting how it locates **(see illustration)**.

Panniers

4 Unlock and raise the pannier lever **(see illustration)**. Lift and remove the pannier, noting how it locates on the lock bracket and the back of the footrest bracket.

Installation

5 Installation is the reverse of removal, noting the following:
- To adjust the height of the rider's seat draw the adjuster bar back and raise or lower it as required at the front – there are three positions **(see illustration)**.
- Make sure the tab on the front of the rider's seat locates correctly under the adjuster bar **(see illustration 3.3)**, and the rear supports locate in the holes of the correct step according to the adjuster position **(see illustration)**.
- Make sure the centre tab at the front of the

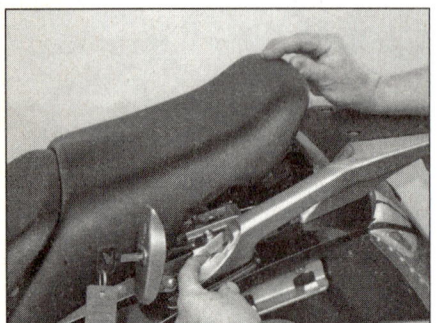

3.1a Pull the lever to release the seat . . .

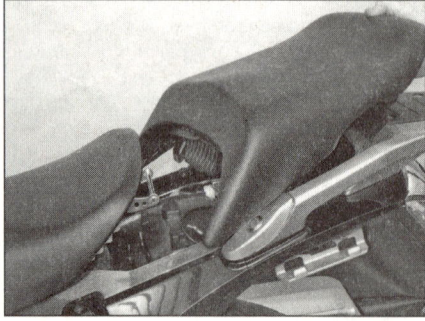

3.1b . . . then draw it back and remove it

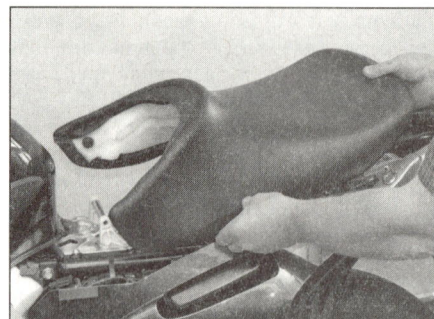

3.3 Draw the rider's seat up and back

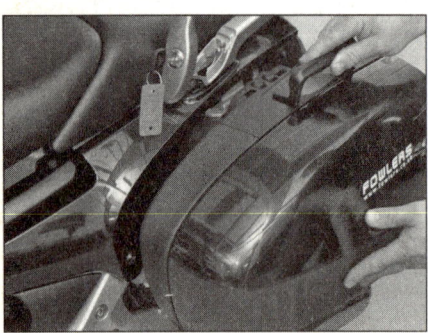

3.4 Unlock the lever and remove the pannier

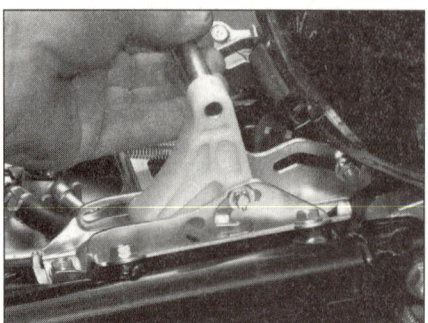

3.5a The adjuster can set in three positions

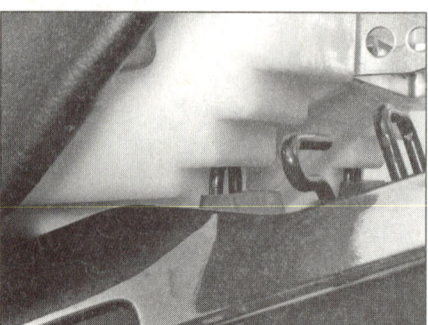

3.5b Make sure the rear supports locate correctly

Bodywork 7•3

4.3a Undo the screws (arrowed) . . .

4.3b . . . release the peg(s) from the grommet(s) (later type shown) . . .

passenger seat locates correctly between the back of the rider's seat and the bar, and the side tabs locate under the hooks on the rear sub-frame, then push down on the back of the seat to engage the latch **(see illustration 3.1b)**.
- Make sure the front of the pannier seats correctly over the rear of the footrest bracket and the top seats correctly on the lock bracket **(see illustration 3.4)**.

4 Side covers

4.3c . . . and pull the lifting lever out

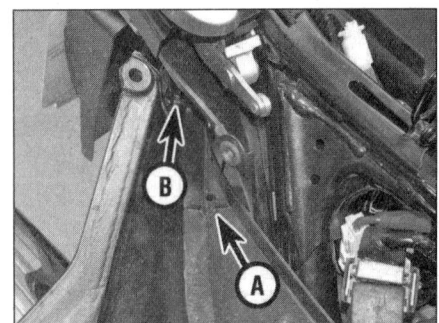

4.4 Note how the peg (A) and tab (B) locate

1 Remove both seats (see Section 3).
2 On 2002 to 2007 models undo the three screws, then free the peg at the back from the grommet and remove the panel, noting how the tab at the back locates, pulling the lifting lever out when removing the left-hand panel **(see illustrations 4.3a and c)**.
3 On 2008-on models, to remove the left-hand side cover, undo the three screws, then carefully pull the bottom edge away to release the pegs from the grommet, and pull the lifting lever out and draw the panel off the lever and pre-load adjuster, noting how the peg and tab at the back locate **(see illustrations)**.
4 On 2008-on models, to remove the right-hand side cover, undo the three screws and remove the cover, noting how the peg and tab at the back locate **(see illustration)**.
5 To remove the battery cover on the left-hand side, release the fuseholder and its wiring from the top of the battery cover **(see illustration)**. On 2002 to 2007 models release the tabs, two on the bottom and one at the top and remove the cover. On 2008-on models pull the bottom of the cover away to release the pegs from the grommets **(see illustrations)**.

6 Installation is the reverse of removal. Make sure the grommets are in good condition and correctly seated, and the pegs locate correctly in them.

5 Access panels and trim covers

Access panel removal

1 Release and remove the trim clip (see Section 2, Step 4) and remove the

4.5a Release the fuseholder

4.5b Pull the bottom away . . .

4.5c . . . to release the pegs (arrowed) from the grommets

7•4 Bodywork

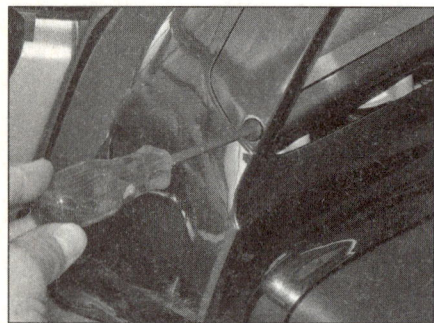

5.1a Release the trim clip . . .

5.1b . . . and remove the panel, noting how the tabs (arrowed) locate

5.3a Lift the cover to free the peg from the grommet . . .

5.3b . . . then release the hooks and remove the cover

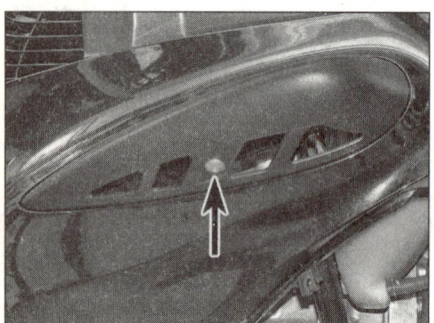

5.4a Undo the screw (arrowed) . . .

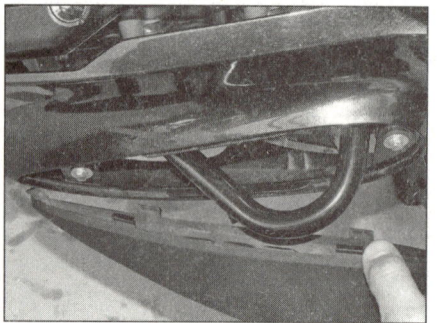

5.4b . . . push the top edge down and the bottom edge up to release the tabs

panel, noting how the tabs locate (see illustrations).

Valve cover trim removal

2 Remove the access panel (see Step 1).
3 Lift the rear of the trim cover from the top of the valve cover to release the grommet from its peg, then disengage the hooks from the front and remove the cover (see illustrations).

Engine guard cover removal

4 Undo the screw on the underside, then release the tabs along the top and bottom and at the front and remove the cover (see illustrations).

Installation

5 Installation is the reverse of removal. Make sure valve cover trim grommet is in good condition and correctly seated, and the peg locates correctly in it. Make sure the access panel and engine guard cover tabs locate correctly.

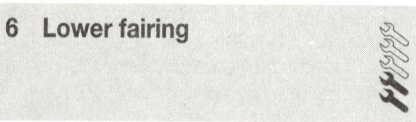

6 Lower fairing

Removal

Note: *Remove each side of the lower fairing individually. If access is only required to one side of the bike, the other panel can be left in place.*

1 Release the trim clips (see Section 2, Step 3) securing the sections together on the underside (see illustration).
2 Release the trim clip (see Section 2, Step 4) securing the lower fairing to the rear of the fairing side panel (see illustration).
3 Undo the five screws securing the

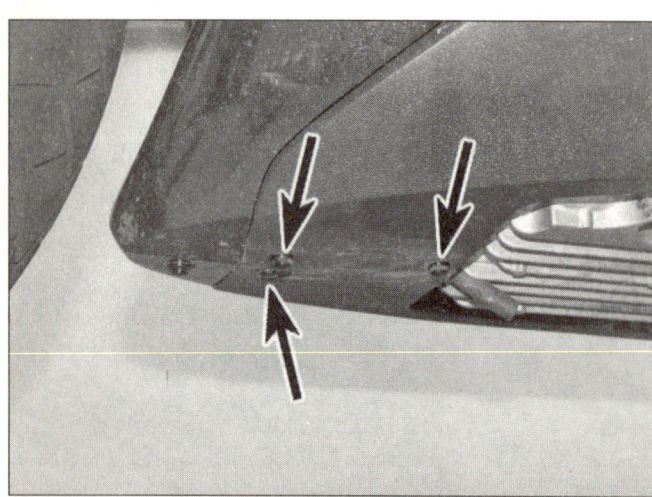

6.1 Release the trim clips (arrowed) . . .

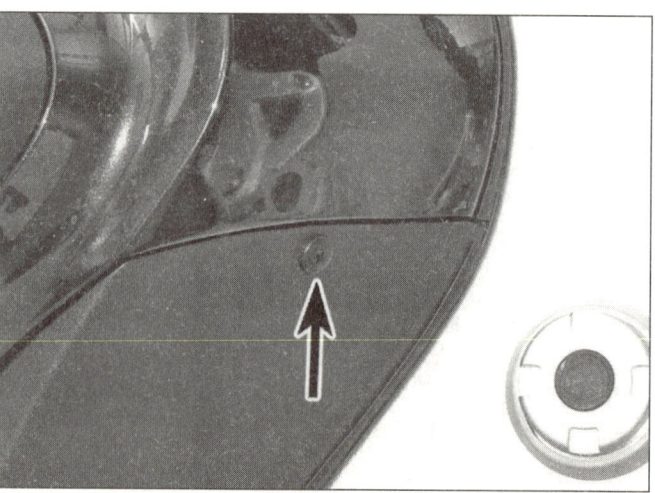

6.2 . . . and the trim clip (arrowed)

Bodywork 7•5

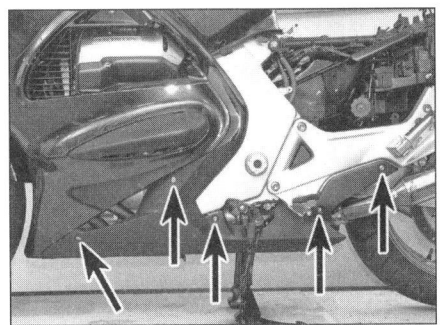

6.3a Undo the screws (arrowed) . . .

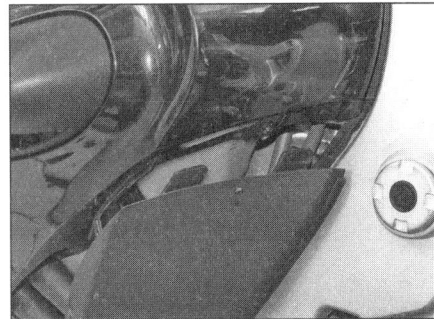

6.3b . . . then release the tabs . . .

6.3c . . . and remove the panel

lower fairing, noting which fits where **(see illustration)**. Release the panel, noting how the tabs locate, and remove it **(see illustrations)**.

Installation

4 Installation is the reverse of removal. Make sure the screws are returned to their correct positions; there are two different screw types – two which go in the front mountings and three which go in the rear mountings.

7 Fairing side panels

7.4a Release the trim clips (arrowed) in the cockpit . . .

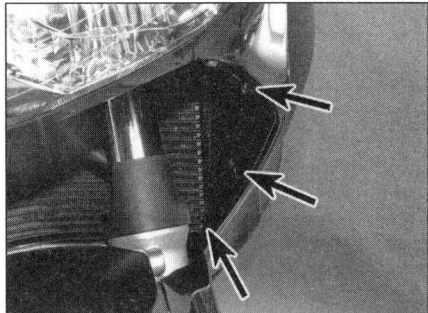

7.4b . . . the trim clips (arrowed) into the fairing side panel . . .

Removal

1 Remove the lower fairing (see Section 6).
2 Remove the engine guard cover (see Section 5).
3 Remove the mirror cover (see Section 9).
4 Release the trim clips (see Section 2) and undo the screw securing the inner panel **(see illustrations)**. Release the panel and manoeuvre it out – on the right-hand panel disconnect the ambient temperature sensor wiring connector when accessible **(see illustrations)**.
5 Release the trim clip on the underside **(see illustration)**.
6 Release the trim clip and undo the screw joining the panel to the centre section **(see illustration)** – if one side panel has already been removed you can now remove the centre section.

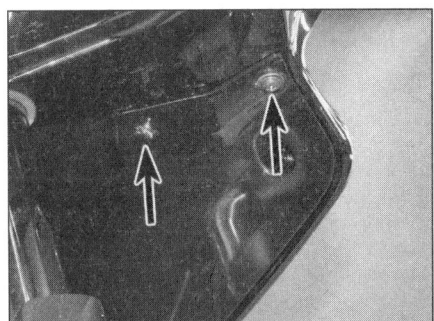

7.4c . . . and the trim clip and screw (arrowed) into the fairing

7.4d Remove the inner panel . . .

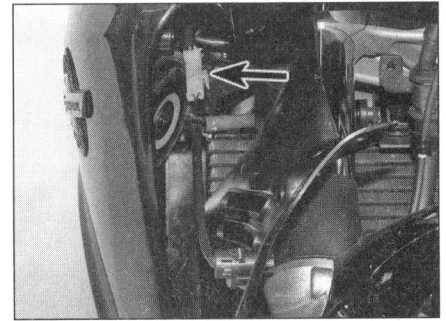

7.4e . . . on the right-hand side disconnecting the sensor wiring connector (arrowed)

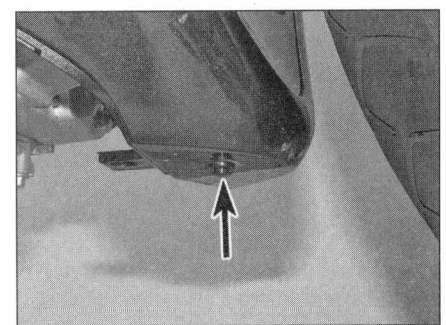

7.5 Release the trim clip (arrowed)

7.6 Release the trim clip and undo the screw (arrowed)

7•6 Bodywork

7.7a Undo the screws below the mirror (arrowed) . . .

7.7b . . . and the screws in the glove compartment (arrowed)

7.8 Unscrew the bolts (arrowed)

7.9a Release the peg (arrowed) from the grommet . . .

7.9b . . . and the tabs (arrowed) from the fairing . . .

7.9c . . . and on the left release the wiring connector

7 Undo the two screws below the mirror **(see illustration)**. Open the glove compartment and undo the two screws **(see illustration)**.
8 Unscrew the three bolts, noting the collars with the lower ones **(see illustration)**.
9 Carefully pull the rear of the panel away to release the peg from the grommet, then release the front from the fairing, noting how the tabs locate **(see illustrations)** – when removing the left-hand panel also release the front loom wiring connector from its holder **(see illustration)**.

Installation

10 Installation is the reverse of removal.

8 Fairing

Removal

1 Remove the windshield and inner cowl (see Section 10).
2 Remove the fairing side panels (see Section 7).
3 Undo the screw on each side **(see illustration)**. Push the turn signal wiring connector through the hole.

4 Remove the mirrors (see Section 9).
5 Carefully draw the fairing forwards, noting how the pegs locate in the grommets in the stay **(see illustration)**.
6 Disconnect the headlight aim adjuster wiring connector **(see illustration)**. Disconnect the headlight wiring connectors and pull each sidelight bulbholder out **(see illustrations)**. Unscrew the lean angle sensor bolts and displace the sensor **(see illustration)** – you can now remove the fairing **(see illustration)**.
7 With the fairing removed the instrument panel is fairly insecure, so it is best to disconnect the wiring connector and remove

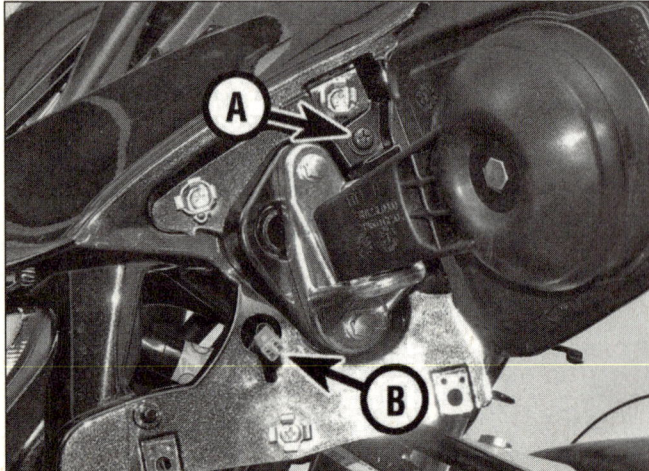

8.3 Undo the screw (A) and push the wiring connector (B) through the hole

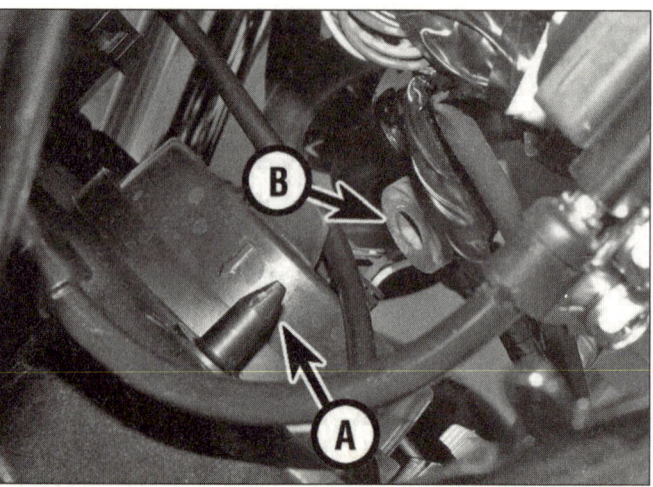

8.5 Note how the peg (A) on each side locates in the grommet (B)

Bodywork

8.6a Disconnect the aiming motor wiring connector . . .

8.6b . . . and the headlight wiring connectors . . .

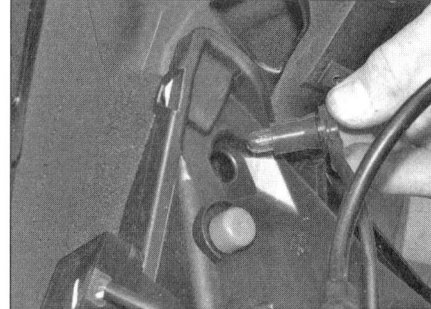

8.6c . . . and withdraw the sidelights

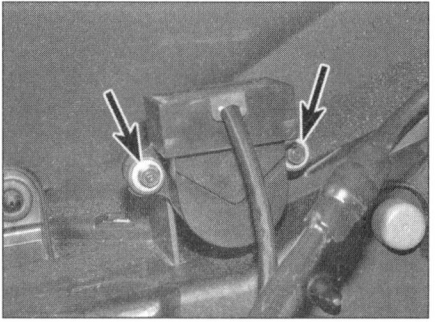

8.6d Unscrew the bolts (arrowed) and displace the sensor . . .

8.6e . . . and remove the fairing

8.7a Disconnect the wiring connectors and remove the instrument panel . . .

the panel **(see illustrations)** – note how the peg locates in the grommet.

8 If required remove the headlight assembly from the fairing (see Chapter 8).

Installation

9 Installation is the reverse of removal.
- Make sure the sensor is fitted with its UP mark facing upwards and with the wiring facing back **(see illustration)**.
- Make sure the fairing pegs locate correctly in the grommets on the fairing stay **(see illustration 8.5)**, and all wiring connectors are secure.

- Check the operation of the headlights, sidelights and turn signals before riding.

9 Mirror covers and mirrors

Mirror cover removal

1 Ease the mirror cover locating pegs out of their sockets **(see illustration)**.

8.7b . . . noting how the peg locates in the grommet (arrowed)

8.9 Make sure the sensor is fitted as described

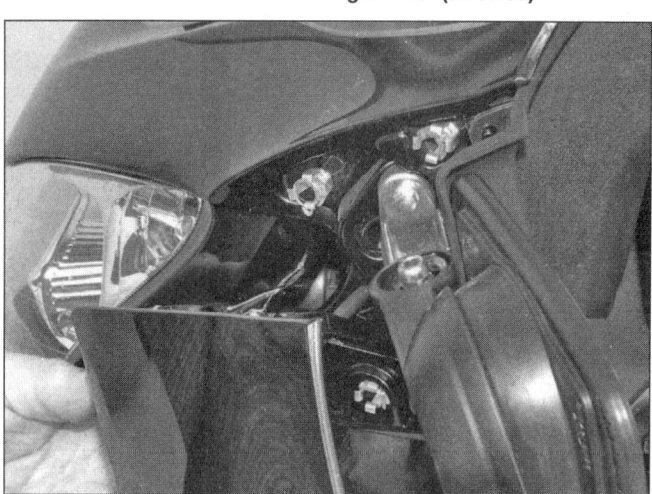

9.1 Ease the mirror cover off . . .

7•8 Bodywork

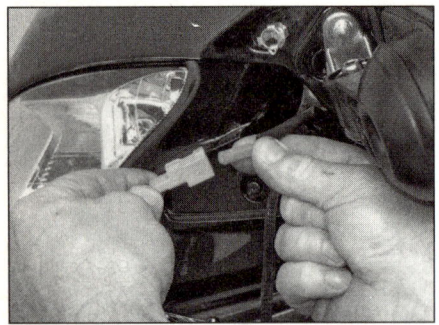

9.2 ... then disconnect the wiring connector ...

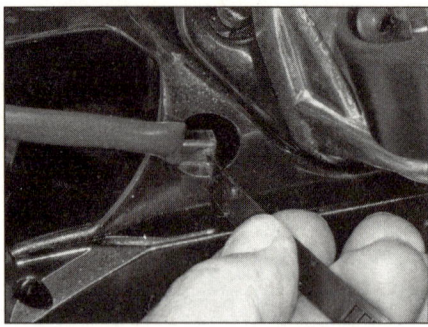

9.3 ... and free the retaining strap

9.4a Release and remove the rubber trim ...

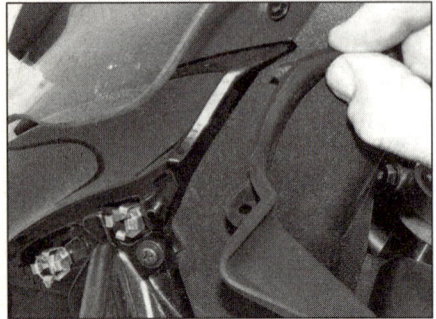

9.4b ... noting how it locates

9.7 Unscrew the two bolts and remove the mirror

2 Disconnect the turn signal wiring connector **(see illustration)**.
3 Free the retaining strap from its cut-out and remove the cover **(see illustration)**.
4 Free the rubber trim from between the mirror and instrument panel, noting how it locates **(see illustrations)**.
5 If required remove the turn signal from the cover (see Chapter 8).

Mirror removal

6 Remove the mirror cover (Steps 1 to 4).
7 Unscrew the bolts and remove the mirror **(see illustration)**.

Installation

8 Installation is the reverse of removal. When fitting the mirror cover make sure the peg on the rubber trim locates in the cut-out **(see illustration)**.

10 Windshield and inner cowl

Note: *The windshield height adjuster mechanism is covered in Chapter 8.*

Windshield removal

1 Undo the windshield holder cover screws and remove the covers, noting how they hold the rubber trim pieces around the holders under the windshield **(see illustration)**.
2 Unscrew the windshield bolts, noting the collars and washers, and lift the windshield off, noting the rubber strips **(see illustrations)**.

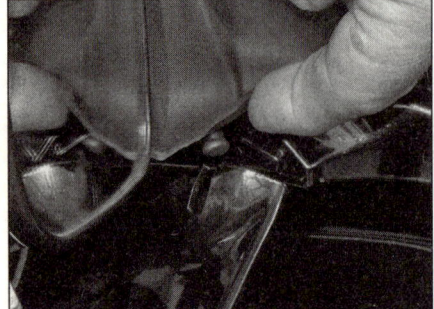

9.8 Locate the peg in the cut-out

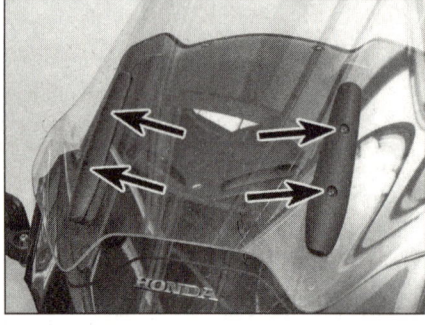

10.1 Undo the screws (arrowed) and remove the covers

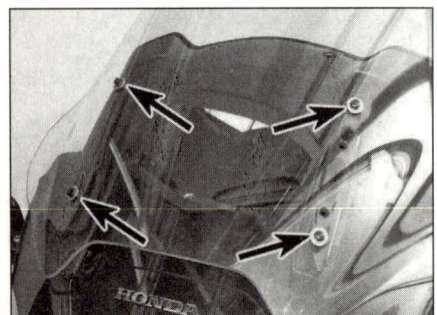

10.2a Unscrew the bolts (arrowed) ...

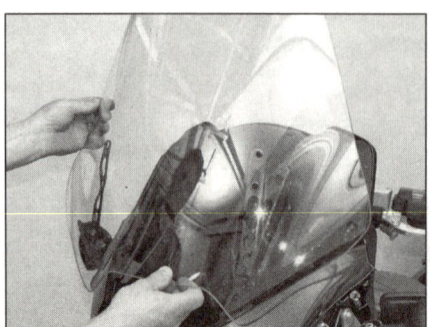

10.2b ... and remove the windshield ...

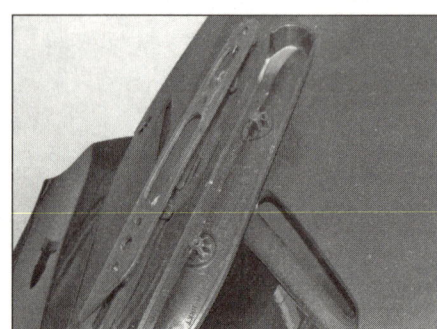

10.2c ... and the trim pieces

Bodywork 7•9

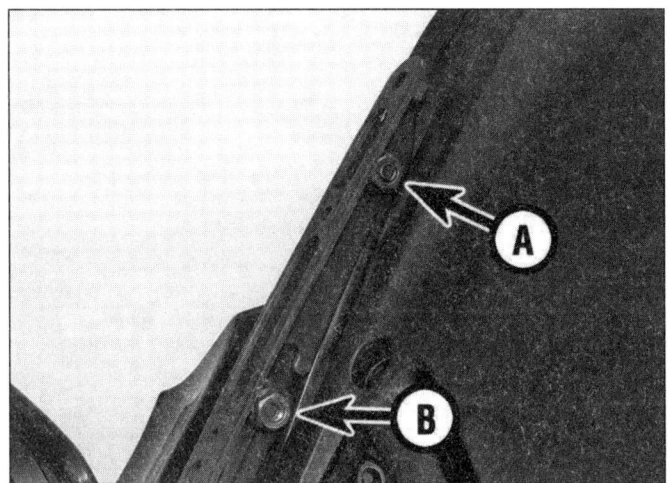

10.3a Slacken the nut (A) and remove the nut (B) . . .

10.3b . . . and remove the holder

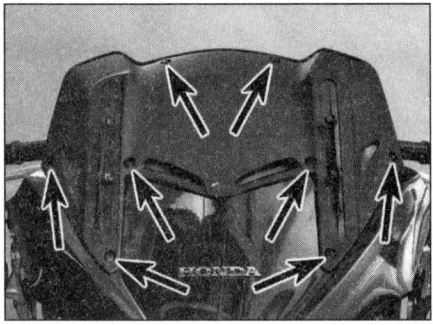

10.5a Release the trim clips (arrowed) . . .

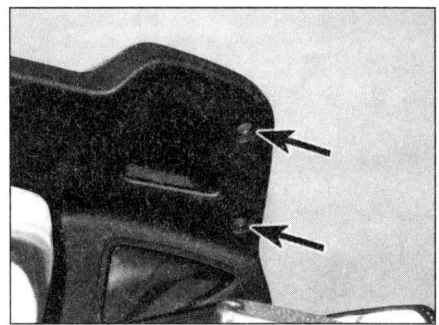

10.5b . . . undo the screws (arrowed) on each side . . .

10.5c . . . and remove the cowl

Remove the rubber trim pieces from around the holders.

3 Slacken the upper nuts securing the holders and remove the lower nuts, then release the holders from the brackets, noting in which position they locate **(see illustrations)** – they have two different positions for height adjustment.

Inner cowl removal

4 Remove the windshield and holders.

5 Release all the trim clips (see Section 2) on the front of the cowl **(see illustration)**. Undo the four screws on the rear and remove the cowl, noting how it locates **(see illustrations)**.

Installation

6 Installation is the reverse of removal. Make sure both holders are set in either the lower position **(see illustration 10.3b)** or the higher position **(see illustration)**. When fitting the windshield covers make sure the rubber

trim pieces are correctly in position **(see illustration)**.

11 Mudguards

Front mudguard removal

1 Unscrew the brake hose holder bolt from each side of the mudguard **(see illustration)**.

10.6a Higher set position for the holder

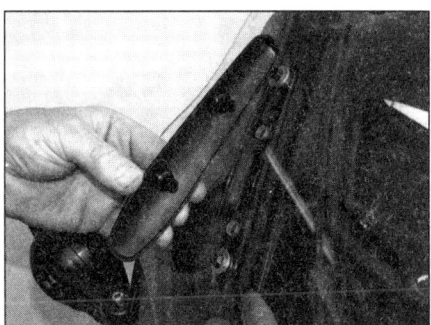

10.6b Hold the trim pieces in place when fitting the covers

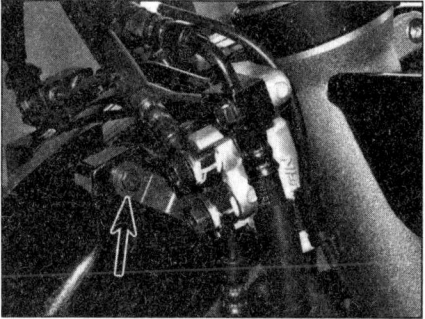

11.1 Unscrew the brake hose holder bolt (arrowed) on each side . . .

7•10 Bodywork

11.2 ... and the mudguard bolts (arrowed) on each side ...

11.3 ... and draw the front mudguard forwards

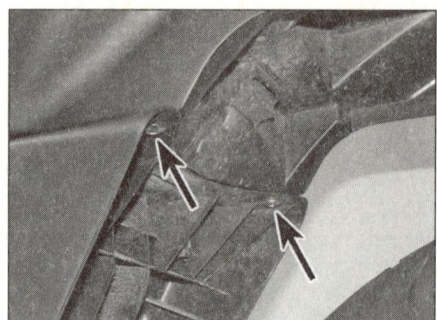

11.4a Undo the screws at the front (arrowed) ...

2 Unscrew the bolts securing each side of the mudguard to each fork **(see illustration)**.

3 Carefully draw the mudguard forwards and remove it **(see illustration)** – note that there are captive nuts for each bolt on the inner sides of the mudguard – take care not to lose them.

Rear mudguard removal

4 Undo the rear mudguard screws and remove the mudguard **(see illustrations)**.

Installation

5 Installation is the reverse of removal. Make sure the captive nuts are correctly positioned on each inner side of the front mudguard **(see illustration)**.

11.4b ... and at the rear (arrowed) ...

11.4c ... and remove the rear mudguard

12 Rear cowl

Removal

1 Remove the panniers and passenger seat (see Section 3).
2 Remove the side covers (see Section 4).
3 Unscrew the luggage rack trim bolts, noting the spacers and captive nuts on the front bolts and the collars and nuts on the rear bolts **(see illustrations)**. Remove the trim.
4 Undo the seat lock mechanism screw, then release the cable holder from its slot **(see illustration)**.

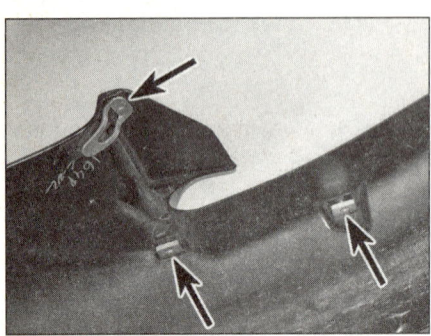

11.5 Make sure the captive nuts (arrowed) are correctly in place

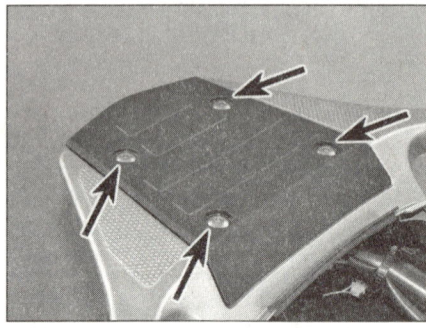

12.3a Unscrew the bolts (arrowed) ...

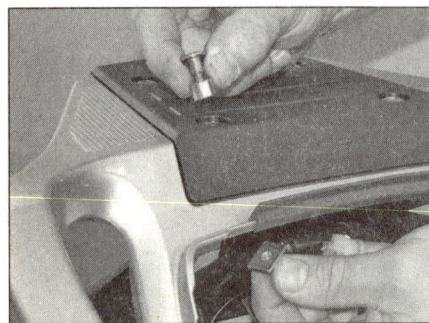

12.3b ... noting the front bolt spacers and captive nuts ...

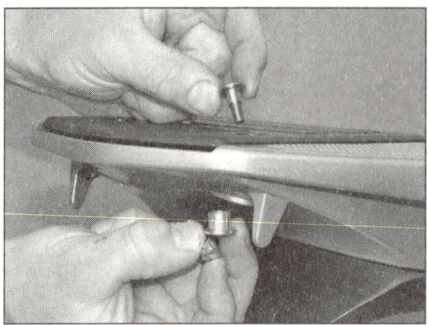

12.3c ... and the rear bolt collars and nuts

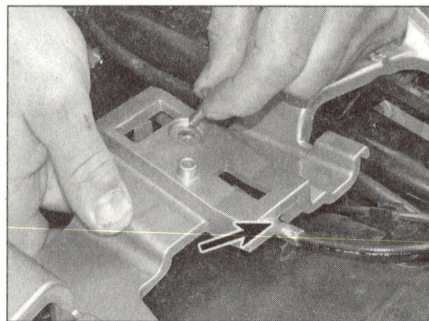

12.4 Undo the screw and release the cable from the slot (arrowed)

Bodywork 7•11

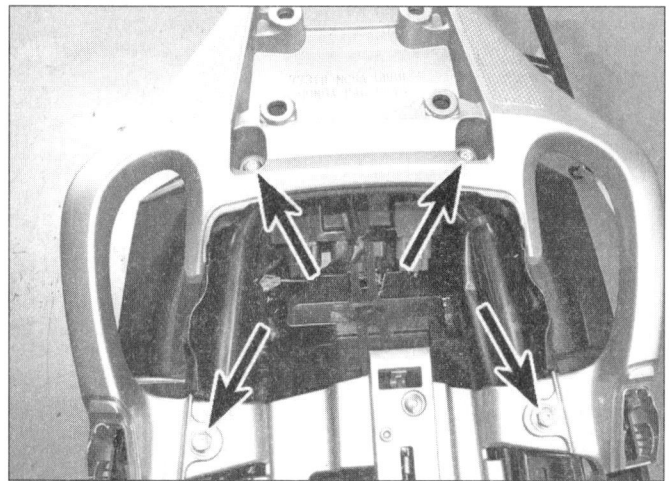

12.5a Unscrew the bolts . . .

12.5b . . . and remove the spacers

12.6 Detach the cable from the lock if required

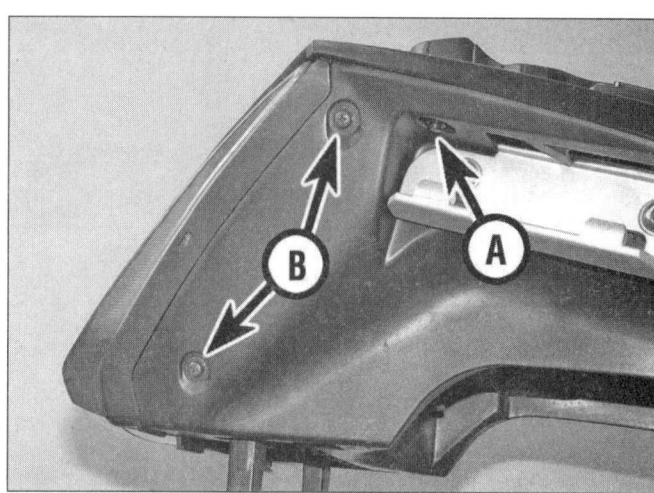

12.7a Release the trim clip (A) and undo the screws (B)

5 Unscrew the four bolts, noting the washers and spacers **(see illustrations)**.

6 Lift the luggage rack off and detach the seat lock, noting how the peg locates in the hole. If required free the cable end from the lock and remove it **(see illustration)**.

7 Release the trim clip (see Section 2) and undo the two screws on each side **(see illustration)**. Detach the rear cowl, noting how it locates over the seat release lever on the left-hand side, and release the bulb holders from the tail light **(see illustrations)**.

8 If required remove the tail light from the cover (see Chapter 8).

Installation

9 Installation is the reverse of removal. Make sure all spacers, collars and captive nuts are correctly positioned.

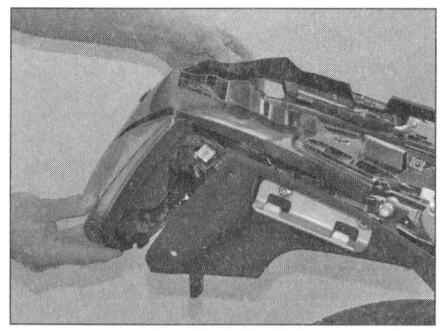

12.7b Detach the cowl . . .

12.7c . . . lifting it over the lever . . .

12.7d . . . and release the bulb holders

Notes

Chapter 8
Electrical system

Contents

	Section
Alternator/regulator/rectifier	29
Battery charging	4
Battery removal and maintenance	3
Brake light switches	14
Brake/tail light bulbs	9
Charging system testing	28
Clutch switch	22
Diode block	23
Electrical system fault finding	2
Fuses	5
General information	1
Handlebar switches	19
Headlight	8
Headlight bulbs and sidelight bulbs	7
Horn	24
Ignition switch	18

	Section
Ignition system components	see Chapter 4
Instrument check and replacement	16
Instrument cluster removal and installation	15
Lighting system check	6
Neutral switch	20
Oil pressure switch	17
Sidestand switch	21
Starter motor overhaul	27
Starter motor removal and installation	26
Starter relay	25
Tail light	10
Turn signal assemblies	13
Turn signal bulbs	12
Turn signal circuit check and relay	11
Windshield height adjuster mechanism	30

Degrees of difficulty

Easy, suitable for novice with little experience	Fairly easy, suitable for beginner with some experience	Fairly difficult, suitable for competent DIY mechanic	Difficult, suitable for experienced DIY mechanic	Very difficult, suitable for expert DIY or professional

Specifications

Battery
Capacity	12V, 11Ah
Voltage	
Fully-charged	13.0 to 13.2V
Uncharged	below 12.3V
Charging rate	
Normal	0.9A for 5 to 10 hrs
Quick	4.5A for 0.5 hr
Current leakage	2.5mA (max)

Alternator
Rotor coil resistance	0.1 to 1.0 ohms
Stator coil resistance	0.1 to 1.0 ohms
Output	
2002 to 2007 models	742W @ 5000 rpm
2008-on models	675W @ 5000 rpm
Regulated voltage output	max. 15.5V @ 5000 rpm
Slip ring OD	
Standard	14.4 mm
Service limit	12.0 mm

Starter motor
Brush length	
Standard	12 to 13 mm
Service limit (min)	6.5 mm

8•2 Electrical system

Fuses
Main A	30A
Main B	65A
Others	30A, 20A, 15A, 10A (see *Wiring Diagrams*)

Bulbs
Headlights	
Europe	60/55W x 2 halogen H7
US and Canada	45/45W x 2 halogen H7
Sidelight	5W x 2
Brake/tail light	21/5W x 2
Turn signal lights	
Europe	21W x 4
US and Canada	
Front	21/5W x 2
Rear	21W x 2
Instrument and warning lights	LED

Torque settings
Engine protection bar bolts/nut	
Front bolt	39 Nm
Rear and lower bolts/nut	26 Nm
Engine side mounting bracket bolts	
Front bolt	39 Nm
Rear bolt	26 Nm
Footrest bracket bolts	
Front bolts (to main frame)	64 Nm
Rear bolts (to sub-frame)	42 Nm
Fork clamp bolts (top yoke)	26 Nm
Ignition switch bolts	25 Nm
Neutral switch	12 Nm
Oil pressure switch	12 Nm
Sidestand switch bolt	10 Nm
Steering stem nut	103 Nm

1 General information

All models have a 12 volt electrical system charged by a three-phase alternator with integral regulator/rectifier.

The regulator maintains the charging system output within the specified range to prevent overcharging, and the rectifier converts the ac (alternating current) output of the alternator to dc (direct current) to power the lights and other components and to charge the battery. The alternator rotor is gear driven and mounted on the top of the engine.

The starter motor is mounted on the back of the engine. The starting system includes the motor, the battery, the relay and the various wires and switches. Some of the switches are part of a starter interlock system which prevents the engine from being started if the sidestand is down and the engine is in gear. The engine can be started with the sidestand up when it is in gear as long as the clutch lever is pulled in. The system will also cut the engine should the sidestand extend while the engine is running and in gear – see Chapter 1 for further information and checks on the system.

Note: *Keep in mind that electrical parts, once purchased, often cannot be returned. To avoid unnecessary expense, make very sure the faulty component has been positively identified before buying a replacement part.*

2 Electrical system fault finding

1 A typical electrical circuit consists of an electrical component, the switches, relays, etc, related to that component and the wiring and connectors that link the component to the battery and the frame.

2 Before tackling any troublesome electrical circuit, first study the wiring diagram thoroughly to get a complete picture of what makes up that individual circuit. Trouble spots, for instance, can often be narrowed down by noting if other components related to that circuit are operating properly or not. If several components or circuits fail at one time, chances are the fault lies either in the fuse or in a common earth (ground) connection, as several circuits are often routed through the same fuse and earth (ground) connections **(see illustration)**.

3 Electrical problems often stem from simple causes, such as loose or corroded connections or a blown fuse. Prior to any electrical fault finding, always visually check the condition of the fuse, wires and connections in the problem circuit. Intermittent failures can be especially frustrating, since you can't always duplicate the failure when it's convenient to test. In such situations, a good practice is to clean all connections in the affected circuit, whether or not they appear to be good – where possible use a dedicated electrical cleaning spray along with emery cloth, wire wool or other abrasive material to remove corrosion, and a dedicated electrical protection spray to prevent further problems. All of the connections and wires should also be wiggled to check for looseness which can cause intermittent failure.

4 If you don't have a multimeter it is highly advisable to obtain one – they are not expensive and will enable a full range of electrical tests to be made **(see illustration)**. Go for a modern digital one with LCD display

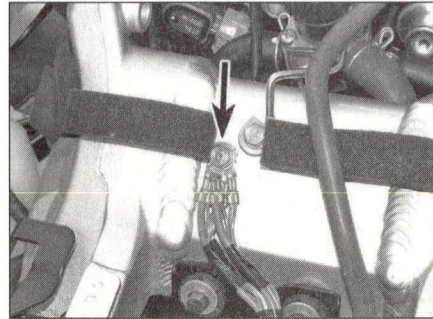

2.2 Common earth point (arrowed) – raise the fuel tank for access

Electrical system 8•3

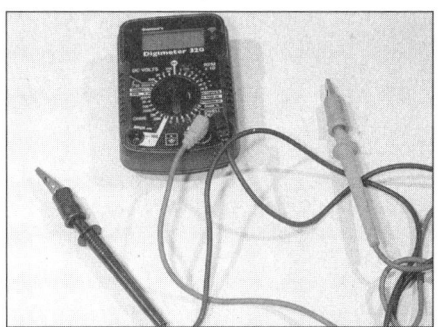

2.4a A digital multimeter can be used for all electrical tests

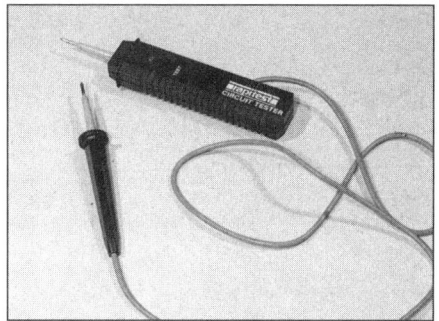

2.4b A battery-powered continuity tester

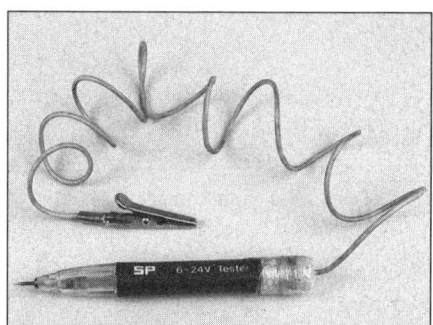

2.4c A simple test light is useful for voltage tests

as they are easier to use. A continuity tester and/or test light are useful for certain electrical checks as an alternative, though are limited in their usefulness compared to a multimeter **(see illustrations)**.

Continuity checks

5 The term continuity describes the uninterrupted flow of electricity through an electrical circuit. Continuity can be checked with a multimeter set either to its continuity function (a beep is emitted when continuity is found), or to the resistance (ohms / Ω) function, or with a dedicated continuity tester. Both instruments are powered by an internal battery, therefore the checks are made with the ignition OFF. As a safety precaution, always disconnect the battery negative (-) lead before making continuity checks, particularly if ignition switch checks are being made.

6 If using a multimeter, select the continuity function if it has one, or the resistance (ohms) function. Touch the meter probes together and check that a beep is emitted or the meter reads zero, which indicates continuity. If there is no continuity there will be no beep or the meter will show infinite resistance. After using the meter, always switch it OFF to conserve its battery.

7 A continuity tester can be used in the same way – its light should come on or it should beep to indicate continuity in the switch ON position, but should be off or silent in the OFF position.

8 Note that the polarity of the test probes doesn't matter for continuity checks, although care should be taken to follow specific test procedures if a diode or solid-state component is being checked.

Switch continuity checks

9 If a switch is at fault, trace its wiring to the wiring connectors. Separate the connectors and inspect them for security and condition. A build-up of dirt or corrosion here will most likely be the cause of the problem – clean up and apply a water dispersant such as WD40, or alternatively use a dedicated contact cleaner and protection spray.

10 If using a multimeter, select the continuity function if it has one, or the resistance (ohms) function, and connect its probes to the terminals in the connector **(see illustration)**. Simple ON/OFF type switches, such as brake light switches, only have two wires whereas combination switches, like the handlebar switches, have many wires. Study the wiring diagram to ensure that you are connecting to the correct pair of wires. Continuity should be indicated with the switch ON and no continuity with it OFF.

Wiring continuity checks

11 Many electrical faults are caused by damaged wiring, often due to incorrect routing or chaffing on frame components. Loose, wet or corroded wire connectors can also be the cause of electrical problems.

12 A continuity check can be made on a single length of wire by disconnecting it at each end and connecting the meter or continuity tester probes to each end of the wire **(see illustration)**. Continuity (low or no resistance – 0 ohms) should be indicated if the wire is good. If no continuity (high resistance) is shown, suspect a broken wire.

13 To check for continuity to earth in any earth wire connect one probe of your meter or tester to the earth wire terminal in the connector and the other to the frame, engine, or battery earth (-) terminal. Continuity (low or no resistance – 0 ohms) should be indicated if the wire is good. If no continuity (high resistance) is shown, suspect a broken wire or corroded or loose earth point (see below).

Voltage checks

14 A voltage check can determine whether power is reaching a component. Use a multimeter set to the dc voltage scale, or a test light. The test light is the cheaper component, but the meter has the advantage of being able to give a voltage reading.

15 Connect the meter or test light in parallel, i.e. across the load **(see illustration)**.

16 First identify the relevant wiring circuit by referring to the wiring diagram at the end of this manual. If other electrical components share the same power supply (i.e. are fed from the same fuse), take note whether they are working correctly – this is useful information in deciding where to start checking the circuit.

17 If using a meter, check first that the meter leads are plugged into the correct terminals

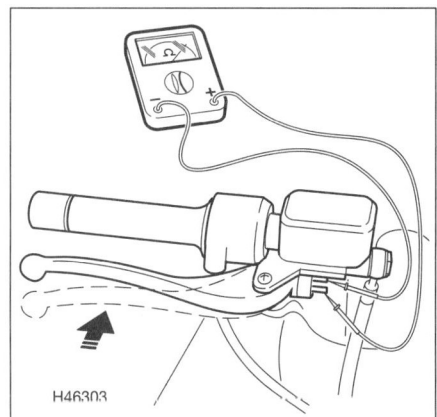

2.10 Continuity should be indicated across switch terminals when lever is operated

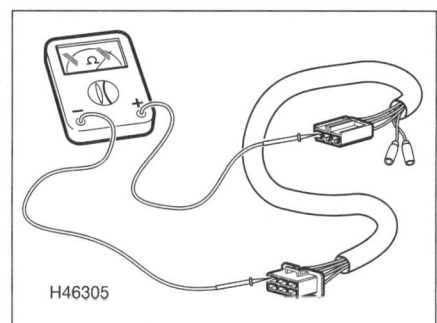

2.12 Wiring continuity check. Connect the meter probes across each end of the same wire

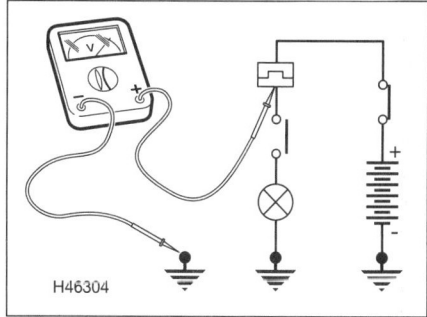

2.15 Voltage check. Connect the meter positive probe to the component and the negative probe to earth

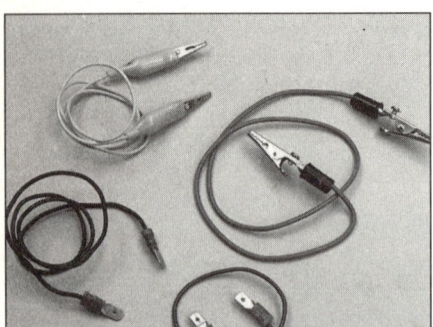

2.23 A selection of insulated jumper wires

3.2a Disconnect the negative lead first...

3.2b ... then disconnect the positive lead

on the meter (red to positive (+), black to negative (-). Set the meter to the dc volts function, where necessary at a range suitable for the battery voltage – 0 to 20 vdc. Connect the meter red probe (+) to the power supply wire and the black probe to a good metal earth (ground) on the motorcycle's frame or directly to the battery negative terminal. Battery voltage should be shown on the meter with the ignition switch, and if necessary any other relevant switch, ON.

18 If using a test light, connect its positive (+) probe to the power supply terminal and its negative (-) probe to a good earth (ground) on the motorcycle's frame. With the switch, and if necessary any other relevant switch, ON, the test light should illuminate.

19 If no voltage is indicated, work back towards the fuse continuing to check for voltage. When you reach a point where there is voltage, you know the problem lies between that point and your last check point.

Earth (ground) checks

20 Earth connections are made either directly to the engine or frame via the mounting of the component, or by a separate wire into the earth circuit of the wiring harness. Alternatively a short earth wire is sometimes run from the component directly to the motorcycle's frame.

21 Corrosion is a common cause of a poor earth connection, as is a loose earth terminal fastener.

22 If total or multiple component failure is experienced, check the security of the main earth lead from the negative (-) terminal of the battery, the earth lead bolted to the engine, and the main earth point(s) on the frame. If corroded, dismantle the connection and clean all surfaces back to bare metal. Remake the connection and prevent further corrosion from forming by smearing battery terminal grease over the connection.

23 To check the earth of a component, use an insulated jumper wire to temporarily bypass its earth connection **(see illustration)** – connect one end of the jumper wire to the earth terminal or metal body of the component and the other end to the motorcycle's frame. If the circuit works with the jumper wire installed, the earth circuit is faulty.

24 To check an earth wire first check for corroded or loose connections, then check the wiring for continuity (Step 13) between each connector in the circuit in turn, and then to its earth point, to locate the break.

3 Battery removal and maintenance

Caution: *Be extremely careful when handling or working around the battery. The electrolyte is very caustic and an explosive gas (hydrogen) is given off when the battery is charging.*

Removal and installation

1 Make sure the ignition is switched OFF. Remove the right-hand side cover and battery cover (see Chapter 7).

2 Unscrew the negative (–) terminal bolt first and disconnect the lead from the battery **(see illustration)**. Lift up the red insulating cover to access the positive (+) terminal, then unscrew the bolt and disconnect the lead **(see illustration)**.

3 Undo the screw securing the top of the battery retainer and remove the retainer **(see illustration)**. Remove the battery from the bike **(see illustration)**.

4 Installation is the reverse of removal. Clean the battery terminals and lead ends with a wire brush, emery paper or steel wool. Reconnect the leads, connecting the positive (+) terminal first.

> **HAYNES HINT** *Battery corrosion can be kept to a minimum by applying a layer of battery terminal grease or petroleum jelly (Vaseline) to the terminals after the leads have been connected. DO NOT use a mineral based grease.*

Inspection and maintenance

5 The battery is of the maintenance free (sealed) type, therefore requiring no regular maintenance. However, the following checks should still be performed. **Note:** *Do not attempt to remove the battery caps to check the electrolyte level or battery specific gravity. Removal will damage the caps, resulting in electrolyte leakage and battery damage.*

6 Check the battery terminals and leads are tight and free of corrosion. If corrosion is evident, clean the terminals as described in Step 4, then protect them from further corrosion (see **Haynes Hint**).

7 Look for cracks in the case and replace the battery with a new one if any are found. If acid has been spilled on the frame or battery box, neutralise it with a baking soda and water solution, dry it thoroughly, then touch up any damaged paint.

8 If the motorcycle sits unused for long periods of time, disconnect the cables from the battery terminals, negative (–) terminal first. Refer to Section 4 and charge the battery once every month to six weeks.

9 Check the condition of the battery by

3.3a Undo the screw at the top and remove the retainer ...

3.3b ... and remove the battery

Electrical system 8•5

measuring the voltage present at the battery terminals **(see illustration)**. Connect the voltmeter positive (+) probe to the battery positive (+) terminal, and the negative (–) probe to the battery negative (–) terminal. When fully-charged there should be 13.0 to 13.2 volts present. If the voltage falls below 12.3 volts remove the battery (see above), and recharge it as described in Section 4.

4 Battery charging

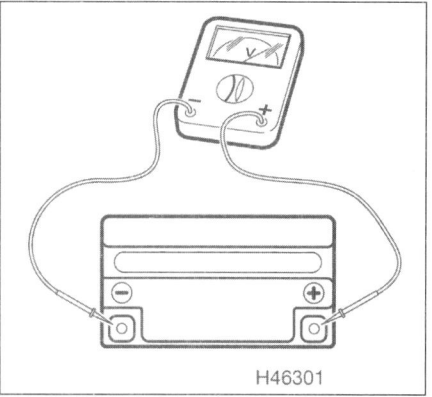

3.9 Checking battery voltage

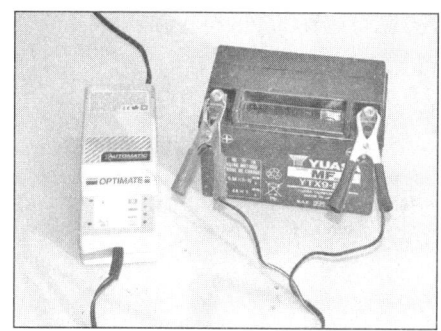

4.2 Battery connected to a charger

Caution: Be extremely careful when handling or working around the battery. The electrolyte is very caustic and an explosive gas (hydrogen) is given off when the battery is charging.

1 Remove the battery (see Section 3). Connect the charger to the battery, making sure that the positive (+) lead on the charger is connected to the positive (+) terminal on the battery, and the negative (–) lead is connected to the negative (–) terminal.

2 Honda recommend that the battery is charged at the normal rate specified at the beginning of the Chapter. A higher 'quick charge' rate that can be used if absolutely necessary is also specified, but note that exceeding this could cause the battery to overheat, buckling the plates and rendering it useless. Few owners will have access to an expensive current controlled charger, so if a normal domestic charger is used check that after a possible initial peak, the charge rate falls to a safe level. If the battery becomes hot during charging **stop**. Further charging will cause damage. Note that there are many bike-specific chargers available from good suppliers that are designed for the maintenance and recovery of motorcycle batteries, in particular catering for the requirements of heavily discharged MF batteries **(see illustration)**. They are a worthwhile investment, especially if the bike is not used over winter. Follow the manufacturer's instructions.

3 If the recharged battery discharges rapidly if left disconnected it is likely that an internal short caused by physical damage or sulphation has occurred. A new battery will be required. A sound item will tend to lose its charge at about 1% per day.

4 Install the battery (see Section 3).

5 If the motorcycle sits unused for long periods of time, charge the battery once every month to six weeks and leave it disconnected.

5 Fuses

1 The electrical system is protected by fuses of different ratings. All except the main fuses are housed in two fuseboxes, located behind the left-hand side cover **(see illustrations)** – remove the side cover to access them (see Chapter 7). The main fuse A is integral with the starter relay, and the main fuse B is in a holder on the top of the battery cover **(see illustration)** – remove the right-hand side cover to access them (see Chapter 7).

2 To access the fusebox fuses unclip the fusebox lid **(see illustration)**. To access the main fuse A, disconnect the starter relay wiring connector **(see illustration 5.1b)**. To access the main fuse B unclip the holder from the top of the battery cover **(see illustration 5.1c)**, then unclip the fuse cover **(see illustration)**.

3 With the exception of main fuse B the fuses can be removed and checked visually – if you can't pull the fuse out with your fingertips, use

5.1a Fuseboxes (arrowed)

5.1b Main fuse A (arrowed) is under the starter relay wiring connector

5.1c Main fuse B is in the holder (arrowed) on the top of the battery

5.2a Unclip the lids to access the fuses

5.2b Remove the cover to access the main fuse B (arrowed)

8•6 Electrical system

a pair of suitable pliers (see illustration). The main fuse B is secured by two screws (see illustration). A blown fuse is easily identified by a break in the element (see illustration). Each fuse is clearly marked with its rating and must only be replaced by a fuse of the correct rating. A spare fuse of each rating except the main fuses is housed in the fusebox, and a spare main fuse A is housed in the starter relay holder (see illustration). There is no spare main fuse B. If a spare fuse is used, always replace it with a new one so that a spare of each rating is carried on the bike at all times.

⚠ **Warning:** *Never put in a fuse of a higher rating or bridge the terminals with any other substitute, however temporary it may be. Serious damage may be done to the circuit, or a fire may start.*

4 If the new fuse blows immediately check the wiring circuit very carefully for evidence of a short-circuit. Look for bare wires and chafed, melted or burned insulation.

5 Occasionally a fuse will blow or cause an open-circuit for no obvious reason. Corrosion of the fuse ends and fusebox terminals may occur and cause poor fuse contact. If this happens, remove the corrosion with a wire brush or emery paper, then spray the fuse end and terminals with electrical contact cleaner.

5.3a Remove the fuses using pliers

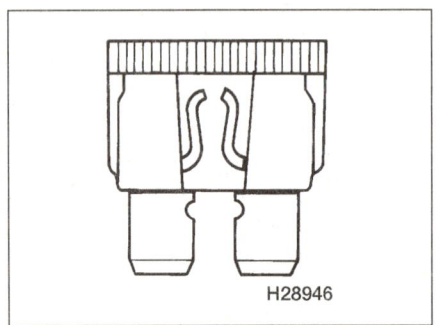

5.3c A blown fuse can be identified by a break in its element

5.3b Undo the screws (arrowed) to remove the main fuse B

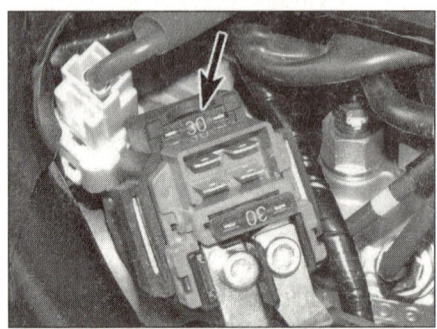

5.3d Spare main fuse A (arrowed)

6 Lighting system check

1 If a light fails first check the bulb (see relevant Section), and the bulb terminals in the holder. If none of the lights work, check the battery (see Section 3). Low battery voltage indicates either a faulty battery or a defective charging system. Refer to Section 3 for battery checks and Section 28 for charging system tests. Also, check the fuses (Section 5) – if there is more than one problem at the same time, it is likely to be a fault relating to a multi-function component, such as one of the fuses governing more than one circuit, or the ignition switch. When checking for a blown filament in a bulb, it is advisable to back up a visual check with a continuity test of the filament as it is not always apparent that a bulb has blown.

Headlight

2 All models have two twin filament bulbs. If all headlight beams fail to work, check the headlight fuse (see Section 5). If either both LO beams or both HI beams fail to work first check the relevant relay (see Step 3). If only one beam in one bulb fails check the bulb (see Section 7). If all seems good, the problem lies in the wiring or connectors, the light switch where fitted, or the dimmer switch. Refer to Section 19 for the switch testing procedures.

3 If a relay is suspected of being faulty, swap the HI and LO beam relays and see if the problem transfers with the relay. Remove the left-hand side cover to access the relays (see Chapter 7) – displace the relays and disconnect the wiring connectors (see illustration). To confirm a relay is faulty it can be tested as follows (see illustration): displace the relay, disconnect its wiring connector and move it to the bench for testing. Set a multimeter to the ohms x 1 scale and connect it across the relay's A and B (black/red and blue/black on the HI beam relay, or black/red and white/black on the LO beam relay) wire terminals. There

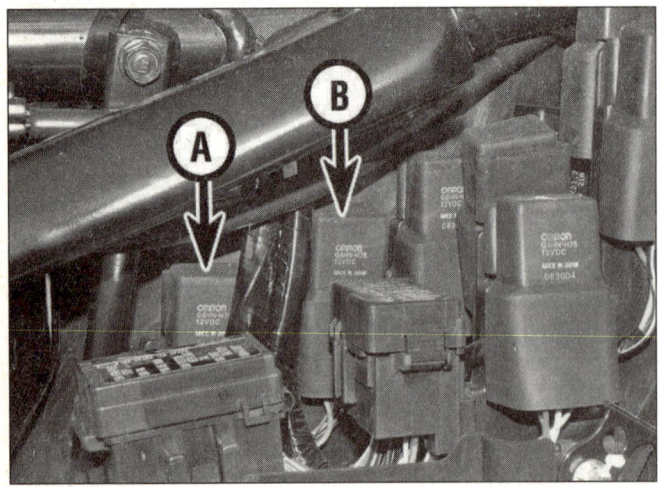

6.3a LO beam relay (A), HI beam relay (B)

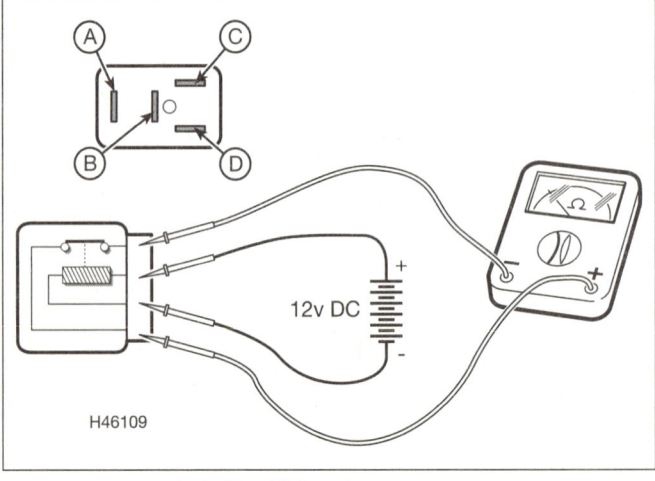

6.3b Headlight relay test set-up

Electrical system 8•7

6.7 Power relay (arrowed)

7.2a Disconnect the wiring connector . . .

7.2b . . . and remove the dust cover

should be no continuity (infinite resistance). Using a fully-charged 12 volt battery and two insulated jumper wires, connect the positive (+) terminal of the battery to the C (blue on the HI beam relay, or white on the LO beam relay) wire terminal on the relay, and the negative (–) terminal to the D (green) wire terminal. At this point the relay should be heard to click and the meter read 0 ohms (continuity). If this is the case the relay is good. If the relay does not click when battery voltage is applied and indicates no continuity (infinite resistance) across its terminals, it is faulty and must be replaced with a new one.

4 If the relays are good, check there is battery voltage at the black/red wire terminal on the relay wiring connector with the ignition ON. If there is no voltage, check the wiring between the relay wiring connector and the ignition switch, via the fusebox, and check the light switch where fitted and the dimmer switch (see Section 19), and the ignition switch (see Section 18). If voltage is present, check all wires between the relay connectors, the headlight connectors and the dimmer switch for continuity, and check there is continuity to earth (ground) in the green wire from the headlight connector. Repair or renew the wiring or connectors as necessary.

Tail lights

5 If one tail light fails to work, check the bulb (see Section 9); if both lights fail check the tail light fuse (see Section 5). If they are good, remove the rear mudguard (see Chapter 7). Release the relevant bulbholder by turning it anti-clockwise, then disconnect the wiring connector **(see illustration 9.2)**. Check there is battery voltage at the brown/white wire terminal in the connector with the ignition switch ON. If voltage is present, check there is continuity to earth (ground) in the green wire from the wiring connector. If no voltage is indicated, check the wiring and connectors between the tail light and the fusebox.

Brake light

6 If one brake light fails to work, check the bulb (see Section 9); if both lights fail check the stop light fuse (see Section 5). If they are good, remove the rear mudguard (see Chapter 7). Release the relevant bulbholder by turning it anti-clockwise, then disconnect the wiring connector **(see illustration 9.2)**. Check there is battery voltage at the green/yellow wire terminal on the loom side of the connector with the ignition ON, and first with the front brake lever on, then with the rear brake pedal on. If voltage is present with one brake on but not the other, then the switch or its wiring is faulty. If voltage is present in both cases, check there is continuity to earth (ground) in the green wire from the wiring connector. If no voltage is indicated, check the wiring and connectors between the brake light and the brake switches, the power relay, the fusebox, and the ignition switch, then check the brake light switches themselves. Refer to Section 14 for the switch testing procedures.

7 If all is good, check the power relay as follows: remove the left-hand side cover (see Chapter 7). Displace the relay and disconnect the wiring connector **(see illustration)**. Set a multimeter to the ohms x 1 scale and connect it across the relay's A and B (white and white/green wire) terminals **(see illustration 6.3b)**. There should be no continuity (infinite resistance). Using a fully-charged 12 volt battery and two insulated jumper wires, connect the positive (+) terminal of the battery to the C (red/black wire) terminal on the relay, and the negative (–) terminal to the D (green wire) terminal on the relay. At this point the relay should be heard to click and the multimeter read 0 ohms (continuity). If this is the case the relay is proved good. If the relay does not click when battery voltage is applied and still indicates no continuity (infinite resistance) across its terminals, it is faulty and must be replaced with a new one.

Sidelight

8 If one sidelight fails to work, check the bulb (see Section 7); if both sidelights fail check the position light fuse (see Section 5). If they are good, check there is battery voltage at the brown/white wire terminal on the loom side of the wiring connector with the ignition switch ON. If voltage is present, check there is continuity to earth (ground) in the green wire from the wiring connector. If no voltage is indicated, check the wiring and connectors between the tail light and the fusebox.

Turn signals

9 See Section 11.

7 Headlight bulbs and sidelight bulbs

Note: *The headlight bulbs are of the quartz-halogen type. Do not touch the bulb glass as skin acids will shorten the bulb's service life. If the bulb is accidentally touched, it should be wiped carefully when cold with a rag soaked in methylated spirit and dried before fitting.*

Headlight

1 For best access remove the relevant fairing side panel (see Chapter 7).
2 Disconnect the wiring connector from the bulb in question. Remove the rubber dust cover, noting how it fits **(see illustrations)**.
3 Release the bulb retaining clip, noting how it fits, then remove the bulb bearing in mind the information in the **Note** above **(see illustrations)**.

7.3a Release the clip . . .

7.3b . . . and remove the headlight bulb

8•8 Electrical system

7.8 Pull the sidelight bulbholder out . . .

4 Fit the new bulb into the headlight, making sure it locates correctly, and secure it in position with the retaining clip **(see illustrations 7.3b and a)**.

 **Haynes Hint**: *Always use a paper towel or dry cloth when handling new bulbs to prevent injury if the bulb should break and to increase bulb life.*

5 Fit the dust cover, making sure it is correctly seated and with the arrow at the top, and connect the wiring connector **(see illustrations 7.2b and a)**.
6 Check the operation of the headlight.

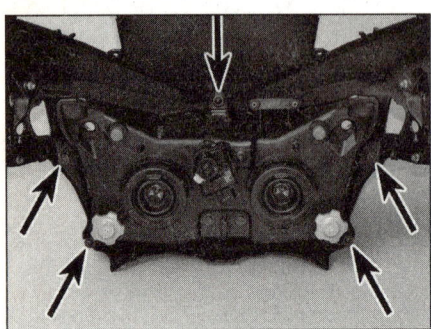

8.2 Undo the screws (arrowed) and remove the headlight from the fairing

7.9 . . . then pull the bulb out of the holder

Sidelight

7 For best access remove the relevant fairing side panel (see Chapter 7).
8 Carefully pull the bulbholder out of the headlight **(see illustration)**.
9 Carefully pull the bulb out of the holder **(see illustration)**.
10 Fit the new bulb in the bulbholder, then fit the bulbholder into the headlight – make sure the rubber seal is in good condition and correctly seated.
11 Check the operation of the sidelight.

8 Headlight

Removal

1 Remove the fairing (see Chapter 7).
2 Undo the screws securing the headlight assembly to the fairing, and lift it out, releasing the grommet from the peg **(see illustration)**.
3 If required remove the headlight bulbs (see Section 7).

Installation

4 Installation is the reverse of removal. Check the operation of the headlights and sidelights. Check the headlight aim (see Chapter 1).

Headlight aim adjuster mechanism

Check

5 If the vertical aim adjuster does not work remove the fairing (see Chapter 7). Check the adjuster motor wiring connector for loose or broken wires and corroded or broken terminals.
6 Check for battery voltage at the black/brown wire terminal in the motor connector with the ignition switch ON. If no voltage is indicated, check the wiring and connectors between the connector and the fusebox. If voltage is present, check there is continuity to earth (ground) in the green wire from the wiring connector.
7 If all is good check for a variable voltage – between 1.2 and 10.8 volts as you turn the adjuster knob – at the light green wire terminal in the motor connector with the ignition switch ON. If voltage is present, replace the aiming motor with a new one.
8 If no voltage is indicated, disconnect the instrument cluster 16-pin wiring connector (if not already done after removing the fairing). Check the connector for loose or broken wires and corroded or broken terminals. Check there is continuity in the light green wire between the motor and instrument connectors. Check there is continuity to earth in the green/yellow wire in the instrument cluster connector. Disconnect the instrument cluster 20-pin wiring connector. Check for battery voltage at the black/brown wire terminal in the connector with the ignition switch ON. If no voltage is indicated, check the wiring and connectors between the connector and the fusebox. If all is good replace the adjuster unit in the instrument cluster with a new one.

Adjuster motor removal and installation

9 Remove the fairing (see Chapter 7).
10 Pull the body of the motor slightly away from the headlight and turn it about 1/8 turn anti-clockwise **(see illustration)**.
11 Turn the adjuster anti-clockwise until it threads out of its socket and remove the motor **(see illustrations)**.
12 Installation is the reverse of removal

8.10 Pull and turn the adjuster motor as described

8.11a Turn the adjuster fully anti-clockwise . . .

8.11b . . . and remove the motor

Electrical system 8•9

8.12 The peg locates in the hole in the motor (arrowed)

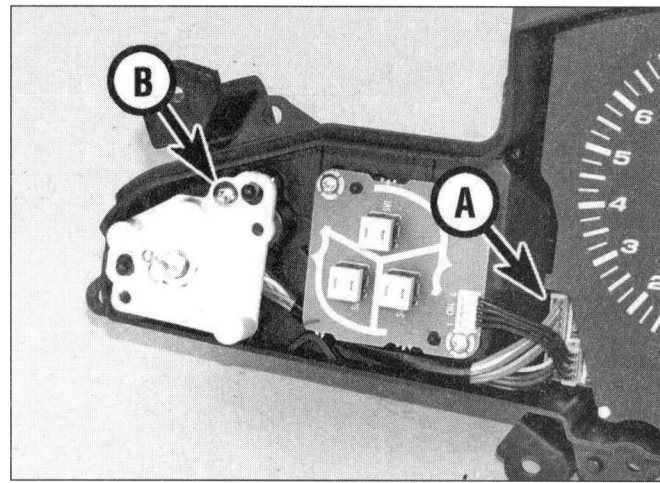

8.14 Disconnect the wiring connector (A), then undo the screw (B)

– when refitting the motor, turn it 1/8 turn clockwise until the peg aligns with the hole then push the motor in so the peg locates in the hole **(see illustration)**. Check headlight aim after installing the fairing (see Chapter 1).

Adjuster unit removal and installation

13 Remove the instrument cluster (see Section 15), then remove the front cover from it (see Section 16, Steps 25 and 26).
14 Disconnect the wiring connector, then undo the screw and remove the unit, noting how it locates **(see illustration)**.
15 Installation is the reverse of removal.

9 Brake/tail light bulbs

Note: *It is a good idea to use a paper towel or dry cloth when handling the new bulb to prevent injury if it breaks, and to increase bulb life.*

1 Remove the rear mudguard (see Chapter 7).
2 Turn the bulbholder anti-clockwise to release it **(see illustration)**. Carefully pull the bulb out of the holder. Check the socket terminals for corrosion and clean them if necessary.

3 Fit the new bulb, then fit the bulbholder and turn it clockwise.
4 Install the rear mudguard (see Chapter 7).

10 Tail light

1 Remove the rear cowl (see Chapter 7).
2 Undo the screws securing the tail light in the cowl and lift it out, noting the washers and collars **(see illustration)**.
3 Installation is the reverse of removal. Make sure the rubber wellnuts are in good condition. Check the operation of the tail and brake lights.

11 Turn signal circuit check and relay

Note: *On US and Canada models the front turn signals also function as running lights and have dual filament bulbs. When checking for faults, refer to the wiring diagram at the end of this Chapter.*

1 Most turn signal problems are the result of a burned out bulb or corroded socket. This is especially true when the turn signals function properly in one direction, but fail to flash in the other direction. If this is the case, first check the bulbs, the sockets and the wiring connectors (see Section 12). If all four turn signals fail to work, check the fuse (see Section 5), and then the relay (see Steps 2 to 4). If they are good, the problem lies in the wiring or connectors, or the switch. Refer to Section 19 for the switch testing procedures, and also to the wiring diagrams at the end of this Chapter.

2 To check the relay, remove the left-hand side cover (see Chapter 7).
3 Displace the relay and disconnect the wiring connector **(see illustration)**. Check for battery voltage at the red/green wire terminal on the loom side of the connector with the ignition ON. If no voltage is present, check the wiring from the relay to the ignition switch via the fusebox for continuity. Refer to electrical system fault finding in Section 2 and to the wiring diagrams at the end of this Chapter.

4 If voltage was present, short between the red/green and grey wire terminals on the connector using a jumper wire. Turn the ignition ON and operate the turn signal switch. If the lights come on, the relay is faulty and must be replaced with a new one.

9.2 Release the tail light bulbholder then pull the bulb from it

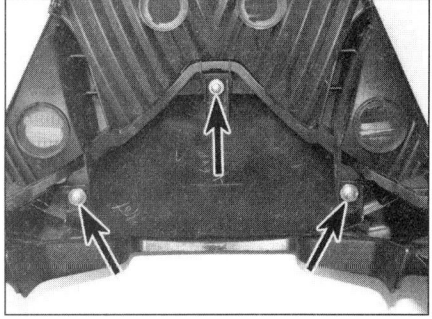

10.2 Undo the screws (arrowed) and remove the tail light

11.3 Turn signal relay (arrowed)

12.2a Release the front turn signal bulbholder . . .

12.2b . . . then pull the bulb from it

13 Turn signal assemblies

1 Remove the mirror cover (see Chapter 7).
2 Undo the screws and remove the turn signal **(see illustration)**.
3 See Section 10 for the rear turn signals.

14 Brake light switches

Circuit check

1 Before checking the switches, and if not already done, check the brake light circuit (see Section 6).
2 The front brake light switch is mounted on the underside of the brake master cylinder. Disconnect the wiring connectors from the switch **(see illustration)**. Using a continuity tester, connect the probes to the terminals of the switch. With the brake lever at rest, there should be no continuity. With the brake lever applied, there should be continuity. If the switch does not behave as described, replace it with a new one.
3 The rear brake light switch is mounted on the inside of the right-hand rider's footrest bracket. Remove the right-hand fairing side panel (see Chapter 7) to access the wiring connector and disconnect it **(see illustration)**. Using a continuity tester, connect the probes to the terminals on the switch side of the wiring connector. With the brake pedal at rest, there should be no continuity. With the brake pedal applied, there should be continuity. If the switch does not behave as described, replace it with a new one, although check first that the spring has not broken and the switch is adjusted correctly (see Chapter 1, Section 2).
4 If the switches are good, refer back to Section 6, Step 7 and check the power relay.

Switch replacement

Front brake lever switch

5 The switch is mounted on the underside of the brake master cylinder. Disconnect

12.6a Release the rear turn signal bulb holder (left-hand side arrowed) . . .

12.6b . . . then pull the bulb from it

5 If the lights do not come on, check the grey wire for continuity to the left-hand switch housing, and repair or renew the wiring or connectors as required.
6 If all is good so far, or if the lights came on one side but not the other, check the wiring between the left-hand switch housing and the turn signals themselves. Repair or renew the wiring or connectors as necessary.

12 Turn signal bulbs

Front turn signals

1 Displace the mirror cover (see Chapter 7).
2 Turn the bulbholder anti-clockwise to

release it **(see illustration)**. Carefully pull the bulb out of the holder **(see illustration)**. Check the socket terminals for corrosion and clean them if necessary.
3 Fit the new bulb, then fit the bulbholder and turn it clockwise.
4 Fit the mirror cover.

Rear turn signals

5 Remove the passenger seat (see Chapter 7).
6 Turn the bulbholder anti-clockwise to release it **(see illustration)**. Carefully pull the bulb out of the holder **(see illustration)**. Check the socket terminals for corrosion and clean them if necessary.
7 Fit the new bulb, then fit the bulbholder and turn it clockwise.
8 Install the seat.

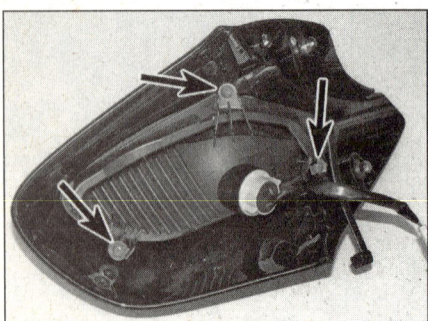

13.2 Front turn signal screws (arrowed)

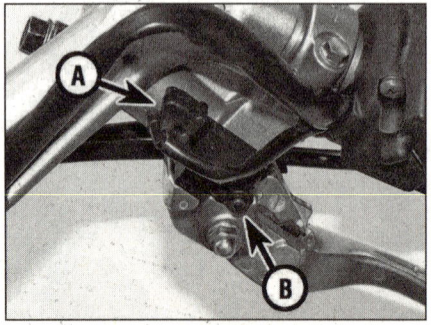

14.2 Front brake switch wiring connectors (A) and mounting screw (B)

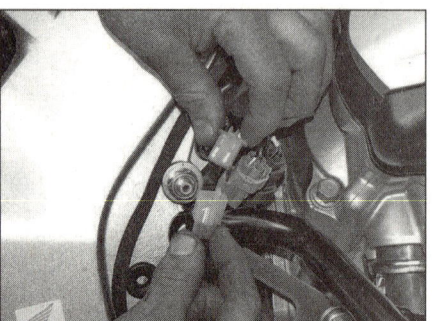

14.3 Disconnect the rear brake light switch wiring connector

Electrical system 8•11

14.9a Unscrew the exhaust bolt . . .

14.9b . . . and the battery tray bolt (arrowed)

14.10 Unscrew the bolts (arrowed) and displace the footrest bracket

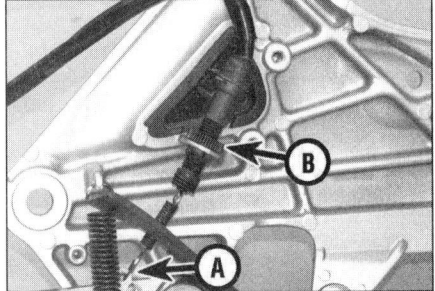

14.11 Detach the spring from the pedal (A), then thread the switch out of the adjuster nut (B)

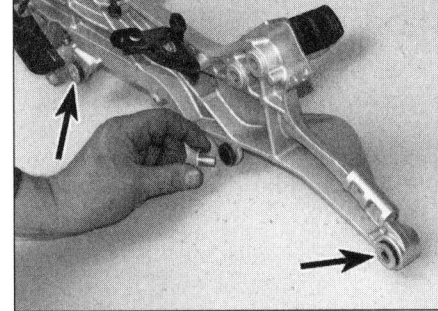

14.12 Make sure the collars are in place

15.1 Pull the boot back and disconnect the wiring connectors

the wiring connectors from the switch (see illustration 14.2).

6 Undo the single screw securing the switch to the master cylinder and remove the switch.
7 Installation is the reverse of removal. Make sure the peg on the switch is correctly located in its hole before tightening the screw. The switch isn't adjustable.

Rear brake pedal switch

8 The rear brake light switch is mounted on the inside of the rider's right-hand footrest bracket. Remove the fairing right-hand side panel (see Chapter 7) to access the wiring connector and disconnect it (see illustration 14.3). Feed the wiring down to the switch, noting its routing and releasing it from any ties.
9 Remove the battery (see Section 3). Remove the right-hand silencer (see Chapter 4). Unscrew the bolt securing the rear of the downpipe assembly (see illustration).

Unscrew the bolt in the battery tray (see illustration).
10 Unscrew the footrest bracket bolts, then displace the assembly and turn it so the inside is accessible, supporting it you don't strain the brake hoses or brake light switch wiring (see illustration).
11 Detach the end of the switch spring from the brake pedal (see illustration). Thread the switch out of its adjuster nut, then pull the nut out of the bracket.
12 Installation is the reverse of removal, noting the following:
• Make sure none of the collars have fallen out of the exhaust mounting rubbers (see illustration).
• Tighten the footrest bracket bolts to the torque settings specified at the beginning of the Chapter.
• Make sure the brake light is activated just before the rear brake pedal takes effect.

If adjustment is necessary, refer to Chapter 1, Section 2.

15 Instrument cluster removal and installation

Removal

1 Remove the windshield and inner cowl (see Chapter 7). Disconnect the instrument cluster wiring connectors (see illustration).
2 Remove the mirror covers (see Chapter 7). Undo the screw on each side (see illustration).
3 Open the storage compartment lids. Undo the two screws in each compartment (see illustration).
4 Remove the instrument panel, noting how the peg locates in the grommet (see illustration).

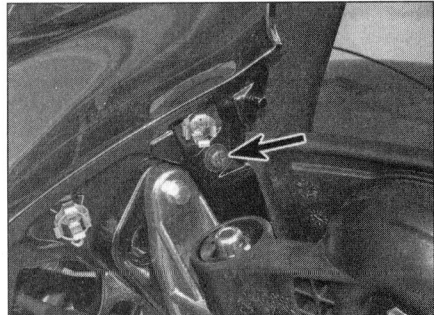

15.2 Undo the screw (arrowed) on each side

15.3 Undo the screws (arrowed) in each compartment

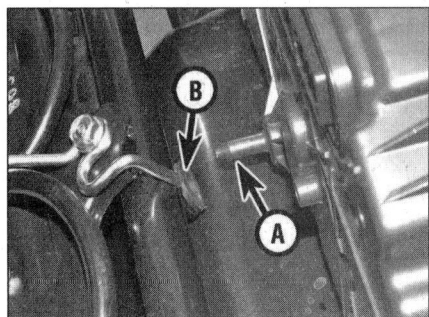

15.4 Note how the peg (A) locates in the grommet (B)

8•12 Electrical system

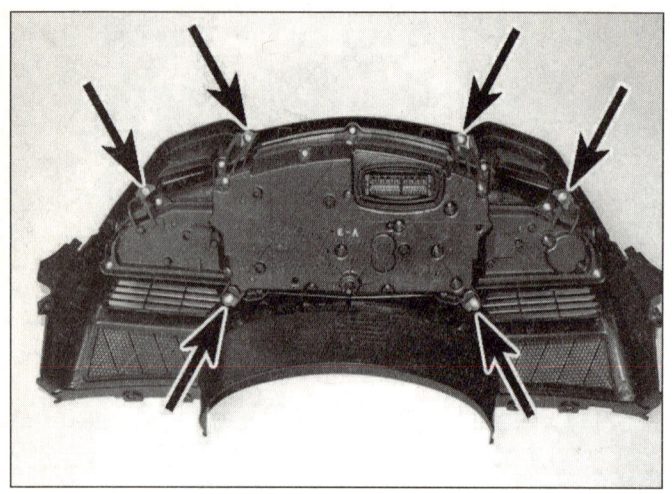

15.5 Instrument cluster screws (arrowed)

16.9 Disconnect the speed sensor wiring connector (arrowed)

5 Undo the screws and remove the instrument cluster from the panel **(see illustration)**.

Installation

6 Installation is the reverse of removal. Check the rubber grommet and replace it with a new one if necessary. Make sure the peg locates correctly in the grommet. Make sure that the wiring connectors are secure.

16 Instrument check and replacement

Check

Instrument cluster power check

1 If none of the instruments or displays are working, first check the meter fuse (see Section 5).
2 If the fuse is good, remove the windshield and inner cowl (see Chapter 7). Check the instrument cluster wiring connectors for loose or broken connections **(see illustration 15.1)**.
3 To check the power input wire, check for battery voltage between the black/brown wire terminal on the wiring loom side of the 20-pin connector and a good earth (ground) with the ignition switch ON. There should be battery voltage. If there is no voltage, refer to the wiring diagrams and check the wire between the instrument cluster and the fusebox for loose or broken connections or a damaged wire.
4 To check the back-up power wire, check for battery voltage between the red/green wire terminal on the wiring loom side of the connector and a good earth (ground) with the ignition switch OFF. There should be battery voltage. If there is no voltage, refer to the wiring diagrams and check the red/green wire between the instrument cluster and the fusebox for loose or broken connections or a damaged wire, then check the red wire from the fusebox to the main fuse and battery.
5 If there is voltage, and to check the earth (ground) wire, check for continuity between the green wire terminal on the loom side of the 16-pin wiring connector and earth (ground). If there is no continuity, check the circuit for loose or broken connections or a damaged wire and repair as necessary.
6 If all power input and earth wires are good, but there is no display or instrument function, then the printed circuit board (PCB), which contains the LCD display, is faulty. Disassemble the instrument cluster and replace the PCB with a new one (see Steps 24 to 29).

Speedometer and speed sensor

7 First check the meter fuse (see Section 5).
8 If the fuse is good, remove the windshield and the inner cowl (see Chapter 7). Check the instrument cluster wiring connectors for loose or broken connections **(see illustration 15.1)**.
9 Remove the right-hand fairing side panel (see Chapter 7). Disconnect the speed sensor 3-pin black wiring connector **(see illustration)**. Check the connector for loose terminals. With the ignition switch ON, check for battery voltage between the black/brown (+) and green/black (–) wire terminals on the wiring loom side of the connector. If there is no voltage refer to the wiring diagrams and check the wires for continuity and repair any loose or broken connection or damaged wire.
10 If there is voltage, reconnect the wiring connector, then place the bike on its centrestand so the rear wheel is off the ground. Connect a voltmeter between the pink (+) and green (–) wire terminals in the sensor side of the connector – make sure the probes make good contact when inserted into the connector. With the ignition switch ON, turn the rear wheel by hand and check that a fluctuating voltage reading between 0 and 5 volts is obtained. If no reading is obtained, the speed sensor is faulty and must be replaced with a new one (see Steps 42 to 45).
11 If a reading is obtained, repeat the check in Step 10, but connect the meter between the yellow/green and green wire terminals on the loom side of the cluster 16-pin wiring connector. If no fluctuating voltage is obtained, check there is continuity in the yellow/green wire to the ECM (refer to Chapter 4 for access), and in the pink/green wire from the ECM to the speed sensor connector, and check there is continuity to earth in the green/black wire from the sensor connector, referring to the wiring diagrams.
12 If the wiring is all good, the printed circuit board (PCB) is faulty. Disassemble the instrument cluster and replace the PCB with a new one (see Steps 24 to 29).

Tachometer

13 Check that when the ignition is switched on the tachometer needle makes a full swing around the dial and returns to zero. If not check the power input (see Steps 1 to 6).
14 Remove the windshield and inner cowl (see Chapter 7). Pull the rubber boot off the instrument cluster wiring connectors, but leave them connected **(see illustration)**. Connect the positive (+) lead of a voltmeter to the yellow/green wire terminal in the 16-pin wiring connector and the negative (–) lead to the green/black wire terminal. Start the engine and measure the tachometer input voltage, which should fluctuate between 0 and 5 volts. If the voltage is normal the tachometer is faulty. Disassemble the instrument cluster and replace the PCB with a new one (see Steps 24 to 29).

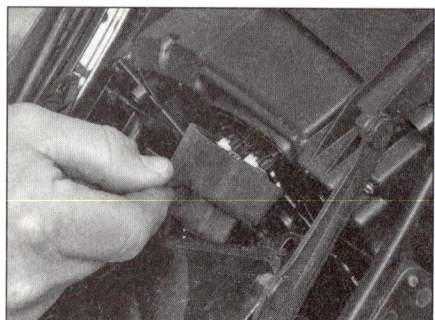

16.14 Pull the boot off the wiring connectors

Electrical system 8•13

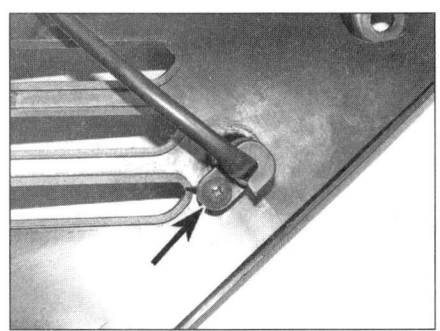

16.18 Ambient temperature sensor is secure by a screw (arrowed)

16.25 Pull the headlight adjuster knob off

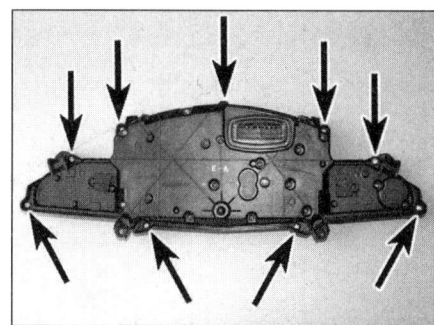

16.26a Undo the screws (arrowed) . . .

15 If there is no reading, check there is continuity to earth in the green/black wire. If there is remove the rear cowl (see Chapter 7), and disconnect the ECM 26-pin black wiring connector (see Chapter 4). Check there is continuity in the yellow/green wire between the ECM wiring connector and the instrument cluster wiring connector. If there is no continuity there is a break in the wire or faulty connector. Refer to the wiring diagrams and trace and rectify the fault. If the wiring is good the ECM could be faulty (see Chapter 4).

LCD display

16 If the display is not working at all, the printed circuit board (PCB), which contains the LCD display, is faulty. Disassemble the instrument cluster and replace the PCB with a new one (see Steps 24 to 29).

17 If an individual display is not working, refer to Chapter 3 for the coolant temperature display and Chapter 4 for the fuel level display. If the clock doesn't work, first check the battery/clock fuse (see Section 5).

18 If the ambient temperature display does not work, remove the inner panel from the right-hand fairing side panel (see Chapter 7). Check the resistance of the sensor by connecting an ohmmeter across the terminals on the sensor connector – there should be 4.8 to 5.2 ohms at 25°C. If not replace the sensor with a new one (see illustration). If it is good, check the connectors between the sensor connector and the instrument cluster 16-pin connector, and check there is continuity in each wire.

19 If any fault points to the LCD unit being faulty, replace the instrument cluster PCB with a new one (see Steps 24 to 29).

Indicator light board

20 If the display is not working at all, disassemble the instrument cluster (see below) and check the wiring and connectors – remove the light board and PCB from the cover to inspect the underside if required. If they are good, either the indicator light board or the main instrument PCB is faulty – take the instrument cluster to a Honda dealer for assessment.

21 If an individual indicator light is not working, refer to Section 6 for the HI beam light, Section 20 for the neutral switch, Section 17 for the oil pressure switch and Chapter 4 for the FI and HISS lights. If the particular component and its circuit are good see Step 23.

Multi-function button board

22 If one or more of the buttons do not work, disassemble the instrument cluster (see below) and check the wiring and connectors – remove the button board and PCB from the cover to inspect the underside if required. If they are good, either the button board or the main instrument PCB is faulty – take the instrument cluster to a Honda dealer for assessment.

Replacement

Instrument and warning lights

23 All instrument and warning lights are LEDs, which are part of the instrument cluster printed circuit board and are not available individually. If one of the LEDs fails disassemble the instrument cluster and replace the PCB or indicator board with a new one (see Steps 24 to 29).

Instrument PCB replacement

24 Remove the instrument cluster (see Section 15).

25 Pull the headlight adjuster knob off (see illustration).

26 Undo the screws on the back, then turn the instruments over and lift the front cover off (see illustrations).

27 Disconnect the indicator light board wiring connector (see illustration 16.33b), multi-function button board wiring connector (see illustration 16.39), and headlight aim adjuster unit wiring connector (see illustration 8.14).

28 Undo the PCB screws and lift the board out of the rear cover (see illustration).

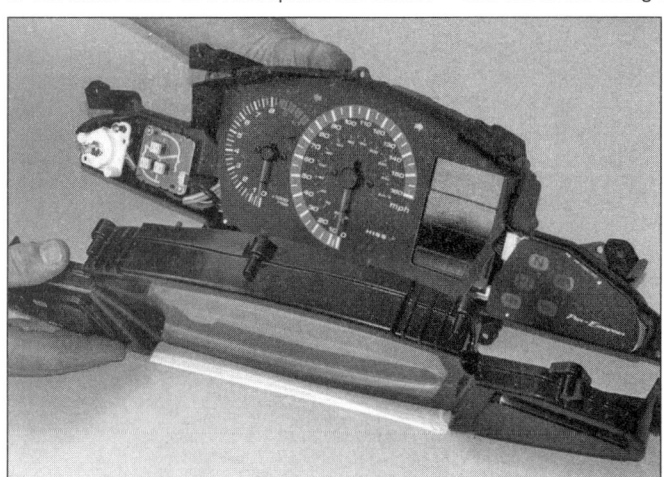

16.26b . . . and remove the front cover

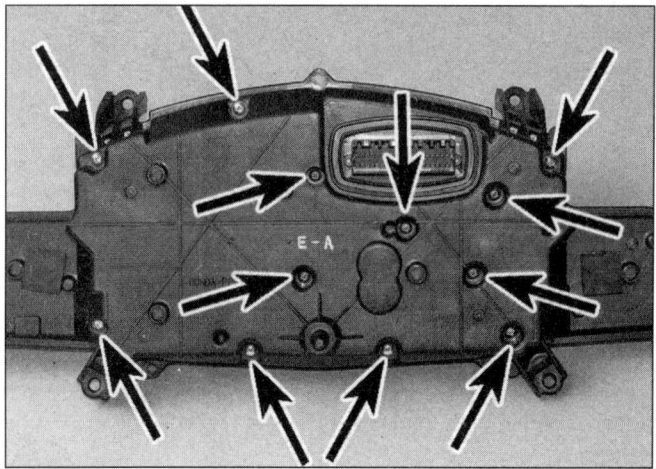

16.28 Undo the screws (arrowed) and remove the instrument board

8•14 Electrical system

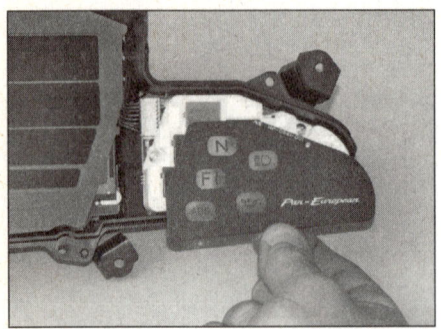

16.33a Remove the lens cover

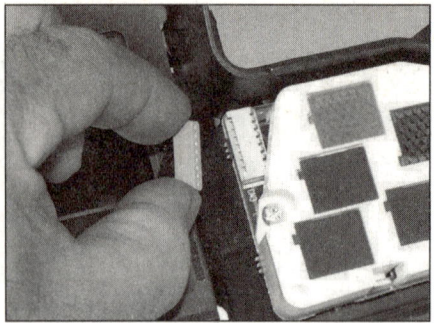

16.33b Disconnect the indicator light board wiring connector

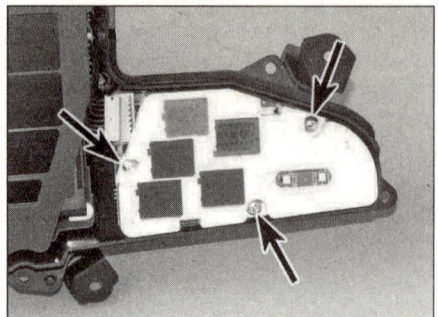

16.34 Undo the screws (arrowed) and remove the light board

29 Installation is the reverse of removal. Do not over-tighten the screws.

Indicator light board

30 Remove the instrument cluster (see Section 15).
31 Pull the headlight adjuster knob off **(see illustration 16.25)**.
32 Undo the screws on the back, then turn the instruments over and lift the front cover off **(see illustrations 16.26a and b)**.
33 Remove the lens cover **(see illustration)**. Disconnect the indicator light board wiring connector **(see illustration)**.
34 Undo the screws and lift the board out of the rear cover **(see illustration)**.
35 Installation is the reverse of removal. Do not over-tighten the screws.

Multi-function button board

36 Remove the instrument cluster (see Section 15).
37 Pull the headlight adjuster knob off **(see illustration 16.25)**.
38 Undo the screws on the back, then turn the instruments over and lift the front cover off **(see illustrations 16.26a and b)**.
39 Disconnect the multi-function board wiring connector **(see illustration)**.
40 Undo the screws and lift the board out of the rear cover **(see illustration)**.
41 Installation is the reverse of removal. Do not over-tighten the screws.

Speed sensor

42 The speed sensor is mounted on the back of the engine, low down between the oil filter and the gearchange linkage arm **(see illustration)**. Access is restricted, but is best from below.
43 Remove the right-hand fairing side panel (see Chapter 7). Disconnect the speed sensor 3-pin black wiring connector inside the boot behind the cylinder head **(see illustration)**. Feed the wiring down to the sensor, noting its routing and freeing it from any ties.
44 Unscrew the sensor mounting bolts and remove the sensor **(see illustration)**. Check the condition of its O-ring and replace it with a new one if it is damaged or there is evidence of leakage around it **(see illustration)**. While the sensor is removed plug the orifice with clean rag.
45 Installation is the reverse of removal, using a new O-ring if necessary.

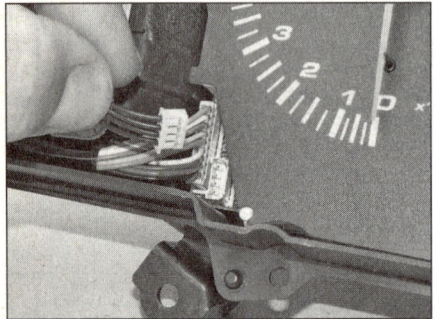

16.39 Disconnect the multi-function board wiring connector

16.40 Undo the screws (arrowed) and remove the multi-function board

16.42 Speed sensor (arrowed)

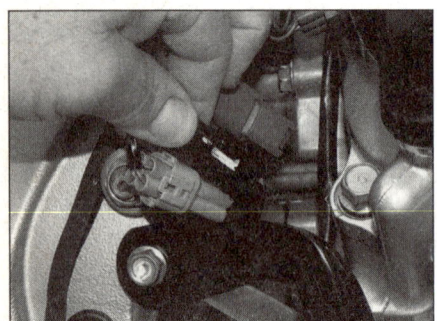

16.43 Draw the boot off the connectors and disconnect the black one

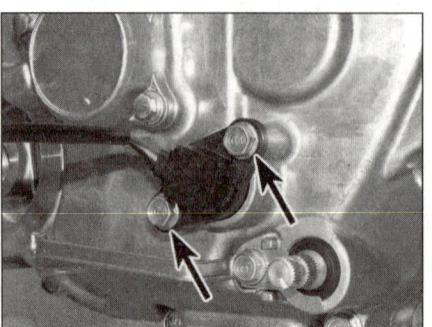

16.44a Speed sensor mounting bolts (arrowed)

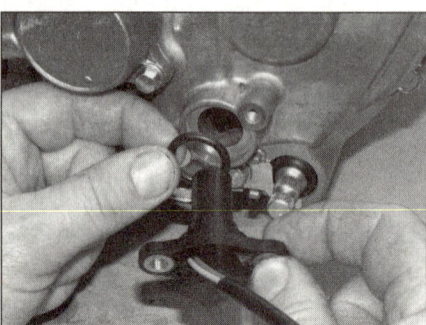

16.44b Replace the O-ring with a new one if necessary

17 Oil pressure switch

Check

1 The oil pressure warning light should come on when the ignition switch is turned ON and go out a few seconds after the engine is started. If the oil pressure warning light does not go out or comes on whilst the engine is running, stop the engine immediately and carry out an oil level check (see *Pre-ride checks*), and if the level is correct, an oil pressure check (see Chapter 2).

2 If the oil pressure warning light does not come on when the ignition is turned ON, but the indicator light board otherwise appears to be functioning, test it as follows.

3 Remove the thermostat housing (see Chapter 3). The oil pressure switch is screwed into the top of the crankcase. Pull the rubber cover off the switch and undo the screw securing the wiring connector **(see illustration)**. With the ignition switched ON, earth (ground) the wire on the crankcase and check that the warning light comes on. If the light comes on, the switch is defective and must be replaced with a new one.

4 If the light still does not come on, check for voltage at the wire terminal with the ignition ON. If there is no voltage present, remove the windshield and inner cowl (see Chapter 7) and check there is continuity in the blue/red wire between the switch and the instrument cluster 20-pin connector.

5 If the warning light does not go out when the engine is started or comes on whilst the engine is running, yet the oil pressure is satisfactory, detach the wire from the oil pressure switch (see above). With the wire detached and the ignition switched ON the light should be out. If it is illuminated, the wire between the switch and instrument cluster is earthed (grounded) at some point. If the wiring is good, the switch must be assumed faulty and replaced with a new one.

Removal

6 The oil pressure switch is screwed into the top of the crankcase. Remove the thermostat housing for access (see Chapter 3). If required for better access refer to Section 29 and disconnect the alternator lead and wiring connector.

7 Pull the rubber cover off the switch, then undo the screw securing the wiring connector **(see illustration 17.3)**.

8 Unscrew and remove the switch.

Installation

9 Apply a suitable sealant to the upper portion of the switch threads near the switch body, leaving the bottom 3 to 4 mm of thread clean. Thread the switch into the crankcase and tighten it to the torque setting specified at the beginning of the Chapter. Attach the wiring connector and secure it with the screw, then fit the rubber cover.

10 Install the thermostat housing (see Chapter 3).

11 Run the engine and check that the switch operates correctly and without leakage.

18 Ignition switch

> **Warning:** To prevent the risk of short circuits, disconnect the battery negative (–) lead before making any ignition switch checks.

Check

1 Remove the left-hand fairing side panel (see Chapter 7). Trace the wiring from the ignition switch and disconnect it at the 4-pin white connector **(see illustration)**.

2 Using an ohmmeter or a continuity tester, check

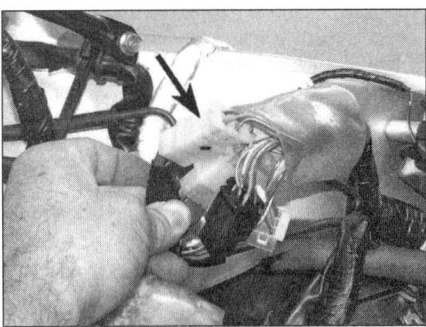

18.1 Ignition switch wiring connector (arrowed)

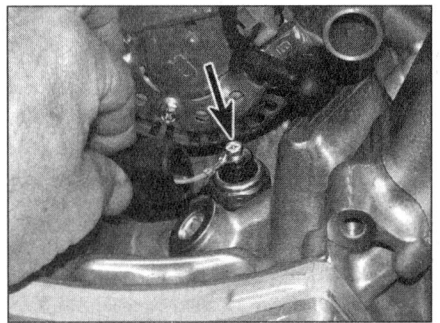

17.3 Pull back the rubber cover then undo the terminal screw (arrowed) and detach the wiring

the continuity of the connector terminal pairs (see the wiring diagrams at the end of this Chapter). Continuity should exist between the terminals connected by a solid line on the diagram when the switch is in the indicated position.

3 If the switch fails any of the tests, replace it with a new one.

Removal

4 Remove left-hand fairing side panel and the fairing (see Chapter 7).

5 Trace the wiring from the ignition switch and disconnect it at the 4-pin white connector **(see illustration 18.1)**. Feed the wiring back to the switch, freeing it from any clips and ties and noting its routing.

6 On models fitted with the HISS immobiliser system, undo the screws securing the receiver around the ignition switch and displace it, noting how it fits **(see illustration)**.

18.7a Ignition switch one-way security bolts (arrowed)

18.7b Slacken the clamp bolt (arrowed) on each side ...

18.6 Undo the screws (arrowed) and displace the HISS receiver

18.7c ... then unscrew the nut and lift the yoke up off the forks

8•16 Electrical system

7 One-way security bolts (which can be done up but not undone using conventional tools) are fitted **(see illustration)** – drive the heads around using a cold chisel. If you can't get to the bolts to do this displace the handlebars from the top yoke (see Chapter 5), then detach the cable and hose guide and free the wiring. Slacken the fork clamp bolts, unscrew the steering stem nut, and move the yoke to a bench **(see illustrations)**.

8 If required separate the contact plate from the bottom of the switch – it is available separately from the main body of the switch.

Installation

9 Installation is the reverse of removal. Tighten the ignition switch bolts to the torque setting specified at the beginning of the Chapter, using new ones if necessary. Also tighten the steering stem nut and then the fork clamp bolts to the specified torque. Make sure the wiring connector is correctly routed and securely connected, and all hoses, cables and wiring are correctly routed. Refer to Chapter 5 for the handlebars if required.

19 Handlebar switches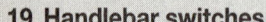

Check

1 Generally speaking, the switches are reliable and trouble-free. Most troubles, when they do occur, are caused by dirty or corroded contacts, but wear and breakage of internal parts is a possibility that should not be overlooked. If breakage does occur, the entire switch and related wiring harness will have to be replaced with a new one, as individual parts are not available.

2 The switches can be checked for continuity using an ohmmeter or a continuity test light. Always disconnect the battery negative (–) lead, which will prevent the possibility of a short circuit, before making the checks.

3 To access the connector for the right-hand switch assembly remove the right-hand fairing

19.3a Right-hand switch wiring connector (arrowed)

side panel (see Chapter 7). To access the connectors for the left-hand switch assembly remove the left-hand fairing side panel (see Chapter 7). Trace the wiring from the switch and disconnect it at the connector(s) **(see illustrations)**.

4 Check for continuity between the terminals of the switch connector with the switch in the various positions (i.e. switch off – no continuity, switch on – continuity) – see the wiring diagram for your model at the end of this Chapter. Continuity should exist between the terminals connected by a solid line on the diagram when the switch is in the indicated position.

5 If the continuity check indicates a problem exists, displace the switch housing (Step 8 or 9), and spray the switch contacts with electrical contact cleaner **(see illustration)** (there is no need to remove the switch completely). If they are accessible, the contacts can be scraped clean with a knife or polished with crocus cloth. If switch components are damaged or broken, it will be obvious when the switch is disassembled.

Removal and installation

6 To access the connector for the right-hand switch assembly remove the right-hand fairing side panel (see Chapter 7). To access the connectors for the left-hand switch assembly remove the left-hand fairing side panel (see Chapter 7). Trace the wiring from the switch and disconnect it at the connector(s) **(see illustration 19.3a or b)**. Feed the wiring back

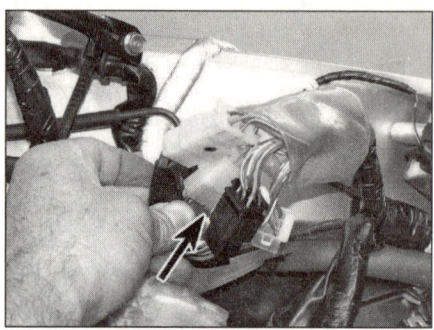

19.3b Left-hand switch wiring connectors (arrowed)

to the switch, freeing it from any clips and ties and noting its routing.

7 If removing the right-hand switch disconnect the wires from the brake light switch **(see illustration 14.2)**. If removing the left-hand switch disconnect the wires from the clutch switch **(see illustration 22.2)**.

8 To remove the left-hand switch housing undo the screws and free the switch from the handlebar by separating the halves **(see illustration)**.

9 To remove the right-hand switch housing refer to Chapter 4; the procedure is included in the throttle cable section.

10 Installation is the reverse of removal. Make sure the locating pin in the switch housing locates in the hole in the handlebar **(see illustration)**.

20 Neutral switch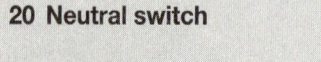

Check

1 The neutral switch light should come whenever the ignition switch is ON and the transmission is in neutral. The switch is located in the right-hand side of the engine.

2 If the light does not come on when it should, but the indicator light board otherwise appears to be functioning, remove the right-hand section of the lower fairing (see Chapter 7). Unscrew the nut and detach

19.5 Open the switch housing and spray the contacts

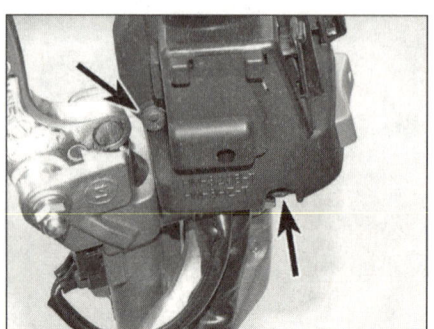

19.8 Left-hand switch housing screws (arrowed)

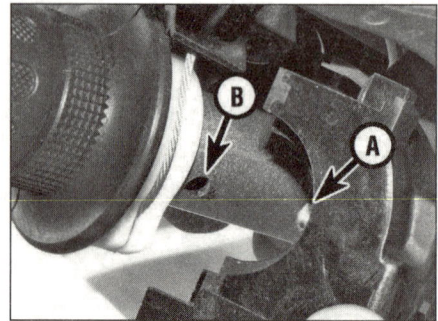

19.10 Locate the pin (A) in the hole (B)

Electrical system 8•17

20.2 Unscrew the nut (arrowed) and detach the wiring connector

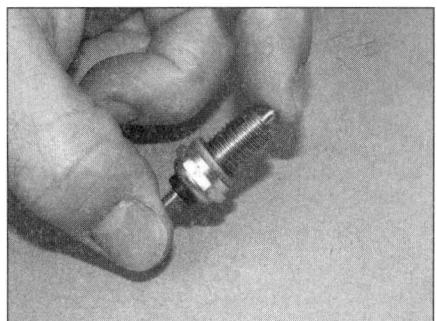
20.3 Make sure the plunger moves in and out smoothly and freely

20.8 Use a new sealing washer

the wiring connector from the switch (see illustration). With the wire detached and the ignition switched ON the light should be out. If it is illuminated, the wire between the switch and instrument cluster is earthed (grounded) at some point. Earth (ground) the wire on the crankcase and check that the warning light comes on. If the light comes on, the wiring circuit is proved good. If not, see Step 4.

3 Check for continuity between the switch terminal and the crankcase. With the transmission in neutral, there should be continuity. With the transmission in gear, there should be no continuity. If not, then remove the switch (see below) and check whether the plunger is bent or damaged, or just stuck (see illustration). Replace the switch with a new one if necessary.

4 If the switch is good, check the other components (clutch switch, sidestand switch, diode block) in the starter safety circuit, and check the wiring between them for continuity, and the connectors for loose or broken connections.

Removal and installation

5 The switch is located in the right-hand side of the engine. Remove the right-hand section of the lower fairing for access (see Chapter 7).
6 Unscrew the nut and detach the wiring connector from the switch (see illustration 20.2).
7 Clean the area around the switch, then unscrew it from the crankcase (see illustration 20.8). Discard the sealing washer as a new one should be used.
8 Install the switch using a new washer and tighten it to the torque setting specified at the beginning of the Chapter (see illustration).
9 Connect the wiring connector and check the operation of the neutral light (see illustration 20.2).

21 Sidestand switch

Check

1 The sidestand switch is mounted on the stand pivot. The switch is part of the starter interlock safety circuit which prevents or stops the engine running if the transmission is in gear whilst the sidestand is down, and prevents the engine from starting if the transmission is in gear unless the sidestand is up and the clutch is pulled in.
2 Remove the left-hand side cover (see Chapter 7). Trace the wiring from the switch and disconnect at the green wiring connector (see illustration).
3 Check the operation of the switch using an ohmmeter or continuity test light. Connect the meter between the terminals on the switch side of the connector. With the sidestand up there should be continuity (zero resistance) between the terminals, and with the stand down there should be no continuity (infinite resistance).
4 If the switch does not perform as expected, it is faulty and must be replaced with a new one.
5 If the switch is good, check the other components (clutch switch, neutral switch, diode block) in the starter safety circuit, and check the wiring between them for continuity, and the connectors for loose or broken connections.

Removal

6 The sidestand switch is mounted on the stand pivot. Remove the left-hand side cover (see Chapter 7), then trace the wiring from the switch and disconnect at the green wiring connector (see illustration 21.2). Feed the wiring back to the switch, freeing it from any clips and ties and noting its routing.
7 Unscrew the switch bolt and remove the switch from the stand, noting how it fits (see illustration). Honda specify that the switch

21.2 Sidestand switch wiring connector (arrowed)

21.7 Sidestand switch mounting bolt (arrowed)

8•18 Electrical system

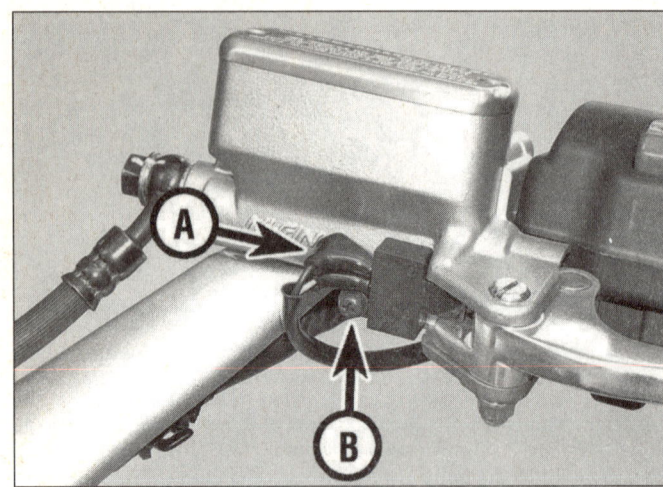

22.2 Clutch switch wiring connectors (A) and mounting screw (B)

23.2 The diode block (arrowed)

bolt be replaced with a new one every time it is disturbed – the new bolt has a locking compound already applied to its threads. However there is nothing to stop you cleaning up the threads on the old bolt and applying a suitable non-permanent thread locking compound on installation.

Installation

8 Fit the new switch onto the sidestand, making sure the pin locates in the hole, and the lug on the stand bracket locates into the cut-out in the switch body. Secure the switch with a new or cleaned and threadlocked bolt and tighten it to the torque setting specified at the beginning of the Chapter **(see illustration 21.7)**.
9 Feed the wiring up to its connector, making sure it is correctly routed and secured by any clips.
10 Reconnect the wiring connector and check the operation of the sidestand switch **(see illustration 21.2)**.

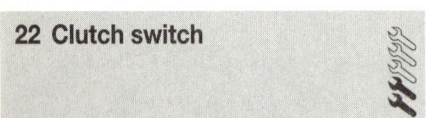

22 Clutch switch

Check

1 The clutch switch is mounted on the front of the master cylinder. The switch is part of the starter interlock safety circuit which prevents or stops the engine running if the transmission is in gear whilst the sidestand is down, and prevents the engine from starting if the transmission is in gear unless the sidestand is up and the clutch lever is pulled in. The switch isn't adjustable.
2 To check the switch, disconnect the wiring connectors from it **(see illustration)**. Connect the probes of an ohmmeter or a continuity tester to the two switch terminals. With the clutch lever pulled in, continuity should be indicated. With the clutch lever out, no continuity (infinite resistance) should be indicated.
3 If the switch is good, check the other components (sidestand switch, neutral switch, diode block) in the starter safety circuit, and check the wiring between them for continuity, and the connectors for loose or broken connections.

Removal and installation

4 The clutch switch is mounted on the front of the master cylinder.
5 Disconnect the wiring connectors from the switch **(see illustration 22.2)**.
6 Undo the single screw securing the switch and remove it, noting how it fits.
7 Installation is the reverse of removal. Make sure the switch is correctly located before tightening its screw.

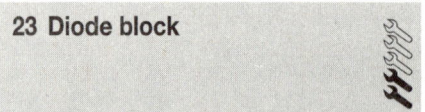

23 Diode block

1 The diode block plugs into a connector in the front fusebox, which is located behind the left-hand side cover **(see illustration 5.1a)**. The diode block contains two diodes which are part of the starter interlock safety circuit that prevents or stops the engine running if the transmission is in gear whilst the sidestand is down, and prevents the engine from starting if the transmission is in gear unless the sidestand is up and the clutch lever is pulled in.
2 Remove the side cover (see Chapter 7), then open the left-hand fusebox lid **(see illustration)**. Pull the diode block out of its socket.
3 Using an ohmmeter or continuity tester, connect the positive (+) probe to one of the outer terminals of the diode block and the negative (−) probe to the middle terminal of the block **(see illustration)**. The diode being tested should show continuity. Now reverse the probes. The diode should show no continuity. Repeat the tests between the other outer terminal and the middle terminal. The same results should be achieved. If it doesn't behave as stated, replace the diode block with a new one.
4 If the diode block is good, push it back into its socket, then check the other components (sidestand switch, neutral switch, clutch switch) in the starter safety circuit, and check the wiring between them for continuity, and the connectors for loose or broken connections.

24 Horn

Check

1 The horn is mounted in the front of the right-hand fairing side panel – remove the inner panel from the side panel for access (see Chapter 7).
2 Disconnect the wiring connectors from the

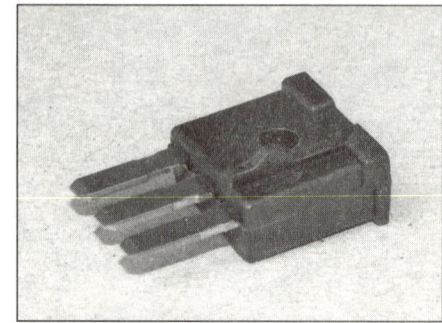

23.3 Test the diode as described

Electrical system 8•19

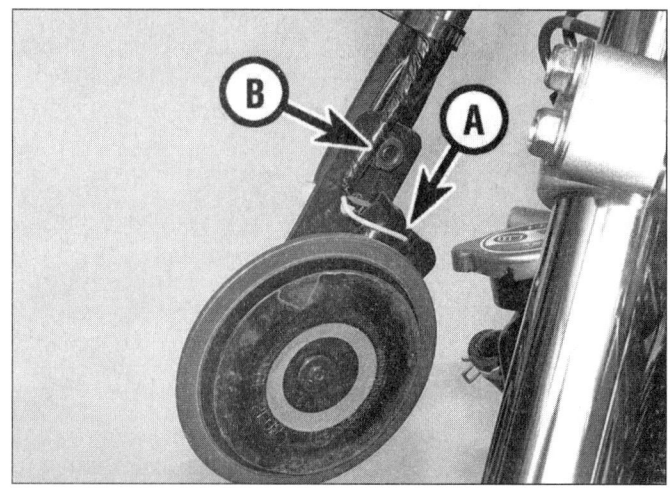

24.2 Disconnect the wiring connectors (A). Horn mounting bolt nut (B)

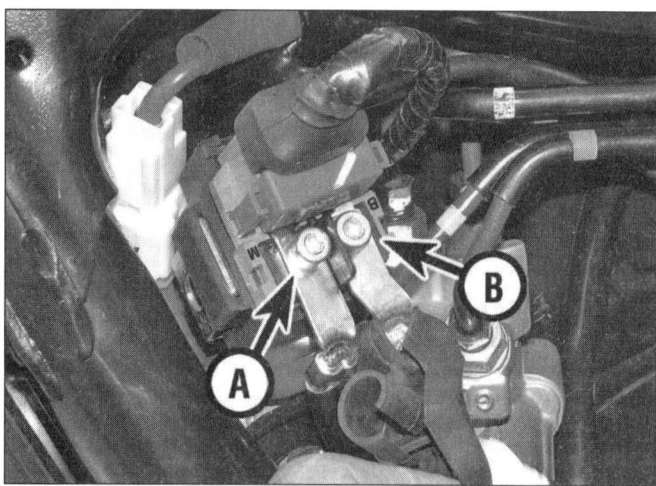

25.3 Lift the rubber cover to access the starter motor lead terminal (A) and battery lead terminal (B)

horn (see illustration). Check them for loose wires. Using two jumper wires, apply voltage from a fully-charged 12V battery directly to the terminals on the horn. If the horn doesn't sound, replace it with a new one.

3 If there is no sound check for voltage at the light green wire connector with the ignition ON and the horn button pressed. If voltage is present, check the green wire for continuity to earth. Refer to electrical system fault finding in Section 2 and to the wiring diagrams at the end of this Chapter.

4 If no voltage was present, check the light green wire for continuity between the horn and the button in the left-hand handlebar switch. Next, with the ignition switch ON, check that there is voltage at the white/green wire to the horn button. If there is, the problem lies between the button and the horn, or in the button itself. Check the button contacts in the switch housing (see Section 19).

5 If there isn't voltage at the white/green wire, check the wire from the switch to the power relay, then all wiring and connectors from the relay to the fusebox, and the ignition switch.

6 If all is good, check the power relay as described in Section 6, Step 7.

Replacement

7 The horn is mounted in the front of the

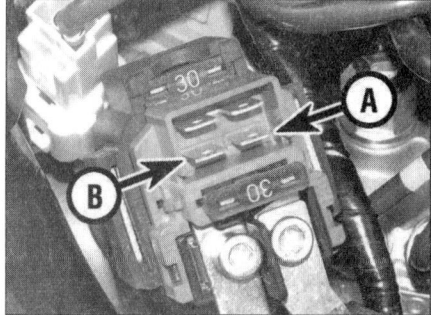

25.5 Connect the battery + lead to terminal A and the – lead to terminal B

right-hand fairing side panel – remove the inner panel from the side panel for access (see Chapter 7).

8 Unplug the wiring connectors from the horn (see illustration 24.2). Unscrew the nut and withdraw the bolt securing the horn.

9 Fit the horn, insert the bolt and tighten the nut. Connect the wiring to the horn. Check that it works. Install the fairing inner panel (see Chapter 7).

25 Starter relay

Check

1 If the starter circuit is faulty, first check the starter fuse (see Section 5).
2 The starter relay is located behind the right-hand side cover – remove the cover (see Chapter 7).
3 Lift the rubber terminal cover and unscrew the bolt securing the starter motor lead, identified by the letter M (the other lead, marked B, is the battery lead) (see illustration); position the lead away from the relay terminal. With the ignition switch ON, the engine kill switch in the RUN position, and the transmission in neutral, press the starter switch. The relay should be heard to click.
4 If the relay doesn't click, switch off the ignition and remove the relay as described below; test it as follows:
5 Set a multimeter to the ohms x 1 scale and connect it across the relay's starter motor and battery lead terminals (see illustration 25.3). There should be no continuity. Using a fully-charged 12 volt battery and two insulated jumper wires, connect the positive (+) terminal of the battery to the yellow/red wire terminal of the relay, and the negative (–) terminal to the green/red wire terminal of the relay (see illustration). At this point the relay should

be heard to click and the multimeter read 0 ohms (continuity). If this is the case the relay is proved good. If the relay does not click when battery voltage is applied and indicates no continuity (infinite resistance) across its terminals, it is faulty and must be replaced with a new one.

6 If the relay is good, check for continuity in the main lead from the battery to the relay. Also check that the terminals and connectors at each end of the lead are tight and corrosion-free.

7 Next check for battery voltage at the yellow/red wire terminal on the relay wiring connector with the ignition ON, the kill switch in the RUN position and the starter button pressed. If there is no voltage, check the wiring between the relay wiring connector and the starter button.

8 If voltage is present, check that there is continuity to earth in the green/red wire with the transmission in neutral (note that there will be a very slight resistance due to the diodes in the starter interlock circuit. If not check the wiring and connectors between the relay, the fusebox and the neutral switch, then if that is good check the switch itself and the diode block.

9 Now shift the transmission into gear, raise the sidestand and pull the clutch lever in and check for continuity to earth again. If there is no continuity, check the clutch switch and sidestand switch as described in the relevant sections of this Chapter. If all components are good, check the wiring between the various components (see the wiring diagrams at the end of this Chapter).

Replacement

10 The starter relay is located behind the right-hand side cover – remove the cover (see Chapter 7).
11 Disconnect the battery terminals, remembering to disconnect the negative (–) terminal first.
12 Disconnect the relay wiring connector

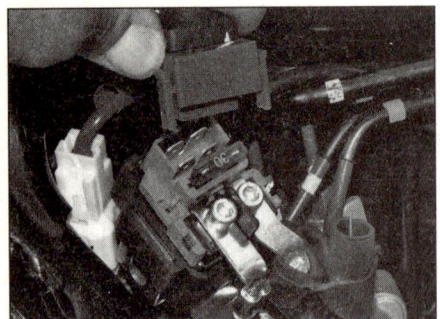

25.12 Disconnect the relay wiring connector

26.3 Unscrew the nut (arrowed)

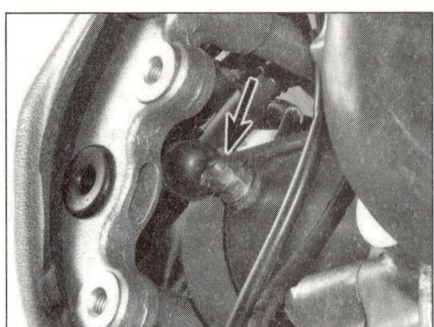

26.4 Pull back the terminal cover then unscrew the nut (arrowed) and detach the lead

(see illustration). Lift the insulating cover and unscrew the bolts securing the starter motor and battery leads to the relay and detach the leads **(see illustration 25.3)**. Remove the relay from its rubber sleeve. If the relay is being replaced with a new one, remove the main fuse and fit it into the new relay **(see illustration 5.1b)**. If you are fitting a new rubber sleeve remove the spare main fuse from its pocket and fit it into the new sleeve **(see illustration 5.3d)**.

13 Installation is the reverse of removal. Connect the red lead from the battery to the terminal marked B and the black lead from the starter motor to the terminal marked M, and make sure the terminal bolts are securely tightened **(see illustration 25.3)**. Do not forget to fit the main fuse into the relay and the spare into the rubber sleeve, if removed. Connect the negative (–) lead last when reconnecting the battery.

26 Starter motor removal and installation

Removal

1 Remove the rear shock absorber (see Chapter 5). The starter motor is mounted on the right-hand side of the crankcase behind the cylinders.
2 Unscrew the right-hand engine protection bar and side mounting bracket nut/bolts and remove the bar and bracket, on 2004-on models also removing the stiffening plate, noting how it fits **(see illustrations 26.11e, d, c, b and a)**.
3 Unscrew the nut on the brake pipe joint assembly **(see illustration)**.
4 Peel back the rubber terminal cover on the starter motor **(see illustration)**. Unscrew the nut and detach the lead.
5 Unscrew the two bolts securing the starter motor to the crankcase, noting the earth lead **(see illustration)** – if you don't have the correct tools to get onto the bolts with only the rear shock removed, also remove the rear wheel (see Chapter 6). Slide the starter motor out, using a screwdriver as leverage if required, and pushing the brake pipe joint assembly stud in so it does not interfere **(see illustrations)**.
6 Remove the O-ring on the end of the starter motor and discard it as a new one must be used **(see illustration 26.7)**.

Installation

7 Fit a new O-ring onto the end of the starter motor, making sure it is seated in its groove **(see illustration)**. Apply a smear of engine oil to the O-ring.
8 Manoeuvre the motor into position and slide it into the crankcase **(see illustration 26.5b)**. Ensure that the starter motor teeth mesh correctly with those of the starter idle/reduction gear. Install the mounting bolts, not forgetting to secure the earth lead, and tighten them **(see illustration 26.5a)**.
9 Connect the starter lead to the motor and secure it with the nut **(see illustration 26.4)**. Fit the rubber cover over the terminal.
10 Fit the brake pipe joint assembly nut **(see illustration 26.3)**.
11 Fit the right-hand engine bracket and engine protection bar, and on 2004-on models the stiffening plate, in that order, and tighten

26.5a Unscrew the two bolts (arrowed), noting the earth lead

26.5b Ease the starter motor out and manoeuvre it back . . .

26.5c . . . pushing the stud in to give better clearance . . .

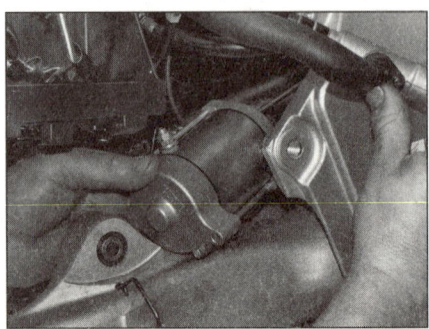

26.5d . . . and remove the starter motor

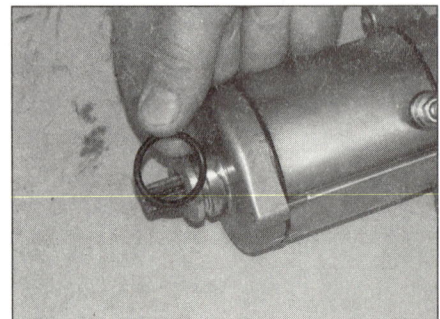

26.7 Fit a new O-ring and lubricate it

Electrical system 8•21

26.11a Fit the bracket and the lower rear bolt . . .

the nut/bolts finger-tight **(see illustrations)**. Tighten the front bolt on the mounting bracket to the torque setting specified at the beginning of the Chapter, then tighten the rear bolt to the specified torque. Tighten the rear bolt on the engine protection bar, then the front bolt, and finally the nut, again to the specified torques.

12 Install the shock absorber (see Chapter 5).

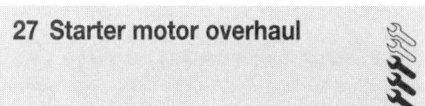

27 Starter motor overhaul

Check

1 Remove the starter motor (see Section 26). Cover the body in some rag and clamp the motor in a soft-jawed vice – do not overtighten it.
2 Using a fully-charged 12 volt battery and two insulated jumper wires, connect the

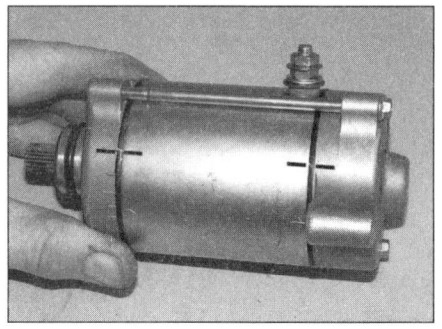

27.4 Note the alignment marks between the housing and the covers or make your own as shown if preferred

27.5b . . . then remove the front cover, noting the sealing ring (arrowed)

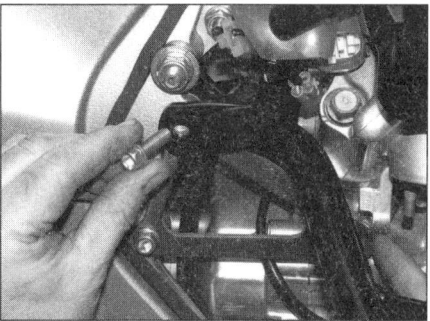

26.11b . . . then fit the engine bar and its rear bolt . . .

26.11d . . . then where fitted locate the stiffening plate and fit the bracket front bolt . . .

positive (+) terminal of the battery to the protruding terminal on the starter motor, and the negative (–) terminal to one of the motor's

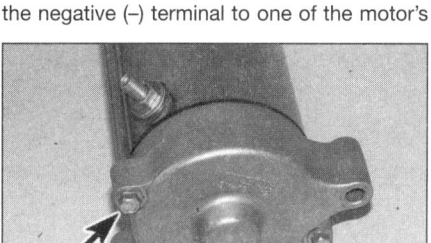

27.5a Unscrew and remove the two bolts (arrowed) . . .

27.5c Remove the tabbed washer . . .

26.11c . . . and front bolt . . .

26.11e . . . and the engine bar lower nut

mounting lugs. At this point the starter motor should spin. If this is the case the motor is proved good, though it is worth disassembling it and checking it if you suspect it of not working properly under load.

Disassembly

3 Remove the starter motor (see Section 26).
4 Note any alignment marks between the main housing and the front and rear covers, or make your own if they aren't clear **(see illustration)**.
5 Unscrew the two long bolts and remove the front cover **(see illustrations)**. Note the sealing ring and remove it if required. Remove the tabbed washer from the cover and slide the insulating washer and shim(s) from the front end of the armature, noting the number of shims and their correct fitted order **(see illustrations)**.

27.5d . . . and the insulating washer and shim(s)

27.6 Remove the rear cover, noting the sealing ring (arrowed)

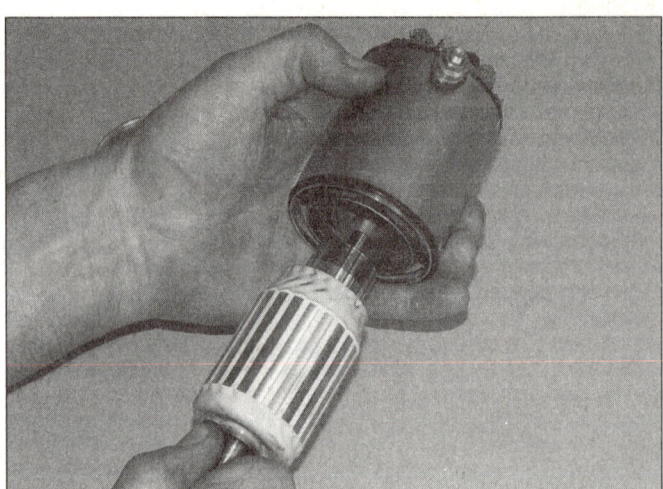

27.7 Withdraw the armature from the housing

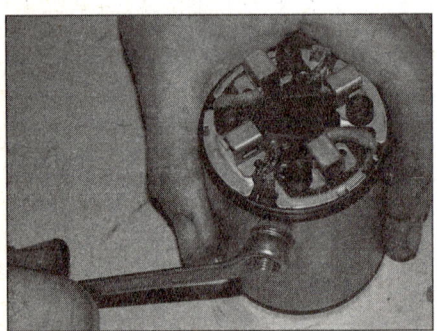

27.9a Unscrew the nut and remove the plain washer and the large and small insulating washers

6 Remove the rear cover **(see illustration)**. Note the sealing ring and remove it if required. Remove the shim(s) from the rear end of the armature noting how many are fitted **(see illustration 27.23a)**.

7 Withdraw the armature from the main housing noting that there will some resistance from the pull of the magnets set in the housing **(see illustration)**.

8 At this stage check for continuity between the terminal bolt and each insulated brush – there should be continuity (zero resistance). Check for continuity between the terminal bolt and the housing – there should be no continuity (infinite resistance).

9 Noting the correct fitted location of each component, unscrew the nut from the terminal bolt and remove the plain washer, the one large and two small insulating washers **(see illustration)**. Remove the brushplate assembly, noting how it locates **(see illustration)**. Remove the O-ring and insulator piece from the terminal bolt, then remove the bolt.

10 Remove the brush piece seat from the housing **(see illustration 27.18a)**.

Inspection

11 The parts of the starter motor that are most likely to require attention are the brushes. Measure the length of each brush and compare the results to the length listed in this Chapter's Specifications **(see illustration)**. If any of the brushes are worn beyond the service limit, fit a new brush set and brushplate. If the brushes are not worn excessively, nor cracked, chipped, or otherwise damaged, they may be reused.

12 Inspect the commutator bars on the armature for scoring, scratches and discoloration. The commutator can be cleaned and polished with crocus cloth, but do not use sandpaper or emery paper. After cleaning, wipe away any residue with a cloth soaked in electrical system cleaner or denatured alcohol.

13 Using an ohmmeter or a continuity test light, check for continuity between the

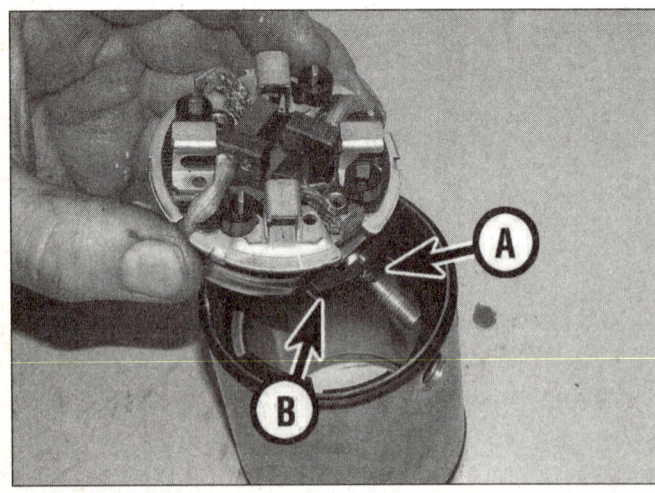

27.9b Remove the brushplate assembly then remove the O-ring (A) and the insulator (B) from the bolt and remove the bolt

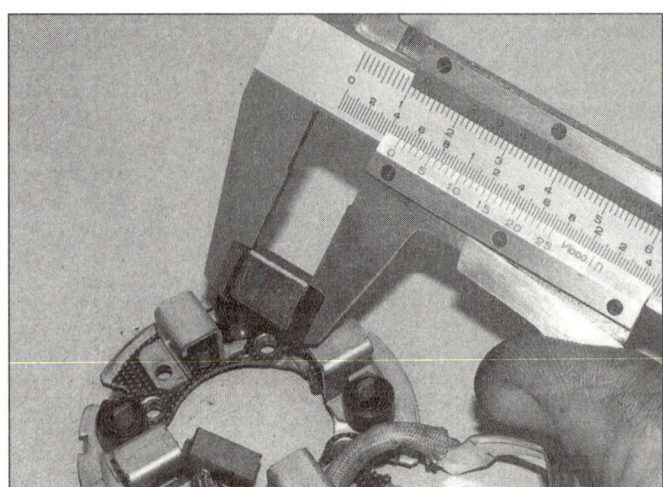

27.11 Measure the length of each brush

Electrical system 8•23

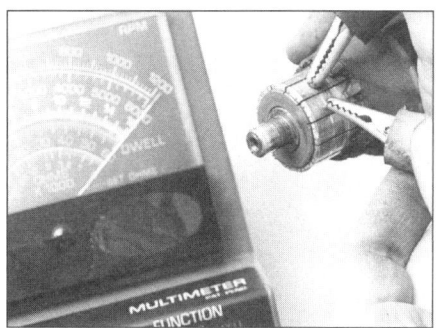

27.13a There should be continuity between the bars . . .

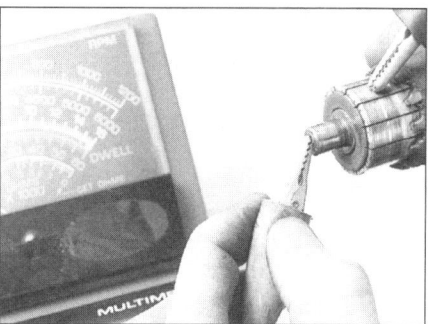

27.13b . . . and no continuity between the bars and the shaft

commutator bars **(see illustration)**. Continuity should exist between each bar and all of the others. Also, check for continuity between the commutator bars and the armature shaft **(see illustration)**. There should be no continuity (infinite resistance) between the commutator and the shaft. If the checks indicate otherwise, the armature is defective and a new starter motor must be obtained – the armature is not available separately.

14 Check the front end of the armature shaft for worn, cracked, chipped and broken teeth. If any are found check the teeth of the idle/reduction gear via the starter orifice in the back of the engine. If the shaft is damaged or worn, a new starter motor must be obtained – the armature is not available separately.

15 Inspect the front and rear covers for signs of cracks or wear. Check the oil seal and the needle bearing in the front cover and the bush in the rear cover for wear and damage **(see illustration)** – the seal, bearing, bush and covers are not listed as being available separately so if necessary a new starter motor must be fitted.

16 Inspect the magnets in the main housing and the housing itself for cracks.

17 Check the housing sealing rings for signs of deformation and deterioration and replace them with new ones if necessary.

Reassembly

18 Fit the brush piece seat into the housing, then locate the insulator piece **(see illustrations)**.

19 Push the brushes all the way back into their housings and locate the brush spring ends onto the tops of the brushes so they are held retracted **(see illustration)**.

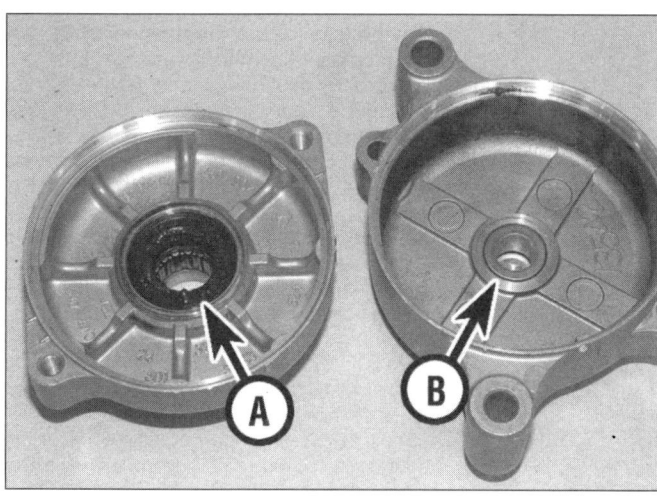

27.15 Check the bearing and seal (A) in the front cover and the bush (B) in the rear cover

27.18a Fit the brush piece seat . . .

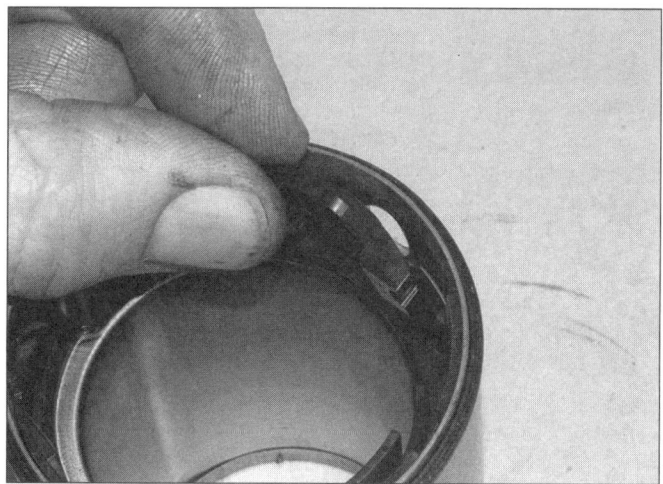

27.18b . . . and the insulator piece

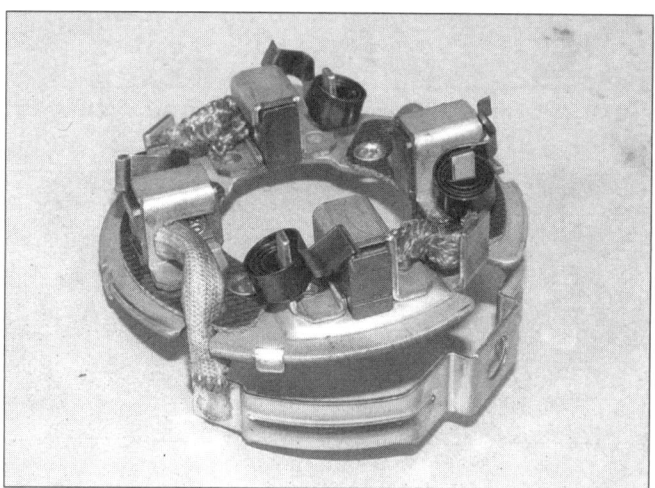

27.19 Fit the brushes into their housings and locate the spring ends as shown to hold the brushes

8•24 Electrical system

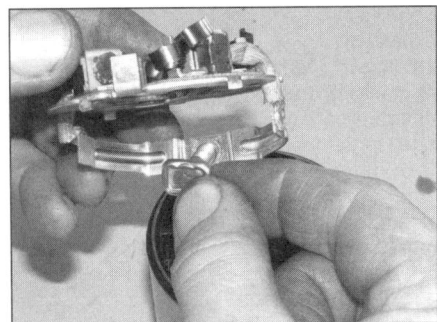

27.20a Fit the bolt into the brush piece ...

27.20b ... then fit the brushplate into the housing, seating the brush piece in its seat ...

27.20c ... and locating the wires in their cut-outs (A) and the tab in its cut-out (B)

20 Fit the terminal bolt through the brush piece, locating its base in the recess **(see illustration)**. Fit the brushplate, locating the brush piece in its seat, the brush wires in their cut-outs and the locating tab in its cut-out **(see illustrations)**.

21 Fit the O-ring down over the bolt and press it into place between the bolt and the cover **(see illustration)**. Slide the small insulating washers onto the terminal bolt, followed by the large insulating washer and the plain washer **(see illustration)**. Fit the nut onto the terminal bolt and tighten it securely.

22 Carefully insert the armature into the housing, keeping a strong hold on both against the draw of the magnets, and keeping the brushplate in position as the commutator fits through it **(see illustration 27.7)**. Lift the brush springs off the brushes, push the brushes against the commutator, and set the spring ends against the brushes **(see illustration)**. Check the armature turns.

23 Fit the shim(s) onto the rear of the armature shaft **(see illustration)**. Fit the sealing ring onto the rear of the housing if removed, using a new one if necessary **(see illustration)**. Apply a smear of grease to the end of the shaft. Fit the rear cover, aligning the marks between the cover and housing.

24 Apply a smear of grease to the front cover oil seal lip. Fit the tabbed washer into the cover so that its teeth are correctly located between the cover ribs **(see illustration 27.5c)**.

25 Fit the sealing ring onto the front of the housing if removed, using a new one if necessary **(see illustration)**. Slide the shim(s) onto the front end of the armature shaft then fit the insulating washer **(see illustration 27.5d)**. Slide the front cover into position, aligning the marks made on removal **(see illustration 27.5b)**.

26 Check the marks made on removal are correctly aligned then fit the long bolts and tighten them **(see illustration)**.

27 Install the starter motor (see Section 26).

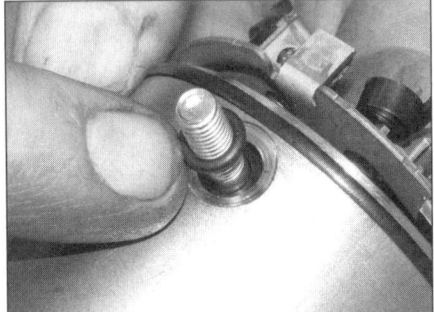

27.21a Fit the O-ring over the bolt and press it into the gap between the bolt and the housing

27.21b Fit the insulating washers, plain washer and the nut

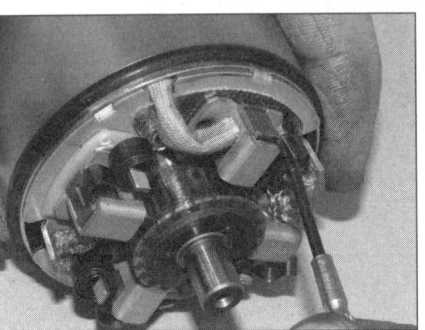

27.22 Seat the brush springs onto the brushes

27.23b Fit the sealing ring (arrowed) if removed, then fit the rear cover

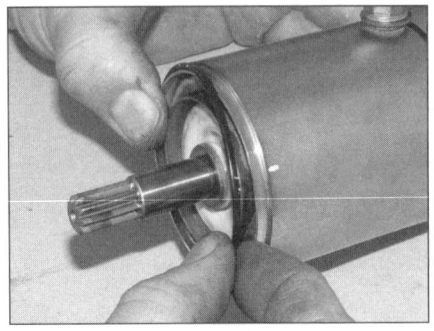

27.25 Fit the sealing ring onto the front of the housing

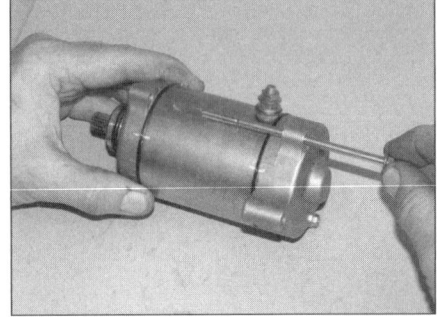

27.26 Fit the long bolts with their O-rings

Electrical system 8•25

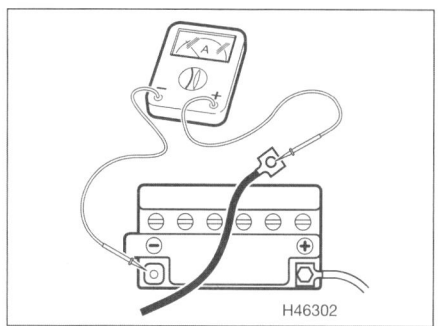

28.5 Checking the charging system leakage rate – connect the meter as shown

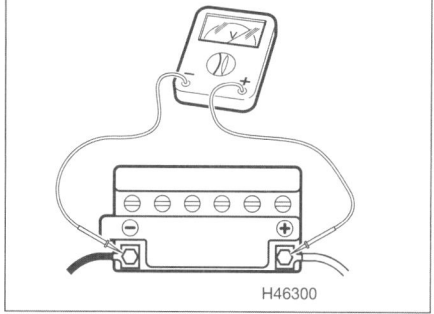

28.9 Checking the charging system output rate – connect the meter as shown

10 Slowly increase the engine speed to 5000 rpm and note the reading obtained. Compare the result with the Specification at the beginning of this Chapter. If the regulated voltage output is outside the specification, check the alternator/regulator/rectifier (see Section 29).

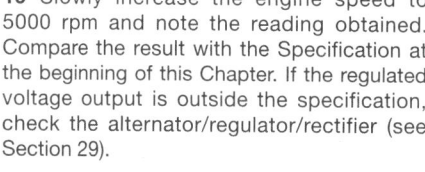 **Clues to a faulty regulator are constantly blowing bulbs, with brightness varying considerably with engine speed, and battery overheating.**

28 Charging system testing

1 If the performance of the charging system is suspect, the system as a whole should be checked first, followed by testing of the individual components. **Note:** *Before beginning the checks, make sure the battery is fully charged and that all system connections are clean and tight.*
2 Checking the output of the charging system and the performance of the various components within the charging system requires the use of a multimeter (with voltage, current, resistance checking facilities). If a multimeter is not available, the job of checking the charging system should be left to a Honda dealer.
3 When making the checks, follow the procedures carefully to prevent incorrect connections or short circuits resulting in irreparable damage to electrical system components.

Leakage test

Caution: *Always connect an ammeter in series, never in parallel with the battery, otherwise it will be damaged. Do not turn the ignition ON or operate the starter motor when the ammeter is connected – a sudden surge in current will blow the meter's fuse.*

4 Ensure the ignition is OFF. Remove the right-hand side cover (see Chapter 7). Disconnect the battery negative (-) lead (see Section 3).
5 Set the multimeter to the Amps function and connect its negative (-) probe to the battery negative (-) terminal, and positive (+) probe to the disconnected negative (-) lead **(see illustration)**. Always set the meter to a high amps range initially and then bring it down to the mA (milli Amps) range; if there is a high current flow in the circuit it may blow the meter's fuse.
6 Battery current leakage should not exceed the maximum limit (see Specifications). If a higher leakage rate is shown there is a short circuit in the wiring, although if an after-market alarm is fitted its current draw should be taken into account. Disconnect the meter and reconnect the battery negative (-) lead.
7 If leakage is indicated, refer to Wiring Diagrams at the end of this Chapter to systematically disconnect individual electrical components and repeat the test until the source is identified.

Output test

8 Remove the right-hand side cover (see Chapter 7). Start the engine and warm it up.
9 To check the regulated (DC) voltage output, allow the engine to idle with the headlight main beam (HI) turned ON. Connect a multimeter set to the 0-20 volts DC scale across the terminals of the battery with the positive (+) meter probe to battery positive (+) terminal and the negative (-) meter probe to battery negative (-) terminal (see Section 3) **(see illustration)**.

29 Alternator/regulator/rectifier

Check

Power check

1 Ensure the ignition is OFF. Remove the right-hand side cover (see Chapter 7). Disconnect the battery negative (-) lead (see Section 3).
2 Remove the thermostat housing (see Chapter 3).
3 Peel back the rubber terminal cover on the alternator **(see illustration)**. Unscrew the nut and detach the lead. Disconnect the wiring connector. Reconnect the battery negative (-) lead (see Section 3).
4 Connect the positive (+) probe of a voltmeter to the alternator lead and touch the negative probe to the engine. There should be battery voltage at all times (i.e. ignition switch OFF).
5 Turn the ignition ON, and make sure the kill switch is set to RUN. Connect the positive (+) probe of the voltmeter to the wire terminal in the connector and touch the negative probe to the engine. There should be battery voltage.

Brushes and slip rings

6 Remove the alternator (see Steps 13 to 17). Remove the cover and brush holder (Steps 19 and 20).
7 Remove the cover from the brush holder **(see illustration)**. Inspect the holder for any signs of damage. Check the brush lengths and replace the brush assembly with a new one if the brushes are worn to the wear indicators **(see illustration)**.

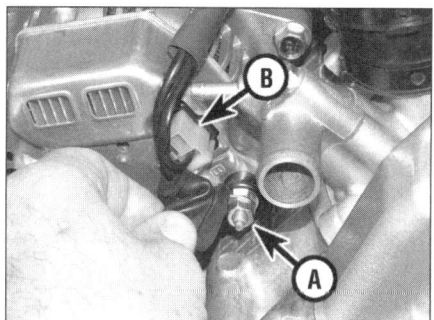

29.3 Pull the rubber cover back then unscrew the nut (A) and detach the lead, and disconnect the wiring connector (B)

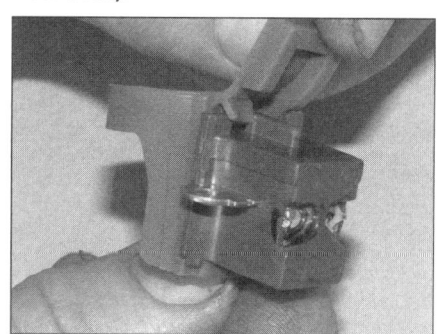

29.7a Remove the rubber cover . . .

29.7b . . . and check the brushes

29.8 Clean the slip rings (arrowed) and check them for wear and damage

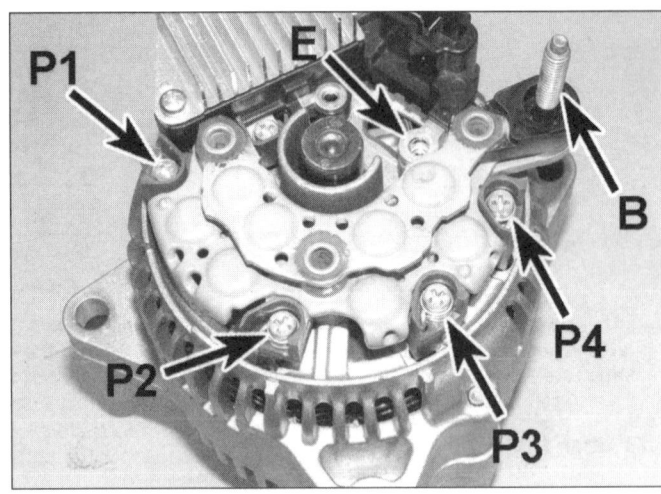

29.11 Test the rectifier by connecting between the terminals as stated and shown

8 Clean the slip rings with a rag moistened with some solvent and check them for wear and damage **(see illustration)**. If required remove the rotor from the alternator housing (Step 23), then measure the diameter of each slip ring. If they are worn below the limit specified replace the rotor with a new one.

Rotor and stator coils

9 Clean the slip rings with a rag moistened with some solvent **(see illustration 29.8)**. Measure the rotor coil resistance between the slip rings – it should be as specified at the beginning of the Chapter. If not, replace the rotor with a new one (Step 23). Check for continuity between each slip ring and the end of the shaft. There should be no continuity (infinite resistance). If there is continuity, replace the rotor with a new one.

10 Measure the stator coil resistance between each pair of terminals on the stator, taking six readings in all, and compare the readings to that specified at the beginning of the Chapter. Check for continuity between each terminal and the alternator housing. There should be no continuity (infinite resistance).

Replace the alternator with a new one if necessary.

Rectifier

11 To test the rectifier, use a multimeter set to the ohms x 1 scale to check its diodes, connecting between the terminal pairs given in the list below and as shown **(see illustration)**. Each diode is checked in both directions by reversing the meter probes. Continuity should exist in one direction only; if no continuity is shown in both directions, or continuity is shown if both directions, the diode is faulty and the rectifier must be replaced with a new one.

B to P1	P1 to B
B to P2	P2 to B
B to P3	P3 to B
B to P4	P4 to B
E to P1	P1 to E
E to P2	P2 to E
E to P3	P3 to E
E to P4	P4 to E

Regulator

12 There are no specific tests for the regulator. If the charging system output test in Section 28 shows a higher voltage output

than specified, and bulb brightness varies and bulbs blow, the regulator is faulty and must be replaced with a new one.

Removal

13 Ensure the ignition is OFF. Remove the right-hand side cover (see Chapter 7). Disconnect the battery negative (-) lead (see Section 3).
14 Remove the thermostat housing (see Chapter 3).
15 Remove the oil pressure switch (see Section 17).
16 Peel back the rubber terminal cover on the alternator **(see illustration 29.3)**. Unscrew the nut and detach the lead. Disconnect the wiring connector.
17 Unscrew the three bolts – you need a universal drive on a socket extension to get to the lower bolt **(see illustrations)**. Draw the alternator out and remove it **(see illustration)**. Discard the O-ring as a new one must be used.
18 To remove the alternator driven gear assembly refer to Chapter 2.

Disassembly

19 To access the brush holder, regulator and

29.17a Unscrew the bolts (arrowed) . . .

29.17b . . . using a universal drive to unscrew the lower bolt . . .

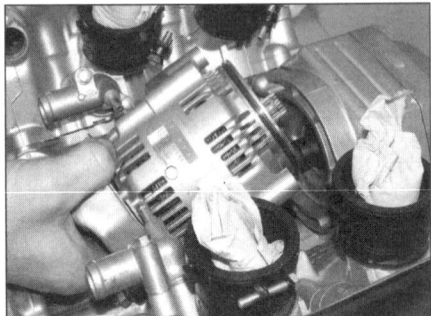

29.17c . . . and remove the alternator as shown

Electrical system 8•27

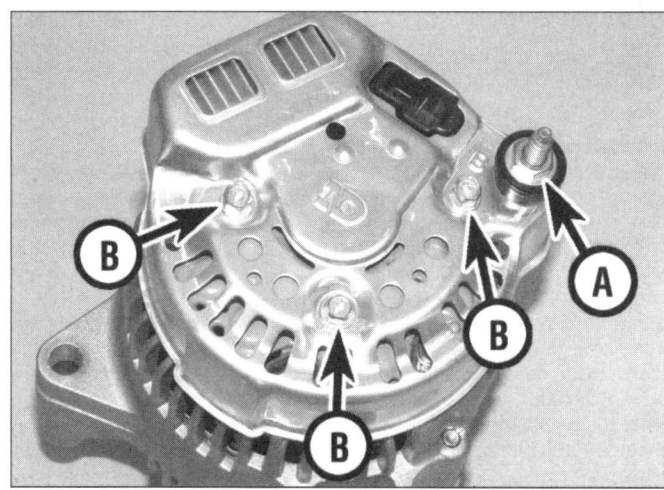

29.19 Unscrew the nut (A) and remove the insulator beneath it, then unscrew the bolts (B) and remove the cover

29.20 Brush holder screws (arrowed)

rectifier, unscrew the terminal nut and remove the insulator **(see illustration)**. Unscrew the three bolts and remove the front cover.

20 To remove the brush holder undo the screws and remove the holder, noting how it fits **(see illustration)**.

21 To remove the regulator first remove the brush holder. Undo the screws securing the regulator and lift it off **(see illustration)**.

22 To remove the rectifier, first remove the regulator. Undo the four screws securing the wires and bend them straight **(see illustration)**. Undo the remaining screw and carefully lift the rectifier up off the wires.

23 To access the rotor and bearings, first remove the brush holder (Steps 19 and 20). Unscrew the nuts securing the rear cover and remove the cover **(see illustration)**. Draw the rotor out of the main housing/stator assembly.

24 Check the condition of the alternator shaft bearings – one in the rear cover and one on the shaft. Also check the oil seal in the rear cover. Refer to *Tools and Workshop Tips* in the Reference Section for information on bearing checks.

25 To remove the bearing in the rear cover undo the four screws and remove the bearing cover. Lever the oil seal out – a new one must be fitted. Drive the bearing out using a socket. Remove the spacer. Check the bearing housing for damage. Fit the spacer, then drive the new bearing in using a driver or socket that bears only on the outer race. Fit the retainer and tighten the screws. Press a new seal into the cover with its marked side facing out.

26 To remove the bearing on the shaft use a puller, locating the legs behind the outer race, and pull the insulator bush off with it. Remove the retainer ring from the bearing. Drive the new bearing onto the shaft using a suitable tube that bears on the inner race, and take great care to support the shaft properly and not damage the slip rings. Fit the retainer into its grove and fit the insulator bush.

27 Reassemble the alternator in a reverse of the above procedure. Smear the rear cover oil seal lips with grease. If the rectifier

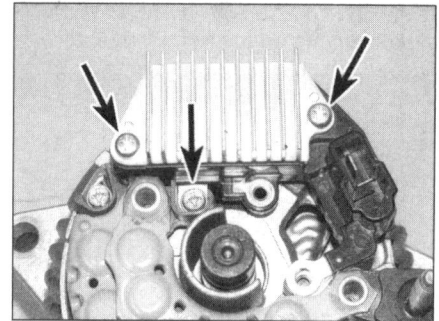

29.21 Regulator screws (arrowed)

was removed make sure all four wires locate correctly in their holes and are secured by the screws.

Installation

28 If removed install the alternator driven gear assembly (see Chapter 2).

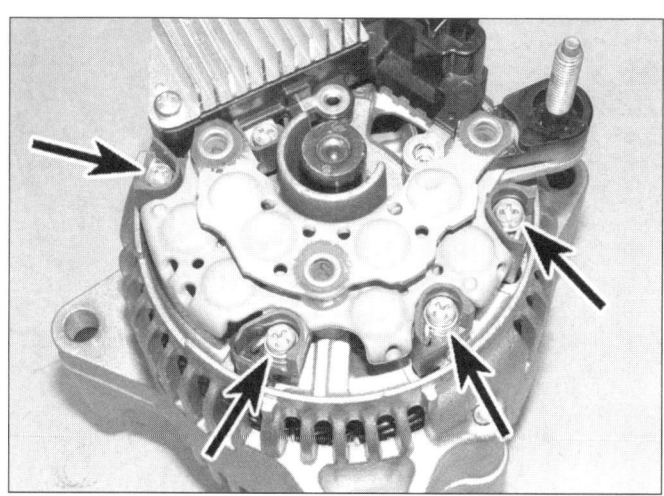

29.22 Rectifier screws (arrowed)

29.23 Rear cover nuts (arrowed)

8•28 Electrical system

29 Fit a new O-ring into the groove in the rear cover and smear it with oil. Install the alternator, aligning the shaft splines, and tighten the bolts securely **(see illustrations 29.17c, b and a)**.
30 Connect the wiring connector and fit the lead on the terminal, making sure the nut is secure **(see illustration 29.3)**.
31 Install the oil pressure switch (Section 17).
32 Install the thermostat housing (see Chapter 3). Connect the battery.

30 Windshield height adjuster mechanism

Note: *The windshield has two base-setting heights built into the mounting bracket assembly, one low, one high. From either of these positions the electrical system can be used through its range. Refer to Chapter 7, Section 10 to check and adjust the base setting of the windshield if an optimum position cannot be obtained through the electric adjuster.*

Check

1 The height adjuster motor has an in-built circuit breaker – if the mechanism stops working completely during adjustment wait a few minutes and try again. If the adjuster still does not work check the screen fuse (see Section 5). If that is good remove the fairing (see Chapter 7). Disconnect the adjuster motor green wiring connector and check it for loose or broken wires and corroded or broken terminals **(see illustration)**. Note that if the screen moves up but not down then your tests can be restricted to the relevant circuit.
2 Connect a 12 volt battery to the terminals on the motor side of the connector – if the motor does not work replace it with a new one.
3 If the motor worked refer to Section 19, Step 3 and disconnect the white wiring connector for the left-hand switch housing. Also disconnect the adjuster motor grey wiring connector **(see illustration)**. Check both connectors for loose or broken wires and corroded or broken terminals. Check for continuity in the light green/blue wire and the light green/yellow wire between the connectors. There should be continuity – if not repair the wiring. If the wiring is good check the switch itself (see Section 19).
4 If all is good disconnect the wiring connector from the screen UP and DOWN relays **(see illustration)**. Check for continuity in the pink/yellow and pink/blue wires between the connectors. There should be continuity – if not repair the wiring.
5 If all is good check for continuity in the orange/black and orange/blue wires between the relay and motor green connectors. There should be continuity – if not repair the wiring.
6 If all is good disconnect the switch housing black wiring connector (see Section 19), and check for battery voltage at the pink wire terminal on the loom side of the connector with the ignition ON. If no voltage is indicated check the wiring and connectors between the connector and the screen main relay, located behind the left-hand side cover **(see illustration)** – remove the cover for access

30.1 Disconnect the green wiring connector (arrowed)

30.3 Disconnect the grey wiring connector (arrowed)

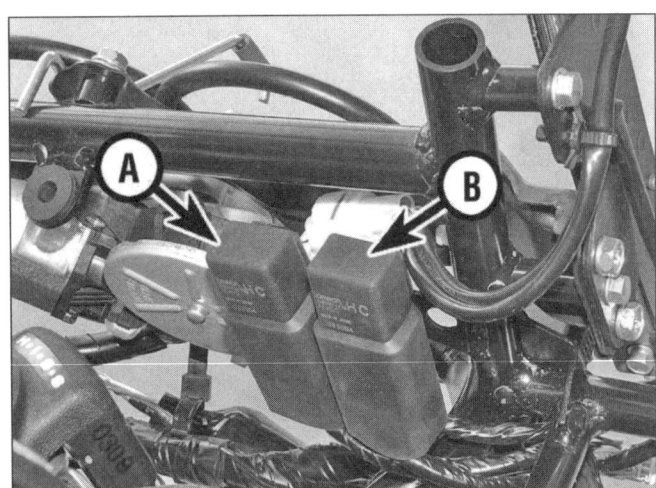

30.4 Screen UP relay (A), screen DOWN relay (B)

30.6 Screen main relay (arrowed)

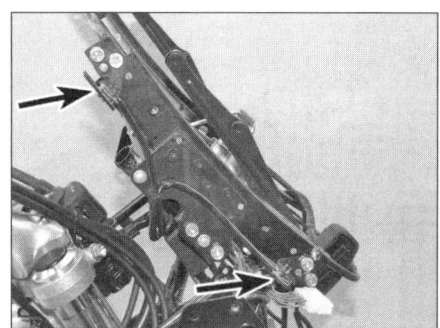

30.9 Check the switches (arrowed) for damage

(see Chapter 7). If they are good check the main relay (see Step 8).

7 If all is good check for continuity to earth in the green wire from the UP and DOWN relay connectors. If continuity exists the relay could be faulty – the best way to check is by substituting with the other one. If the fault transfers to the other circuit the relay is confirmed faulty.

8 To check the main relay displace it from its bracket and disconnect the wiring connector **(see illustration 30.6)**. Set a multimeter to the ohms x 1 scale and connect it across the relay's pink and pink/blue wire terminals **(see illustration 6.3b)**. There should be no continuity (infinite resistance). If there is the relay is faulty. Using a fully-charged 12 volt battery and two insulated jumper wires, connect the positive (+) terminal of the battery to the red/black wire terminal on the relay, and the negative (–) terminal to the green wire terminal on the relay. At this point the relay should be heard to click and the multimeter read 0 ohms (continuity). If this is the case the relay is proved good. If the relay does not click when battery voltage is applied and still indicates no continuity (infinite resistance) across its terminals, it is faulty and must be replaced with a new one.

9 Check the UP and DOWN switches for damage to the contacts and for broken wires **(see illustration)**. To check the switches, disconnect the grey wiring connector and check for continuity in the pink/yellow and light green/yellow wire terminals on the assembly side of the connector for the UP switch and the pink/blue and light green/blue wire terminals for the down switch – each switch should show no continuity with the screen in its fully up or fully down position according to the switch being tested. If you need to move the screen connect the battery to the green connector wire terminals as in Step 2.

Removal and installation

10 Remove the fairing (see Chapter 7).
11 Disconnect the green and grey wiring connectors **(see illustrations 30.1 and 30.3)**.
12 Unscrew the bolts securing the complete screen adjuster assembly to the main front bracket and remove it.
13 Installation is the reverse of removal.

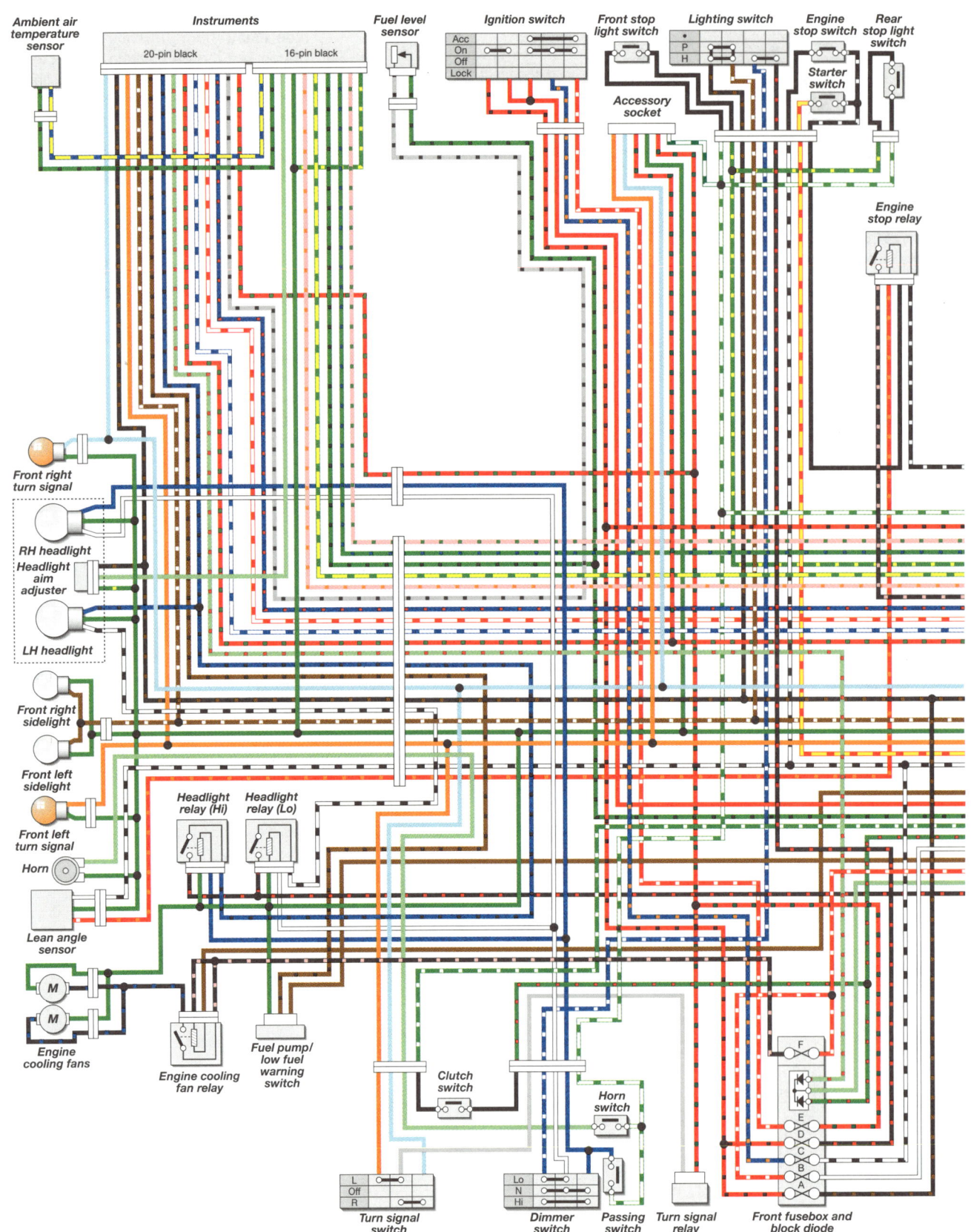

Europe ST1300-2 and ST1300-3

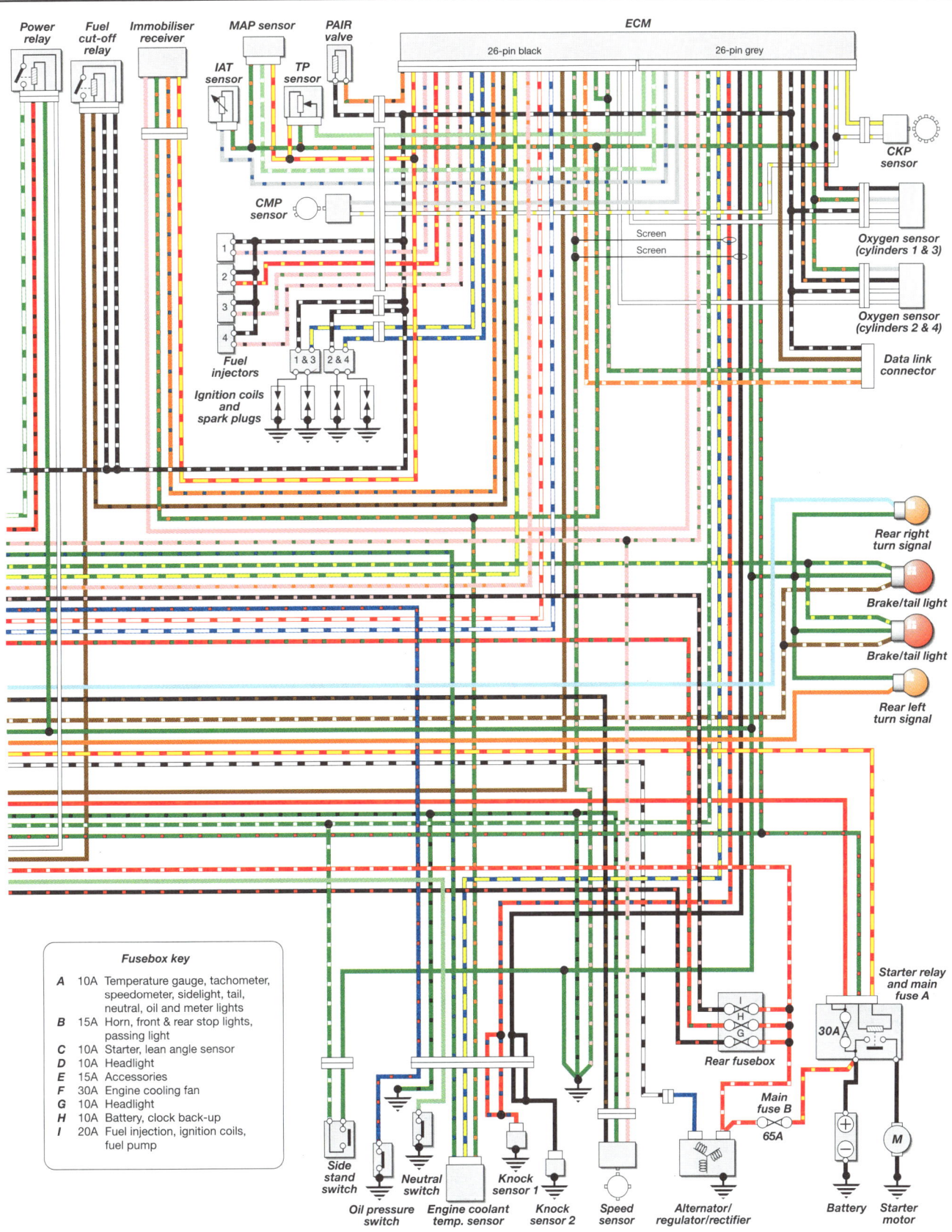

Wiring diagrams 8•31

Europe ST1300-2 and ST1300-3

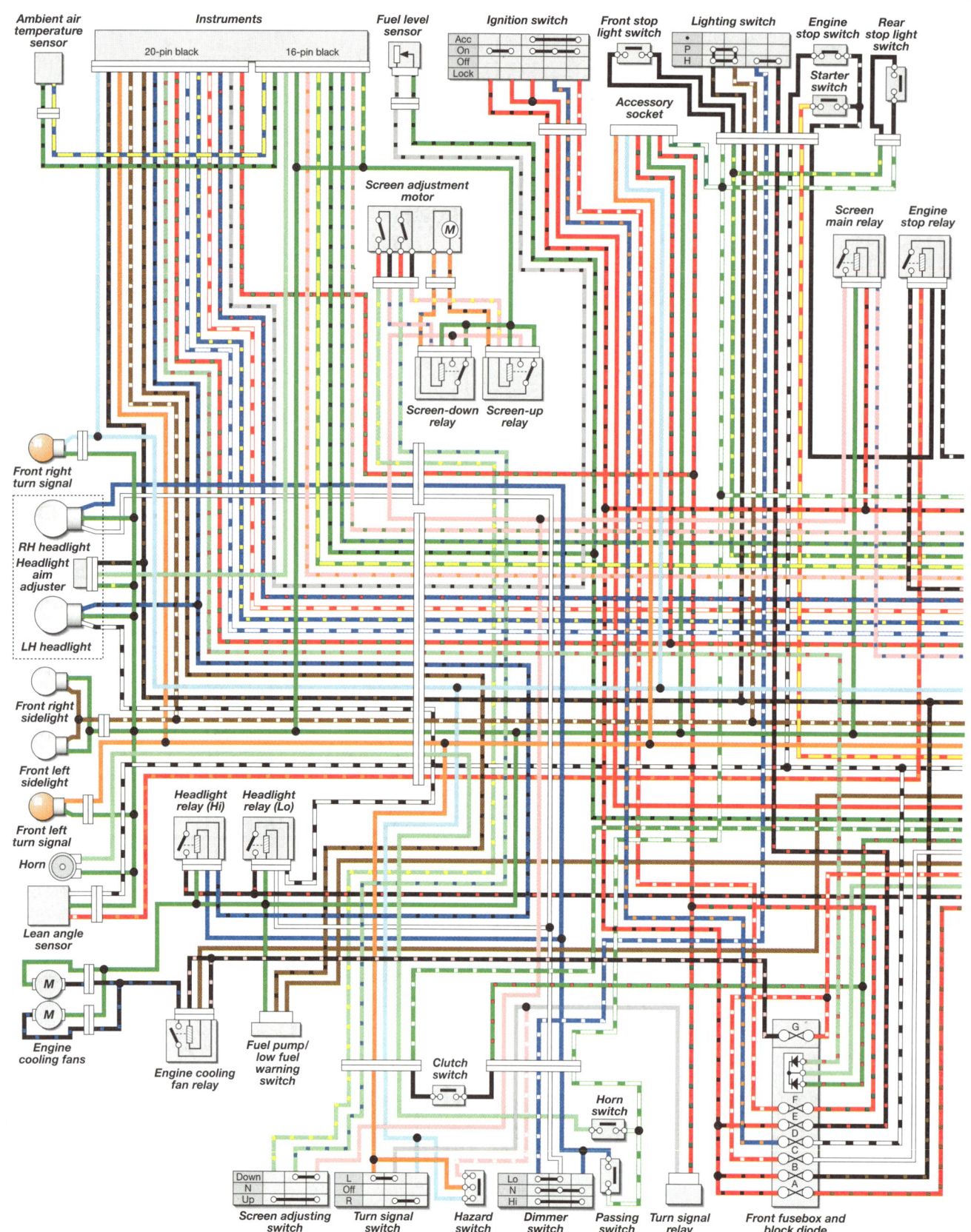

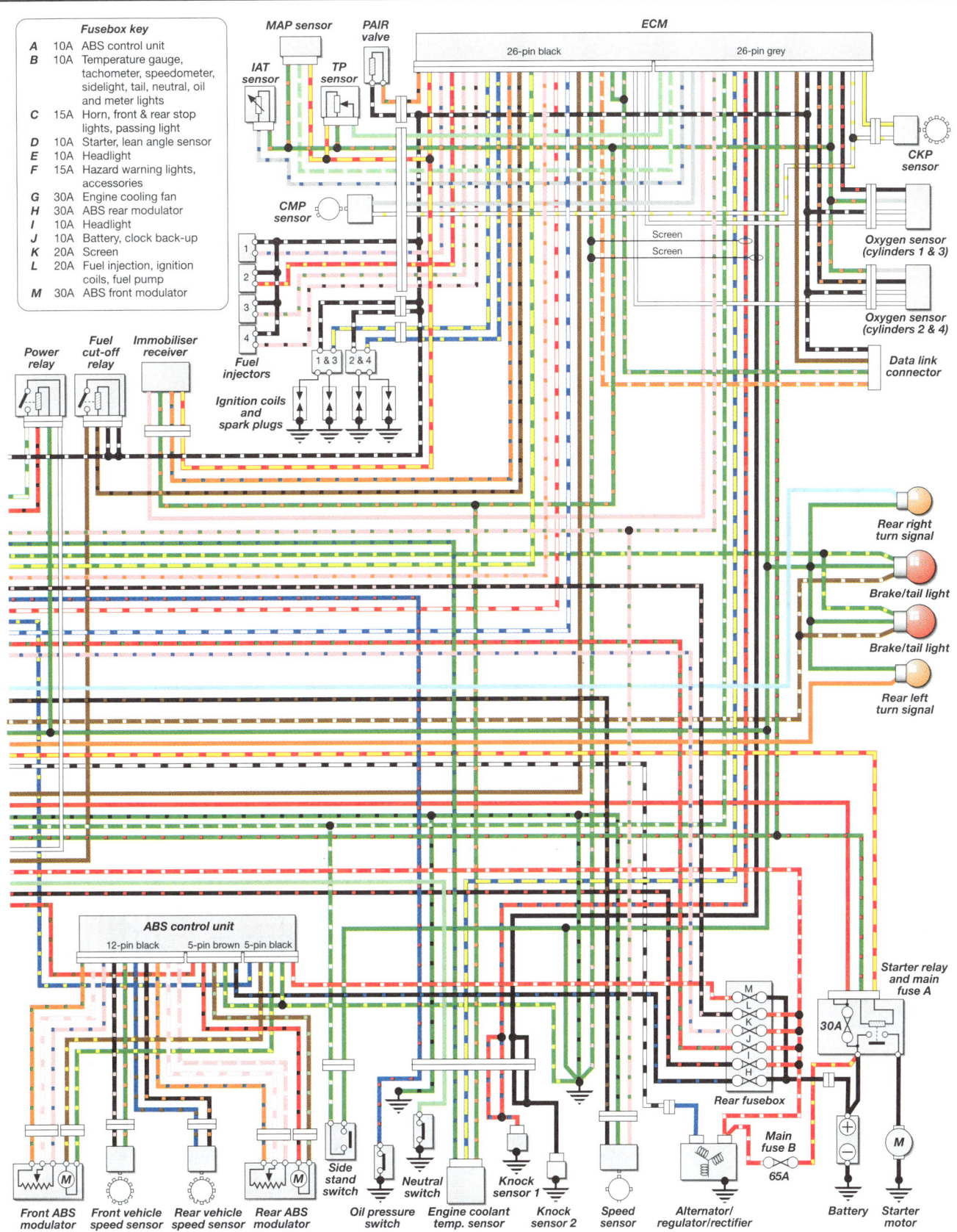

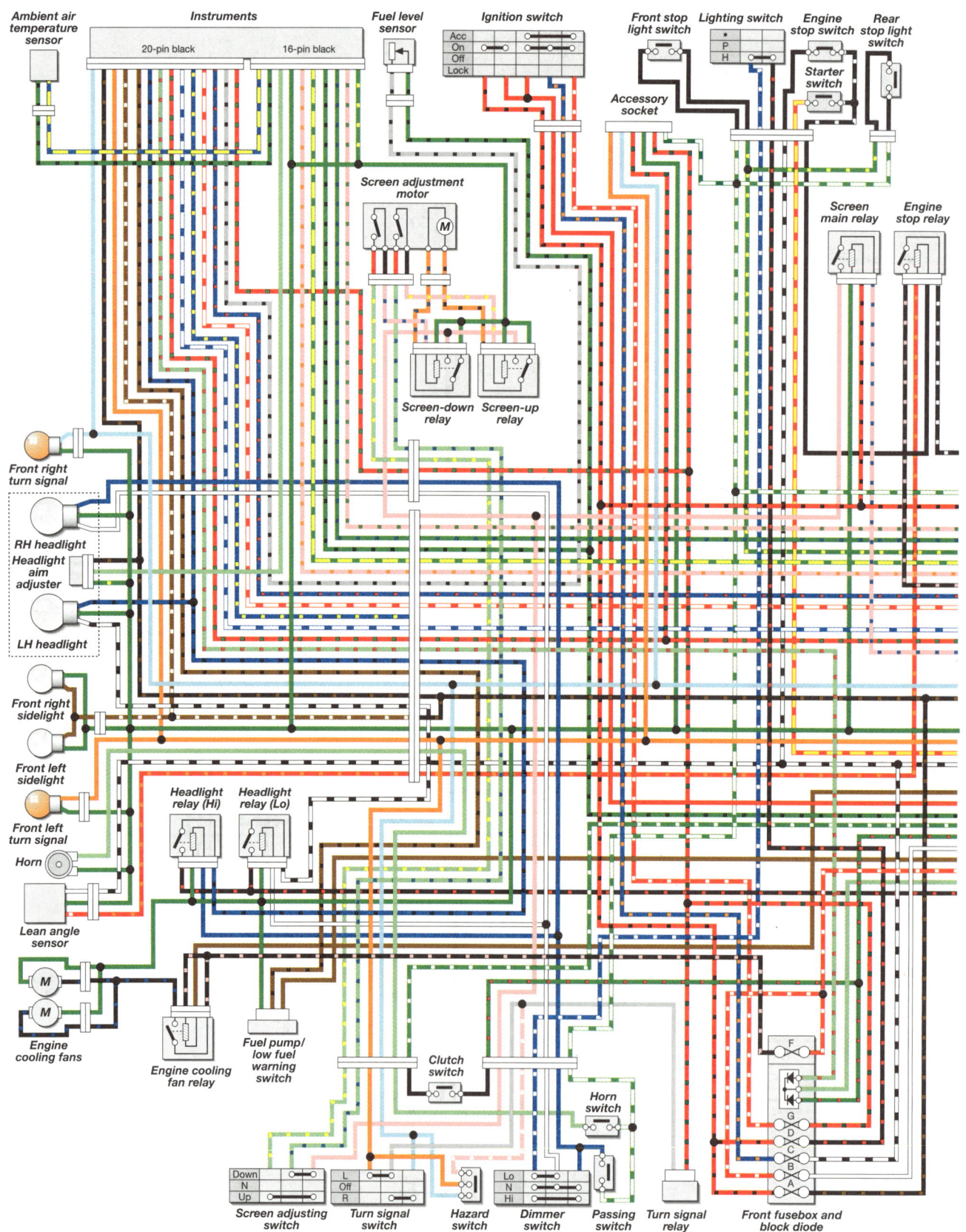

Wiring diagrams

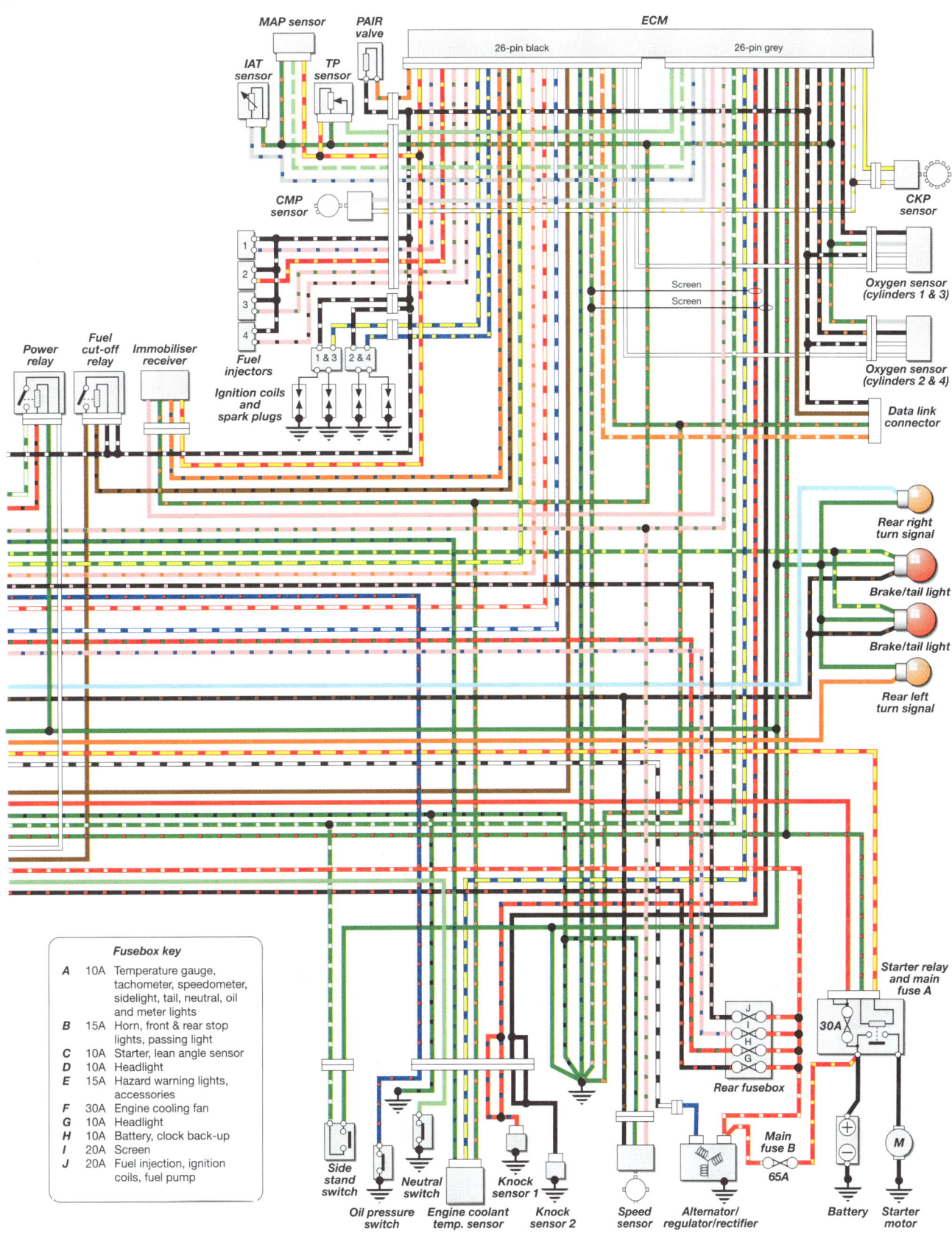

Europe ST1300-4 onwards

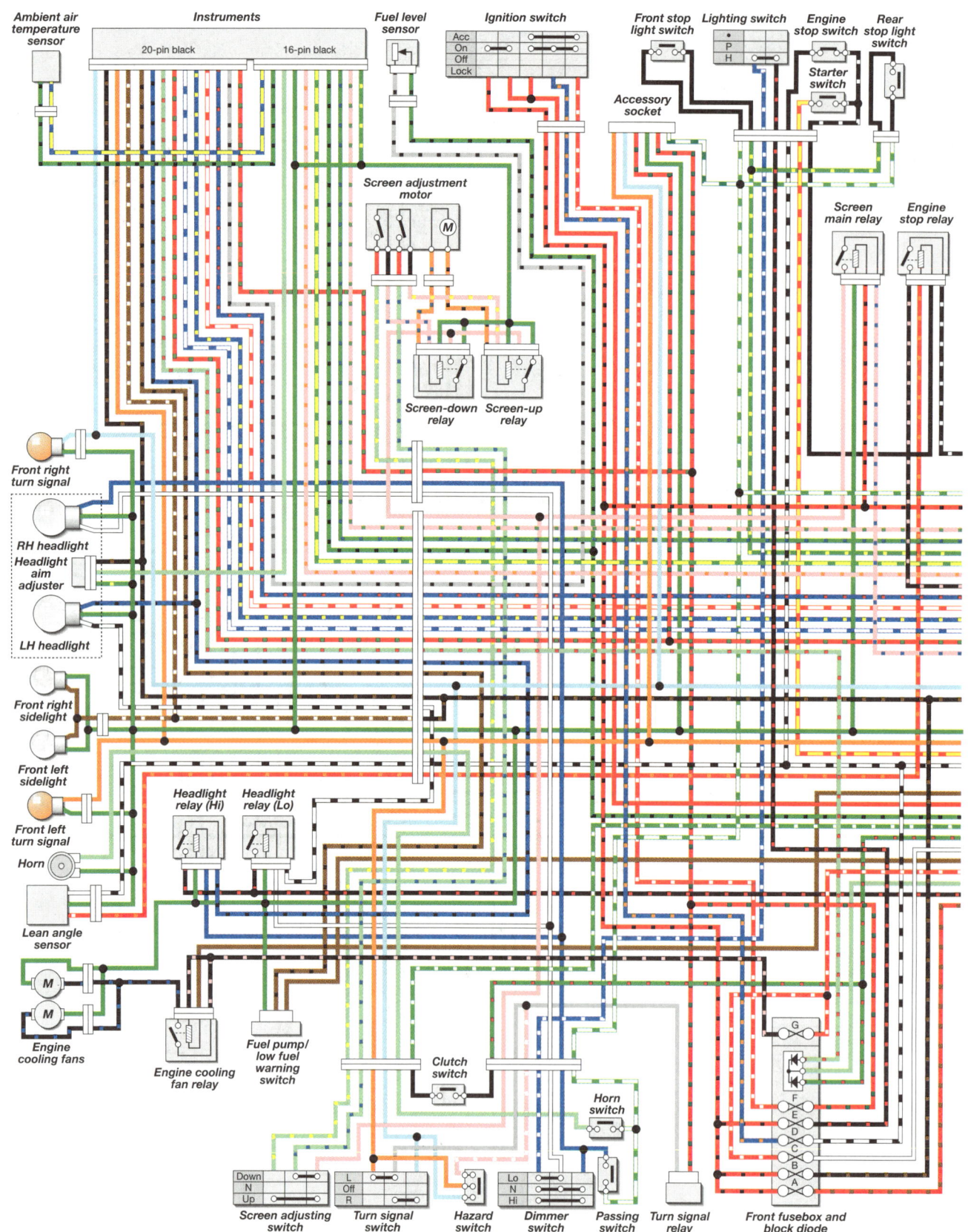

8•36 Wiring diagrams

Europe ST1300A-4 onwards

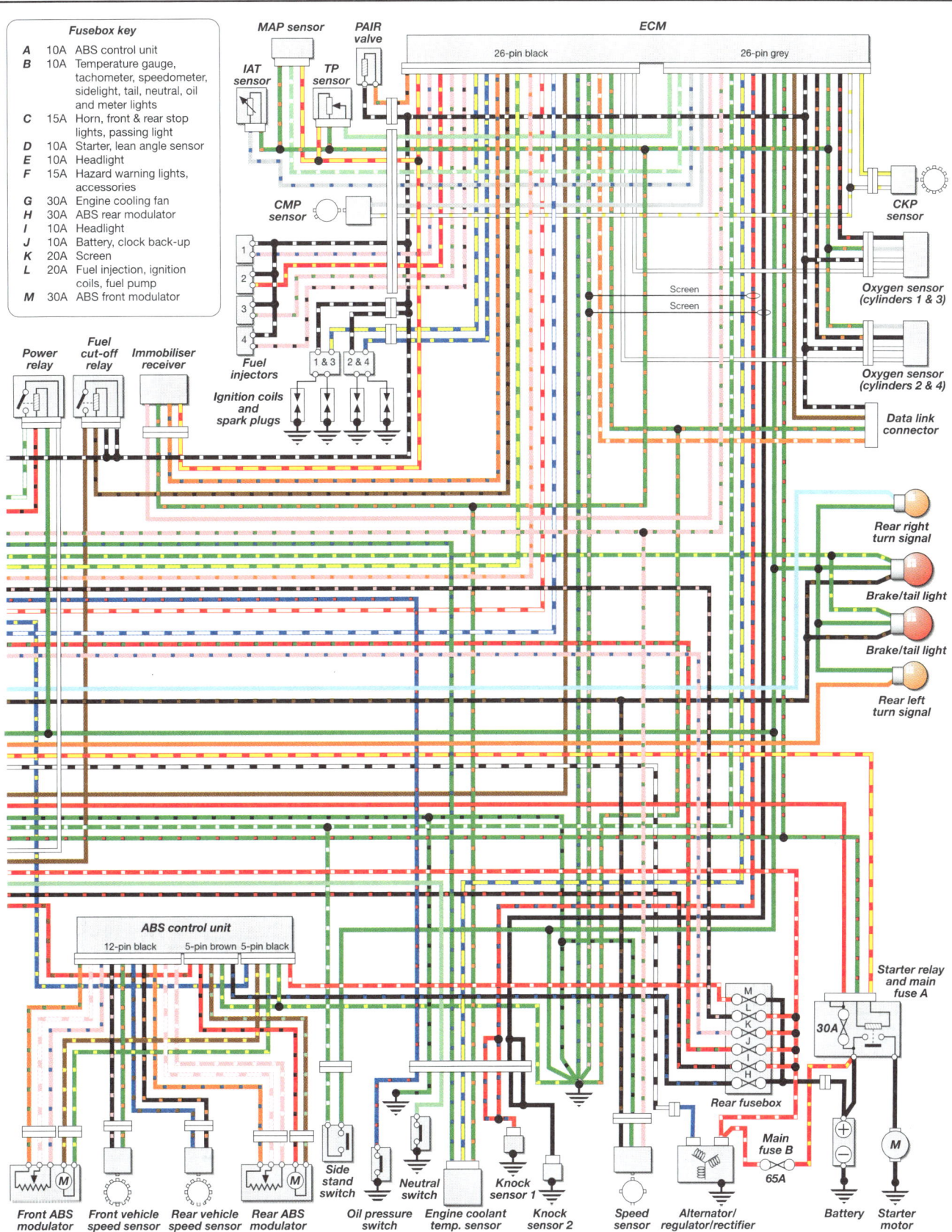

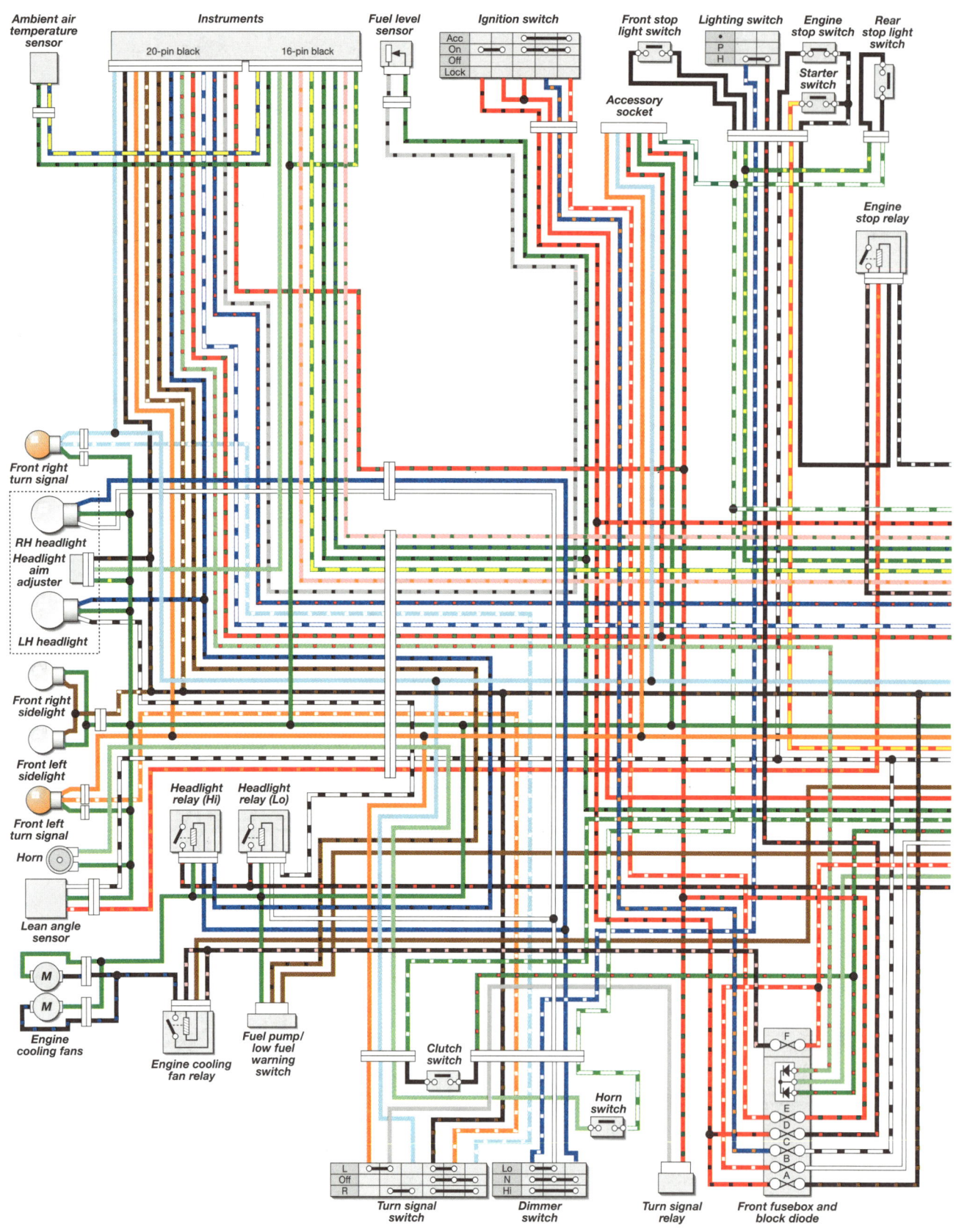

Wiring diagrams 8•39

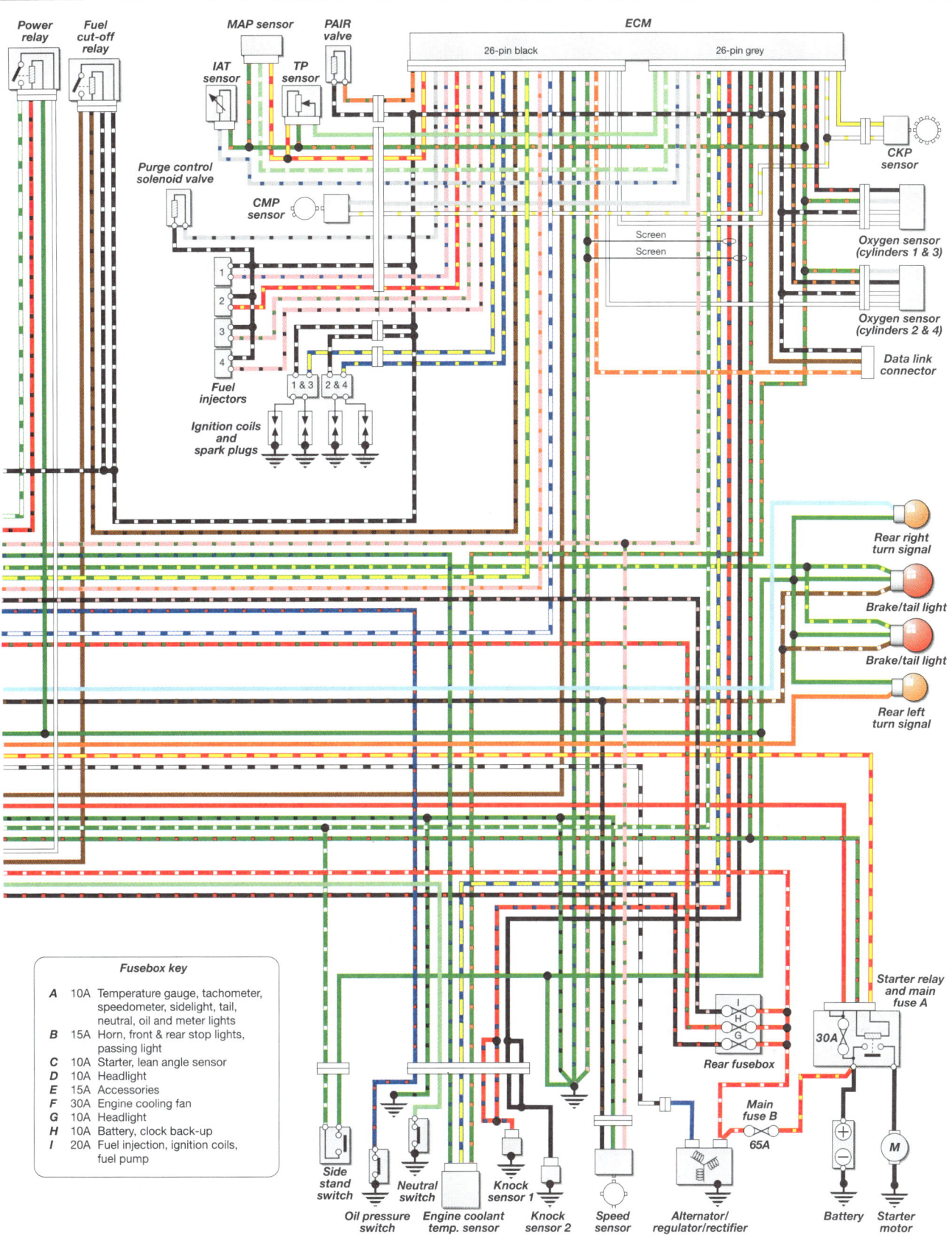

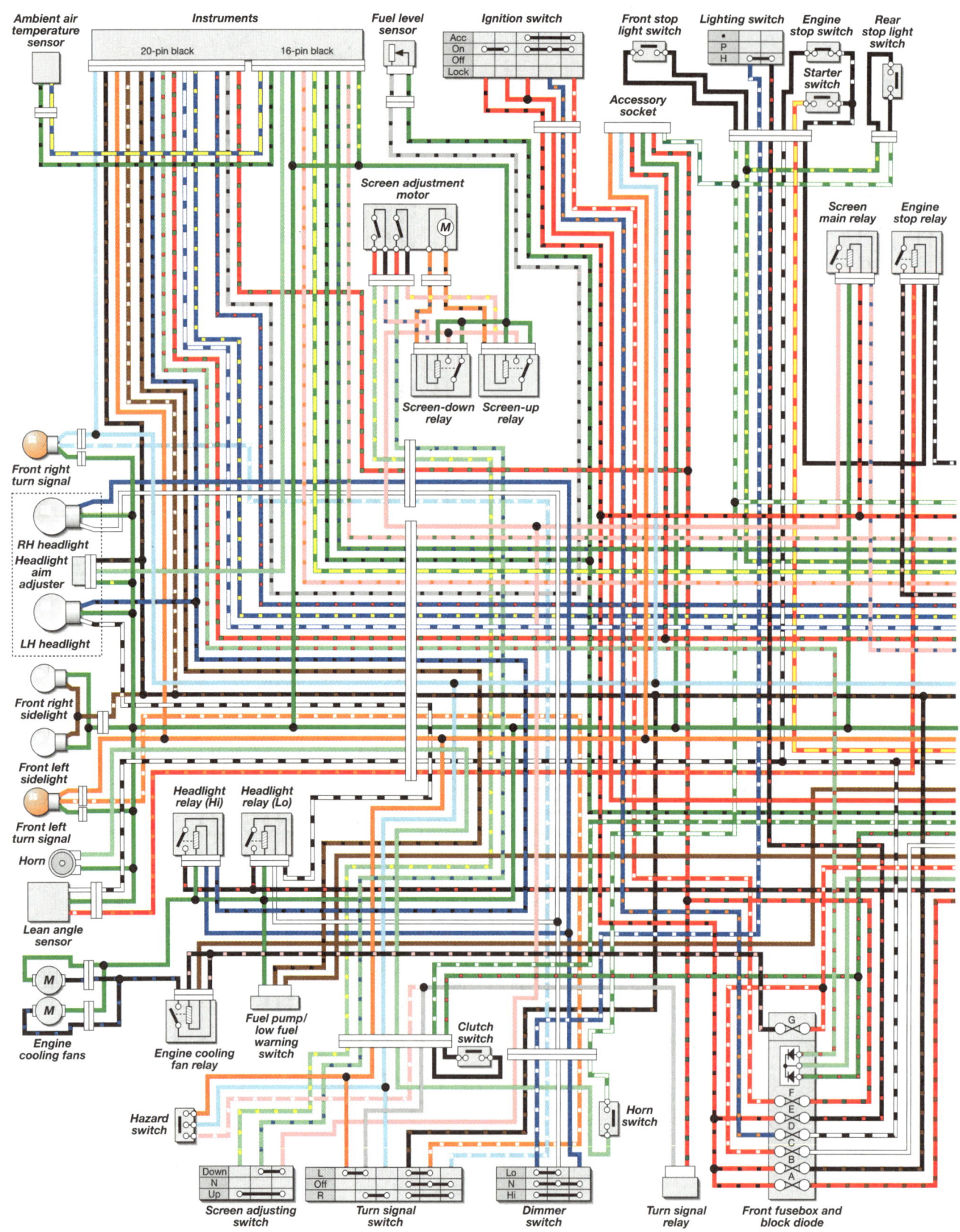

Wiring diagrams

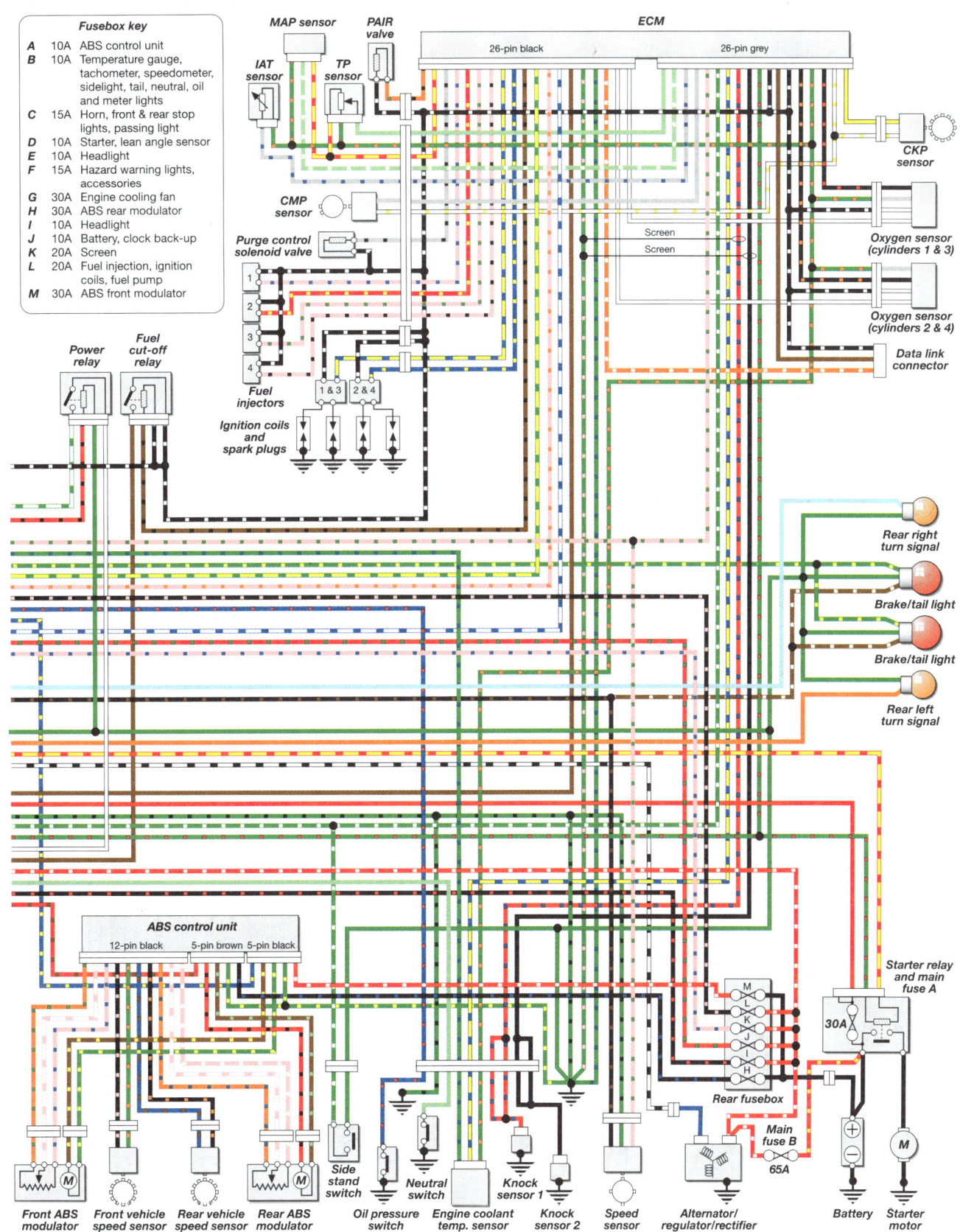

US ST1300A-3

8•42 Wiring diagrams

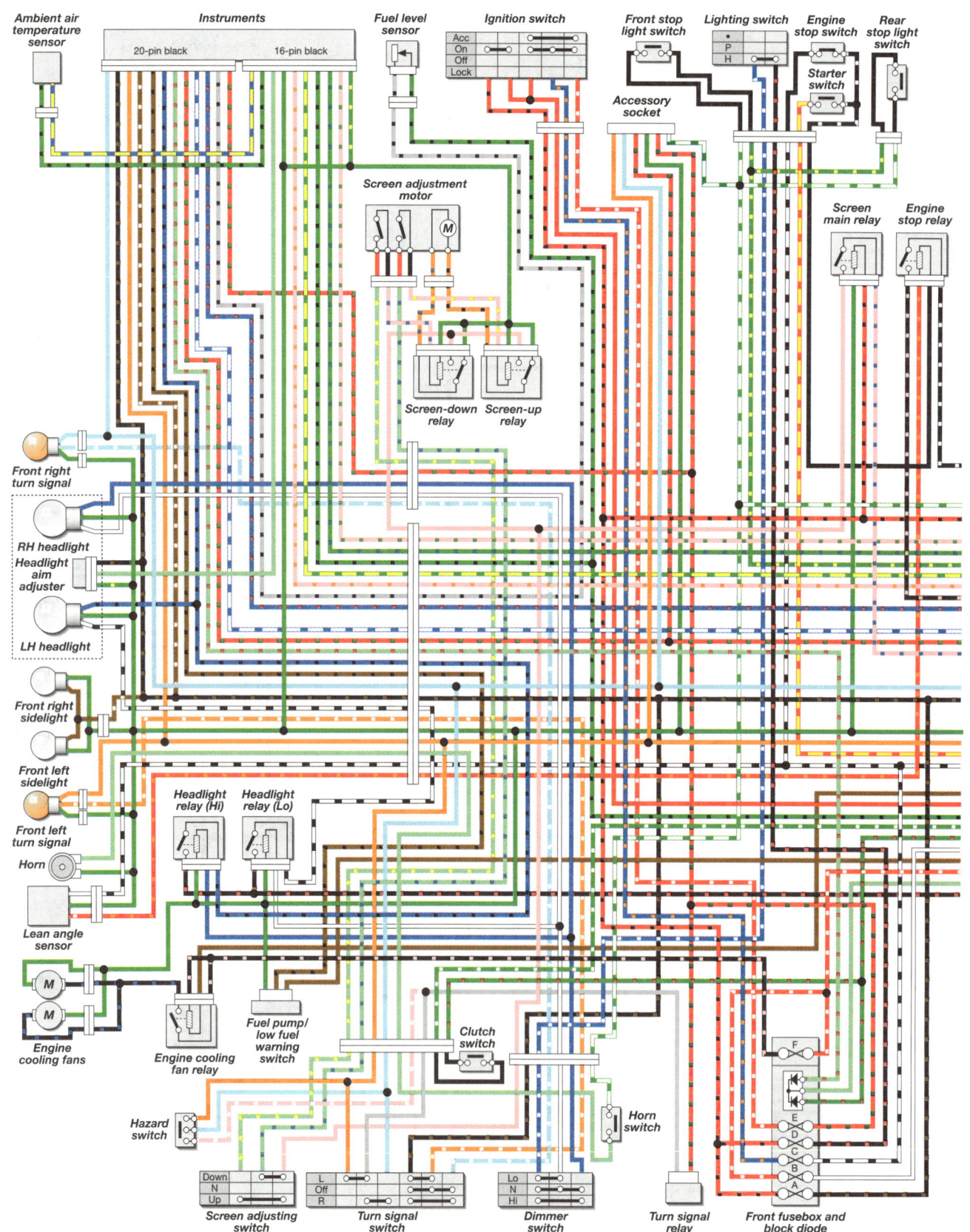

US ST1300-4 to ST1300-7

Wiring diagrams 8•43

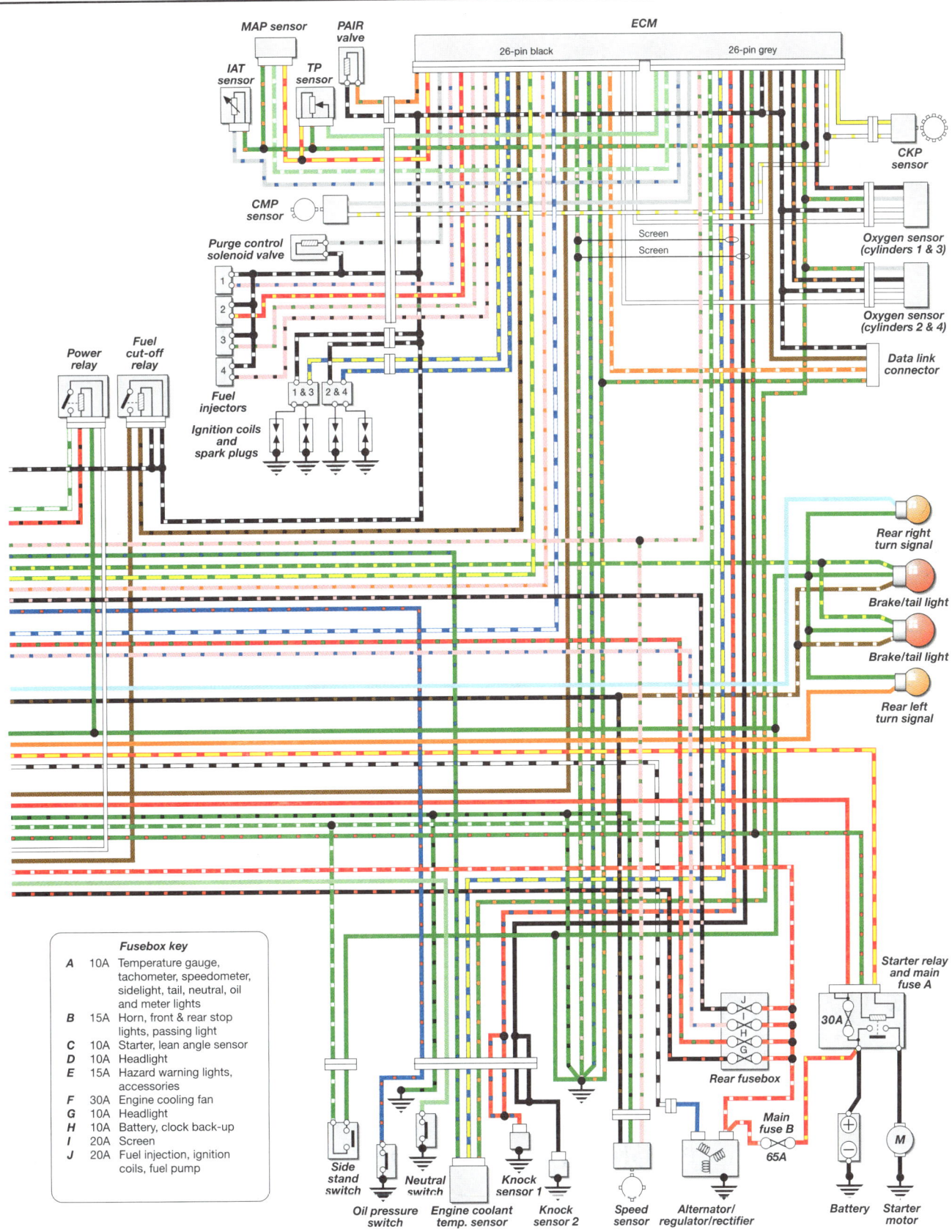

US ST1300-4 to ST1300-7

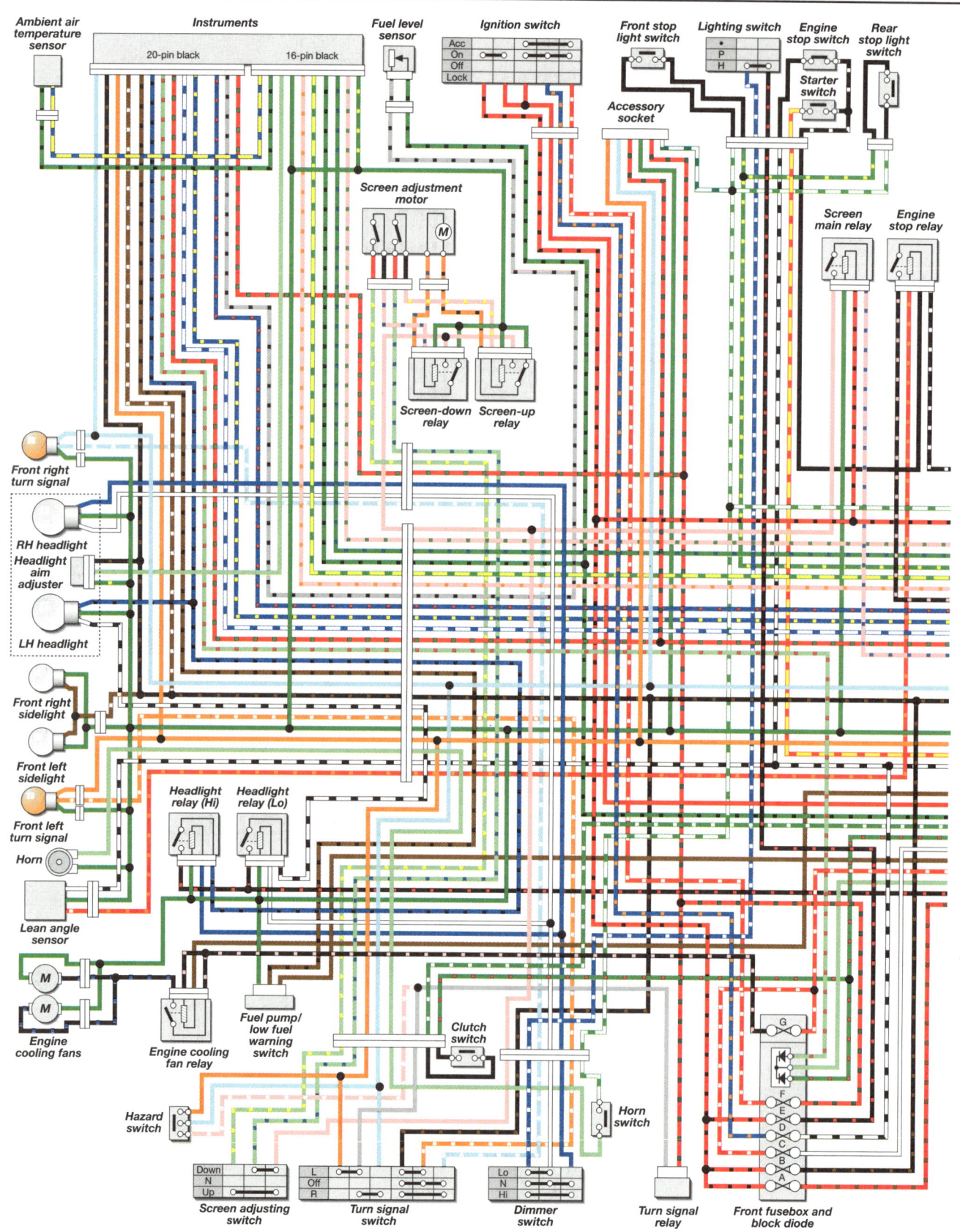

Wiring diagrams 8•45

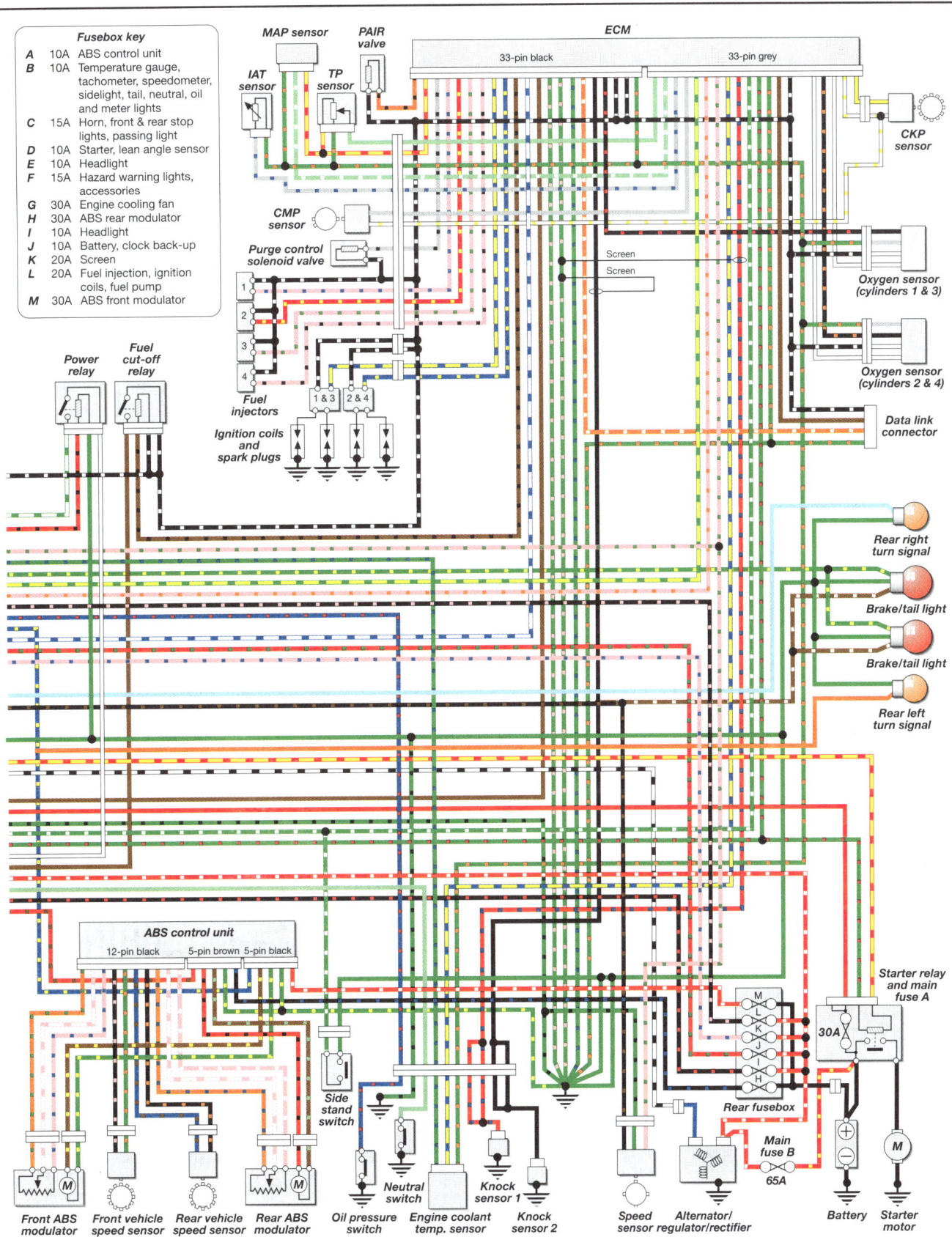

US ST1300A-4 to ST1300A-7

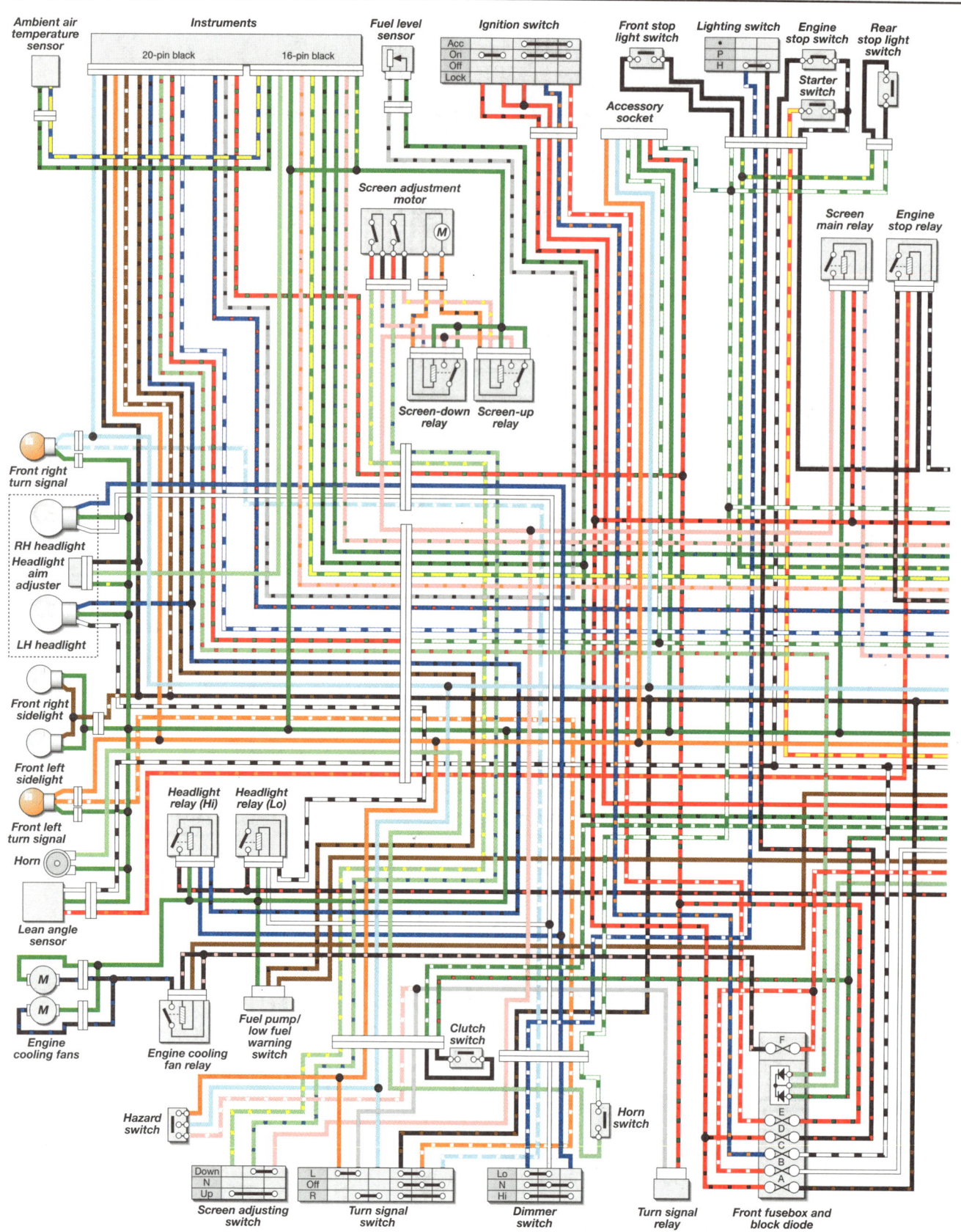

Wiring diagrams 8•47

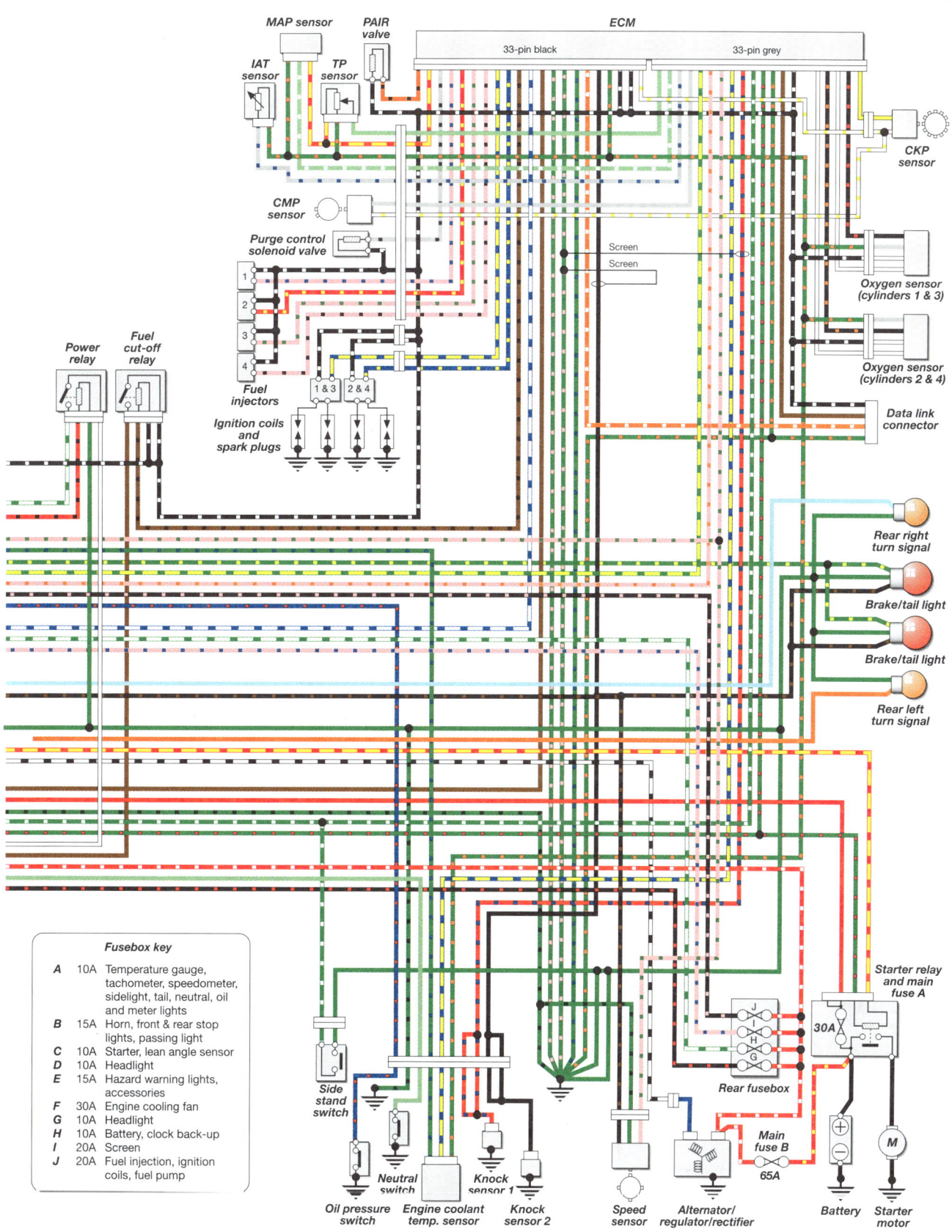

US ST1300-8 onwards

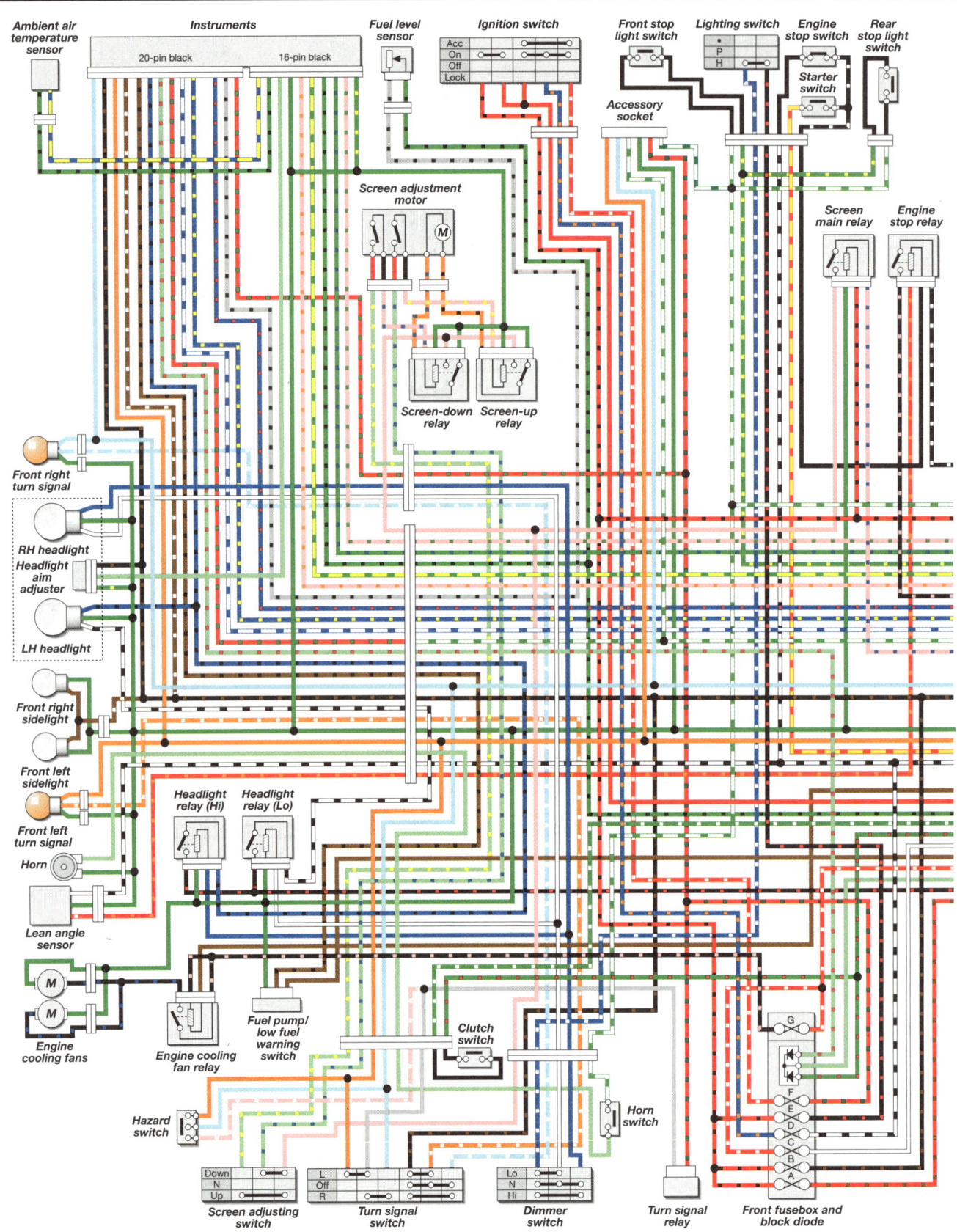

Wiring diagrams 8•49

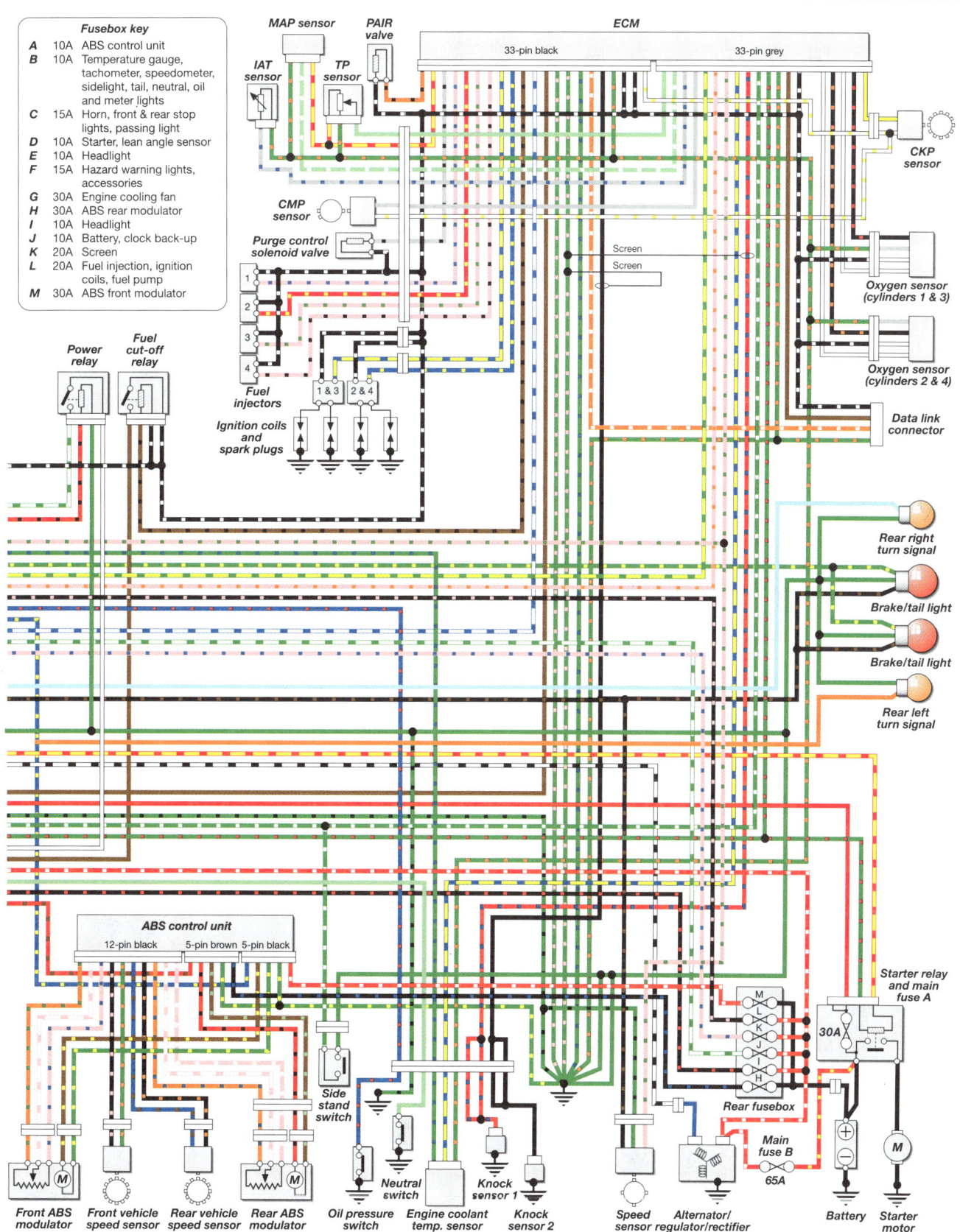

US ST1300A-8 onwards

Notes

Reference

Tools and Workshop Tips — REF•2

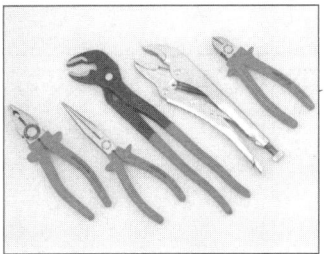

- Building up a tool kit and equipping your workshop
- Using tools
- Understanding bearing, seal, fastener and chain sizes and markings
- Repair techniques

Security — REF•20

- Locks and chains
- U-locks
- Disc locks
- Alarms and immobilisers
- Security marking systems
- Tips on how to prevent bike theft

Lubricants and fluids — REF•23

- Engine oils
- Transmission (gear) oils
- Coolant/anti-freeze
- Fork oils and suspension fluids
- Brake/clutch fluids
- Spray lubes, degreasers and solvents

Conversion Factors — REF•26

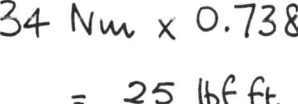

- Formulae for conversion of the metric (SI) units used throughout the manual into Imperial measures

MOT Test Checks — REF•27

- A guide to the UK MOT test
- Which items are tested
- How to prepare your motorcycle for the test and perform a pre-test check

Storage — REF•32

- How to prepare your motorcycle for going into storage and protect essential systems
- How to get the motorcycle back on the road

Fault Finding — REF•35

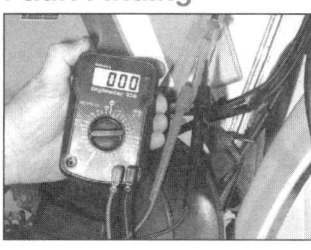

- Common faults and their likely causes

Technical Terms Explained — REF•44

- Component names, technical terms and common abbreviations explained

Index — REF•48

Tools and Workshop Tips

Buying tools

A toolkit is a fundamental requirement for servicing and repairing a motorcycle. Although there will be an initial expense in building up enough tools for servicing, this will soon be offset by the savings made by doing the job yourself. As experience and confidence grow, additional tools can be added to enable the repair and overhaul of the motorcycle. Many of the specialist tools are expensive and not often used so it may be preferable to hire them, or for a group of friends or motorcycle club to join in the purchase.

As a rule, it is better to buy more expensive, good quality tools. Cheaper tools are likely to wear out faster and need to be renewed more often, nullifying the original saving.

> **Warning: To avoid the risk of a poor quality tool breaking in use, causing injury or damage to the component being worked on, always aim to purchase tools which meet the relevant national safety standards.**

The following lists of tools do not represent the manufacturer's service tools, but serve as a guide to help the owner decide which tools are needed for this level of work. In addition, items such as an electric drill, hacksaw, files, soldering iron and a workbench equipped with a vice, may be needed. Although not classed as tools, a selection of bolts, screws, nuts, washers and pieces of tubing always come in useful.

For more information about tools, refer to the Haynes *Motorcycle Workshop Practice Techbook* (Bk. No. 3470).

Manufacturer's service tools

Inevitably certain tasks require the use of a service tool. Where possible an alternative tool or method of approach is recommended, but sometimes there is no option if personal injury or damage to the component is to be avoided. Where required, service tools are referred to in the relevant procedure.

Service tools can usually only be purchased from a motorcycle dealer and are identified by a part number. Some of the commonly-used tools, such as rotor pullers, are available in aftermarket form from mail-order motorcycle tool and accessory suppliers.

Maintenance and minor repair tools

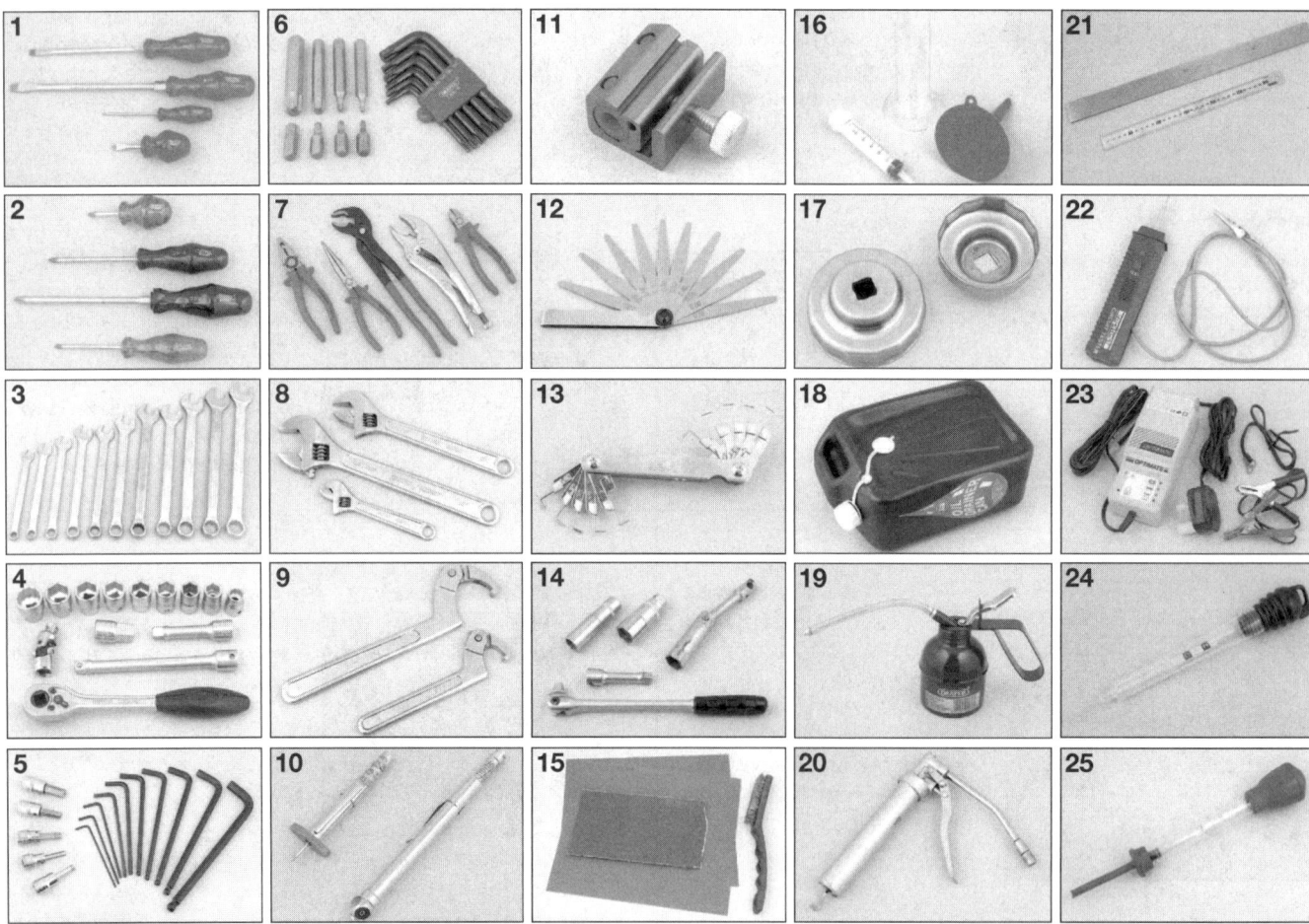

1 Set of flat-bladed screwdrivers
2 Set of Phillips head screwdrivers
3 Combination open-end and ring spanners
4 Socket set (3/8 inch or 1/2 inch drive)
5 Set of Allen keys or bits
6 Set of Torx keys or bits
7 Pliers, cutters and self-locking grips (Mole grips)
8 Adjustable spanners
9 C-spanners
10 Tread depth gauge and tyre pressure gauge
11 Cable oiler clamp
12 Feeler gauges
13 Spark plug gap measuring tool
14 Spark plug spanner or deep plug sockets
15 Wire brush and emery paper
16 Calibrated syringe, measuring vessel and funnel
17 Oil filter adapters
18 Oil drainer can or tray
19 Pump type oil can
20 Grease gun
21 Straight-edge and steel rule
22 Continuity tester
23 Battery charger
24 Hydrometer (for battery specific gravity check)
25 Anti-freeze tester (for liquid-cooled engines)

Tools and Workshop Tips

Repair and overhaul tools

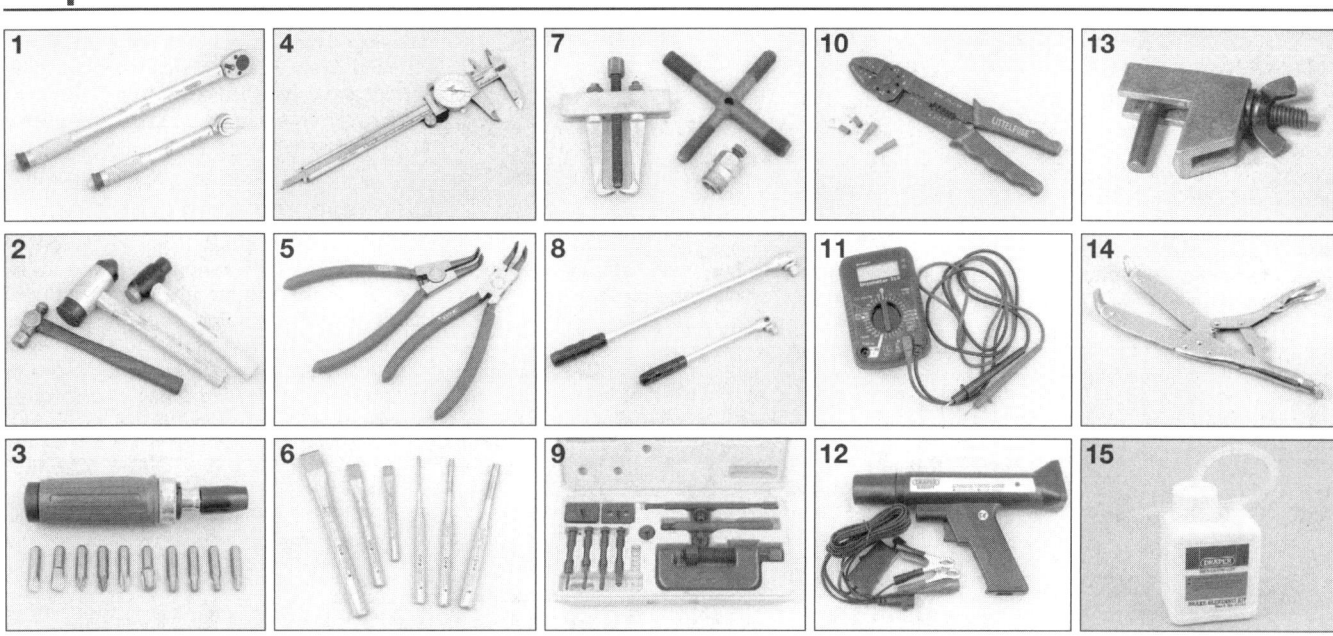

1. Torque wrench (small and mid-ranges)
2. Conventional, plastic or soft-faced hammers
3. Impact driver set
4. Vernier gauge
5. Circlip pliers (internal and external, or combination)
6. Set of cold chisels and punches
7. Selection of pullers
8. Breaker bars
9. Chain breaking/riveting tool set
10. Wire stripper and crimper tool
11. Multimeter (measures amps, volts and ohms)
12. Stroboscope (for dynamic timing checks)
13. Hose clamp (wingnut type shown)
14. Clutch holding tool
15. One-man brake/clutch bleeder kit

Specialist tools

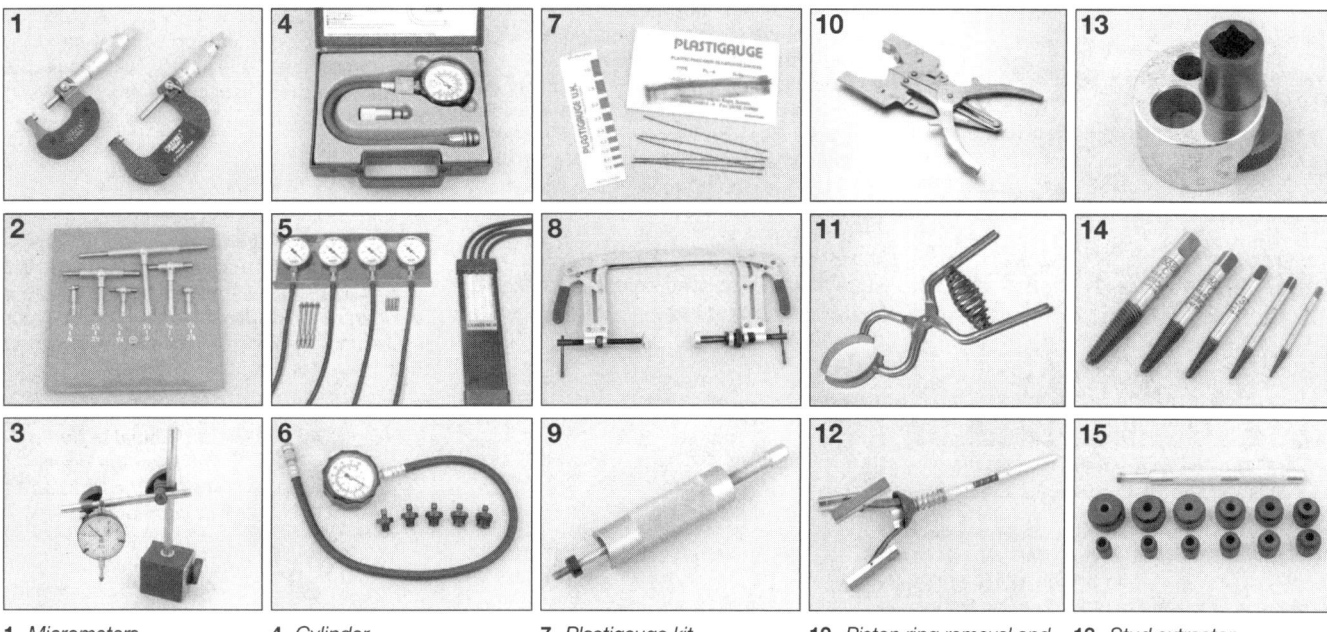

1. Micrometers (external type)
2. Telescoping gauges
3. Dial gauge
4. Cylinder compression gauge
5. Vacuum gauges (left) or manometer (right)
6. Oil pressure gauge
7. Plastigauge kit
8. Valve spring compressor (4-stroke engines)
9. Piston pin drawbolt tool
10. Piston ring removal and installation tool
11. Piston ring clamp
12. Cylinder bore hone (stone type shown)
13. Stud extractor
14. Screw extractor set
15. Bearing driver set

REF•4 Tools and Workshop Tips

1 Workshop equipment and facilities

The workbench

- Work is made much easier by raising the bike up on a ramp - components are much more accessible if raised to waist level. The hydraulic or pneumatic types seen in the dealer's workshop are a sound investment if you undertake a lot of repairs or overhauls **(see illustration 1.1)**.

1.1 Hydraulic motorcycle ramp

- If raised off ground level, the bike must be supported on the ramp to avoid it falling. Most ramps incorporate a front wheel locating clamp which can be adjusted to suit different diameter wheels. When tightening the clamp, take care not to mark the wheel rim or damage the tyre - use wood blocks on each side to prevent this.
- Secure the bike to the ramp using tie-downs **(see illustration 1.2)**. If the bike has only a sidestand, and hence leans at a dangerous angle when raised, support the bike on an auxiliary stand.

1.2 Tie-downs are used around the passenger footrests to secure the bike

- Auxiliary (paddock) stands are widely available from mail order companies or motorcycle dealers and attach either to the wheel axle or swingarm pivot **(see illustration 1.3)**. If the motorcycle has a centrestand, you can support it under the crankcase to prevent it toppling whilst either wheel is removed **(see illustration 1.4)**.

1.3 This auxiliary stand attaches to the swingarm pivot

1.4 Always use a block of wood between the engine and jack head when supporting the engine in this way

Fumes and fire

- Refer to the Safety first! page at the beginning of the manual for full details. Make sure your workshop is equipped with a fire extinguisher suitable for fuel-related fires (Class B fire - flammable liquids) - it is not sufficient to have a water-filled extinguisher.
- Always ensure adequate ventilation is available. Unless an exhaust gas extraction system is available for use, ensure that the engine is run outside of the workshop.
- If working on the fuel system, make sure the workshop is ventilated to avoid a build-up of fumes. This applies equally to fume build-up when charging a battery. Do not smoke or allow anyone else to smoke in the workshop.

Fluids

- If you need to drain fuel from the tank, store it in an approved container marked as suitable for the storage of petrol (gasoline) **(see illustration 1.5)**. Do not store fuel in glass jars or bottles.

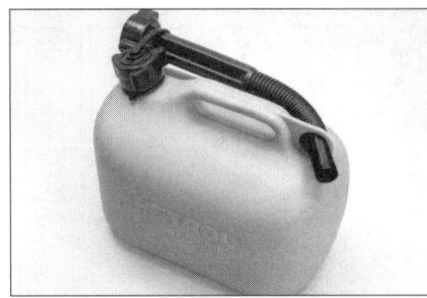

1.5 Use an approved can only for storing petrol (gasoline)

- Use proprietary engine degreasers or solvents which have a high flash-point, such as paraffin (kerosene), for cleaning off oil, grease and dirt - never use petrol (gasoline) for cleaning. Wear rubber gloves when handling solvent and engine degreaser. The fumes from certain solvents can be dangerous - always work in a well-ventilated area.

Dust, eye and hand protection

- Protect your lungs from inhalation of dust particles by wearing a filtering mask over the nose and mouth. Many frictional materials still contain asbestos which is dangerous to your health. Protect your eyes from spouts of liquid and sprung components by wearing a pair of protective goggles **(see illustration 1.6)**.

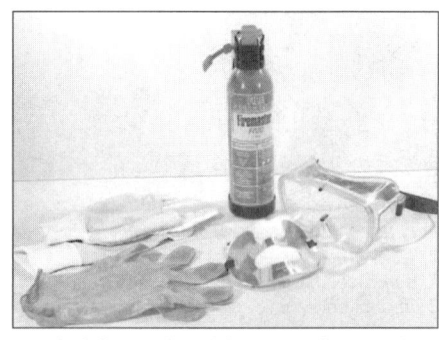

1.6 A fire extinguisher, goggles, mask and protective gloves should be at hand in the workshop

- Protect your hands from contact with solvents, fuel and oils by wearing rubber gloves. Alternatively apply a barrier cream to your hands before starting work. If handling hot components or fluids, wear suitable gloves to protect your hands from scalding and burns.

What to do with old fluids

- Old cleaning solvent, fuel, coolant and oils should not be poured down domestic drains or onto the ground. Package the fluid up in old oil containers, label it accordingly, and take it to a garage or disposal facility. Contact your local authority for location of such sites or ring the oil care hotline.

Note: It is illegal and anti-social to dump oil down the drain. To find the location of your local oil recycling bank in the UK, call 08708 506 506 or visit www.oilbankline.org.uk

In the USA, note that any oil supplier must accept used oil for recycling.

Tools and Workshop Tips REF•5

2 Fasteners - screws, bolts and nuts

Fastener types and applications

Bolts and screws

● Fastener head types are either of hexagonal, Torx or splined design, with internal and external versions of each type **(see illustrations 2.1 and 2.2)**; splined head fasteners are not in common use on motorcycles. The conventional slotted or Phillips head design is used for certain screws. Bolt or screw length is always measured from the underside of the head to the end of the item **(see illustration 2.11)**.

2.1 Internal hexagon/Allen (A), Torx (B) and splined (C) fasteners, with corresponding bits

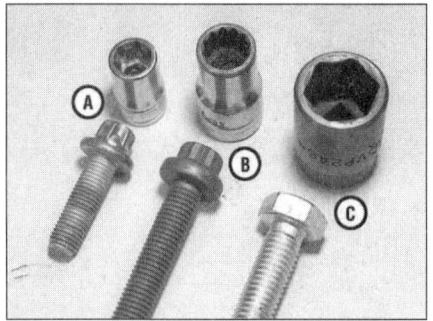

2.2 External Torx (A), splined (B) and hexagon (C) fasteners, with corresponding sockets

● Certain fasteners on the motorcycle have a tensile marking on their heads, the higher the marking the stronger the fastener. High tensile fasteners generally carry a 10 or higher marking. Never replace a high tensile fastener with one of a lower tensile strength.

Washers (see illustration 2.3)

● Plain washers are used between a fastener head and a component to prevent damage to the component or to spread the load when torque is applied. Plain washers can also be used as spacers or shims in certain assemblies. Copper or aluminium plain washers are often used as sealing washers on drain plugs.

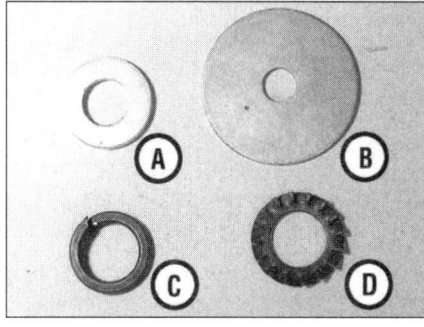

2.3 Plain washer (A), penny washer (B), spring washer (C) and serrated washer (D)

● The split-ring spring washer works by applying axial tension between the fastener head and component. If flattened, it is fatigued and must be renewed. If a plain (flat) washer is used on the fastener, position the spring washer between the fastener and the plain washer.
● Serrated star type washers dig into the fastener and component faces, preventing loosening. They are often used on electrical earth (ground) connections to the frame.
● Cone type washers (sometimes called Belleville) are conical and when tightened apply axial tension between the fastener head and component. They must be installed with the dished side against the component and often carry an OUTSIDE marking on their outer face. If flattened, they are fatigued and must be renewed.
● Tab washers are used to lock plain nuts or bolts on a shaft. A portion of the tab washer is bent up hard against one flat of the nut or bolt to prevent it loosening. Due to the tab washer being deformed in use, a new tab washer should be used every time it is disturbed.
● Wave washers are used to take up endfloat on a shaft. They provide light springing and prevent excessive side-to-side play of a component. Can be found on rocker arm shafts.

Nuts and split pins

● Conventional plain nuts are usually six-sided **(see illustration 2.4)**. They are sized by thread diameter and pitch. High tensile nuts carry a number on one end to denote their tensile strength.

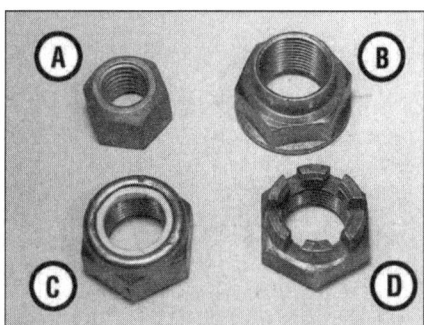

2.4 Plain nut (A), shouldered locknut (B), nylon insert nut (C) and castellated nut (D)

● Self-locking nuts either have a nylon insert, or two spring metal tabs, or a shoulder which is staked into a groove in the shaft - their advantage over conventional plain nuts is a resistance to loosening due to vibration. The nylon insert type can be used a number of times, but must be renewed when the friction of the nylon insert is reduced, ie when the nut spins freely on the shaft. The spring tab type can be reused unless the tabs are damaged. The shouldered type must be renewed every time it is disturbed.
● Split pins (cotter pins) are used to lock a castellated nut to a shaft or to prevent slackening of a plain nut. Common applications are wheel axles and brake torque arms. Because the split pin arms are deformed to lock around the nut a new split pin must always be used on installation - always fit the correct size split pin which will fit snugly in the shaft hole. Make sure the split pin arms are correctly located around the nut **(see illustrations 2.5 and 2.6)**.

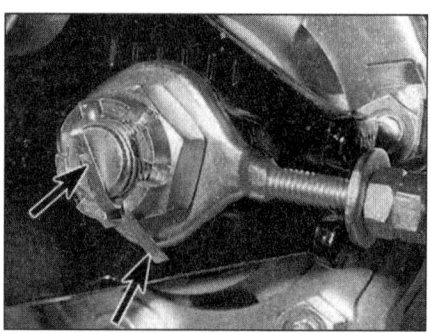

2.5 Bend split pin (cotter pin) arms as shown (arrows) to secure a castellated nut

2.6 Bend split pin (cotter pin) arms as shown to secure a plain nut

Caution: If the castellated nut slots do not align with the shaft hole after tightening to the torque setting, tighten the nut until the next slot aligns with the hole - never slacken the nut to align its slot.

● R-pins (shaped like the letter R), or slip pins as they are sometimes called, are sprung and can be reused if they are otherwise in good condition. Always install R-pins with their closed end facing forwards **(see illustration 2.7)**.

REF•6 Tools and Workshop Tips

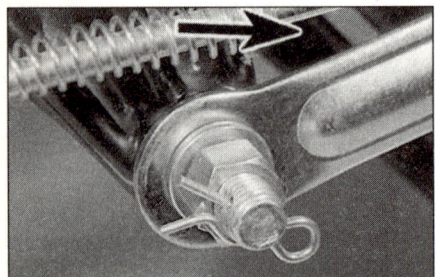

2.7 Correct fitting of R-pin. Arrow indicates forward direction

Circlips (see illustration 2.8)

● Circlips (sometimes called snap-rings) are used to retain components on a shaft or in a housing and have corresponding external or internal ears to permit removal. Parallel-sided (machined) circlips can be installed either way round in their groove, whereas stamped circlips (which have a chamfered edge on one face) must be installed with the chamfer facing away from the direction of thrust load **(see illustration 2.9)**.

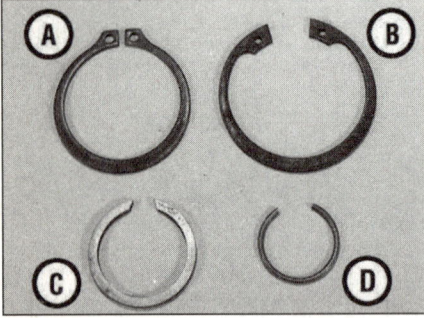

2.8 External stamped circlip (A), internal stamped circlip (B), machined circlip (C) and wire circlip (D)

● Always use circlip pliers to remove and install circlips; expand or compress them just enough to remove them. After installation, rotate the circlip in its groove to ensure it is securely seated. If installing a circlip on a splined shaft, always align its opening with a shaft channel to ensure the circlip ends are well supported and unlikely to catch **(see illustration 2.10)**.

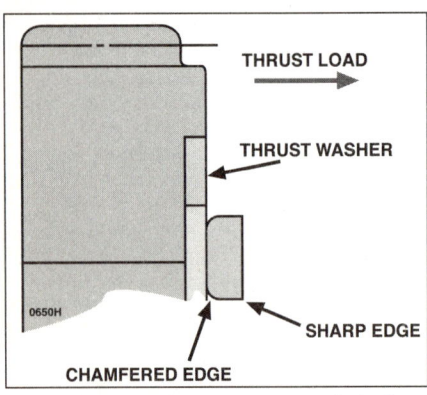

2.9 Correct fitting of a stamped circlip

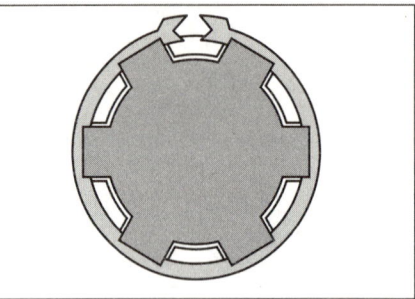

2.10 Align circlip opening with shaft channel

● Circlips can wear due to the thrust of components and become loose in their grooves, with the subsequent danger of becoming dislodged in operation. For this reason, renewal is advised every time a circlip is disturbed.

● Wire circlips are commonly used as piston pin retaining clips. If a removal tang is provided, long-nosed pliers can be used to dislodge them, otherwise careful use of a small flat-bladed screwdriver is necessary. Wire circlips should be renewed every time they are disturbed.

Thread diameter and pitch

● Diameter of a male thread (screw, bolt or stud) is the outside diameter of the threaded portion **(see illustration 2.11)**. Most motorcycle manufacturers use the ISO (International Standards Organisation) metric system expressed in millimetres, eg M6 refers to a 6 mm diameter thread. Sizing is the same for nuts, except that the thread diameter is measured across the valleys of the nut.

● Pitch is the distance between the peaks of the thread **(see illustration 2.11)**. It is expressed in millimetres, thus a common bolt size may be expressed as 6.0 x 1.0 mm (6 mm thread diameter and 1 mm pitch). Generally pitch increases in proportion to thread diameter, although there are always exceptions.

● Thread diameter and pitch are related for conventional fastener applications and the accompanying table can be used as a guide. Additionally, the AF (Across Flats), spanner or socket size dimension of the bolt or nut **(see illustration 2.11)** is linked to thread and pitch specification. Thread pitch can be measured with a thread gauge **(see illustration 2.12)**.

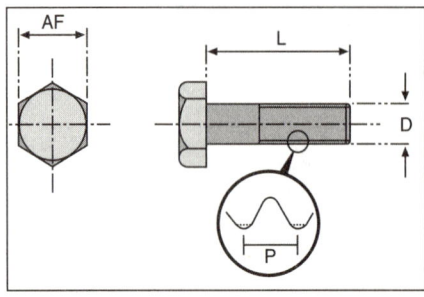

2.11 Fastener length (L), thread diameter (D), thread pitch (P) and head size (AF)

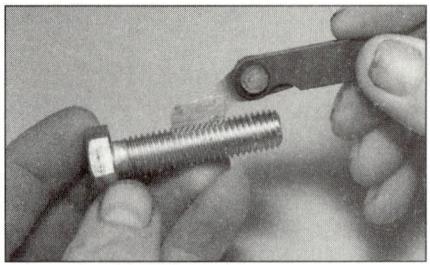

2.12 Using a thread gauge to measure pitch

AF size	Thread diameter x pitch (mm)
8 mm	M5 x 0.8
8 mm	M6 x 1.0
10 mm	M6 x 1.0
12 mm	M8 x 1.25
14 mm	M10 x 1.25
17 mm	M12 x 1.25

● The threads of most fasteners are of the right-hand type, ie they are turned clockwise to tighten and anti-clockwise to loosen. The reverse situation applies to left-hand thread fasteners, which are turned anti-clockwise to tighten and clockwise to loosen. Left-hand threads are used where rotation of a component might loosen a conventional right-hand thread fastener.

Seized fasteners

● Corrosion of external fasteners due to water or reaction between two dissimilar metals can occur over a period of time. It will build up sooner in wet conditions or in countries where salt is used on the roads during the winter. If a fastener is severely corroded it is likely that normal methods of removal will fail and result in its head being ruined. When you attempt removal, the fastener thread should be heard to crack free and unscrew easily - if it doesn't, stop there before damaging something.

● A smart tap on the head of the fastener will often succeed in breaking free corrosion which has occurred in the threads **(see illustration 2.13)**.

● An aerosol penetrating fluid (such as WD-40) applied the night beforehand may work its way down into the thread and ease removal. Depending on the location, you may be able to make up a Plasticine well around the fastener head and fill it with penetrating fluid.

2.13 A sharp tap on the head of a fastener will often break free a corroded thread

Tools and Workshop Tips

- If you are working on an engine internal component, corrosion will most likely not be a problem due to the well lubricated environment. However, components can be very tight and an impact driver is a useful tool in freeing them **(see illustration 2.14)**.

2.14 Using an impact driver to free a fastener

- Where corrosion has occurred between dissimilar metals (eg steel and aluminium alloy), the application of heat to the fastener head will create a disproportionate expansion rate between the two metals and break the seizure caused by the corrosion. Whether heat can be applied depends on the location of the fastener - any surrounding components likely to be damaged must first be removed **(see illustration 2.15)**. Heat can be applied using a paint stripper heat gun or clothes iron, or by immersing the component in boiling water - wear protective gloves to prevent scalding or burns to the hands.

2.15 Using heat to free a seized fastener

- As a last resort, it is possible to use a hammer and cold chisel to work the fastener head unscrewed **(see illustration 2.16)**. This will damage the fastener, but more importantly extreme care must be taken not to damage the surrounding component.

Caution: Remember that the component being secured is generally of more value than the bolt, nut or screw - when the fastener is freed, do not unscrew it with force, instead work the fastener back and forth when resistance is felt to prevent thread damage.

2.16 Using a hammer and chisel to free a seized fastener

Broken fasteners and damaged heads

- If the shank of a broken bolt or screw is accessible you can grip it with self-locking grips. The knurled wheel type stud extractor tool or self-gripping stud puller tool is particularly useful for removing the long studs which screw into the cylinder mouth surface of the crankcase or bolts and screws from which the head has broken off **(see illustration 2.17)**. Studs can also be removed by locking two nuts together on the threaded end of the stud and using a spanner on the lower nut **(see illustration 2.18)**.

2.17 Using a stud extractor tool to remove a broken crankcase stud

2.18 Two nuts can be locked together to unscrew a stud from a component

- A bolt or screw which has broken off below or level with the casing must be extracted using a screw extractor set. Centre punch the fastener to centralise the drill bit, then drill a hole in the fastener **(see illustration 2.19)**. Select a drill bit which is approximately half to three-quarters the

2.19 When using a screw extractor, first drill a hole in the fastener . . .

diameter of the fastener and drill to a depth which will accommodate the extractor. Use the largest size extractor possible, but avoid leaving too small a wall thickness otherwise the extractor will merely force the fastener walls outwards wedging it in the casing thread.

- If a spiral type extractor is used, thread it anti-clockwise into the fastener. As it is screwed in, it will grip the fastener and unscrew it from the casing **(see illustration 2.20)**.

2.20 . . . then thread the extractor anti-clockwise into the fastener

- If a taper type extractor is used, tap it into the fastener so that it is firmly wedged in place. Unscrew the extractor (anti-clockwise) to draw the fastener out.

 **Warning: Stud extractors are very hard and may break off in the fastener if care is not taken - ask an engineer about spark erosion if this happens.**

- Alternatively, the broken bolt/screw can be drilled out and the hole retapped for an oversize bolt/screw or a diamond-section thread insert. It is essential that the drilling is carried out squarely and to the correct depth, otherwise the casing may be ruined - if in doubt, entrust the work to an engineer.
- Bolts and nuts with rounded corners cause the correct size spanner or socket to slip when force is applied. Of the types of spanner/socket available always use a six-point type rather than an eight or twelve-point type - better grip

Tools and Workshop Tips

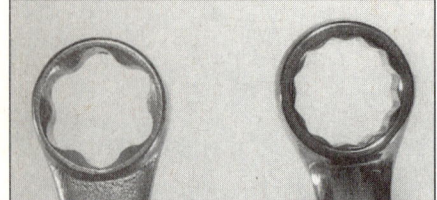

2.21 Comparison of surface drive ring spanner (left) with 12-point type (right)

is obtained. Surface drive spanners grip the middle of the hex flats, rather than the corners, and are thus good in cases of damaged heads **(see illustration 2.21)**.

● Slotted-head or Phillips-head screws are often damaged by the use of the wrong size screwdriver. Allen-head and Torx-head screws are much less likely to sustain damage. If enough of the screw head is exposed you can use a hacksaw to cut a slot in its head and then use a conventional flat-bladed screwdriver to remove it. Alternatively use a hammer and cold chisel to tap the head of the fastener around to slacken it. Always replace damaged fasteners with new ones, preferably Torx or Allen-head type.

HAYNES HiNT

A dab of valve grinding compound between the screw head and screwdriver tip will often give a good grip.

Thread repair

● Threads (particularly those in aluminium alloy components) can be damaged by overtightening, being assembled with dirt in the threads, or from a component working loose and vibrating. Eventually the thread will fail completely, and it will be impossible to tighten the fastener.

● If a thread is damaged or clogged with old locking compound it can be renovated with a thread repair tool (thread chaser) **(see illustrations 2.22 and 2.23)**; special thread

2.22 A thread repair tool being used to correct an internal thread

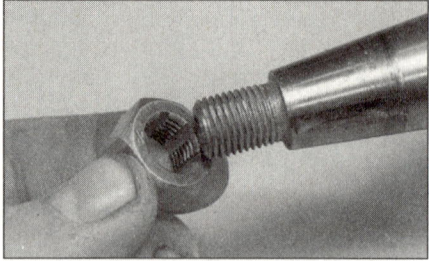

2.23 A thread repair tool being used to correct an external thread

chasers are available for spark plug hole threads. The tool will not cut a new thread, but clean and true the original thread. Make sure that you use the correct diameter and pitch tool. Similarly, external threads can be cleaned up with a die or a thread restorer file **(see illustration 2.24)**.

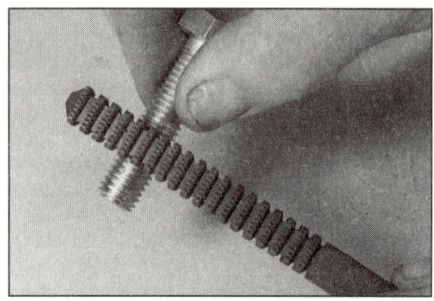

2.24 Using a thread restorer file

● It is possible to drill out the old thread and retap the component to the next thread size. This will work where there is enough surrounding material and a new bolt or screw can be obtained. Sometimes, however, this is not possible - such as where the bolt/screw passes through another component which must also be suitably modified, also in cases where a spark plug or oil drain plug cannot be obtained in a larger diameter thread size.

● The diamond-section thread insert (often known by its popular trade name of Heli-Coil) is a simple and effective method of renewing the thread and retaining the original size. A kit can be purchased which contains the tap, insert and installing tool **(see illustration 2.25)**. Drill out the damaged thread with the size drill specified **(see illustration 2.26)**. Carefully retap the thread **(see illustration 2.27)**. Install the

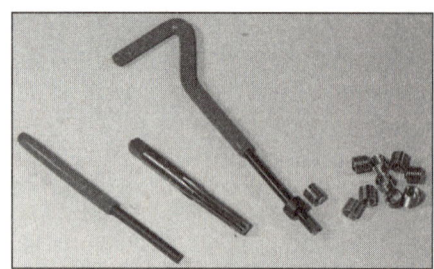

2.25 Obtain a thread insert kit to suit the thread diameter and pitch required

2.26 To install a thread insert, first drill out the original thread . . .

2.27 . . . tap a new thread . . .

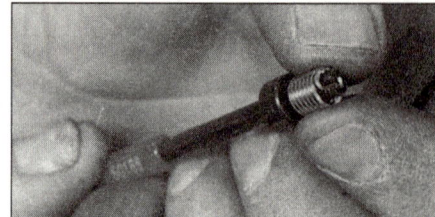

2.28 . . . fit insert on the installing tool . . .

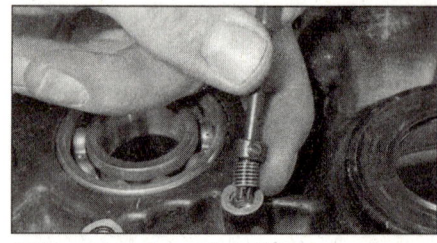

2.29 . . . and thread into the component . . .

2.30 . . . break off the tang when complete

insert on the installing tool and thread it slowly into place using a light downward pressure **(see illustrations 2.28 and 2.29)**. When positioned between a 1/4 and 1/2 turn below the surface withdraw the installing tool and use the break-off tool to press down on the tang, breaking it off **(see illustration 2.30)**.

● There are epoxy thread repair kits on the market which can rebuild stripped internal threads, although this repair should not be used on high load-bearing components.

Tools and Workshop Tips

Thread locking and sealing compounds

● Locking compounds are used in locations where the fastener is prone to loosening due to vibration or on important safety-related items which might cause loss of control of the motorcycle if they fail. It is also used where important fasteners cannot be secured by other means such as lockwashers or split pins.

● Before applying locking compound, make sure that the threads (internal and external) are clean and dry with all old compound removed. Select a compound to suit the component being secured - a non-permanent general locking and sealing type is suitable for most applications, but a high strength type is needed for permanent fixing of studs in castings. Apply a drop or two of the compound to the first few threads of the fastener, then thread it into place and tighten to the specified torque. Do not apply excessive thread locking compound otherwise the thread may be damaged on subsequent removal.

● Certain fasteners are impregnated with a dry film type coating of locking compound on their threads. Always renew this type of fastener if disturbed.

● Anti-seize compounds, such as copper-based greases, can be applied to protect threads from seizure due to extreme heat and corrosion. A common instance is spark plug threads and exhaust system fasteners.

3 Measuring tools and gauges

Feeler gauges

● Feeler gauges (or blades) are used for measuring small gaps and clearances **(see illustration 3.1)**. They can also be used to measure endfloat (sideplay) of a component on a shaft where access is not possible with a dial gauge.

● Feeler gauge sets should be treated with care and not bent or damaged. They are etched with their size on one face. Keep them clean and very lightly oiled to prevent corrosion build-up.

3.1 Feeler gauges are used for measuring small gaps and clearances - thickness is marked on one face of gauge

● When measuring a clearance, select a gauge which is a light sliding fit between the two components. You may need to use two gauges together to measure the clearance accurately.

Micrometers

● A micrometer is a precision tool capable of measuring to 0.01 or 0.001 of a millimetre. It should always be stored in its case and not in the general toolbox. It must be kept clean and never dropped, otherwise its frame or measuring anvils could be distorted resulting in inaccurate readings.

● External micrometers are used for measuring outside diameters of components and have many more applications than internal micrometers. Micrometers are available in different size ranges, eg 0 to 25 mm, 25 to 50 mm, and upwards in 25 mm steps; some large micrometers have interchangeable anvils to allow a range of measurements to be taken. Generally the largest precision measurement you are likely to take on a motorcycle is the piston diameter.

● Internal micrometers (or bore micrometers) are used for measuring inside diameters, such as valve guides and cylinder bores. Telescoping gauges and small hole gauges are used in conjunction with an external micrometer, whereas the more expensive internal micrometers have their own measuring device.

External micrometer

Note: *The conventional analogue type instrument is described. Although much easier to read, digital micrometers are considerably more expensive.*

● Always check the calibration of the micrometer before use. With the anvils closed (0 to 25 mm type) or set over a test gauge (for

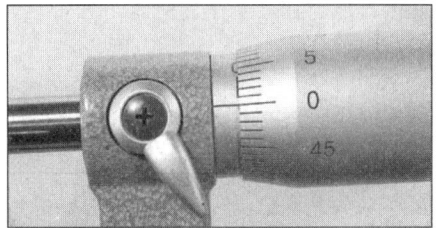

3.2 Check micrometer calibration before use

the larger types) the scale should read zero **(see illustration 3.2)**; make sure that the anvils (and test piece) are clean first. Any discrepancy can be adjusted by referring to the instructions supplied with the tool. Remember that the micrometer is a precision measuring tool - don't force the anvils closed, use the ratchet (4) on the end of the micrometer to close it. In this way, a measured force is always applied.

● To use, first make sure that the item being measured is clean. Place the anvil of the micrometer (1) against the item and use the thimble (2) to bring the spindle (3) lightly into contact with the other side of the item **(see illustration 3.3)**. Don't tighten the thimble down because this will damage the micrometer - instead use the ratchet (4) on the end of the micrometer. The ratchet mechanism applies a measured force preventing damage to the instrument.

● The micrometer is read by referring to the linear scale on the sleeve and the annular scale on the thimble. Read off the sleeve first to obtain the base measurement, then add the fine measurement from the thimble to obtain the overall reading. The linear scale on the sleeve represents the measuring range of the micrometer (eg 0 to 25 mm). The annular scale

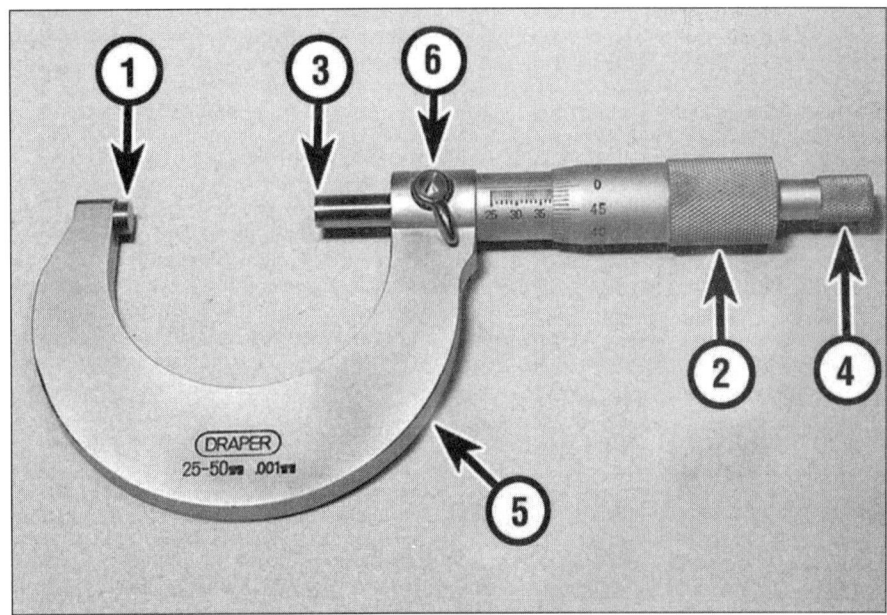

3.3 Micrometer component parts

1 Anvil
2 Thimble
3 Spindle
4 Ratchet
5 Frame
6 Locking lever

REF•10 Tools and Workshop Tips

on the thimble will be in graduations of 0.01 mm (or as marked on the frame) - one full revolution of the thimble will move 0.5 mm on the linear scale. Take the reading where the datum line on the sleeve intersects the thimble's scale. Always position the eye directly above the scale otherwise an inaccurate reading will result.

In the example shown the item measures 2.95 mm (see illustration 3.4):

Linear scale	2.00 mm
Linear scale	0.50 mm
Annular scale	0.45 mm
Total figure	**2.95 mm**

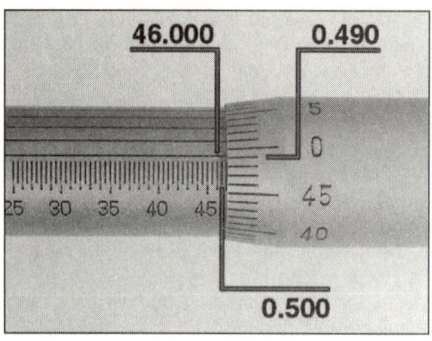

3.5 Micrometer reading of 46.99 mm on linear and annular scales . . .

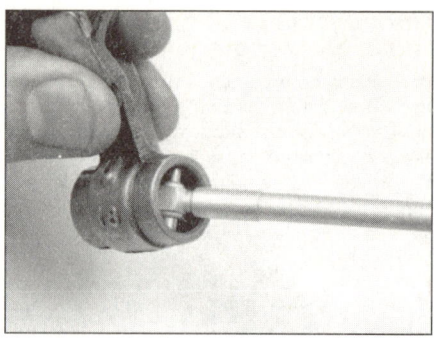

3.7 Expand the telescoping gauge in the bore, lock its position . . .

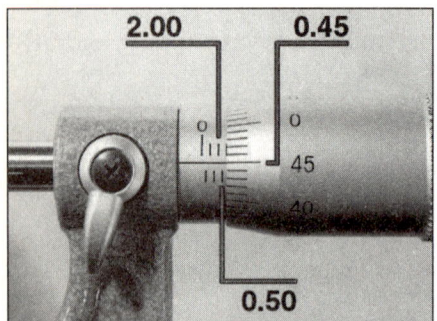

3.4 Micrometer reading of 2.95 mm

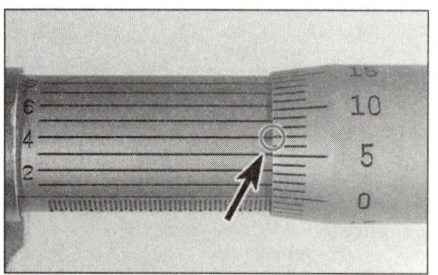

3.6 . . . and 0.004 mm on vernier scale

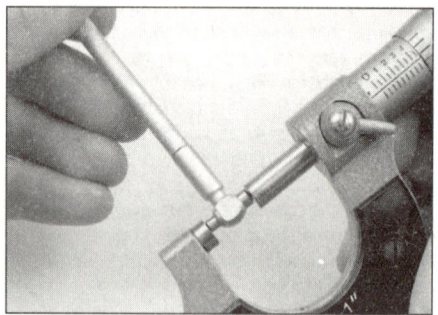

3.8 . . . then measure the gauge with a micrometer

- Most micrometers have a locking lever (6) on the frame to hold the setting in place, allowing the item to be removed from the micrometer.
- Some micrometers have a vernier scale on their sleeve, providing an even finer measurement to be taken, in 0.001 increments of a millimetre. Take the sleeve and thimble measurement as described above, then check which graduation on the vernier scale aligns with that of the annular scale on the thimble **Note:** *The eye must be perpendicular to the scale when taking the vernier reading - if necessary rotate the body of the micrometer to ensure this.* Multiply the vernier scale figure by 0.001 and add it to the base and fine measurement figures.

In the example shown the item measures 46.994 mm (see illustrations 3.5 and 3.6):

Linear scale (base)	46.000 mm
Linear scale (base)	00.500 mm
Annular scale (fine)	00.490 mm
Vernier scale	00.004 mm
Total figure	**46.994 mm**

Internal micrometer

- Internal micrometers are available for measuring bore diameters, but are expensive and unlikely to be available for home use. It is suggested that a set of telescoping gauges and small hole gauges, both of which must be used with an external micrometer, will suffice for taking internal measurements on a motorcycle.
- Telescoping gauges can be used to measure internal diameters of components. Select a gauge with the correct size range, make sure its ends are clean and insert it into the bore. Expand the gauge, then lock its position and withdraw it from the bore **(see illustration 3.7)**. Measure across the gauge ends with a micrometer **(see illustration 3.8)**.
- Very small diameter bores (such as valve guides) are measured with a small hole gauge. Once adjusted to a slip-fit inside the component, its position is locked and the gauge withdrawn for measurement with a micrometer **(see illustrations 3.9 and 3.10)**.

Vernier caliper

Note: *The conventional linear and dial gauge type instruments are described. Digital types are easier to read, but are far more expensive.*

- The vernier caliper does not provide the precision of a micrometer, but is versatile in being able to measure internal and external diameters. Some types also incorporate a depth gauge. It is ideal for measuring clutch plate friction material and spring free lengths.
- To use the conventional linear scale vernier, slacken off the vernier clamp screws (1) and set its jaws over (2), or inside (3), the item to be measured **(see illustration 3.11)**. Slide the jaw into contact, using the thumbwheel (4) for fine movement of the sliding scale (5) then tighten the clamp screws (1). Read off the main scale (6) where the zero on the sliding scale (5) intersects it, taking the whole number to the left of the zero; this provides the base measurement. View along the sliding scale and select the division which

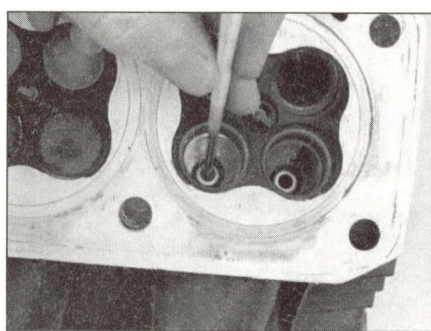

3.9 Expand the small hole gauge in the bore, lock its position . . .

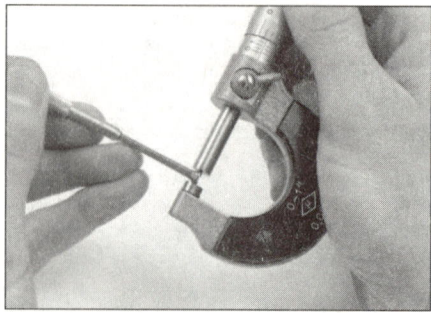

3.10 . . . then measure the gauge with a micrometer

lines up exactly with any of the divisions on the main scale, noting that the divisions usually represents 0.02 of a millimetre. Add this fine measurement to the base measurement to obtain the total reading.

Tools and Workshop Tips

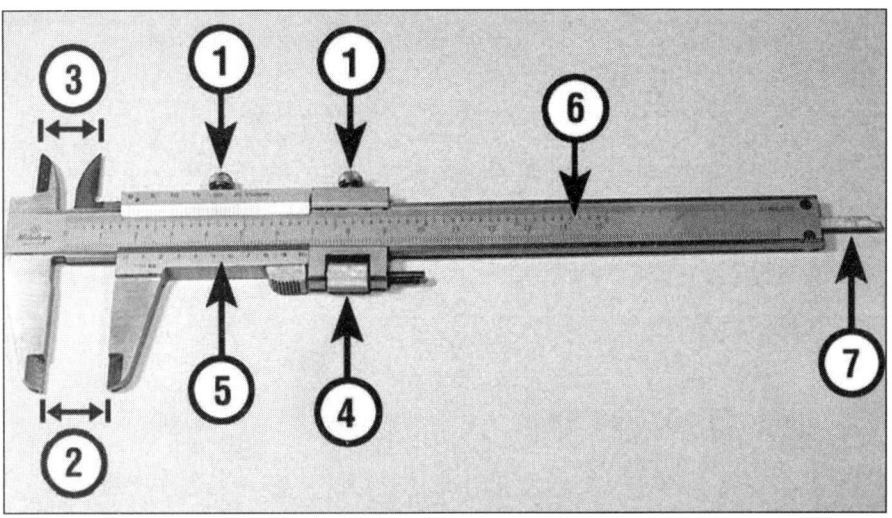

3.11 Vernier component parts (linear gauge)

1 Clamp screws
2 External jaws
3 Internal jaws
4 Thumbwheel
5 Sliding scale
6 Main scale
7 Depth gauge

In the example shown the item measures 55.92 mm **(see illustration 3.12)**:

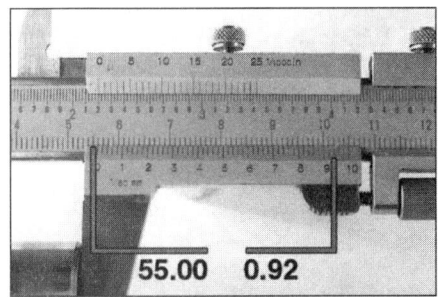

3.12 Vernier gauge reading of 55.92 mm

Base measurement	55.00 mm
Fine measurement	00.92 mm
Total figure	**55.92 mm**

● Some vernier calipers are equipped with a dial gauge for fine measurement. Before use, check that the jaws are clean, then close them fully and check that the dial gauge reads zero. If necessary adjust the gauge ring accordingly. Slacken the vernier clamp screw (1) and set its jaws over (2), or inside (3), the item to be measured **(see illustration 3.13)**. Slide the jaws into contact, using the thumbwheel (4) for fine movement. Read off the main scale (5) where the edge of the sliding scale (6) intersects it, taking the whole number to the left of the zero; this provides the base measurement. Read off the needle position on the dial gauge (7) scale to provide the fine measurement; each division represents 0.05 of a millimetre. Add this fine measurement to the base measurement to obtain the total reading.

In the example shown the item measures 55.95 mm **(see illustration 3.14)**:

Base measurement	55.00 mm
Fine measurement	00.95 mm
Total figure	**55.95 mm**

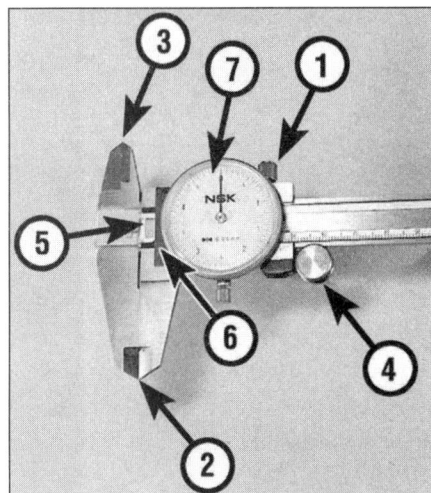

3.13 Vernier component parts (dial gauge)

1 Clamp screw
2 External jaws
3 Internal jaws
4 Thumbwheel
5 Main scale
6 Sliding scale
7 Dial gauge

3.14 Vernier gauge reading of 55.95 mm

Plastigauge

● Plastigauge is a plastic material which can be compressed between two surfaces to measure the oil clearance between them. The width of the compressed Plastigauge is measured against a calibrated scale to determine the clearance.

● Common uses of Plastigauge are for measuring the clearance between crankshaft journal and main bearing inserts, between crankshaft journal and big-end bearing inserts, and between camshaft and bearing surfaces. The following example describes big-end oil clearance measurement.

● Handle the Plastigauge material carefully to prevent distortion. Using a sharp knife, cut a length which corresponds with the width of the bearing being measured and place it carefully across the journal so that it is parallel with the shaft **(see illustration 3.15)**. Carefully install both bearing shells and the connecting rod. Without rotating the rod on the journal tighten its bolts or nuts (as applicable) to the specified torque. The connecting rod and bearings are then disassembled and the crushed Plastigauge examined.

3.15 Plastigauge placed across shaft journal

● Using the scale provided in the Plastigauge kit, measure the width of the material to determine the oil clearance **(see illustration 3.16)**. Always remove all traces of Plastigauge after use using your fingernails.

Caution: Arriving at the correct clearance demands that the assembly is torqued correctly, according to the settings and sequence (where applicable) provided by the motorcycle manufacturer.

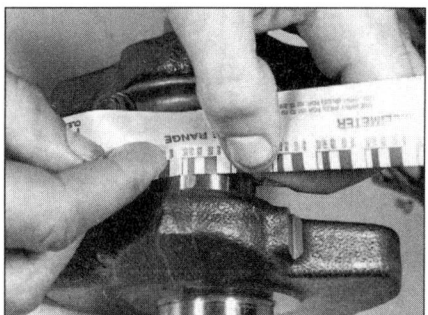

3.16 Measuring the width of the crushed Plastigauge

Tools and Workshop Tips

Dial gauge or DTI (Dial Test Indicator)

● A dial gauge can be used to accurately measure small amounts of movement. Typical uses are measuring shaft runout or shaft endfloat (sideplay) and setting piston position for ignition timing on two-strokes. A dial gauge set usually comes with a range of different probes and adapters and mounting equipment.

● The gauge needle must point to zero when at rest. Rotate the ring around its periphery to zero the gauge.

● Check that the gauge is capable of reading the extent of movement in the work. Most gauges have a small dial set in the face which records whole millimetres of movement as well as the fine scale around the face periphery which is calibrated in 0.01 mm divisions. Read off the small dial first to obtain the base measurement, then add the measurement from the fine scale to obtain the total reading.

In the example shown the gauge reads 1.48 mm (see illustration 3.17):

Base measurement	1.00 mm
Fine measurement	0.48 mm
Total figure	**1.48 mm**

3.17 Dial gauge reading of 1.48 mm

● If measuring shaft runout, the shaft must be supported in vee-blocks and the gauge mounted on a stand perpendicular to the shaft. Rest the tip of the gauge against the centre of the shaft and rotate the shaft slowly whilst watching the gauge reading (see illustration 3.18). Take several measurements along the length of the shaft and record the maximum gauge reading as the amount of runout in the shaft. **Note:** *The reading obtained will be total runout at that point - some manufacturers specify that the runout figure is halved to compare with their specified runout limit.*

● Endfloat (sideplay) measurement requires that the gauge is mounted securely to the surrounding component with its probe touching the end of the shaft. Using hand pressure, push and pull on the shaft noting the maximum endfloat recorded on the gauge (see illustration 3.19).

3.19 Using a dial gauge to measure shaft endfloat

● A dial gauge with suitable adapters can be used to determine piston position BTDC on two-stroke engines for the purposes of ignition timing. The gauge, adapter and suitable length probe are installed in the place of the spark plug and the gauge zeroed at TDC. If the piston position is specified as 1.14 mm BTDC, rotate the engine back to 2.00 mm BTDC, then slowly forwards to 1.14 mm BTDC.

Cylinder compression gauges

● A compression gauge is used for measuring cylinder compression. Either the rubber-cone type or the threaded adapter type can be used. The latter is preferred to ensure a perfect seal against the cylinder head. A 0 to 300 psi (0 to 20 Bar) type gauge (for petrol/gasoline engines) will be suitable for motorcycles.

● The spark plug is removed and the gauge either held hard against the cylinder head (cone type) or the gauge adapter screwed into the cylinder head (threaded type) (see illustration 3.20). Cylinder compression is measured with the engine turning over, but not running - carry out the compression test as described in *Fault Finding Equipment*. The gauge will hold the reading until manually released.

Oil pressure gauge

● An oil pressure gauge is used for measuring engine oil pressure. Most gauges come with a set of adapters to fit the thread of the take-off point (see illustration 3.21). If the take-off point specified by the motorcycle manufacturer is an external oil pipe union, make sure that the specified replacement union is used to prevent oil starvation.

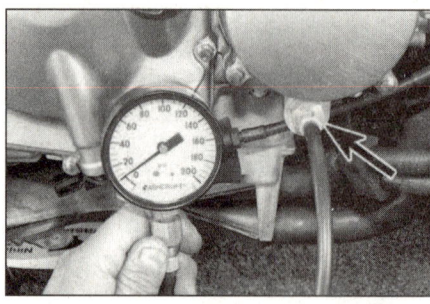

3.21 Oil pressure gauge and take-off point adapter (arrow)

● Oil pressure is measured with the engine running (at a specific rpm) and often the manufacturer will specify pressure limits for a cold and hot engine.

Straight-edge and surface plate

● If checking the gasket face of a component for warpage, place a steel rule or precision straight-edge across the gasket face and measure any gap between the straight-edge and component with feeler gauges (see illustration 3.22). Check diagonally across the component and between mounting holes (see illustration 3.23).

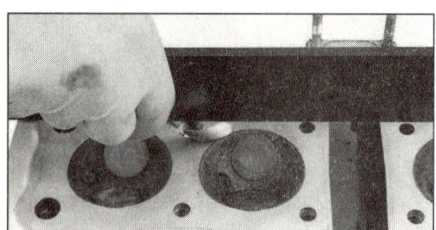

3.22 Use a straight-edge and feeler gauges to check for warpage

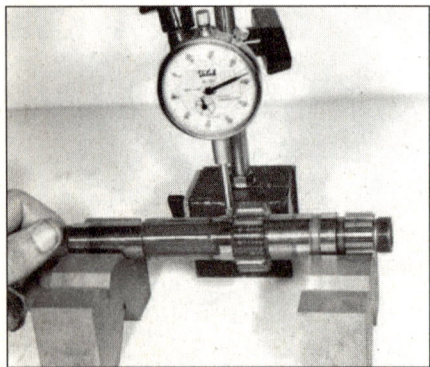

3.18 Using a dial gauge to measure shaft runout

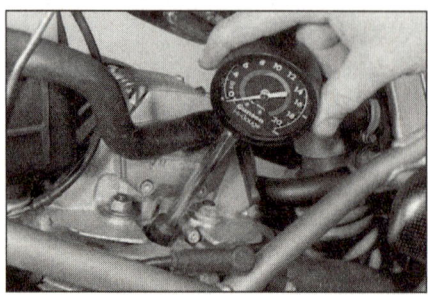

3.20 Using a rubber-cone type cylinder compression gauge

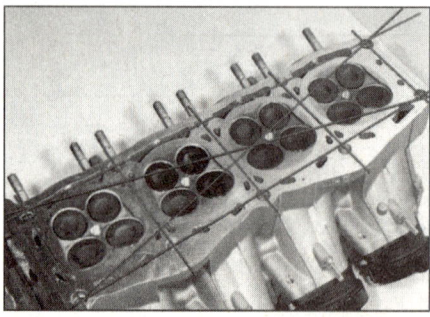

3.23 Check for warpage in these directions

Tools and Workshop Tips

● Checking individual components for warpage, such as clutch plain (metal) plates, requires a perfectly flat plate or piece or plate glass and feeler gauges.

4 Torque and leverage

What is torque?

● Torque describes the twisting force about a shaft. The amount of torque applied is determined by the distance from the centre of the shaft to the end of the lever and the amount of force being applied to the end of the lever; distance multiplied by force equals torque.

● The manufacturer applies a measured torque to a bolt or nut to ensure that it will not slacken in use and to hold two components securely together without movement in the joint. The actual torque setting depends on the thread size, bolt or nut material and the composition of the components being held.

● Too little torque may cause the fastener to loosen due to vibration, whereas too much torque will distort the joint faces of the component or cause the fastener to shear off. Always stick to the specified torque setting.

Using a torque wrench

● Check the calibration of the torque wrench and make sure it has a suitable range for the job. Torque wrenches are available in Nm (Newton-metres), kgf m (kilograms-force metre), lbf ft (pounds-feet), lbf in (inch-pounds). Do not confuse lbf ft with lbf in.

● Adjust the tool to the desired torque on the scale **(see illustration 4.1)**. If your torque wrench is not calibrated in the units specified, carefully convert the figure (see *Conversion Factors*). A manufacturer sometimes gives a torque setting as a range (8 to 10 Nm) rather than a single figure - in this case set the tool midway between the two settings. The same torque may be expressed as 9 Nm ± 1 Nm. Some torque wrenches have a method of locking the setting so that it isn't inadvertently altered during use.

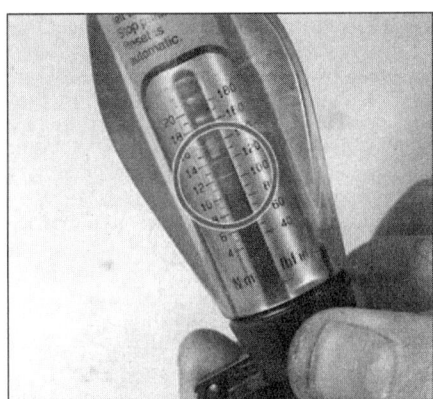

4.1 Set the torque wrench index mark to the setting required, in this case 12 Nm

● Install the bolts/nuts in their correct location and secure them lightly. Their threads must be clean and free of any old locking compound. Unless specified the threads and flange should be dry - oiled threads are necessary in certain circumstances and the manufacturer will take this into account in the specified torque figure. Similarly, the manufacturer may also specify the application of thread-locking compound.

● Tighten the fasteners in the specified sequence until the torque wrench clicks, indicating that the torque setting has been reached. Apply the torque again to double-check the setting. Where different thread diameter fasteners secure the component, as a rule tighten the larger diameter ones first.

● When the torque wrench has been finished with, release the lock (where applicable) and fully back off its setting to zero - do not leave the torque wrench tensioned. Also, do not use a torque wrench for slackening a fastener.

Angle-tightening

● Manufacturers often specify a figure in degrees for final tightening of a fastener. This usually follows tightening to a specific torque setting.

● A degree disc can be set and attached to the socket **(see illustration 4.2)** or a protractor can be used to mark the angle of movement on the bolt/nut head and the surrounding casting **(see illustration 4.3)**.

4.2 Angle tightening can be accomplished with a torque-angle gauge ...

4.3 ... or by marking the angle on the surrounding component

Loosening sequences

● Where more than one bolt/nut secures a component, loosen each fastener evenly a little at a time. In this way, not all the stress of the joint is held by one fastener and the components are not likely to distort.

● If a tightening sequence is provided, work in the REVERSE of this, but if not, work from the outside in, in a criss-cross sequence **(see illustration 4.4)**.

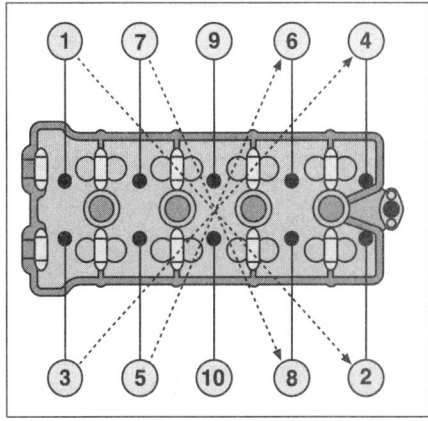

4.4 When slackening, work from the outside inwards

Tightening sequences

● If a component is held by more than one fastener it is important that the retaining bolts/nuts are tightened evenly to prevent uneven stress build-up and distortion of sealing faces. This is especially important on high-compression joints such as the cylinder head.

● A sequence is usually provided by the manufacturer, either in a diagram or actually marked in the casting. If not, always start in the centre and work outwards in a criss-cross pattern **(see illustration 4.5)**. Start off by securing all bolts/nuts finger-tight, then set the torque wrench and tighten each fastener by a small amount in sequence until the final torque is reached. By following this practice,

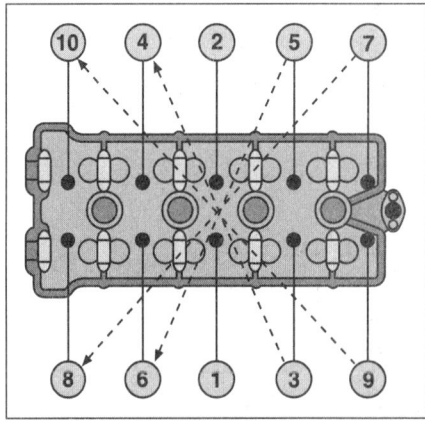

4.5 When tightening, work from the inside outwards

REF•14 Tools and Workshop Tips

the joint will be held evenly and will not be distorted. Important joints, such as the cylinder head and big-end fasteners often have two- or three-stage torque settings.

Applying leverage

● Use tools at the correct angle. Position a socket wrench or spanner on the bolt/nut so that you pull it towards you when loosening. If this can't be done, push the spanner without curling your fingers around it **(see illustration 4.6)** - the spanner may slip or the fastener loosen suddenly, resulting in your fingers being crushed against a component.

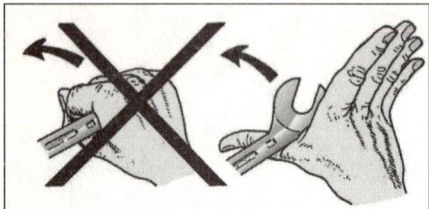

4.6 If you can't pull on the spanner to loosen a fastener, push with your hand open

● Additional leverage is gained by extending the length of the lever. The best way to do this is to use a breaker bar instead of the regular length tool, or to slip a length of tubing over the end of the spanner or socket wrench.
● If additional leverage will not work, the fastener head is either damaged or firmly corroded in place (see *Fasteners*).

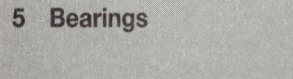

5 Bearings

Bearing removal and installation

Drivers and sockets

● Before removing a bearing, always inspect the casing to see which way it must be driven out - some casings will have retaining plates or a cast step. Also check for any identifying markings on the bearing and if installed to a certain depth, measure this at this stage. Some roller bearings are sealed on one side - take note of the original fitted position.
● Bearings can be driven out of a casing using a bearing driver tool (with the correct size head) or a socket of the correct diameter. Select the driver head or socket so that it contacts the outer race of the bearing, not the balls/rollers or inner race. Always support the casing around the bearing housing with wood blocks, otherwise there is a risk of fracture. The bearing is driven out with a few blows on the driver or socket from a heavy mallet. Unless access is severely restricted (as with wheel bearings), a pin-punch is not recommended unless it is moved around the bearing to keep it square in its housing.

● The same equipment can be used to install bearings. Make sure the bearing housing is supported on wood blocks and line up the bearing in its housing. Fit the bearing as noted on removal - generally they are installed with their marked side facing outwards. Tap the bearing squarely into its housing using a driver or socket which bears only on the bearing's outer race - contact with the bearing balls/rollers or inner race will destroy it **(see illustrations 5.1 and 5.2)**.
● Check that the bearing inner race and balls/rollers rotate freely.

5.1 Using a bearing driver against the bearing's outer race

5.2 Using a large socket against the bearing's outer race

Pullers and slide-hammers

● Where a bearing is pressed on a shaft a puller will be required to extract it **(see illustration 5.3)**. Make sure that the puller clamp or legs fit securely behind the bearing and are unlikely to slip out. If pulling a bearing

5.3 This bearing puller clamps behind the bearing and pressure is applied to the shaft end to draw the bearing off

off a gear shaft for example, you may have to locate the puller behind a gear pinion if there is no access to the race and draw the gear pinion off the shaft as well **(see illustration 5.4)**.

> **Caution:** Ensure that the puller's centre bolt locates securely against the end of the shaft and will not slip when pressure is applied. Also ensure that puller does not damage the shaft end.

5.4 Where no access is available to the rear of the bearing, it is sometimes possible to draw off the adjacent component

● Operate the puller so that its centre bolt exerts pressure on the shaft end and draws the bearing off the shaft.
● When installing the bearing on the shaft, tap only on the bearing's inner race - contact with the balls/rollers or outer race with destroy the bearing. Use a socket or length of tubing as a drift which fits over the shaft end **(see illustration 5.5)**.

5.5 When installing a bearing on a shaft use a piece of tubing which bears only on the bearing's inner race

● Where a bearing locates in a blind hole in a casing, it cannot be driven or pulled out as described above. A slide-hammer with knife-edged bearing puller attachment will be required. The puller attachment passes through the bearing and when tightened expands to fit firmly behind the bearing **(see illustration 5.6)**. By operating the slide-hammer part of the tool the bearing is jarred out of its housing **(see illustration 5.7)**.
● It is possible, if the bearing is of reasonable weight, for it to drop out of its housing if the casing is heated as described opposite. If this

Tools and Workshop Tips REF•15

5.6 Expand the bearing puller so that it locks behind the bearing . . .

5.7 . . . attach the slide hammer to the bearing puller

method is attempted, first prepare a work surface which will enable the casing to be tapped face down to help dislodge the bearing - a wood surface is ideal since it will not damage the casing's gasket surface. Wearing protective gloves, tap the heated casing several times against the work surface to dislodge the bearing under its own weight **(see illustration 5.8)**.

5.8 Tapping a casing face down on wood blocks can often dislodge a bearing

● Bearings can be installed in blind holes using the driver or socket method described above.

Drawbolts

● Where a bearing or bush is set in the eye of a component, such as a suspension linkage arm or connecting rod small-end, removal by drift may damage the component. Furthermore, a rubber bushing in a shock absorber eye cannot successfully be driven out of position. If access is available to a engineering press, the task is straightforward. If not, a drawbolt can be fabricated to extract the bearing or bush.

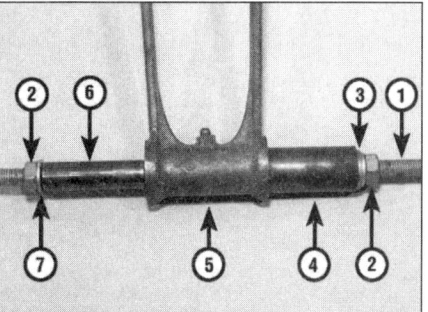

5.9 Drawbolt component parts assembled on a suspension arm

1 Bolt or length of threaded bar
2 Nuts
3 Washer (external diameter greater than tubing internal diameter)
4 Tubing (internal diameter sufficient to accommodate bearing)
5 Suspension arm with bearing
6 Tubing (external diameter slightly smaller than bearing)
7 Washer (external diameter slightly smaller than bearing)

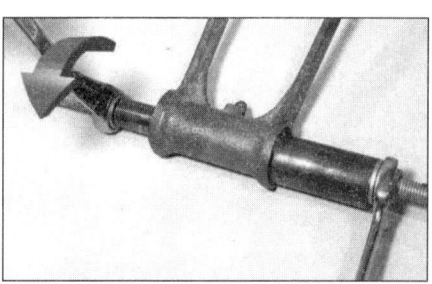

5.10 Drawing the bearing out of the suspension arm

● To extract the bearing/bush you will need a long bolt with nut (or piece of threaded bar with two nuts), a piece of tubing which has an internal diameter larger than the bearing/bush, another piece of tubing which has an external diameter slightly smaller than the bearing/bush, and a selection of washers **(see illustrations 5.9 and 5.10)**. Note that the pieces of tubing must be of the same length, or longer, than the bearing/bush.

● The same kit (without the pieces of tubing) can be used to draw the new bearing/bush back into place **(see illustration 5.11)**.

5.11 Installing a new bearing (1) in the suspension arm

Temperature change

● If the bearing's outer race is a tight fit in the casing, the aluminium casing can be heated to release its grip on the bearing. Aluminium will expand at a greater rate than the steel bearing outer race. There are several ways to do this, but avoid any localised extreme heat (such as a blow torch) - aluminium alloy has a low melting point.

● Approved methods of heating a casing are using a domestic oven (heated to 100°C) or immersing the casing in boiling water **(see illustration 5.12)**. Low temperature range localised heat sources such as a paint stripper heat gun or clothes iron can also be used **(see illustration 5.13)**. Alternatively, soak a rag in boiling water, wring it out and wrap it around the bearing housing.

> ⚠ **Warning:** *All of these methods require care in use to prevent scalding and burns to the hands. Wear protective gloves when handling hot components.*

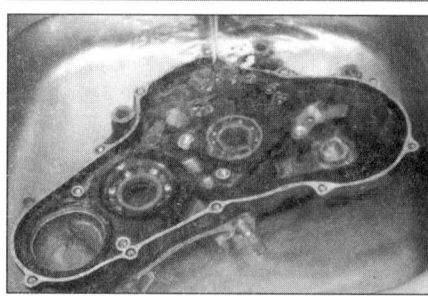

5.12 A casing can be immersed in a sink of boiling water to aid bearing removal

5.13 Using a localised heat source to aid bearing removal

● If heating the whole casing note that plastic components, such as the neutral switch, may suffer - remove them beforehand.

● After heating, remove the bearing as described above. You may find that the expansion is sufficient for the bearing to fall out of the casing under its own weight or with a light tap on the driver or socket.

● If necessary, the casing can be heated to aid bearing installation, and this is sometimes the recommended procedure if the motorcycle manufacturer has designed the housing and bearing fit with this intention.

REF•16 Tools and Workshop Tips

● Installation of bearings can be eased by placing them in a freezer the night before installation. The steel bearing will contract slightly, allowing easy insertion in its housing. This is often useful when installing steering head outer races in the frame.

Bearing types and markings

● Plain shell bearings, ball bearings, needle roller bearings and tapered roller bearings will all be found on motorcycles **(see illustrations 5.14 and 5.15)**. The ball and roller types are usually caged between an inner and outer race, but uncaged variations may be found.

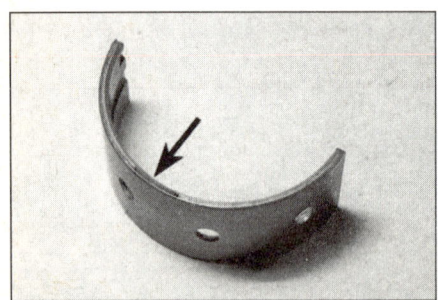

5.14 Shell bearings are either plain or grooved. They are usually identified by colour code (arrow)

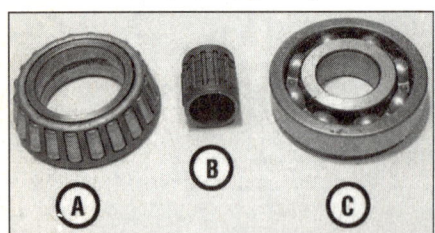

5.15 Tapered roller bearing (A), needle roller bearing (B) and ball journal bearing (C)

● Shell bearings (often called inserts) are usually found at the crankshaft main and connecting rod big-end where they are good at coping with high loads. They are made of a phosphor-bronze material and are impregnated with self-lubricating properties.

● Ball bearings and needle roller bearings consist of a steel inner and outer race with the balls or rollers between the races. They require constant lubrication by oil or grease and are good at coping with axial loads. Taper roller bearings consist of rollers set in a tapered cage set on the inner race; the outer race is separate. They are good at coping with axial loads and prevent movement along the shaft - a typical application is in the steering head.

● Bearing manufacturers produce bearings to ISO size standards and stamp one face of the bearing to indicate its internal and external diameter, load capacity and type **(see illustration 5.16)**.

● Metal bushes are usually of phosphor-bronze material. Rubber bushes are used in suspension mounting eyes. Fibre bushes have also been used in suspension pivots.

5.16 Typical bearing marking

Bearing fault finding

● If a bearing outer race has spun in its housing, the housing material will be damaged. You can use a bearing locking compound to bond the outer race in place if damage is not too severe.

● Shell bearings will fail due to damage of their working surface, as a result of lack of lubrication, corrosion or abrasive particles in the oil **(see illustration 5.17)**. Small particles of dirt in the oil may embed in the bearing material whereas larger particles will score the bearing and shaft journal. If a number of short journeys are made, insufficient heat will be generated to drive off condensation which has built up on the bearings.

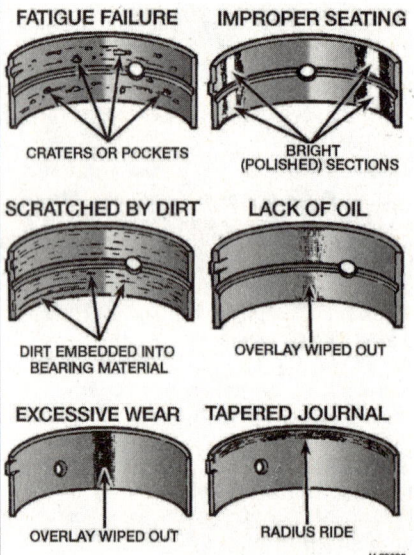

5.17 Typical bearing failures

● Ball and roller bearings will fail due to lack of lubrication or damage to the balls or rollers. Tapered-roller bearings can be damaged by overloading them. Unless the bearing is sealed on both sides, wash it in paraffin (kerosene) to remove all old grease then allow it to dry. Make a visual inspection looking to dented balls or rollers, damaged cages and worn or pitted races **(see illustration 5.18)**.

● A ball bearing can be checked for wear by listening to it when spun. Apply a film of light oil to the bearing and hold it close to the ear - hold the outer race with one hand and spin the inner race with the other hand **(see illustration 5.19)**. The bearing should be almost silent when spun; if it grates or rattles it is worn.

5.18 Example of ball journal bearing with damaged balls and cages

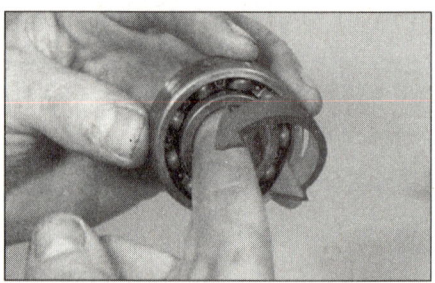

5.19 Hold outer race and listen to inner race when spun

6 Oil seals

Oil seal removal and installation

● Oil seals should be renewed every time a component is dismantled. This is because the seal lips will become set to the sealing surface and will not necessarily reseal.

● Oil seals can be prised out of position using a large flat-bladed screwdriver **(see illustration 6.1)**. In the case of crankcase seals, check first that the seal is not lipped on the inside, preventing its removal with the crankcases joined.

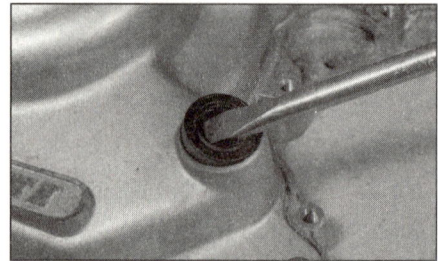

6.1 Prise out oil seals with a large flat-bladed screwdriver

● New seals are usually installed with their marked face (containing the seal reference code) outwards and the spring side towards the fluid being retained. In certain cases, such as a two-stroke engine crankshaft seal, a double lipped seal may be used due to there being fluid or gas on each side of the joint.

Tools and Workshop Tips

- Use a bearing driver or socket which bears only on the outer hard edge of the seal to install it in the casing - tapping on the inner edge will damage the sealing lip.

Oil seal types and markings

- Oil seals are usually of the single-lipped type. Double-lipped seals are found where a liquid or gas is on both sides of the joint.
- Oil seals can harden and lose their sealing ability if the motorcycle has been in storage for a long period - renewal is the only solution.
- Oil seal manufacturers also conform to the ISO markings for seal size - these are moulded into the outer face of the seal (see illustration 6.2).

6.2 These oil seal markings indicate inside diameter, outside diameter and seal thickness

7 Gaskets and sealants

Types of gasket and sealant

- Gaskets are used to seal the mating surfaces between components and keep lubricants, fluids, vacuum or pressure contained within the assembly. Aluminium gaskets are sometimes found at the cylinder joints, but most gaskets are paper-based. If the mating surfaces of the components being joined are undamaged the gasket can be installed dry, although a dab of sealant or grease will be useful to hold it in place during assembly.
- RTV (Room Temperature Vulcanising) silicone rubber sealants cure when exposed to moisture in the atmosphere. These sealants are good at filling pits or irregular gasket faces, but will tend to be forced out of the joint under very high torque. They can be used to replace a paper gasket, but first make sure that the width of the paper gasket is not essential to the shimming of internal components. RTV sealants should not be used on components containing petrol (gasoline).
- Non-hardening, semi-hardening and hard setting liquid gasket compounds can be used with a gasket or between a metal-to-metal joint. Select the sealant to suit the application: universal non-hardening sealant can be used on virtually all joints; semi-hardening on joint faces which are rough or damaged; hard setting sealant on joints which require a permanent bond and are subjected to high temperature and pressure. **Note:** Check first if the paper gasket has a bead of sealant impregnated in its surface before applying additional sealant.
- When choosing a sealant, make sure it is suitable for the application, particularly if being applied in a high-temperature area or in the vicinity of fuel. Certain manufacturers produce sealants in either clear, silver or black colours to match the finish of the engine. This has a particular application on motorcycles where much of the engine is exposed.
- Do not over-apply sealant. That which is squeezed out on the outside of the joint can be wiped off, whereas an excess of sealant on the inside can break off and clog oilways.

Breaking a sealed joint

- Age, heat, pressure and the use of hard setting sealant can cause two components to stick together so tightly that they are difficult to separate using finger pressure alone. Do not resort to using levers unless there is a pry point provided for this purpose (see illustration 7.1) or else the gasket surfaces will be damaged.
- Use a soft-faced hammer (see illustration 7.2) or a wood block and conventional hammer to strike the component near the mating surface. Avoid hammering against cast extremities since they may break off. If this method fails, try using a wood wedge between the two components.

Caution: If the joint will not separate, double-check that you have removed all the fasteners.

7.1 If a pry point is provided, apply gently pressure with a flat-bladed screwdriver

7.2 Tap around the joint with a soft-faced mallet if necessary - don't strike cooling fins

Removal of old gasket and sealant

- Paper gaskets will most likely come away complete, leaving only a few traces stuck on

Most components have one or two hollow locating dowels between the two gasket faces. If a dowel cannot be removed, do not resort to gripping it with pliers - it will almost certainly be distorted. Install a close-fitting socket or Phillips screwdriver into the dowel and then grip the outer edge of the dowel to free it.

the sealing faces of the components. It is imperative that all traces are removed to ensure correct sealing of the new gasket.

- Very carefully scrape all traces of gasket away making sure that the sealing surfaces are not gouged or scored by the scraper (see illustrations 7.3, 7.4 and 7.5). Stubborn deposits can be removed by spraying with an aerosol gasket remover. Final preparation of

7.3 Paper gaskets can be scraped off with a gasket scraper tool . . .

7.4 . . . a knife blade . . .

7.5 . . . or a household scraper

REF•18 Tools and Workshop Tips

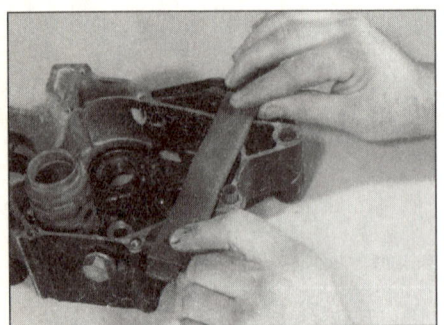

7.6 Fine abrasive paper is wrapped around a flat file to clean up the gasket face

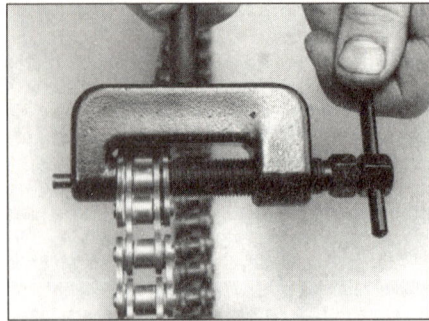

8.1 Tighten the chain breaker to push the pin out of the link . . .

8.4 Insert the new soft link, with O-rings, through the chain ends . . .

7.7 A kitchen scourer can be used on stubborn deposits

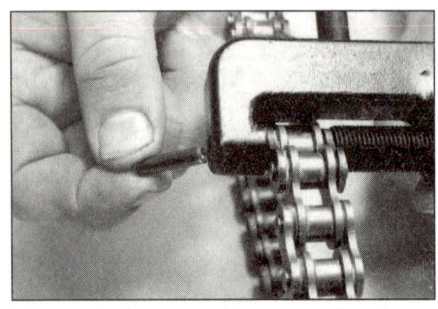

8.2 . . . withdraw the pin, remove the tool . . .

8.5 . . . install the O-rings over the pin ends . . .

8.6 . . . followed by the sideplate

the gasket surface can be made with very fine abrasive paper or a plastic kitchen scourer **(see illustrations 7.6 and 7.7)**.
● Old sealant can be scraped or peeled off components, depending on the type originally used. Note that gasket removal compounds are available to avoid scraping the components clean; make sure the gasket remover suits the type of sealant used.

8 Chains

Breaking and joining final drive chains

● Drive chains for all but small bikes are continuous and do not have a clip-type connecting link. The chain must be broken using a chain breaker tool and the new chain securely riveted together using a new soft rivet-type link. Never use a clip-type connecting link instead of a rivet-type link, except in an emergency. Various chain breaking and riveting tools are available, either as separate tools or combined as illustrated in the accompanying photographs - read the instructions supplied with the tool carefully.

> **Warning: The need to rivet the new link pins correctly cannot be overstressed - loss of control of the motorcycle is very likely to result if the chain breaks in use.**

● Rotate the chain and look for the soft link. The soft link pins look like they have been

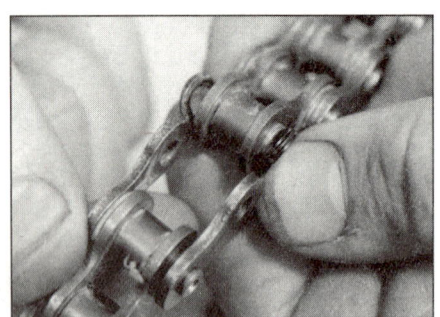

8.3 . . . and separate the chain link

deeply centre-punched instead of peened over like all the other pins **(see illustration 8.9)** and its sideplate may be a different colour. Position the soft link midway between the sprockets and assemble the chain breaker tool over one of the soft link pins **(see illustration 8.1)**. Operate the tool to push the pin out through the chain **(see illustration 8.2)**. On an O-ring chain, remove the O-rings **(see illustration 8.3)**. Carry out the same procedure on the other soft link pin.

> **Caution: Certain soft link pins (particularly on the larger chains) may require their ends to be filed or ground off before they can be pressed out using the tool.**

● Check that you have the correct size and strength (standard or heavy duty) new soft link - do not reuse the old link. Look for the size marking on the chain sideplates **(see illustration 8.10)**.
● Position the chain ends so that they are engaged over the rear sprocket. On an O-ring chain, install a new O-ring over each pin of the link and insert the link through the two chain ends **(see illustration 8.4)**. Install a new O-ring over the end of each pin, followed by the sideplate (with the chain manufacturer's marking facing outwards) **(see illustrations 8.5 and 8.6)**. On an unsealed chain, insert the link through the two chain ends, then install the sideplate with the chain manufacturer's marking facing outwards.
● Note that it may not be possible to install the sideplate using finger pressure alone. If using a joining tool, assemble it so that the plates of the tool clamp the link and press the sideplate over the pins **(see illustration 8.7)**. Otherwise, use two small sockets placed over

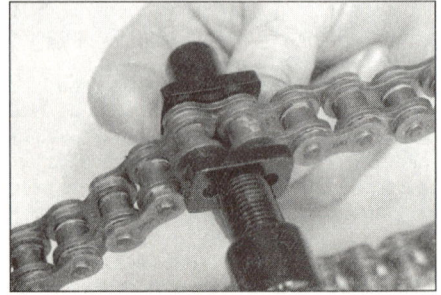

8.7 Push the sideplate into position using a clamp

Tools and Workshop Tips

8.8 Assemble the chain riveting tool over one pin at a time and tighten it fully

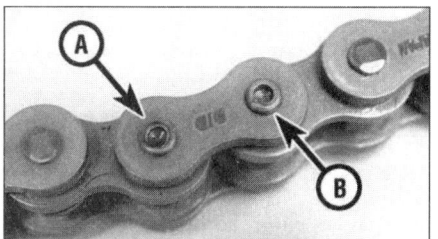

8.9 Pin end correctly riveted (A), pin end unriveted (B)

the rivet ends and two pieces of the wood between a G-clamp. Operate the clamp to press the sideplate over the pins.

● Assemble the joining tool over one pin (following the maker's instructions) and tighten the tool down to spread the pin end securely **(see illustrations 8.8 and 8.9)**. Do the same on the other pin.

> **Warning: Check that the pin ends are secure and that there is no danger of the sideplate coming loose. If the pin ends are cracked the soft link must be renewed.**

Final drive chain sizing

● Chains are sized using a three digit number, followed by a suffix to denote the chain type **(see illustration 8.10)**. Chain type is either standard or heavy duty (thicker sideplates), and also unsealed or O-ring/X-ring type.

● The first digit of the number relates to the pitch of the chain, ie the distance from the centre of one pin to the centre of the next pin **(see illustration 8.11)**. Pitch is expressed in eighths of an inch, as follows:

8.10 Typical chain size and type marking

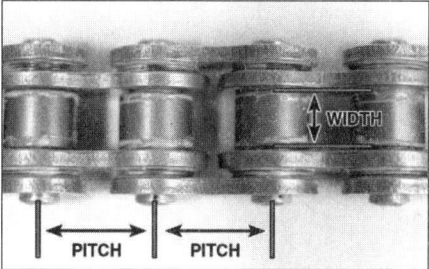

8.11 Chain dimensions

Sizes commencing with a 4 (eg 428) have a pitch of 1/2 inch (12.7 mm)

Sizes commencing with a 5 (eg 520) have a pitch of 5/8 inch (15.9 mm)

Sizes commencing with a 6 (eg 630) have a pitch of 3/4 inch (19.1 mm)

● The second and third digits of the chain size relate to the width of the rollers, again in imperial units, eg the 525 shown has 5/16 inch (7.94 mm) rollers **(see illustration 8.11)**.

9 Hoses

Clamping to prevent flow

● Small-bore flexible hoses can be clamped to prevent fluid flow whilst a component is worked on. Whichever method is used, ensure that the hose material is not permanently distorted or damaged by the clamp.

a) A brake hose clamp available from auto accessory shops **(see illustration 9.1)**.
b) A wingnut type hose clamp **(see illustration 9.2)**.

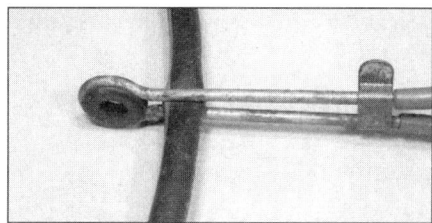

9.1 Hoses can be clamped with an automotive brake hose clamp . . .

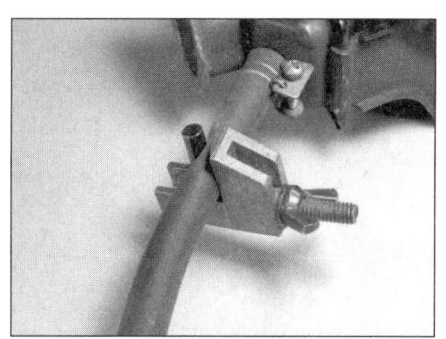

9.2 . . . a wingnut type hose clamp . . .

c) Two sockets placed each side of the hose and held with straight-jawed self-locking grips **(see illustration 9.3)**.
d) Thick card each side of the hose held between straight-jawed self-locking grips **(see illustration 9.4)**.

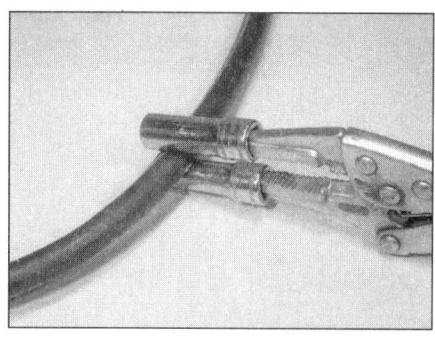

9.3 . . . two sockets and a pair of self-locking grips . . .

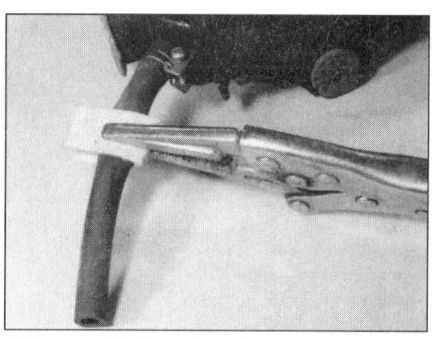

9.4 . . . or thick card and self-locking grips

Freeing and fitting hoses

● Always make sure the hose clamp is moved well clear of the hose end. Grip the hose with your hand and rotate it whilst pulling it off the union. If the hose has hardened due to age and will not move, slit it with a sharp knife and peel its ends off the union **(see illustration 9.5)**.

● Resist the temptation to use grease or soap on the unions to aid installation; although it helps the hose slip over the union it will equally aid the escape of fluid from the joint. It is preferable to soften the hose ends in hot water and wet the inside surface of the hose with water or a fluid which will evaporate.

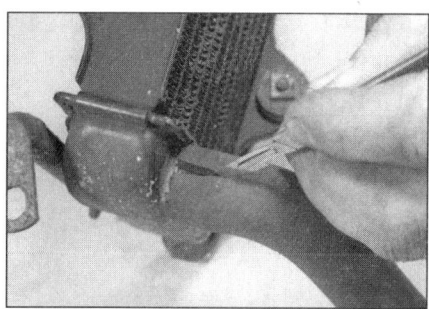

9.5 Cutting a coolant hose free with a sharp knife

Security

Introduction

In less time than it takes to read this introduction, a thief could steal your motorcycle. Returning only to find your bike has gone is one of the worst feelings in the world. Even if the motorcycle is insured against theft, once you've got over the initial shock, you will have the inconvenience of dealing with the police and your insurance company.

The motorcycle is an easy target for the professional thief and the joyrider alike and the official figures on motorcycle theft make for depressing reading; on average a motorcycle is stolen every 16 minutes in the UK!

Motorcycle thefts fall into two categories, those stolen 'to order' and those taken by opportunists. The thief stealing to order will be on the look out for a specific make and model and will go to extraordinary lengths to obtain that motorcycle. The opportunist thief on the other hand will look for easy targets which can be stolen with the minimum of effort and risk.

Whilst it is never going to be possible to make your machine 100% secure, it is estimated that around half of all stolen motorcycles are taken by opportunist thieves. Remember that the opportunist thief is always on the look out for the easy option: if there are two similar motorcycles parked side-by-side, they will target the one with the lowest level of security. By taking a few precautions, you can reduce the chances of your motorcycle being stolen.

Security equipment

There are many specialised motorcycle security devices available and the following text summarises their applications and their good and bad points.

Once you have decided on the type of security equipment which best suits your needs, we recommended that you read one of the many equipment tests regularly carried out by the motorcycle press. These tests compare the products from all the major manufacturers and give impartial ratings on their effectiveness, value-for-money and ease of use.

No one item of security equipment can provide complete protection. It is highly recommended that two or more of the items described below are combined to increase the security of your motorcycle (a lock and chain plus an alarm system is just about ideal). The more security measures fitted to the bike, the less likely it is to be stolen.

Ensure the lock and chain you buy is of good quality and long enough to shackle your bike to a solid object

Lock and chain

Pros: *Very flexible to use; can be used to secure the motorcycle to almost any immovable object. On some locks and chains, the lock can be used on its own as a disc lock (see below).*

Cons: *Can be very heavy and awkward to carry on the motorcycle, although some types will be supplied with a carry bag which can be strapped to the pillion seat.*

● Heavy-duty chains and locks are an excellent security measure **(see illustration 1)**. Whenever the motorcycle is parked, use the lock and chain to secure the machine to a solid, immovable object such as a post or railings. This will prevent the machine from being ridden away or being lifted into the back of a van.

● When fitting the chain, always ensure the chain is routed around the motorcycle frame or swingarm **(see illustrations 2 and 3)**. Never merely pass the chain around one of the wheel rims; a thief may unbolt the wheel and lift the rest of the machine into a van, leaving you with just the wheel! Try to avoid having excess chain free, thus making it difficult to use cutting tools, and keep the chain and lock off the ground to prevent thieves attacking it with a cold chisel. Position the lock so that its lock barrel is facing downwards; this will make it harder for the thief to attack the lock mechanism.

Pass the chain through the bike's frame, rather than just through a wheel . . .

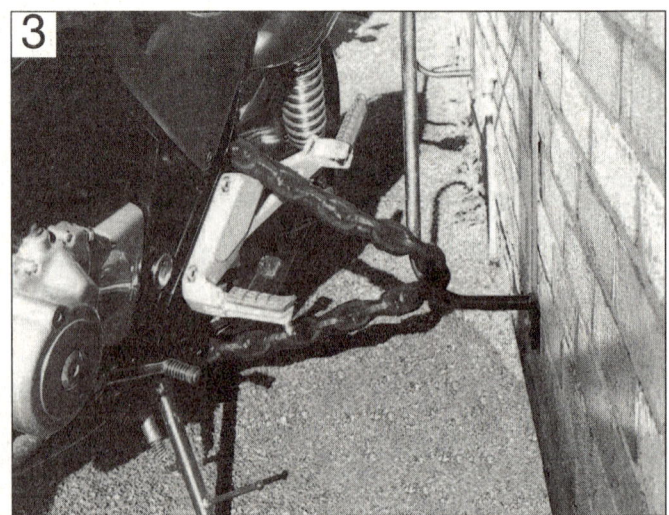

. . . and loop it around a solid object

Security

U-locks

Pros: *Highly effective deterrent which can be used to secure the bike to a post or railings. Most U-locks come with a carrier which allows the lock to be easily carried on the bike.*

Cons: *Not as flexible to use as a lock and chain.*

- These are solid locks which are similar in use to a lock and chain. U-locks are lighter than a lock and chain but not so flexible to use. The length and shape of the lock shackle limit the objects to which the bike can be secured **(see illustration 4)**.

U-locks can be used to secure the bike to a solid object – ensure you purchase one which is long enough

Disc locks

Pros: *Small, light and very easy to carry; most can be stored underneath the seat.*

Cons: *Does not prevent the motorcycle being lifted into a van. Can be very embarrassing if you forget to remove the lock before attempting to ride off!*

- Disc locks are designed to be attached to the front brake disc. The lock passes through one of the holes in the disc and prevents the wheel rotating by jamming against the fork/brake caliper **(see illustration 5)**. Some are equipped with an alarm siren which sounds if the disc lock is moved; this not only acts as a theft deterrent but also as a handy reminder if you try to move the bike with the lock still fitted.

- Combining the disc lock with a length of cable which can be looped around a post or railings provides an additional measure of security **(see illustration 6)**.

Alarms and immobilisers

Pros: *Once installed it is completely hassle-free to use. If the system is 'Thatcham' or 'Sold Secure-approved', insurance companies may give you a discount.*

Cons: *Can be expensive to buy and complex to install. No system will prevent the motorcycle from being lifted into a van and taken away.*

- Electronic alarms and immobilisers are available to suit a variety of budgets. There are three different types of system available: pure alarms, pure immobilisers, and the more expensive systems which are combined alarm/immobilisers **(see illustration 7)**.
- An alarm system is designed to emit an audible warning if the motorcycle is being tampered with.
- An immobiliser prevents the motorcycle being started and ridden away by disabling its electrical systems.
- When purchasing an alarm/immobiliser system, check the cost of installing the system unless you are able to do it yourself. If the motorcycle is not used regularly, another consideration is the current drain of the system. All alarm/immobiliser systems are powered by the motorcycle's battery; purchasing a system with a very low current drain could prevent the battery losing its charge whilst the motorcycle is not being used.

A typical disc lock attached through one of the holes in the disc

A disc lock combined with a security cable provides additional protection

A typical alarm/immobiliser system

REF•22 Security

Indelible markings can be applied to most areas of the bike – always apply the manufacturer's sticker to warn off thieves

Chemically-etched code numbers can be applied to main body panels . . .

. . . again, always ensure that the kit manufacturer's sticker is applied in a prominent position

Security marking kits

Pros: Very cheap and effective deterrent. Many insurance companies will give you a discount on your insurance premium if a recognised security marking kit is used on your motorcycle.

Cons: Does not prevent the motorcycle being stolen by joyriders.

● There are many different types of security marking kits available. The idea is to mark as many parts of the motorcycle as possible with a unique security number **(see illustrations 8, 9 and 10)**. A form will be included with the kit to register your personal details and those of the motorcycle with the kit manufacturer. This register is made available to the police to help them trace the rightful owner of any motorcycle or components which they recover should all other forms of identification have been removed. Always apply the warning stickers provided with the kit to deter thieves.

Ground anchors, wheel clamps and security posts

Pros: An excellent form of security which will deter all but the most determined of thieves.

Cons: Awkward to install and can be expensive.

● Whilst the motorcycle is at home, it is a good idea to attach it securely to the floor or a solid wall, even if it is kept in a securely locked garage. Various types of ground anchors, security posts and wheel clamps are available for this purpose **(see illustration 11)**. These security devices are either bolted to a solid concrete or brick structure or can be cemented into the ground.

Permanent ground anchors provide an excellent level of security when the bike is at home

Security at home

A high percentage of motorcycle thefts are from the owner's home. Here are some things to consider whenever your motorcycle is at home:

✔ Where possible, always keep the motorcycle in a securely locked garage. Never rely solely on the standard lock on the garage door, these are usual hopelessly inadequate. Fit an additional locking mechanism to the door and consider having the garage alarmed. A security light, activated by a movement sensor, is also a good investment.

✔ Always secure the motorcycle to the ground or a wall, even if it is inside a securely locked garage.

✔ Do not regularly leave the motorcycle outside your home, try to keep it out of sight wherever possible. If a garage is not available, fit a motorcycle cover over the bike to disguise its true identity.

✔ It is not uncommon for thieves to follow a motorcyclist home to find out where the bike is kept. They will then return at a later date. Be aware of this whenever you are returning home on your motorcycle. If you suspect you are being followed, do not return home, instead ride to a garage or shop and stop as a precaution.

✔ When selling a motorcycle, do not provide your home address or the location where the bike is normally kept. Arrange to meet the buyer at a location away from your home. Thieves have been known to pose as potential buyers to find out where motorcycles are kept and then return later to steal them.

Security away from the home

As well as fitting security equipment to your motorcycle here are a few general rules to follow whenever you park your motorcycle.

✔ Park in a busy, public place.
✔ Use car parks which incorporate security features, such as CCTV.
✔ At night, park in a well-lit area, preferably directly underneath a street light.
✔ Engage the steering lock.
✔ Secure the motorcycle to a solid, immovable object such as a post or railings with an additional lock. If this is not possible, secure the bike to a friend's motorcycle. Some public parking places provide security loops for motorcycles.
✔ Never leave your helmet or luggage attached to the motorcycle. Take them with you at all times.

Lubricants and fluids

A wide range of lubricants, fluids and cleaning agents is available for motor-cycles. This is a guide as to what is available, its applications and properties.

Four-stroke engine oil

● Engine oil is without doubt the most important component of any four-stroke engine. Modern motorcycle engines place a lot of demands on their oil and choosing the right type is essential. Using an unsuitable oil will lead to an increased rate of engine wear and could result in serious engine damage. Before purchasing oil, always check the recommended oil specification given by the manufacturer. The manufacturer will state a recommended 'type or classification' and also a specific 'viscosity' range for engine oil.

● The oil 'type or classification' is identified by its API (American Petroleum Institute) rating. The API rating will be in the form of two letters, e.g. SG. The S identifies the oil as being suitable for use in a petrol (gasoline) engine (S stands for spark ignition) and the second letter, ranging from A to J, identifies the oil's performance rating. The later this letter, the higher the specification of the oil; for example API SG oil exceeds the requirements of API SF oil. **Note:** *On some oils there may also be a second rating consisting of another two letters, the first letter being C, e.g. API SF/CD. This rating indicates the oil is also suitable for use in a diesel engines (the C stands for compression ignition) and is thus of no relevance for motorcycle use.*

● The 'viscosity' of the oil is identified by its SAE (Society of Automotive Engineers) rating. All modern engines require multigrade oils and the SAE rating will consist of two numbers, the first followed by a W, e.g. 10W/40. The first number indicates the viscosity rating of the oil at low temperatures (W stands for winter – tested at –20°C) and the second number represents the viscosity of the oil at high temperatures (tested at 100°C). The lower the number, the thinner the oil. For example an oil with an SAE 10W/40 rating will give better cold starting and running than an SAE 15W/40 oil.

● As well as ensuring the 'type' and 'viscosity' of the oil match the recommendations, another consideration to make when buying engine oil is whether to purchase a standard mineral-based oil, a semi-synthetic oil (also known as a synthetic blend or synthetic-based oil) or a fully-synthetic oil. Although all oils will have a similar rating and viscosity, their cost will vary considerably; mineral-based oils are the cheapest, the fully-synthetic oils the most expensive with the semi-synthetic oils falling somewhere in-between. This decision is very much up to the owner, but it should be noted that modern synthetic oils have far better lubricating and cleaning qualities than traditional mineral-based oils and tend to retain these properties for far longer. Bearing in mind the operating conditions inside a modern, high-revving motorcycle engine it is highly recommended that a fully synthetic oil is used. The extra expense at each service could save you money in the long term by preventing premature engine wear.

● As a final note always ensure that the oil is specifically designed for use in motorcycle engines. Engine oils designed primarily for use in car engines sometimes contain additives or friction modifiers which could cause clutch slip on a motorcycle fitted with a wet-clutch.

Two-stroke engine oil

● Modern two-stroke engines, with their high power outputs, place high demands on their oil. If engine seizure is to be avoided it is essential that a high-quality oil is used. Two-stroke oils differ hugely from four-stroke oils. The oil lubricates only the crankshaft and piston(s) (the transmission has its own lubricating oil) and is used on a total-loss basis where it is burnt completely during the combustion process.

● The Japanese have recently introduced a classification system for two-stroke oils, the JASO rating. This rating is in the form of two letters, either FA, FB or FC – FA is the lowest classification and FC the highest. Ensure the oil being used meets or exceeds the recommended rating specified by the manufacturer.

● As well as ensuring the oil rating matches the recommendation, another consideration to make when buying engine oil is whether to purchase a standard mineral-based oil, a semi-synthetic oil (also known as a synthetic blend or synthetic-based oil) or a fully-synthetic oil. The cost of each type of oil varies considerably; mineral-based oils are the cheapest, the fully-synthetic oils the most expensive with the semi-synthetic oils falling somewhere in-between. This decision is very much up to the owner, but it should be noted that modern synthetic oils have far better lubricating properties and burn cleaner than traditional mineral-based oils. It is therefore recommended that a fully synthetic oil is used. The extra expense could save you money in the long term by preventing premature engine wear, engine performance will be improved, carbon deposits and exhaust smoke will be reduced.

REF•24 Lubricants and fluids

● Always ensure that the oil is specifically designed for use in an injector system. Many high quality two-stroke oils are designed for competition use and need to be pre-mixed with fuel. These oils are of a much higher viscosity and are not designed to flow through the injector pumps used on road-going two-stroke motorcycles.

Transmission (gear) oil

● On a two-stroke engine, the transmission and clutch are lubricated by their own separate oil bath which must be changed in accordance with the Maintenance Schedule.
● Although the engine and transmission units of most four-strokes use a common lubrication supply, there are some exceptions where the engine and gearbox have separate oil reservoirs and a dry clutch is used.
● Motorcycle manufacturers will either recommend a monograde transmission oil or a four-stroke multigrade engine oil to lubricate the transmission.
● Transmission oils, or gear oils as they are often called, are designed specifically for use in transmission systems. The viscosity of these oils is represented by an SAE number, but the scale of measurement applied is different to that used to grade engine oils. As a rough guide a SAE90 gear oil will be of the same viscosity as an SAE50 engine oil.

Shaft drive oil

● On models equipped with shaft final drive, the shaft drive gears are will have their own oil supply. The manufacturer will state a recommended 'type or classification' and also a specific 'viscosity' range in the same manner as for four-stroke engine oil.
● Gear oil classification is given by the number which follows the API GL (GL standing for gear lubricant) rating, the higher the number, the higher the specification of the oil, e.g. API GL5 oil is a higher specification than API GL4 oil. Ensure the oil meets or exceeds the classification specified and is of the correct viscosity. The viscosity of gear oils is also represented by an SAE number but the scale of measurement used is different to that used to grade engine oils. As a rough guide an SAE90 gear oil will be of the same viscosity as an SAE50 engine oil.
● If the use of an EP (Extreme Pressure) gear oil is specified, ensure the oil purchased is suitable.

Fork oil and suspension fluid

● Conventional telescopic front forks are hydraulic and require fork oil to work. To ensure the forks function correctly, the fork oil must be changed in accordance with the Maintenance Schedule.
● Fork oil is available in a variety of viscosities, identified by their SAE rating; fork oil ratings vary from light (SAE 5) to heavy (SAE 30). When purchasing fork oil, ensure the viscosity rating matches that specified by the manufacturer.
● Some lubricant manufacturers also produce a range of high-quality suspension fluids which are very similar to fork oil but are designed mainly for competition use. These fluids may have a different viscosity rating system which is not to be confused with the SAE rating of normal fork oil. Refer to the manufacturer's instructions if in any doubt.

Brake and clutch fluid

● All disc brake systems and some clutch systems are hydraulically operated. To ensure correct operation, the hydraulic fluid must be changed in accordance with the Maintenance Schedule.
● Brake and clutch fluid is classified by its DOT rating with most motorcycle manufacturers specifying DOT 3 or 4 fluid. Both fluid types are glycol-based and can be mixed together without adverse effect; DOT 4 fluid exceeds the requirements of DOT 3 fluid. Although it is safe to use DOT 4 fluid in a system designed for use with DOT 3 fluid, never use DOT 3 fluid in a system which specifies the use of DOT 4 as this will adversely affect the system's performance. The type required for the system will be marked on the fluid reservoir cap.
● Some manufacturers also produce a DOT 5 hydraulic fluid. DOT 5 hydraulic fluid is silicone-based and is not compatible with the glycol-based DOT 3 and 4 fluids. Never mix DOT 5 fluid with DOT 3 or 4 fluid as this will seriously affect the performance of the hydraulic system.

Coolant/antifreeze

● When purchasing coolant/antifreeze, always ensure it is suitable for use in an aluminium engine and contains corrosion inhibitors to prevent possible blockages of the internal coolant passages of the system. As a general rule, most coolants are designed to be used neat and should not be diluted whereas antifreeze can be mixed with distilled water to provide a coolant solution of the required strength. Refer to the manufacturer's instructions on the bottle.
● Ensure the coolant is changed in accordance with the Maintenance Schedule.

Chain lube

● Chain lube is an aerosol-type spray lubricant specifically designed for use on motorcycle final drive chains. Chain lube has two functions, to minimise friction between the final drive chain and sprockets and to prevent corrosion of the chain. Regular use of a good-quality chain lube will extend the life of the drive chain and sprockets and thus maximise the power being transmitted from the transmission to the rear wheel.
● When using chain lube, always allow some time for the solvents in the lube to evaporate before riding the motorcycle. This will minimise the amount of lube which will

Lubricants and fluids

'fling' off from the chain when the motorcycle is used. If the motorcycle is equipped with an 'O-ring' chain, ensure the chain lube is labelled as being suitable for use on 'O-ring' chains.

Degreasers and solvents

● There are many different types of solvents and degreasers available to remove the grime and grease which accumulate around the motorcycle during normal use. Degreasers and solvents are usually available as an aerosol-type spray or as a liquid which you apply with a brush. Always closely follow the manufacturer's instructions and wear eye protection during use. Be aware that many solvents are flammable and may give off noxious fumes; take adequate precautions when using them (see Safety First!).

● For general cleaning, use one of the many solvents or degreasers available from most motorcycle accessory shops. These solvents are usually applied then left for a certain time before being washed off with water.

Brake cleaner is a solvent specifically designed to remove all traces of oil, grease and dust from braking system components. Brake cleaner is designed to evaporate quickly and leaves behind no residue.

Carburettor cleaner is an aerosol-type solvent specifically designed to clear carburettor blockages and break down the hard deposits and gum often found inside carburettors during overhaul.

Contact cleaner is an aerosol-type solvent designed for cleaning electrical components. The cleaner will remove all traces of oil and dirt from components such as switch contacts or fouled spark plugs and then dry, leaving behind no residue.

Gasket remover is an aerosol-type solvent designed for removing stubborn gaskets from engine components during overhaul. Gasket remover will minimise the amount of scraping required to remove the gasket and therefore reduce the risk of damage to the mating surface.

Spray lubricants

● Aerosol-based spray lubricants are widely available and are excellent for lubricating lever pivots and exposed cables and switches. Try to use a lubricant which is of the dry-film type as the fluid evaporates, leaving behind a dry-film of lubricant. Lubricants which leave behind an oily residue will attract dust and dirt which will increase the rate of wear of the cable/lever.

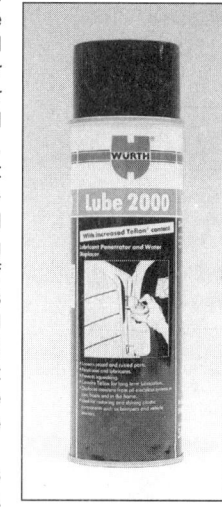

● Most lubricants also act as a moisture dispersant and a penetrating fluid. This means they can also be used to 'dry out' electrical components such as wiring connectors or switches as well as helping to free seized fasteners.

Greases

● Grease is used to lubricate many of the pivot-points. A good-quality multi-purpose grease is suitable for most applications but some manufacturers will specify the use of specialist greases for use on components such as swingarm and suspension linkage bushes. These specialist greases can be purchased from most motorcycle (or car) accessory shops; commonly specified types include molybdenum disulphide grease, lithium-based grease, graphite-based grease, silicone-based grease and high-temperature copper-based grease.

Gasket sealing compounds

● Gasket sealing compounds can be used in conjunction with gaskets, to improve their sealing capabilities, or on their own to seal metal-to-metal joints. Depending on their type, sealing compounds either set hard or stay relatively soft and pliable.

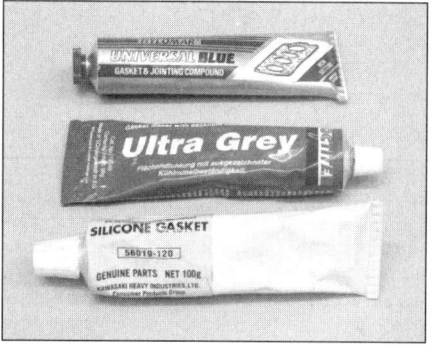

● When purchasing a gasket sealing compound, ensure that it is designed specifically for use on an internal combustion engine. General multi-purpose sealants available from DIY stores may appear visibly similar but they are not designed to withstand the extreme heat or contact with fuel and oil encountered when used on an engine (see 'Tools and Workshop Tips' for further information).

Thread locking compound

● Thread locking compounds are used to secure certain threaded fasteners in position to prevent them from loosening due to vibration. Thread locking compounds can be purchased from most motorcycle (and car) accessory shops. Ensure the threads of the both components are completely clean and dry before sparingly applying the locking compound (see 'Tools and Workshop Tips' for further information).

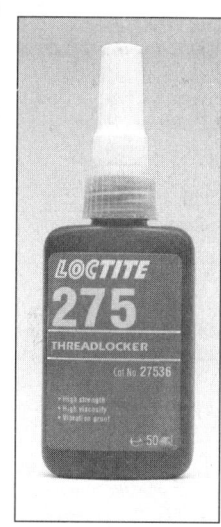

Fuel additives

● Fuel additives which protect and clean the fuel system components are widely available. These additives are designed to remove all traces of deposits that build up on the carburettors/injectors and prevent wear, helping the fuel system to operate more efficiently. If a fuel additive is being used, check that it is suitable for use with your motorcycle, especially if your motorcycle is equipped with a catalytic converter.

● Octane boosters are also available. These additives are designed to improve the performance of highly-tuned engines being run on normal pump-fuel and are of no real use on standard motorcycles.

Conversion factors

Length (distance)
Inches (in)	x 25.4	= Millimetres (mm)	x 0.0394	= Inches (in)
Feet (ft)	x 0.305	= Metres (m)	x 3.281	= Feet (ft)
Miles	x 1.609	= Kilometres (km)	x 0.621	= Miles

Volume (capacity)
Cubic inches (cu in; in^3)	x 16.387	= Cubic centimetres (cc; cm^3)	x 0.061	= Cubic inches (cu in; in^3)
Imperial pints (Imp pt)	x 0.568	= Litres (l)	x 1.76	= Imperial pints (Imp pt)
Imperial quarts (Imp qt)	x 1.137	= Litres (l)	x 0.88	= Imperial quarts (Imp qt)
Imperial quarts (Imp qt)	x 1.201	= US quarts (US qt)	x 0.833	= Imperial quarts (Imp qt)
US quarts (US qt)	x 0.946	= Litres (l)	x 1.057	= US quarts (US qt)
Imperial gallons (Imp gal)	x 4.546	= Litres (l)	x 0.22	= Imperial gallons (Imp gal)
Imperial gallons (Imp gal)	x 1.201	= US gallons (US gal)	x 0.833	= Imperial gallons (Imp gal)
US gallons (US gal)	x 3.785	= Litres (l)	x 0.264	= US gallons (US gal)

Mass (weight)
Ounces (oz)	x 28.35	= Grams (g)	x 0.035	= Ounces (oz)
Pounds (lb)	x 0.454	= Kilograms (kg)	x 2.205	= Pounds (lb)

Force
Ounces-force (ozf; oz)	x 0.278	= Newtons (N)	x 3.6	= Ounces-force (ozf; oz)
Pounds-force (lbf; lb)	x 4.448	= Newtons (N)	x 0.225	= Pounds-force (lbf; lb)
Newtons (N)	x 0.1	= Kilograms-force (kgf; kg)	x 9.81	= Newtons (N)

Pressure
Pounds-force per square inch (psi; lbf/in^2; lb/in^2)	x 0.070	= Kilograms-force per square centimetre (kgf/cm^2; kg/cm^2)	x 14.223	= Pounds-force per square inch (psi; lbf/in^2; lb/in^2)
Pounds-force per square inch (psi; lbf/in^2; lb/in^2)	x 0.068	= Atmospheres (atm)	x 14.696	= Pounds-force per square inch (psi; lbf/in^2; lb/in^2)
Pounds-force per square inch (psi; lbf/in^2; lb/in^2)	x 0.069	= Bars	x 14.5	= Pounds-force per square inch (psi; lbf/in^2; lb/in^2)
Pounds-force per square inch (psi; lbf/in^2; lb/in^2)	x 6.895	= Kilopascals (kPa)	x 0.145	= Pounds-force per square inch (psi; lbf/in^2; lb/in^2)
Kilopascals (kPa)	x 0.01	= Kilograms-force per square centimetre (kgf/cm^2; kg/cm^2)	x 98.1	= Kilopascals (kPa)
Millibar (mbar)	x 100	= Pascals (Pa)	x 0.01	= Millibar (mbar)
Millibar (mbar)	x 0.0145	= Pounds-force per square inch (psi; lbf/in^2; lb/in^2)	x 68.947	= Millibar (mbar)
Millibar (mbar)	x 0.75	= Millimetres of mercury (mmHg)	x 1.333	= Millibar (mbar)
Millibar (mbar)	x 0.401	= Inches of water (inH$_2$O)	x 2.491	= Millibar (mbar)
Millimetres of mercury (mmHg)	x 0.535	= Inches of water (inH$_2$O)	x 1.868	= Millimetres of mercury (mmHg)
Inches of water (inH$_2$O)	x 0.036	= Pounds-force per square inch (psi; lbf/in^2; lb/in^2)	x 27.68	= Inches of water (inH$_2$O)

Torque (moment of force)
Pounds-force inches (lbf in; lb in)	x 1.152	= Kilograms-force centimetre (kgf cm; kg cm)	x 0.868	= Pounds-force inches (lbf in; lb in)
Pounds-force inches (lbf in; lb in)	x 0.113	= Newton metres (Nm)	x 8.85	= Pounds-force inches (lbf in; lb in)
Pounds-force inches (lbf in; lb in)	x 0.083	= Pounds-force feet (lbf ft; lb ft)	x 12	= Pounds-force inches (lbf in; lb in)
Pounds-force feet (lbf ft; lb ft)	x 0.138	= Kilograms-force metres (kgf m; kg m)	x 7.233	= Pounds-force feet (lbf ft; lb ft)
Pounds-force feet (lbf ft; lb ft)	x 1.356	= Newton metres (Nm)	x 0.738	= Pounds-force feet (lbf ft; lb ft)
Newton metres (Nm)	x 0.102	= Kilograms-force metres (kgf m; kg m)	x 9.804	= Newton metres (Nm)

Power
Horsepower (hp)	x 745.7	= Watts (W)	x 0.0013	= Horsepower (hp)

Velocity (speed)
Miles per hour (miles/hr; mph)	x 1.609	= Kilometres per hour (km/hr; kph)	x 0.621	= Miles per hour (miles/hr; mph)

Fuel consumption*
Miles per gallon (mpg)	x 0.354	= Kilometres per litre (km/l)	x 2.825	= Miles per gallon (mpg)

Temperature

Degrees Fahrenheit = (°C x 1.8) + 32   Degrees Celsius (Degrees Centigrade; °C) = (°F - 32) x 0.56

It is common practice to convert from miles per gallon (mpg) to litres/100 kilometres (l/100km), where mpg x l/100 km = 282

MOT Test Checks

About the MOT Test

In the UK, all vehicles more than three years old are subject to an annual test to ensure that they meet minimum safety requirements. A current test certificate must be issued before a machine can be used on public roads, and is required before a road fund licence can be issued. Riding without a current test certificate will also invalidate your insurance.

For most owners, the MOT test is an annual cause for anxiety, and this is largely due to owners not being sure what needs to be checked prior to submitting the motorcycle for testing. The simple answer is that a fully roadworthy motorcycle will have no difficulty in passing the test.

This is a guide to getting your motorcycle through the MOT test. Obviously it will not be possible to examine the motorcycle to the same standard as the professional MOT tester, particularly in view of the equipment required for some of the checks. However, working through the following procedures will enable you to identify any problem areas before submitting the motorcycle for the test.

It has only been possible to summarise the test requirements here, based on the regulations in force at the time of printing. Test standards are becoming increasingly stringent, although there are some exemptions for older vehicles. More information about the MOT test can be obtained from the TSO publications, *How Safe is your Motorcycle* and *The MOT Inspection Manual for Motorcycle Testing*.

Many of the checks require that one of the wheels is raised off the ground. If the motorcycle doesn't have a centre stand, note that an auxiliary stand will be required. Additionally, the help of an assistant may prove useful.

Certain exceptions apply to machines under 50 cc, machines without a lighting system, and Classic bikes - if in doubt about any of the requirements listed below seek confirmation from an MOT tester prior to submitting the motorcycle for the test.

Check that the frame number is clearly visible.

Electrical System

Lights, turn signals, horn and reflector

✔ With the ignition on, check the operation of the following electrical components. **Note:** *The electrical components on certain small-capacity machines are powered by the generator, requiring that the engine is run for this check.*

a) Headlight and tail light. Check that both illuminate in the low and high beam switch positions.
b) Position lights. Check that the front position (or sidelight) and tail light illuminate in this switch position.
c) Turn signals. Check that all flash at the correct rate, and that the warning light(s) function correctly. Check that the turn signal switch works correctly.
d) Hazard warning system (where fitted). Check that all four turn signals flash in this switch position.
e) Brake stop light. Check that the light comes on when the front and rear brakes are independently applied. Models first used on or after 1st April 1986 must have a brake light switch on each brake.
f) Horn. Check that the sound is continuous and of reasonable volume.

✔ Check that there is a red reflector on the rear of the machine, either mounted separately or as part of the tail light lens.
✔ Check the condition of the headlight, tail light and turn signal lenses.

Headlight beam height

✔ The MOT tester will perform a headlight beam height check using specialised beam setting equipment **(see illustration 1)**. This equipment will not be available to the home mechanic, but if you suspect that the headlight is incorrectly set or may have been maladjusted in the past, you can perform a rough test as follows.
✔ Position the bike in a straight line facing a brick wall. The bike must be off its stand, upright and with a rider seated. Measure the height from the ground to the centre of the headlight and mark a horizontal line on the wall at this height. Position the motorcycle 3.8 metres from the wall and draw a vertical line up the wall central to the centreline of the motorcycle. Switch to dipped beam and check that the beam pattern falls slightly lower than the horizontal line and to the left of the vertical line **(see illustration 2)**.

Headlight beam height checking equipment

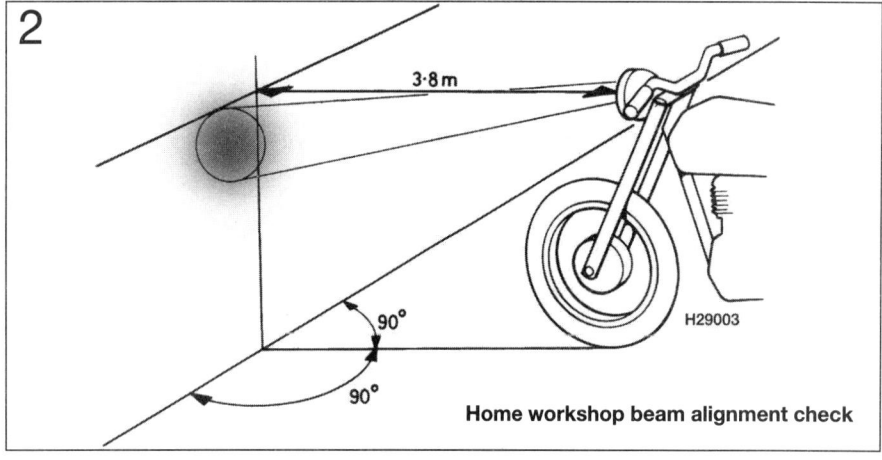

Home workshop beam alignment check

REF•28 MOT Test Checks

Exhaust System and Final Drive

Exhaust

✔ Check that the exhaust mountings are secure and that the system does not foul any of the rear suspension components.
✔ Start the motorcycle. When the revs are increased, check that the exhaust is neither holed nor leaking from any of its joints. On a linked system, check that the collector box is not leaking due to corrosion.
✔ Note that the exhaust decibel level ("loudness" of the exhaust) is assessed at the discretion of the tester. If the motorcycle was first used on or after 1st January 1985 the silencer must carry the BSAU 193 stamp, or a marking relating to its make and model, or be of OE (original equipment) manufacture. If the silencer is marked NOT FOR ROAD USE, RACING USE ONLY or similar, it will fail the MOT.

Final drive

✔ On chain or belt drive machines, check that the chain/belt is in good condition and does not have excessive slack. Also check that the sprocket is securely mounted on the rear wheel hub. Check that the chain/belt guard is in place.
✔ On shaft drive bikes, check for oil leaking from the drive unit and fouling the rear tyre.

Steering and Suspension

Steering

✔ With the front wheel raised off the ground, rotate the steering from lock to lock. The handlebar or switches must not contact the fuel tank or be close enough to trap the rider's hand. Problems can be caused by damaged lock stops on the lower yoke and frame, or by the fitting of non-standard handlebars.
✔ When performing the lock to lock check, also ensure that the steering moves freely without drag or notchiness. Steering movement can be impaired by poorly routed cables, or by overtight head bearings or worn bearings. The tester will perform a check of the steering head bearing lower race by mounting the front wheel on a surface plate, then performing a lock to lock check with the weight of the machine on the lower bearing (see illustration 3).
✔ Grasp the fork sliders (lower legs) and attempt to push and pull on the forks (see

Front wheel mounted on a surface plate for steering head bearing lower race check

illustration 4). Any play in the steering head bearings will be felt. Note that in extreme cases, wear of the front fork bushes can be misinterpreted for head bearing play.
✔ Check that the handlebars are securely mounted.
✔ Check that the handlebar grip rubbers are secure. They should by bonded to the bar left end and to the throttle cable pulley on the right end.

Front suspension

✔ With the motorcycle off the stand, hold the front brake on and pump the front forks up and down (see illustration 5). Check that they are adequately damped.

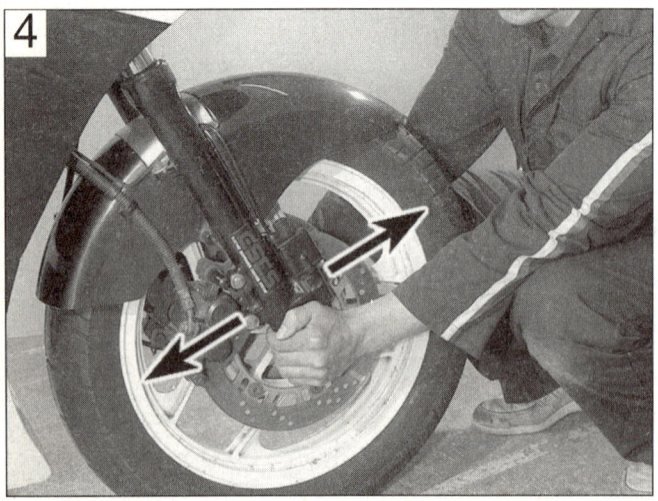

Checking the steering head bearings for freeplay

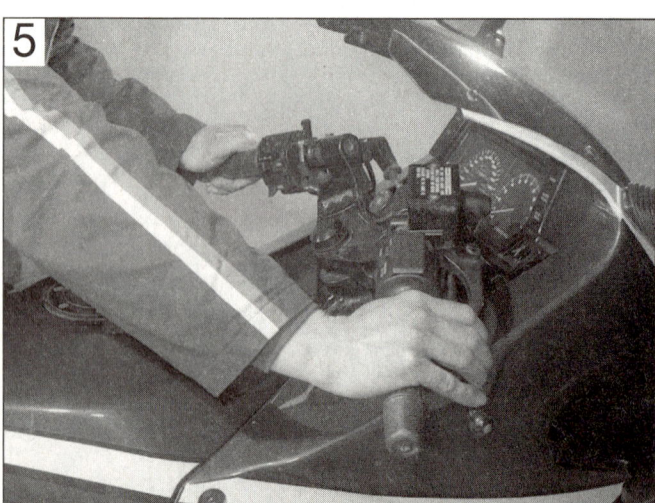

Hold the front brake on and pump the front forks up and down to check operation

MOT Test Checks REF•29

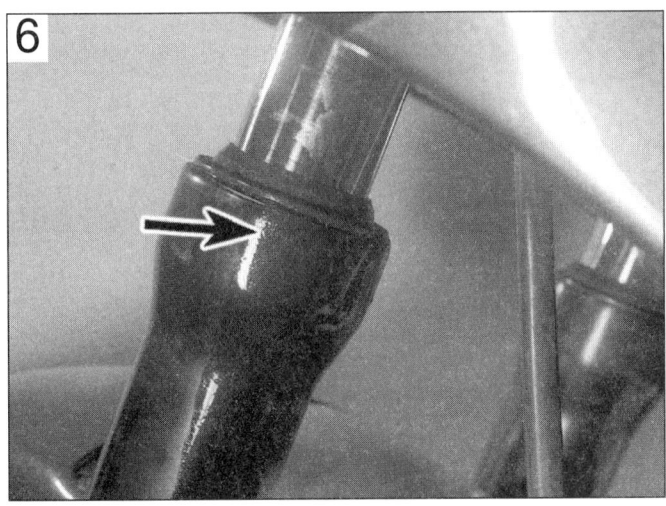

Inspect the area around the fork dust seal for oil leakage (arrow)

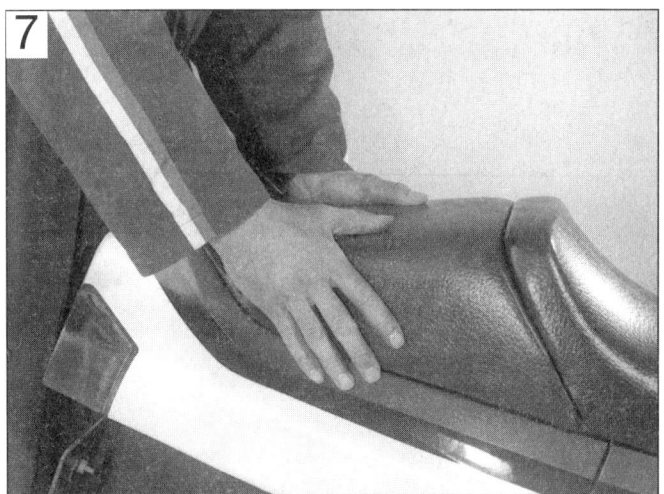

Bounce the rear of the motorcycle to check rear suspension operation

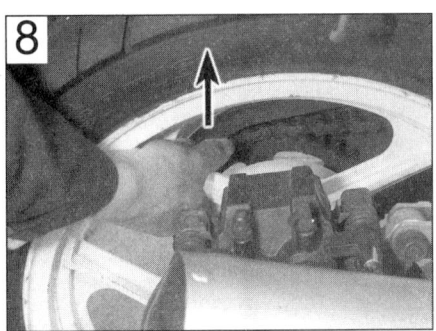

Checking for rear suspension linkage play

✔ Inspect the area above and around the front fork oil seals **(see illustration 6)**. There should be no sign of oil on the fork tube (stanchion) nor leaking down the slider (lower leg). On models so equipped, check that there is no oil leaking from the anti-dive units.

✔ On models with swingarm front suspension, check that there is no freeplay in the linkage when moved from side to side.

Rear suspension

✔ With the motorcycle off the stand and an assistant supporting the motorcycle by its handlebars, bounce the rear suspension **(see illustration 7)**. Check that the suspension components do not foul on any of the cycle parts and check that the shock absorber(s) provide adequate damping.

✔ Visually inspect the shock absorber(s) and check that there is no sign of oil leakage from its damper. This is somewhat restricted on certain single shock models due to the location of the shock absorber.

✔ With the rear wheel raised off the ground, grasp the wheel at the highest point and attempt to pull it up **(see illustration 8)**. Any play in the swingarm pivot or suspension linkage bearings will be felt as movement.

Note: *Do not confuse play with actual suspension movement.* Failure to lubricate suspension linkage bearings can lead to bearing failure **(see illustration 9)**.

✔ With the rear wheel raised off the ground, grasp the swingarm ends and attempt to move the swingarm from side to side and forwards and backwards - any play indicates wear of the swingarm pivot bearings **(see illustration 10)**.

Worn suspension linkage pivots (arrows) are usually the cause of play in the rear suspension

Grasp the swingarm at the ends to check for play in its pivot bearings

REF•30 MOT Test Checks

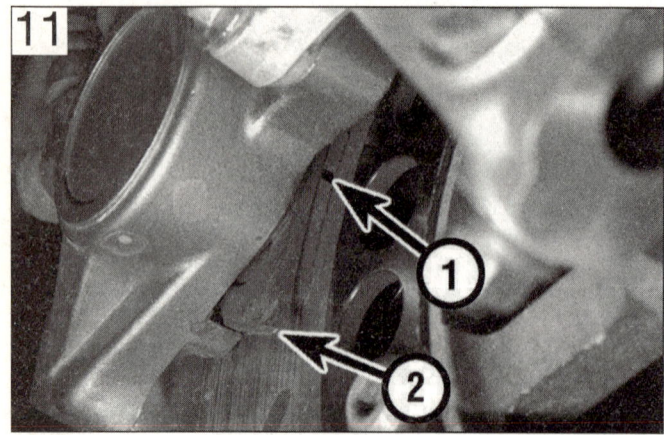

Brake pad wear can usually be viewed without removing the caliper. Most pads have wear indicator grooves (1) and some also have indicator tangs (2)

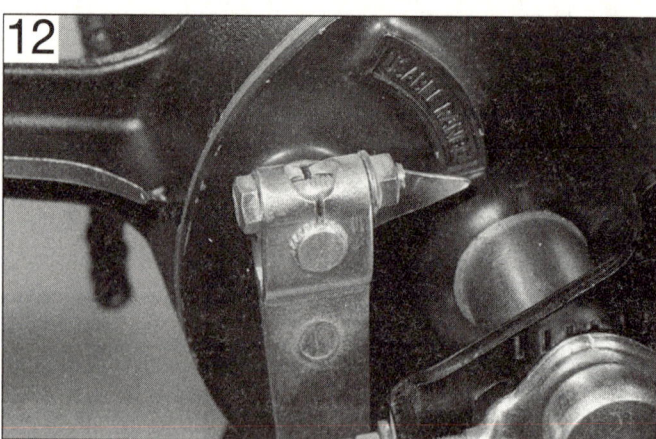

On drum brakes, check the angle of the operating lever with the brake fully applied. Most drum brakes have a wear indicator pointer and scale.

Brakes, Wheels and Tyres

Brakes

✔ With the wheel raised off the ground, apply the brake then free it off, and check that the wheel is about to revolve freely without brake drag.
✔ On disc brakes, examine the disc itself. Check that it is securely mounted and not cracked.
✔ On disc brakes, view the pad material through the caliper mouth and check that the pads are not worn down beyond the limit **(see illustration 11)**.
✔ On drum brakes, check that when the brake is applied the angle between the operating lever and cable or rod is not too great **(see illustration 12)**. Check also that the operating lever doesn't foul any other components.
✔ On disc brakes, examine the flexible hoses from top to bottom. Have an assistant hold the brake on so that the fluid in the hose is under pressure, and check that there is no sign of fluid leakage, bulges or cracking. If there are any metal brake pipes or unions, check that these are free from corrosion and damage. Where a brake-linked anti-dive system is fitted, check the hoses to the anti-dive in a similar manner.
✔ Check that the rear brake torque arm is secure and that its fasteners are secured by self-locking nuts or castellated nuts with split-pins or R-pins **(see illustration 13)**.
✔ On models with ABS, check that the self-check warning light in the instrument panel works.
✔ The MOT tester will perform a test of the motorcycle's braking efficiency based on a calculation of rider and motorcycle weight. Although this cannot be carried out at home, you can at least ensure that the braking systems are properly maintained. For hydraulic disc brakes, check the fluid level, lever/pedal feel (bleed of air if its spongy) and pad material. For drum brakes, check adjustment, cable or rod operation and shoe lining thickness.

Wheels and tyres

✔ Check the wheel condition. Cast wheels should be free from cracks and if of the built-up design, all fasteners should be secure. Spoked wheels should be checked for broken, corroded, loose or bent spokes.
✔ With the wheel raised off the ground, spin the wheel and visually check that the tyre and wheel run true. Check that the tyre does not foul the suspension or mudguards.
✔ With the wheel raised off the ground, grasp the wheel and attempt to move it about the axle (spindle) **(see illustration 14)**. Any play felt here indicates wheel bearing failure.

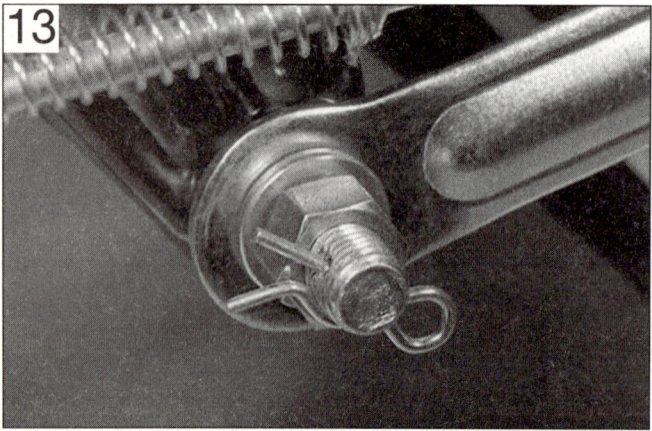

Brake torque arm must be properly secured at both ends

Check for wheel bearing play by trying to move the wheel about the axle (spindle)

MOT Test Checks

Checking the tyre tread depth

Tyre direction of rotation arrow can be found on tyre sidewall

Castellated type wheel axle (spindle) nut must be secured by a split pin or R-pin

Two straightedges are used to check wheel alignment

✔ Check the tyre tread depth, tread condition and sidewall condition **(see illustration 15)**.
✔ Check the tyre type. Front and rear tyre types must be compatible and be suitable for road use. Tyres marked NOT FOR ROAD USE, COMPETITION USE ONLY or similar, will fail the MOT.

✔ If the tyre sidewall carries a direction of rotation arrow, this must be pointing in the direction of normal wheel rotation **(see illustration 16)**.
✔ Check that the wheel axle (spindle) nuts (where applicable) are properly secured. A self-locking nut or castellated nut with a split-pin or R-pin can be used **(see illustration 17)**.
✔ Wheel alignment is checked with the motorcycle off the stand and a rider seated. With the front wheel pointing straight ahead, two perfectly straight lengths of metal or wood and placed against the sidewalls of both tyres **(see illustration 18)**. The gap each side of the front tyre must be equidistant on both sides. Incorrect wheel alignment may be due to a cocked rear wheel (often as the result of poor chain adjustment) or in extreme cases, a bent frame.

General checks and condition

✔ Check the security of all major fasteners, bodypanels, seat, fairings (where fitted) and mudguards.

✔ Check that the rider and pillion footrests, handlebar levers and brake pedal are securely mounted.

✔ Check for corrosion on the frame or any load-bearing components. If severe, this may affect the structure, particularly under stress.

Sidecars

A motorcycle fitted with a sidecar requires additional checks relating to the stability of the machine and security of attachment and swivel joints, plus specific wheel alignment (toe-in) requirements. Additionally, tyre and lighting requirements differ from conventional motorcycle use. Owners are advised to check MOT test requirements with an official test centre.

Storage

Preparing for storage

Before you start

If repairs or an overhaul is needed, see that this is carried out now rather than left until you want to ride the bike again.

Give the bike a good wash and scrub all dirt from its underside. Make sure the bike dries completely before preparing for storage.

Engine

● Remove the spark plug(s) and lubricate the cylinder bores with approximately a teaspoon of motor oil using a spout-type oil can **(see illustration 1)**. Reinstall the spark plug(s). Crank the engine over a couple of times to coat the piston rings and bores with oil. If the bike has a kickstart, use this to turn the engine over. If not, flick the kill switch to the OFF position and crank the engine over on the starter **(see illustration 2)**. If the nature on the ignition system prevents the starter operating with the kill switch in the OFF position, remove the spark plugs and fit them back in their caps; ensure that the plugs are earthed (grounded) against the cylinder head when the starter is operated **(see illustration 3)**.

⚠ **Warning: It is important that the plugs are earthed (grounded) away from the spark plug holes otherwise there is a risk of atomised fuel from the cylinders igniting.**

HAYNES HiNT *On a single cylinder four-stroke engine, you can seal the combustion chamber completely by positioning the piston at TDC on the compression stroke.*

● Drain the carburettor(s) otherwise there is a risk of jets becoming blocked by gum deposits from the fuel **(see illustration 4)**.

● If the bike is going into long-term storage, consider adding a fuel stabiliser to the fuel in the tank. If the tank is drained completely, corrosion of its internal surfaces may occur if left unprotected for a long period. The tank can be treated with a rust preventative especially for this purpose. Alternatively, remove the tank and pour half a litre of motor oil into it, install the filler cap and shake the tank to coat its internals with oil before draining off the excess. The same effect can also be achieved by spraying WD40 or a similar water-dispersant around the inside of the tank via its flexible nozzle.

● Make sure the cooling system contains the correct mix of antifreeze. Antifreeze also contains important corrosion inhibitors.

● The air intakes and exhaust can be sealed off by covering or plugging the openings. Ensure that you do not seal in any condensation; run the engine until it is hot,

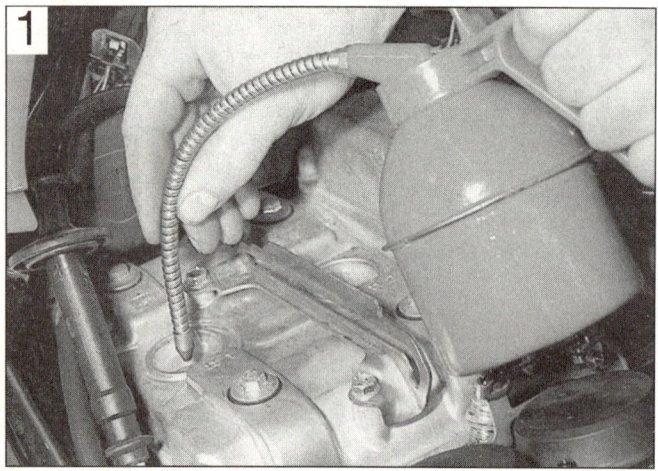

Squirt a drop of motor oil into each cylinder

Flick the kill switch to OFF . . .

. . . and ensure that the metal bodies of the plugs (arrows) are earthed against the cylinder head

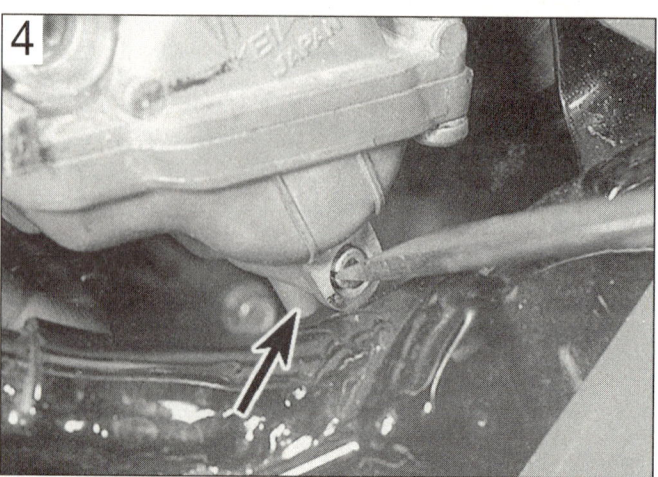

Connect a hose to the carburettor float chamber drain stub (arrow) and unscrew the drain screw

Storage

Exhausts can be sealed off with a plastic bag

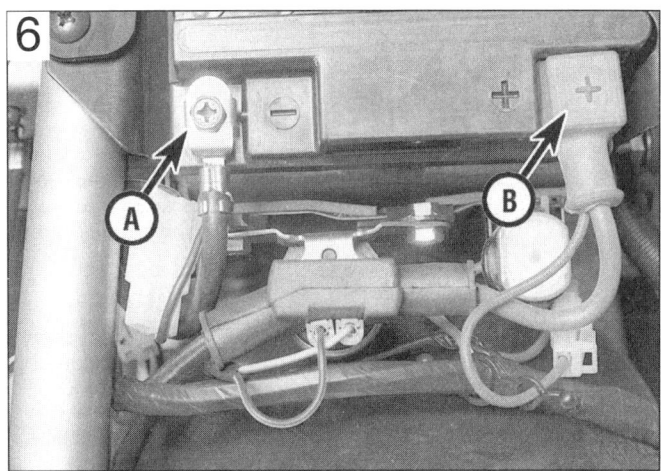

Disconnect the negative lead (A) first, followed by the positive lead (B)

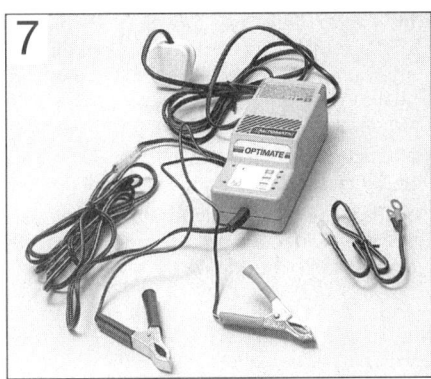

Use a suitable battery charger - this kit also assess battery condition

then switch off and allow to cool. Tape a piece of thick plastic over the silencer end(s) **(see illustration 5)**. Note that some advocate pouring a tablespoon of motor oil into the silencer(s) before sealing them off.

Battery

● Remove it from the bike - in extreme cases of cold the battery may freeze and crack its case **(see illustration 6)**.

● Check the electrolyte level and top up if necessary (conventional refillable batteries). Clean the terminals.
● Store the battery off the motorcycle and away from any sources of fire. Position a wooden block under the battery if it is to sit on the ground.
● Give the battery a trickle charge for a few hours every month **(see illustration 7)**.

Tyres

● Place the bike on its centrestand or an auxiliary stand which will support the motorcycle in an upright position. Position wood blocks under the tyres to keep them off the ground and to provide insulation from damp. If the bike is being put into long-term storage, ideally both tyres should be off the ground; not only will this protect the tyres, but will also ensure that no load is placed on the steering head or wheel bearings.
● Deflate each tyre by 5 to 10 psi, no more or the beads may unseat from the rim, making subsequent inflation difficult on tubeless tyres.

Pivots and controls

● Lubricate all lever, pedal, stand and footrest pivot points. If grease nipples are fitted to the rear suspension components, apply lubricant to the pivots.
● Lubricate all control cables.

Cycle components

● Apply a wax protectant to all painted and plastic components. Wipe off any excess, but don't polish to a shine. Where fitted, clean the screen with soap and water.
● Coat metal parts with Vaseline (petroleum jelly). When applying this to the fork tubes, do not compress the forks otherwise the seals will rot from contact with the Vaseline.
● Apply a vinyl cleaner to the seat.

Storage conditions

● Aim to store the bike in a shed or garage which does not leak and is free from damp.
● Drape an old blanket or bedspread over the bike to protect it from dust and direct contact with sunlight (which will fade paint). This also hides the bike from prying eyes. Beware of tight-fitting plastic covers which may allow condensation to form and settle on the bike.

Getting back on the road

Engine and transmission

● Change the oil and replace the oil filter. If this was done prior to storage, check that the oil hasn't emulsified - a thick whitish substance which occurs through condensation.
● Remove the spark plugs. Using a spout-type oil can, squirt a few drops of oil into the cylinder(s). This will provide initial lubrication as the piston rings and bores comes back into contact. Service the spark plugs, or fit new ones, and install them in the engine.

● Check that the clutch isn't stuck on. The plates can stick together if left standing for some time, preventing clutch operation. Engage a gear and try rocking the bike back and forth with the clutch lever held against the handlebar. If this doesn't work on cable-operated clutches, hold the clutch lever back against the handlebar with a strong elastic band or cable tie for a couple of hours **(see illustration 8)**.
● If the air intakes or silencer end(s) were blocked off, remove the bung or cover used.
● If the fuel tank was coated with a rust

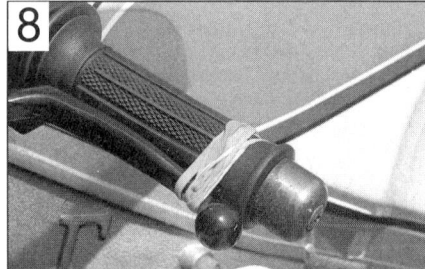

Hold clutch lever back against the handlebar with elastic bands or a cable tie

Storage

preventative, oil or a stabiliser added to the fuel, drain and flush the tank and dispose of the fuel sensibly. If no action was taken with the fuel tank prior to storage, it is advised that the old fuel is disposed of since it will go off over a period of time. Refill the fuel tank with fresh fuel.

Frame and running gear

- Oil all pivot points and cables.
- Check the tyre pressures. They will definitely need inflating if pressures were reduced for storage.
- Lubricate the final drive chain (where applicable).
- Remove any protective coating applied to the fork tubes (stanchions) since this may well destroy the fork seals. If the fork tubes weren't protected and have picked up rust spots, remove them with very fine abrasive paper and refinish with metal polish.
- Check that both brakes operate correctly. Apply each brake hard and check that it's not possible to move the motorcycle forwards, then check that the brake frees off again once released. Brake caliper pistons can stick due to corrosion around the piston head, or on the sliding caliper types, due to corrosion of the slider pins. If the brake doesn't free after repeated operation, take the caliper off for examination. Similarly drum brakes can stick due to a seized operating cam, cable or rod linkage.
- If the motorcycle has been in long-term storage, renew the brake fluid and clutch fluid (where applicable).
- Depending on where the bike has been stored, the wiring, cables and hoses may have been nibbled by rodents. Make a visual check and investigate disturbed wiring loom tape.

Battery

- If the battery has been previously removal and given top up charges it can simply be reconnected. Remember to connect the positive cable first and the negative cable last.
- On conventional refillable batteries, if the battery has not received any attention, remove it from the motorcycle and check its electrolyte level. Top up if necessary then charge the battery. If the battery fails to hold a charge and a visual checks show heavy white sulphation of the plates, the battery is probably defective and must be renewed. This is particularly likely if the battery is old. Confirm battery condition with a specific gravity check.
- On sealed (MF) batteries, if the battery has not received any attention, remove it from the motorcycle and charge it according to the information on the battery case - if the battery fails to hold a charge it must be renewed.

Starting procedure

- If a kickstart is fitted, turn the engine over a couple of times with the ignition OFF to distribute oil around the engine. If no kickstart is fitted, flick the engine kill switch OFF and the ignition ON and crank the engine over a couple of times to work oil around the upper cylinder components. If the nature of the ignition system is such that the starter won't work with the kill switch OFF, remove the spark plugs, fit them back into their caps and earth (ground) their bodies on the cylinder head. Reinstall the spark plugs afterwards.
- Switch the kill switch to RUN, operate the choke and start the engine. If the engine won't start don't continue cranking the engine - not only will this flatten the battery, but the starter motor will overheat. Switch the ignition off and try again later. If the engine refuses to start, go through the fault finding procedures in this manual. **Note:** *If the bike has been in storage for a long time, old fuel or a carburettor blockage may be the problem. Gum deposits in carburettors can block jets - if a carburettor cleaner doesn't prove successful the carburettors must be dismantled for cleaning.*
- Once the engine has started, check that the lights, turn signals and horn work properly.
- Treat the bike gently for the first ride and check all fluid levels on completion. Settle the bike back into the maintenance schedule.

Fault Finding

This Section provides an easy reference-guide to the more common faults that are likely to afflict your machine. Obviously, the opportunities are almost limitless for faults to occur as a result of obscure failures, and to try and cover all eventualities would require a book. Indeed, a number have been written on the subject.

Successful troubleshooting is not a mysterious 'black art' but the application of a bit of knowledge combined with a systematic and logical approach to the problem. Approach any troubleshooting by first accurately identifying the symptom and then checking through the list of possible causes, starting with the simplest or most obvious and progressing in stages to the most complex.

Take nothing for granted, but above all apply liberal quantities of common sense.

The main symptom of a fault is given in the text as a major heading below which are listed the various systems or areas which may contain the fault. Details of each possible cause for a fault and the remedial action to be taken are given, in brief, in the paragraphs below each heading. Further information should be sought in the relevant Chapter.

1 Engine doesn't start or is difficult to start
- [ ] Starter motor doesn't rotate
- [ ] Starter motor rotates but engine does not turn over
- [ ] Starter works but engine won't turn over (seized)
- [ ] No fuel flow
- [ ] Engine flooded
- [ ] No spark or weak spark
- [ ] Compression low
- [ ] Stalls after starting
- [ ] Rough idle

2 Poor running at low speed
- [ ] Spark weak
- [ ] Fuel/air mixture incorrect
- [ ] Compression low
- [ ] Poor acceleration

3 Poor running or no power at high speed
- [ ] Firing incorrect
- [ ] Fuel/air mixture incorrect
- [ ] Compression low
- [ ] Knocking or pinking
- [ ] Miscellaneous causes

4 Overheating
- [ ] Engine overheats
- [ ] Firing incorrect
- [ ] Fuel/air mixture incorrect
- [ ] Compression too high
- [ ] Engine load excessive
- [ ] Lubrication inadequate
- [ ] Miscellaneous causes

5 Clutch problems
- [ ] Clutch slipping
- [ ] Clutch not disengaging completely

6 Gearchange problems
- [ ] Doesn't go into gear, or lever doesn't return
- [ ] Jumps out of gear
- [ ] Overselects

7 Abnormal engine noise
- [ ] Knocking or pinking
- [ ] Piston slap or rattling
- [ ] Valve noise
- [ ] Other noise

8 Abnormal driveline noise
- [ ] Clutch noise
- [ ] Transmission noise
- [ ] Final drive noise

9 Abnormal frame and suspension noise
- [ ] Front end noise
- [ ] Shock absorber noise
- [ ] Brake noise

10 Oil pressure warning light comes on
- [ ] Engine lubrication system
- [ ] Electrical system

11 Excessive exhaust smoke
- [ ] White smoke
- [ ] Black smoke
- [ ] Brown smoke

12 Poor handling or stability
- [ ] Handlebar hard to turn
- [ ] Handlebar shakes or vibrates excessively
- [ ] Handlebar pulls to one side
- [ ] Poor shock absorbing qualities

13 Braking problems
- [ ] Brakes are spongy, don't hold
- [ ] Brake lever or pedal pulsates
- [ ] Brakes drag

14 Electrical problems
- [ ] Battery dead or weak
- [ ] Battery overcharged

REF•36 Fault Finding

1 Engine doesn't start or is difficult to start

Starter motor doesn't rotate
- [ ] Engine kill switch OFF.
- [ ] Fuse blown. Check main fuse and FI fuse (Chapter 8).
- [ ] Battery voltage low. Check and recharge battery (Chapter 8).
- [ ] Starter motor defective. Make sure the wiring to the starter is secure. Make sure the starter relay clicks when the start button is pushed. If the relay clicks, then the fault is in the wiring or motor (see Chapter 8).
- [ ] Starter switch not contacting. The contacts could be wet, corroded or dirty. Disassemble and clean the switch (Chapter 8).
- [ ] Wiring open or shorted. Check all wiring connections and harnesses to make sure that they are dry, tight and not corroded. Also check for broken or frayed wires that can cause a short to ground (earth) (see *Wiring diagrams*, Chapter 8).
- [ ] Ignition switch defective. Check the switch and replace with a new one if it is defective (see Chapter 8).
- [ ] Engine kill switch defective. Check for wet, dirty or corroded contacts. Clean or replace the switch with a new one as necessary (see Chapter 8).
- [ ] Faulty neutral switch, sidestand switch or clutch switch. Check the wiring to each switch and the switch itself (see Chapter 8).
- [ ] Faulty diode (Chapter 8).
- [ ] Fuel injection system shutdown due to system fault (Chapter 4).
- [ ] Immobiliser fault (models with HISS) (Chapter 4).

Starter motor rotates but engine does not turn over
- [ ] Starter clutch defective. Inspect and repair or replace with a new one (see Chapter 2).
- [ ] Damaged idler or starter gears. Inspect and replace the damaged parts (see Chapter 2).

Starter works but engine won't turn over (seized)
- [ ] Seized engine caused by one or more internally damaged components. Failure due to wear, abuse or lack of lubrication. Damage can include seized valves, followers, camshafts, pistons, crankshaft, connecting rod, transmission gears or bearings. Refer to Chapter 2 for engine disassembly.

No fuel flow
- [ ] No fuel in tank.
- [ ] Fuel tank breather hose obstructed.
- [ ] Faulty fuel cut-off relay. Check the relay (see Chapter 4).
- [ ] Fuel pump faulty, or the fuel filter is blocked (see Chapter 4).
- [ ] Fuel hose clogged. Remove the fuel hose and carefully blow through it. Check the fuel filter for damage.
- [ ] Fuel rail or injector clogged. For all of the injectors to be clogged, either a very bad batch of fuel with an unusual additive has been used, or some other foreign material has entered the tank. Check the fuel filter. In some cases, if a machine has been unused for several months, the fuel turns to a varnish-like liquid which can cause an injector needle to stick to its seat. Drain the tank and fuel system (Chapter 4).

Engine flooded
- [ ] Injector needle valve worn or stuck open. A piece of dirt, rust or other debris can cause the needle to seat improperly, causing excess fuel to be admitted to the throttle body. In this case, the injector should be cleaned and the needle and seat inspected (see Chapter 4). If the needle and seat are worn, then the leaking will persist and the parts should be renewed.
- [ ] Starting technique incorrect. Under normal circumstances (i.e. if all the components of the fuel injection system are good) the machine should start with the throttle closed.

No spark or weak spark
- [ ] Ignition switch OFF.
- [ ] Engine kill switch turned to the OFF position or engine stop relay defective.
- [ ] Ignition or kill switch shorted. This is usually caused by water, corrosion, damage or excessive wear. The switches can be disassembled and cleaned with electrical contact cleaner. If cleaning does not help, replace the switches (see Chapter 8).
- [ ] Battery voltage low. Check and recharge the battery as necessary (Chapter 8).
- [ ] Spark plug caps not making good contact. Make sure that the caps fit snugly over the plugs.
- [ ] Spark plugs dirty, defective or worn out. Locate reason for fouled plugs using spark plug condition chart on the inside back cover and follow the plug maintenance procedures (see Chapter 1).
- [ ] Incorrect spark plugs. Wrong type or heat range. Check and install correct plugs (see Chapter 1).
- [ ] Ignition coil defective. Test and replace with new one if necessary (Chapter 4).
- [ ] Fuel injection system shutdown due to system fault (Chapter 4).
- [ ] Camshaft position (CMP) sensor defective (see Chapter 4).
- [ ] Crankshaft position (CKP) sensor defective (see Chapter 4).
- [ ] Engine control module (ECM) defective (see Chapter 4).
- [ ] Wiring shorted or broken between:
    a) *Ignition switch and engine kill switch (or blown fuse)*
    b) *ECM and engine kill switch*
    c) *ECM and ignition coils*
    d) *ECM and CKP*
- [ ] Make sure that all wiring connections are clean, dry and tight. Look for chafed and broken wires (see Chapters 4 and 8).

Compression low
- [ ] Spark plug(s) loose. Remove the plugs and inspect their threads. Reinstall and tighten securely (see Chapter 1).
- [ ] Cylinder head not sufficiently tightened down. If a cylinder head is suspected of being loose, then there's a chance that the gasket or head is damaged if the problem has persisted for any length of time. The head bolts should be tightened to the proper torque and in the correct sequence (Chapter 2).
- [ ] Improper valve clearance. This means that the valve is not closing completely and compression pressure is leaking past the valve. Check and adjust the valve clearances (Chapter 1).
- [ ] Cylinder and/or piston worn. Excessive wear will cause compression pressure to leak past the rings. This is usually accompanied by worn rings as well. A top-end overhaul is necessary (Chapter 2).
- [ ] Piston rings worn, weak, broken, or sticking. Broken or sticking piston rings usually indicate a lubrication or fuelling problem that causes excess carbon deposits to form on the pistons and rings. Top-end overhaul is necessary (Chapter 2).
- [ ] Piston ring-to-groove clearance excessive. This is caused by excessive wear of the piston ring lands. Piston renewal is necessary (Chapter 2).
- [ ] Cylinder head gasket damaged. If a head is allowed to become loose, or if excessive carbon build-up on the piston crown and combustion chamber causes extremely high compression, the head gasket may leak. Retorquing the head is not always sufficient to restore the seal, so a new gasket is necessary (Chapter 2).
- [ ] Cylinder head warped. This is caused by overheating or improperly tightened head bolts. Machine shop resurfacing or head renewal is necessary (Chapter 2).
- [ ] Valve spring broken or weak. Caused by component failure or wear; the springs must be renewed (Chapter 2).
- [ ] Valve not seating properly. This is caused by a bent valve (from over-revving or improper valve adjustment), burned valve or seat (improper fuelling) or an accumulation of carbon deposits on the seat. The valves must be cleaned and/or renewed and the seats serviced (Chapter 2).

Fault Finding REF•37

1 Engine doesn't start or is difficult to start (continued)

Stalls after starting
- [ ] Faulty fast idle system. Check the operation of the wax unit and starter valves (see Chapter 4).
- [ ] Engine idle speed incorrect. Turn idle adjusting screw until the engine idles at the specified rpm (Chapter 1).
- [ ] Ignition malfunction (see Chapter 4).
- [ ] Fuel injection system malfunction (see Chapter 4).
- [ ] Fuel contaminated. The fuel can be contaminated with either dirt or water, or can change chemically if the machine has been unused for several months. Drain the tank and fuel system (Chapter 4).
- [ ] Intake air leak. Check for loose throttle body-to-intake manifold connections, loose or damaged PAIR vacuum hose or loose vacuum hoses on the throttle body (Chapter 4).

Rough idle
- [ ] Idle speed incorrect (see Chapter 1).
- [ ] Ignition fault (see Chapter 4).
- [ ] Starter valves not synchronised. Adjust them as described in Chapter 4.
- [ ] Fuel injection system malfunction (see Chapter 4).
- [ ] Fuel contaminated. The fuel can be contaminated with either dirt or water, or can change chemically if the machine has been unused for several months. Drain the tank and the fuel system (Chapter 4).
- [ ] Intake air leak. Check for loose throttle body-to-intake manifold connections, loose or damaged PAIR vacuum hose or loose vacuum hoses on the throttle body (Chapter 4).
- [ ] Air filter clogged. Clean the air filter element or replace it with a new one (Chapter 1).

2 Poor running at low speeds

Spark weak
- [ ] Battery voltage low. Check and recharge battery (see Chapter 8).
- [ ] Spark plug caps not making good contact. Make sure that the caps fit snugly over the plugs.
- [ ] Spark plugs dirty, defective or worn out. Locate reason for fouled plugs using spark plug condition chart on the inside back cover and follow the plug maintenance procedures (see Chapter 1).
- [ ] Incorrect spark plugs. Wrong type or heat range. Check and install correct plugs (see Chapter 1).
- [ ] Ignition coil defective. Test and replace with new one if necessary (Chapter 4).

Fuel/air mixture incorrect
- [ ] Fuel tank breather hose obstructed.
- [ ] Fuel pump faulty, or the fuel filter is blocked (see Chapter 4).
- [ ] Fuel hose clogged. Remove the fuel hose and carefully blow through it. Check the fuel filter for damage.
- [ ] Fuel rail or injector clogged. For all of the injectors to be clogged, either a very bad batch of fuel with an unusual additive has been used, or some other foreign material has entered the tank. Check the fuel filter. In some cases, if a machine has been unused for several months, the fuel turns to a varnish-like liquid which can cause an injector needle to stick to its seat. Drain the tank and fuel system (Chapter 4).
- [ ] Intake air leak. Check for loose throttle body-to-intake manifold connections, loose or damaged PAIR vacuum hose or loose vacuum hoses on throttle body (Chapter 4).
- [ ] Air filter clogged. Clean the air filter elements or renew them (Chapter 1).

Compression low
- [ ] Spark plug(s) loose. Remove the plugs and inspect their threads. Reinstall and tighten securely (see Chapter 1).
- [ ] Cylinder head not sufficiently tightened down. If a cylinder head is suspected of being loose, then there's a chance that the gasket or head is damaged if the problem has persisted for any length of time. The head bolts should be tightened to the proper torque and in the correct sequence (Chapter 2).
- [ ] Improper valve clearance. This means that the valve is not closing completely and compression pressure is leaking past the valve. Check and adjust the valve clearances (Chapter 1).
- [ ] Cylinder and/or piston worn. Excessive wear will cause compression pressure to leak past the rings. This is usually accompanied by worn rings as well. A top-end overhaul is necessary (Chapter 2).
- [ ] Piston rings worn, weak, broken, or sticking. Broken or sticking piston rings usually indicate a lubrication or fuelling problem that causes excess carbon deposits to form on the pistons and rings. Top-end overhaul is necessary (Chapter 2).
- [ ] Piston ring-to-groove clearance excessive. This is caused by excessive wear of the piston ring lands. Piston renewal is necessary (Chapter 2).
- [ ] Cylinder head gasket damaged. If the head is allowed to become loose, or if excessive carbon build-up on the piston crown and combustion chamber causes extremely high compression, the head gasket may leak. Retorquing the head is not always sufficient to restore the seal, so a new gasket is necessary (Chapter 2).
- [ ] Cylinder head warped. This is caused by overheating or improperly tightened head bolts. Machine shop resurfacing or head renewal is necessary (Chapter 2).
- [ ] Valve spring broken or weak. Caused by component failure or wear; the springs must be renewed (Chapter 2).
- [ ] Valve not seating properly. This is caused by a bent valve (from over-revving or improper valve adjustment), burned valve or seat (improper fuelling) or an accumulation of carbon deposits on the seat (from fuelling or lubrication problems). The valves must be cleaned and/or renewed and the seats serviced (Chapter 2).

Poor acceleration
- [ ] Timing not advancing. The crankshaft position sensor (CKP) or the engine control module (ECM) may be defective (see Chapter 4). If so, they must be renewed.
- [ ] Engine oil viscosity too high. Using a heavier oil than that recommended in Chapter 1 can damage the oil pump or lubrication system and cause drag on the engine.
- [ ] Brakes dragging. Usually caused by debris which has entered the brake caliper piston seals, or from a warped disc or bent axle (see Chapter 6).

REF•38 Fault Finding

3 Poor running or no power at high speed

Firing incorrect

- [ ] Spark plug caps not making good contact. Make sure that the caps fit snugly over the plugs.
- [ ] Spark plugs dirty, defective or worn out. Locate reason for fouled plugs using spark plug condition chart on the inside back cover and follow the plug maintenance procedures (see Chapter 1).
- [ ] Incorrect spark plugs. Wrong type or heat range. Check and install correct plugs (see Chapter 1).
- [ ] Ignition coil defective. Test and replace with new one if necessary (Chapter 4).
- [ ] Faulty ECM (engine control module) (see Chapter 4).

Fuel/air mixture incorrect

- [ ] Fuel tank breather hose obstructed.
- [ ] Fuel pump faulty, or the fuel filter is blocked (see Chapter 4).
- [ ] Fuel hose clogged. Remove the fuel hose and carefully blow through it. Check the fuel filter for damage.
- [ ] Fuel rail or injector clogged. For all of the injectors to be clogged, either a very bad batch of fuel with an unusual additive has been used, or some other foreign material has entered the tank. Check the fuel filter. In some cases, if a machine has been unused for several months, the fuel turns to a varnish-like liquid which can cause an injector needle to stick to its seat. Drain the tank and fuel system (Chapter 4).
- [ ] Intake air leak. Check for loose throttle body-to-intake manifold connections, loose or damaged PAIR vacuum hose or loose vacuum hoses on throttle body (Chapter 4).
- [ ] Air filter clogged. Clean the air filter element or replace it with a new one (Chapter 1).

Compression low

- [ ] Spark plug(s) loose. Remove the plugs and inspect their threads. Reinstall and tighten securely (see Chapter 1).
- [ ] Cylinder head not sufficiently tightened down. If a cylinder head is suspected of being loose, then there's a chance that the gasket or head is damaged if the problem has persisted for any length of time. The head bolts should be tightened to the proper torque and in the correct sequence (Chapter 2).
- [ ] Improper valve clearance. This means that the valve is not closing completely and compression pressure is leaking past the valve. Check and adjust the valve clearances (Chapter 1).
- [ ] Cylinder and/or piston worn. Excessive wear will cause compression pressure to leak past the rings. This is usually accompanied by worn rings as well. A top-end overhaul is necessary (Chapter 2).
- [ ] Piston rings worn, weak, broken, or sticking. Broken or sticking piston rings usually indicate a lubrication or fuelling problem that causes excess carbon deposits to form on the pistons and rings. Top-end overhaul is necessary (Chapter 2).
- [ ] Piston ring-to-groove clearance excessive. This is caused by excessive wear of the piston ring lands. Piston renewal is necessary (Chapter 2).
- [ ] Cylinder head gasket damaged. If a head is allowed to become loose, or if excessive carbon build-up on the piston crown and combustion chamber causes extremely high compression, the head gasket may leak. Retorquing the head is not always sufficient to restore the seal, so a new gasket is necessary (Chapter 2).
- [ ] Cylinder head warped. This is caused by overheating or improperly tightened head bolts. Machine shop resurfacing or head renewal is necessary (Chapter 2).
- [ ] Valve spring broken or weak. Caused by component failure or wear; the springs must be replaced with new ones (Chapter 2).
- [ ] Valve not seating properly. This is caused by a bent valve (from over-revving or improper valve adjustment), burned valve or seat (improper fuelling) or an accumulation of carbon deposits on the seat (from fuelling or lubrication problems). The valves must be cleaned and/or renewed and the seats serviced (Chapter 2).

Knocking or pinking

- [ ] Carbon build-up in combustion chamber. Use of a fuel additive that will dissolve the adhesive bonding the carbon particles to the piston crown and chamber is the easiest way to remove the build-up. Otherwise, the cylinder heads will have to be removed and decarbonised (Chapter 2).
- [ ] Incorrect or poor quality fuel. Old or improper grades of fuel can cause detonation. This causes the piston to rattle, thus the knocking or pinking sound. Drain old fuel and always use the recommended fuel grade.
- [ ] Spark plug heat range incorrect. Uncontrolled detonation indicates the plug heat range is too hot. The plug in effect becomes a glow plug, raising cylinder temperatures. Install the proper heat range plug (Chapter 1).
- [ ] Improper air/fuel mixture. This will cause the cylinders to run hot, which leads to detonation. A blockage in the fuel system or an air leak can cause this imbalance (see Chapter 4).

Miscellaneous causes

- [ ] Throttle valve doesn't open fully. Adjust the throttle twistgrip freeplay (see Chapter 1).
- [ ] Clutch slipping due loose or worn clutch components (see Chapter 2).
- [ ] Timing not advancing. The crankshaft position sensor (CKP) or the engine control module (ECM) may be defective (see Chapter 4). If so, they must be replaced with new ones.
- [ ] Engine oil viscosity too high. Using a heavier oil than the one recommended in Chapter 1 can damage the oil pump or lubrication system and cause drag on the engine.
- [ ] Brakes dragging. Usually caused by debris which has entered the brake caliper piston seals, or from a warped disc or bent axle (see Chapter 6).

Fault Finding

4 Overheating

Engine overheats
- [ ] Coolant level low. Check and add coolant (see *Pre-ride checks*).
- [ ] Leak in cooling system. Check cooling system hoses and radiator for leaks and other damage. Repair or renew parts as necessary (see Chapter 3).
- [ ] Faulty thermostat. Check and renew as described in Chapter 3.
- [ ] Faulty radiator cap. Remove the cap and have it pressure tested.
- [ ] Coolant passages clogged. Have the entire system drained and flushed, then refill with fresh coolant.
- [ ] Water pump defective. Remove the pump and check the components (see Chapter 3).
- [ ] Clogged or damaged radiator fins (see Chapter 3).
- [ ] Faulty cooling fan, ECT sensor or fan relay (see Chapter 3).

Firing incorrect
- [ ] Wrongly connected ignition coil wiring.
- [ ] Spark plugs dirty, defective or worn out. Locate reason for fouled plugs using spark plug condition chart on the inside back cover and follow the plug maintenance procedures (see Chapter 1).
- [ ] Incorrect spark plugs. Wrong type or heat range. Check and install correct plugs (see Chapter 1).
- [ ] Ignition coil defective. Test and replace with a new one if necessary (see Chapter 5).
- [ ] Faulty ECM (engine control module) (see Chapter 4).

Fuel/air mixture incorrect
- [ ] Fuel tank breather hose obstructed.
- [ ] Fuel pump faulty, or the fuel filter blocked (see Chapter 4).
- [ ] Fuel hose clogged. Remove the fuel hose and carefully blow through it. Check the fuel filter for damage.
- [ ] Fuel rail or injector clogged. For all of the injectors to be clogged, either a very bad batch of fuel with an unusual additive has been used, or some other foreign material has entered the tank. Check the fuel filter. In some cases, if a machine has been unused for several months, the fuel turns to a varnish-like liquid which can cause an injector needle to stick to its seat. Drain the tank and fuel system (Chapter 4).
- [ ] Intake air leak. Check for loose throttle body-to-intake manifold connections, loose or damaged PAIR vacuum hose or loose vacuum hoses on throttle body (Chapter 4).
- [ ] Air filter clogged. Clean the air filter elements or renew them (Chapter 1).

Compression too high
- [ ] Carbon build-up in combustion chamber. Use of a fuel additive that will dissolve the adhesive bonding the carbon particles to the piston crown and chamber is the easiest way to remove the build-up. Otherwise, the cylinder heads will have to be removed and decarbonised (Chapter 2).
- [ ] Improperly machined head surface or installation of incorrect gasket during engine assembly.

Engine load excessive
- [ ] Clutch slipping due loose or worn clutch components (see Chapter 2).
- [ ] Engine oil level too high. Too much oil will cause pressurisation of the crankcase and inefficient engine operation. Check Specifications and drain to proper level (see *Pre-ride checks*).
- [ ] Engine oil viscosity too high. Using a heavier oil than the one recommended in Chapter 1 can damage the oil pump or lubrication system as well as cause drag on the engine.
- [ ] Brakes dragging. Usually caused by debris which has entered the brake caliper piston seals, or from a warped disc or bent axle (see Chapter 6).

Lubrication inadequate
- [ ] Engine oil level too low. Friction caused by intermittent lack of lubrication or from oil that is overworked can cause overheating. The oil provides a definite cooling function in the engine. Check the oil level (see *Pre-ride checks*).
- [ ] Low engine oil pressure. Check the pressure (see Chapter 2).
- [ ] Blocked oil filter or strainer (see Chapter 1).
- [ ] Poor quality engine oil or incorrect viscosity or type. Oil is rated not only according to viscosity but also according to type. Some oils are not rated high enough for use in this engine. Check the Specifications section and change to the correct oil (Chapter 1).

5 Clutch problems

Clutch slipping
- [ ] Clutch plates worn or warped. Overhaul the clutch assembly (see Chapter 2).
- [ ] Clutch springs broken or weak. Old or heat-damaged (from slipping clutch) springs should be renewed (Chapter 2).
- [ ] Clutch centre or housing unevenly worn. This causes improper engagement of the plates. Replace the damaged or worn parts (see Chapter 2).
- [ ] Clutch release mechanism fault. Check the pushrod and release cylinder components (see Chapter 2).
- [ ] Incorrect type of oil. Use of oils designed for car engines which include friction modifiers can cause clutch slip in a wet clutch application.

Clutch not disengaging completely
- [ ] Clutch fluid level low (see *Pre-ride checks*).
- [ ] Clutch master cylinder seals or release cylinder seals worn (see Chapter 2).
- [ ] Clutch plates warped or damaged. This will cause clutch drag, which in turn will cause the machine to creep. Overhaul the clutch assembly (see Chapter 2).
- [ ] Clutch springs fatigued or broken. Check and renew the springs (see Chapter 2).
- [ ] Engine oil deteriorated. Old, thin oil will not provide proper lubrication for the plates, causing the clutch to drag. Renew the oil and filter (see Chapter 1).
- [ ] Engine oil viscosity too high. Using a heavier oil than recommended in Chapter 1 can cause the plates to stick together. Change to the correct weight oil.
- [ ] Clutch housing bearing seized on the transmission input shaft. Lack of lubrication, severe wear or damage can cause the bearing to seize. Overhaul of the clutch, and perhaps transmission, may be necessary to repair the damage (see Chapter 2).
- [ ] Loose clutch centre nut. Causes housing and centre misalignment putting a drag on the engine. Engagement adjustment continually varies. Overhaul the clutch assembly (see Chapter 2).

REF•40 Fault Finding

6 Gearchange problems

Doesn't go into gear or lever doesn't return
- [ ] Clutch not disengaging (see above).
- [ ] Gearchange mechanism stopper arm spring weak or broken, or arm roller broken or worn. Replace the spring or arm with a new one (see Chapter 2).
- [ ] Selector fork(s) bent, worn or seized. Renew the forks (see Chapter 2).
- [ ] Gear(s) stuck on shaft. Most often caused by a lack of lubrication or excessive wear in transmission bearings and bushes. Strip and rebuild the transmission shafts (see Chapter 2).
- [ ] Selector drum binding. Caused by lubrication failure or excessive wear. Replace the drum and/or its bearing with a new one (see Chapter 2).
- [ ] Gearchange mechanism centralising spring weak or broken (see Chapter 2).
- [ ] Gearchange lever linkage rod incorrectly adjusted (see Chapter 6).

Jumps out of gear
- [ ] Selector fork(s) worn (see Chapter 2).
- [ ] Selector fork groove(s) in selector drum worn (see Chapter 2).
- [ ] Selector pawls or pins worn (see Chapter 2).
- [ ] Gear pinion dogs or dog slots worn or damaged. Strip and rebuild the transmission shafts (see Chapter 2).

Overselects
- [ ] Gearchange mechanism stopper arm spring weak or broken, or arm roller broken or worn. Renew the spring or arm (see Chapter 2).
- [ ] Gearchange mechanism centralising spring weak or broken (see Chapter 2).

7 Abnormal engine noise

Knocking or pinking
- [ ] Carbon build-up in combustion chamber. Use of a fuel additive that will dissolve the adhesive bonding the carbon particles to the piston crown and chamber is the easiest way to remove the build-up. Otherwise, the cylinder head will have to be removed and decarbonised (Chapter 2).
- [ ] Incorrect or poor quality fuel. Old or improper grades of fuel can cause detonation. This causes the piston to rattle, thus the knocking or pinking sound. Drain old fuel and always use the recommended fuel grade.
- [ ] Spark plug heat range incorrect. Uncontrolled detonation indicates the plug heat range is too hot. The plug in effect becomes a glow plug, raising cylinder temperatures. Install the proper heat range plug (Chapter 1).
- [ ] Improper air/fuel mixture. This will cause the cylinders to run hot, which leads to detonation. A blockage in the fuel system or an air leak can cause this imbalance (see Chapter 4).

Piston slap or rattling
- [ ] Cylinder-to-piston clearance excessive. Cylinder and/or piston worn, usually accompanied by worn rings as well. Inspect and measure components and rebore if necessary (see Chapter 2).
- [ ] Piston ring(s) worn, broken or sticking. Overhaul the top-end (see Chapter 2).
- [ ] Piston pin, piston pin bore or connecting rod small-end worn from high mileage or seized due to lack of lubrication (see Chapter 2).
- [ ] Piston seizure damage. Usually from lack of lubrication or overheating. Inspect the piston and bores and rebore if necessary (see Chapter 2).
- [ ] Connecting rod big-end clearance excessive. Caused by excessive wear or lack of lubrication. Replace worn parts.
- [ ] Connecting rod bent. Caused by over-revving, trying to start a badly flooded engine or from ingesting a foreign object into the combustion chamber. Replace the damaged parts (Chapter 2).

Valve noise
- [ ] Incorrect valve clearances – check and adjust (see Chapter 1).
- [ ] Valve spring broken or weak. Check and replace weak valve springs with new ones (see Chapter 2).
- [ ] Camshaft or camshaft journals in the cylinder head worn or damaged. Lubrication failure at high rpm is usually the cause of damage due to insufficient oil or failure to change the oil at the recommended intervals. Since there are no replaceable bearings in the head, the head itself will have to be replaced with a new one (see Chapter 2).

Other noise
- [ ] Cylinder head gasket leaking. Check around the joint for blowing with the engine running.
- [ ] Exhaust pipe leaking at cylinder head connection. Caused by incorrect fit of pipe(s), loose exhaust flange or damaged gasket. All exhaust system fasteners should be tightened evenly and carefully to avoid leaks (see Chapter 4).
- [ ] Crankshaft runout excessive. Caused by a bent crankshaft (from over-revving) or damage from an upper cylinder component failure.
- [ ] Engine mounting bolts loose – ensure all the bolts are tightened to the specified torque settings (see Chapter 2).
- [ ] Crankshaft bearings worn (see Chapter 2).
- [ ] Cam chain rattle, due to worn chain or defective tensioner. Also worn chain tensioner/guide blades (see Chapter 2).
- [ ] Gear whine or clatter from the front of the engine. Too little or too much backlash between the balancer shaft gear and its drive gear on the crankshaft. Carry out the dynamic backlash adjustment procedure (see Chapter 2).

Fault Finding REF•41

8 Abnormal driveline noise

Clutch noise
- [ ] Clutch housing/friction plate clearance excessive (see Chapter 2).
- [ ] Wear between the clutch housing splines and primary damper shaft splines (see Chapter 2).
- [ ] Worn release bearing (see Chapter 2).

Transmission noise
- [ ] Bearings worn. Also includes the possibility that the shafts are worn. Overhaul the transmission (see Chapter 2).
- [ ] Gears worn or chipped (see Chapter 2).
- [ ] Metal chips jammed in gear teeth. Probably pieces from a broken clutch, gear or selector mechanism that were picked up by the gears. This will cause early bearing failure (see Chapter 2).
- [ ] Engine oil level too low. Causes a howl from transmission. Also affects engine power and clutch operation (see *Pre-ride checks*).

Final drive noise
- [ ] Final drive oil level low (Chapter 1).
- [ ] Rear wheel coupling worn or damaged (Chapter 6).
- [ ] Final drive gears worn or damaged (Chapter 6).
- [ ] Final drive bearings worn (Chapter 6).
- [ ] Driveshaft splines worn and slipping (Chapter 6).

9 Abnormal frame and suspension noise

Front end noise
- [ ] Low fluid level or improper viscosity oil in forks. This can sound like spurting and is usually accompanied by irregular fork action (Chapter 5).
- [ ] Spring weak or broken. Makes a clicking or scraping sound. Fork oil, when drained, will have a lot of metal particles in it (Chapter 5).
- [ ] Steering head bearings loose or damaged. Clicks when braking. Check and adjust or replace with new ones as necessary (Chapters 1 and 5).
- [ ] Fork yoke clamp bolts loose – ensure all the bolts are tightened to the specified torque (Chapter 6).
- [ ] Forks bent. Good possibility if machine has been dropped. Replace the fork tubes with new ones as required (Chapter 5).
- [ ] Front axle or axle pinch bolts loose. Tighten them to the specified torque (Chapter 6).
- [ ] Loose or worn wheel bearings. Check and replace with new ones as needed (Chapters 1 and 6).
- [ ] Faulty steering damper (see Chapter 5).

Shock absorber noise
- [ ] Fluid level incorrect. Indicates a leak caused by defective seal. Shock will be covered with oil. Replace shock with a new one or seek advice on repair from a suspension specialist (Chapter 5).
- [ ] Defective shock absorber with internal damage. This is in the body of the shock and can't be remedied. The shock must be replaced with a new one or returned to a suspension specialist for rebuild (Chapter 5).
- [ ] Bent or damaged shock body. Replace the shock with a new one (Chapter 5).
- [ ] Loose or worn shock mountings. Check and replace as necessary (Chapter 5).

Brake noise
- [ ] Squeal caused by pad shim not installed or positioned correctly (where fitted) (Chapter 6).
- [ ] Squeal caused by dust on brake pads. Usually found in combination with glazed pads. Renew the pads (Chapter 6).
- [ ] Pads glazed. Caused by excessive heat from prolonged hard use or from contamination. DO NOT use sandpaper, emery cloth, carborundum cloth or any other abrasive to roughen the pad surfaces as abrasives will stay in the pad material and damage the disc. A very fine flat file can be used, but new pads is the best remedy (Chapter 6).
- [ ] Contamination of brake pads. Oil or brake fluid can cause the brake pads to chatter or squeal. Fit new pads. Identify the cause of the contamination, especially check the caliper piston seals for leaking fluid. Clean disc thoroughly with brake system cleaner (Chapter 6).
- [ ] Disc warped. Can cause a chattering, clicking or intermittent squeal. Usually accompanied by a pulsating lever and uneven braking. Replace the disc(s) (Chapter 6).
- [ ] Loose or worn wheel bearings. Check and replace (Chapters 1 and 6).

10 Oil pressure warning light comes on

Engine lubrication system
- [ ] Engine oil level low. Inspect for leak or other problem causing low oil level and add recommended oil (see *Pre-ride checks*).
- [ ] Engine oil pump defective, blocked oil strainer gauze or failed pressure regulator. Carry out an oil pressure check (Chapter 2).
- [ ] Engine oil viscosity too low. Very old, thin oil or an improper weight of oil used in the engine. Change to correct oil (Chapter 1).
- [ ] Camshaft or crankshaft journals worn. Excessive wear causing drop in oil pressure. Abnormal wear could be caused by oil starvation at high rpm from low oil level or improper weight or type of oil (Chapter 1).

Electrical system
- [ ] Oil pressure switch defective. Check the switch according to the procedure in Chapter 8. Replace it with a new one it if is defective.
- [ ] Oil pressure warning LED or symbol defective. Check for pinched, shorted, disconnected or damaged wiring (Chapter 8).

Fault Finding

11 Excessive exhaust smoke

White smoke

- ☐ Piston rings worn or broken, causing oil from the crankcase to be pulled past the piston into the combustion chamber. Replace the rings with new ones (Chapter 2).
- ☐ Cylinders worn or scored. Caused by overheating or oil starvation. Rebore the cylinders (Chapter 2).
- ☐ Valve stem oil seal damaged or worn. Replace the oil seals with new ones (Chapter 2).
- ☐ Valve guide worn. Perform a complete valve job (Chapter 2).
- ☐ Engine oil level too high, which causes the oil to be forced past the rings. Drain oil to the proper level (see *Pre-ride checks*).
- ☐ Head gasket broken between oil return and cylinder. Causes oil to be pulled into the combustion chamber. Replace the head gasket with a new one and check the head for warpage (Chapter 2).
- ☐ Abnormal crankcase pressurisation which forces oil past the rings, usually caused by a clogged breather.

Black smoke

- ☐ Air filter clogged. Clean the air filter elements or renew them (Chapter 1).
- ☐ Fuel injection system malfunction (Chapter 4).

Brown smoke

- ☐ Air filters poorly sealed or not installed (Chapter 1).
- ☐ Fuel injection system malfunction (Chapter 4).

12 Poor handling or stability

Handlebar hard to turn

- ☐ Steering head bearing adjuster nut too tight. Check adjustment as described in Chapter 1.
- ☐ Bearings damaged. Roughness can be felt as the bars are turned from side-to-side. Replace the bearings with new ones (Chapter 5).
- ☐ Races dented or worn. Denting results from wear in only one position (e.g., straight ahead), from a collision or hitting a pothole or from dropping the machine. Replace the bearings with new ones (Chapter 5).
- ☐ Steering stem lubrication inadequate. Causes are grease getting hard from age or being washed out by high pressure car washes. Disassemble steering head and repack bearings (Chapter 5).
- ☐ Steering stem bent. Caused by a collision, hitting a pothole or by dropping the machine. Replace damaged part. Don't try to straighten the steering stem (Chapter 5).
- ☐ Front tyre air pressure too low (see *Pre-ride checks*).

Handlebar shakes or vibrates excessively

- ☐ Tyres worn or out of balance (*Pre-ride checks* and Chapter 6).
- ☐ Swingarm bearings worn. Replace the bearings with new ones (Chapter 5).
- ☐ Wheel rim(s) warped or damaged. Inspect wheels for runout (Chapter 6).
- ☐ Wheel bearings worn. Worn front or rear wheel bearings can cause poor tracking. Worn front bearings will cause wobble (Chapters 1 and 6).
- ☐ Fork yoke clamp bolts or handlebar clamp bolts loose. Tighten them to the specified torque (Chapter 5).
- ☐ Engine mounting bolts loose. Will cause excessive vibration with increased engine rpm – ensure all the bolts are tightened to the specified torque settings (see Chapter 2).

Machine pulls to one side

- ☐ Frame bent. Definitely suspect this if the machine has been dropped. May or may not be accompanied by cracking near the steering head, swingarm mountings or engine mountings. Replace the frame with a new one (Chapter 5).
- ☐ Wheels out of alignment. Bent steering stem or frame following accident damage.
- ☐ Forks bent. Disassemble the forks and replace the damaged parts (Chapter 5).
- ☐ Swingarm bent or twisted. Replace the arm with a new one (Chapter 5).
- ☐ Fork oil level uneven. Check and add or drain as necessary (Chapter 5).

Poor shock absorbing qualities

- ☐ Too hard:
    - a) Suspension settings incorrect (Chapter 5).
    - b) Fork oil level excessive (Chapter 5).
    - c) Fork oil viscosity too high. Use a lighter oil (see the Specifications in Chapter 5).
    - d) Fork tube bent. Causes a harsh, sticking feeling (Chapter 5).
    - e) Fork internal damage (Chapter 5).
    - f) Shock shaft or body bent or damaged (Chapter 5).
    - g) Shock internal damage (Chapter 5).
    - h) Tyre pressure too high (Pre-ride checks).
- ☐ Too soft:
    - a) Suspension settings incorrect (Chapter 5).
    - b) Fork oil level too low (Chapter 5).
    - c) Fork oil viscosity too light (Chapter 5).
    - d) Fork springs weak or broken (Chapter 5).
    - e) Fork or shock oil leaking (Chapter 5).
    - f) Shock internal damage (Chapter 5).

Fault Finding REF•43

13 Braking problems

Brakes are spongy, don't hold
- [ ] Low brake fluid level (see *Pre-ride checks*).
- [ ] Air in hydraulic system. Caused by inattention to master cylinder fluid level or by leakage. Locate problem and bleed brakes (Chapter 6).
- [ ] Pads or disc worn (Chapters 1 and 6).
- [ ] Contaminated pads. Caused by contamination with oil, grease, brake fluid, etc. Fit new pads. Identify the cause of the contamination, especially check the caliper piston seals for leaking fluid. Clean disc thoroughly with brake system cleaner (Chapter 6).
- [ ] Brake fluid deteriorated. Fluid is old or contaminated. Drain system, replenish with new fluid and bleed the system (Chapter 6).
- [ ] Master cylinder internal seals worn or damaged causing fluid to bypass (Chapter 6).
- [ ] Master cylinder bore scratched by foreign material or broken spring. Fit a new master cylinder (Chapter 6).
- [ ] Disc warped. Replace disc(s) (Chapter 6).
- [ ] ABS system faulty (Chapter 6).

Brake lever or pedal pulsates
- [ ] Disc warped. Replace disc with new one (Chapter 6).
- [ ] Brake caliper bolts loose – tighten the bolts to the specified torque (Chapter 6).
- [ ] Wheel warped or otherwise damaged (Chapter 6).
- [ ] Wheel bearings damaged or worn (Chapters 1 and 6).
- [ ] ABS system faulty (Chapter 6).

Brakes drag
- [ ] Master cylinder piston seized. Caused by wear or damage to piston or cylinder bore (Chapter 6).
- [ ] Lever balky or stuck. Check pivot and lubricate (Chapter 5).
- [ ] Brake caliper piston seized in bore. Caused by corrosion or ingestion of dirt past deteriorated seal (Chapter 6).
- [ ] Brake caliper slider pins sticking (Chapter 6).
- [ ] Pads improperly installed (Chapter 6).
- [ ] Brake caliper incorrectly installed (Chapter 6).
- [ ] ABS system faulty (Chapter 6).

14 Electrical problems

Battery dead or weak
- [ ] Battery faulty. Caused by sulphated plates which are shorted through sedimentation. Confirm with battery condition check (Chapter 8).
- [ ] Broken battery terminal making only occasional contact.
- [ ] Battery leads making poor contact (Chapter 8).
- [ ] Load excessive. Caused by addition of high wattage lights or other electrical accessories.
- [ ] Ignition switch defective. Switch either grounds (earths) internally or fails to shut off system. Renew the switch (Chapter 8).
- [ ] Regulator/rectifier defective (Chapter 8).
- [ ] Alternator stator coil open or shorted (Chapter 8).
- [ ] Charging system fault. Check for excessive current leakage (Chapter 8).
- [ ] Wiring faulty. Wiring grounded (earthed) or connections loose in ignition, charging or lighting circuits (Chapter 8).

Battery overcharged
- [ ] Regulator/rectifier defective. Overcharging is noticed when battery gets excessively warm (Chapter 8).
- [ ] Battery faulty. Confirm with battery condition check (Chapter 8).
- [ ] Battery amperage too low, wrong type or size of battery. Install manufacturer's specified amp-hour battery to handle charging load (Chapter 8).

Technical Terms Explained

A

ABS (Anti-lock braking system) A system, usually electronically controlled, that senses incipient wheel lockup during braking and relieves hydraulic pressure at wheel which is about to skid.
Aftermarket Components suitable for the motorcycle, but not produced by the motorcycle manufacturer.
Allen key A hexagonal wrench which fits into a recessed hexagonal hole.
Alternating current (ac) Current produced by an alternator. Requires converting to direct current by a rectifier for charging purposes.
Alternator Converts mechanical energy from the engine into electrical energy to charge the battery and power the electrical system.
Ampere (amp) A unit of measurement for the flow of electrical current. Current = Volts ÷ Ohms.
Ampere-hour (Ah) Measure of battery capacity.
Angle-tightening A torque expressed in degrees. Often follows a conventional tightening torque for cylinder head or main bearing fasteners **(see illustration)**.

Angle-tightening cylinder head bolts

Antifreeze A substance (usually ethylene glycol) mixed with water, and added to the cooling system, to prevent freezing of the coolant in winter. Antifreeze also contains chemicals to inhibit corrosion and the formation of rust and other deposits that would tend to clog the radiator and coolant passages and reduce cooling efficiency.
Anti-dive System attached to the fork lower leg (slider) to prevent fork dive when braking hard.
Anti-seize compound A coating that reduces the risk of seizing on fasteners that are subjected to high temperatures, such as exhaust clamp bolts and nuts.
API American Petroleum Institute. A quality standard for 4-stroke motor oils.
Asbestos A natural fibrous mineral with great heat resistance, commonly used in the composition of brake friction materials. Asbestos is a health hazard and the dust created by brake systems should never be inhaled or ingested.
ATF Automatic Transmission Fluid. Often used in front forks.
ATU Automatic Timing Unit. Mechanical device for advancing the ignition timing on early engines.
ATV All Terrain Vehicle. Often called a Quad.
Axial play Side-to-side movement.
Axle A shaft on which a wheel revolves. Also known as a spindle.

B

Backlash The amount of movement between meshed components when one component is held still. Usually applies to gear teeth.
Ball bearing A bearing consisting of a hardened inner and outer race with hardened steel balls between the two races.
Bearings Used between two working surfaces to prevent wear of the components and a build-up of heat. Four types of bearing are commonly used on motorcycles: plain shell bearings, ball bearings, tapered roller bearings and needle roller bearings.
Bevel gears Used to turn the drive through 90°. Typical applications are shaft final drive and camshaft drive **(see illustration)**.

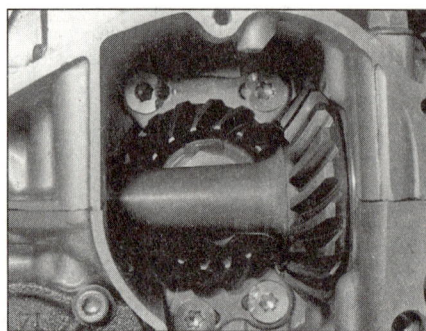

Bevel gears are used to turn the drive through 90°

BHP Brake Horsepower. The British measurement for engine power output. Power output is now usually expressed in kilowatts (kW).
Bias-belted tyre Similar construction to radial tyre, but with outer belt running at an angle to the wheel rim.
Big-end bearing The bearing in the end of the connecting rod that's attached to the crankshaft.
Bleeding The process of removing air from an hydraulic system via a bleed nipple or bleed screw.
Bottom-end A description of an engine's crankcase components and all components contained there-in.
BTDC Before Top Dead Centre in terms of piston position. Ignition timing is often expressed in terms of degrees or millimetres BTDC.
Bush A cylindrical metal or rubber component used between two moving parts.
Burr Rough edge left on a component after machining or as a result of excessive wear.

C

Cam chain The chain which takes drive from the crankshaft to the camshaft(s).
Canister The main component in an evaporative emission control system (California market only); contains activated charcoal granules to trap vapours from the fuel system rather than allowing them to vent to the atmosphere.
Castellated Resembling the parapets along the top of a castle wall. For example, a castellated wheel axle or spindle nut.
Catalytic converter A device in the exhaust system of some machines which converts certain pollutants in the exhaust gases into less harmful substances.
Charging system Description of the components which charge the battery, ie the alternator, rectifier and regulator.
Circlip A ring-shaped clip used to prevent endwise movement of cylindrical parts and shafts. An internal circlip is installed in a groove in a housing; an external circlip fits into a groove on the outside of a cylindrical piece such as a shaft. Also known as a snap-ring.
Clearance The amount of space between two parts. For example, between a piston and a cylinder, between a bearing and a journal, etc.
Coil spring A spiral of elastic steel found in various sizes throughout a vehicle, for example as a springing medium in the suspension and in the valve train.
Compression Reduction in volume, and increase in pressure and temperature, of a gas, caused by squeezing it into a smaller space.
Compression damping Controls the speed the suspension compresses when hitting a bump.
Compression ratio The relationship between cylinder volume when the piston is at top dead centre and cylinder volume when the piston is at bottom dead centre.
Continuity The uninterrupted path in the flow of electricity. Little or no measurable resistance.
Continuity tester Self-powered bleeper or test light which indicates continuity.
Cp Candlepower. Bulb rating commonly found on US motorcycles.
Crossply tyre Tyre plies arranged in a criss-cross pattern. Usually four or six plies used, hence 4PR or 6PR in tyre size codes.
Cush drive Rubber damper segments fitted between the rear wheel and final drive sprocket to absorb transmission shocks **(see illustration)**.

Cush drive rubbers dampen out transmission shocks

D

Degree disc Calibrated disc for measuring piston position. Expressed in degrees.
Dial gauge Clock-type gauge with adapters for measuring runout and piston position. Expressed in mm or inches.
Diaphragm The rubber membrane in a master cylinder or carburettor which seals the upper chamber.
Diaphragm spring A single sprung plate often used in clutches.
Direct current (dc) Current produced by a dc generator.

Technical Terms Explained

Decarbonisation The process of removing carbon deposits - typically from the combustion chamber, valves and exhaust port/system.
Detonation Destructive and damaging explosion of fuel/air mixture in combustion chamber instead of controlled burning.
Diode An electrical valve which only allows current to flow in one direction. Commonly used in rectifiers and starter interlock systems.
Disc valve (or rotary valve) A induction system used on some two-stroke engines.
Double-overhead camshaft (DOHC) An engine that uses two overhead camshafts, one for the intake valves and one for the exhaust valves.
Drivebelt A toothed belt used to transmit drive to the rear wheel on some motorcycles. A drivebelt has also been used to drive the camshafts. Drivebelts are usually made of Kevlar.
Driveshaft Any shaft used to transmit motion. Commonly used when referring to the final driveshaft on shaft drive motorcycles.

E

Earth return The return path of an electrical circuit, utilising the motorcycle's frame.
ECU (Electronic Control Unit) A computer which controls (for instance) an ignition system, or an anti-lock braking system.
EGO Exhaust Gas Oxygen sensor. Sometimes called a Lambda sensor.
Electrolyte The fluid in a lead-acid battery.
EMS (Engine Management System) A computer controlled system which manages the fuel injection and the ignition systems in an integrated fashion.
Endfloat The amount of lengthways movement between two parts. As applied to a crankshaft, the distance that the crankshaft can move side-to-side in the crankcase.
Endless chain A chain having no joining link. Common use for cam chains and final drive chains.
EP (Extreme Pressure) Oil type used in locations where high loads are applied, such as between gear teeth.
Evaporative emission control system Describes a charcoal filled canister which stores fuel vapours from the tank rather than allowing them to vent to the atmosphere. Usually only fitted to California models and referred to as an EVAP system.
Expansion chamber Section of two-stroke engine exhaust system so designed to improve engine efficiency and boost power.

F

Feeler blade or gauge A thin strip or blade of hardened steel, ground to an exact thickness, used to check or measure clearances between parts.
Final drive Description of the drive from the transmission to the rear wheel. Usually by chain or shaft, but sometimes by belt.
Firing order The order in which the engine cylinders fire, or deliver their power strokes, beginning with the number one cylinder.
Flooding Term used to describe a high fuel level in the carburettor float chambers, leading to fuel overflow. Also refers to excess fuel in the combustion chamber due to incorrect starting technique.

Free length The no-load state of a component when measured. Clutch, valve and fork spring lengths are measured at rest, without any preload.
Freeplay The amount of travel before any action takes place. The looseness in a linkage, or an assembly of parts, between the initial application of force and actual movement. For example, the distance the rear brake pedal moves before the rear brake is actuated.
Fuel injection The fuel/air mixture is metered electronically and directed into the engine intake ports (indirect injection) or into the cylinders (direct injection). Sensors supply information on engine speed and conditions.
Fuel/air mixture The charge of fuel and air going into the engine. See **Stoichiometric ratio**.
Fuse An electrical device which protects a circuit against accidental overload. The typical fuse contains a soft piece of metal which is calibrated to melt at a predetermined current flow (expressed as amps) and break the circuit.

G

Gap The distance the spark must travel in jumping from the centre electrode to the side electrode in a spark plug. Also refers to the distance between the ignition rotor and the pickup coil in an electronic ignition system.
Gasket Any thin, soft material - usually cork, cardboard, asbestos or soft metal - installed between two metal surfaces to ensure a good seal. For instance, the cylinder head gasket seals the joint between the block and the cylinder head.
Gauge An instrument panel display used to monitor engine conditions. A gauge with a movable pointer on a dial or a fixed scale is an analogue gauge. A gauge with a numerical readout is called a digital gauge.
Gear ratios The drive ratio of a pair of gears in a gearbox, calculated on their number of teeth.
Glaze-busting see **Honing**
Grinding Process for renovating the valve face and valve seat contact area in the cylinder head.
Gudgeon pin The shaft which connects the connecting rod small-end with the piston. Often called a piston pin or wrist pin.

H

Helical gears Gear teeth are slightly curved and produce less gear noise that straight-cut gears. Often used for primary drives.

Installing a Helicoil thread insert in a cylinder head

Helicoil A thread insert repair system. Commonly used as a repair for stripped spark plug threads **(see illustration)**.
Honing A process used to break down the glaze on a cylinder bore (also called glaze-busting). Can also be carried out to roughen a rebored cylinder to aid ring bedding-in.
HT (High Tension) Description of the electrical circuit from the secondary winding of the ignition coil to the spark plug.
Hydraulic A liquid filled system used to transmit pressure from one component to another. Common uses on motorcycles are brakes and clutches.
Hydrometer An instrument for measuring the specific gravity of a lead-acid battery.
Hygroscopic Water absorbing. In motorcycle applications, braking efficiency will be reduced if DOT 3 or 4 hydraulic fluid absorbs water from the air - care must be taken to keep new brake fluid in tightly sealed containers.

I

lbf ft Pounds-force feet. An imperial unit of torque. Sometimes written as ft-lbs.
lbf in Pound-force inch. An imperial unit of torque, applied to components where a very low torque is required. Sometimes written as in-lbs.
IC Abbreviation for Integrated Circuit.
Ignition advance Means of increasing the timing of the spark at higher engine speeds. Done by mechanical means (ATU) on early engines or electronically by the ignition control unit on later engines.
Ignition timing The moment at which the spark plug fires, expressed in the number of crankshaft degrees before the piston reaches the top of its stroke, or in the number of millimetres before the piston reaches the top of its stroke.
Infinity (∞) Description of an open-circuit electrical state, where no continuity exists.
Inverted forks (upside down forks) The sliders or lower legs are held in the yokes and the fork tubes or stanchions are connected to the wheel axle (spindle). Less unsprung weight and stiffer construction than conventional forks.

J

JASO Quality standard for 2-stroke oils.
Joule The unit of electrical energy.
Journal The bearing surface of a shaft.

K

Kickstart Mechanical means of turning the engine over for starting purposes. Only usually fitted to mopeds, small capacity motorcycles and off-road motorcycles.
Kill switch Handebar-mounted switch for emergency ignition cut-out. Cuts the ignition circuit on all models, and additionally prevent starter motor operation on others.
km Symbol for kilometre.
kmh Abbreviation for kilometres per hour.

L

Lambda (λ) sensor A sensor fitted in the exhaust system to measure the exhaust gas oxygen content (excess air factor).

Technical Terms Explained

Lapping see **Grinding**.
LCD Abbreviation for Liquid Crystal Display.
LED Abbreviation for Light Emitting Diode.
Liner A steel cylinder liner inserted in a aluminium alloy cylinder block.
Locknut A nut used to lock an adjustment nut, or other threaded component, in place.
Lockstops The lugs on the lower triple clamp (yoke) which abut those on the frame, preventing handlebar-to-fuel tank contact.
Lockwasher A form of washer designed to prevent an attaching nut from working loose.
LT Low Tension Description of the electrical circuit from the power supply to the primary winding of the ignition coil.

M

Main bearings The bearings between the crankshaft and crankcase.
Maintenance-free (MF) battery A sealed battery which cannot be topped up.
Manometer Mercury-filled calibrated tubes used to measure intake tract vacuum. Used to synchronise carburettors on multi-cylinder engines.
Micrometer A precision measuring instrument that measures component outside diameters **(see illustration)**.

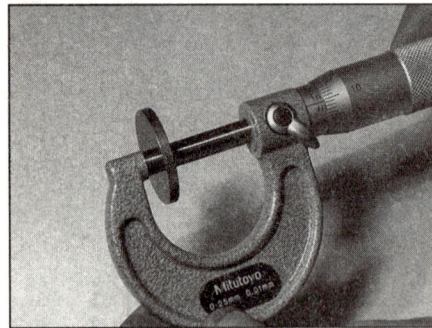

Tappet shims are measured with a micrometer

MON (Motor Octane Number) A measure of a fuel's resistance to knock.
Monograde oil An oil with a single viscosity, eg SAE80W.
Monoshock A single suspension unit linking the swingarm or suspension linkage to the frame.
mph Abbreviation for miles per hour.
Multigrade oil Having a wide viscosity range (eg 10W40). The W stands for Winter, thus the viscosity ranges from SAE10 when cold to SAE40 when hot.
Multimeter An electrical test instrument with the capability to measure voltage, current and resistance. Some meters also incorporate a continuity tester and buzzer.

N

Needle roller bearing Inner race of caged needle rollers and hardened outer race. Examples of uncaged needle rollers can be found on some engines. Commonly used in rear suspension applications and in two-stroke engines.
Nm Newton metres.
NOx Oxides of Nitrogen. A common toxic pollutant emitted by petrol engines at higher temperatures.

O

Octane The measure of a fuel's resistance to knock.
OE (Original Equipment) Relates to components fitted to a motorcycle as standard or replacement parts supplied by the motorcycle manufacturer.
Ohm The unit of electrical resistance. Ohms = Volts ÷ Current.
Ohmmeter An instrument for measuring electrical resistance.
Oil cooler System for diverting engine oil outside of the engine to a radiator for cooling purposes.
Oil injection A system of two-stroke engine lubrication where oil is pump-fed to the engine in accordance with throttle position.
Open-circuit An electrical condition where there is a break in the flow of electricity - no continuity (high resistance).
O-ring A type of sealing ring made of a special rubber-like material; in use, the O-ring is compressed into a groove to provide the sealing action.
Oversize (OS) Term used for piston and ring size options fitted to a rebored cylinder.
Overhead cam (sohc) engine An engine with single camshaft located on top of the cylinder head.
Overhead valve (ohv) engine An engine with the valves located in the cylinder head, but with the camshaft located in the engine block or crankcase.
Oxygen sensor A device installed in the exhaust system which senses the oxygen content in the exhaust and converts this information into an electric current. Also called a Lambda sensor.

P

Plastigauge A thin strip of plastic thread, available in different sizes, used for measuring clearances. For example, a strip of Plastigauge is laid across a bearing journal. The parts are assembled and dismantled; the width of the crushed strip indicates the clearance between journal and bearing.
Polarity Either negative or positive earth (ground), determined by which battery lead is connected to the frame (earth return). Modern motorcycles are usually negative earth.
Pre-ignition A situation where the fuel/air mixture ignites before the spark plug fires. Often due to a hot spot in the combustion chamber caused by carbon build-up. Engine has a tendency to 'run-on'.
Pre-load (suspension) The amount a spring is compressed when in the unloaded state. Preload can be applied by gas, spacer or mechanical adjuster.
Premix The method of engine lubrication on older two-stroke engines. Engine oil is mixed with the petrol in the fuel tank in a specific ratio. The fuel/oil mix is sometimes referred to as "petroil".
Primary drive Description of the drive from the crankshaft to the clutch. Usually by gear or chain.
PS Pfedestärke - a German interpretation of BHP.
PSI Pounds-force per square inch. Imperial measurement of tyre pressure and cylinder pressure measurement.
PTFE Polytetrafluroethylene. A low friction substance.
Pulse secondary air injection system A process of promoting the burning of excess fuel present in the exhaust gases by routing fresh air into the exhaust ports.

Q

Quartz halogen bulb Tungsten filament surrounded by a halogen gas. Typically used for the headlight **(see illustration)**.

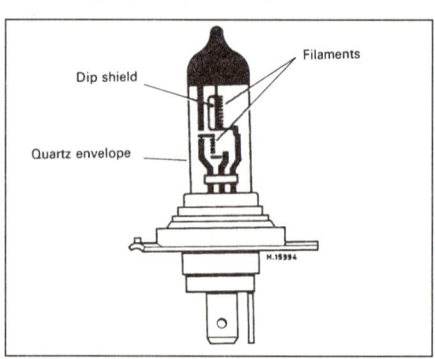

Quartz halogen headlight bulb construction

R

Rack-and-pinion A pinion gear on the end of a shaft that mates with a rack (think of a geared wheel opened up and laid flat). Sometimes used in clutch operating systems.
Radial play Up and down movement about a shaft.
Radial ply tyres Tyre plies run across the tyre (from bead to bead) and around the circumference of the tyre. Less resistant to tread distortion than other tyre types.
Radiator A liquid-to-air heat transfer device designed to reduce the temperature of the coolant in a liquid cooled engine.
Rake A feature of steering geometry - the angle of the steering head in relation to the vertical **(see illustration)**.

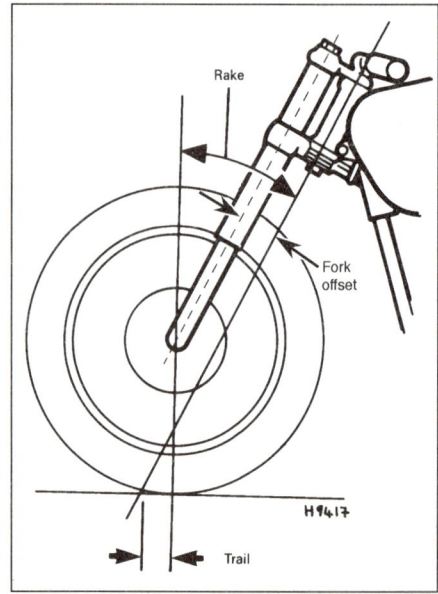

Steering geometry

Technical Terms Explained

Rebore Providing a new working surface to the cylinder bore by boring out the old surface. Necessitates the use of oversize piston and rings.

Rebound damping A means of controlling the oscillation of a suspension unit spring after it has been compressed. Resists the spring's natural tendency to bounce back after being compressed.

Rectifier Device for converting the ac output of an alternator into dc for battery charging.

Reed valve An induction system commonly used on two-stroke engines.

Regulator Device for maintaining the charging voltage from the generator or alternator within a specified range.

Relay A electrical device used to switch heavy current on and off by using a low current auxiliary circuit.

Resistance Measured in ohms. An electrical component's ability to pass electrical current.

RON (Research Octane Number) A measure of a fuel's resistance to knock.

rpm revolutions per minute.

Runout The amount of wobble (in-and-out movement) of a wheel or shaft as it's rotated. The amount a shaft rotates 'out-of-true'. The out-of-round condition of a rotating part.

S

SAE (Society of Automotive Engineers) A standard for the viscosity of a fluid.

Sealant A liquid or paste used to prevent leakage at a joint. Sometimes used in conjunction with a gasket.

Service limit Term for the point where a component is no longer useable and must be renewed.

Shaft drive A method of transmitting drive from the transmission to the rear wheel.

Shell bearings Plain bearings consisting of two shell halves. Most often used as big-end and main bearings in a four-stroke engine. Often called bearing inserts.

Shim Thin spacer, commonly used to adjust the clearance or relative positions between two parts. For example, shims inserted into or under tappets or followers to control valve clearances. Clearance is adjusted by changing the thickness of the shim.

Short-circuit An electrical condition where current shorts to earth (ground) bypassing the circuit components.

Skimming Process to correct warpage or repair a damaged surface, eg on brake discs or drums.

Slide-hammer A special puller that screws into or hooks onto a component such as a shaft or bearing; a heavy sliding handle on the shaft bottoms against the end of the shaft to knock the component free.

Small-end bearing The bearing in the upper end of the connecting rod at its joint with the gudgeon pin.

Spalling Damage to camshaft lobes or bearing journals shown as pitting of the working surface.

Specific gravity (SG) The state of charge of the electrolyte in a lead-acid battery. A measure of the electrolyte's density compared with water.

Straight-cut gears Common type gear used on gearbox shafts and for oil pump and water pump drives.

Stanchion The inner sliding part of the front forks, held by the yokes. Often called a fork tube.

Stoichiometric ratio The optimum chemical air/fuel ratio for a petrol engine, said to be 14.7 parts of air to 1 part of fuel.

Sulphuric acid The liquid (electrolyte) used in a lead-acid battery. Poisonous and extremely corrosive.

Surface grinding (lapping) Process to correct a warped gasket face, commonly used on cylinder heads.

T

Tapered-roller bearing Tapered inner race of caged needle rollers and separate tapered outer race. Examples of taper roller bearings can be found on steering heads.

Tappet A cylindrical component which transmits motion from the cam to the valve stem, either directly or via a pushrod and rocker arm. Also called a cam follower.

TCS Traction Control System. An electronically-controlled system which senses wheel spin and reduces engine speed accordingly.

TDC Top Dead Centre denotes that the piston is at its highest point in the cylinder.

Thread-locking compound Solution applied to fastener threads to prevent slackening. Select type to suit application.

Thrust washer A washer positioned between two moving components on a shaft. For example, between gear pinions on gearshaft.

Timing chain See **Cam Chain**.

Timing light Stroboscopic lamp for carrying out ignition timing checks with the engine running.

Top-end A description of an engine's cylinder block, head and valve gear components.

Torque Turning or twisting force about a shaft.

Torque setting A prescribed tightness specified by the motorcycle manufacturer to ensure that the bolt or nut is secured correctly. Undertightening can result in the bolt or nut coming loose or a surface not being sealed. Overtightening can result in stripped threads, distortion or damage to the component being retained.

Torx key A six-point wrench.

Tracer A stripe of a second colour applied to a wire insulator to distinguish that wire from another one with the same colour insulator. For example, Br/W is often used to denote a brown insulator with a white tracer.

Trail A feature of steering geometry. Distance from the steering head axis to the tyre's central contact point.

Triple clamps The cast components which extend from the steering head and support the fork stanchions or tubes. Often called fork yokes.

Turbocharger A centrifugal device, driven by exhaust gases, that pressurises the intake air. Normally used to increase the power output from a given engine displacement.

TWI Abbreviation for Tyre Wear Indicator. Indicates the location of the tread depth indicator bars on tyres.

U

Universal joint or U-joint (UJ) A double-pivoted connection for transmitting power from a driving to a driven shaft through an angle. Typically found in shaft drive assemblies.

Unsprung weight Anything not supported by the bike's suspension (ie the wheel, tyres, brakes, final drive and bottom (moving) part of the suspension).

V

Vacuum gauges Clock-type gauges for measuring intake tract vacuum. Used for carburettor synchronisation on multi-cylinder engines.

Valve A device through which the flow of liquid, gas or vacuum may be stopped, started or regulated by a moveable part that opens, shuts or partially obstructs one or more ports or passageways. The intake and exhaust valves in the cylinder head are of the poppet type.

Valve clearance The clearance between the valve tip (the end of the valve stem) and the rocker arm or tappet/follower. The valve clearance is measured when the valve is closed. The correct clearance is important - if too small the valve won't close fully and will burn out, whereas if too large noisy operation will result.

Valve lift The amount a valve is lifted off its seat by the camshaft lobe.

Valve timing The exact setting for the opening and closing of the valves in relation to piston position.

Vernier caliper A precision measuring instrument that measures inside and outside dimensions. Not quite as accurate as a micrometer, but more convenient.

VIN Vehicle Identification Number. Term for the bike's engine and frame numbers.

Viscosity The thickness of a liquid or its resistance to flow.

Volt A unit for expressing electrical "pressure" in a circuit. Volts = current x ohms.

W

Water pump A mechanically-driven device for moving coolant around the engine.

Watt A unit for expressing electrical power. Watts = volts x current.

Wear limit see **Service limit**

Wet liner A liquid-cooled engine design where the pistons run in liners which are directly surrounded by coolant **(see illustration)**.

Wet liner arrangement

Wheelbase Distance from the centre of the front wheel to the centre of the rear wheel.

Wiring harness or loom Describes the electrical wires running the length of the motorcycle and enclosed in tape or plastic sheathing. Wiring coming off the main harness is usually referred to as a sub harness.

Woodruff key A key of semi-circular or square section used to locate a gear to a shaft. Often used to locate the alternator rotor on the crankshaft.

Wrist pin Another name for gudgeon or piston pin.

Index

A
About this Manual – 0•8
ABS – 6•4
  components – 6•26
  fault diagnosis – 6•22
  operation – 6•21
Access panels and trim covers – 7•3
Acknowledgements – 0•8
Air filter – 1•22
  housing – 4•7
Alternator – 8•25
  drive, middle and driven gears – 2•45
Antifreeze – 1•2
  level – 0•12
Asbestos – 0•11

B
Balancer shafts – 2•74
Battery – 0•11, 1•26
  charging – 8•5
  removal and maintenance – 8•4
Bearing seal lips lubricant – 1•2
Bike spec – 0•9
Bleeding
  brake system – 6•20
  clutch release mechanism – 2•36
Bodywork – 7•1 *et seq*
  engine guard cover – 7•4
  fairing – 7•6
  fairing side panels – 7•5
  lower fairing – 7•4
  mirror covers and mirrors – 7•7
  mudguards – 7•9
  panniers – 7•2
  rear cowl – 7•10
  seats – 7•2
  side covers – 7•3
  trim clips – 7•1
  valve cover trim – 7•4
  windshield and inner cowl – 7•8
Bolts – 1•22
Brake calipers – 6•7, 6•15
  seals – 1•8
  slider pins and boots lubricant – 1•2
Brake discs – 6•9, 6•16
Brake fluid – 1•2
  change – 1•8
  levels – 0•13
Brake hoses – 1•8, 6•20
Brake lever – 5•8
  pivot and pushrod lubricant – 1•2
  switch – 8•10
Brake light – 8•7
  circuit check – 8•10
  switches – 8•10
Brake master cylinder – 6•10, 6•16
  pushrod and boot lubricant – 1•2
  seals – 1•8
Brake pads – 6•5, 6•14
  wear check – 1•6
Brake pedal – 5•3
  lubricant – 1•2
  switch – 8•11
Brake system – 1•6
  check – 1•7
Brake/tail light bulbs – 8•2, 8•9
Brakes, wheels and final drive – 6•1 *et seq*
  ABS – 6•4
  ABS control unit – 6•27
  ABS fault codes – 6•22
  ABS fault diagnosis – 6•22
  ABS modulator – 6•26, 6•27
  ABS operation – 6•21
  ABS pulse ring – 6•26
  ABS wheel sensor – 6•26
  brake calipers – 6•7, 6•15
  brake discs – 6•9, 6•16
  brake hoses and fittings – 6•20
  brake master cylinder – 6•10, 6•16
  brake pads – 6•5, 6•14
  brake system bleeding and fluid change – 6•20
  driveshaft – 6•33
  Dual Combined Braking System – 6•4
  final drive housing and driveshaft – 6•33
  proportional control valve – 6•13
  rear wheel drive coupling – 6•31
  rear wheel drive coupling bearings – 6•32
  secondary master cylinder – 6•12
  tyres – 6•33
  wheel alignment check – 6•28
  wheel bearings – 6•31
  wheel inspection and repair – 6•27
Buying spare parts – 0•10

C
Cables
  lubricant – 1•2
  lubrication – 1•21
  throttle – 1•10, 4•26
Calipers – 6•7, 6•15
  seals – 1•8
  slider pins and boots lubricant – 1•2
Cam chains, tensioner blades and guides – 2•17, 2•24
Camshaft position (CMP) sensor – 4•14
Camshafts and followers – 2•18
Catalytic converters – 4•31
Centrestand – 1•17, 5•5
Charcoal canister – 4•31
Charging system testing – 8•25
Clutch – 1•8, 2•29
  check – 1•8
  fluid – 1•2
  fluid change – 1•8
  fluid level – 0•15
  hoses – 1•8
  lever pivot and pushrod lubricant – 1•2, 5•8
  master cylinder – 2•34
  master cylinder seals – 1•8
  release cylinder – 2•35
  release cylinder seals – 1•8
  release mechanism – 2•33, 2•36
  switch – 8•18
Coils – 4•32
Connecting rods – 2•69
  bearings – 2•66, 2•69
  bearing shell selection – 2•71
Continuity checks – 8•3
Control unit (ABS) – 6•27
Conversion factors – REF•26
Coolant – 1•2
  hoses – 1•16, 3•8
  level – 0•12
  reservoir – 3•8
Cooling system – 1•14, 3•1 *et seq*
  coolant hoses and unions – 3•8
  coolant reservoir – 3•8
  cooling fan – 3•2
  cooling fan relay – 3•2
  ECT sensor – 3•3
  pressure cap check – 3•6
  radiator – 3•5
  temperature display – 3•3
  thermostat – 3•4
  thermostat housing – 3•5
  water pump – 3•6
Cowl – 7•9, 7•10

Crankcase separation and reassembly – 2•63
Crankcases – 2•66
Crankshaft – 2•67
Crankshaft position (CKP) sensor – 4•14
Cylinder bores – 2•66
Cylinder compression check – 2•7
Cylinder head
  overhaul – 2•26
  removal and installation – 2•25

D
Delay valve – 6•13
Diode block – 8•18
Discs – 6•9, 6•16
Downpipe assembly – 4•28
Driveshaft – 6•33
Dual Combined Braking System – 6•4

E
Earth (ground) checks – 8•4
ECT sensor – 3•3
Electrical system – 8•1 *et seq*
  alternator/regulator/rectifier – 8•25
  battery charging – 8•5
  battery removal and maintenance – 8•4
  brake lever switch – 8•10
  brake light – 8•7
  brake light switches – 8•10
  brake pedal switch – 8•11
  brake/tail light bulbs – 8•9
  charging system testing – 8•25
  circuit check – 8•10
  clutch switch – 8•18
  continuity checks – 8•3
  diode block – 8•18
  earth (ground) checks – 8•4
  fault finding – 8•2
  fuses – 8•5
  handlebar switches – 8•16
  headlight – 8•6, 8•7, 8
  headlight aim adjuster mechanism – 8•8
  horn – 8•18
  ignition switch – 8•15
  indicator light board – 8•13, 8•14
  instrument and warning lights – 8•13
  instrument check and replacement – 8•12
  instrument cluster power check – 8•12
  instrument cluster removal and installation – 8•11
  instrument PCB – 8•13
  LCD display – 8•13
  leakage test – 8•25
  lighting system check – 8•6
  multi-function button board – 8•13, 8•14
  neutral switch – 8•16
  oil pressure switch – 8•15
  output test – 8•25
  sidelight – 8•7, 8•8
  sidestand switch – 8•17
  speed sensor – 8•12, 8•14
  speedometer – 8•12
  starter motor overhaul – 8•21
  starter motor removal and installation – 8•20
  starter relay – 8•19
  switch replacement – 8•10
  tachometer – 8•12
  tail lights – 8•7, 8•9
  turn signal assemblies – 8•10
  turn signal bulbs – 8•10
  turn signal circuit check and relay – 8•9
  turn signals – 8•7
  voltage checks – 8•3
  warning lights – 8•13
  windshield height adjuster mechanism – 8•28
  wiring diagrams – 8•30 *et seq*

Index

Electricity – 0•11
Engine control module (ECM) – 4•16
Engine coolant temperature (ECT) sensor – 4•12
Engine guard cover – 7•4
Engine management system – 4•1 et seq
 air filter housing – 4•7
 camshaft position (CMP) sensor – 4•14
 catalytic converters – 4•31
 charcoal canister – 4•31
 crankshaft position (CKP) sensor – 4•14
 engine control module (ECM) – 4•16
 engine coolant temperature (ECT) sensor – 4•12
 engine stop relay – 4•15
 evaporative emission control (EVAP) system – 4•30
 exhaust system – 4•28
 fast idle system wax unit – 4•21
 fault diagnosis – 4•9, 4•35
 fuel consumption readout – 4•25
 fuel cut-off relay – 4•16
 fuel gauge and level sensor – 4•25
 fuel pressure check – 4•22
 fuel pressure regulator – 4•22
 fuel pump and filter – 4•22
 fuel rails and injectors – 4•11
 fuel system – 4•2, 4•9
 fuel system fault diagnosis – 4•9
 fuel system hoses – 4•29
 fuel tanks – 4•3
 ignition coils – 4•32
 ignition system – 4•2
 ignition system check – 4•32
 ignition timing – 4•33
 immobiliser system – 4•34
 injectors – 4•11
 intake air temperature (IAT) sensor – 4•13
 knock sensors – 4•17
 lean angle sensor – 4•15
 level sensor and low fuel warning switch – 4•25
 manifold absolute pressure (MAP) sensor – 4•13
 oxygen sensors – 4•16
 pulse secondary air (PAIR) system – 4•30
 purge control valve – 4•31
 speed sensor – 4•15
 starter valves – 4•19
 throttle bodies – 4•17
 throttle cables – 4•26
 throttle position (TP) sensor – 4•12
 troubleshooting procedure – 4•36
Engine numbers – 0•10
Engine oil – 1•12
 level – 0•14
 pressure check – 2•7
Engine stop relay – 4•15
Engine, clutch and transmission – 2•1 et seq
 alternator drive, middle and driven gears – 2•45
 balancer shafts – 2•74
 cam chains, tensioner blades and guides – 2•17, 2•24
 camshafts and followers – 2•18
 clutch – 2•29
 clutch release mechanism – 2•33
 connecting rod bearings – 2•66, 2•69
 connecting rods – 2•69
 crankcases – 2•63, 2•66
 crankshaft – 2•67
 cylinder bores – 2•66
 compression check – 2•7
 cylinder head and valve overhaul – 2•26
 cylinder head removal and installation – 2•25
 engine overhaul information – 2•15
 engine removal and installation – 2•8
 engine wear assessment – 2•7
 final output shaft and gears – 2•40
 gearchange mechanism – 2•47
 input shaft – 2•54
 main bearings – 2•66, 2•67
 oil cooler – 2•16
 oil pressure check – 2•7
 oil pump and pressure relief valve – 2•60
 oil sump and strainers – 2•59
 operations possible with the engine in the frame – 2•7
 operations requiring engine removal – 2•7
 output shaft – 2•56
 piston rings – 2•73
 pistons – 2•72
 primary damper shaft – 2•39
 primary drive gear – 2•37
 running-in procedure – 2•77
 selector drum and forks – 2•50
 starter clutch and gears – 2•44
 transmission assembly removal and installation – 2•49
 transmission shaft and bearing removal and installation – 2•52
 valve covers – 2•16
 valve overhaul – 2•26
EVAP (Evaporative emission control) system (California models) – 1•23
Evaporative emission control (EVAP) system – 4•30
Exhaust system – 4•28

F

Fairing – 7•6
 side panels – 7•5
Fans – 3•2
Fast idle system wax unit – 4•21
Fault codes
 ABS – 6•22
 immobiliser system – 4•35, 4•36
Fault Finding – REF•35 et seq
 electrical system – 8•2
 fuel injection system – 4•9
 immobiliser system – 4•35
Filter
 air – 1•22, 4•7
 fuel – 1•10, 4•22
 oil – 1•12
Final drive – 0•15
 housing and driveshaft – 6•33
 oil – 1•2, 1•14
Final output shaft and gears – 2•40
Fire – 0•11
Fluids – 1•2, REF•23 et seq
Followers – 2•18
Footrest pivots lubricant – 1•2
Footrests – 5•3
Forks
 oil – 1•19, 5•1
 oil change – 5•9
 overhaul – 5•11
 removal and installation – 5•8
Frame and suspension – 5•1 et seq
 brake pedal – 5•3
 centrestand – 5•5
 footrests – 5•3
 fork oil – 5•1
 fork oil change – 5•9
 fork overhaul – 5•11
 fork removal and installation – 5•8
 frame inspection and repair – 5•2
 gearchange lever and linkage – 5•4
 handlebars and levers – 5•6
 rear shock absorber – 5•18
 sidestand – 5•5
 steering head bearings – 5•16
 steering stem – 5•14
 suspension adjustment – 5•20
 swingarm removal and installation – 5•20
Frame inspection and repair – 5•2
Frame numbers – 0•10
Fuel checks – 0•16
Fuel consumption readout – 4•25
Fuel cut-off relay – 4•16
Fuel gauge and level sensor – 4•25
Fuel injection system – 1•9, 4•2, 4•9
 components – 4•10
 fault diagnosis – 4•9
Fuel pressure check – 4•22
Fuel pressure regulator – 4•22
Fuel pump and filter – 4•22
Fuel rails and injectors – 4•11
Fuel strainer and filter – 1•10
Fuel system hoses – 1•9, 4•29
Fuel tanks – 4•3
 repair – 4•7
Fumes – 0•11
Fuses – 8•2, 8•5

G

Gearchange lever and linkage – 5•4
 lubricant – 1•2
Gearchange mechanism – 2•47

H

Handlebars – 5•6
 holder – 5•7
 switches – 8•16
 weights – 5•7
Headlight – 8•6, 8•7, 8•8
 aim – 1•17
 aim adjuster mechanism – 8•8
Horn – 8•18
Hoses
 brake – 1•8, 6•20
 clutch – 1•8
 coolant – 1•16, 3•8
 fuel system – 1•9, 4•29

I

Identification numbers – 0•10
Idle speed – 1•6
Ignition coils – 4•32
Ignition switch – 8•15
Ignition system – 4•2
 check – 4•32
Ignition timing – 4•33
Immobiliser system – 4•34
Indicator light board – 8•13, 8•14
Injectors – 4•11
Inner cowl – 7•9
Input shaft – 2•54
Instrument
 check and replacement – 8•12
 cluster power check – 8•12
 cluster removal and installation – 8•11
 PCB – 8•13
 warning lights – 8•13
Intake air temperature (IAT) sensor – 4•13

K

Key registration procedure – 4•34
Knock sensors – 4•17

L

LCD display – 8•13
Leakage test – 8•25
Lean angle sensor – 4•15
Legal checks – 0•16
Level sensor and low fuel warning switch – 4•25
Lever pivots lubrication – 1•21
Levers – 5•8
 brake – 8•10
 clutch – 8•18
Lighting checks – 0•16, 8•6
Lower fairing – 7•4
Lubricants and fluids – 1•2, REF•23 et seq
Luggage locking plates lubricant – 1•2

Index

M
Main bearings – 2•66, 2•67
  shell selection – 2•68
Main fuel tank – 4•3
Maintenance schedule – 1•3
Manifold absolute pressure (MAP)
  sensor – 4•13
Master cylinder
  brake – 6•10, 6•12, 6•16
  clutch – 2•34
  pushrod and boot lubricant – 1•2
  seals – 1•8
Mirror covers and mirrors – 7•7
Model development – 0•9
Modulator (ABS) – 6•26, 6•27
MOT Test Checks – REF•27 *et seq*
Mudguards – 7•9
Multi-function button board – 8•13, 8•14

N
Neutral switch – 8•16
Nuts – 1•22

O
Oil
  engine – 0•14, 1•12
  forks – 1•19, 5•1, 5•9
  final drive – 1•2, 1•14
Oil cooler – 2•16
Oil filter – 1•12
Oil pressure check – 2•7
Oil pressure switch – 8•15
Oil pump and pressure relief valve – 2•60
Oil sump and strainers – 2•59
Output shaft – 2•56
Output test (charging system) – 8•25
Oxygen sensors – 4•16

P
Pads – 6•5, 6•14
  wear check – 1•6
PAIR (Pulse secondary air supply) system – 1•17
Panniers – 7•2
Parts – 0•10
Pedal
  brake – 1•8, 5•3, 8•11
Piston rings – 2•73
Pistons – 2•72
Pre-ride checks – 0•12 *et seq*
  brake fluid levels – 0•13
  clutch fluid level – 0•15
  coolant level – 0•12
  engine oil level – 0•14
  final drive – 0•15
  fuel checks – 0•16
  legal checks – 0•16
  lighting checks – 0•16
  safety checks – 0•16
  signalling checks – 0•16
  steering – 0•15
  suspension – 0•15
  tyres – 0•16
Pressure cap check – 3•6
Primary damper shaft – 2•39
Primary drive gear – 2•37
Proportional control valve – 6•12
Pulse ring (ABS) – 6•26
Pulse secondary air (PAIR) system – 4•30
Purge control valve – 4•31

R
Radiator – 3•5
  pressure cap check – 3•6
Rear cowl – 7•10
Rear wheel drive coupling – 6•31
  bearings – 6•32

Relays
  cooling fan – 3•2
  engine stop – 4•15
  fuel cut-off – 4•16
  headlight – 8•6
  power – 8•7
  starter – 8•19
  turn signal circuit – 8•9
  windshield height adjuster – 8•28
Release cylinder (clutch) – 2•35
  seals – 1•8
Reservoir coolant – 3•8
Routine maintenance and servicing – 1•1 *et seq*
  air filter – 1•22
  battery – 1•26
  bolts – 1•22
  brake system – 1•6
  cable lubrication – 1•21
  centrestand – 1•17
  clutch – 1•8
  cooling system – 1•15
  engine oil and filter – 1•12
  EVAP (evaporative emission control) system
    (California models) – 1•23
  final drive gear oil – 1•14
  fork oil change – 1•19
  fuel system – 1•9
  headlight aim – 1•17
  idle speed – 1•6
  lever pivots lubrication – 1•21
  lubricants and fluids – 1•2
  maintenance schedule – 1•3
  nuts – 1•22
  PAIR (Pulse secondary air supply) system – 1•17
  sidestand – 1•17
  spark plugs – 1•2, 1•11
  stands – 1•17
  stands lubrication – 1•21
  starter interlock circuit – 1•17
  steering head bearings – 1•19
  suspension – 1•18
  throttle cables – 1•10
  tyre pressures – 1•2
  tyres – 1•21
  valve clearances – 1•23
  wheels – 1•21
Running-in procedure – 2•77

S
Safety checks – 0•16
Safety First! – 0•11
Seats – 7•2
Secondary fuel tank – 4•5
Secondary master cylinder – 6•12
  cylinder pushrod and boot lubricant – 1•2
Security – REF•20 *et seq*
Selector drum and forks – 2•50
Shock absorber – 5•18
  adjustment – 5•20
  pivot bearings lubricant – 1•2
Side covers – 7•3
Sidelight – 8•7, 8•8
Sidestand – 1•17, 5•5
  switch – 8•17
Signalling checks – 0•16
Silencers – 4•28
Spare parts – 0•10
Spark plugs – 1•2, 1•11
Speed sensor – 4•15, 8•12, 8•14
Speedometer – 8•12
Stands – 1•17
  lubrication – 1•21
  pivots lubricant – 1•2
Starter clutch and gears – 2•44
Starter interlock circuit – 1•17
Starter motor
  overhaul – 8•21
  removal and installation – 8•20

Starter relay – 8•19
Starter valves – 4•19
Steering – 0•15
Steering head bearings – 1•19, 5•16
  lubricant – 1•2
Steering stem – 5•14
Storage – REF•32 *et seq*
Suspension – 0•15, 1•18
  adjustment – 5•20
  bearing lubrication – 1•19
Swingarm
  pivot bearings lubricant – 1•2
  removal and installation – 5•20
Switches
  brake lever – 8•10
  brake light – 8•10
  brake pedal – 8•11
  continuity checks – 8•3
  handlebar – 8•16
  ignition – 8•15
  low fuel warning – 4•25
  neutral – 8•16
  oil pressure – 8•15
  sidestand – 8•17

T
Tachometer – 8•12
Tail lights – 8•2, 8•7, 8•9
Technical Terms Explained – REF•44 *et seq*
Temperature display – 3•3
Thermostat – 3•4
  housing – 3•5
Throttle bodies – 4•17
Throttle cables – 1•10, 4•26
  lubricant – 1•2
Throttle position (TP) sensor – 4•12
Throttle twistgrip lubricant – 1•2
Timing ignition – 4•33
Tools and Workshop Tips – REF•2 *et seq*
**Transmission assembly removal and
  installation** – 2•49
**Transmission shaft and bearing removal and
  installation** – 2•52
Transmission shaft overhaul – 2•53
Trim clips – 7•1
Trim covers – 7•3
**Troubleshooting procedure immobiliser
  system** – 4•36
Turn signals – 8•7, 8•10
  bulbs – 8•2, 8•10
  circuit check and relay – 8•9
Tyres – 0•16, 1•21, 6•33
  care – 0•16
  pressures – 0•16, 1•2
  tread depth – 0•16

V
Valves
  clearances – 1•2, 1•23
  overhaul – 2•26
Valve covers – 2•16
  trim – 7•4
Voltage checks – 8•3

W
Warning lights – 8•13
Water pump – 3•6
  seal and bearing replacement – 3•6
Wheels – 1•21
  alignment check – 6•28
  bearings – 6•31
  inspection and repair – 6•27
Wheel sensor (ABS) – 6•26
Windshield – 7•8
  height adjuster mechanism – 8•28
  sliders lubricant – 1•2
Wiring continuity checks – 8•3
Wiring diagrams – 8•30 *et seq*

Haynes Motorcycle Manuals – The Complete List

Title	Book No
APRILIA RS50 (99 - 06) & RS125 (93 - 06)	4298
Aprilia RSV1000 Mille (98 - 03)	♦ 4255
Aprilia SR50	4755
BMW 2-valve Twins (70 - 96)	♦ 0249
BMW F650	♦ 4761
BMW K100 & 75 2-valve Models (83 - 96)	♦ 1373
BMW R850, 1100 & 1150 4-valve Twins (93 - 04)	♦ 3466
BMW R1200 (04 - 06)	♦ 4598
BSA Bantam (48 - 71)	0117
BSA Unit Singles (58 - 72)	0127
BSA Pre-unit Singles (54 - 61)	0326
BSA A7 & A10 Twins (47 - 62)	0121
BSA A50 & A65 Twins (62 - 73)	0155
Chinese Scooters	4768
DUCATI 600, 620, 750 and 900 2-valve V-Twins (91 - 05)	♦ 3290
Ducati MK III & Desmo Singles (69 - 76)	◊ 0445
Ducati 748, 916 & 996 4-valve V-Twins (94 - 01)	♦ 3756
GILERA Runner, DNA, Ice & SKP/Stalker (97 - 07)	4163
HARLEY-DAVIDSON Sportsters (70 - 08)	♦ 2534
Harley-Davidson Shovelhead and Evolution Big Twins (70 - 99)	♦ 2536
Harley-Davidson Twin Cam 88 (99 - 03)	♦ 2478
HONDA NB, ND, NP & NS50 Melody (81 - 85)	◊ 0622
Honda NE/NB50 Vision & SA50 Vision Met-in (85 - 95)	◊ 1278
Honda MB, MBX, MT & MTX50 (80 - 93)	0731
Honda C50, C70 & C90 (67 - 03)	0324
Honda XR80/100R & CRF80/100F (85 - 04)	2218
Honda XL/XR 80, 100, 125, 185 & 200 2-valve Models (78 - 87)	0566
Honda H100 & H100S Singles (80 - 92)	◊ 0734
Honda CB/CD125T & CM125C Twins (77 - 88)	◊ 0571
Honda CG125 (76 - 07)	◊ 0433
Honda NS125 (86 - 93)	◊ 3056
Honda CBR125R (04 - 07)	4620
Honda MBX/MTX125 & MTX200 (83 - 93)	◊ 1132
Honda CD/CM185 200T & CM250C 2-valve Twins (77 - 85)	0572
Honda XL/XR 250 & 500 (78 - 84)	0567
Honda XR250L, XR250R & XR400R (86 - 03)	2219
Honda CB250 & CB400N Super Dreams (78 - 84)	◊ 0540
Honda CR Motocross Bikes (86 - 01)	2222
Honda CRF250 & CRF450 (02 - 06)	2630
Honda CB400RR Fours (88 - 99)	◊ 3552
Honda VFR400 (NC30) & RVF400 (NC35) V-Fours (89 - 98)	◊ ♦ 3496
Honda CB500 (93 - 02) & CBF500 03 - 08	♦ 3753
Honda CB400 & CB550 Fours (73 - 77)	0262
Honda CX/GL500 & 650 V-Twins (78 - 86)	0442
Honda CBX550 Four (82 - 86)	◊ 0940
Honda XL600R & XR600R (83 - 08)	♦ 2183
Honda XL600/650V Transalp & XRV750 Africa Twin (87 to 07)	♦ 3919
Honda CBR600F1 & 1000F Fours (87 - 96)	♦ 1730
Honda CBR600F2 & F3 Fours (91 - 98)	♦ 2070
Honda CBR600F4 (99 - 06)	♦ 3911
Honda CB600F Hornet & CBF600 (98 - 06)	◊ ♦ 3915
Honda CBR600RR (03 - 06)	♦ 4590
Honda CB650 sohc Fours (78 - 84)	0665
Honda NTV600 Revere, NTV650 and NT650V Deauville (88 - 05)	◊ ♦ 3243
Honda Shadow VT600 & 750 (USA) (88 - 03)	2312
Honda CB750 sohc Four (69 - 79)	0131
Honda V45/65 Sabre & Magna (82 - 88)	0820
Honda VFR750 & 700 V-Fours (86 - 97)	♦ 2101
Honda VFR800 V-Fours (97 - 01)	♦ 3703
Honda VFR800 V-Tec V-Fours (02 - 05)	♦ 4196
Honda CB750 & CB900 dohc Fours (78 - 84)	0535
Honda VTR1000 (FireStorm, Super Hawk) & XL1000V (Varadero) (97 - 08)	♦ 3744
Honda CBR900RR FireBlade (92 - 99)	♦ 2161
Honda CBR900RR FireBlade (00 - 03)	♦ 4060
Honda CBR1000RR Fireblade (04 - 07)	♦ 4604
Honda CBR1100XX Super Blackbird (97 - 07)	♦ 3901
Honda ST1100 Pan European V-Fours (90 - 02)	♦ 3384
Honda Shadow VT1100 (USA) (85 - 98)	2313
Honda GL1000 Gold Wing (75 - 79)	0309

Title	Book No
Honda GL1100 Gold Wing (79 - 81)	0669
Honda Gold Wing 1200 (USA) (84 - 87)	2199
Honda Gold Wing 1500 (USA) (88 - 00)	2225
KAWASAKI AE/AR 50 & 80 (81 - 95)	1007
Kawasaki KC, KE & KH100 (75 - 99)	1371
Kawasaki KMX125 & 200 (86 - 02)	◊ 3046
Kawasaki 250, 350 & 400 Triples (72 - 79)	0134
Kawasaki 400 & 440 Twins (74 - 81)	0281
Kawasaki 400, 500 & 550 Fours (79 - 91)	0910
Kawasaki EN450 & 500 Twins (Ltd/Vulcan) (85 - 07)	2053
Kawasaki EX500 (GPZ500S) & ER500 (ER-5) (87 - 08)	♦ 2052
Kawasaki ZX600 (ZZ-R600 & Ninja ZX-6) (90 - 06)	♦ 2146
Kawasaki ZX-6R Ninja Fours (95 - 02)	♦ 3541
Kawasaki ZX-6R (03 - 06)	♦ 4742
Kawasaki ZX600 (GPZ600R, GPX600R, Ninja 600R & RX) & ZX750 (GPX750R, Ninja 750R)	♦ 1780
Kawasaki 650 Four (76 - 78)	0373
Kawasaki Vulcan 700/750 & 800 (85 - 04)	♦ 2457
Kawasaki 750 Air-cooled Fours (80 - 91)	0574
Kawasaki ZR550 & 750 Zephyr Fours (90 - 97)	♦ 3382
Kawasaki Z750 & Z1000 (03 - 08)	♦ 4762
Kawasaki ZX750 (Ninja ZX-7 & ZXR750) Fours (89 - 96)	♦ 2054
Kawasaki Ninja ZX-7R & ZX-9R (94 - 04)	♦ 3721
Kawasaki 900 & 1000 Fours (73 - 77)	0222
Kawasaki ZX900, 1000 & 1100 Liquid-cooled Fours (83 - 97)	♦ 1681
KTM EXC Enduro & SX Motocross (00 - 07)	♦ 4629
MOTO GUZZI 750, 850 & 1000 V-Twins (74 - 78)	0339
MZ ETZ Models (81 - 95)	◊ 1680
NORTON 500, 600, 650 & 750 Twins (57 - 70)	0187
Norton Commando (68 - 77)	0125
PEUGEOT Speedfight, Trekker & Vivacity Scooters (96 - 08)	◊ 3920
PIAGGIO (Vespa) Scooters (91 - 06)	◊ 3492
SUZUKI GT, ZR & TS50 (77 - 90)	◊ 0799
Suzuki TS50X (84 - 00)	◊ 1599
Suzuki 100, 125, 185 & 250 Air-cooled Trail bikes (79 - 89)	0797
Suzuki GP100 & 125 Singles (78 - 93)	◊ 0576
Suzuki GS, GN, GZ & DR125 Singles (82 - 05)	◊ 0888
Suzuki GSX-R600/750 (06 - 09)	♦ 4790
Suzuki 250 & 350 Twins (68 - 78)	0120
Suzuki GT250X7, GT200X5 & SB200 Twins (78 - 83)	◊ 0469
Suzuki GS/GSX250, 400 & 450 Twins (79 - 85)	0736
Suzuki GS500 Twin (89 - 06)	♦ 3238
Suzuki GS550 (77 - 82) & GS750 Fours (76 - 79)	0363
Suzuki GS/GSX550 4-valve Fours (83 - 88)	1133
Suzuki SV650 & SV650S (99 - 08)	♦ 3912
Suzuki GSX-R600 & 750 (96 - 00)	♦ 3553
Suzuki GSX-R600 (01 - 03), GSX-R750 (00 - 03) & GSX-R1000 (01 - 02)	♦ 3986
Suzuki GSX-R600/750 (04 - 05) & GSX-R1000 (03 - 06)	♦ 4382
Suzuki GSF600, 650 & 1200 Bandit Fours (95 - 06)	♦ 3367
Suzuki Intruder, Marauder, Volusia & Boulevard (85 - 06)	♦ 2618
Suzuki GS850 Fours (78 - 88)	0536
Suzuki GS1000 Four (77 - 79)	0484
Suzuki GSX-R750, GSX-R1100 (85 - 92), GSX600F, GSX750F, GSX1100F (Katana) Fours	♦ 2055
Suzuki GSX600/750F & GSX750 (98 - 02)	♦ 3987
Suzuki GS/GSX1000, 1100 & 1150 4-valve Fours (79 - 88)	0737
Suzuki TL1000S/R & DL1000 V-Strom (97 - 04)	♦ 4083
Suzuki GSF650/1250 (05 - 09)	♦ 4798
Suzuki GSX1300R Hayabusa (99 - 04)	♦ 4184
Suzuki GSX1400 (02 - 07)	♦ 4758
TRIUMPH Tiger Cub & Terrier (52 - 68)	0414
Triumph 350 & 500 Unit Twins (58 - 73)	0137
Triumph Pre-Unit Twins (47 - 62)	0251
Triumph 650 & 750 2-valve Unit Twins (63 - 83)	0122
Triumph Trident & BSA Rocket 3 (69 - 75)	0136
Triumph Bonneville (01 - 07)	♦ 4364
Triumph Daytona, Speed Triple, Sprint & Tiger (97 - 05)	♦ 3755
Triumph Triples and Fours (carburettor engines) (91 - 04)	♦ 2162
VESPA P/PX125, 150 & 200 Scooters (78 - 09)	0707
Vespa Scooters (59 - 78)	0126
YAMAHA DT50 & 80 Trail Bikes (78 - 95)	◊ 0800
Yamaha T50 & 80 Townmate (83 - 95)	◊ 1247

Title	Book No
Yamaha YB100 Singles (73 - 91)	◊ 0474
Yamaha RS/RXS100 & 125 Singles (74 - 95)	0331
Yamaha RD & DT125LC (82 - 95)	◊ 0887
Yamaha TZR125 (87 - 93) & DT125R (88 - 07)	◊ 1655
Yamaha TY50, 80, 125 & 175 (74 - 84)	◊ 0464
Yamaha XT & SR125 (82 - 03)	◊ 1021
Yamaha YBR125	4797
Yamaha Trail Bikes (81 - 00)	2350
Yamaha 2-stroke Motocross Bikes 1986 - 2006	2662
Yamaha YZ & WR 4-stroke Motocross Bikes (98 - 08)	2689
Yamaha 250 & 350 Twins (70 - 79)	0040
Yamaha XS250, 360 & 400 sohc Twins (75 - 84)	0378
Yamaha RD250 & 350LC Twins (80 - 82)	0803
Yamaha RD350 YPVS Twins (83 - 95)	1158
Yamaha RD400 Twin (75 - 79)	0333
Yamaha XT, TT & SR500 Singles (75 - 83)	0342
Yamaha XZ550 Vision V-Twins (82 - 85)	0821
Yamaha FJ, FZ, XJ & YX600 Radian (84 - 92)	2100
Yamaha XJ600S (Diversion, Seca II) & XJ600N Fours (92 - 03)	♦ 2145
Yamaha YZF600R Thundercat & FZS600 Fazer (96 - 03)	♦ 3702
Yamaha FZ-6 Fazer (04 - 07)	♦ 4751
Yamaha YZF-R6 (99 - 02)	♦ 3900
Yamaha YZF-R6 (03 - 05)	♦ 4601
Yamaha 650 Twins (70 - 83)	0341
Yamaha XJ650 & 750 Fours (80 - 84)	0738
Yamaha XS750 & 850 Triples (76 - 85)	0340
Yamaha TDM850, TRX850 & XTZ750 (89 - 99)	◊ ♦ 3540
Yamaha YZF750R & YZF1000R Thunderace (93 - 00)	♦ 3720
Yamaha FZR600, 750 & 1000 Fours (87 - 96)	♦ 2056
Yamaha XV (Virago) V-Twins (81 - 03)	♦ 0802
Yamaha XVS650 & 1100 Drag Star/V-Star (97 - 05)	♦ 4195
Yamaha XJ900F Fours (83 - 94)	♦ 3239
Yamaha XJ900S Diversion (94 - 01)	♦ 3739
Yamaha YZF-R1 (98 - 03)	♦ 3754
Yamaha YZF-R1 (04 - 06)	♦ 4605
Yamaha FZS1000 Fazer (01 - 05)	♦ 4287
Yamaha FJ1100 & 1200 Fours (84 - 96)	♦ 2057
Yamaha XJR1200 & 1300 (95 - 06)	♦ 3981
Yamaha V-Max (85 - 03)	♦ 4072
ATVs	
Honda ATC70, 90, 110, 185 & 200 (71 - 85)	0565
Honda Rancher, Recon & TRX250EX ATVs	2553
Honda TRX300 Shaft Drive ATVs (88 - 00)	2125
Honda Foreman (95 - 07)	2465
Honda TRX300EX, TRX400EX & TRX450ER ATVs (93 - 06)	2318
Kawasaki Bayou 220/250/300 & Prairie 300 ATVs (86 - 03)	2351
Polaris ATVs (85 - 97)	2302
Polaris ATVs (98 - 06)	2508
Yamaha YFS200 Blaster ATV (88 - 06)	2317
Yamaha YFB250 Timberwolf ATVs (92 - 00)	2217
Yamaha YFM350 & YFM400 (ER and Big Bear) ATVs (87 - 03)	2126
Yamaha Banshee and Warrior ATVs (87 - 03)	2314
Yamaha Kodiak and Grizzly ATVs (93 - 05)	2567
ATV Basics	10450
TECHBOOK SERIES	
Twist and Go (automatic transmission) Scooters Service and Repair Manual	4082
Motorcycle Basics TechBook (2nd Edition)	3515
Motorcycle Electrical TechBook (3rd Edition)	3471
Motorcycle Fuel Systems TechBook	3514
Motorcycle Maintenance TechBook	4071
Motorcycle Modifying	4272
Motorcycle Workshop Practice TechBook (2nd Edition)	3470

◊ = not available in the USA   ♦ = Superbike

The manuals on this page are available through good motorcycle dealers and accessory shops.
In case of difficulty, contact: **Haynes Publishing**
(UK) **+44 1963 442030**   (USA) **+1 805 498 6703**
(SV) **+46 18 124016**
(Australia/New Zealand) **+61 3 9763 8100**

Preserving Our Motoring Heritage

The Model J Duesenberg Derham Tourster. Only eight of these magnificent cars were ever built – this is the only example to be found outside the United States of America

Almost every car you've ever loved, loathed or desired is gathered under one roof at the Haynes Motor Museum. Over 300 immaculately presented cars and motorbikes represent every aspect of our motoring heritage, from elegant reminders of bygone days, such as the superb Model J Duesenberg to curiosities like the bug-eyed BMW Isetta. There are also many old friends and flames. Perhaps you remember the 1959 Ford Popular that you did your courting in? The magnificent 'Red Collection' is a spectacle of classic sports cars including AC, Alfa Romeo, Austin Healey, Ferrari, Lamborghini, Maserati, MG, Riley, Porsche and Triumph.

A Perfect Day Out

Each and every vehicle at the Haynes Motor Museum has played its part in the history and culture of Motoring. Today, they make a wonderful spectacle and a great day out for all the family. Bring the kids, bring Mum and Dad, but above all bring your camera to capture those golden memories for ever. You will also find an impressive array of motoring memorabilia, a comfortable 70 seat video cinema and one of the most extensive transport book shops in Britain. The Pit Stop Cafe serves everything from a cup of tea to wholesome, home-made meals or, if you prefer, you can enjoy the large picnic area nestled in the beautiful rural surroundings of Somerset.

John Haynes O.B.E., Founder and Chairman of the museum at the wheel of a Haynes Light 12.

The 1936 490cc sohc-engined International Norton – well known for its racing success

The Museum is situated on the A359 Yeovil to Frome road at Sparkford, just off the A303 in Somerset. It is about 40 miles south of Bristol, and 25 minutes drive from the M5 intersection at Taunton.
Open 9.30am - 5.30pm (10.00am - 4.00pm Winter) 7 days a week, *except Christmas Day, Boxing Day and New Years Day*
Special rates available for schools, coach parties and outings Charitable Trust No. 292048